Contemporary Cryptography

For quite a long time, computer security was a rather narrow field of study that was populated mainly by theoretical computer scientists, electrical engineers, and applied mathematicians. With the proliferation of open systems in general, and of the Internet and the World Wide Web (WWW) in particular, this situation has changed fundamentally. Today, computer and network practitioners are equally interested in computer security, since they require technologies and solutions that can be used to secure applications related to electronic commerce. Against this background, the field of computer security has become very broad and includes many topics of interest. The aim of this series is to publish state-of-the-art, high standard technical books on topics related to computer security. Further information about the series can be found on the WWW at the following URL:

http://www.esecurity.ch/serieseditor.html

Also, if you'd like to contribute to the series by writing a book about a topic related to computer security, feel free to contact either the Commissioning Editor or the Series Editor at Artech House.

For a listing of recent titles in the *Artech House Computer Security Library,*
turn to the back of this book.

Contemporary Cryptography

Rolf Oppliger

ARTECH
HOUSE

BOSTON | LONDON
artechhouse.com

Library of Congress Cataloging-in-Publication Data
Oppliger, Rolf.
    Contemporary cryptography/Rolf Oppliger.
      p. cm. —(Artech House computer security series)
    Includes bibliographical references and index.
    ISBN 1-58053-642-5
    1. Cryptography. I. Title. II. Series.

    Z103.O66 2005   2005043576
    652'.8–dc22

British Library Cataloguing in Publication Data
Oppliger, Rolf
    Contemporary cryptography. —(Artech House computer security series)
    1. Data encryption (Computer science) 2. Cryptography
    I. Title
    005.8'2

ISBN 1-58053-642-5
Cover design by Yekaterina Ratner

International Standard Book Number: 1-58053-642-5

10 9 8 7 6 5 4 3 2 1

To my family

Contents

III   SECRET KEY CRYPTOSYSTEMS   227

IV PUBLIC KEY CRYPTOSYSTEMS 331

Foreword

Assume for a moment that everything in this book was known for decades but not widely published. If I owned this book in the early 1980s, some governments would consider me dangerous (certainly more dangerous than anyone reasonably considers me now). The reason? Cryptography—the ability to encipher messages—was considered an instrument of war and espionage. Some countries (the USA included) considered export of cryptographic mechanisms to be in the same category of crime as smuggling nuclear weapons! This was despite the fact that cryptology has been studied and practiced for thousands of years around the world.

In 2005, a mere twenty years later, things are somewhat less extreme, and I have shelves full of books on cryptography. However, many governments still fear the spread of encryption and thus severely restrict (or prohibit) its use within their borders. This is despite its regular use billions of times per day in everything from banking networks to medical records to cable TV systems to Internet commerce over the WWW, as well as governmental uses.

Why is knowledge of cryptography so often feared by those in authority? One explanation may be that it is because cryptography can be used to hide criminal behavior, espionage, and political activities. More generally, it helps to remove information from the purview of the state, and this can be threatening to governments whose survival is based on restricting citizens' knowledge. Information can be used or misused in so many ways it is no wonder that protecting it is of widespread interest.

At its heart, cryptography is concerned with information, whether stored as data, or communicated to others. In turn, information and communication undergird nearly everything we do. Commerce is driven by communication of finance and sales, research is based on data acquisition and reference, and government functions on the collection and processing of records. Entertainment is encoded information, whether presented as music, paintings, or the performance of a play. Civilization is enabled by our ability to communicate information to each other, and to store it for later use. Even something as commonplace as currency would be useless unless it conveyed meaning of denomination and validity. Of course, personal relationships also require some level of communication, too—imagine conveying "I love you" to those people special in your life without any shared means of communication!

At its very heart, life itself is based on information storage and processing: the DNA in genes encodes information governing how organisms are constructed and operate. Recently, there were reports from the world of physics about new conjectures on the permanence of black holes that revolved around their effect on information.[1] Some students of psychology and philosophy believe that consciousness and behavior are predetermined by the events of the past—basically, the complex processing of information. Others believe that if we can simply capture the "information state" of the brain in an appropriately-advanced computer, we can transfer our "minds" outside our bodies.[2]

The more deeply you pursue this trail of information, the more connections one finds. It is clear that our ability to store and communicate information is fundamental to much more than most of us realize. Furthermore, knowing some of that information at the right time can provide tremendous advantage, whether it is in personal relationships, commercial enterprise, or acts by nation-state leaders. It therefore follows that means of protecting that information from disclosure or alteration are often as valuable as the information itself—if not more so.

It is here that cryptography comes into play. With good cryptography, we may be able to protect sensitive information; without it, we are all disadvantaged. It should thus be no surprise that so many organizations have tried to restrict cryptography such that they were the sole practitioners. History continues to show that such efforts seem destined to (eventually) fail. For uses good and ill, cryptography is around to stay.

You hold in your hands a multifarious work that exists against that backdrop. As with the role of information, the more you examine this book, the more facets you will discover.

For instance, if you read this book carefully, you will find it to be a comprehensive and detailed tutorial on cryptographic algorithms and protocols, along with supporting mathematics and statistics. As such, you can expand your knowledge of an important area that is also related to computing and communications. What's more, you can inform yourself about a broad range of issues, from historically significant ciphers to very current research results.

As with other works by Rolf Oppliger, this book is nicely organized and the contents are clearly presented. Each section of the book contains numerous references to important related literature. This combination provides an outstanding

---

1 See, for instance, "Hawking cracks black hole paradox" by Jenny Hogan in *New Scientist*, July 14, 2004.
2 cf. *In the Age of Spiritual Machines: When Computers Exceed Human Intelligence* by Ray Kurzweil, Penguin Putnam, 2000.

reference work for anyone pursuing scholarly work in the field. Thus, this book is one that will occupy a spot on your bookshelf—and ensure that it doesn't collect dust while there, as I have found so many other books do.

If you're a teacher, you now have a powerful textbook that can be used to prepare students for everything from basic comprehension of cryptographic concepts to reasonably advanced research in the field. As such, this is a much-needed instrument of pedagogy. This is the book colleagues and I wish we had over the last decade when teaching our graduate cryptography class; luckily, now we have it, and you do too.

Cryptography can be an enabler of subversion, of civil disobedience, and of criminal enterprise. It can also be used to safeguard protection of basic human rights, promote privacy, and enhance lawful commerce. Cryptography is an incredibly powerful set of technologies. A sound understanding of cryptographic techniques is not sufficient to guarantee information protection, but it is necessary, whether in computer processing, telecommunications, or database management. As our reliance on computing and network grows, our need for sound cryptography will also grow, and we all will need to have a better understanding of its uses and limitations.

When Rolf set out to write this book, I doubt he considered how it might be used by readers to do so many things. When you started reading it, you probably didn't have wide-ranging motives, either. And when I agreed to write the foreword, I was unsure what the book would be like. But now I know what you will shortly discover: Rolf has done a wonderful job of making so much important information accessible. He is thus a dangerous person, at least in the sense of "dangerous" that I employed at the beginning of this essay, and we should congratulate him for it. Enjoy.

—Gene Spafford[3]
January 2005

---

3   Eugene H. Spafford is the Executive Director of the Center for Education and Research in Information Assurance and Security at Purdue University in the USA. He is also a professor of Computer Sciences, a professor of Electrical and Computer Engineering, a professor of Philosophy (courtesy), and a professor of Communication (courtesy).

Preface

Necessity is the mother of invention,
and computer networks are the mother of modern cryptography.

— Ronald L. Rivest[4]

With the current ubiquity of computer networks and distributed systems in general, and the Internet in particular, cryptography has become an enabling technology to secure the information infrastructure(s) we are building, using, and counting on in daily life. This is particularly true for modern cryptography.[5] The important role of (modern) cryptography is, for example, pointed out by the quote given above. As explained later in this book, the quoted cryptographer—Ronald L. Rivest—is one of the pioneers of modern cryptography and has coinvented the widely deployed Rivest, Shamir, Adleman (RSA) public key cryptosystem.

Due to its important role, computer scientists, electrical engineers, and applied mathematicians should all be educated in the basic principles and applications of cryptography. Cryptography is a tool, and as such it can provide security only if it is used properly. If it is not used properly, then it may fail to provide security in the first place. It may even be worse than not using it at all, because users think that they are protected, whereas in reality this is not the case (this may lead to incorrect user behavior).

There are several books that can be used for educational purposes (e.g., [1–16] itemized in chronological order). Among these books, I particularly recommend [5, 9, 10, 12, 14] to teach classes,[6] [3] to serve as a handy reference for cryptographic algorithms and protocols (also available electronically on the Internet),[7] and [16] to provide an overview about practically relevant cryptographic standards. After having

---

4   In: "Cryptography as Duct Tape," a short note written to the Senate Commerce and Judiciary Committees in opposition to mandatory key recovery proposals on June 12, 1997 (the note is available electronically at http://theory.lcs.mit.edu/~rivest/ducttape.txt).

5   In Chapter 1, we explain what modern cryptography really means and how it differs from classical cryptography.

6   Prior to this book, I used to recommend [10] as a textbook for cryptography.

7   http://www.cacr.math.uwaterloo.ca/hac.

spent a considerable amount of time compiling and writing a manuscript that can be used to lecture and teach classes on contemporary cryptography, I decided to turn the manuscript into a book and to publish it in Artech House's computer security series.[8] The present book is the result of this endevour.

More often than not, mathematicians care about theoretical concepts and models without having applications in mind. On the other side, computer scientists and electrical engineers often deal with applications without having studied and properly understood the underlying mathematical fundamentals and principles. Against this background, *Contemporary Cryptography* tries to build a bridge and fill the gap between these two communities. As such, it is intended to serve the needs of mathematicians who want to be educated in contemporary cryptography as a possible application of their field(s) of study, as well as computer scientists and electrical engineers who want to be educated in the relevant mathematical fundamentals and principles. Consequently, the target audience for *Contemporary Cryptography* includes all of them: mathematicians, computer scientists, and electrical engineers, both in research and practice. Furthermore, computer practitioners, consultants, and information officers should also gain insight into the fascinating and quickly evolving field.

Contemporary Cryptography is written to be comprehensive and tutorial in nature. The book starts with two chapters that introduce the topic and briefly overview the cryptographic systems (or cryptosystems) in use today. After a thorough introduction of the mathematical fundamentals and principles that are at the heart of contemporary cryptography (Part I), the cryptographic systems are addressed in detail and defined in a mathematically precise sense. The cryptographic systems are discussed in three separate parts, addressing unkeyed cryptosystems (Part II), secret key cryptosystems (Part III), and public key cryptosystems (Part IV). Part IV also includes cryptographic protocols that make use of public key cryptography. Finally, the book finishes with an epilogue (Part V) and two appendixes.

Each chapter is intended to be comprehensive (on its own) and includes a list of references that can be used for further study. Where necessary and appropriate, I have also added some uniform resource locators (URLs) as footnotes to the text. The URLs point to corresponding information pages on the World Wide Web (WWW). While care has been taken to ensure that the URLs are valid now, unfortunately—due to the dynamic nature of the Internet and the WWW—I cannot guarantee that these URLs and their contents remain valid forever. In regard to the URLs, I apologize for any information page that may have been removed or replaced since the writing and publishing of the book. To make the problem less severe, I have not included URLs I expect to be removed or replaced anytime soon.

---

8   http://www.esecurity.ch/serieseditor.html.

Readers who like to experiment with cryptographic systems are invited to download, install, and play around with some of the many software packages that have been written and are available for demonstrational and educational purposes. Among these packages, I particularly recommend *CrypTool*. CrypTool is a demonstration and reference program for cryptography that is publicly and freely available[9] and that provides insight into the basic working principles of the cryptographic algorithms and protocols in use today.

If you want to implement and market some of the cryptographic techniques or systems addressed in this book, then you must must be very cautious and note that the entire field of cryptography is tied up in patents and corresponding patent claims. Consequently, you must make sure that you have an appropriate license or a good lawyer (or both).

In either case, regulations for the use and export of cryptographic products (see, for example, Bert-Jaap Koops' Crypto Law Survey)[10] differ in different countries. For example, France had regulations for the use of cryptographic techniques until recently, and some countries—especially in the Far East—still have. On the other side, some countries require specific data to be encrypted according to certain standards or best practices. This is particularly true for personal and medical data. With regard to the export of cryptographic products, the situation is even more involved. For example, since 1996 the U.S. export controls on cryptographic products are administered by the Bureau of Industry and Security (BIS) of the Department of Commerce (DoC). Rules governing exports and reexports of cryptographic products are found in the Export Administration Regulations (EAR). If a U.S. company wants to sell a cryptographic product overseas, it must have export approval according to the EAR. In January 2000, the DoC published a regulation implementing the White House's announcement of a new framework for U.S. export controls on encryption items.[11] The policy was in response to the changing global market, advances in technology, and the need to give U.S. industry better access to these markets, while continuing to provide essential protections for national security. The regulation enlarged the use of license exceptions, implemented the changes agreed to at

---

9 http://www.cryptool.com or http://www.cryptool.org.
10 http://rechten.uvt.nl/koops/cryptolaw.
11 The announcement was made on September 16, 1999.

the Wassenaar Arrangement[12] on export controls for conventional arms and dual-use goods and technologies in December 1998, and eliminated the deemed export rule for encryption technology. In addition, new license exception provisions were created for certain types of encryption, such as source code and toolkits. Some countries are exempted from the regulation (i.e., Cuba, Iran, Iraq, Libya, North Korea, Sudan, and Syria). We are not going to address legal issues regarding the use and export of cryptographic products in this book.[13] But note again that you may talk to a lawyer before you use and/or export cryptographic products.

Last, but not least, it is important to note that *Contemporary Cryptography* addresses only the materials that are published and available in the open literature. These materials are, for example, presented and discussed at the conferences[14] held by the International Association for Cryptologic Research (IACR).[15] There may (or may not) be additional and complementary materials available in the backyards of secret services and intelligence agencies. These materials are subject to speculations and rumors; sometimes they even provide the starting point for bestselling books and movies. *Contemporary Cryptography* does not speculate about these materials. It is, however, important to note and always keep in mind that these materials may still exist and that their mere existence may make this book or parts of it obsolete (once their existence becomes publicly known). For example, the notion of public key cryptography was invented by employees of a British intelligence agency a few years before it was published in the open literature (see Section 1.3). Also, the data encryption standard (DES) was designed to make it resistant against differential cryptanalysis—a cryptanalytical attack against symmetric encryption systems that was discussed in the public literature almost two decades after the standardization of the DES (see Section 10.2.1.4). There are certainly many other (undocumented) examples to illustrate this point.

12 The Wassenaar Arrangement is a treaty originally negotiated in July 1996 and signed by 31 countries to restrict the export of dual-use goods and technologies to specific countries considered to be dangerous. The countries that have signed the Wassenaar Arrangement include the former Coordinating Committee for Multilateral Export Controls (COCOM) member and cooperating countries, as well as some new countries such as Russia. The COCOM was an international munitions control organization that also restricted the export of cryptography as a dual-use technology. It was formally dissolved in March 1994. More recently, the Wassenaar Arrangement was updated. The participating countries of the Wassenaar Arrangement are Argentina, Australia, Austria, Belgium, Bulgaria, Canada, Czech Republic, Denmark, Finland, France, Germany, Greece, Hungary, Ireland, Italy, Japan, Luxembourg, The Netherlands, New Zealand, Norway, Poland, Portugal, Republic of Korea, Romania, Russian Federation, Slovakia, Spain, Sweden, Switzerland, Turkey, Ukraine, the United Kingdom, and the United States. Further information on the Wassenaar Arrangement can be found at http://www.wassenaar.org.

13 There are usually no regulations for the import of cryptographic products.

14 The three major annual conferences are CRYPTO, EUROCRYPT, and ASIACRYPT.

15 http://www.iacr.org.

I hope that *Contemporary Cryptography* serves your needs. Also, I would like to take the opportunity to invite you as a reader to let me know your opinions and thoughts. If you have something to correct or add, please let me know. If I have not expressed myself clearly, please let me know. I appreciate and sincerely welcome any comment or suggestion in order to update the book in future editions and to turn it into an appropriate reference book that can be used for educational purposes. The best way to reach me is to send a message to rolf.oppliger@esecurity.ch. You can also visit the book's home page at http://www.esecurity.ch/Books/cryptography.html. I use this page to periodically post errata lists, additional information, and complementary material related to the topic of the book (e.g., slides that can be used to lecture and teach introductory courses on contemporary cryptography). I'm looking forward to hearing from you in one way or another.

References

[1] Koblitz, N.I., *A Course in Number Theory and Cryptography*, 2nd edition. Springer-Verlag, New York, 1994.

[2] Schneier, B., *Applied Cryptography: Protocols, Algorithms, and Source Code in C*, 2nd edition. John Wiley & Sons, New York, 1996.

[3] Menezes, A., P. van Oorschot, and S. Vanstone, *Handbook of Applied Cryptography*. CRC Press, Boca Raton, FL, 1996.

[4] Luby, M., *Pseudorandomness and Cryptographic Applications*. Princeton Computer Science Notes, Princeton, NJ, 1996.

[5] Buchmann, J.A., *Introduction to Cryptography*. Springer-Verlag, New York, 2000.

[6] Garrett, P.B., *Making, Breaking Codes: Introduction to Cryptology*. Prentice Hall PTR, Upper Saddle River, NJ, 2001.

[7] Mollin, R.A., *An Introduction to Cryptography*. Chapman & Hall/CRC, Boca Raton, FL, 2001.

[8] Goldreich, O., *Foundations of Cryptography: Volume 1, Basic Tools*. Cambridge University Press, Cambridge, UK, 2001.

[9] Delfs, H., and H. Knebl, *Introduction to Cryptography: Principles and Applications*. Springer-Verlag, New York, 2002.

[10] Stinson, D., *Cryptography: Theory and Practice*, 2nd edition. Chapman & Hall/CRC, Boca Raton, FL, 2002.

[11] Mollin, R.A., *RSA and Public-Key Cryptography*. Chapman & Hall/CRC, Boca Raton, FL, 2002.

[12] Smart, N., *Cryptography, An Introduction*. McGraw-Hill Education, UK, 2003.

[13] Ferguson, N., and B. Schneier, *Practical Cryptography*. John Wiley & Sons, New York, 2003.

[14] Mao, W., *Modern Cryptography: Theory and Practice.* Prentice Hall PTR, Upper Saddle River, NJ, 2003.

[15] Goldreich, O., *Foundations of Cryptography: Volume 2, Basic Applications.* Cambridge University Press, Cambridge, UK, 2004.

[16] Dent, A.W., and C.J. Mitchell, *User's Guide to Cryptography and Standards.* Artech House Publishers, Norwood, MA, 2004.

Acknowledgments

There are many people involved in the writing and publication of a book. I thank all of them. In particular, I thank Kurt Bauknecht, Dieter Hogrefe, Hansjürg Mey, and Günther Pernul for their ongoing interest and support for my scientific work; Daniel Bleichenbacher, Pascal Junod, Javier Lopez, Rafal Lukawiecki, Ueli Maurer, Hans Oppliger, Ruedi Rytz, Peter Stadlin for answering specific questions, reading parts of the manuscript, and discussing some interesting questions with me; Ed Dawson for reviewing the entire manuscript; and Gene Spafford for providing the foreword. Once again, the staff at Artech House was enormously helpful in producing and promoting the book. Among these people, I am particularly grateful to Julie Lancashire, Tim Pitts, Tiina Ruonamaa, and Wayne Yuhasz. My most important thanks go to my family—my wife Isabelle and our beloved children Lara and Marc. Without their encouragement, support, patience, and love, this book would not exist.

Chapter 1

Introduction

In this chapter, we introduce the topic of the book (i.e., contemporary cryptography) at a high level of abstraction. More specifically, we elaborate on cryptology (including cryptography) in Section 1.1, address cryptographic systems (or cryptosystems) in Section 1.2, provide some historical background information in Section 1.3, and outline the rest of the book in Section 1.4.

1.1 CRYPTOLOGY

The term *cryptology* is derived from the Greek words "kryptós," standing for "hidden," and "lógos," standing for "word." Consequently, the meaning of the term cryptology is best paraphrased as "hidden word." This paraphrase refers to the original intent of cryptology, namely to hide the meaning of specific words and to protect their confidentiality and secrecy accordingly. As will (hopefully) become clear throughout the rest of the book, this viewpoint is far too narrow, and the term cryptology is nowadays used for many other security-related purposes and applications (in addition to the protection of the confidentiality and secrecy of messages).

More specifically, cryptology refers to the mathematical science and field of study that comprises both cryptography and cryptanalysis.

- The term *cryptography* is derived from the Greek words "kryptós" (see above) and "gráphein," standing for "write." Consequently, the meaning of the term cryptography is best paraphrased as "hidden writing." According to Request for Comments (RFC) 2828 [1], cryptography refers to the "mathematical science that deals with transforming data to render its meaning unintelligible

1

(i.e., to hide its semantic content), prevent its undetected alteration, or prevent its unauthorized use. If the transformation is reversible, cryptography also deals with restoring encrypted data to intelligible form." Consequently, cryptography refers to the process of protecting data in a very broad sense.

- The term *cryptanalysis* is derived from the Greek words "kryptós" (see above) and "analýein," standing for "to loosen." Consequently, the meaning of the term can be paraphrased as "loosen the hidden word." This paraphrase refers to the process of destroying the cryptographic protection, or—more generally—to study the security properties and possibilities to break cryptographic techniques and systems. Again referring to RFC 2828 [1], the term cryptanalysis is used to refer to the "mathematical science that deals with analysis of a cryptographic system in order to gain knowledge needed to break or circumvent the protection that the system is designed to provide." As such, the cryptanalyst is the antagonist of the cryptographer, meaning that his or her job is to break or at least circumvent the protection the cryptographer has designed and implemented in the first place.

Many other definitions for the terms cryptology, cryptography, and cryptanalysis are available and can be found in the relevant literature (or on the Internet, respectively). For example, the term cryptography is sometimes said to refer to the study of mathematical techniques related to all aspects of information security (e.g., [2]). These aspects include (but are not restricted to) data confidentiality, data integrity, entity authentication, data origin authentication, and/or nonrepudiation. Again, this definition is very broad and comprises anything that is directly or indirectly related to information security.

In some literature, the term cryptology is even said to include steganography (in addition to cryptography and cryptanalysis).

- The term *steganography* is derived from the Greek words "steganos," standing for "impenetrable," and "gráphein (see above). Consequently, the meaning of the term is best paraphrased as "impenetrable writing." According to Request for Comments (RFC) 2828 [1], the term steganography refers to "methods of hiding the existence of a message or other data. This is different than cryptography, which hides the meaning of a message but does not hide the message itself." An example of a formerly used steganographic method is invisible ink. Contemporary methods are more sophisticated and try to hide additional information in electronic files. In general, this information is arbitrary. It may, however, also be used to name the owner of a file or the recipient thereof. In the first case, one refers to *digital watermarking*, whereas in the second case one refers to *digital fingerprinting*. Digital watermarking and fingerprinting are currently very active areas of steganographic research and development.

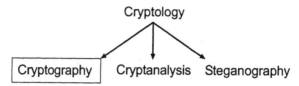

Figure 1.1 The relationship between cryptology, cryptography, cryptanalysis, and steganography.

The relationship between cryptology, cryptography, cryptanalysis, and steganography is overviewed in Figure 1.1. In this book, we address cryptography in a rather narrow sense (this narrow sense is illustrated with a box in Figure 1.1). We elaborate on cryptanalysis only where necessary and appropriate, and we do not address steganography at all. There are many other books that provide useful information about steganography and steganographic technologies and techniques in general (e.g., [3, 4]), and digital watermarking and digital fingerprinting in particular (e.g., [5, 6]).

1.2 CRYPTOGRAPHIC SYSTEMS

According to RFC 2828 [1], the term *cryptographic system* (or *cryptosystem* in short) refers to "a set of cryptographic algorithms together with the key management processes that support use of the algorithms in some application context." Again, this definition is fairly broad and comprises all kinds of cryptographic algorithms (and protocols).

In some literature, the term *cryptographic scheme* is used to refer to a cryptographic system. Unfortunately, it is seldom explained what the difference(s) between a (cryptographic) scheme and a system really is (are). So for the purpose of this book, we don't make a distinction, and we use the term cryptographic system to refer to either of them. We hope that this simplification is not too confusing. In the realm of digital signatures, for example, people frequently talk about digital signature schemes. In this book, however, we are talking about digital signature systems and actually mean the same thing.

If one is talking about a cryptographic system, then one is often talking about one or several algorithms. The term algorithm,[1] in turn, is best defined as suggested in Definition 1.1.

Definition 1.1 (Algorithm) *An* algorithm *is a well-defined computational procedure that takes a variable input and generates a corresponding output.*

Consequently, an algorithm is simply a computational procedure that is well defined and that turns a variable input into a corresponding output (according to the computational procedure it defines). It is sometimes also required that an algorithm halts within a reasonable amount of time (for any meaningful definition of "reasonable"). In either case, Definition 1.1 is rather vague and mathematically unprecise. It neither says what the computational model for the algorithm is, nor does it say anything about the problem the algorithm is supposed to solve (e.g., computing a mathematical function). Consequently, from a theoretical viewpoint, an algorithm can be more precisely defined as a well-defined computational procedure for a well-defined computational model for solving a well-defined problem. This definition, however, is a little bit clumsy, and we use the simpler (and more intuitive) definition given in Definition 1.1.

In either case, it is important to distinguish between deterministic and probabilistic algorithms:

- An algorithm is *deterministic* if its behavior is completely determined by the input. Consequently, the algorithm always generates the same output for the same input (if it is executed multiple times).

- An algorithm is *probabilistic* (or *randomized*) if its behavior is not completely determined by the input, meaning that the algorithm internally uses and takes advantage of some randomly (or pseudo-randomly) generated values. Consequently, a probabilistic algorithm may generate a different output each time it is executed with the same input (if it is executed multiple times). There are different types of probabilistic algorithms, and in Section 6.6.3 we distinguish between Las Vegas, Monte Carlo, and Atlantic City algorithms.

An algorithm may be implemented by a computer program that is written in a specific programming language (e.g., Pascal, C, or Java). Whenever we describe algorithms in this book, we don't use a specific programming language; we use a formal notation instead. The notation used to describe algorithms is sketched in Algorithm 1.1. The input and output parameters of an algorithm are written in brackets at the beginning and at the end of the algorithm description. The body of

---

1   The term *algorithm* is derived from the name of the mathematician Mohammed ibn-Musa al-Khwarizmi, who was part of the royal court in Baghdad and lived from about 780 to 850.

the algorithm consists of a set of arbitrary computational steps that are executed sequentially.

Algorithm 1.1 The notation used to describe algorithms.

(input parameters)
...
computational step
...
(output parameters)

If more than one entity is involved in an algorithm (or the computational procedure it defines, respectively), then one is in the realm of protocols.[2] As suggested in Definition 1.2, a protocol can be viewed as a distributed algorithm.

Definition 1.2 (Protocol) A protocol *is a distributed algorithm in which two or more entities take part.*

Alternatively, one could also define a protocol as a distributed algorithm in which a set of entities takes part. In this case, it becomes immediately clear that an algorithm also represents a protocol, namely one that is degenerated in a certain sense (i.e., the set consists of only one entity). Hence, an algorithm can always be viewed as a special case of a protocol. The major distinction between an algorithm and a protocol is that only one entity is involved in the former, whereas typically two or more entities are involved in the latter. This distinguishing fact is important and must be kept in mind when one talks about algorithms and protocols (not only cryptographic ones).

Similar to an algorithm, a protocol may be *deterministic* or *probabilistic* (depending on whether the protocol internally uses and takes advantage of random values). In fact, many protocols overviewed and discussed in this book are probabilistic in nature.

In this book, we are mainly interested in cryptographic algorithms and protocols as suggested in Definitions 1.3 and 1.4.

Definition 1.3 (Cryptographic algorithm) A cryptographic algorithm *is an algorithm that employs and makes use of cryptographic techniques and mechanisms.*

Definition 1.4 (Cryptographic protocol) A cryptographic protocol *is a protocol that employs and makes use of cryptographic techniques and mechanisms.*

---

2   The term protocol originates from diplomacy.

Remember the definition for a cryptographic system (or cryptosystem) given in RFC 2828 and quoted on page 3. According to this definition, a cryptosystem may comprise more than one algorithm, and the algorithms may not necessarily be executed by the same entity (i.e., they may be executed by multiple entities in a distributed way). Consequently, this notion of a cryptosystem comprises the notion of a cryptographic protocol as suggested in Definition 1.4. Hence, another way to look at cryptographic algorithms and protocols is to say that a cryptographic algorithm is a *single-entity cryptosystem*, whereas a cryptographic protocol is a *multientity* or *multiple entities cryptosystem*. These terms, however, are less frequently used in the literature. We don't use them in this book either.

In either case, it is important to note that cryptographic applications may consist of multiple (sub)protocols, that these (sub)protocols and their concurrent executions may interact in some subtle ways, and that these interactions and interdependencies may be exploited by various chosen-protocol attacks (see, for example, [7] for the notion of a chosen-protocol attack). As of this writing, we are just at the beginning of properly understanding chosen-protocol attacks and what they can be used for in cryptanalysis. These attacks are not further addressed in this book.

In the cryptographic literature, it is quite common to use human names to refer to the entities that take part and participate in a cryptographic protocol (e.g., a Diffie-Hellman key exchange). For example, in a two-party protocol the participating entities are usually called *Alice* and *Bob*. This is a convenient way of making things unambiguous with relatively few words, since the pronoun *she* can then be used for Alice, and *he* can be used for Bob. The disadvantage of this naming scheme is that people assume that the names are referring to people. This need not be the case, and Alice, Bob, and all other entities may be computer systems, cryptographic devices, or anything else. In this book, we don't follow the tradition of using Alice, Bob, and the rest of the gang. Instead, we use single-letter characters, such as A, B, C, ... , to refer to the entities that take part and participate in a cryptographic protocol. This is less fun (I guess), but more appropriate (I hope).

The cryptographic literature is also full of examples of more or less useful cryptographic protocols. Some of these protocols are overviewed, discussed, and put into perspective in this book. To formally describe a (cryptographic) protocol in which two parties (i.e., A and B) take part, we use the notation sketched in Protocol 1.1. Some input parameters may be required on either side of the protocol (note that the input parameters are not necessarily the same). The protocol then includes a set of computational and communicational steps. Each computational step may occur only on one side of the protocol, whereas each communicational step requires data to be transferred from one side to the other. In this case, the direction of the data transmission is indicated with a directed arrow. Finally, some parameters may be output on either side of the protocol. These output parameters actually represent

Protocol 1.1 The notation used for protocols.

A	B
(input parameters)	(input parameters)
...	...
computational step	computational step
...	...

$$\longrightarrow$$
...
$$\longleftarrow$$

...	...
computational step	computational step
...	...
(output parameters)	(output parameters)

the result of the protocol execution. Similar to the input parameters, the output parameters must not necessarily be the same on either side of the protocol execution. In many cases, however, the output parameters are the same (and represent the result and the common output of the protocol execution).

1.2.1 Classes of Cryptographic Systems

Cryptographic systems may or may not use secret parameters (e.g., cryptographic keys). Furthermore, if secret parameters are used, then they may or may not be shared between the participating entities. Consequently, there are at least three classes of cryptographic systems that can be distinguished,[3] and these classes are characterized in Definitions 1.5–1.7.

Definition 1.5 (Unkeyed cryptosystem) *An* unkeyed cryptosystem *is a cryptographic system that uses no secret parameter.*

Definition 1.6 (Secret key cryptosystem) *A* secret key cryptosystem *is a cryptographic system that uses secret parameters that are shared between the participating entities.*

Definition 1.7 (Public key cryptosystem) *A* public key cryptosystem *is a cryptographic system that uses secret parameters that are not shared between the participating entities.*

In Chapter 2, we introduce and briefly overview some representatives of unkeyed, secret key, and public key cryptosystems. These representatives are further

---

3   This classification scheme is due to Ueli Maurer.

addressed in Parts II (unkeyed cryptosystems), III (secret key cryptosystems), and IV (public key cryptosystems) of this book. In these parts, we also provide definitions that are mathematically more precise.

1.2.2 Secure Cryptographic Systems

The goal of cryptography is to design, implement, deploy, and make use of cryptographic systems that are secure in some meaningful way. In order to make precise statements about the security of a cryptographic system, one must formally define what the term "security" really means. Unfortunately, reality looks a little bit different, and the literature is full of cryptographic systems that are claimed to be secure without providing an appropriate definition for the term *security*. This is unfortunate, because anything can be claimed to be secure, unless its meaning is defined and precisely nailed down.

In general, a security definition must answer (at least) the following two questions:

1. *What are the capabilities of the adversary?* An answer to this question must specifiy, for example, the adversary's computing power, available memory, available time, types of feasible attacks, and access to a priori or side information. For some of these parameters, it must be specified whether they are finite or not. Most importantly, it may be reasonable to assume that there are adversaries with infinite computing power at their disposal, meaning that they can perform infinitely many computations in a given amount of time. The alternative is to consider adversaries with finite computing power at their disposal. Obviously, these adversaries can only perform a finite number of computations in a given amount of time. A similar distinction can be made with respect to the available memory and available time. Note, however, that it is reasonable to assume that no adversary has an infinite amount of time at disposal. Furthermore, the types of feasible attacks depend on the cryptographic system in question. For example, in Sections 10.1 and 14.1 we say that ciphertext-only, known-plaintext, (adaptive) chosen-plaintext, and (adaptive) chosen-ciphertext attacks are relevant for (symmetric and asymmetric) encryption systems. Other cryptosystems may be subject to other types of attacks.

2. *What is the task the adversary must solve in order to be successful (i.e., to break the security of the system)?* In a typical setting, the adversary's task is to find (i.e., compute, guess, or otherwise determine) one or several pieces of information he or she should not be able to know. For example, if the adversary is able to determine the cryptographic key used to encrypt

a message, then he or she must certainly be considered to be successful. There are, however, also weaker notions of successful attacks. For example, in modern cryptography one usually defines a theoretically perfect ideal system and says that the adversary is successful if he or she can tell it apart from a real system (i.e., decide whether he or she is interacting with a real system or an ideal system). If he or she cannot tell the systems apart, then the real system has all relevant properties of the ideal system (at least for a computationally bounded observer), and hence the real system is arguably as secure as the ideal one. Many security proofs follow this line of argumentation.

Strong security definitions are obtained when the adversary is assumed to be as powerful as possible, whereas the task he or she must solve is assumed to be as simple as possible. Taking these notes into account, a secure cryptographic system can be defined as suggested in Definition 1.8.

Definition 1.8 (Secure cryptographic system) *A cryptographic system is* secure *if an adversary with specified capabilities is not able to break it, meaning that he or she is not able to solve the specified task.*

Depending on the adversary's capabilities, there are two basic notions of security for a cryptographic system.

Unconditional security: If the adversary is not able to solve the task even with infinite computing power, then we talk about *unconditional* or *information-theoretic security*. The mathematical theories behind this type of security are probability theory and information theory, as briefly introduced in Chapters 4 and 5.

Conditional security: If the adversary is theoretically able to solve the task, but it is computationally infeasible for him or her (meaning that he or she is not able to solve the task given his or her resources, capabilities, and access to a priori or side information), then we talk about *conditional* or *computational security*. The mathematical theory behind this type of security is computational complexity theory, as briefly introduced in Chapter 6.

Interestingly, there are cryptosystems known to be secure in the strong sense (i.e., unconditionally secure), whereas there are no cryptosystems known to be secure in the weak sense (i.e., computationally secure). Not even the existence of conditionally or computationally secure cryptosystems has formally been proven so far. The underlying problem is that it is generally not possible to prove lower bounds for the computational complexity of a problem (this is an inherent weakness of complexity theory as we know and use it today).

In some literature, *provable security* is mentioned as yet another notion of security (e.g., [8]). The idea of provable security goes back to the early days of public key cryptography, when Whitfield Diffie and Martin E. Hellman proposed a complexity-based proof (for the security of a public key cryptosystem) in their seminal paper entitled "New Directions in Cryptography" [9].[4] The idea is to show that breaking a cryptosystem is computationally equivalent to solving a hard problem. This means that one must prove the following two directions:

- If the hard problem can be solved, then the cryptosystem can be broken;

- If the cryptosystem can be broken, then the hard problem can be solved.

Diffie and Hellman proved the first direction for their key exchange protocol (see Section 16.3). They did not prove the second direction.[5] This is unfortunate, because the second direction is the important direction from a security perspective. If we can prove that an adversary who is able to break a cryptosystem is also able to solve the hard problem, then we can argue that it is very unlikely that such an adversary really exists and hence that the cryptosystem in question is likely to be secure. Michael O. Rabin was the first person who found and proposed a cryptosystem that can be proven to be computationally equivalent to a hard problem (i.e., the integer factorization problem as captured in Definition 7.11) [11]. The Rabin public key cryptosystem is further addressed in Section 14.2.2.

The notion of (provable) security has fueled a lot of research since the late 1970s and early 1980s. In fact, there are many (public key) cryptosystems shown to be provably secure in exactly this sense. It is, however, important to note that a complexity-based proof is not absolute and that it is only relative to the (assumed) intractability of the underlying mathematical problem(s). This is a similar situation to proving that a given problem is $\mathcal{NP}$-complete. It proves that the problem is at least as difficult as any other $\mathcal{NP}$-complete problem, but it does not provide an absolute proof of the computational difficulty of the problem.[6]

More recently (i.e., since about the 1990s), people have come up with a methodology for designing cryptographic systems (typically security protocols) that are provably secure in the "reductionist" sense mentioned earlier, and that consists of the following two steps:

---

4   This paper is the one that officially gave birth to public key cryptography. There is a companion paper entitled "Multiuser Cryptographic Techniques" that was presented by the same authors at the National Computer Conference that took place on June 7–10, 1976, in New York City.

5   Ueli M. Maurer made the first serious attempt to prove the second direction [10].

6   Refer to Section 6.6.2.2 to get a more detailed overview about $\mathcal{NP}$-completeness and $\mathcal{NP}$-complete problems.

- First, an ideal system is designed in which all parties (including the adversary) have access to a *random function* (also known as *random oracle*).[7] This ideal system is then proven to be secure in the sense given earlier.

- Second, one replaces the random oracle with a "good" and "appropriately chosen" cryptographic hash function, such as MD5 or SHA-1, and provides all parties (again, including the adversary) with a specification of this function.

Consequently, one obtains an implementation of the ideal system in the real world where random oracles do not exist. Due to its use of random oracles, the design methodology is commonly referred to as *random oracle methodology*. It yields cryptographic systems that are provably secure in the *random oracle model*. Unfortunately, it has been shown that it is possible to construct cryptographic systems that are provably secure in the random oracle model, but that become insecure whenever the cryptographic hash function used in the protocol (to replace the random oracle) is specified and nailed down. This theoretical result is worrisome, and since its publication many researchers have started to think controversially about the random oracle methodology in general, and the random oracle model in particular. At least it must be noted that formal analyses in the random oracle model are not strong security proofs (because of the underlying ideal assumptions about the randomness properties of the cryptographic hash functions). The random oracle model is further addressed in Section 13.3. For the purpose of this book, we don't consider provable security (with or without the random oracle model) as a security notion of its own; instead we treat it as a special case of conditional security.

In the past, we have seen many examples in which people have tried to improve the security of a cryptographic system by keeping secret its design and internal working principles. This approach is sometimes referred to as "security through obscurity." Many of these systems do not work and can be broken trivially.[8] This insight has a long tradition in cryptography, and there is a well-known cryptographic principle—the *Kerckhoffs' principle*[9]—that basically says that a cryptographic system should be designed so as to be secure when the adversary knows all details of the system, except for the values explicitly declared to be secret, such as a secret cryptographic key [12]. We follow this principle in this book, and hence we only address cryptosystems for which we can assume that the adversary knows all of the details of the system.

The design of a secure cryptographic system is a difficult and challenging task. One can neither rely on intuitions regarding the "typical" state of the environment in

---

7   The notion of a random function is introduced in Section 13.1.
8   Note that "security through obscurity" may work well outside the realm of cryptography.
9   The principle is named after Auguste Kerckhoffs who lived from 1835 to 1903.

which the system operates (because the adversary will try to manipulate the environment into "untypical" states), nor can one be content with countermeasures designed to withstand specific attacks (because the adversary will try to attack the systems in ways that are different from the ones the designer envisioned). Cryptographic systems that are based on make-believe, adhoc approaches and heuristics are typically broken sooner or later. Consequently, the design of a secure cryptographic system should be based on firm foundations. It typically consists of the following two steps:

1. In the *definitional step*, the problem the cryptographic system is intended to solve must be identified, precisely defined, and formally specified.

2. In the *constructive step*, a cryptographic system that satisfies the definition distilled in step one, possibly while relying on intractability assumptions, must be designed.

Again, it is important to note that most parts of modern cryptography rely on intractability assumptions and that relying on such assumptions seems to be unavoidable today (see Chapter 21). Still, there is a huge difference between relying on an explicitly stated intractability assumption and just assuming (or rather hoping) that an ad hoc construction satisfies some unspecified or vaguely specified goals.

1.2.3 Side Channel and Related Attacks

It is important to note (and always keep in mind) that an implementation of a secure cryptographic system may not necessarily be secure. In fact, many attacks can be mounted against a particular implementation of a (secure) cryptographic system (rather than its mathematical properties). For example, there are attacks that take advantage of and try to exploit the side channel information that a particular implementation may leak. These attacks are called *side channel attacks*. Since about the middle of the 1990s, people have found and come up with many possibilities to mount side channel attacks. The following list is not comprehensive.

- *Timing attacks* take advantage of and try to exploit the correlation between a cryptographic key and the running time of a (cryptographic) operation that employs this key [13]. Consider, for example, the square-and-multiply algorithm (i.e., Algorithm 3.3) that is frequently used in public key cryptography to decrypt data or digitally sign messages. The running time of this algorithm mainly depends on the number of ones in the argument that represents the (private) exponent and key; hence the running time of the algorithm provides some side channel information about the particular key in use. This is a very general problem, and there are basically two possibilities to protect against timing attacks. The first possibility is to make sure that a specific operation always takes a fixed amount of time (or at least an amount of time that is not related to the cryptographic key in use). The second possibility is to pseudo-randomly and reversably transform the data on which the cryptographic operation is applied (i.e., the data is blinded). Both possibilities have the disadvantage that they lead to performance penalties.

- *Differential fault analysis* takes advantage of and exploits the fact that errors on cryptographic operations that depend on a particular cryptographic key may also leak some information about the key in use. The errors, in turn, can be random, latent (e.g., due to a buggy implementation), or—most interestingly—induced. In fact, people have tried all kinds of physical pressure to induce such errors, and they have been surprisingly successful in analyzing them (e.g., [14, 15]). Protection against differential fault analysis seems to be more involved than protection against timing attacks.

- A conceptually similar but still very different side-channel attack is sometimes called *failure analysis*. Failure analysis takes advantage of and exploits the fact that many implementations of cryptographic operations return notifications (e.g., error messages) if they fail. Consequently, these implementations provide a one-bit oracle that depends on the cryptographic operation and key in use. It has been shown that such an oracle—when invoked a very large number of times—can eventually be used to misuse the key (e.g., [16]). Designing and implementing cryptographic systems in a way that is resistant to failure analysis is a currently very active area of research and development.

- *Differential power analysis* exploits the fact that any hardware device consumes power, because this power consumption can be monitored and analyzed while a cryptographic operation is going on. Based on the fact that the power consumption varies significantly during the different steps of a cryptographic operation, it may be possible to derive information about the cryptographic key in use (e.g., [17]). In general, the smaller and the more specialized a hardware device is, the more successful a differential power analysis is likely to be. For example, differential power analysis has been shown to be particularly successful against smartcards. There are a couple of possibilities to protect against differential power analysis, such as keeping the power consumption stable or blinding the data before the cryptographic operations are applied.

In addition to these side-channel attacks, many other attacks (against tamper resistant hardware devices) employ invasive measuring techniques (e.g., [18, 19]). This field of study has a long tradition in computer security. For example, the U.S. government has invested a lot of time and money in the classified TEMPEST program[10] to prevent sensitive information from leaking through electromagnetic emanation. More recently, people have tried to exploit and employ diffuse visible light from cathode-ray tube (CRT) displays[11] and acoustic emanation[12] for cryptanalytical purposes. From a practical point of view, all of the earlier mentioned types of attacks (and many others that will be developed in the future) are relevant and must be considered with care (e.g., [20]). For the purpose of this book, however, we only mention some of the more important attacks, but we do not address them in detail. You may refer to the referenced literature to get more information about them.

1.3 HISTORICAL BACKGROUND INFORMATION

Cryptography has a long and thrilling history that is addressed in many books (e.g., [21–23]). Since the very beginning of the spoken and—even more important—written word, people have tried to transform "data to render its meaning unintelligible (i.e., to hide its semantic content), prevent its undetected alteration, or prevent its unauthorized use" [1]. According to this definition, these people have always employed cryptography and cryptographic techniques. The mathematics behind these early systems may not have been very sophisticated, but they still employed cryptography and cryptographic techniques. For example, Gaius Julius Caesar[13] used an encryption system in which every letter in the Latin alphabet was substituted with the letter that is found three positions afterwards in the lexical order (i.e., "A" is substituted with "D," "B" is substituted with "E," and so on). This simple additive cipher is known as *Caesar cipher* (see Section 10.1.1). Later on, people employed encryption systems that use more involved mathematical transformations. Many books on cryptography contain numerous examples of historically relevant encryption systems—they are not repeated in this book.

Until World War II, cryptography was considered to be an art (rather than a science) and was primarily used in the military and diplomacy. The following two developments and scientific achievements turned cryptography from an art into a science:

- During World War II, Claude E. Shannon[14] developed a mathematical theory of communication [24] and a related communication theory of secrecy

---

10 http://www.eskimo.com/~joelm/tempest.html.
11 http://www.cl.cam.ac.uk/TechReports/UCAM-CL-TR-577.pdf.
12 http://www.wisdom.weizmann.ac.il/~tromer/acoustic.
13 Gaius Julius Caesar was a Roman emperor who lived from 102 BC to 44 BC.
14 Claude E. Shannon was a mathematician who lived from 1916 to 2001.

systems [25] when he was working at AT&T Laboratories.[15] After their publication, the two theories started a new branch of research that is commonly referred to as *information theory* (refer to Chapter 5 for a brief introduction on information theory).

- As mentioned earlier, Diffie and Hellman developed and proposed the idea of public key cryptography at Stanford University in the 1970s.[16] Their vision was to employ trapdoor functions to encrypt and digitally sign electronic documents. Informally speaking, a trapdoor function is a function that is easy to compute but hard to invert, unless one knows and has access to some specific trapdoor information. This information is the private key that must be held by only one person. Diffie and Hellman's work culminated in a key agreement protocol (i.e., the Diffie-Hellman key exchange protocol described in Section 16.3) that allows two parties that share no prior secret to exchange a few messages over a public channel and to establish a shared (secret) key. This key can then be used as a session key.

After Diffie and Hellman published their discovery, a number of public key cryptosystems were developed and proposed. Some of these systems are still in use today, such as the RSA [27] and ElGamal [28] public key cryptosystems. Other systems, such as a number of public key cryptosystems based on the knapsack problem[17] have been broken and are no longer in use today. Some public key cryptosystems are overviewed and discussed in Part IV of this book.

Since around the early 1990s, we have seen a wide deployment and massive commercialization of cryptography. Today, many companies develop, market, and sell cryptographic techniques, mechanisms, services, and products (implemented in hardware or software) on a global scale. There are cryptography-related conferences

---

15 Similar studies were done by Norbert Wiener who lived from 1894 to 1964.

16 Similar ideas were pursued by Ralph C. Merkle at the University of California at Berkeley [26]. More recently, the British government announced that public key cryptography, including the Diffie-Hellman key agreement protocol and the RSA public key cryptosystem, was invented at the Government Communications Headquarters (GCHQ) in Cheltenham in the early 1970s by James H. Ellis, Clifford Cocks, and Malcolm J. Williamson under the name *non-secret encryption* (NSE). You may refer to the note "The Story of Non-Secret Encryption" written by Ellis in 1997 (available at http://citeseer.nj.nec.com/ellis97story.html) to get the story. Being part of the world of secret services and intelligence agencies, Ellis, Cocks, and Williamson were not allowed to openly talk about their invention.

17 The *knapsack problem* is a well-known problem in computational complexity theory and applied mathematics. Given a set of items, each with a cost and a value, determine the number of each item to include in a collection so that the total cost is less than some given cost and the total value is as large as possible. The name derives from the scenario of choosing treasures to stuff into your knapsack when you can only carry so much weight.

and trade shows[18] one can attend to learn more about products that implement cryptographic techniques, mechanisms, and services. The major goal of this book is to provide some basic understanding for what is currently going on. If you want to learn more about the practical use of cryptography to secure Internet and WWW applications, you may refer to [29–31] or any other book about Internet and Web security.[19] These practical applications of cryptography are not addressed (repeated) in this book.

1.4 OUTLINE OF THE BOOK

The rest of this book is organized as follows:

- In Chapter 2, *Cryptographic Systems*, we introduce, briefly overview, and put into perspective the three classes of cryptographic systems (i.e., unkeyed cryptosystems, secret key cryptosystems, and public key cryptosystems) and some major representatives.

- In Chapter 3, *Discrete Mathematics*, we begin the part on mathematical fundamentals (i.e., Part I) by discussing the aspects of discrete mathematics that are relevant for contemporary cryptography.

- In Chapter 4, *Probability Theory*, we elaborate on probability theory as far as it is relevant for contemporary cryptography.

- In Chapter 5, *Information Theory*, we use probability theory to quantify information and to introduce the aspects of information theory that are used in contemporary cryptography.

- In Chapter 6, *Complexity Theory*, we provide a brief introduction to complexity theory as far as it is relevant for contemporary cryptography.

- In Chapter 7, *One-Way Functions*, we begin the part on unkeyed cryptosystems (i.e., Part II) by elaborating on one-way functions and discussing some candidate one-way functions that are frequently used in cryptography.

- In Chapter 8, *Cryptographic Hash Functions*, we overview and discuss cryptographic hash functions and their use in contemporary cryptography.

- In Chapter 9, *Random Bit Generators*, we elaborate on random bit generators and discuss some possible realizations and implementations.

---

18   The most important trade show is the RSA Conference held annually in ths United States, Europe, and Asia. Refer to http://www.rsaconference.com for more information.

19   http://www.esecurity.ch/bookstore.html

- In Chapter 10, *Symmetric Encryption Systems*, we begin the part on secret key cryptosystems (i.e., Part III) by overviewing and discussing some symmetric encryption systems.

- In Chapter 11, *Message Authentication Codes*, we address message authentication and explain how secret key cryptography can be used to generate and verify message authentication codes (MACs).

- In Chapter 12, *Pseudorandom Bit Generators*, we explore the notion and elaborate on possible constructions for pseudorandom bit generators (PRBGs).

- In Chapter 13, *Pseudorandom Functions*, we introduce, discuss, and put into perspective pseudorandom functions (PRFs).

- In Chapter 14, *Asymmetric Encryption Systems*, we begin the part on public key cryptosystems (i.e., Part IV) by overviewing and discussing some asymmetric encryption systems.

- In Chapter 15, *Digital Signature Systems*, we elaborate on digital signatures and digital signature systems (DSSs) as an increasingly important application of public key cryptography.

- In Chapter 16, *Key Establishment*, we address key establishment and elaborate on corresponding key distribution and key agreement protocols.

- In Chapter 17, *Entity Authentication*, we elaborate on entity authentication in general and (cryptographic) authentication protocols that implement a proof by knowledge in particular.

- In Chapter 18, *Secure Multiparty Computation*, we address the problem of how mutually distrusting parties can compute a function without revealing their individual arguments to one another.

- In Chapter 19, *Key Management*, we begin the epilogue (i.e., Part V) by discussing some aspects related to key management.

- In Chapter 20, *Conclusions*, we conclude with some remarks about the current state of the art in cryptography.

- In Chapter 21, *Outlook*, we provide an outlook about possible and likely developments and trends in the future.

Last but not least, the book includes two appendixes (i.e., a list of abbreviations and acronyms and a summary of the mathematical notation used in the book), a page about the author, and an index.

Note that cryptography is a field of study that is far too broad to be addressed in a single book and that you have to refer to additional material, such as the literature referenced at the end of each chapter, if you want to learn more about a particular topic. The aims of this book are to provide an overview, to give an introduction into each of the previously mentioned topics and areas of research and development, and to put everything into perspective. Most importantly, we want to ensure that you no longer cannot see the forest for the trees.

References

[1] Shirey, R., *Internet Security Glossary*, Request for Comments 2828, May 2000.

[2] Menezes, A., P. van Oorschot, and S. Vanstone, *Handbook of Applied Cryptography*. CRC Press, Boca Raton, FL, 1996.

[3] Wayner, P., *Disappearing Cryptography*, 2nd edition. Morgan Kaufmann Publishers, San Francisco, CA, 2002.

[4] Cole, E., *Hiding in Plain Sight: Steganography and the Art of Covert Communication*. John Wiley & Sons, New York, 2003.

[5] Katzenbeisser, S., and F. Petitcolas (Eds.), *Information Hiding Techniques for Steganography and Digital Watermarking*. Artech House Publishers, Norwood, MA, 2000.

[6] Arnold, M., M. Schmucker, and S.D. Wolthusen, *Techniques and Applications of Digital Watermarking and Content Protection*. Artech House Publishers, Norwood, MA, 2003.

[7] Kelsey, J., B. Schneier, and D. Wagner, "Protocol Interactions and the Chosen Protocol Attack," *Proceedings of the 5th International Workshop on Security Protocols*, Springer-Verlag, 1997, pp. 91–104.

[8] Stinson, D., *Cryptography: Theory and Practice*, 2nd edition. Chapman & Hall/CRC, Boca Raton, FL, 2002.

[9] Diffie, W., and M.E. Hellman, "New Directions in Cryptography," *IEEE Transactions on Information Theory*, IT-22(6), 1976, pp. 644–654.

[10] Maurer, U.M., "Towards the Equivalence of Breaking the Diffie-Hellman Protocol and Computing Discrete Logarithms," *Proceedings of CRYPTO '94*, Springer-Verlag, LNCS 839, 1994, pp. 271–281.

[11] Rabin, M.O., "Digitalized Signatures and Public-Key Functions as Intractable as Factorization," MIT Laboratory for Computer Science, MIT/LCS/TR-212, 1979.

[12] Kerckhoffs, A., "La Cryptographie Militaire," *Journal des Sciences Militaires*, Vol. IX, January 1883, pp. 5-38, February 1883, pp. 161-191.

[13] Kocher, P., "Timing Attacks on Implementations of Diffie-Hellman, RSA, DSS, and other Systems," *Proceedings of CRYPTO '96*, Springer-Verlag, LNCS 1109, 1996, pp. 104–113.

[14] Boneh, D., R. DeMillo, and R. Lipton, "On the Importance of Checking Cryptographic Protocols for Faults," *Proceedings of EUROCRYPT '97*, Springer-Verlag, LNCS 1233, 1997, pp. 37–51.

[15] Biham, E., and A. Shamir, "Differential Fault Analysis of Secret Key Cryptosystems," *Proceedings of CRYPTO '97*, Springer-Verlag, LNCS 1294, 1997, pp. 513–525.

[16] Bleichenbacher, D., "Chosen Ciphertext Attacks Against Protocols Based on the RSA Encryption Standard PKCS #1," *Proceedings of CRYPTO '98*, Springer-Verlag, LNCS 1462, 1998, pp. 1–12.

[17] Kocher, P., J. Jaffe, and B. Jun, "Differential Power Analysis," *Proceedings of CRYPTO '99*, Springer-Verlag, LNCS 1666, 1999, pp. 388–397.

[18] Anderson, R., and M. Kuhn, "Tamper Resistance — A Cautionary Note," *Proceedings of the 2nd USENIX Workshop on Electronic Commerce*, November 1996, pp. 1–11.

[19] Anderson, R., and M. Kuhn, "Low Cost Attacks on Tamper Resistant Devices," *Proceedings of the 5th International Workshop on Security Protocols*, Springer-Verlag, LNCS 1361, 1997, pp. 125–136.

[20] Anderson, R., "Why Cryptosystems Fail," *Communications of the ACM*, Vol. 37, No. 11, November 1994, pp. 32–40.

[21] Kahn, D., *The Codebreakers: The Comprehensive History of Secret Communication from Ancient Times to the Internet.* Scribner, New York, 1996.

[22] Bauer, F.L., *Decrypted Secrets: Methods and Maxims of Cryptology*, 2nd edition. Springer-Verlag, New York, 2000.

[23] Levy, S., *Crypto: How the Code Rebels Beat the Government—Saving Privacy in the Digital Age.* Viking Penguin, New York, 2001.

[24] Shannon, C.E., "A Mathematical Theory of Communication," *Bell System Technical Journal*, Vol. 27, No. 3/4, July/October 1948, pp. 379–423/623–656.

[25] Shannon, C.E., "Communication Theory of Secrecy Systems," *Bell System Technical Journal*, Vol. 28, No. 4, October 1949, pp. 656–715.

[26] Merkle, R.C., "Secure Communication over Insecure Channels," *Communications of the ACM*, 21(4), April 1978 (submitted in 1975), pp. 294–299.

[27] Rivest, R.L., A. Shamir, and L. Adleman, "A Method for Obtaining Digital Signatures and Public-Key Cryptosystems," *Communications of the ACM*, 21(2), February 1978, pp. 120–126.

[28] ElGamal, T., "A Public Key Cryptosystem and a Signature Scheme Based on Discrete Logarithm," *IEEE Transactions on Information Theory*, IT-31(4), 1985, pp. 469–472.

[29] Oppliger, R., *Secure Messaging with PGP and S/MIME.* Artech House Publishers, Norwood, MA, 2001.

[30] Oppliger, R., *Internet and Intranet Security*, 2nd edition. Artech House Publishers, Norwood, MA, 2002.

[31] Oppliger, R., *Security Technologies for the World Wide Web*, 2nd edition. Artech House Publishers, Norwood, MA, 2003.

Chapter 2

Cryptographic Systems

As mentioned in Section 1.2.1, there are three major classes of cryptographic systems: unkeyed cryptosystems, secret key cryptosystems, and public key cryptosystems. In this chapter, we briefly introduce and provide some preliminary definitions for the most important representatives of these classes in Sections 2.1–2.3 (the definitions are partly revised and refined in later parts of the book). We conclude with some final remarks in Section 2.4.

2.1 UNKEYED CRYPTOSYSTEMS

According to Definition 1.5, unkeyed cryptosystems use no secret parameter. Examples include one-way functions, cryptographic hash functions, and random bit generators. Let us have a preliminary look at these systems.

2.1.1 One-Way Functions

The notion of a one-way function plays a central role in contemporary cryptography. Informally speaking, a function $f : X \to Y$ is one way if it is easy to compute but hard to invert. In accordance with the terminology used in complexity theory (see Chapter 6), the term *easy* means that the computation can be done efficiently, whereas the term *hard* means that the computation is not known to be feasible in an efficient way (i.e., no efficient algorithm to do the computation is known to exist).[1] Consequently, one can define a *one-way function* as suggested in Definition 2.1 and illustrated in Figure 2.1.

---

1   Note that it is not impossible that such an algorithm exists; it is just not known.

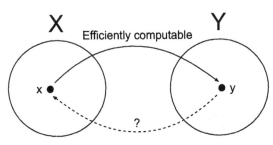

Figure 2.1   A one-way function.

Definition 2.1 (One-way function) *A function* $f : X \rightarrow Y$ *is* one way *if* $f(x)$ *can be computed efficiently for all* $x \in X$, *but* $f^{-1}(y)$ *cannot be computed efficiently for* $y \in_R Y$.

   In this definition, X represents the domain of the function f, Y represents the range, and the expression $y \in_R Y$ stands for "a y that is randomly chosen from Y." Consequently, it must be possible to efficiently compute $f(x)$ for all $x \in X$, whereas it must not—or only with a negligible probability—be possible to compute $f^{-1}(y)$ for a randomly chosen $y \in Y$. To be more precise, one must say that it may be possible to compute $f^{-1}(y)$, but that the entity that wants to do the computation does not know how to actually do it. In either case, Definition 2.1 is not precise in a mathematically strong sense, because we have not yet defined what an efficient computation really is. This must be postponed to somewhere after Chapter 6, when we have introduced the fundamentals and basic principles of complexity theory. In the meantime, it is sufficient to know that a computation is said to be efficient, if the (expected) running time of the algorithm that does the computation is bounded by a polynomial in the length of the input. The algorithm itself may be probabilistic. Otherwise (i.e., if the expected running time is not bounded by a polynomial), the algorithm requires super-polynomial (e.g., exponential) time and is said to be inefficient. This notion of efficiency (and the distinction between polynomial and super-polynomial running time algorithms) is fairly broad. It is, however, the best we have at hand to work with.

   An everyday example of a one-way function is a telephone book. Using such a book, the function that assigns a telephone number to a name is easy to compute (because the names are sorted alphabetically) but hard to invert (because the telephone numbers are not sorted numerically). Furthermore, many physical processes are inherently one way. If, for example, we smash a bottle into pieces, it is generally infeasible (or at least prohibitively difficult) to put the pieces together and reconstruct the bottle. Similarly, if we drop a bottle from a bridge, it falls down.

The reverse process does not frequently occur in the real world. Last but not least, life is one way, and it is (currently) not known how to travel back in time.

In contrast to the real world, the idealized world of mathematics is less rich with one-way functions. In fact, there are only a couple of functions conjectured to be one way. As overviewed and discussed in Section 7.2, examples include the discrete exponentiation function, the modular power function, and the modular square function. But note that none of these functions has been shown to be one way and that it is theoretically not even known whether one-way functions really exist. These facts should be kept in mind when one discusses the usefulness and actual use of one-way functions in cryptography.

There is a class of one-way functions that can be inverted efficiently if and—as it is hoped—only if some extra information is known. This brings us to the notion of a *trapdoor (one-way) function* as suggested in Definition 2.2.

Definition 2.2 (Trapdoor function) *A one-way function $f : X \to Y$ is a* trapdoor function *(or a* trapdoor one-way function, *respectively) if there exists some extra information (i.e., the* trapdoor*) with which f can be inverted efficiently (i.e., $f^{-1}(y)$ can be computed efficiently for $y \in_R Y$).*

The mechanical analog of a trapdoor (one-way) function is a padlock. It can be closed by everybody (if it is in an unlocked state), but it can be opened only by somebody who holds or has access to the proper key. In this analogy, a padlock without a keyhole would represent a one-way function (without trapdoor). This may not be a very useful construct in the real world.

One-way functions and trapdoor functions are frequently used in public key cryptography. In fact, they yield all kinds of asymmetric encryption systems, DSSs, and key agreement protocols. They are further addressed in Chapter 7. We then also explain why one has to consider families of such functions to be mathematically correct (so a one-way or trapdoor function actually refers to a family of such functions).

2.1.2 Cryptographic Hash Functions

Hash functions are frequently used and have many applications in computer science. Informally speaking, a hash function is an efficiently computable function that takes an arbitrarily sized input (string) and generates an output (string) of fixed size. This idea is captured in Defintion 2.3.

Definition 2.3 (Hash function) *Let Σ_{in} be an input alphabet and Σ_{out} be an output alphabet. Any function $h : \Sigma_{in}^* \to \Sigma_{out}^n$ that can be computed efficiently is said to be a* hash function. *It generates hash values of length n.*

In this definition, the domain of the hash function is Σ_{in}^*. This means that it consists of all strings over Σ. In theory, these strings can be infinitely long. In practice, however, one usually has to assume a maximum string length n_{max} for technical reasons. In this case, a hash function is formally expressed as

$$h : \Sigma_{in}^{n_{max}} \rightarrow \Sigma_{out}^n.$$

In either case, note that the hash function must be efficiently computable and that we further explain the notion of an "efficient computation" in the context of complexity theory in Chapter 6. Also, note that the two alphabets Σ_{in} and Σ_{out} can be (and typically are) the same. In this case, Σ is used to refer to either of them. In a typical (cryptographic) setting, Σ is the binary alphabet (i.e., $\Sigma = \{0, 1\}$) and n is 128 or 160 bits. In such a setting, a hash function h generates binary strings of 128 or 160 bits.

```
This is a file that includes some important but long statements.
Consequently, we may need a short representation of this file.
```

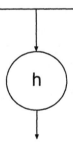

E4 23 AB 7D 17 67 D1 3E F6 EA EA 69 80

Figure 2.2   A cryptographic hash function.

In cryptography, we are mainly interested in hash functions with specific properties. Some of these properties (i.e., preimage resistance, second-preimage resistance, and collision resistance) are formally introduced and discussed in Chapter 8. A *one-way hash function* is then a hash function that is preimage resistant and second-preimage resistant (or weak collision resistant), whereas a *collision resistant hash function* is a hash function that is preimage resistant and collision resistant (or strong collision resistant). As suggested in Definition 2.4, either of these functions is called *cryptographic* and can be used for cryptographic purposes (e.g., for data integrity protection, message authentication, and digital signatures).

Definition 2.4 (Cryptographic hash function) *A hash function* $h : \Sigma_{in}^* \rightarrow \Sigma_{out}^n$ *is* cryptographic *if it is one way or collision resistant.*

Most of the time, a cryptographic hash function h is used to hash arbitrarily sized messages to binary strings of fixed size. This is illustrated in Figure 2.2, where the ASCII-encoded message "This is a file that includes some important but long statements. Consequently, we may need a short representation of this file." is hashed to 0xE423AB7D1767D13EF6EAEA6980 (in hexadecimal notation). The resulting hash value represents a *fingerprint* or *digest* that is characteristic for the message and uniquely identifies it. The collision resistance property implies that it is difficult—or computationally infeasible—to find another message that hashes to the same fingerprint.

Examples of cryptographic hash functions in widespread use today are MD5 (as used in Figure 2.2) and SHA-1. Cryptographic hash functions and their underlying design principles are further addressed in Chapter 8.

2.1.3 Random Bit Generators

Randomness is one of the most fundamental ingredients of and prerequisites for the security of a cryptographic system. In fact, the generation of secret and unpredictable random quantities (i.e., random bits or random numbers) is at the heart of most practically relevant cryptographic systems. The frequency and volume of these quantities vary from system to system. If, for example, we consider secret key cryptography, then we must have random quantities that can be used as secret keys. In the most extreme case, we must have a random bit for every bit that we want to encrypt in a perfectly secure way (see Section 10.4). If we consider public key cryptography, then we must have random quantities to generate public key pairs. In either case, a cryptographic system may be probabilistic, meaning that random quantities must be generated for every use of the system. The required quantities must then be random in the sense that the probability of any particular value being selected must be sufficiently small to preclude an adversary from gaining advantage through optimizing a search strategy based on such probability. This is where the notion of a *random bit generator* as introduced in Definition 2.5 and illustrated in Figure 2.3 comes into play.

Definition 2.5 (Random bit generator) *A* random bit generator *is a device or algorithm that outputs a sequence of statistically independent and unbiased bits.*

Alternatively, a random bit generator is sometimes also defined as an idealized model of a device that generates and outputs a sequence of statistically independent and unbiased bits. In either case, it is important to note that a random bit generator

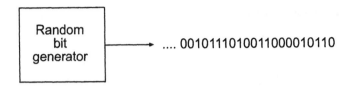

Figure 2.3 A random bit generator.

has no input (i.e., it only generates an output), and that because the output of the random bit generator is a sequence of statistically independent and unbiased bits, the bits occur with the same probability (i.e., $\Pr[0] = \Pr[1] = 1/2$), or—more generally—all 2^k different k-tuples occur approximately equally often for all $k \in \mathbb{N}^+$. There are many statistical tests that can be used to verify the (randomness) properties of a given random bit generator.

There is no known deterministic (i.e., computational) realization or implementation of a random bit generator. There are, however, many nondeterministic realizations and implementations. Many of these realizations and implementations make use of physical events and phenomena. In fact, it is fair to say that a (true) random bit generator requires a naturally occuring source of randomness.[2] Designing and implementing a device or algorithm that exploits this source of randomness to generate binary sequences that are free of biases and correlations is a challenging and highly demanding (engineering) task. As further addressed in Chapter 9, there are solutions for this task. To be useful for cryptographic applications, the resulting random bit generators must also be resistant to various types of passive and active attacks.

2.2 SECRET KEY CRYPTOSYSTEMS

According to Definition 1.6, secret key cryptosystems use secret parameters that are shared between the participating entities. Examples include symmetric encryption systems, MACs, PRBGs, and PRFs. Again, let us have a preliminary look at these systems.

---

2 See, for example, the leading quote of John von Neumann in Chapter 12.

2.2.1 Symmetric Encryption Systems

When one talks about cryptography, one is often referring to confidentiality protection using symmetric encryption systems (to encrypt and decrypt data). *Encryption* is the process that turns a *plaintext message* into a *ciphertext*, and *decryption* is the reverse process (i.e., the process that turns a ciphertext into a plaintext message).

As suggested in Definition 2.6, a *symmetric encryption system* consists of a set of possible plaintext messages (i.e., the plaintext message space), a set of possible ciphertexts (i.e., the ciphertext space), a set of possible keys (i.e., the key space), as well as two families of encryption and decryption functions (or algorithms) that are inverse to each other.

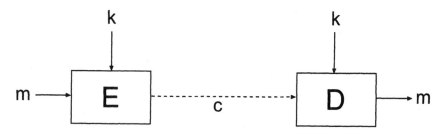

Figure 2.4 The working principle of a symmetric encryption system.

Definition 2.6 (Symmetric encryption system) *A symmetric encryption system or cipher consists of the following five components:*

- *A plaintext message space $\mathcal{M}$;*[3]
- *A ciphertext space $\mathcal{C}$;*
- *A key space $\mathcal{K}$;*
- *A family $E = \{E_k : k \in \mathcal{K}\}$ of encryption functions $E_k : \mathcal{M} \to \mathcal{C}$;*
- *A family $D = \{D_k : k \in \mathcal{K}\}$ of decryption functions $D_k : \mathcal{C} \to \mathcal{M}$.*

For every key $k \in \mathcal{K}$ and every message $m \in \mathcal{M}$, the functions D_k and E_k must be inverse to each other (i.e., $D_k(E_k(m)) = E_k(D_k(m)) = m$).

---

3   In some literature, the plaintext message space is denoted by $\mathcal{P}$. In this book, however, we conventionally use the letter "P" to refer to a probability distribution.

In either case, the encryption functions may be probabilistic in the sense that they also take into account some random input data (not expressed in Definition 2.6). Typically, $\mathcal{M} = \mathcal{C} = \{0,1\}^*$ (i.e., the set of binary strings of arbitrary but finite length), and $\mathcal{K} = \{0,1\}^l$ for some fixed key length l (e.g., $l = 128$). The notion of a function family (or family of functions, respectively) is formally introduced in Section 3.1.1. In the meantime, it is sufficient to have an intuitive understanding for the term.

The working principle of a symmetric encryption system is illustrated in Figure 2.4. On the left side, the sender encrypts the message $m \in \mathcal{M}$ with his or her implementation of the encryption function E (parametrized with the secret key k). The resulting ciphertext $E_k(m) = c \in \mathcal{C}$ is sent to the recipient over a potentially unsecure channel (drawn as a dotted line in Figure 2.4). On the right side, the recipient decrypts c with his or her implementation of the decryption function D (again, parametrized with the secret key k). If the decryption is successful, then the recipient is able to recover the plaintext message m.

Many examples of symmetric encryption systems are described in the literature. Some of these systems are relevant and used in practice, whereas others are not (i.e., they are only theoretically or historically relevant, or they are used only in small and typically closed communities). In Chapter 10, we overview and discuss two symmetric encryption systems that are in widespread use today: the DES and the *advanced encryption standard* (AES). We use them as examples and note that many other symmetric encryption systems can be used instead. Unfortunately, all practically relevant symmetric encryption systems are only conditionally or computationally secure. We also elaborate on symmetric encryption systems that are unconditionally or information-theoretically secure. These systems, however, are not used in practice, because most of them require keys that are at least as long as the plaintext messages that are encrypted. The key management of such a system is prohibitively expensive for practical use.

2.2.2   Message Authentication Codes

It is not always necessary to encrypt messages and to protect their confidentiality. Sometimes, it is sufficient to protect their authenticity and integrity, meaning that it must be possible for the recipient of a message to verify its authenticity and integrity (note that authenticity and integrity properties always go together when one considers messages). In this case, one can add an *authentication tag* to a message and have the recipient verify the tag before he or she accepts the message as being genuine. A message and a tag computed from it are illustrated in Figure 2.5.

One possibility to compute and verify an authentication tag is to use public key cryptography in general, and a DSS in particular (as explained later in this book).

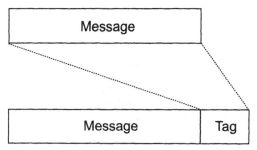

Figure 2.5 A message and a tag computed from it.

This is, however, neither always necessary nor always desired, and sometimes one wishes to use more lightweight mechanisms based on secret key cryptography. This is where the notion of a MAC as suggested in Definition 2.7 comes into play.[4]

Definition 2.7 (Message authentication code) *A MAC is an authentication tag that can be computed and verified with a secret parameter (e.g., a secret crypto-graphic key).*

In the case of a message that is sent from one sender to a single recipient, the secret parameter must be shared between the two entities. If, however, a message is sent to multiple recipients, then the secret parameter must be shared between the sender and all receiving entities. In this case, the distribution and management of the secret parameter is a major issue (and probably the Achilles' heel of the entire encryption system).

Similar to a symmetric encryption system, one can introduce and formally define a system to compute and verify MACs. In this book, we use the term *message authentication system* to refer to such a system (contrary to most other terms used in this book, this term is not widely used in the literature). As captured in Definition 2.8, a message authentication system consists of a set of possible messages (i.e., the message space), a set of possible authentication tags (i.e., the tag space), a set of possible keys (i.e., the key space), as well as two families of related message authentication and verification functions.

Definition 2.8 (Message authentication system) *A message authentication system consists of the following five components:*

- *A message space $\mathcal{M}$;*

---

4   In some literature, the term *message integrity code* (MIC) is used synonymously and interchangeably with MAC. However, this term is not used in this book.

- *A* tag space $\mathcal{T}$;

- *A* key space $\mathcal{K}$;

- *A family* $A = \{A_k : k \in \mathcal{K}\}$ *of* authentication functions $A_k : \mathcal{M} \to \mathcal{T}$;

- *A family* $V = \{V_k : K \in \mathcal{K}\}$ *of* verification functions $V_k : \mathcal{M} \times \mathcal{T} \to \{valid, invalid\}$. $V_k(m, t)$ *must yield valid if t is a valid authentication tag for message m and key k (i.e., $t = A_k(m)$).*

For every key $k \in \mathcal{K}$ and every message $m \in \mathcal{M}$, $V_K(m, A_K(m))$ must yield valid.

Typically, $\mathcal{M} = \{0,1\}^*$, $\mathcal{T} = \{0,1\}^{l_{tag}}$ for some fixed tag length l_{tag}, and $\mathcal{K} = \{0,1\}^{l_{key}}$ for some fixed key length l_{key} (e.g., $l_{tag} = l_{key} = 128$).

Many message authentication systems have been developed and proposed in the literature. Some of these systems are unconditionally (i.e., information-theoretically) secure, but most of them are conditionally (i.e., computationally) secure. The most important message authentication systems are overviewed, discussed, and put into perspective in Chapter 11.

2.2.3   PRBGs

In Section 2.1.3 we mentioned that random bit generators are important building blocks for many cryptographic systems, and that there is no deterministic (computational) realization or implementation of such a generator, but that there are non-deterministic realizations and implementations making use of physical events and phenomena. Unfortunately, these realizations and implementations are not always appropriate, and there are situations in which one needs to deterministically generate binary sequences that appear to be random (e.g., if one needs a random bit generator but none is available, or if one must make statistical simulations or experiments that can be repeated as needed). Also, one may have a short random bit sequence that must be stretched into a long sequence. This is where the notion of a PRBG as illustrated in Figure 2.6 and introduced in Definition 2.9 comes into play.[5] Again, the definition is not precise in a mathematically strong sense, because we have neither defined the notion of an efficient algorithm nor have we specified what we really mean by saying that a binary sequence "appears to be random."

Definition 2.9 (Pseudorandom bit generator) *A PRBG is an efficient deterministic algorithm that takes as input a random binary sequence of length k (i.e., the seed) and generates as output another binary sequence (i.e., the pseudorandom bit sequence) of length $l \gg k$ that appears to be random.*

5   Note the subtle difference between Figures 2.3 and 2.5. Both generators output a binary sequence. The random bit generator has no input, whereas the PRBG has a seed that serves as input.

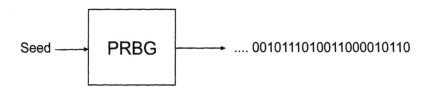

Figure 2.6 A PRBG.

Note that the pseudorandom bit sequence a PRBG outputs may be of infinite length (i.e., $l = \infty$). Also note that in contrast to a random bit generator, a PRBG represents a deterministic algorithm (i.e., an algorithm that can be implemented in a deterministic way). This suggests that a PRBG is implemented as a finite state machine and that the sequence of generated bits must be cyclic (with a potentially very large cycle). This is why we cannot require that the bits in a pseudorandom sequence are truly random, we can only require that they appear to be so (for a computationally bounded adversary). Again, many statistical tests can be used to verify the randomness properties of a binary sequence. Note, however, that passing all of these tests is a necessary but usually not sufficient condition for a binary sequence to be securely used for cryptographic applications.

PRBGs have many applications in cryptography. Examples include additive stream ciphers, as well as cryptographic key generation and expansion. In fact, the title of [1] suggests that the notion of pseudorandomness and (modern) cryptography are closely related and deeply intertwined. The notion of a PRBG and some possible constructions for cryptographically secure PRBGs are further addressed in Chapter 12.

2.2.4 PRFs

Contrary to PRBGs, PRFs do not generate an output that meets specific (randomness) requirements. Instead, PRFs try to model the input-output behavior of a random function (i.e., a function $f : X \rightarrow Y$ that is randomly chosen from the set of all mappings from domain X to range Y). Random functions are also known as random oracles. For input value $x \in X$, a PRF computes an arbitrary output value $y = f(x) \in f(X) \subseteq Y$. The only requirement is that the same input value x must always be mapped to the same output value y. PRBGs and (families of) PRFs are closely related to each other in the sense that a PRF family can be used to construct a PRBG, and a PRBG can be used to construct a PRF family (the corresponding constructions are given in Section 13.2).

Because the notion and use of PRFs is a more advanced topic, we don't provide an informal definition at this point. Instead, we refer to Chapter 13, where we introduce, discuss, and put into perspective random functions, PRFs, and some applications of PRFs in modern cryptography.

2.3 PUBLIC KEY CRYPTOSYSTEMS

According to Definition 1.7, public key cryptosystems use secret parameters that are not shared between the participating entities. Instead, each entity holds a set of secret parameters (collectively referred to as the *private key*) and publishes another set of parameters (collectively referred to as the *public key*) that don't have to be secret and can be published at will.[6] A necessary (but usually not sufficient) condition for a public key cryptosystem to be secure is that it is computationally infeasible to compute the private key from the public key. In this book, k is frequently used to refer to a public key, whereas k^{-1} is used to refer to the corresponding private key. Because public key cryptography is computationally less efficient than secret key cryptography, public key cryptosystems are mainly used for authentication and key management. The resulting cryptosystems combine secret and public key cryptography and are often called *hybrid*. In fact, hybrid cryptosystems are very frequently used in practice.

Note that the fact that public key cryptosystems use secret parameters that are not shared between the participating entities implies that the corresponding algorithms must be executed by different entities. Consequently, such cryptosystems are typically defined as sets of algorithms (that may be executed by different entities). We adopt this viewpoint in this book. Examples of public key cryptosystems include asymmetric encryption systems and DSSs, as well as cryptographic protocols for key agreement, entity authentication, and secure multiparty computation. We have a preliminary look at these examples.

2.3.1 Asymmetric Encryption Systems

Similar to a symmetric encryption system, an asymmetric encryption system can be used to encrypt and decrypt (plaintext) messages. The major difference between a symmetric and an asymmetric encryption system is that the former employs secret

---

6   It depends on the cryptosystem, whether it matters which set of parameters is used to represent the private key and which set of parameters is used to represent the public key.

key cryptography and corresponding techniques, whereas the latter employs public key cryptography and corresponding techniques.

As already mentioned in Section 2.1.1, an asymmetric encryption system requires a family of trapdoor functions. Each public key pair yields a public key that represents a one-way function and a private key that represents the inverse of this function. To send a secret message to a recipient, the sender must look up the recipient's public key, apply the corresponding one-way function to the message, and send the resulting ciphertext to the recipient. The recipient, in turn, is the only person who is supposed to know the trapdoor (information) necessary to invert the one-way function. Consequently, he or she is the only person who is able to properly decrypt the ciphertext and to recover the original (plaintext) message accordingly.

In the literature, the encryption (decryption) algorithm is often denoted as E (D), and subscripts are used to refer to the entities that hold the appropriate keys. For example, E_A refers to the encryption algorithm fed with the public key of A, whereas D_A refers to the decryption algorithm fed with the private key of A. Consequently, it is implicitly assumed that the public key is used for encryption and the private key is used for decryption. If the use of the keys is not clear, then the keys in use may be subscript to E and D. In this case, for example, E_{k_A} refers to the encryption algorithm fed with A's public key, whereas $D_{k_A^{-1}}$ refers to the decryption algorithm fed with A's private key.

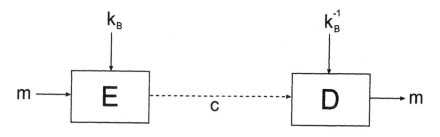

Figure 2.7   The working principle of an asymmetric encryption system.

The working principle of an asymmetric encryption system is illustrated in Figure 2.7. On the left side, the sender applies the recipient B's one-way function (implemented by the encryption algorithm E parametrized with B's public key k_B) to the plaintext message m, and sends the resulting ciphertext

$$c = E_B(m) = E_{k_B}(m)$$

to B. On the right side, B knows his or her private key k_B^{-1} (representing the trapdoor information) and can use this key to invert the one-way function and decrypt

$$m = D_B(c) = D_{k_B^{-1}}(c).$$

An asymmetric encryption system is a public key cryptosystem. As such, it can be specified by a set of three algorithms. This is done in Definition 2.10 and illustrated in Figure 2.8.

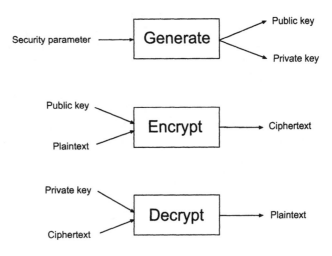

Figure 2.8   The three algorithms of an asymmetric encryption system.

Definition 2.10 (Asymmetric encryption system) *An* asymmetric encryption system *consists of the following three efficiently computable algorithms:*

- Generate(1^n) *is a probabilistic key generation algorithm that takes as input a security parameter 1^n and generates as output a public key pair (consisting of a public key k and a corresponding private key k^{-1}).*[7]

---

7   In most literature, the security parameter is denoted by 1^k (i.e., k written in unary representation). Because this notation may provide some confusion between k standing for the security parameter and k standing for the public key, we don't use it in this book. Instead, we use 1^n to refer to the security parameter.

- Encrypt(k, m) *is a deterministic or probabilistic encryption algorithm that takes as input a public key k and a plaintext message m, and that generates as output a ciphertext c (i.e., $c =$ Encrypt(k, m)).*

- Decrypt(k^{-1}, c) *is a deterministic decryption algorithm that takes as input a private key k^{-1} and a ciphertext c, and that generates as output a plaintext message m (i.e., $m =$ Decrypt(k^{-1}, c)).*

For every public key pair (k, k^{-1}) and every plaintext message m, the algorithms Encrypt$(k, \cdot)$ *and* Decrypt$(k^{-1}, \cdot)$ *must be inverse to each other, meaning that*

$$\text{Decrypt}(k^{-1}, \text{Encrypt}(k, m)) = m.$$

If k and k^{-1} do not correspond to each other, then the ciphertext must decrypt to gibberish.

In summary, an asymmetric encryption system can be fully specified by a triple that consists of the algorithms Generate, Encrypt, and Decrypt. Many such systems have been developed, proposed, and published in the literature. The most important and widely deployed examples are overviewed, discussed, and put into perspective in Chapter 14.

2.3.2 DSSs

Digital signatures can be used to protect the authenticity and integrity of data objects. According to RFC 2828, a *digital signature* refers to "a value computed with a cryptographic algorithm and appended to a data object in such a way that any recipient of the data can use the signature to verify the data's origin and integrity" [2]. Similarly, the term digital signature is defined as "data appended to, or a cryptographic transformation of, a data unit that allows a recipient of the data unit to prove the source and integrity of the data unit and protect against forgery, e.g. by the recipient" in ISO/IEC 7498-2 [3].

According to the last definition, there are two classes of digital signatures that should be distinguished.

- If data representing the digital signature is appended to a data unit (or message) then one refers to a *digital signature with appendix*.

- If a data unit is cryptographically transformed in a way that it represents both the data unit (or message) that is signed and the digital signature, then one refers to a *digital signature with message recovery*. In this case, the data unit is recovered when the signature is verified.

Digital signatures with appendix are, for example, specified in ISO/IEC 14888, whereas digital signatures with message recovery are specified in ISO/IEC 9796. Both ISO/IEC standards consist of multiple parts. They are not further addressed in this book.

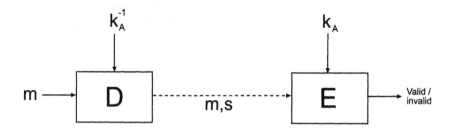

Figure 2.9   The working principle of a DSS.

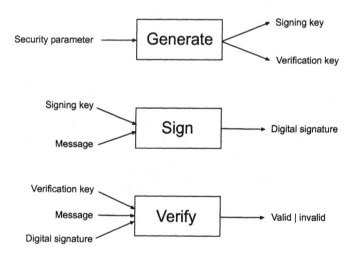

Figure 2.10   The three algorithms of a DSS with appendix.

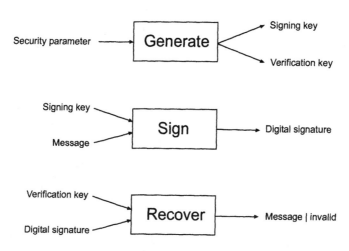

Figure 2.11   The three algorithms of a DSS with message recovery.

A DSS can be used to digitally sign messages and verify digital signatures accordingly.[8] A *DSS with appendix* is used to generate and verify digital signatures with appendix, whereas a *DSS with message recovery* is used to generate and verify digital signatures giving message recovery. Note that any DSS with message recovery can be turned into a DSS with appendix by hashing the message and then signing the hash value.

In either case, the entity that digitally signs data units or messages is sometimes called *signer* or *signatory*, whereas the entity that verifies the digital signatures is called *verifier*. In a typical setting, both the signatory and the verifier are computing devices that are operated on behalf of human users.

The working principle of a DSS (with appendix or message recovery) is illustrated in Figure 2.9. Having in mind the notion of a trapdoor function, it is simple and straightforward to explain what is going on. On the left side, the signatory A uses its private key k_A^{-1} to invert the one-way function for message m and to compute the digital signature s as follows:

$$s = D_A(m) = D_{k_A^{-1}}(m)$$

The signatory sends s to the verifier (if the digital signature is with appendix, then m must also be sent along with s). On the right side, the verifier must use the

---

8   In the literature, a DSS is often called *digital signature scheme* (with the same abbreviation).

signatory's public key (i.e., k_A) to compute the one-way function for s and to either verify the digital signature (if the DSS is with appendix) or recover the original message (if the DSS is giving message recovery). In either case, it is important to note that only A can compute s (because only A is assumed to know k_A^{-1}), whereas everybody can verify s or recover m (because everybody has access to k_A). In fact, public verifiability is a basic property of digital signatures and corresponding DSSs.

Similar to an asymmetric encryption system, a DSS can be defined as a set of three efficiently computable algorithms. A DSS with appendix is defined in Definition 2.11, and its three algorithms are illustrated in Figure 2.10.

Definition 2.11 (DSS with appendix) *A DSS with appendix consists of the following three efficiently computable algorithms:*

- Generate(1^n) *is a probabilistic key generation algorithm that takes as input a security parameter 1^n and generates as output a signing key k^{-1} and a corresponding verification key k. Both keys represent the public key pair (k, k^{-1}).*

- Sign(k^{-1}, m) *is a deterministic or probabilistic signature generation algorithm that takes as input a signing key k^{-1} and a message m (i.e., the message to be signed), and that generates as output a digital signature s for m.[9]*

- Verify(k, m, s) *is a deterministic signature verification algorithm that takes as input a verification key k, a message m, and a purported digital signature s for m, and that generates as output a binary decision (i.e., whether the digital signature is valid). In fact, Verify(k, m, s) must yield valid if and only if s is a valid digital signature for message m and verification key k.*

So for every public key pair (k, k^{-1}) and every possible message m,

$$\text{Verify}(k, m, \text{Sign}(k^{-1}, m))$$

must yield valid.

Similarly, a DSS giving message recovery is defined in Definition 2.12, and its three algorithms are illustrated in Figure 2.11.

Definition 2.12 (DSS with message recovery) *A DSS giving message recovery consists of the following three efficiently computable algorithms:*

9   Optionally, the signing algorithm may also output a new (i.e., updated) signing key. Note, however, that in a memoryless DSS, the signing key always remains the same. Consequently, this optional output is not illustrated in Figure 2.10.

- Generate(1^n) *is a probabilistic key generation algorithm that takes as input a security parameter 1^n and generates as output a signing key k^{-1} and a verification key k. Again, both keys represent the public key pair (k, k^{-1}).*

- Sign(k^{-1}, m) *is a deterministic or probabilistic signature generation algorithm that takes as input a signing key k^{-1} and a message m, and that generates as output a digital signature s giving message recovery.*

- Recover(k, s) *is a deterministic message recovery algorithm that takes as input a verification key k and a digital signature s, and that generates as output either the message that is digitally signed or a notification indicating that the digital signature is invalid. This means that* Recover(k, s) *must yield m if and only if s is a valid digital signature for message m and verification key k.*

So for every public key pair (k, k^{-1}) and every possible message m,

$$\text{Recover}(k, \text{Sign}(k^{-1}, m))$$

must yield m.

Note that the Generate algorithms are basically the same for both a DSS with appendix and a DSS giving message recovery, and that the Sign algorithms are at least structurally the same. The major difference is with the Verify and Recover algorithms.

With the proliferation of the Internet in general, and Internet-based electronic commerce in particular, digital signatures and the legislation thereof have become important and very timely topics. In fact, many DSSs with specific and unique properties have been developed, proposed, and published in the literature. The most important examples are overviewed, discussed, and put into perspective in Chapter 15. Unfortunately, digital signatures (and their mathematical properties) are sometimes also overrated as proofs or pieces of evidence.

2.3.3 Key Agreement

If two or more entities want to employ and make use of secret key cryptography, then they must share a secret parameter or cryptographic key. Consequently, in a large system many secret keys must typically be generated, stored, managed, and destroyed in a highly secure way. If, for example, n entities want to securely communicate with each other, then there are

$$\binom{n}{2} = \frac{n(n-1)}{1 \cdot 2} = \frac{n^2 - n}{2}$$

secret keys that must be generated, stored, managed, and destroyed. This number grows in the order of n^2, and hence the establishment of secret keys is a major practical problem (and probably the Achilles' heel) for the large-scale deployment of secret key cryptography. For example, if $n = 1,000$ entities want to securely communicate with each other, then there are

$$\binom{1,000}{2} = \frac{1,000^2 - 1,000}{2} = 499,500$$

secret keys. Even for moderately large n, the generation, storage, and management of so many keys is prohibitively expensive, and the predistribution of the keys is infeasible.

Things get even more involved when one considers that keys are often used in dynamic environments, where new entities join and other entities leave at will, and that it is usually impossible, impractical, or simply too expensive to transmit keys over secure channels (e.g., by a trusted courier). Consequently, one typically faces a key establishment problem in computer networks and distributed systems. There are basically two approaches to address (and hopefully solve) the key establishment problem in computer networks and distributed systems:

- The use of a key distribution center (KDC);
- The use of a key establishment protocol.

A prominent and widely deployed example of a KDC is the Kerberos authentication and key distribution system (see, for example, [4]). Unfortunately, KDCs have many disadvantages. The most important disadvantage is that each entity must unconditionally trust the KDC and share a secret master key with it. There are situations in which this level of trust is neither justified nor can be accepted by the communicating entities. Consequently, the use of key establishment protocols (that typically make use of public key cryptography in some way or another) provides a viable alternative in many situations.

In a simple key establishment protocol, an entity randomly generates a key and uses a secure channel to transmit it to the communicating peer entity (or entities). This protocol is simple and straightforward; it is basically what a Web browser does when it establishes a cryptographic key to be shared with a secure Web server.[10] From a security point of view, however, one may face the problem that the security of the secret key cryptographic system that is used with the cryptographic key is then bound by the quality and the security of the key generation process (which is typically a PRBG). Consequently, it is advantageous to have a mechanism in place in which two or more entities can establish and agree on a commonly shared secret key. This is where the notion of a key agreement protocol comes into play (as opposed to a key distribution protocol). The single most important key agreement protocol for two entities was suggested by Diffie and Hellman [6]. Key establishment protocols (including, for example, the Diffie-Hellman key agreement protocol) are further addressed in Chapter 16. They play a central role in many cryptographic security protocols for the Internet.

2.3.4 Entity Authentication

In computer networks and distributed systems it is often required that entities must authenticate each other. In theory, many technologies can be used for entity authentication. In computer networks and distributed systems, however, entity authentication is most often implemented as a proof by knowledge. This means that the entity that is authenticated knows something (e.g., a password, a passphrase, or a cryptographic key) that allows him or her to prove his or her identity to another entity. An entity authentication protocol is used for this purpose. More often than not, an entity authentication protocol is combined with a key distribution protocol (yielding an entity authentication and key distribution protocol).

In Chapter 17, we elaborate on entity authentication and corresponding protocols. Among these protocols, we mainly focus on the ones that have the zero-knowledge property. Zero-knowledge authentication protocols are interesting, because it can be shown in a mathematically precise sense that they do not leak any (partial) information about the secret that is used in the proof by knowledge. This protects the prover against a verifier trying to illegitimately derive information about the prover's secret.

2.3.5 Secure Multiparty Computation

Let us assume that multiple entities want to compute the result of a function evaluation without having to reveal their (local) input values to each other. There are basically two cases to distinguish:

---

10 A *secure Web server* is a server that implements the secure sockets layer (SSL) or transport layer security (TLS) protocol (see, for example, Chapter 6 of [5]).

- If the entities have a trusted party at their disposal, then there is a trivial solution for the problem: all entities securely transmit their input values to the trusted party, and the trusted party, in turn, evaluates the function and provides the result to all entities (it goes without saying that all communications must take place over secure channels).

- If, however, the entities have no trusted party at their disposal, then the situation is more involved. In this case, it is not at all obvious that the problem can be solved at all.

In the second case, we are in the realm of secure multiparty computation. We ask for cryptographic protocols that can be used by the entities to evaluate a function and to effectively simulate a trusted party. Such protocols can be found and have many (potential) applications, such as electronic voting and mental game playing (i.e., playing a game over a communication network). In Chapter 18, we briefly touch on secure multiparty computation and the major results that have been found in theory.

2.4 FINAL REMARKS

In this chapter, we briefly introduced and provided some preliminary definitions for the most important representatives of the three major classes of cryptosystems distinguished in this book (i.e., unkeyed cryptosystems, secret key cryptosystems, and public key cryptosystems). We want to note (again) that this classification scheme is somewhat arbitrary, and that other classification schemes may be used instead.

In either case, the cryptosystems that are preliminarily defined in this chapter are refined, more precisely defined (in a mathematical sense), discussed, and put into perspective in the later parts of the book. For all of these systems, we also elaborate on the notion of security and try to find appropriate definitions and evaluation criteria for secure systems. In fact, a major theme in contemporary cryptography is to better understand and formally express the notion of security, and to prove that a particular cryptosystem is secure in exactly this sense. In many cases, the cryptographic community has been surprisingly successful in doing so. This is what the rest of this book is basically all about. We have to begin with some mathematical fundamentals first.

References

[1]   Luby, M., *Pseudorandomness and Cryptographic Applications*. Princeton Computer Science Notes, Princeton, NJ, 1996.

[2] Shirey, R., *Internet Security Glossary*, Request for Comments 2828, May 2000.

[3] ISO/IEC 7498-2, *Information Processing Systems—Open Systems Interconnection Reference Model—Part 2: Security Architecture*, 1989.

[4] Oppliger, R., *Authentication Systems for Secure Networks*. Artech House Publishers, Norwood, MA, 1996.

[5] Oppliger, R., *Security Technologies for the World Wide Web*, 2nd edition. Artech House Publishers, Norwood, MA, 2003.

[6] Diffie, W., and M.E. Hellman, "New Directions in Cryptography," *IEEE Transactions on Information Theory*, IT-22(6), 1976, pp. 644–654.

Part I

MATHEMATICAL FUNDAMENTALS

Chapter 3

Discrete Mathematics

In this chapter, we begin the part on the mathematical fundamentals by discussing the aspects of discrete mathematics that are relevant for contemporary cryptography. More specifically, we introduce algebraic basics in Section 3.1, elaborate on integer and modular arithmetic in Sections 3.2 and 3.3, introduce elliptic curves in Section 3.4, and conclude with some final remarks in Section 3.5. Note that this chapter is intentionally kept short, and that many facts are stated without a proof. There are many (introductory) books on discrete mathematics and algebra that contain the missing proofs, put the facts into perspective, and provide much more background information (e.g., [1–5]). Most importantly, Victor Shoup's book about number theory and algebra [6] is electronically available[1] and is recommended reading for anybody interested in discrete mathematics.

3.1 ALGEBRAIC BASICS

The term *algebra* refers to the mathematical field of study that deals with sets of elements (e.g., sets of numbers) and operations on these elements.[2] The operations must satisfy specific rules (called *axioms*). These axioms are defined abstractly, but most of them are motivated by existing mathematical structures (e.g., the set of integers with the addition and multiplication operations).

---

1   http://www.shoup.net/ntb.
2   For the purpose of this book, we assume familiarity with set theory at a basic level.

3.1.1 Preliminary Remarks

Let S be a nonempty set and $*$ be a binary operation on the elements of this set.[3] For example, S may be one of the following sets of numbers (that are frequently used in mathematics):

- The set $\mathbb{N} := \{0, 1, 2, \ldots\}$ of *natural numbers* (also known as *nonnegative* or *positive integers*). In some literature, the term $\mathbb{N}^+$ is used to refer to $\mathbb{N}$ without zero (i.e., $\mathbb{N}^+ := \mathbb{N} \setminus \{0\}$).

- The set $\mathbb{Z} := \{\ldots, -2, -1, 0, 1, 2, \ldots\}$ of *integer numbers*, or *integers* in short. In addition to the natural numbers, this set also comprises the negative numbers.

- The set $\mathbb{Q}$ of *rational numbers*. Roughly speaking, a rational number is a number that can be written as a ratio of two integers. More specifically, a number is rational if it can be written as a fraction where the numerator and denominator are integers and the denominator is not equal to zero. This can be expressed as follows:

$$\mathbb{Q} := \{\frac{a}{b} \mid a, b \in \mathbb{Z} \text{ and } b \neq 0\}$$

- The set $\mathbb{R}$ of *real numbers*. Each real number can be represented by a converging infinite sequence of rational numbers (i.e., the limit of the sequence refers to the real number). There are two subsets within the set of real numbers: algebraic numbers and transcendental numbers. Roughly speaking, an *algebraic number* is a real number that is the root of a polynomial equation with integer coefficients, whereas a *transcendental number* is a real number that is not the root of a polynomial equation with integer coefficients. Examples of transcendental numbers are π and e. Real numbers are the most general and most frequently used mathematical objects to model real-world phenomena. A real number that is not rational is called *irrational*, and hence the set of irrational numbers is $\mathbb{R} \setminus \mathbb{Q}$. In some literature, the term $\mathbb{R}^+$ is also used to refer to the real numbers that are nonnegative.

- The set $\mathbb{C}$ of *complex numbers*. Each complex number can be specified by a pair (a, b) of real numbers, and hence $\mathbb{C}$ can be expressed as follows:

$$\mathbb{C} := \{a + bi \mid a, b \in \mathbb{R} \text{ and } i = \sqrt{-1}\}$$

3   The choice of the symbol $*$ is arbitrary. The operations most frequently used in algebra are addition (denoted as $+$) and multiplication (denoted as $\cdot$).

The first element of (a, b) is called the *real part* of the complex number, whereas the second element of (a, b) is called the *imaginary part*. This part is usually written as a multiple of $i = \sqrt{-1}$, meaning that the imaginary part of $a + bi$ is written as b (instead of bi).

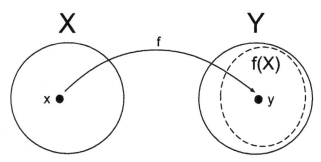

Figure 3.1 A function $f : X \to Y$.

In this book, we assume some familiarity with functions and function families. As illustrated in Figure 3.1, a *function* $f : X \to Y$ is a mapping from a *domain* X to a *codomain* Y assigning to every $x \in X$ a unique $f(x) \in Y$. The *range* of f is the subset of values of Y that are actually reached by the function (i.e., $f(X) \subseteq Y$). A function $f : X \to Y$ may be injective, surjective, or bijective.

- The function f is *injective* (or *one to one*) if for all $x_1, x_2 \in X$ it holds that $x_1 \neq x_2 \Rightarrow f(x_1) \neq f(x_2)$ (i.e., if two preimages are different, then the corresponding images are also different).

- The function f is *surjective* (or *onto*) if for all $y \in Y$ there is an $x \in X$ with $y = f(x)$, meaning that $f(X) = Y$ (i.e., the codomain and the range are the same).

- The function f is *bijective* if it is both injective and surjective.

If we consider a set of functions $f : X \to Y$ that takes a key as an additional input parameter, then we are talking about function families. Formally, a *function family* is a mapping

$$F : K \times X \to Y$$

where X and Y are the domain and codomain of the functions, and K is a set of possible keys. For every $k \in K$, the map $f_k : X \to Y$ is defined as $f_k(x) = f(k, x)$

and represents an instance of the family F. Consequently, F is a collection or ensemble of mappings. Every key $k \in K$ or map f_k occurs with some probability, and hence there is a probability distribution on K. If $K = \{0,1\}^n$ and all keys are uniformly distributed, then

$$k \xleftarrow{u} K$$

refers to an n-bit key k that is randomly chosen from K. Furthermore,

$$f \xleftarrow{u} F$$

refers to a function f_k that is randomly chosen from F. This can be translated into $k \xleftarrow{u} K; f \leftarrow f_k$ (in this sequence). In other words, f is the function f_k, where k is a randomly chosen key.

We sometimes use the term $Rand^{X \to Y}$ to refer to the family of all functions from the domain X to the codomain Y. If $X = Y$, then we are talking about the family of all permutations on X, and we use the term $Perm^{X \to X}$ or $P(X)$ to refer to it. Permutations and families of permutations are further addressed in Section 3.1.4.

The fact that $*$ is a binary operation on S means that it actually defines a function from $S \times S$ into S. If $a, b \in S$, then the use of $*$ can be expressed as follows:

$$\begin{aligned} * : S \times S &\longrightarrow S \\ (a, b) &\longmapsto a * b \end{aligned}$$

This expression suggests that two arbitrary elements $a, b \in S$ are mapped to a new element $a * b \in S$. In this setting, the operation $*$ may have specific properties. We are mainly interested in commutative and associative operations as formally expressed in Definitions 3.1 and 3.2.

Definition 3.1 (Commutative operation) *A binary operation $*$ is* commutative *if $a * b = b * a$ for all $a, b \in S$.*

Definition 3.2 (Associative operation) *A binary operation $*$ is* associative *if $a * (b * c) = (a * b) * c$ for all $a, b, c \in S$.*

A commutative operation $*$ may have (left and right) identity elements as formally introduced in Definitions 3.3–3.5.

Definition 3.3 (Left identity element) *Let S be a set and $*$ a binary operation on S. An element $e \in S$ is called* left identity element *if $e * a = a$ for all $a \in S$.*

Definition 3.4 (Right identity element) *Let S be a set and $*$ a binary operation on S. An element $e \in S$ is called* right identity element *if $a * e = a$ for all $a \in S$.*

Definition 3.5 (Identity element) *Let S be a set and $*$ a binary operation on S. An element $e \in S$ is called* identity element *(or neutral element) if it is both a left identity element and a right identity element (i.e., $e * a = a * e = a$ for all $a \in S$).*

Note that an identity element does not have to exist, but if it exists it must be unique. This can easily be shown by assuming that e_1 and e_2 are both identity elements. It then follows from the definition of an identity element that $e_1 = e_1 * e_2 = e_2$, and hence $e_1 = e_2$. Also note that we don't require the operation $*$ to be commutative. For example, the identity matrix is the identity element of the matrix multiplication, and this operation is not commutative.

If there exists an identity element $e \in S$ with respect to $*$, then some elements of S may also have inverse elements. This is captured in Definition 3.6.

Definition 3.6 (Inverse element) *Let S be a set, $*$ be a binary operation with an identity element e, and a be an element of S. If there exists an element $b \in S$ with $a * b = b * a = e$, then a is* invertible *and b is the* inverse element *(or inverse) of a.*

Note that not all elements in a given set must be invertible and have inverse elements with respect to the operation under consideration. As discussed below, the question whether all elements are invertible is the distinguishing feature between a group and a monoid or between a field and a ring, respectively.

3.1.2 Algebraic Structures

An *algebraic structure*[4] consists of a nonempty set S and one or more binary operations. For the sake of simplicity, we sometimes omit the operation(s) and use S to denote the entire structure. In this section, we overview and briefly discuss the algebraic structures that are most frequently used in algebra. Among these structures, groups, rings, and (finite) fields are particularly important for cryptography in general, and public key cryptography in particular.

3.1.2.1 Semigroups

The simplest algebraic structure is a semigroup as formally introduced in Definition 3.7.

---

4   In some literature, an algebraic structure is also called *algebra* or *algebraic system*.

Definition 3.7 (Semigroup) *A semigroup is an algebraic structure* $\langle S, * \rangle$ *that consists of a nonempty set S and an associative binary operation* $*$. *The semigroup must be closed (i.e., for all* $a, b \in S$, $a * b$ *must also be an element of S).*

Note that this definition does not require a semigroup to have an identity element. For example, the set of even integers (i.e., $\{\ldots, -4, -2, 0, 2, 4, \ldots\}$) with the multiplication operation is a semigroup without identity element.[5]

3.1.2.2   Monoids

As suggested in Definition 3.8, a monoid is a semigroup with the additional property (or requirement) that it must have an identity element.

Definition 3.8 (Monoid) *A monoid is a semigroup* $\langle S, * \rangle$ *that has an identity element* $e \in S$ *with respect to* $*$.

For example, $\langle \mathbb{N}, \cdot \rangle$, $\langle \mathbb{Z}, \cdot \rangle$, $\langle \mathbb{Q}, \cdot \rangle$, and $\langle \mathbb{R}, \cdot \rangle$ are monoids with the identity element 1. Also, the set of even integers with the addition operation and the identity element 0, as well as the set of all binary sequences of nonnegative and finite length with the string concatenation operation and the empty string representing the identity element, are monoids. If the empty string is excluded from the set in the second case, then the resulting algebraic structure is only a semigroup.

3.1.2.3   Groups

As suggested in Definition 3.9, a group is a monoid in which every element is invertible (and has an inverse element accordingly).

Definition 3.9 (Group) *A group is a monoid* $\langle S, * \rangle$ *in which every element* $a \in S$ *has an inverse element in S (i.e., every element* $a \in S$ *is invertible).*

Because $\langle S, * \rangle$ is a group and the operation $*$ is associative, one can easily show that the inverse element of an element must be unique (i.e., every element has exactly one inverse element). Assume that b and c are both inverse elements of a. It then follows that $b = b * e = b * (a * c) = (b * a) * c = e * c = c$, and hence the two inverse elements of a must be the same.

Considering everything said so far, a group can also be defined as an algebraic structure $\langle S, * \rangle$ that satisfies the following four axioms:

1. *Closure axiom:* $\forall\, a, b \in S : a * b \in S$;

---

5   The identity element with respect to multiplication would be 1 (which is not even).

2. *Associativity axiom:* $\forall a, b, c \in S : a * (b * c) = (a * b) * c$;

3. *Identity axiom:* $\exists$ a unique identity element $e \in S$ such that $\forall a \in S : a * e = e * a = a$;

4. *Inverse axiom:* $\forall a \in S : \exists$ a unique inverse element $a^{-1} \in S$ such that $a * a^{-1} = a^{-1} * a = e$.

The operations most frequently used in groups are addition $(+)$ and multiplication $(\cdot)$. Such groups are called *additive groups* and *multiplicative groups*. For multiplicative groups, the symbol $\cdot$ is often omitted, and $a \cdot b$ is written as ab. For additive and multiplicative groups, the identity elements are usually denoted as 0 and 1, whereas the inverse elements of element a are usually denoted as $-a$ and a^{-1}. Consequently, a multiplicative group is assumed in the fourth axiom given here.

Commutative Groups

A distinction is often made between commutative and noncommutative groups. The notion of a commutative group is formally introduced in Definition 3.10.

Definition 3.10 (Commutative group) *A group $\langle S, * \rangle$ is* commutative *if the operation $*$ is commutative (i.e., $a * b = b * a$ for all $a, b \in S$).*

In the literature, commutative groups are also called *Abelian* groups. If a group is not commutative, then it is called *noncommutative* or *non-Abelian*. For example, $\langle \mathbb{Z}, + \rangle$, $\langle \mathbb{Q}, + \rangle$, and $\langle \mathbb{R}, + \rangle$ are commutative groups with the identity element 0. The inverse element of a is $-a$. Similarly, $\langle \mathbb{Q} \setminus \{0\}, \cdot \rangle$ and $\langle \mathbb{R} \setminus \{0\}, \cdot \rangle$ are commutative groups with the identity element 1. In this case, the inverse element of a is a^{-1}. Furthermore, the set of real-valued $n \times n$ matrices is a commutative group with respect to matrix addition, whereas the subset of nonsingular (i.e., invertible) matrices is a noncommutative group with respect to matrix multiplication.

Finite Groups

Groups can be finite or infinite (depending on the number of elements). Finite groups as captured in Definition 3.11 play a fundamental role in (public key) cryptography.

Definition 3.11 (Finite group) *A group $\langle S, * \rangle$ is* finite *if it contains only finitely many elements.*

The order of a finite group $\langle S, * \rangle$ equals the cardinality of the set S (i.e., $|S|$). Hence, another way to define a finite group is to say that $\langle S, * \rangle$ is finite if $|S| < \infty$. For example, the set of permutations of n elements is finite and has $n!$ elements.

It is a noncommutative group with respect to the composition of permutations (see Section 3.1.4). More interestingly, $\langle \mathbb{Z}_n, + \rangle$ and $\langle \mathbb{Z}_n^*, \cdot \rangle$ are finite groups that have many cryptographic applications. As explained later in this chapter, $\mathbb{Z}_n$ consists of all integers from 0 to $n-1$, whereas $\mathbb{Z}_n^*$ consists of all integers between 1 and $n-1$ that have no common divisor with n greater than 1.[6]

If $\langle S, * \rangle$ is a group, then for any element $a \in S$ and for any positive integer $i \in \mathbb{N}$, $a^i \in S$ denotes the following element in S:

$$\underbrace{a * a * \ldots * a}_{i \text{ times}}$$

Due to the closure axiom (i.e., axiom 1), this element must again be in S. Note that we use a^i only as a shorthand representation for the element, and that the operation between the group element a and the integer i is not the group operation. For additive groups, a^i is sometimes also written as $i \cdot a$ (or ia, respectively). But note again that $i \cdot a$ only represents the resulting group element and that $\cdot$ is not the group operation.

Cyclic Groups

If $\langle S, * \rangle$ is a finite group with identity element e (with respect to $*$), then the order of an element $a \in S$, denoted as $ord(a)$, is the least positive integer n such that $a^{ord(a)}$ equals e. This can be formally expressed as follows:

$$\underbrace{a * a * \ldots * a}_{ord(a) \text{ times}} = e.$$

Alternatively speaking, the order of an element $a \in S$ (in a multiplicative group) is defined as follows:

$$ord(a) := min\{n \geq 1 \mid a^n = e\}$$

If there exists an element $a \in S$ such that the elements

$$a$$

---

6   Note that the star used in $\mathbb{Z}_n^*$ has nothing to do with the star used in Definition 3.11. In the second case, the star represents an arbitrary binary operation.

$$a * a$$

$$a * a * a$$

$$\ldots$$

$$\underbrace{a * a * \ldots * a}_{n \text{ times}}$$

are different and represent all elements of S, then the group $\langle S, * \rangle$ is called *cyclic* and a is called a *generator* of the group (or a *primitive root* of the group's identity element, respectively). If a generates the group (in the sense that a is a generator of the group), then we may write $S = \langle a \rangle$. If a finite group is cyclic, then there are typically many generators. In fact, there are $\phi(n - 1)$ generators if n refers to the order of the group.[7]

For example, $\langle \mathbb{Z}_n, + \rangle$ is a cyclic group with generator 1. This basically means that every number of $\{0, 1, 2, 3, \ldots, n - 1\}$ can be generated by adding 1 modulo n a certain number of times:

$$0 \;\; = \;\; \underbrace{1 + 1 + \ldots + 1}_{n \text{ times}}$$

$$1 \;\; = \;\; 1$$

$$2 \;\; = \;\; 1 + 1$$

$$3 \;\; = \;\; 1 + 1 + 1$$

$$\ldots$$

$$n - 1 \;\; = \;\; \underbrace{1 + 1 + \ldots + 1}_{n-1 \text{ times}}$$

As illustrated in Figure 3.2, $\langle \mathbb{Z}_7^*, \cdot \rangle$ is a cyclic group with generator 3 (i.e., $\langle \mathbb{Z}_7^*, \cdot \rangle = \langle 3 \rangle$). This means that every element of $\mathbb{Z}_7^* = \{1, 2, \ldots, 6\}$ can be represented by 3 to the power of another element of $\mathbb{Z}_7^*$.

In either case, it is important to note that not all finite groups must be cyclic (and hence not all finite groups must have a generator), but that all cyclic groups must be Abelian. The converse of the second fact is not true, meaning that an Abelian group must not necessarily be cyclic.

---

7   The function ϕ is called Euler's totient function and is formally introduced in Section 3.2.6.

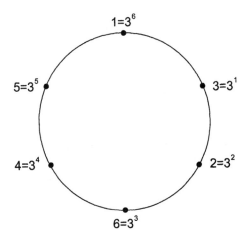

Figure 3.2   The cyclic group $\langle \mathbb{Z}_7^*, \cdot \rangle$.

Subgroups

When we elaborate on groups and their basic properties, it is sometimes useful to consider subgroups. The notion of a subgroup is formally introduced in Definition 3.12.

Definition 3.12 (Subgroup) *A subset H of a group G is a* subgroup *of G if it is closed under the operation of G and also forms a group.*

For example, the integers are a subgroup both of the rational and real numbers (with respect to the addition operation). Furthermore, $\{0, 2, 4\}$ is a subgroup of $\langle \mathbb{Z}_6, + \rangle$ with regard to addition modulo 6, and $\{0\}$ and $\{1\}$ are (trivial) subgroups of every additive and multiplicative group.

An important class of subgroups of a finite group are those generated by an element a, denoted as $\langle a \rangle := \{a^j \mid j \geq 0\}$. The subgroup $\langle a \rangle$ has $ord(a)$ elements. Furthermore, we need the notion of cosets as captured in Definitions 3.13–3.15.

Definition 3.13 (Left coset) *Let G be a group and $H \subseteq G$ be a subset of G. For all $a \in G$, the sets $a * H := \{a * h \mid h \in H\}$ are called* left *cosets of H.*

Definition 3.14 (Right coset) *Let G be a group and $H \subseteq G$ be a subset of G. For all $a \in G$, the sets $H * a := \{a * h \mid h \in H\}$ are called* right *cosets of H.*

Definition 3.15 (Coset) *Let G be a (commutative) group and $H \subseteq G$. For all $a \in G$, the sets $a * H$ and $H * a$ are equal and are called cosets of H.*

In the example given earlier (i.e., $G = \langle \mathbb{Z}_6, + \rangle$ and $H = \{0, 2, 4\}$), the elements of G are partitioned into the following two left cosets of H:

$$1 + H = 3 + H = \{1, 3, 5\}$$
$$2 + H = 4 + H = \{2, 4, 6\}$$

The notion of a coset is important to prove Theorem 3.1 that is due to Lagrange.[8]

Theorem 3.1 (Lagrange's Theorem) *If H is a subgroup of G, then $|H| \mid |G|$ (i.e., the order of H divides the order of G).*

Proof. If $H = G$, then $|H| \mid |G|$ holds trivially. Consequently, we only consider the case in which $H \subset G$. For any $a \in G \backslash H$, the coset $a * H$ is a subset of G. The following can be shown:
 i) For any $a \neq a'$, if $a \notin a' * H$ then $(a * H) \cap (a' * H) = \emptyset$;
 ii) $|a * H| = |H|$.
  For (i), suppose there exists a $b \in (a * H) \cap (a' * H)$. Then there exist $c, c' \in H$ such that $a * c = b = a' * c'$. Applying various group axioms, we have $a = a * e = a * (c * c^{-1}) = b * c^{-1} = (a' * c') * c^{-1} = a' * (c' * c^{-1}) \in a' * H$. This contradicts our assumption (that $a \notin a' * H$).
  For (ii), $|a * H| \leq |H|$ holds trivially (by the definition of a coset). Suppose that the inequality is rigorous. This is only possible if there are $b, c \in H$ with $b \neq c$ and $a * b = a * c$. Applying the inverse element of a on either side of the equation, we get $b = c$, contradicting to $b \neq c$.
  In summary, G is partitioned by H and the family of its mutually disjoint cosets, each has the size $|H|$, and hence $|H| \mid |G|$. This proves the theorem.

$\square$

Quotient Groups

Let G be a (commutative) group and $H \subseteq G$ a subgroup of G. The quotient group of G modulo H, denoted by G/H, is the set of all cosets $a * H$ with a ranging over G, and with the identity element being $e * H$. For example, for every positive integer $n \in \mathbb{N}^+$, the set $\{0, \pm n, \pm 2n, \ldots\}$ is a subgroup of $\mathbb{Z}$ under integer addition. The quotient group

---

8   Joseph Louis Lagrange was a French mathematician who lived from 1736 to 1813.

$$\mathbb{Z}/n\mathbb{Z} = \{x + n\mathbb{Z} \mid x \in \mathbb{Z}\}$$

has the following n elements:

$$
\begin{aligned}
0 &+ n\mathbb{Z} \\
1 &+ n\mathbb{Z} \\
2 &+ n\mathbb{Z} \\
&\cdots \\
n-1 &+ n\mathbb{Z}
\end{aligned}
$$

$\mathbb{Z}/n\mathbb{Z}$ is the formal and standard notation for the quotient group of $\mathbb{Z}$ modulo $n\mathbb{Z}$. However, for presentation convenience, we use the shorthand notation $\mathbb{Z}_n$ in place of $\mathbb{Z}/n\mathbb{Z}$ for the purpose of this book.

As corollaries of Lagrange's Theorem, one can show that the order of the quotient group G/H equals $|G|/|H|$ and that in a finite group the order of every element divides the group order. Fermat's Little Theorem (see Theorem 3.7) and Euler's Theorem (see Theorem 3.8) take advantage of the second fact and form the mathematical basis for the widely deployed RSA public key cryptosystem.

There are two important algebraic structures that comprise two operations: rings and fields. They are addressed next.

3.1.2.4 Rings

The simpler algebraic structure that comprises two operations is the ring. It is formally introduced in Definition 3.16.

Definition 3.16 (Ring) *A ring is an algebraic structure $\langle S, *_1, *_2 \rangle$ with a set S and two associative binary operations $*_1$ and $*_2$ that fulfill the following requirements:*

1. *$\langle S, *_1 \rangle$ is a commutative group with identity element e_1;*

2. *$\langle S, *_2 \rangle$ is a monoid with identity element e_2;*

3. *The operation $*_2$ is distributive over the operation $*_1$. This means that for all $a, b, c \in S$ the following two distributive laws must hold:*

$$
\begin{aligned}
a *_2 (b *_1 c) &= (a *_2 b) *_1 (a *_2 c) \\
(b *_1 c) *_2 a &= (b *_2 a) *_1 (c *_2 a)
\end{aligned}
$$

According to the first requirement, the operation $*_1$ must be commutative (this is not required for the operation $*_2$). The ring is called *commutative (noncommutative)* if the operation $*_2$ is (not) commutative.

For example, $\langle \mathbb{Z}, +, \cdot \rangle$ and $\langle \mathbb{Z}_n, +, \cdot \rangle$ are commutative rings that are further addressed in Sections 3.2 (entitled "Integer Arithmetic") and 3.3 (entitled "Modular Arithmetic").[9] Similarly, $\langle \mathbb{Q}, +, \cdot \rangle$ and $\langle \mathbb{R}, +, \cdot \rangle$ are commutative rings. Also, the set of real-valued $n \times n$ matrices form a ring with the zero matrix as the identity element of addition and the identity matrix as the identity element of multiplication. Contrary to the previous examples, this ring is noncommutative.

3.1.2.5 Fields

If we have a ring $\langle S, *_1, *_2 \rangle$ and require that $\langle S \setminus \{e_1\}, *_2 \rangle$ is a group (instead of a monoid), then we have a *field*. This is formally expressed in Definition 3.17.

Definition 3.17 (Field) *A ring $\langle S, *_1, *_2 \rangle$ in which $\langle S \setminus \{e_1\}, *_2 \rangle$ is a group is a field.*

Another way of saying that $\langle S \setminus \{e_1\}, *_2 \rangle$ is a group is that every nonidentity element (with respect to $*_1$) must have an inverse element (with respect to $*_2$).

A field $\langle S, *_1, *_2 \rangle$ is *finite* if it contains only finitely many elements (i.e., $|S| < \infty$). Finite fields have many applications in cryptography. For example, they are frequently used in public key cryptography. More surprisingly, they are also used in new symmetric encryption systems, such as the AES addressed in Section 10.2.2.

All finite fields with n elements can be shown to be structurally equivalent or isomorphic (see Section 3.1.3 for the notion of isomorphic algebraic structures). Consequently, it is sufficient to consider and thoroughly examine only one finite field with n elements. This field is called *Galois field*,[10] denoted by $\mathbb{F}_n$ or $GF(n)$. For every prime number p, there is a finite field with p elements (i.e., $\mathbb{F}_p$) and a series of finite fields with p^n elements for every positive integer n (see Section 3.3.6). In the simplest case, $p = 2$ and $\mathbb{F}_2$ consists of only two elements, namely the identity elements of the two binary operations (i.e., the zero element and the unity element).

Similar to Definition 3.12, we can introduce the notion of a subfield as suggested in Definition 3.18.

Definition 3.18 (Subfield) *A subset H of a field F is a subfield of F if it closed under the operations of F and also forms a field.*

---

9   If n is prime, then $\langle \mathbb{Z}_n, +, \cdot \rangle$ is a field.

10   The term was chosen in honor of Evariste Galois, who lived from 1811 to 1832. Galois is said to have found all finite fields.

Using the notion of a subfield, we can introduce the notion of a prime field. This is suggested in Definition 3.19.

Definition 3.19 (Prime field) *A prime field is a field that contains no proper subfield.*

For example, $\mathbb{Q}$ is a(n infinite) prime field, whereas $\mathbb{R}$ is not a prime field (note that $\mathbb{Q}$ is a proper subfield of $\mathbb{R}$). If we only consider finite fields, then a prime field must contain a prime number of elements, meaning that it must have a prime order.

3.1.3 Homomorphisms and Isomorphisms

In algebraic discussions and analyses, one often uses the notion of a homomorphism or isomorphism as formally introduced in Definitions 3.20 and 3.21.

Definition 3.20 (Homomorphism) *Let A and B be two algebraic structures. A mapping $f : A \rightarrow B$ is called a homomorphism of A into B if it preserves the operations of A. That is, if $\circ$ is an operation of A and $\bullet$ an operation of B, then $f(x \circ y) = f(x) \bullet f(y)$ must hold for all $x, y \in A$.*

Definition 3.21 (Isomorphism) *A homomorphism $f : A \rightarrow B$ is an isomorphism if it is injective ("one to one"). In this case, we say that A and B are isomorphic and we write $A \cong B$.*

Another way of saying that two algebraic structures are isomorphic is to say that they are structurally equivalent. Furthermore, if an isomorphism of an algebraic structure onto itself is considered, then one frequently uses the term automorphism as formally introduced in Definition 3.22.

Definition 3.22 (Automorphism) *An isomorphism $f : A \rightarrow A$ is an automorphism.*

Against this background, a *group homomorphism* is a mapping f between two groups $\langle S_1, *_1 \rangle$ and $\langle S_2, *_2 \rangle$ such that the group operation is preserved (i.e., $f(a *_1 b) = f(a) *_2 f(b)$ for all $a, b \in S_1$) and the identity element e_1 of $\langle S_1, *_1 \rangle$ is mapped to the identity element e_2 of $\langle S_2, *_2 \rangle$ (i.e., $f(e_1) = e_2$). If $f : \langle S_1, *_1 \rangle \rightarrow \langle S_2, *_2 \rangle$ is injective ("one to one"), then the group homomorphism is a group isomorphism (i.e., $\langle S_1, *_1 \rangle \cong \langle S_2, *_2 \rangle$).

It can be shown that every cyclic group with order n is isomorphic to $\langle \mathbb{Z}_n, + \rangle$. Hence, if we know $\langle \mathbb{Z}_n, + \rangle$, then we know all structural properties of every cyclic group of order n. Furthermore, it can be shown that $\langle \mathbb{Z}_n^*, \cdot \rangle$ is cyclic if and only if n is a prime, a power of a prime > 2, or twice the power of a prime > 2 (see Definition

3.26 for the notion of a prime). For example, $\langle \mathbb{Z}_{11}^*, \cdot \rangle$ is a cyclic group, but $\langle \mathbb{Z}_{12}^*, \cdot \rangle$ is not (i.e., it can be shown that no element of $\mathbb{Z}_{12}^*$ generates the entire group and hence that the group has no generator). In either case, $\langle \mathbb{Z}_p^*, \cdot \rangle$ is a cyclic group for every prime number p, and this group is isomorphic to $\langle \mathbb{Z}_{p-1}, + \rangle$. For example, the function $f(x) = g^x \pmod{p}$ defines an isomorphism between $\langle \mathbb{Z}_{p-1}, + \rangle$ and $\langle \mathbb{Z}_p^*, \cdot \rangle$. This isomorphism is reflected by the equation $g^{x+y} = g^x \cdot g^y$.

3.1.4 Permutations

Permutations are important mathematical building blocks for symmetric encryption systems in general, and block ciphers in particular (in Section 10.2 we argue that a block cipher represents a family of permutations). In short, a permutation is a bijective map whose domain and range are the same. This is formally expressed in Definition 3.23.

Definition 3.23 (Permutation) *Let S be a set. A map $f : S \to S$ is a permutation if f is bijective (i.e., injective and surjective). The set of all permutations of S is denoted by $Perm^{S \to S}$, or $P(S)$ in short.*

If, for example, $S = \{1, 2, 3, 4, 5\}$, then an exemplary permutation of S can be expressed as follows:

$$\begin{pmatrix} 1 & 2 & 3 & 4 & 5 \\ 5 & 3 & 4 & 2 & 1 \end{pmatrix}$$

This permutation maps every element in the first row of the matrice to the corresponding element in the second row (i.e., 1 is mapped to 5, 2 is mapped to 3, and so on). Using this notation, it is possible to specify any permutation of a finite set S.

In what follows, we use S_n to refer to $\{1, 2, \ldots, n\}$ for any integer n, and we use P_n to refer to $Perm^{S_n \to S_n}$ or $P(S_n)$. If $\circ$ represents the concatenation operator,[11] then $\langle P_n, \circ \rangle$ is a noncommutative group for $n \geq 3$. For example, P_2 has the two elements

$$\begin{pmatrix} 1 & 2 \\ 1 & 2 \end{pmatrix}$$

and

---

11 The permutation $A \circ B$ is the permutation that results by applying B and A (in this order).

$$\begin{pmatrix} 1 & 2 \\ 2 & 1 \end{pmatrix}$$

As can be shown, $|P_n| = n! = 1 \cdot 2 \cdot \ldots \cdot n$. For the first position, we have n possibilities. For the second position, we have $n-1$ possibilities. This continues until the last position, where we have only one possibility left. Consequently, there are $n \cdot n-1 \cdot \ldots \cdot 1$ possibilities, and this value is equal to $|P_n| = n!$. More specifically, the formula is proven by induction over n. Because P_1 has $1! = 1$ element, the formula is correct for $n = 1$. We assume that the formula is correct for $n - 1$ (i.e., $|P_{n-1}| = (n - 1)!$) and show that the formula is then also correct for n. Therefore, we look at the permutations of P_n that map 1 to an arbitrary $x \in S_n$. By using such a permutation, the numbers $2, 3, \ldots, n$ are mapped to $1, 2, \ldots, x - 1, x + 1, \ldots, n$, and this function is bijective. There are $(n - 1)!$ such functions. Furthermore, there are n possibilities to map 1 to an x (i.e., $x = 1, \ldots, n$). Consequently, there is a total of $|P_n| = n(n - 1)! = n!$ permutations of S_n.

Let $S = \{0, 1\}^n$ be the set of all binary strings of length n. A permutation of S in which the bit positions are permuted is said to be a *bit permutation*. To specify a bit permutation f, we must select a $\pi \in P_n$ and set

$$f : \{0, 1\}^n \longrightarrow \{0, 1\}^n$$
$$b_0 \ldots b_{n-1} \longmapsto b_{\pi(0)} \ldots b_{\pi(n-1)}.$$

Every bit permutation can be described in this way, and hence there are $n!$ possible bit permutations for binary strings of length n.

There are bit permutations that are frequently used in cryptography, such as *cyclic shift left* and *cyclic shift right*. A cyclic shift left for i positions maps the bit string $(b_0, b_1, \ldots, b_{n-1})$ into

$$(b_{i \bmod n}, b_{(i+1) \bmod n}, \ldots, b_{(i+n-1) \bmod n}).$$

A cyclic shift right is defined similarly.

Last but not least, we sometimes use the notion of a family of permutations. Roughly speaking, F is a *family of permutations* if the domain and range are the same and each f_k is a permutation (according to Definition 3.23).

3.2 INTEGER ARITHMETIC

Mathematics is the queen of sciences and number theory is the queen of mathematics.

— Carl Friedrich Gauss[12]

As mentioned earlier, integer arithmetic elaborates on the ring $\langle \mathbb{Z}, +, \cdot \rangle$ and its basic properties.[13] This special (and comparably narrow) field of study is sometimes also referred to as *number theory*. According to the quote given above, number theory is a very important and fundamental mathematical topic that has had (and continues to have) a deep impact on natural sciences. One fascinating aspect of number theory is that many of its problems and theorems can be easily expressed and understood even by nonmathematicians, but they are hard to solve (generally without being able to prove the hardness property). This is in contrast to many other areas of mathematics (where the relevant problems cannot easily be understood by nonexperts). For example, the integer factorization problem (see Section 7.2.2) is explained in a few words, whereas number theorists have tried to solve it without success for several centuries.

In this section, we look at the aspects of integer arithmetic or number theory that are relevant for the topic of this book. More specifically, we address integer division, common divisors and multiples, Euclidean algorithms, prime numbers, factorization, and Euler's totient function.

3.2.1 Integer Division

In an algebraic structure with the multiplication operation, one usually divides two elements by multiplying the first element with the (multiplicatively) inverse element of the second. This can be formally expressed as follows:

$$\frac{a}{b} = ab^{-1}$$

Obviously, this construction requires that element b has an inverse element. This is always the case in a group (or field). If, however, the algebraic structure is only a monoid (or ring), then there are elements that have no inverse, and hence it

---

12 Carl Friedrich Gauss was a German mathematician who lived from 1777 to 1855.
13 What makes the integers unique (as compared to other rings and integral domains) is the order relation $\leq$.

may not be possible to divide two arbitrarily chosen elements. For example, in the ring $\langle \mathbb{Z}, +, \cdot \rangle$ it is possible to divide 6 by 2, but it is not possible to divide 2 by 3.

For $a, b \in \mathbb{Z}$, we say that a *divides* b, denoted as $a|b$, if there exists a $c \in \mathbb{Z}$ such that $b = ac$. Alternatively speaking, a is a *divisor* of b and b is said to be a *multiple* of a. In the examples given earlier $2|6$, because $6 = 2 \cdot 3$, but 3 does not divide 2. Also, 1 divides every integer and the largest divisor of any integer $a \in \mathbb{Z} \setminus \{0\}$ is $|a|$. Furthermore, every integer $a \in \mathbb{Z}$ divides 0; thus 0 has no largest divisor. Theorem 3.2 enumerates some rules that can be used to compute with divisors.

Theorem 3.2 *For all $a, b, c, d, e \in \mathbb{Z}$, the following rules apply:*

1. *If $a|b$ and $b|c$, then $a|c$.*

2. *If $a|b$, then $ac|bc$ for all c.*

3. *If $c|a$ and $c|b$, then $c|da + eb$ for all d and e.*

4. *If $a|b$ and $b \neq 0$, then $|a| \leq |b|$.*

5. *If $a|b$ and $b|a$, then $|a| = |b|$.*

Proofs.

1. If $a|b$ and $b|c$, then there exist $f, g \in \mathbb{Z}$ with $b = af$ and $c = bg$. Consequently, we can write $c = bg = (af)g = a(fg)$ to express c as a multiple of a. The claim (i.e., $a|c$) follows directly from this equation.

2. If $a|b$, then there exists $f \in \mathbb{Z}$ with $b = af$. Consequently, we can write $bc = (af)c = f(ac)$ to express bc as a multiple of ac. The claim (i.e., $ac|bc$) follows directly from this equation.

3. If $c|a$ and $c|b$, then there exist $f, g \in \mathbb{Z}$ with $a = fc$ and $b = gc$. Consequently, we can write $da + eb = dfc + egc = (df + eg)c$ to express $da + eb$ as a multiple of c. The claim (i.e., $c|da + eb$) follows directly from this equation.

4. If $a|b$ and $b \neq 0$, then there exists $0 \neq f \in \mathbb{Z}$ with $b = af$. Consequently, $|b| = |af| \geq |a|$ and the claim (i.e., $|a| \leq |b|$) follows immediately.

5. Let us assume that $a|b$ and $b|a$. If $a = 0$ then $b = 0$, and vice versa. If $a, b \neq 0$, then it follows from 4. that $|a| \leq |b|$ and $|b| \leq |a|$, and hence $|b| = |a|$.

$\square$

Theorem 3.3 elaborates on the division operation and is commonly known as Euclid's division theorem for integers. We don't prove the theorem in this book.

Theorem 3.3 (Euclid's division theorem) *For all $n, d \in \mathbb{Z} \setminus \{0\}$ there exist unique and efficiently computable $q, r \in \mathbb{Z}$ such that $n = qd + r$ and $0 \le r < |d|$.*

In this setting, d is called the *divisor* (i.e., n is divided by d), q the *quotient*, and r the *remainder*. The remainder r can also be written as $R_d(n)$, and we sometimes use this notation.

For example, $R_7(16) = 2$ (because $16 = 2 \cdot 7 + 2$), $R_7(-16) = 5$ (because $-16 = -3 \cdot 7 + 5$), and $R_{25}(104) = 4$ (because $104 = 4 \cdot 25 + 4$). Obviously, $R_d(n) = 0$ means that d divides n (with remainder zero), and hence d is a divisor of n. Furthermore, $R_d(n + id)$ is equal to $R_d(n)$ for all $i \in \mathbb{Z}$, and hence $R_7(1) = R_7(8) = R_7(15) = R_7(22) = R_7(29) = \ldots = 1$.

3.2.2 Common Divisors and Multiples

Two integers can have many common divisors, but only one of them can be the greatest. Quite naturally, this divisor is called *greatest common divisor*. It is formally introduced in Definition 3.24.

Definition 3.24 (Common divisors and greatest common divisor) *For $a, b \in \mathbb{Z} \setminus \{0\}$, $c \in \mathbb{Z}$ is a* common divisor *of a and b if $c|a$ and $c|b$. Furthermore, c is the* greatest common divisor, *denoted $\gcd(a, b)$, if it is the largest integer that divides a and b.*

Another possibility to define the greatest common divisor of a and b is to say that $c = \gcd(a, b)$ if any common divisor of a and b also divides c. $\gcd(0, 0) = 0$, and $\gcd(a, 0) = |a|$ for all $a \in \mathbb{Z} \setminus \{0\}$. If $a, b \in \mathbb{Z} \setminus \{0\}$, then $1 \le \gcd(a, b) \le \min\{|a|, |b|\}$ and $\gcd(a, b) = \gcd(\pm|a|, \pm|b|)$. Consequently, the greatest common divisor of two integers can never be negative (even if one or both integers are negative). Furthermore, two integers $a, b \in \mathbb{Z} \setminus \{0\}$ are *relatively prime* or *co-prime* if their greatest common divisor is 1 (i.e., if $\gcd(a, b) = 1$).

Similar to the (greatest) common divisor, it is possible to define the (least) common multiple of two integers. This is formally introduced in Definition 3.25.

Definition 3.25 (Common multiples and least common multiple) *For $a, b \in \mathbb{Z} \setminus \{0\}$, $c \in \mathbb{Z}$ is a* common multiple *of a and b if $a|c$ and $b|c$. Furthermore, c is the* least common multiple, *denoted $\text{lcm}(a, b)$, if it is the smallest integer that is divided by a and b.*

Another possibility to define the least common multiple of a and b is to say that $c = \text{lcm}(a, b)$ if c divides any common multiple of a and b.

The *gcd* and *lcm* operators can be generalized to more than two arguments. In fact, $\gcd(a_1, \ldots, a_k)$ is the largest integer that divides all a_i ($i = 1, \ldots, k$) and $\text{lcm}(a_1, \ldots, a_k)$ is the smallest integer that is divided by all a_i ($i = 1, \ldots, k$).

3.2.3   Euclidean Algorithms

In Section 3.2.5 we see how one can compute the greatest common divisor of two integers if their prime factorization is known. It is, however, not necessary to know the prime factorization of two integers to compute their greatest common divisor. In fact, the *Euclidean algorithm* (or *Euclid's algorithm*) can be used to compute the greatest common divisor of two integers $a, b \in \mathbb{Z} \setminus \{0\}$ with unknown prime factorization.[14]

Theorem 3.3 says that for two nonzero integers $a \geq b$, we can always write

$$a = bq + r$$

for some quotient $q \neq 0$ and remainder $0 \leq r < b$. Because by definition, $gcd(a, b)$ divides both a and b, the above equation shows that it must also divide r. Consequently, $gcd(a, b)$ equals $gcd(b, r)$, and because the remainder r of a divided by b is denoted by $a \bmod b$, we can say

$$gcd(a, b) = gcd(b, a \bmod b) = gcd(b, R_b(a)).$$

This equation can be recursively applied to compute $gcd(a, b)$. For example, $gcd(100, 35)$ can be computed as follows:

$$
\begin{aligned}
gcd(100, 35) &= gcd(35, R_{35}(100)) \\
&= gcd(35, 30) \\
&= gcd(30, R_{30}(35)) \\
&= gcd(30, 5) \\
&= gcd(5, R_5(30)) \\
&= gcd(5, 0) \\
&= 5.
\end{aligned}
$$

This way of computing $gcd(a, b)$ is at the core of the Euclidean algorithm. If we consider the following series of k equations:

$$a \quad = \quad bq_1 + r_1$$

---

[14]   The Euclidean algorithm is one of the oldest algorithms known; it appeared in Euclid's *Elements* around 300 B.C.

$$b = r_1 q_2 + r_2$$
$$r_1 = r_2 q_3 + r_3$$
$$\cdots$$
$$r_{k-3} = r_{k-2} q_{k-1} + r_{k-1}$$
$$r_{k-2} = r_{k-1} q_k + r_k$$

All quotients and remainders are integers. At the end, r_k is equal to zero and $q_1, q_2, \ldots, q_k, r_1, r_2, \ldots, r_{k-1}$ are nonzero. If $r_k = 0$, then the last equation implies that r_{k-1} divides r_{k-2}. The last-but-one equation implies that it also divides r_{k-3}. This line of argumentation can be continued until the first equation, and hence r_{k-1} divides a and b. None of the other remainders $r_{k-2}, r_{k-3}, \ldots, r_1$ has this property.[15] Consequently, r_{k-1} is the greatest common divisor of a and b, meaning that $r_{k-1} = gcd(a, b)$.

Algorithm 3.1 The Euclidean algorithm to compute the greatest common divisor of a and b.

$$\underline{(a, b \in \mathbb{Z}, |a| \geq |b|, a \neq 0)}$$
$a \leftarrow |a|$
$b \leftarrow |b|$
while $b \neq 0$ do
$\quad t \leftarrow a$
$\quad a \leftarrow b$
$\quad b \leftarrow t \bmod b$
return a
$$\overline{(gcd(a, b))}$$

The Euclidean algorithm is illustrated in Algorithm 3.1. It takes as input two integers a and b with $|a| \geq |b|$ and $a \neq 0$, and computes as output $gcd(a, b)$. First it replaces a and b with their absolute values (note that this does not change the greatest common divisor). Then the previously mentioned rule that $gcd(a, b) = gcd(b, a \bmod b)$ is applied until b reaches zero. At this point in time, a represents the greatest common divisor and is returned by the algorithm. Note that the loop can also be represented by a recursive function call.

The Euclidean algorithm explained so far can be used to compute the greatest common divisor of two integers a and b. During its execution, all intermediate results (in particular all quotients q_i and remainders r_i) are discarded. This makes the algorithm simple to implement in the first place. If, however, one does not throw all intermediate results away but accumulates them during the execution of the

---

15 That's why they are called remainders in the first place (not divisors). Only r_{k-1} is a divisor in the last equation.

algorithm, then one may obtain more information than simply the greatest common divisor. In fact, the *extended Euclidean algorithm* can be used to compute two integers x and y that satisfy (3.1):

$$xa + yb = gcd(a, b) \tag{3.1}$$

Note that the first equation of the previously mentioned series of k equations can be written as

$$a + b(-q_1) = r_1$$

If we multiply both sides of this equation with q_2, we get

$$aq_2 + b(-q_1q_2) = r_1q_2.$$

Combining this equation with the second equation of the series, we get

$$a(-q_2) + b(1 + q_1q_2) = r_2.$$

A similar calculation can be used to express each r_i for $i = 1, 2, \ldots, k$ as a linear combination of a and b. In fact,

$$ax_i + by_i = r_i \tag{3.2}$$

where x_i and y_i are some integers. As explained earlier, we eventually reach the point where $r_k = 0$ and r_{k-1} represents $gcd(a, b)$:

$$ax_{k-1} + by_{k-1} = r_{k-1} = gcd(a, b).$$

In essence, the extended Euclidean algorithm specifies a way to accumulate the intermediate quotients to compute x_{k-1} and y_{k-1}. Like the Euclidean algorithm, the extended Euclidean algorithm takes as input two integers a and b with $|a| \geq |b|$ and $a \neq 0$, and computes as output two integers x and y that satisfy (3.1).

If we set $r_{-1} = a$, $r_0 = b$, $x_{-1} = 1$, $y_{-1} = 0$, $x_0 = 0$, and $y_0 = 1$, then the ith equation of the previously mentioned series of k equations relates r_{i-1}, r_i, and r_{i+1} in the following way:

$$r_{i+1} = r_{i-1} - r_i q_{i+1}$$

Replacing r_{i-1} and r_i in the right-hand side of this equation using (3.2), we get

$$r_{i+1} = a(x_{i-1} - q_{i+1}x_i) + b(y_{i-1} - q_{i+1}y_i).$$

Algorithm 3.2 The extended Euclidean algorithm.

$(a, b \in \mathbb{Z}, |a| \geq |b|, a \neq 0)$

$i \leftarrow 0$
$r_{-1} \leftarrow a$
$r_0 \leftarrow b$
$x_{-1} \leftarrow 1$
$y_{-1} \leftarrow 0$
$x_0 \leftarrow 0$
$y_0 \leftarrow 1$
while $(r_i = ax_i + by_i \neq 0)$ do
$\quad q \leftarrow r_{i-1} \text{ div } r_i$
$\quad x_{i+1} \leftarrow x_{i-1} - qx_i$
$\quad y_{i+1} \leftarrow y_{i-1} - qy_i$
$\quad i \leftarrow i + 1$
return (x_{i-1}, y_{i-1})

$(x$ and y with $xa + yb = gcd(a, b))$

Comparing this equation with (3.2), we obtain

$$
\begin{aligned}
x_{i+1} &= x_{i-1} - q_{i+1}x_i \\
y_{i+1} &= y_{i-1} - q_{i+1}y_i
\end{aligned}
$$

for $i = 0, 1, \ldots, k - 1$, and this pair of equations provides us with a general method for accumulating the intermediate quotients while computing the greatest common divisor of a and b. The resulting extended Euclidean algorithm is illustrated in Algorithm 3.2.

For example, the extended Euclidean algorithm can be used to determine x and y that satisfy $gcd(100, 35) = 5 = x \cdot 100 + y \cdot 35$ in the example given earlier.

In this case, $a = 100$ and $b = 35$. After the initialization phase of the algorithm, we come to the first incarnation of the while-loop with $i = 0$. We compute

$$r_0 = ax_0 + by_0 = 100 \cdot 0 + 35 \cdot 1 = 35.$$

Because this value is not equal to 0, we enter the loop. The variable q is set to r_{-1} div r_0. In our example, this integer division yields 100 div 35 = 2. Using $q = 2$, we compute the following pair of values:

$$
\begin{aligned}
x_1 &= x_{-1} - qx_0 = 1 - 2 \cdot 0 = 1 \\
y_1 &= y_{-1} - qy_0 = 0 - 2 \cdot 1 = -2
\end{aligned}
$$

After having incremented i with 1, we have $i = 1$ and come back to the second incarnation of the while-loop. We compute

$$r_1 = ax_1 + by_1 = 100 \cdot 1 + 35 \cdot (-2) = 100 - 70 = 30.$$

Because this value is again not equal to 0, we enter the loop again. This time, the variable q is set to r_0 div $r_1 = 35$ div 30 = 1. Using $q = 1$, we then compute the following pair of values:

$$
\begin{aligned}
x_2 &= x_0 - qx_1 = 0 - 1 = -1 \\
y_2 &= y_0 - qy_1 = 1 - (1 \cdot (-2)) = 1 + 2 = 3
\end{aligned}
$$

After having incremented i with 1, we have $i = 2$ and come back to the third incarnation of the while-loop. We compute

$$r_2 = ax_2 + by_2 = 100 \cdot (-1) + 35 \cdot 3 = -100 + 105 = 5.$$

Because this value is not equal to 0, we enter the loop. This time, the variable q is set to r_1 div $r_2 = 30$ div 5 = 6. Using $q = 6$, we compute the following pair of values:

$$x_3 = x_1 - qx_2 = 1 + 6 = 7$$
$$y_3 = y_1 - qy_2 = -2 - 6 \cdot 3 = -20$$

Finally, we increment i and come back to the fourth incarnation of the while-loop with $i = 3$. When we compute

$$r_3 = 100 \cdot 7 + (-20) \cdot 35$$

we immediately realize that this value equals 0. Consequently, we don't enter the while-loop anymore, but return $(x, y) = (x_2, y_2) = (-1, 3)$ as the result of the algorithm. It can easily be verified that this result is correct, because $gcd(100, 35) = 5 = -1 \cdot 100 + 3 \cdot 35$.

3.2.4 Prime Numbers

Prime numbers (or primes) as formally introduced in Definition 3.26 are frequently used in mathematics.[16]

Definition 3.26 (Prime number) *A natural number* $1 < n \in \mathbb{N}$ *is called a* prime number *(or* prime*) if it divisible only by 1 and itself.*

Contrary to that, a natural number $1 < n \in \mathbb{N}$ that is not prime is called *composite* (note that 1 is neither prime nor composite). In this book, the set of all prime numbers is denoted as $\mathbf{P}$. The set $\mathbf{P}$ is infinitely large (i.e., $|\mathbf{P}| = \infty$), and its first 8 elements are $2, 3, 5, 7, 11, 13, 17$, and 19.

Suppose that you want to find the set that consists of all primes less than a certain threshold n (e.g., $n = 20$). In the third century B.C., Eratosthenes proposed an algorithm to systematically find these primes, and this algorithm introduced the notion of a *sieve*. The sieve starts by writing down the set of all natural numbers between 2 and n. In our example $n = 20$, this may look as follows:

$$\{2, 3, 4, 5, 6, 7, 8, 9, 10, 11, 12, 13, 14, 15, 16, 17, 18, 19, 20\}$$

Next, all numbers bigger than 2 (i.e., the smallest prime) which are multiples of 2 are removed from the set (this means that all even numbers are removed). The following set remains:

---

16 The first recorded definition of a prime was again given by Euclid. There is even some evidence that the concept of primality was known earlier to Aristotle and Pythagoras.

$$\{2, 3, 5, 7, 9, 11, 13, 15, 17, 19\}$$

This step is repeated for every prime number not bigger than $\sqrt{n}$. In our example, $\sqrt{20} \approx 4.472$. This basically means that the step must be repeated only for the prime number 3. The following set remains:

$$\{2, 3, 5, 7, 11, 13, 17, 19\}$$

What is left is the set of prime numbers less than 20. In this example, the cardinality of the prime number set is 8. In general, the cardinality of the prime number set is measured by the prime counting function $\pi(n)$. This function is introduced next.

3.2.4.1 Prime Counting Function

As mentioned earlier, the prime counting function $\pi(n)$ counts the number of primes that are less or equal to $n \in \mathbb{N}$. This statement can be defined as follows:

$$\pi(n) := |\{p \in \mathbf{P} \mid p \leq n\}|$$

The following table illustrates the first couple of values of the prime counting function $\pi(n)$. Note that the function grows monotonically.

n	2	3	4	5	6	7	8	9	10	11	12	13	14	...
$\pi(n)$	1	2	2	3	3	4	4	4	4	5	5	6	6	...

In public key cryptography, one often uses very large prime numbers. Consequently, one may ask whether there are arbitrarily sized prime numbers. This question can be answered in the affirmative. In fact, it is easy to proof that there are infinitely many primes. Assume that there are only finitely many primes, and let them be $p_1 \cdots p_n$. Consider the number $m = p_1 \cdots p_n + 1$. Because m is bigger than any prime, it must be composite, and hence it must be divisible by some prime. We note, however, that m is not divisible by p_1, as when we divide m by p_1 we get the quotient $p_2 \cdots p_n$ and a remainder of 1. Similarly, m is not divisible by any p_i for $i = 2, \ldots, n$. Consequently, we get a contradiction and hence the assumption (i.e., that there are only finitely many primes) must be wrong. This proves that there are infinitely many primes.

Although there are infinitely many primes, it may still be the case that they are sparse and that finding a large prime is prohibitively difficult. Consequently, a somehow related question asks for the density of prime numbers. How likely does an interval of a given size comprise a prime number? We can use the prime density theorem addressed next to answer questions of this type.

3.2.4.2 Prime Density Theorem

Theorem 3.4 is called the *prime density theorem*. It says that arbitrarily sized prime numbers do in fact exist, and that finding them is not difficult (even for very large numbers). We give the theorem without a proof.

Theorem 3.4 (Prime density theorem)

$$\lim_{n \to \infty} \frac{\pi(n) \ln(n)}{n} = 1$$

In essence, the prime density theorem says that for sufficiently large n the value $\pi(n)$ is about $n/\ln(n)$ and that roughly every $\ln(n)^{th}$ number of the size of n is prime. For example, $\ln(10^{100}) \approx 230$. This means that about 1 in 230 (115) integers (odd integers) with 100 decimal digits is a prime. More specifically, it is known that

$$\pi(n) \geq \frac{n}{\ln(n)}$$

for $2 < n \in \mathbb{N}$ and that

$$\pi(n) \leq 1.10555 \frac{n}{\ln(n)}$$

for $17 \leq n \in \mathbb{N}$. Consequently, $\pi(n) \approx n/\ln(n)$ is indeed a very good approximation for almost all $n \in \mathbb{N}$.

There are several open conjectures on prime numbers. For example, it is conjectured that there exist infinitely many twin primes (i.e., primes p for which $p + 2$ is also prime), and that every even number is the sum of two primes. We don't elaborate on these issues in this book.

3.2.4.3 Generating Large Primes

In cryptographic applications, one often needs large primes, and there are two methods for generating them:

- One can construct provable primes;

- One can randomly choose large odd numbers and apply primality (or compositeness) tests.

There are only a few algorithms to construct provable primes (e.g., [7]), and in practice one randomly chooses large odd numbers and applies primality (or compositeness) tests. If a number turns out to be composite, then it is discarded and the next odd number is taken into consideration. The primality decision problem as captured in Definition 3.27 has attracted many mathematicians in the past.

Definition 3.27 (Primality decision problem) *Given a positive integer* $n \in \mathbb{N}$, *decide whether* $n \in \mathbf{P}$ *(i.e., n is prime) or not (i.e., n is composite).*

There are a couple of algorithms to address the primality decision problem. Most of them are probabilistic.[17] Only a few deterministic primality testing algorithms are efficient (i.e., run in polynomial time). They are, however, much less efficient than their probabilistic counterparts. From a theoretical viewpoint, however, knowing efficient deterministic primality testing algorithms means that the primality decision problem is in the complexity class $\mathcal{P}$ (as introduced in Definition 6.6) This fact was proven in 2002.[18]

Numbers that are not truly known to be prime, but which have passed some probabilistic primality tests, are called *probable primes* or *pseudoprimes*. Sometimes, the term "pseudoprime" is also used to refer to a nonprime (i.e., a composite number) that has nevertheless passed a probabilistic primality test. For the purpose of this book, however, a pseudoprime is a (prime or composite) number n that has passed some specified probabilistic primality tests. Each of these tests makes use of one or several randomly chosen auxiliary numbers $1 < a < n$. If such an a tells us that a is likely prime (composite), then a is a *witness* to the primality (compositeness) of n. A problem is that a significant fraction of numbers between 2 and $n - 1$ may be false witnesses (sometimes called *liars*) to the primality of n, meaning that they tell us n is prime when it's not. Thus, part of the issue is to be sure that a large fraction of the numbers a in the range $1 < a < n$ are true witnesses to either the primality or the compositeness of n. As discussed later, the fatal flaw in the Fermat test is that there are composite numbers for which there are no witnesses. The other two probabilistic primality tests have no such flaw.

Trial Division

The simplest (deterministic) primality testing algorithm for a positive integer $n \in \mathbb{N}$ is to test whether there exists a prime between 2 and $\sqrt{n}$ that divides n. If such a number exists, then n is not prime (i.e., it is composite) and the algorithm can abort. If, however, such a number does not exist, then n is prime. In the literature, this algorithm is commonly referred to as *trial division*. It requires a list of known prime numbers between 2 and $\sqrt{n}$. As a consequence of the prime density theorem (i.e., Theorem 3.4), one must perform

$$\frac{\sqrt{n}}{\ln \sqrt{n}}$$

trial divisions to show that n is a prime. For example, in a typical cryptographic setting, n is larger than 10^{75}. In this case, one must perform

$$\frac{\sqrt{10^{75}}}{\ln \sqrt{10^{75}}} > 3.5 \cdot 10^{35}$$

trial divisions. This is computationally infeasible, and hence the trial division algorithm cannot be used for numbers of a certain size. All major primality testing algorithms that work for large numbers are probabilistic.

Fermat Test

In the 17th century, Pierre de Fermat[19] proved Theorem 3.7 (also known as Fermat's Little Theorem), which can be turned into a simple primality testing algorithm. Fermat's Little Theorem states that for any prime number p and any number a not divisible by p, the equivalence $a^{p-1} \equiv 1 \pmod{p}$ must hold. Consequently, one can test the primality—or rather the compositeness—of n by randomly choosing a value for a (not divisible by n) and computing $a^{n-1} \pmod{n}$. If this value is not equal to 1, then n is definitively not a prime (and we have found a witness for the compositeness of n, respectively). Unfortunately, the converse is not true and finding an a for which $a^{n-1} \equiv 1 \pmod{n}$ does not imply that n is prime.[20] In fact, there is an entire class of composite numbers for which $a^{n-1} \equiv 1 \pmod{n}$ holds

---

19 Pierre de Fermat was a French mathematician who lived from 1607 to 1665.
20 For this reason, the Fermat test (and the two other tests mentioned later) is referred to as a compositeness test.

for all a. These numbers are called *Carmichael numbers*.[21] Because it is not able to correctly handle Carmichael numbers, the Fermat test is not widely deployed in practice. Instead, either the Solovay-Strassen test or the Miller-Rabin test is used.

Solovay-Strassen Test

The Solovay-Strassen test is a probabilistic compositeness testing algorithm that was developed by Robert Solovay and Volker Strassen in 1976. It can prove the compositeness of a large number n with certainty, but it can prove the primality of n only with a certain probability.

The Solovay-Strassen test makes use of some facts related to quadratic residuosity that we introduce in Section 3.3.7. More specifically, the test employs and takes advantage of the fact that if n is prime, then the Legendre symbol

$$\left(\frac{a}{n}\right)$$

and

$$a^{\frac{n-1}{2}} \pmod{n}$$

must be equal for every $1 \leq a \leq n - 1$ (according to Euler's criterion stated in Theorem 3.9 on page 93). Consequently, if one finds an a for which the two values are different, then n must be composite (and a is a witness for the compositeness of n, respectively). Let n be a large odd number for which we want to decide whether it is prime or composite. We execute the Solovay-Strassen test multiple times. In each execution, we randomly choose an integer a between 1 and $n - 1$ and compute both the Legendre symbol $(a|n)$ and $a^{n-1/2} \pmod{n}$. If the two values are not the same, then n is composite and a is a witness for the compositeness of n. In this case, the algorithm can abort. Otherwise (i.e., if the two computed values are the same), the algorithm must continue with the next value of a. If we execute the test k times and two computed values are the same for all k values of a, then we can say that n is prime with probability at least $1 - 2^{-k}$.

Miller-Rabin Test

The Miller-Rabin test is another probabilistic compositeness testing algorithm that was developed by Gary Miller and Michael O. Rabin in the late 1970s. Similar

---

21 It can be shown that a Carmichael number must be odd, square free, and divisible by at least 3 prime numbers. For example, the smallest Carmichael number is $561 = 3 \cdot 11 \cdot 17$.

to the Fermat and Solovay-Strassen tests, the Miller-Rabin test can prove the compositeness of a large number n with certainty, but it can prove the primality of n only with a certain probability.

The underlying idea of the Miller-Rabin test is that if n is a prime, then 1 should have only 2 square roots in $\mathbb{Z}_n$, namely ± 1. Alternatively speaking, if n is nonprime, then there are at least 2 elements x of $\mathbb{Z}_n$ with $x^2 \equiv 1 \pmod{n}$ but $x \neq \pm 1$. That is, there will be more square roots of 1 than there should be. The Miller-Rabin test itself is based on the properties of strong pseudoprimes. If we want to test the primality of a large odd number $n = 2^r s + 1$, then we randomly choose an integer a between 1 and $n - 1$. If

$$a^s \equiv 1 \pmod{n}$$

or

$$a^{2^j s} \equiv -1 \pmod{n}$$

for some $0 \leq j \leq r - 1$, then n passes the test for this value of a (i.e., a is not a witness for the compositeness of n). Unfortunately, a number that passes the test is not necessarily prime. In fact, it can be shown that a composite number passes the test for at most $1/4$ of the possible values for a. Consequently, if k tests are performed on a composite number n, then the probability that it passes each test is at most $1/4^k$. This means that the error probability can be made arbitrarily small.

Note that the operation of the Miller-Rabin test is quite simple, though— even simpler than that of the Solovay-Strassen test. Consequently, the Miller-Rabin test is the primality (or compositeness) testing algorithm of choice for all practical purposes.

3.2.5 Factorization

First of all, it can be shown that a prime p that divides the product ab of two natural numbers a and b divides at least one of the two factors (i.e., a or b). To prove this fact, we assume that p divides ab but not a and show that p must then divide b. Because p is a prime, we have $gcd(a, p) = 1$ and hence there exist $x, y \in N$ with $gcd(a, p) = 1 = ax + py$ [refer to (3.1)]. This equation can be multiplied with b to get $b = abx + pby$. Obviously, p divides abx and pby (the right side of the equation), so p must also divide b (the left side of the equation).

This result can be generalized to more than two factors. In fact, if p divides a product

$$\prod_{i=1}^{k} q_i$$

of prime factors, then p must be equal to one of the prime factors $q_1, \ldots, q_k$. This result can be proven by induction over k (using the result given earlier).

One of the fundamental theorems of integer arithmetic says that every natural number $n \in \mathbb{N}$ has a unique prime factorization. This is Theorem 3.5, and it was first proved by Gauss in 1801. We provide the theorem without a proof.

Theorem 3.5 (Unique factorization) *Every natural number $n \in \mathbb{N}$ can be factored uniquely (up to a permutation of the prime factors):*

$$n = \prod_{p \in \mathbf{P}} p^{e_p(n)}$$

In this formula, $e_p(n)$ refers to the exponent of p in the factorization of n. For almost all $p \in \mathbf{P}$ this value is zero, and only for finitely many primes p the value $e_p(n)$ is greater than zero.

Theorem 3.5 says only that every natural number $n \in \mathbb{N}$ can be factored. Its proof comprises an existence proof and a uniqueness proof. The existence proof is a consequence of the definition of a prime number; it gives no clue about how to efficiently find the prime factors. As further addressed in Section 7.3, no efficient (i.e., polynomial time) is currently known to factorize integers.

Using this notation, the greatest common divisor and least common multiple can be defined as follows:

$$gcd(a, b) = \prod_{p \in \mathbf{P}} p^{min(e_p(a), e_p(b))}$$

$$lcm(a, b) = \prod_{p \in \mathbf{P}} p^{max(e_p(a), e_p(b))}$$

The algorithms we learn in school to compute greatest common divisors and least common multiples are directly derived from these equations. Note, however, that these algorithms can only be used if the prime factorizations of a and b are known.

Last but not least, the notion of a smooth integer is sometimes used, especially in the realm of integer factorization algorithms. Informally speaking, an integer is said to be *smooth* if it is the product of only small prime factors. More specifically, we must say what a "small prime factor" is, and hence one has to define smoothness with respect to a certain bound B. The notion of a B-*smooth* integer is captured in Definition 3.28.

Definition 3.28 (B-smooth integer) *Let B be an integer. An integer n is* B-smooth *if every prime factor of n is less than B.*

For example, the integer $n = 4^3 \cdot 5^{2345} \cdot 17^2$ is 18-smooth (because 17 is the largest prime factor of n).

3.2.6 Euler's Totient Function

Euler's totient function was first proposed by Leonhard Euler[22] as a function that counts the numbers that are smaller than n and have no other common divisor with n other than 1 (i.e., they are co-prime with n). The function is formally defined as follows:

$$\phi(n) = |\{a \in \{0, \ldots, n-1\} \mid gcd(a, n) = 1\}|$$

The Euler's totient function has the following properties:

- If p is prime, then every number smaller than p is co-prime with p. Consequently, the equation $\phi(p) = p - 1$ holds for every prime number.

- If p is prime and $1 \leq k \in \mathbb{Z}$, then $\phi(p^k) = p^k - p^k/p$. This is because every p^{th} number between 1 and p^k is not co-prime with p^k (because p is a common divisor of p^i (for $i = 1, \ldots, k-1$) and p^k) and we have to subtract p^k/p from p^k accordingly. Note that $p^k - p^k/p = p^k - p^{k-1} = p^{k-1}(p-1)$, and hence $\phi(p^k) = (p-1)p^{k-1}$ (this is the equation that is often found in textbooks).

- If n is the product of two primes p and q (i.e., $n = pq$), then $\phi(n) = \phi(p)\phi(q) = (p-1)(q-1)$. This is because the numbers $0, p, 2p, \ldots, (q-1)p, q, 2q, \ldots, (p-1)q$ are not co-prime with n, and there are $1 + (q-1) + (p-1) = p+q-1$ of these numbers (they are all different from each other if $p \neq q$). Consequently, $\phi(n) = pq - (p+q-1) = pq - p - q + 1 = (p-1)(q-1)$.

Putting the results together, we can determine $\phi(n)$ for any integer n that has a known prime factorization (i.e., $n = \prod_i q_i^{k_i}$):

22 Leonhard Euler was a Swiss mathematician who lived from 1707 to 1783.

$$\phi(n) = \prod_i (q_i - 1)q_i^{k_i-1}$$

For example, in order to compute $\phi(45)$ we compute the factorization $45 = 3^2 \cdot 5$ and apply the formula given earlier. In fact, we have

$$
\begin{aligned}
\phi(45) &= (3-1) \cdot 3^{2-1} \cdot (5-1)^{1-1} \\
&= 2 \cdot 3^1 \cdot 4 \cdot 5^0 \\
&= 2 \cdot 3 \cdot 4 \cdot 1 \\
&= 24.
\end{aligned}
$$

A final word is due to the difficulty of computing $\phi(n)$ as compared to finding the factorization of n. For simplicity, we assume n to be the product of two primes p and q (i.e., $n = pq$). In this case, we can show that computing $\phi(n)$ is equally difficult to finding p and q. This means that if we can compute $\phi(n)$ for any n, then we can also factor n.

Starting with $\phi(pq) = (p-1)(q-1) = pq - (p+q) + 1 = n - (p+q) + 1$, we can state (3.3):

$$p + q = n - \phi(pq) + 1 \tag{3.3}$$

On the other hand, we can state that $(p-q)^2 = p^2 - 2pq + q^2 = p^2 + 2pq + q^2 - 4pq = (p+q)^2 - 4pq = (p+q)^2 - 4n$. Computing the square root on either side of this equation, we get $p - q = \sqrt{(p+q)^2 - 4n}$. In this equation, we can substitute $p + q$ with the right side of (3.3). The result is (3.4):

$$p - q = \sqrt{(n - \phi(pq) + 1)^2 - 4n} \tag{3.4}$$

By adding (3.3) and (3.4), we get the following formula to compute $(p+q) + (p-q) = p + q + p - q = 2p$:

$$2p = n - \phi(pq) + 1 + \sqrt{(n - \phi(pq) + 1)^2 - 4n}$$

This means that we can compute $2p$ and—more interestingly—p if we know $\phi(n)$. Assuming the difficulty of factorization, we can assume that computing $\phi(n)$ for any n with unknown factorization is also difficult (otherwise we could construct an efficient factorization algorithm by first computing $\phi(n)$). This property is used, for example, in the RSA public key cryptosystem.

3.3 MODULAR ARITHMETIC

Modular arithmetic elaborates on the ring[23] $\langle \mathbb{Z}_n, +, \cdot \rangle$ that consists of a complete residue system modulo n (denoted as $\mathbb{Z}_n$) and the two operations $+$ and $\cdot$. In this setting, $+$ refers to the addition modulo n, and $\cdot$ refers to the multiplication modulo n. In this section, we look at the aspects of modular arithmetic that are relevant for contemporary cryptography.

3.3.1 Modular Congruence

Two integers are *congruent* modulo a given natural number if they represent the same value when computed modulo this number. This is formally expressed in Definition 3.29.

Definition 3.29 *Let $a, b \in \mathbb{Z}$ and $n \in \mathbb{N}$. a is* congruent to b modulo n, *denoted $a \equiv b \pmod{n}$, if n divides $a - b$ (i.e., $n | a - b$).*

For example, $7 \equiv 12 \pmod 5$, $4 \equiv -1 \pmod 5$, $12 \equiv 0 \pmod 2$, and $-2 \equiv 19 \pmod{21}$.

It can be shown that congruence modulo n defines an *equivalence relation* over $\mathbb{Z}$. This means that for all $n \in \mathbb{N}$ and $a, b, c \in \mathbb{Z}$

1. $a \equiv a \pmod{n}$ (i.e., the relation is *reflexive*);

2. If $a \equiv b \pmod{n}$, then $b \equiv a \pmod{n}$ (i.e., the relation is *symmetric*);

3. If $a \equiv b \pmod{n}$ and $b \equiv c \pmod{n}$, then $a \equiv c \pmod{n}$ (i.e., the relation is *transitive*).

It is well known that an equivalence relation over a set (e.g., $\mathbb{Z}$) partitions the set into *equivalence classes*. In the case of $\mathbb{Z}$, the equivalence classes are also referred to as *residue classes*. Every $a \in \mathbb{Z}$ is congruent modulo n to some $b \in \{0, \ldots, n - 1\}$, and hence $R_n(a)$ defines a residue class that consists of all $x \in \mathbb{Z}$ that are congruent to a modulo n. This can be formally expressed as follows:

---

23 Note that $\langle \mathbb{Z}_n, +, \cdot \rangle$ is a field if n is a prime.

$$R_n(a) := \{x \in \mathbb{Z} \mid a \equiv x \pmod{n}\}$$

In the literature, $\bar{a}$ or $a + n\mathbb{Z}$ are sometimes also used to refer to $R_n(a)$. Furthermore, one frequently uses the term residue to actually refer to a residue class. For example, the residue (class) of 0 modulo 2 is the set of even integers, whereas the residue (class) of 1 modulo 2 is the set of odd integers. Similarly, the residue classes modulo 4 are defined as follows:

$$\bar{0} = 0 + 4\mathbb{Z} = R_4(0) = \{0, 0 \pm 4, 0 \pm 2 \cdot 4, \ldots\} = \{0, -4, 4, -8, 8, \ldots\}$$
$$\bar{1} = 1 + 4\mathbb{Z} = R_4(1) = \{1, 1 \pm 4, 1 \pm 2 \cdot 4, \ldots\} = \{1, -3, 5, -7, 9, \ldots\}$$
$$\bar{2} = 2 + 4\mathbb{Z} = R_4(2) = \{2, 2 \pm 4, 2 \pm 2 \cdot 4, \ldots\} = \{2, -2, 6, -6, 10, \ldots\}$$
$$\bar{3} = 3 + 4\mathbb{Z} = R_4(3) = \{3, 3 \pm 4, 3 \pm 2 \cdot 4, \ldots\} = \{3, -1, 7, -5, 11, \ldots\}$$

As already mentioned in Section 3.1.2.3, $\mathbb{Z}_n$ is used to represent $\mathbb{Z}/n\mathbb{Z}$, and $\mathbb{Z}/n\mathbb{Z}$ is used to represent the quotient group of $\mathbb{Z}$ modulo $n\mathbb{Z}$. It consists of all residue classes modulo n (there are n such classes, because all residues $0, 1, \ldots, n - 1$ can occur in the division with n). In fact, the set $\{0, \ldots, n - 1\}$ is called a *complete residue system modulo n*. Note that other elements could also be used to get a complete residue system modulo n, but that the ones mentioned earlier simplify things considerably.

The modulo n operator defines a mapping $f : \mathbb{Z} \to \mathbb{Z}_n$, and this mapping represents a homomorphism from $\mathbb{Z}$ onto $\mathbb{Z}_n$. This means that we can add and multiply residues (or residue classes, respectively) similar to integers. The corresponding rules are as follows:

$$R_n(a + b) = R_n(R_n(a) + R_n(b))$$
$$R_n(a \cdot b) = R_n(R_n(a) \cdot R_n(b))$$

Consequently, intermediate results of a modular computation can be reduced (i.e., computed modulo m) at any time without changing the result. The following examples are to make this point more clear.

$$R_7(12 + 18) = R_7(R_7(12) + R_7(18))$$

$$
\begin{aligned}
&= R_7(5+4) \\
&= R_7(9) = 2
\end{aligned}
$$

$$
\begin{aligned}
R_7(12 \cdot 18) &= R_7(R_7(12) \cdot R_7(18)) \\
&= R_7(5 \cdot 4) \\
&= R_7(20) = 6
\end{aligned}
$$

$$
\begin{aligned}
R_7(8^{37} + 9^4) &= R_7(1^{37} + 2^4) \\
&= R_7(1 + 16) \\
&= R_7(17) = 3
\end{aligned}
$$

On the other hand, the fact that $\langle \mathbb{Z}_n, +, \cdot \rangle$ is (only) a ring implies that not all elements of $\mathbb{Z}_n$ must have inverse elements with regard to multiplication. For example, the inverse element of 3 modulo 10 is 7 (i.e., $3 \cdot 7 = 21 \equiv 1 \pmod{10}$, but the inverse of 4 modulo 10 does not exist.[24] If there exists a $b \in \mathbb{Z}_n$ such that $ab \equiv 1 \pmod{n}$, then b is called the *multiplicative inverse* of a modulo n and is denoted as $b = a^{-1} \pmod{n}$. One can show that a has a multiplicative inverse modulo n if and only if $gcd(a, n) = 1$, meaning that a and n must be co-prime. In this case, the multiplicative inverse modulo n can be computed using the extended Euclidean algorithm (see Algorithm 3.2). If one replaces b with n in (3.1), then one gets

$$
xa + yn = gcd(a, n) = 1. \tag{3.5}
$$

This equation is equivalent to $xa \equiv 1 \pmod{n}$, and hence x is the multiplicative inverse of a modulo n. Contrary to that, if $gcd(a, n) = k > 1$, then one can show that a cannot have an inverse modulo n.

If we look at all elements in $\mathbb{Z}_n$ that are co-prime with n, then we get a subset of $\mathbb{Z}_n$ in which all elements are invertible. This subset is denoted $\mathbb{Z}_n^*$ and is formally defined as follows:

$$
\mathbb{Z}_n^* := \{ x \in \mathbb{Z}_n \mid gcd(x, n) = 1 \}
$$

---

[24] Note that 4 and 10 have a common factor 2, and that $4 \cdot a$ always contains a factor 2 and cannot be 1 (for all $a \in \mathbb{Z}_n$).

$\langle \mathbb{Z}_n^*, \cdot \rangle$ is a commutative group that is frequently written as $\mathbb{Z}_n^*$. If n is prime, then $\mathbb{Z}_n \setminus \{0\} = \mathbb{Z}_n^*$, and hence $\langle \mathbb{Z}_n \setminus \{0\}, \cdot \rangle$ is a group. Furthermore, the order of $\mathbb{Z}_n^*$ (i.e., $|\mathbb{Z}_n^*|$) is equal to $\phi(n)$. This means that it can be computed using Euler's totient function (see Section 3.2.6).

3.3.2 Modular Exponentiation

A frequently used computation in cryptography is modular exponentiation. If, for example, we want to compute

$$a^b \ (\text{mod } n)$$

for $a \in \mathbb{Z}_n^*$ and $b \in \mathbb{N}$, then the simplest algorithm is to iteratively multiply a modulo n b times. If $b = 23$, then the following sequence of equations yields the correct result with 22 modular multiplications:

$$
\begin{aligned}
R_n(a^2) &= R_n(a \cdot a) \\
R_n(a^3) &= R_n(a \cdot R_n(a^2)) \\
R_n(a^4) &= R_n(a \cdot R_n(a^3)) \\
&\cdots \\
R_n(a^{23}) &= R_n(a \cdot R_n(a^{22}))
\end{aligned}
$$

This can be simplified considerably, and the following sequence of equations yields the correct result but requires only 7 modular multiplications:

$$
\begin{aligned}
R_n(a^2) &= R_n(a \cdot a) \\
R_n(a^4) &= R_n(R_n(a^2) \cdot R_n(a^2)) \\
R_n(a^5) &= R_n(a \cdot R_n(a^4)) \\
R_n(a^{10}) &= R_n(R_n(a^5) \cdot R_n(a^5)) \\
R_n(a^{11}) &= R_n(a \cdot R_n(a^{10})) \\
R_n(a^{22}) &= R_n(R_n(a^{11}) \cdot R_n(a^{11})) \\
R_n(a^{23}) &= R_n(a \cdot R_n(a^{22}))
\end{aligned}
$$

This method can be generalized and the resulting *square-and-multiply algorithm* as captured in Algorithm 3.3 works for modular exponentiation in any (multiplicative) group. Let $\langle G, \cdot \rangle$ be such a group, a an element in the group, and b a positive integer (i.e., $b \in \mathbb{N}$). If we want to compute a^b in G, then we must have a binary representation of the exponent b (i.e., $b = b_{k-1} \ldots b_1 b_0$) and process this string bitwise from one end to the other. More specifically, we process the exponent from the most significant bit (i.e., b_{k-1}) to the least significant bit (i.e., b_0). The other direction is also possible and works similarly. In Algorithm 3.3, the variable s is used to accumulate the result. The variable is initially set to 1. The exponent is then processed from b_{k-1} to b_0. For each exponent bit, the value of s is squared and multiplied with a if the bit is equal to one. Finally, the algorithm returns s, and this value represents a^b in G.

Algorithm 3.3 The square-and-multiply algorithm.

$$\frac{(a \in G, b = b_{k-1} \ldots b_1 b_0 \in \mathbb{N})}{\begin{aligned} &s \leftarrow 1 \\ &\text{for } i = k - 1 \text{ down to } 0 \text{ do} \\ &\quad s \leftarrow s \cdot s \\ &\quad \text{if } b_i = 1 \text{ then } s \leftarrow s \cdot a \\ &\text{return } s \end{aligned}}$$
$$(a^b)$$

Let's have a look at an example. If we consider the group $\mathbb{Z}_{11}$ and want to compute $7^{22} \pmod{11}$, then we must first write the exponent in binary notation (i.e., $b = (22)_{10} = (10110)_2$) and set s to 1. The computation according to Algorithm 3.3 is as follows:

$$
\begin{aligned}
7^{(1)_2} &= 1^2 \cdot 7 \equiv 7 \pmod{11} \\
7^{(10)_2} &= 7^2 \equiv 5 \pmod{11} \\
7^{(101)_2} &= 5^2 \cdot 7 \equiv 3 \cdot 7 \equiv 10 \pmod{11} \\
7^{(1011)_2} &= (10)^2 \cdot 7 \equiv 7 \pmod{11} \\
7^{(10110)_2} &= 7^2 \equiv 5 \pmod{11}
\end{aligned}
$$

In the first iteration, s is squared and multiplied with 7 modulo 11. The result is 7. In the second iteration, this value is squared modulo 11. The result is 5. In the third iteration, this value is squared and multiplied with 7 modulo 11. The result is 10 (or -1). In the fourth iteration, this value is squared and multiplied with 7 modulo

11. The result is again 7. Finally, in the fifth and last iteration, this value is squared modulo 11. The result is 5. Consequently, 7^{22} (mod 11) equals 5.

3.3.3 Chinese Remainder Theorem

One sometimes has a system of congruences for an integer that must all be fulfilled simultaneously. This is where the *Chinese remainder theorem* (CRT) as captured in Theorem 3.6 comes into play (we provide the theorem without a proof).

Theorem 3.6 (Chinese remainder theorem) *Let*

$$x \equiv a_1 \ (\text{mod } n_1)$$
$$x \equiv a_2 \ (\text{mod } n_2)$$
$$\cdots$$
$$x \equiv a_k \ (\text{mod } n_k)$$

be a system of k congruences with pairwise co-prime moduli $n_1, \ldots, n_k$. The system has a unique and efficiently computable solution x in $\mathbb{Z}_n$ with $n = \prod_{i=1}^{k} n_i$.

The fact that the solution is *unique* in $\mathbb{Z}_n$ means that all other solutions are not elements of $\mathbb{Z}_n$. In fact, the set of all solutions is the set of integers y such that $y \equiv x \ (\text{mod } n)$. Furthermore, the fact that there is an *efficiently computable* solution x in $\mathbb{Z}_n$ means that there is an efficient algorithm that finds the solution. This algorithm is sometimes referred to as the *Chinese remainder algorithm* (CRA).

Let $m_i = n/n_i$ for $i = 1, \ldots, k$, and $y_i = m_i^{-1} \ (\text{mod } n_i)$, meaning that y_i is the multiplicative inverse element of m_i modulo n_i. Because all moduli are assumed to be pairwise co-prime, y_i is well defined (for all $i = 1, \ldots, k$). The solution x can then be computed as follows:

$$x \equiv \sum_{i=1}^{k} a_i m_i y_i \ (\text{mod } n)$$

For example, consider the following system of 3 congruences:

$$x \equiv 5 \ (\text{mod } 7)$$
$$x \equiv 3 \ (\text{mod } 11)$$
$$x \equiv 11 \ (\text{mod } 13)$$

In this example, $n_1 = 7$, $n_2 = 11$, $n_3 = 13$ (note that these integers are pairwise co-prime), and $n = 7 \cdot 11 \cdot 13 = 1001$. Furthermore, $a_1 = 5$, $a_2 = 3$, and $a_3 = 10$. To determine the solution x in $\mathbb{Z}_{1001}$, one must compute

$$
\begin{aligned}
m_1 &= 1001/7 = 143 \\
m_2 &= 1001/11 = 91 \\
m_3 &= 1001/13 = 77
\end{aligned}
$$

and

$$
\begin{aligned}
y_1 &\equiv 143^{-1} \,(\mathrm{mod}\ 1001) = 5 \\
y_2 &\equiv 91^{-1} \,(\mathrm{mod}\ 1001) = 4 \\
y_3 &\equiv 77^{-1} \,(\mathrm{mod}\ 1001) = 12
\end{aligned}
$$

After this preparation, the solution x can be computed as follows:

$$
\begin{aligned}
x &\equiv \sum_{i=1}^{k} a_i m_i y_i \,(\mathrm{mod}\ n) \\
&\equiv a_1 m_1 y_1 + a_2 m_2 y_2 + a_3 m_3 y_3 \,(\mathrm{mod}\ n) \\
&\equiv 5 \cdot 143 \cdot 5 + 3 \cdot 91 \cdot 4 + 10 \cdot 77 \cdot 12 \,(\mathrm{mod}\ 1001) \\
&\equiv 3575 + 1092 + 9240 \,(\mathrm{mod}\ 1001) \\
&\equiv 13907 \,(\mathrm{mod}\ 1001) \\
&= 894
\end{aligned}
$$

Consequently, $x = 894$ is the solution in $\mathbb{Z}_{1001}$, and $\{i \in \mathbb{Z} \mid 894 + i \cdot 1001\}$ is the set of all solutions in $\mathbb{Z}$.

The case $k = 2$ is so important in practice that we have a closer look at the corresponding CRA. The system of congruences looks as follows:

$$
\begin{aligned}
x &\equiv a_1 \,(\mathrm{mod}\ n_1) \\
x &\equiv a_2 \,(\mathrm{mod}\ n_2)
\end{aligned}
$$

Again, the moduli n_1 and n_2 must be co-prime (i.e., $gcd(n_1, n_2) = 1$). We compute

$$t \equiv n_2^{-1} \pmod{n_1}$$

and

$$u \equiv (a_2 - a_1)t \pmod{n_1}.$$

The solution x modulo n can then computed as follows:

$$x = a_1 + un_2$$

The CRA can be used to speed up the implementation of many public key cryptosystems, including, for example, the RSA public key cryptosystem.

3.3.4 Fermat's Little Theorem

We have mentioned several times that $\langle \mathbb{Z}_p, +, \cdot \rangle$ represents a field for every prime p (and hence $\langle \mathbb{Z}_p^*, \cdot \rangle$ is a group in which every element is invertible). Theorem 3.7 applies to all elements in $\mathbb{Z}_p^*$. It is due to Pierre de Fermat, and hence it is known as *Fermat's Little Theorem*.

Theorem 3.7 (Fermat's Little Theorem) *If p is a prime and $a \in \mathbb{Z}_p^*$, then $a^{p-1} \equiv 1 \pmod{p}$.*

Proof. Because $\phi(p) = p - 1$ for every prime number p, Fermat's Little Theorem is just a special case of Euler's Theorem.

$\square$

Fermat's Little Theorem has many applications. For example, it can be used to find the multiplicative inverse of a modulo p. If we divide the equivalence $a^{p-1} \equiv 1 \pmod{p}$ by a on either side, we get

$$a^{(p-1)-1} \equiv a^{p-2} \equiv a^{-1} \pmod{p}.$$

This means that one can find the multiplicative inverse element of a modulo p by computing $a^{p-2} \pmod{p}$. For example, if $p = 7$, then the multiplicative inverse of 2 modulo 7 can be computed as follows: $2^{-1} \equiv 2^{7-2} \equiv 2^5 \equiv 25 \pmod{7} = 4$. Another application of Fermat's Little Theorem was already mentioned in Section 3.2.4.3 in the context of primality (or compositeness) testing.

3.3.5 Euler's Theorem

Fermat's Little Theorem was generalized by Leonhard Euler to be applied in any ring $\langle \mathbb{Z}_n, +, \cdot \rangle$ (with n being a composite). The fact that $\langle \mathbb{Z}_n, +, \cdot \rangle$ is a ring implies that $\langle \mathbb{Z}_n, + \rangle$ is a group with identity element 0, and that $\langle \mathbb{Z}_n, \cdot \rangle$ is a monoid with identity element 1. If we restrict the set of numbers to $\mathbb{Z}_n^* = \{a \in \mathbb{Z}_n \mid gcd(a, n) = 1\}$ (i.e., the set of elements of $\mathbb{Z}_n$ that have inverse elements), then $\langle \mathbb{Z}_n^*, \cdot \rangle$ represents a multiplicative group and inverse elements exist for all of its elements. The order of the the group can be computed using Euler's totient function introduced in Section 3.2.6 (i.e., $|\mathbb{Z}_n^*| = \phi(n)$). For example, $\phi(45) = 3 \cdot (3 - 1)^{2-1} \cdot (5 - 1) = 24$, and this value equals $|\mathbb{Z}_{45}^*| = |\{1, 2, 4, 7, 8, 11, 13, 14, 16, 17, 19, 22, 23, 26, 28, 29, 31, 32, 34, 37, 38, 41, 43, 44\}| = 24$.

In essence, Euler's Theorem as stated in Theorem 3.8 says that any element a in $\mathbb{Z}_n^*$ is equivalent to 1 modulo n if it is multiplied $\phi(n)$ times.

Theorem 3.8 (Euler's Theorem) *If $gcd(a, n) = 1$, then $a^{\phi(n)} \equiv 1 \pmod{n}$.*

Proof. Because $gcd(a, n) = 1$, $a \pmod{n}$ must be an element in $\mathbb{Z}_n^*$. Also, $|\mathbb{Z}_n^*| = \phi(n)$. According to a corollary of Lagrange's Theorem, the order of every element (in a finite group) divides the order of the group. Consequently, the order of a (i.e., $ord(a)$ as introduced in Section 3.1.2.3) divides $\phi(n)$, and hence if we multiply a modulo n $\phi(n)$ times we always get a value that is equivalent to 1 modulo n.

$\square$

Because $\phi(n) = n - 1$ if n is a prime, Euler's Theorem is indeed a generalization of Fermat's Little Theorem.

3.3.6 Finite Fields Modulo Irreducible Polynomials

Finite fields modulo irreducible polynomials are frequently used in contemporary cryptography. The notion of a polynomial is introduced in Definition 3.30.

Definition 3.30 (Polynomial) *Let A be an algebraic structure with addition and multiplication (e.g., a ring or a field). A function $p(x)$ is a polynomial in x over A if it is of the form*

$$p(x) = \sum_{i=0}^{n} a_i x^i = a_0 + a_1 x + a_2 x^2 + \ldots + a_n x^n$$

where n is a positive integer (i.e., the degree of $p(x)$, denoted as $deg(p)$), the coefficients a_i ($0 \leq i \leq n$) are elements in A, and x is a symbol not belonging to A.

The set of all polynomials over A is denoted by $A[x]$. The elements of $A[x]$ are polynomials, and one can compute with these polynomials as if they were integers. More specifically, one can add and multiply polynomials. Furthermore, if $f, g \in A[x]$ such that $g \neq 0$, then one can write

$$f = gq + r$$

for $q, r \in A[x]$ and $deg(r) < deg(g)$. This equation reminds us of Euclid's division theorem (see Theorem 3.3), and hence we can also apply the Euclidean algorithms in $A[x]$. In this case, r is the remainder of f divided by g, denoted by $r \equiv f \pmod{g}$. The set of all remainders of all polynomials in $A[x]$ modulo g is denoted by $A[x]_g$.

A polynomial $f \in A[x]$ is *irreducible* over A if the following two conditions are satisfied:

1. f has a positive degree;

2. $f = gh$ with $g, h \in A[x]$ implies that either g or h is a constant polynomial.

Otherwise, f is *reducible* over A. Note that the reducibility of a polynomial depends on the algebraic structure A over which the polynomial is defined (i.e., a polynomial can be reducible over one algebraic structure and irreducible over another).

Against this background, one can show that if F is a field and f is a nonzero polynomial in $F[x]$, then $F[x]_f$ is a ring. Furthermore, one can show that $F[x]_f$ is a field if and only if f is irreducible over F. In this case, the number of elements in the field $F[x]_f$ is p^n (if p represents the number of elements in F and n represents the degree of f). We conclude that for every prime p and every positive integer n, there is a finite field with p^n elements (as mentioned in Section 3.1.2.5), and we denote this field by $\mathbb{F}_p[x]_f$. Under isomorphism, we can say that $\mathbb{F}_p[x]_f$ is the finite field of order p^n.

For example, the polynomial $f(x) = x^8 + x^4 + x^3 + x + 1$ is irreducible over $\mathbb{F}_2$. Consequently, the set of all polynomials modulo f over $\mathbb{F}_2$ forms a field with 2^8 elements (i.e., all polynomials over $\mathbb{F}_2$ of degree less than 8). So any element in the field $\mathbb{F}_2[x]_f$ is of the form

$$b_7 x^7 + b_6 x^6 + b_5 x^5 + b_4 x^4 + b_3 x^3 + b_2 x^2 + b_1 x + b_0$$

where all $b_i \in \mathbb{Z}_2$ $(0 \leq i \leq 7)$. Thus, any element in this field can be represented as a word of 8 binary digits (bits), or a byte. Conversely, any byte can also be viewed as an element in the field $\mathbb{F}_2[x]_f$. For example, the byte 11010111 can be viewed as polynomial $x^6 + x^4 + x^2 + x + 1$.

3.3.7 Quadratic Residuosity

In integer arithmetic, an $x \in \mathbb{Z}$ is a *perfect square* if there is a $y \in \mathbb{Z}$ such that $x = y^2$. If such a y exists, then it is called a *square root* of x. For example, 25 is a square with square root 5, whereas 20 is not a square. Similarly, all negative numbers are not squares. If an integer x is a square, then it has precisely two square roots, and these values can be computed efficiently from x (even if x is very large).

In modular arithmetic, things are more involved. Similar to perfect squares and square roots in $\mathbb{Z}$, we use the terms *quadratic residues* (corresponding to perfect squares) and *square roots* in $\mathbb{Z}_n^*$. Quadratic residues play an important role in number theory. For example, many integer factoring algorithms employ quadratic residues (see Section 7.3), and quadratic residues also have applications in asymmetric encryption systems and cryptographic protocols. The notions of a quadratic residue and a square root are formally introduced in Definition 3.31.

Definition 3.31 (Quadratic residue and square root) *An element* $x \in \mathbb{Z}_n^*$ *is a* quadratic residue *modulo* n *if there exists an element* $y \in \mathbb{Z}_n^*$ *such that* $x = y^2 \pmod{n}$. *If such a* y *exists, then it is called a* square root *of* x *modulo* n.

The resulting set of quadratic residues in $\mathbb{Z}_n^*$, denoted by QR_n, is formally defined as follows:

$$QR_n := \{x \in \mathbb{Z}_n^* \mid \exists y \in \mathbb{Z}_n^* : y^2 \equiv x \pmod{n}\}$$

Note that QR_n is a multiplicative subgroup of $\mathbb{Z}_n^*$. If $x_1, x_2 \in QR_n$ with square roots y_1 and y_2, then the square root of $x_1 x_2$ is $y_1 y_2$ (because $(y_1 y_2)^2 \equiv y_1^2 y_2^2 \equiv x_1 x_2 \pmod{n}$) and the square root of x_1^{-1} is y_1^{-1} (because $(y_1^{-1})^2 \equiv (y_1^2)^{-1} \equiv x_1^{-1} \pmod{n}$). Also note that every element in $\mathbb{Z}_n^*$ is either a quadratic residue or a quadratic nonresidue. Consequently, the set of all quadratic nonresidues in $\mathbb{Z}_n^*$ is the complement of QR_n (with respect to $\mathbb{Z}_n^*$). It is commonly referred to as QNR_n (i.e., $QNR_n = \mathbb{Z}_n^* \setminus QR_n$). In order to further discuss the properties of quadratic residues, one must distinguish the situation in which n is a prime or n is a composite number. These two cases are discussed separately.

3.3.7.1 Prime

For every prime number p, $\langle \mathbb{Z}_p, +, \cdot \rangle$ is a field and $\langle \mathbb{Z}_p^*, \cdot \rangle$ with $\mathbb{Z}_p^* = \mathbb{Z}_p \setminus \{0\}$ is the multiplicative group. In this group, quadratic residuosity is a comparable simple construct that is not too different from integer arithmetic. For example, it can be shown that any polynomial of degree two has at most two solutions, and that in $\mathbb{Z}_p$ every $x \in QR_p$ has exactly two square roots modulo p (if y is one of them, then the other is $-y = p - y$). There are, however, also some things that are different from integer arithmetic. For example, among integers, perfect squares are quite sparse, and they get sparser and sparser for large n (i.e., there are only about $\sqrt{n}$ perfect squares in the interval $[1, n]$). Contrary to that, half of the elements of $\mathbb{Z}_p^*$ are quadratic residues (and elements of QR_p accordingly). In fact, the following equation holds for every odd prime (i.e., for every prime $p > 2$):

$$|QR_p| = \frac{p-1}{2}$$

For example, in $\mathbb{Z}_7^*$ the elements $\{1, 2, 3, 4, 5, 6\}$ can all be set to the power of two to figure out quadratic residues:

x	1	2	3	4	5	6
x^2	1	4	2	2	4	1

Note that only 1, 4, and 2 occur on the second line and represent quadratic residues accordingly. Consequently, $QR_7 = \{1, 2, 4\}$ and $QNR_7 = \mathbb{Z}_7^* \setminus QR_7 = \{3, 5, 6\}$.[25] Using the same algorithm, one can easily determine

$$QR_{19} = \{1, 4, 5, 6, 7, 9, 11, 16, 17\}$$

and

$$QNR_{19} = \mathbb{Z}_{19}^* \setminus QR_{19} = \{2, 3, 8, 10, 12, 13, 14, 15, 18\}$$

---

25   Even though it is known that half of the elements in $\mathbb{Z}_p^*$ are quadratic nonresidues modulo p, there is no deterministic polynomial-time algorithm known for finding one. A randomized algorithm for finding a quadratic nonresidue is to simply select random integers $a \in \mathbb{Z}_p^*$ until one is found (using, for example, Euler's criterion to decide whether a quadratic nonresidue has been found). The expected number of iterations before a nonresidue is found is 2, and hence the algorithm takes expected polynomial time.

for $p = 19$. Consequently, for every prime $p > 2$, $\mathbb{Z}_p^*$ is partitioned into two equal-size subsets QR_p and QNR_p (each subset comprises $(p-1)/2$ elements).

Euler's criterion (Theorem 3.9) can be used to efficiently decide whether an $x \in Z_p^*$ is a quadratic residue modulo p. We don't prove the criterion is this book.

Theorem 3.9 (Euler's criterion) *Let p be a prime number. For any $x \in Z_p^*$, $x \in QR_p$ if and only if*

$$x^{\frac{p-1}{2}} \equiv 1 \pmod{p}.$$

If Euler's Criterion is not met, then

$$x^{\frac{p-1}{2}} \equiv -1 \pmod{p}.$$

Hence, Euler's criterion provides a criterion to decide whether an element $x \in Z_p^*$ is a quadratic residue modulo p. If $x^{(p-1)/2} \equiv 1 \pmod{p}$, then $x \in QR_p$; otherwise if $x^{(p-1)/2} \equiv -1 \pmod{p}$, then $x \in QNR_p$. In either case, the result of Euler's criterion is captured by the *Legendre symbol*. The Legendre symbol of x modulo p is formally defined as follows:

$$\left(\frac{x}{p}\right) = \begin{cases} +1 & \text{if } x \in QR_p \\ -1 & \text{otherwise (i.e., if } x \in QNR_p) \end{cases}$$

For $p > 2$, the Legendre symbol can be computed using Euler's criterion:

$$\left(\frac{x}{p}\right) \equiv x^{\frac{p-1}{2}} \pmod{p}$$

Consequently, $\left(\frac{1}{p}\right) \equiv 1^{\frac{p-1}{2}} \pmod{p} = 1$ and $\left(\frac{-1}{p}\right) \equiv (-1)^{\frac{p-1}{2}}$ for every prime p.

From Euler's criterion we see that

$$\left(\frac{x}{p}\right) = \left(\frac{y}{p}\right)$$

for $x \equiv y \pmod{p}$. Furthermore, we see that the Legendre symbol is multiplicative, meaning that

$$\left(\frac{xy}{p}\right) = \left(\frac{x}{p}\right) \cdot \left(\frac{y}{p}\right)$$

This fact directly results from Euler's criterion:

$$
\begin{aligned}
\left(\frac{xy}{p}\right) &\equiv (xy)^{\frac{p-1}{2}} \pmod{p} \\
&\equiv x^{\frac{p-1}{2}} y^{\frac{p-1}{2}} \pmod{p} \\
&\equiv x^{\frac{p-1}{2}} \pmod{p} \; y^{\frac{p-1}{2}} \pmod{p} \\
&= \left(\frac{x}{p}\right) \cdot \left(\frac{y}{p}\right)
\end{aligned}
$$

For example,

$$\left(\frac{6}{7}\right) = \left(\frac{2}{7}\right) \cdot \left(\frac{3}{7}\right) = 1 \cdot (-1) = -1.$$

In fact, 6 is a quadratic nonresidue (i.e., $6 \in QNR_7$). Furthermore, for any $x \in \mathbb{Z}_p^*$, it holds that $\left(\frac{x^2}{p}\right) = 1$.

There is an efficient randomized algorithm that on input prime p and $x \in \mathbb{Z}_p$ tests whether x is a quadratic residue and, if so, returns the two square roots of x.

Things are getting even simpler if one assumes $p \equiv 3 \pmod 4$. In this case, it is particularly simple to compute the square root from $x \in QR_p$:

$$y = x^{\frac{p+1}{4}} \pmod{p} \tag{3.6}$$

The expression makes sense, because $p \equiv 3 \pmod 4$ and hence $\frac{p+1}{4}$ is an integer. Also, it can be verified that $y^2 \equiv x \pmod p$:

$$
\begin{aligned}
y^2 &\equiv (x^{\frac{p+1}{4}})^2 \pmod{p} \\
&\equiv x^{\frac{p+1}{2}} \pmod{p} \\
&\equiv x^{\frac{p-1}{2}} \cdot x^{\frac{2}{2}} \pmod{p}
\end{aligned}
$$

$$\equiv \quad x^{\frac{p-1}{2}} \cdot x \pmod{p}$$
$$\equiv \quad 1 \cdot x \equiv x \pmod{p}$$

Euler's criterion and the fact that x is a quadratic residue are used in the last step.

If $p \equiv 3 \pmod{4}$, then for some $r \in \mathbb{N}$ $p = 4r + 3$ and $p - 1 = 4r + 2$ (i.e., $\frac{p-1}{2} = \frac{4r+2}{2} = 2r + 1$). Consequently, the Legendre symbol for -1 can be computed using Euler's criterion:

$$\left(\frac{-1}{p} \right) \equiv (-1)^{\frac{p-1}{2}} \equiv (-1)^{2r+1} \equiv -1 \pmod{p}$$

This means that -1 is a quadratic nonresidue modulo p (i.e., $-1 \in QNR_p$).

3.3.7.2 Composite

If n is a composite, then the situation is more involved. First of all, it can be shown that the *quadratic residuosity problem* (QRP) as captured in Definition 3.32 is hard.[26] It is at the core of many cryptographic systems, including, for example, probabilistic encryption as introduced and discussed in Section 14.3.1.

Definition 3.32 (Quadratic residuosity problem) *Let $n \in \mathbb{N}$ be a composite positive integer and $x \in \mathbb{Z}_n^*$. The QRP is to decide whether $x \in QR_n$.*

It is conjectured that no efficient algorithm, on input $n \in \mathbb{N}$ (the product of two large primes) and $x \in \mathbb{Z}_n^*$, can solve the QRP and decide whether x is a quadratic residue modulo n. Furthermore, it can be shown that a square root of x can be computed if and only if the factorization of n is known. This means that computing square roots in $\mathbb{Z}_n^*$ is as hard as factoring n, and hence computing square roots in $\mathbb{Z}_n^*$ and factoring n are computationally equivalent. Hence, if the factorization of n is known, then extracting square roots becomes feasible (remember the discussion in Section 3.3.3, when we said that there are functions modulo n that are simpler to compute modulo the prime factors of n). In fact, one can show that $x \in QR_n$ if and only if $x \in QR_p$ and $x \in QR_q$, and that every $x \in QR_n$ has exactly 4 square roots in $\mathbb{Z}_n^*$.

The *Jacobi symbol* (modulo n) is a generalization of the Legendre symbol modulo p. For $n = pq$, it is defined as follows:

---

26 The QRP is a well-known hard problem in number theory and is one of the four main algorithmic problems discussed by Gauss in his *Disquisitiones Arithmeticae*.

$$\left(\frac{x}{n}\right) = \left(\frac{x}{p}\right) \cdot \left(\frac{x}{q}\right)$$

Contrary to the Legendre symbol, the Jacobi symbol of x modulo n is not only 1 if $x \in QR_n$; it is 1 either if $x \in QR_p$ and $x \in QR_q$ or if $x \notin QR_p$ and $x \notin QR_q$. Among these two possibilities, only the first refers to the situation in which $x \in QR_n$. Consequently, all quadratic residues have Jacobi symbol 1, but the opposite is not necessarily true (as further addressed later).

More generally, let $n \geq 3$ be odd with prime factorization $n = p_1^{e_1} p_2^{e_2} \ldots p_k^{e_k}$. Then the Jacobi symbol $\left(\frac{x}{n}\right)$ is defined as follows:

$$\left(\frac{x}{n}\right) = \left(\frac{x}{p_1}\right)^{e_1} \left(\frac{x}{p_2}\right)^{e_2} \ldots \left(\frac{x}{p_k}\right)^{e_k}$$

Again, note that if n is prime, then the Jacobi symbol is just the Legendre symbol. In any case, $\left(\frac{x}{n}\right)$ is 0, 1, or -1, and $\left(\frac{x}{n}\right) = 0$ if and only if $gcd(x, n) \neq 1$. If $x \equiv y \pmod{n}$, then the equation $\left(\frac{x}{n}\right) = \left(\frac{y}{n}\right)$ holds.

Similar to the Legendre symbol,

$$\left(\frac{1}{n}\right) = 1.$$

Furthermore,

$$\left(\frac{-1}{n}\right) = (-1)^{(n-1)/2}$$

and

$$\left(\frac{2}{n}\right) = (-1)^{(n^2-1)/8}.$$

The Jacobi symbol is multiplicative in both the numerator and the denominator:

$$\left(\frac{xy}{n}\right) = \left(\frac{x}{n}\right) \cdot \left(\frac{y}{n}\right)$$

$$\left(\frac{x}{mn}\right) = \left(\frac{x}{m}\right) \cdot \left(\frac{x}{n}\right)$$

Consequently, for $x \in \mathbb{Z}_n^*$ $\left(\frac{x^2}{n}\right) = \left(\frac{x}{n}\right) \cdot \left(\frac{x}{n}\right) = 1$.

Last but not least, *Gauss' law of quadratic reciprocity* suggests that if $gcd(m, n) = 1$ and $m, n > 2$, then

$$\left(\frac{m}{n}\right)\left(\frac{n}{m}\right) = (-1)^{(m-1)(n-1)/4}.$$

Thanks to these properties, there is an efficient[27] (and recursive) algorithm for computing $\left(\frac{x}{n}\right)$, which does not require the prime factorization of n. We don't elaborate on this algorithm. For the purpose of this book, it is sufficient to know that an efficient algorithm for computing $\left(\frac{x}{n}\right)$ exists.

As mentioned earlier, the fact that the Jacobi symbol of x modulo n is 1 does not necessarily imply that $x \in QR_n$. Let J_n be the set of all elements of $\mathbb{Z}_n^*$ with Jacobi symbol 1:

$$J_n = \{x \in \mathbb{Z}_n^* \mid \left(\frac{x}{n}\right) = 1\}$$

Obviously, $QR_n \subset J_n$ and there are elements $x \in \mathbb{Z}_n^*$ that are quadratic nonresidue, but still have Jacobi symbol 1. These elements are called *pseudosquares* modulo n, denoted as $\widetilde{QR_n}$ (i.e., $\widetilde{QR_n} = J_n \setminus QR_n$).

Let $n = pq$ be the product of two primes. Then $\mathbb{Z}_n^*$ has $\phi(n) = (p-1)(q-1)$ elements, and these elements can be partitioned into two equally large sets. One half of the elements (i.e., J_n) has Jacobi symbol 1, and the other half of the elements has Jacobi symbol -1. J_n can be further partitioned into two equally large sets (i.e., QR_n and $\widetilde{QR_n}$) with $|QR_n| = |\widetilde{QR_n}| = (p-1)(q-1)/4$. For example, if $p = 3$ and $q = 7$, then $n = 3 \cdot 7 = 21$, $\mathbb{Z}_{21}^* = \{1, 2, 4, 5, 8, 10, 11, 13, 16, 17, 19, 20\}$, and $\phi(21) = 2 \cdot 6 = 12$. J_{21} has 6 elements and these elements can be partitioned as follows :

$$
\begin{aligned}
J_{21} &= \{1, 4, 5, 16, 17, 20\} \\
QR_{21} &= \{1, 4, 16\} \\
\widetilde{QR_{21}} &= \{5, 17, 20\}
\end{aligned}
$$

---

27 The algorithm has a running time of $O((\ln n)^3)$ bit operations.

The example is illustrated in Figure 3.3. The elements of $\mathbb{Z}_{21}^*$ are drawn in the circle. Each quarter of the square comprises 3 elements. The upper right quarter represents QR_{21} and the lower left quarter represents $\widetilde{QR_{21}}$. QNR_{21} comprises all elements of $\mathbb{Z}_{21}^*$ that are not elements of QR_{21} (i.e., $QNR_{21} = \{2, 5, 8, 10, 11, 13, 17, 19, 20\}$).

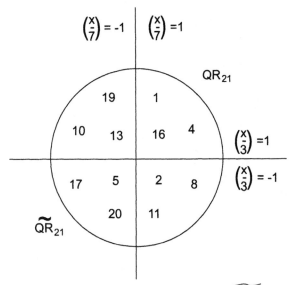

Figure 3.3   The elements of $\mathbb{Z}_{21}^*$, QR_{21}, and $\widetilde{QR_{21}}$.

Consequently, in this example the QRP is to decide whether a particular element of J_{21} is an element of QR_{21} or $\widetilde{QR_{21}}$. It goes without saying that the factorization of 21 must not be known. Many public key cryptosystems take their security from the intractability of the QRP.

3.3.8   Blum Integers

Many (public key) cryptosystems use Blum integers as formally introduced in Definition 3.33.[28]

Definition 3.33 (Blum integer) *A composite number n is a* Blum integer *if $n = pq$ where p and q are distinct prime numbers satisfying $p \equiv q \equiv 3 \pmod 4$.*

---

28   One example is the Rabin asymmetric encryption system addressed in Section 14.2.2.

If n is a Blum integer, then it can be shown that $x \in QR_n$ has precisely four square roots modulo n, exactly one of which is again an element of QR_n. This unique square root of x is called the *principal square root* of x modulo n. If we revisit the example introduced earlier, then it is easy to see that $n = 21 = 3 \cdot 7$ is a Blum integer (i.e., $3 \equiv 7 \equiv 3 \pmod 4$). $\mathbb{Z}_{21}^*$, J_{21}, QR_{21}, and $\widetilde{QR_{21}}$ are specified earlier. If we set $x = 4$, then we can determine the four square roots 2, 5, 16, and 19. Obviously, 16 is the principal square root of 4 modulo 21 (because it is again an element of QR_{21}).

If n is a Blum integer, then the function $f : QR_n \rightarrow QR_n$ defined by $f(x) = x^2 \pmod n$ represents a trapdoor permutation. The trapdoor information is the factorization of n; thus, knowing the prime factors of n, one can efficiently compute the inverse function f^{-1}:

$$f^{-1}(x) = x^{((p-1)(q-1)+4)/8} \pmod n$$

This trapdoor permutation is used, for example, by the Rabin asymmetric encryption system (see Section 14.2.2).

3.4 ELLIPTIC CURVES

Elliptic curve cryptography (ECC) is a hot topic in contemporary cryptography. We elaborate on ECC in Section 7.6. The algebraic structures emplyoyed by ECC are groups of points on elliptic curves defined over a finite field $\mathbb{F}_n$. In applications, n is typically an odd prime or a power of 2 (i.e., 2^m for some m). To keep things as simple as possible, we restrict our explanations to elliptic curves over $\mathbb{Z}_p = \{0, 1, \ldots, p - 1\}$ where p is an odd prime number. Furthermore, we don't look at the general case. We restrict ourselves to a simple case in which an elliptic curve over $\mathbb{Z}_p$ can then be defined as

$$y^2 \equiv x^3 + ax + b \pmod p \tag{3.7}$$

with $a, b \in \mathbb{Z}_p$ and $4a^3 + 27b^2 \not\equiv 0 \pmod p$. For any given a and b in $\mathbb{Z}_p$, (3.7) has pairs of solutions x, y in $\mathbb{Z}_p$ that can be expressed as follows:

$$
\begin{aligned}
E(\mathbb{Z}_p) = \{(x, y) \mid \quad & x, y \in \mathbb{Z}_p \text{ and} \\
& y^2 \equiv x^3 + ax + b \pmod p \text{ and} \\
& 4a^3 + 27b^2 \not\equiv 0 \pmod p\}
\end{aligned}
$$

The resulting set $E(\mathbb{Z}_p)$ consists of all $(x, y) \in \mathbb{Z}_p \times \mathbb{Z}_p = \mathbb{Z}_p^2$ that solve equivalence (3.7). We can graphically interpret (x, y) as a point in the (x, y)-plane (x representing the horizontal axis and y representing the vertical axis). Such an (x, y) is representing a point on the respective elliptic curve $E(\mathbb{Z}_p)$. In addition to the points on the curve, one usually considers a point at infinity (typically denoted by $\mathcal{O}$). If we use $E(\mathbb{Z}_p)$ to refer to an elliptic curve defined over $\mathbb{Z}_p$, then we automatically mean to include $\mathcal{O}$.

Let $p = 23$ and consider the elliptic curve $y^2 \equiv x^3 + x + 1$ defined over $\mathbb{Z}_{23}$. In the notation of equivalence (3.7), a and b are both set to 1. It can easily be verified that $4a^3 + 27b^2 \not\equiv 0 \pmod{p}$, and hence the curve $E(\mathbb{Z}_{23})$ indeed represents an elliptic curve. The points in $E(\mathbb{Z}_{23})$ are $\mathcal{O}$ and the following:

$(0,1)$	$(0,22)$	$(1,7)$	$(1,16)$	$(3,10)$	$(3,13)$	$(4,0)$
$(5,4)$	$(5,19)$	$(6,4)$	$(6,19)$	$(7,11)$	$(7,12)$	$(9,7)$
$(9,16)$	$(11,3)$	$(11,20)$	$(12,4)$	$(12,19)$	$(13,7)$	$(13,16)$
$(17,3)$	$(17,20)$	$(18,3)$	$(18,20)$	$(19,5)$	$(19,18)$	

In order to make use of an elliptic curve, we must define an associative operation. In ECC, this operation is called addition (mainly for historical reasons), meaning that two points on an elliptic curve are said to be added.[29] In the literature, the addition rule is usually explained geometrically. In this book, however, we use a sequence of algebraic formulae to describe the addition of two points:

1. $P + \mathcal{O} = \mathcal{O} + P = P$ for all $P \in E(\mathbb{Z}_q)$.

2. If $P = (x, y) \in E(\mathbb{Z}_q)$, then $(x, y) + (x, -y) = \mathcal{O}$. The point $(x, -y)$ is sometimes also denoted as $-P$ and called the negative of P. Note that $-P$ is indeed a point on the elliptic curve (e.g., $(3, 10) + (3, 13) = \mathcal{O}$).

3. Let $P = (x_1, y_1) \in E(\mathbb{Z}_q)$ and $Q = (x_2, y_2) \in E(\mathbb{Z}_q)$ with $P \neq -Q$, then $P + Q = (x_3, y_3)$ where

$$
\begin{aligned}
x_3 &= \lambda^2 - x_1 - x_2 \\
y_3 &= \lambda(x_1 - x_3) - y_1
\end{aligned}
$$

and

$$
\lambda = \begin{cases} \frac{y_2 - y_1}{x_2 - x_1} & \text{if } P \neq Q \\ \frac{3x_1^2 + a}{2y_1} & \text{if } P = Q \end{cases}
$$

---

29 By contrast, the group operation in $\mathbb{Z}_p^*$ is multiplication. The differences in the resulting additive notation and multiplicative notation can sometimes be confusing.

The geometric interpretation of the plus operator is straightforward: the straight line PQ intersects the elliptic curve at a third point $R' = (x_3, -y_3)$, and $R = P + Q$ is the reflection of R' in the x-axis. Alternatively speaking, if a straight line intersects the elliptic curve at three points P, Q, R, then $P + Q + R = 0$.

Consider the elliptic curve defined earlier. Let $P = (3, 10)$ and $Q = (9, 7)$. Then $P + Q = (x_3, y_3)$ is computed as follows:

$$\lambda = \frac{7 - 10}{9 - 3} = \frac{-3}{6} = \frac{-1}{2} = 11 \in \mathbb{Z}_{23}$$

$$x_3 = 11^2 - 3 - 9 = 6 - 3 - 9 = -6 \equiv 17 \,(\mathrm{mod}\ 23)$$

$$y_3 = 11(3 - (-6)) - 10 = 11(9) - 10 = 89 \equiv 20 \,(\mathrm{mod}\ 23)$$

Consequently, we have $P + Q = (17, 20) \in E(\mathbb{Z}_{23})$.

On the other hand, if we want to add $P = (3, 10)$ to itself, then we have $P + P = 2P = (x_3, y_3)$, and this point is computed as follows:

$$\lambda = \frac{3(3^2) + 1}{20} = \frac{5}{20} = \frac{1}{4} = 6 \in \mathbb{Z}_{23}$$

$$x_3 = 6^2 - 6 = 30 \equiv 7 \,(\mathrm{mod}\ 23)$$

$$y_3 = 6(3 - 7) - 10 = -24 - 10 = -11 \equiv 12 \,(\mathrm{mod}\ 23)$$

Consequently, $2P = (7, 12)$, and the procedure can be iterated to compute arbitrary multiples of point P (i.e., $3P, 4P, \ldots$).

For every elliptic curve $E(\mathbb{Z}_p)$, the group of points on this particular curve together with the point in infinity and the addition operation form a group,[30] and this group can then be used in ECC (see Section 7.6).

3.5 FINAL REMARKS

In this chapter, we overviewed and discussed the aspects of discrete mathematics that are relevant for contemporary cryptography. Most importantly, we elaborated on integer arithmetic and modular arithmetic. We also looked at some algorithms that are frequently used, such as the Euclidean algorithms and the square-and-multiply algorithm. While we elaborated on modular arithmetic, we also came

---

30   This result was proven by Henri Poincaré in 1901.

across Fermat's Little Theorem and Euler's Theorem. Both theorems are based on Lagrange's Theorem and are frequently used in cryptography. Furthermore, they have a straighforward application in the RSA public key cryptosystem. The same is true for quadratic residuosity, which has a direct application in probabilistic encryption and many indirect applications in cryptographic protocols. Last but not least, we introduced the elliptic curves that are used in ECC. While ECC is a hot topic today, it should not be overemphasized. It is useful to speed up implementations and bring down key sizes (of public key cryptosystems). It does not, however, provide cryptosystems that are inherently new or different from the cryptosystems that were known before ECC was proposed and deployed.

References

[1] Koblitz, N.I., *A Course in Number Theory and Cryptography*, 2nd edition. Springer-Verlag, New York, 1994.

[2] Koblitz, N.I., *Algebraic Aspects of Cryptography*. Springer-Verlag, New York, 1998.

[3] Rosen, K.H., *Discrete Mathematics and Its Applications*, 4th edition. McGraw Hill, Hightstown, NJ, 1998.

[4] Johnsonbaugh, R., *Discrete Mathematics*, 5th edition. Prentice Hall, Uppser Saddle River, NJ, 2000.

[5] Dossey, J.A., et al., *Discrete Mathematics*, 4th edition. Addison-Wesley, Reading, MA, 2001.

[6] Shoup, V., *A Computational Introduction to Number Theory and Algebra*. Cambridge University Press, Cambridge, UK, 2005.

[7] Maurer, U.M., "Fast Generation of Prime Numbers and Secure Public-Key Cryptographic Parameters," *Journal of Cryptology*, Vol. 8, No. 3, 1995, pp. 123–155.

Chapter 4

Probability Theory

Probability theory plays a central role in information theory and contemporary cryptography. In fact, the ultimate goal of a cryptographer is to make the probability that an attack against the security of a cryptographic system succeeds equal—or at least close—to zero. Probability theory provides the formalism for this kind of reasoning.

In this chapter, we introduce and overview the basic principles of (discrete) probability theory as far as they are relevant for information theory and contemporary cryptography. More specifically, we introduce basic terms and concepts in Section 4.1, elaborate on random variables in Section 4.2, and conclude with some final remarks in Section 4.3. The chapter is intentionally kept short; further information can be found in any textbook on probability theory (e.g., [1–4]).

4.1 BASIC TERMS AND CONCEPTS

The notion of a discrete probability space as formally introduced in Definiton 4.1 is at the core of probability theory and its application in information theory and contemporary cryptography.

Definition 4.1 (Discrete probability space) *A discrete probability space[1] consists of a finite or countably infinite set Ω called the* sample space *and a probability measure* $\Pr : \Omega \longrightarrow \mathbb{R}^+$ *with* $\sum_{\omega \in \Omega} \Pr[\omega] = 1$.[2]

The elements of the sample space Ω are called *simple events, indecomposable events*, or—as used in this book—*elementary events*.

---

1 In some literature, a discrete probability space is called a *discrete random experiment*.
2 Alternative notations for the probability measure $\Pr[\cdot]$ are $P(\cdot)$, $P[\cdot]$, or $\text{Prob}[\cdot]$.

If we run a (discrete) random experiment in a probability space, then every elementary event of the sample space represents a possible outcome of the experiment. The *probability measure* or *probability distribution* $\Pr[\cdot]$ assigns a nonnegative real value to every elementary event $\omega \in \Omega$, such that all (probability) values sum up to one. There is no general and universally valid requirement on how to assign probability values. In fact, it is often the case that many elementary events of Ω occur with probability zero. If all $|\Omega|$ possible values occur with the same probability (i.e., $\Pr[\omega] = 1/|\Omega|$ for all $\omega \in \Omega$), then the probability distribution is called *uniform*. Uniform probability distributions are frequently used in probability theory and applications thereof.

As mentioned in Definition 4.1, sample spaces are assumed to be finite or countably infinite for the purpose of this book (things get more involved if this assumption is not made). The term *discrete probability theory* is sometimes used to refer to the restriction of probability theory to finite or countably infinite sample spaces. In this book, however, we only focus on discrete probability theory, and hence the terms probability theory and discrete probability theory are used synonymously and interchangeably. Furthermore, we say a "finite" sample space when we actually mean a "finite or countably infinite" sample space.

For example, flipping a coin can be understood as a random experiment taking place in a discrete probability space. The sample space is $\{head, tail\}$ (or $\{0, 1\}$ if 0 and 1 are used to encode *head* and *tail*, respectively) and the probability measure assigns $1/2$ to either *head* or *tail* (i.e., $\Pr[head] = \Pr[tail] = 1/2$). The resulting probability distribution is uniform. If the coin is flipped five times, then the sample space is $\{head, tail\}^5$ (or $\{0, 1\}^5$, respectively) and the probability measure assigns $1/2^5 = 1/32$ to every possible outcome of the experiment. Similarly, rolling a dice can be understood as a random experiment taking place in a discrete probability space. In this case, the sample space is $\{1, \ldots, 6\}$ and the probability measure assigns $1/6$ to every possible outcome of the experiment (i.e., $\Pr[1] = \ldots = \Pr[6] = 1/6$). If the dice is rolled n times (or n dice are rolled simultaneously), then the sample space is $\{1, \ldots, 6\}^n$ and the probability measure assigns $1/6^n$ to every possible outcome of the experiment. In either case, the probability distribution is uniform if the coins are unbiased and if the dice are fair.

Instead of looking at elementary events of a sample space, one may also look at sets of elements. In fact, an *event* refers to a subset $\mathcal{A} \subseteq \Omega$ of the sample space, and its probability equals the sum of the probabilities of the elementary events of which it consists. This is formally expressed as follows:

$$\Pr[\mathcal{A}] = \sum_{\omega \in \mathcal{A}} \Pr[\omega]$$

$\Pr[\Omega]$ is conventionally set to one, and $\Pr[\emptyset]$ is set to zero. Furthermore, one frequently needs the complement of an event $\mathcal{A}$. It consists of all elements of Ω that are not elements of $\mathcal{A}$. The complement of $\mathcal{A}$ is denoted as $\overline{\mathcal{A}}$, and its probability can be computed as follows:

$$\Pr[\overline{\mathcal{A}}] = \sum_{\omega \in \Omega \setminus \mathcal{A}} \Pr[\omega]$$

If we know $\Pr[\mathcal{A}]$, then we can easily compute

$$\Pr[\overline{\mathcal{A}}] = 1 - \Pr[\mathcal{A}]$$

because $\Pr[\mathcal{A}]$ and $\Pr[\overline{\mathcal{A}}]$ must sum up to one.

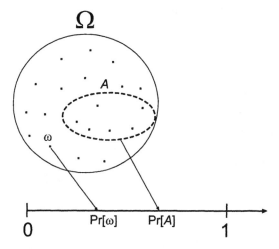

Figure 4.1 A discrete probability space.

A discrete probability space is illustrated in Figure 4.1. There is a sample space Ω and a probability measure $\Pr[\cdot]$ that assign a value between 0 and 1 to every elementary event $\omega \in \Omega$ or event $\mathcal{A} \subseteq \Omega$.

If, for example, we want to compute the probability of the event that, when flipping five coins, we get three heads, then the sample space is $\Omega = \{1, 0\}^5$ and the probability distribution is uniform. This basically means that every element

$\omega \in \Omega$ occurs with the same probability $\Pr[\omega] = 1/2^5 = 1/32$. Let $\mathcal{A}$ be the subset of $\Omega = \{1,0\}^5$ containing strings with exactly three ones and let us ask for the probability $\Pr[\mathcal{A}]$. It can easily be shown that $\mathcal{A}$ consists of the following 10 elements:

00111	10110
01011	10101
01101	11001
01110	11010
10011	11100

Consequently, $\Pr[\mathcal{A}] = 10/32 = 5/16$. The example can be generalized to n flips with a biased coin. If the coin flips are independent and the probability that each coin turns out heads is $0 \le p \le 1$, then the sample space is $\{1,0\}^n$ and the probability for a specific event ω in this space is

$$\Pr[\omega] = p^k(1-p)^{n-k}$$

where k is the number of ones in ω. In the example given earlier, we had $p = 1-p = 1/2$, and the corresponding distribution over $\{1,0\}^n$ was uniform. If $p = 1$ ($p = 0$), then 0^n (1^n) has probability one and all other elements have probability zero. Consequently, the interesting cases occur when p is greater than zero but smaller than one (i.e., $p \in (0,1)$). This brings us to the notion of a *binominal distribution*. If we have such a distribution with parameter p and ask for the probability of the event $\mathcal{A}_k$ that we get a string with k ones, then the probability $\Pr[\mathcal{A}_k]$ can be computed as follows:

$$\Pr[\mathcal{A}_k] = \binom{n}{k} p^k(1-p)^{n-k}$$

In this formula, $\binom{n}{k}$ is read "n choose k" and can be computed as follows:

$$\binom{n}{k} = \frac{n!}{k!(n-k)!}$$

In this notation, $n!$ refers to the factorial of integer n. It is recursively defined with $0! = 1$ and $n! = (n-1)!n$.

More generally, if we have two events $\mathcal{A}, \mathcal{B} \subseteq \Omega$, then the probability of the *union event* $\mathcal{A} \cup \mathcal{B}$ is computed as follows:

$$\Pr[\mathcal{A} \cup \mathcal{B}] = \Pr[\mathcal{A}] + \Pr[\mathcal{B}] - \Pr[\mathcal{A} \cap \mathcal{B}]$$

Consequently, $\Pr[\mathcal{A} \cup \mathcal{B}] \leq \Pr[\mathcal{A}] + \Pr[\mathcal{B}]$ and $\Pr[\mathcal{A} \cup \mathcal{B}] = \Pr[\mathcal{A}] + \Pr[\mathcal{B}]$ if and only if $\mathcal{A} \cap \mathcal{B} = \emptyset$. The former inequality is known as the *union bound*.

Similarly, we may be interested in the *joint event* $\mathcal{A} \cap \mathcal{B}$. Its probability is computed as follows:

$$\Pr[\mathcal{A} \cap \mathcal{B}] = \Pr[\mathcal{A}] + \Pr[\mathcal{B}] - \Pr[\mathcal{A} \cup \mathcal{B}]$$

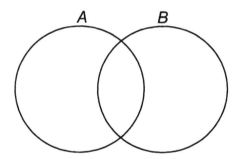

Figure 4.2   A Venn diagram with two events.

Venn diagrams can be used to illustrate the relationship of specific events. A Venn diagram is made up of two or more overlapping circles (each circle represents an event). For example, Figure 4.2 shows a Venn diagram with two events $\mathcal{A}$ and $\mathcal{B}$. The intersection of the two circles represents $\mathcal{A} \cap \mathcal{B}$, whereas the union represents $\mathcal{A} \cup \mathcal{B}$.

The two events $\mathcal{A}$ and $\mathcal{B}$ are *independent* if $\Pr[\mathcal{A} \cap \mathcal{B}] = \Pr[\mathcal{A}] \cdot \Pr[\mathcal{B}]$, meaning that the probability of one event does not influence the probability of the other.

The notion of independence can be generalized to more than two events. In this case, it must be distinguished whether the events are pairwise or mutually independent. Let $\mathcal{A}_1, \dots, \mathcal{A}_n \subseteq \Omega$ be n events in a given sample space Ω.

- $\mathcal{A}_1, \dots, \mathcal{A}_n$ are *pairwise independent* if for every $i, j \in \{1, \dots, n\}$ with $i \neq j$ it holds that $\Pr[\mathcal{A}_i \cap \mathcal{A}_j] = \Pr[\mathcal{A}_i] \cdot \Pr[\mathcal{A}_j]$.

- $A_1, \ldots, A_n$ are *mutually independent* if for every subset of indices $I \subseteq \{1, 2, \ldots, n\}$ with $I \neq \emptyset$ it holds that

$$\Pr[\bigcap_{i \in I} A_i] = \prod_{i \in I} \Pr[A_i].$$

Sometimes it is necessary to compute the probability of an elementary event ω given that an event A with $\Pr[A] > 0$ holds. The resulting *conditional probability* is denoted as $\Pr[\omega | A]$ and can be computed as follows:

$$\Pr[\omega | A] = \begin{cases} \frac{\Pr[\omega]}{\Pr[A]} & \text{if } \omega \in A \\ 0 & \text{otherwise} \end{cases}$$

If $\omega \in A$, then $\Pr[\omega | A]$ must have a value that is proportional to $\Pr[\omega]$, and the factor of proportionality must be $1/\Pr[A]$ (so that all probabilities sum up to one). Otherwise (i.e., if $\omega \notin A$), it is impossible that ω holds, and hence $\Pr[\omega | A]$ must be equal to zero (independent from the probability of A).

The definition of $\Pr[\omega | A]$ can be generalized to arbitrary events. In fact, if A and B are two events, then the probability of event B given that event A holds is the sum of the probabilities of all elementary events $\omega \in B$ given that A holds. This is formally expressed as follows:

$$\Pr[B | A] = \sum_{\omega \in B} \Pr[\omega | A]$$

In the literature, $\Pr[B | A]$ is sometimes also defined as follows:

$$\Pr[B | A] = \frac{\Pr[A \cap B]}{\Pr[A]}$$

Consequently, if two events A and B are independent and $\Pr[A] > 0$ ($\Pr[B] > 0$), then $\Pr[B | A] = \Pr[A \cap B]/\Pr[A] = \Pr[A] \cdot \Pr[B]/\Pr[A] = \Pr[B]$ ($\Pr[A | B] = \Pr[B \cap A]/\Pr[B] = \Pr[B] \cdot \Pr[A]/\Pr[B] = \Pr[A]$). Put in other words: if A and B are independent, then whether A holds or not is not influenced by the knowledge that B holds or not, and vice versa. Consequently, one can also write

$$\Pr[A | B] = \frac{\Pr[B \cap A]}{\Pr[B]} \tag{4.1}$$

and put $\Pr[\mathcal{B}|\mathcal{A}]$ and $\Pr[\mathcal{A}|\mathcal{B}]$ into perspective. In this case, the formula

$$\Pr[\mathcal{A}|\mathcal{B}] = \frac{\Pr[\mathcal{A}]\Pr[\mathcal{B}|\mathcal{A}]}{\Pr[\mathcal{B}]}$$

is known as *Bayes' theorem* and is frequently used in probability theory. Furthermore, one can also formally express a *law of total probability* as suggested in Theorem 4.1.

Theorem 4.1 (Law of total probability) *If the events* $\mathcal{B}_1, \ldots, \mathcal{B}_n$ *represent a partition of the sample space (i.e.,* $\cup_{i=1}^{n} \mathcal{B}_i = \Omega$ *and* $\mathcal{B}_i \cap \mathcal{B}_j = \emptyset$ *for all* $i \neq i$*), then*

$$\Pr[\mathcal{A}] = \sum_{i=1}^{n} \Pr[\mathcal{A}|\mathcal{B}_i] \cdot \Pr[\mathcal{B}_i]$$

must hold for every event $\mathcal{A} \subseteq \Omega$.

Proof. Because

$$\mathcal{A} = \mathcal{A} \cap \Omega = \bigcup_{i=1}^{n} (\mathcal{A} \cap \mathcal{B}_i)$$

where $(\mathcal{A} \cap \mathcal{B}_i)$ and $(\mathcal{A} \cap \mathcal{B}_j)$ are disjoint (and hence mutually exclusive) for $i \neq j$, the probabilities of the right-hand-side sum can be added up, in which each term follows from (4.1).

$\square$

The law of total probability is useful in practice. In fact, it is frequently employed to compute the probability of an event $\mathcal{A}$, which is conditional given some other mutually exclusive events, such as an event $\mathcal{B}$ and its complement $\overline{\mathcal{B}}$.

4.2 RANDOM VARIABLES

If we have a discrete probability space and run a random experiment, then we might be interested in some values that depend on the outcome of the experiment (rather than the outcome itself). If, for example, we roll two dice, then we may be interested in their sum. Similarly, if we run a randomized algorithm, then we may be interested in its output or its running time. This is where the notion of a random variable as formally introduced in Definition 4.2 comes into play.

Definition 4.2 (Random variable) *Let* (Ω, Pr) *be a discrete probabiliy space with sample space* Ω *and probability measure* $\text{Pr}[\cdot]$. *Any function* $X : \Omega \to \mathcal{X}$ *from the sample space to a measurable set* $\mathcal{X}$ *is a* random variable. *The set* $\mathcal{X}$, *in turn, is the* range *of the random variable* X.

Consequently, a random variable is a function that on input an arbitrary element of the sample space of a discrete probability space (or random experiment) outputs an element of the range. In a typical setting, $\mathcal{X}$ is either a subset of the real numbers (i.e., $\mathcal{X} \subseteq \mathbb{R}$) or a subset of the binary strings of a specific length n (i.e., $\mathcal{X} \subseteq \{0,1\}^n$).[3]

If x is in the range of X (i.e., $x \in \mathcal{X}$), then the expression $(X = x)$ refers to the event $\{\omega \in \Omega \mid X(\omega) = x\}$, and hence $\text{Pr}[X = x]$ is defined and something potentially interesting to compute. If only one random variable X is considered, then $\text{Pr}[X = x]$ is sometimes also written as $\text{Pr}[x]$.

If, for example, we roll two fair dice, then the sample space is $\Omega = \{1, 2, \ldots, 6\}^2$ and the probability distribution is uniform (i.e., $\text{Pr}[\omega_1, \omega_2] = 1/6^2 = 1/36$ for every $(\omega_1, \omega_2) \in \Omega$). Let X be the random variable that associates $\omega_1 + \omega_2$ to every $(\omega_1, \omega_2) \in \Omega$. Then the range of the random variable X is $\mathcal{X} = \{2, 3, \ldots, 12\}$. For every element of the range, we can compute the probability that X takes this value. In fact, by counting the number of elements in every possible event, we can easily determine the following probabilities:

$$\text{Pr}[X = 2] = 1/36$$
$$\text{Pr}[X = 3] = 2/36$$
$$\text{Pr}[X = 4] = 3/36$$
$$\text{Pr}[X = 5] = 4/36$$
$$\text{Pr}[X = 6] = 5/36$$
$$\text{Pr}[X = 7] = 6/36$$

The remaining probabilities (i.e., $\text{Pr}[X = 8], \ldots, \text{Pr}[X = 12]$) can be computed by observing that $\text{Pr}[X = x] = \text{Pr}[X = 14 - x]$. Consequently, we have

$$\text{Pr}[X = 8] \quad = \quad \text{Pr}[X = 14 - 8] = \text{Pr}[X = 6] = 5/36$$
$$\text{Pr}[X = 9] \quad = \quad \text{Pr}[X = 14 - 9] = \text{Pr}[X = 5] = 4/36$$

3   In some literature, a random variable is defined as a function $X : \Omega \to \mathbb{R}$.

$$
\begin{aligned}
\Pr[X = 10] &= \Pr[X = 14 - 10] = \Pr[X = 4] = 3/36 \\
\Pr[X = 11] &= \Pr[X = 14 - 11] = \Pr[X = 3] = 2/36 \\
\Pr[X = 12] &= \Pr[X = 14 - 12] = \Pr[X = 2] = 1/36
\end{aligned}
$$

It can easily be verified that all probabilities sum up to one:

$$
\frac{1}{36} + \frac{2}{36} + \frac{3}{36} + \frac{4}{36} + \frac{5}{36} + \frac{6}{36} + \frac{5}{36} + \frac{4}{36} + \frac{3}{36} + \frac{2}{36} + \frac{1}{36} = \frac{36}{36} = 1
$$

We next look at some probability distributions of random variables.

4.2.1 Probability Distributions

If $X : \Omega \rightarrow \mathcal{X}$ is a random variable with sample space Ω and range $\mathcal{X}$, then the *probability distribution* of X (i.e., P_X) is a mapping from $\mathcal{X}$ to $\mathbb{R}^+$. It is formally defined as follows:

$$
\begin{aligned}
P_X : \mathcal{X} &\longrightarrow \mathbb{R}^+ \\
x &\longmapsto P_X(x) = P(X = x) = \sum_{\omega \in \Omega : X(\omega) = x} \Pr[\omega]
\end{aligned}
$$

The probability distribution of a random variable X is illustrated in Figure 4.3. Some events from the sample space Ω (on the left side) are mapped to $x \in \mathcal{X}$ (on the right side), and the probability that x occurs as a map is $P(X = x) = P_X(x)$.

It is possible to define more than one random variable for a discrete random experiment. If, for example, X and Y are two random variables with ranges $\mathcal{X}$ and $\mathcal{Y}$, then $P(X = x, Y = y)$ refers to the probability that X takes on the value $x \in \mathcal{X}$ and Y takes on the value $y \in \mathcal{Y}$. Consequently, the *joint probability distribution* of X and Y (i.e., P_{XY}) is a mapping from $\mathcal{X} \times \mathcal{Y}$ to $\mathbb{R}^+$. It is formally defined as follows:

$$
\begin{aligned}
P_{XY} : \mathcal{X} \times \mathcal{Y} &\longrightarrow \mathbb{R}^+ \\
(x, y) &\longmapsto P_{XY}(x, y) = \\
&\quad P(X = x, Y = y) = \\
&\quad \sum_{\omega \in \Omega : X(\omega) = x; Y(\omega) = y} \Pr[\omega]
\end{aligned}
$$

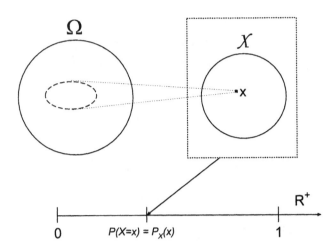

Figure 4.3   The probability distribution of a random variable X.

The joint probability distribution of two random variables X and Y is illustrated in Figure 4.4. Some events from the sample space Ω (on the left side) are mapped to $x \in \mathcal{X}$ and $y \in \mathcal{Y}$ (on the right side), and the probability that x and y occur as maps is $P(X = x, Y = y) = P_{XY}(x, y)$.

Similarly, for n random variables $X_1, \ldots, X_n$ (with ranges $\mathcal{X}_1, \ldots, \mathcal{X}_n$), one can compute the probability that X_i takes on the value $x_i \in \mathcal{X}_i$ for $i = 1, \ldots, n$. In fact, the *joint probability distribution* of $X_1, \ldots, X_n$ (i.e., $P_{X_1 \ldots X_n}$) is a mapping from $\mathcal{X}_1 \times \ldots \times \mathcal{X}_n$ to $\mathbb{R}^+$ that is formally defined as follows:

$$
\begin{aligned}
P_{X_1 \ldots X_n} : \mathcal{X}_1 \times \ldots \times \mathcal{X}_n &\longrightarrow \mathbb{R}^+ \\
(x_1, \ldots, x_n) &\longmapsto P_{X_1 \ldots X_n}(x_1, \ldots, x_n) = \\
&\quad P(X_1 = x_1, \ldots, X_n = x_n) = \\
&\quad \sum_{\omega \in \Omega : X_1(\omega) = x_1; \ldots; X_n(\omega) = x_n} \Pr[\omega]
\end{aligned}
$$

The joint probability distribution of n random variables $X_1, \ldots, X_n$ is illustrated in Figure 4.5. Some events from the sample space Ω (on the left side) are mapped to $x_1 \in \mathcal{X}_1$, $\ldots$, $x_n \in \mathcal{X}_n$ (on the right side), and the probability that $x_1, \ldots, x_n$ actually occur as maps is $P(X_1 = x_1, \ldots, X_n = x_n) = P_{X_1 \ldots X_n}(x_1, \ldots, x_n)$.

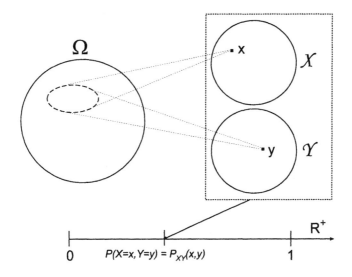

Figure 4.4 The joint probability distribution of two random variables X and Y.

4.2.2 Marginal Distributions

If X and Y are two random variables with joint probability distribution P_{XY}, then the two *marginal distributions* P_X and P_Y are defined as follows:

$$P_X(x) = \sum_{y \in \mathcal{Y}} P_{XY}(x, y)$$

$$P_Y(y) = \sum_{x \in \mathcal{X}} P_{XY}(x, y)$$

Again, the notion of a marginal distribution can be generalized to more than two random variables. If $X_1, \ldots, X_n$ are n random variables with ranges $\mathcal{X}_1, \ldots, \mathcal{X}_n$ and joint probability distribution $P_{X_1 \ldots X_n}$, then for any $m < n$ the marginal distribution $P_{X_1 \ldots X_m}$ is defined as follows:

$$P_{X_1 \ldots X_m}(x_1, \ldots, x_m) = \sum_{(x_{m+1}, \ldots, x_n) \in \mathcal{X}_{m+1} \ldots \mathcal{X}_n} P_{X_1 \ldots X_n}(x_1, \ldots, x_n)$$

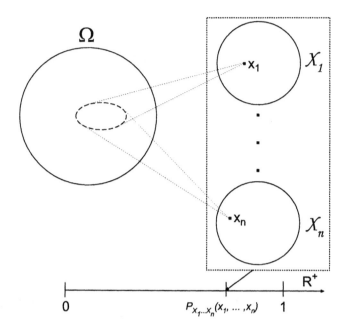

Figure 4.5   The joint probability distribution of n random variables $X_1, \ldots, X_n$.

4.2.3   Conditional Probability Distributions

Let $(\Omega, \Pr)$ be a discrete probability space and $\mathcal{A}$ an event with $\Pr[\mathcal{A}] > 0$. If X is a random variable in that space, then the *conditional probability distribution* $P_{X|\mathcal{A}}$ of X given that event $\mathcal{A}$ holds is defined as follows:

$$P_{X|\mathcal{A}}(x) = \Pr[X = x | \mathcal{A}]$$

Note that $P_{X|\mathcal{A}}$ is a regular probability distribution and hence that the probabilities $P_{X|\mathcal{A}}(x)$ sum up to one:

$$\sum_{x \in \mathcal{X}} P_{X|\mathcal{A}}(x) = 1$$

If the conditioning event involves another random variable Y defined on the same sample space Ω, then the *conditional probability distribution* of X given that Y takes on a value y is defined as

$$P_{X|Y=y}(x) = \frac{P_{XY}(x,y)}{P_Y(y)}$$

whenever $P_Y(y) > 0$. More specifically, the conditional probability distribution $P_{X|Y}$ of X given Y is a two-argument function that is defined as follows:

$$
\begin{aligned}
P_{X|Y} : \mathcal{X} \times \mathcal{Y} &\longrightarrow \mathbb{R}^+ \\
(x,y) &\longmapsto P_{X|Y}(x,y) = P(X = x | Y = y) = \\
&\frac{P(X = x, Y = y)}{P(Y = y)} = \frac{P_{XY}(x,y)}{P_Y(y)}
\end{aligned}
$$

Note that the two-argument function $P_{X|Y}(\cdot, \cdot)$ is not a probability distribution on $\mathcal{X} \times \mathcal{Y}$, but that for every $y \in \mathcal{Y}$, the one-argument function $P_{X|Y}(\cdot, y)$ is a probability distribution, meaning that $\sum_{x \in \mathcal{X}} P_{X|Y}(x,y)$ must sum up to 1 for every y with $P_Y(y) > 0$. Also note that $P_{X|Y}(x,y)$ is defined only for values with $P(Y = y) = P_Y(y) \neq 0$.

4.2.4 Expectation

The expectation of a random variable gives some information about its order of magnitude, meaning that if the expectation is small (large), then large (small) values are unlikely to occur. More formally, let $X : \Omega \rightarrow \mathcal{X}$ be a random variable and $\mathcal{X}$ be a finite subset of the real numbers (i.e., $\mathcal{X} \subset \mathbb{R}$). Then the *expectation* or *mean* of X (denoted as $E[X]$) can be computed as follows:

$$E[X] = \sum_{x \in \mathcal{X}} \Pr[X = x] \cdot x = \sum_{x \in \mathcal{X}} P_X(x) \cdot x \tag{4.2}$$

The expectation is best understood in terms of betting. Let us consider the situation in which a person is playing a game in which one can win one dollar or lose two dollars. Furthermore, there is a $2/3$ probability of winning, a $1/6$ probability of losing, and a $1/6$ probability of a draw. This situation can be modeled using a discrete probability space with a sample space $\Omega = \{W, L, D\}$ (with W standing for "win," L standing for "lose," and D standing for "draw") and a probability measure that assigns $\Pr[W] = 2/3$ and $\Pr[L] = \Pr[D] = 1/6$. Against this background, the random variable X can be used to specify wins and losses—$X(W) = 1$, $X(L) = 2$, and $X(D) = 0$—and one may be interested in the expectation for X. Referring to (4.2), the expectation of X (i.e., $E[X]$) can be computed as follows:

$$E[X] = \frac{1}{6} \cdot (-2) + \frac{1}{6} \cdot 0 + \frac{2}{3} \cdot 1 = \frac{1}{3}$$

Consequently, if one plays the game, then one can reasonably expect to win one third of a dollar in the average (i.e., the game is more than fair). Another typical application of a random variable's expectation is the running time of a randomized algorithm. Remember from Section 1.2 that a randomized algorithm depends on internal random values and that a complete analysis of the algorithm would be a specification of the running time of the algorithm for every possible sequence of random values. This is clearly impractical, and one may analyze the expected running time of the algorithm instead. This refers to a single value that may still provide some useful information about the typical behavior of the algorithm.

In practice, the linearity of expectations is frequently used to compute the expectation of a random variable X. The linearity of expectations basically means that

$$E[aX] = aE[X]$$

for all $a \in \mathbb{R}$. Similarly, if $X_1, X_2, \ldots, X_n$ are random variables over the same sample space, then

$$E[X_1 + X_2 + \ldots + X_n] = E[X_1] + E[X_2] + \ldots + E[X_n].$$

For example, we want to compute the expected number of heads when flipping a coin n times. Without making use of the linearity of expectations, this computation is quite involved. Making use of the linearity of expectations, however, this computation becomes simple and straightforward. We define a random variable X that is the sum of n random variables $X_1, X_2, \ldots, X_n$, where X_i is 1 if the ith coin flip is 1 (X_i is 0 otherwise). Then $E[X_i] = \frac{1}{2} \cdot 0 + \frac{1}{2} \cdot 1 = \frac{1}{2}$ and $E[X] = E[X_1 + X_2 + \ldots + X_n] = E[X_1] + E[X_2] + \ldots + E[X_n] = n \cdot \frac{1}{2} = \frac{n}{2}$.

More generally, if f is a real-valued function whose domain includes $\mathcal{X}$, then $f(X)$ is a real-valued random variable with an expected value that can be computed as follows:

$$E[f(X)] = \sum_{x \in \mathcal{X}} f(x) P_X(x)$$

More specifically, if f is a convex function, then *Jensen's inequality* applies:

$$E[f(X)] \geq f(E[X])$$

Most of the basic inequalities in information theory follow directly from Jensen's inequality.

Last but not least, the *conditional expected value* $E[X|\mathcal{A}]$ of a random variable X given event $\mathcal{A}$ can be computed as follows:

$$E[X|\mathcal{A}] = \sum_{x \in \mathcal{X}} P_{X|\mathcal{A}}(x) \cdot x$$

4.2.5 Independence of Random Variables

Let X and Y be two random variables over the same sample space Ω. X and Y are *independent* if for all $x \in \mathcal{X}$ and $y \in \mathcal{Y}$, the events $(X = x)$ and $(Y = y)$ are independent. This is formally expressed in Definition 4.3.

Definition 4.3 (Independent random variables) *Two random variables X and Y are statistically independent (or independent in short) if and only if $P_{XY}(x, y) = P_X(x) \cdot P_Y(y)$ for all $x \in \mathcal{X}$ and $y \in \mathcal{Y}$.*

Definition 4.3 basically says that the joint probability distribution of two independent random variables X and Y is equal to the product of their marginal distributions.

If two random variables X and Y are independent, then the conditional probability distribution $P_{X|Y}$ of X given Y is

$$P_{X|Y}(x, y) = \frac{P_{XY}(x, y)}{P_Y(y)} = \frac{P_X(x)P_Y(y)}{P_Y(y)} = P_X(x)$$

for all $x \in \mathcal{X}$ and $y \in \mathcal{Y}$ with $P_Y(y) \neq 0$. This basically means that knowing the value of one random variable does not tell anything about the distribution of the other (and vice versa). Furthermore, if X and Y are independent random variables, then

$$E[XY] = E[X] \cdot E[Y].$$

There are two notions of independence for more than two random variables. Roughly speaking, pairwise independence requires two arbitrarily chosen random variables to be independent (see Definition 4.4), whereas mutual independence requires all random variables to be independent (see Definition 4.5). In either case, let $X_1, \ldots, X_n$ be n random variables over the same sample space Ω.

Definition 4.4 (Pairwise independent random variables) $X_1, \ldots, X_n$ *are pairwise independent if for every* $i, j \in \{1, 2, \ldots, n\}$ *with* $i \neq j$, *it holds that the two random variables* X_i *and* X_j *are independent (i.e.,* $P_{X_i X_j}(x_i, x_j) = P_{X_i}(x_i) \cdot P_{X_j}(x_j)$).

Definition 4.5 (Mutually independent random variables) $X_1, \ldots, X_n$ *are mutually independent if for every subset of indices* $I \subseteq \{1, 2, \ldots, n\}$ *with* $I \neq \emptyset$, *it holds that*

$$P_{X_{I_1} \ldots X_{I_m}}(x_{I_1}, \ldots, x_{I_m}) = P_{X_{I_1}}(x_{I_1}) \cdot \ldots \cdot P_{X_{I_m}}(x_{I_m}) = \prod_{i=1}^{m} P_{X_{I_i}}(x_{I_i})$$

Note that the notion of mutual independence is stronger than the notion of pairwise independence. In fact, a collection of random variables that is mutually independent is also pairwise independent, whereas the converse must not be true (i.e., a collection of random variables can be pairwise independent without being mutually independent). For example, consider the situation in which two coins are tossed. The random variable X refers to the result of the first coin, the random variable Y refers to the result of the second coin, and the random variable Z refers to the addition modulo 2 of the results of the two coins. Obviously, all random variables have values of either 0 or 1. Then X, Y, and Z are pairwise independent, but they are not mutually independent (because the value of Z is entirely determined by the values of X and Y).

Similar to the case with two random variables, one can show that if n random variables $X_1, X_2, \ldots, X_n$ are mutually independent, then

$$E[X_1 \cdot X_2 \cdot \ldots \cdot X_n] = E[X_1] \cdot E[X_2] \cdot \ldots \cdot E[X_n].$$

4.2.6   Markov's Inequality

Markov's inequality as specified in Theorem 4.2 puts into perspective the expectation of a random variable X and the probability that its value is larger than a certain threshold value k. We provide the theorem without a proof.

Theorem 4.2 (Markov's inequality) *If X is a nonnegative random variable, then*

$$\Pr[X \geq k] \leq \frac{E[X]}{k}$$

holds for every $k \in \mathbb{R}$.

For example, if $E[X] = 10$, then

$$\Pr[X \geq 1,000,000] \leq \frac{10}{1,000,000} = \frac{1}{100,000}$$

This means that it is very unlikely that the value of X is greater than or equal to $1,000,000$ if its expectation is 10. This result is certainly supported by intuition.

Sometimes the order of magnitude given by Markov's inequality is extremely bad, but the bound is as strong as possible if the only information available about X is its expectation. For example, suppose that X counts the number of heads in a sequence of n coin flips (i.e., $\Omega = \{0,1\}^n$ with uniformly distributed elements). If X is the number of ones in the string, then $E[X] = n/2$. In this example, Markov's inequality provides the following upper bound for $\Pr[X \geq n]$:

$$\Pr[X \geq n] \leq \frac{E[X]}{n} = \frac{n/2}{n} = \frac{1}{2}$$

Obviously, the correct value is 2^{-n}, and the result provided by Markov's inequality is totally off (it does not even depend on n). On the other hand, if n coins are flipped and the flips are glued together (so that the only possible outcomes are n heads or n tails, both with probability $1/2$), then X counts the number of heads and $E[X] = n/2$. In this case, the inequality is tight, and $\Pr[X \geq n]$ is in fact $1/2$. The moral is that Markov's inequality is useful because it applies to every nonnegative random variable with known expectation. According to the examples given earlier, the inequality is accurate when applied to a random variable that typically deviates a lot from its expectation, and it is bad when applied to a random variable that is concentrated around its expectation. In the latter case, more powerful methods are required to achieve more accurate estimations. Most of these methods make use of the variance or standard deviation as introduced next.

4.2.7 Variance and Standard Deviation

For a random variable X, one may consider the complementary random variable

$$X' = |X - E[X]|$$

to provide some information about the likelihood that X deviates a lot from its expectation. More specifically, if X' is expected to be small, then X is not likely to deviate a lot from its expectation. Unfortunately, X' is not easier to analyze than X, and hence X' is not particularly useful to consider as a complementary random variable.

As a viable alternative, one may consider the complementary random variable

$$X'' = (X - E[X])^2.$$

Again, if the expectation of X'' is small, then X is typically close to its expectation. In fact, the expectation of the random variable X'' turns out to be a useful measure in practice. It is called the *variance* of X, denoted as $Var[X]$, and it is formally defined as follows:

$$Var[X] = E[(X - E[X])^2] = \sum_{x \in \mathcal{X}} P_X(x) \cdot (x - E[X])^2$$

Alternatively, the variance of X can also be expressed as follows:

$$
\begin{aligned}
Var[X] &= E[(X - E[X])^2] \\
&= E[X^2 - 2XE[X] + (E[X])^2] \\
&= E[X^2] - 2E[XE[X]] + (E[X])^2 \\
&= E[X^2] - 2E[X]E[X] + (E[X])^2 \\
&= E[X^2] - 2(E[X])^2 + (E[X])^2 \\
&= E[X^2] - (E[X])^2
\end{aligned}
$$

For example, let X be a random variable that is equal to zero with probability $1/2$ and to 1 with probability $1/2$. Then $E[X] = \frac{1}{2} \cdot 0 + \frac{1}{2} \cdot 1 = \frac{1}{2}$, $X = X^2$ (because $0 = 0^2$ and $1 = 1^2$), and

$$Var[X] = E[X^2] - (E[X])^2 = \frac{1}{2} - \frac{1}{4} = \frac{1}{4}.$$

The variance of a random variable is useful because it is often easy to compute, but it still gives rise to sometimes strong estimations on the probability that a random variable deviates a lot from its expectation.

The value $\sigma[X] = \sqrt{Var[X]}$ is called the *standard deviation* of X. In general, one may expect the value of a random variable X to be in the interval $E[X] \pm \sigma[X]$. If X is a random variable, then

$$Var[aX + b] = a^2 Var[X]$$

for every $a, b \in \mathbb{R}$. Similarly, if $X_1, \ldots, X_n$ are pairwise statistically independent random variables over the same sample space, then

$$Var[X_1 + \ldots + X_n] = Var[X_1] + \ldots + Var[X_n].$$

For example, let X be again the random variable that counts the number of heads in a sequence of n independent coin flips (with $E[X] = n/2$). Computing the variance according to the definition given earlier is difficult. If, however, we view the random variable X as the sum $X_1 + \ldots + X_n$ (where all X_i are mutually independent random variables such that for each i, X_i takes the value 1 with probability $1/2$ and the value zero with probability $1/2$), then $Var[X_i] = \frac{1}{4}$, and hence $Var[X] = n \cdot \frac{1}{4} = \frac{n}{4}$.

4.2.8 Chebyshev's Inequality

Chebyshev's inequality as specified in Theorem 4.3 can be used to provide an upper bound for the probability that a random variable X deviates from its expectation more than a certain threshold value $k \in \mathbb{R}$. To make use of Chebyshev's inequality, the variance of X must be known.

Theorem 4.3 (Chebyshev's inequality) *If X is a random variable, then*

$$\Pr[|X - E[X]| \geq k] \leq \frac{Var[X]}{k^2}$$

holds for every $k \in \mathbb{R}$.

Proof.

$$\Pr[|X - E[X]| \geq k] = \Pr[(X - E[X])^2 \geq k^2]$$

$$\leq \frac{E[(X - E[X])^2]}{k^2}$$

$$= \frac{Var[X]}{k^2}$$

In the first step, the argument of the probability function is squared on either side of the relation (this does not change the probability value). In the second step, Markov's inequality is applied (for $X - E[X]$).

$\square$

Let us test Chebyshev's inequality on the example given earlier. X is a random variable defined over the sample space $\Omega = \{0, 1\}^n$, Pr is the uniform distribution, and X counts the number of ones in the elementary event. If we want to compute $\Pr[X \geq n]$ using $Var[X] = n/4$, then we get

$$\Pr[X \geq n] \leq \Pr[|X - E[X]| \geq n/2] \leq \frac{1}{n}.$$

Obviously, this result is much better than the one we get from Markov's inequality. It linearly decreases with n, but it is still far apart from the correct value 2^{-n}.

Using the standard deviation (instead of the variance) and setting $k = c \cdot \sigma[X]$, Chebyshev's inequality can also be expressed as follows:

$$\Pr[|X - E[X]| \geq c \cdot \sigma[X]] \leq \frac{Var[X]}{c^2(\sigma[X])^2} = \frac{(\sigma[X])^2}{c^2(\sigma[X])^2} = \frac{1}{c^2}$$

This form of Chebyshev's inequality is frequently used in cryptography.

4.3 FINAL REMARKS

In this chapter, we introduced and overviewed the basic principles of (discrete) probability theory as far as they are relevant for information theory and contemporary cryptography. First and foremost, we need the notion of a discrete probability space (or random experiment, respectively). Such a space consists of a sample space Ω and a probability measure $\Pr : \Omega \longrightarrow \mathbb{R}^+$ (with $\sum_{\omega \in \Omega} \Pr[\omega] = 1$). We can then define a random variable as a function $X : \Omega \rightarrow \mathcal{X}$ from the sample space to a measurable set $\mathcal{X}$ (i.e., the range of the random variable). Random variables may have probability distributions, and if the range of a random variable is a subset of the real numbers, then the random variable may also have an expectation and a variance (or a standard deviation, respectively). All of these values are put into perspective in some inequalities (e.g., Markov's inequality and Chebyshev's inequality) that are frequently used in probability theory. In the following chapter, we use probability theory and apply it to information theory.

References

[1] Ghahramani, S., *Fundamentals of Probability*, 2nd edition. Prentice-Hall, Upper Saddle River, NJ, 1999.

[2] Chung, K.L., *A Course in Probability Theory*, 2nd edition. Academic Press, New York, 2000.

[3] Ross, S.M., *A First Course in Probability*, 6th edition. Prentice-Hall, Upper Saddle River, NJ, 2001.

[4] Jaynes, E.T., *Probability Theory: The Logic of Science*. Cambridge University Press, Cambridge, UK, 2003.

Chapter 5

Information Theory

As mentioned in Section 1.3, Claude E. Shannon developed a mathematical theory of communication [1] and a related communication theory of secrecy systems [2] that started a new branch of research commonly referred to as *information theory*. Information theory has had (and continues to have) a deep impact on contemporary cryptography.

In this chapter, we briefly overview and discuss the basic principles and results of information theory as far as they are relevant for contemporary cryptography. More specifically, we introduce the topic in Section 5.1, elaborate on the entropy to measure the uncertainty of information in Section 5.2, address the redundancy of languages in Section 5.3, introduce the key equivocation and unicity distance in Section 5.4, and conclude with some final remarks in Section 5.5. Again, this chapter is intentionally kept short; further information can be found in any book about information theory (e.g., [3–5]).

5.1 INTRODUCTION

Information theory is concerned with the analysis of a *communication system* that has traditionally been represented by a block diagram as illustrated in Figure 5.1. The aim of the communication system is to communicate or transfer information (i.e., messages) from a source (on the left side) to a destination (on the right side). The following entities are involved in one way or another:

- The *source* is a person or machine that generates the messages to be communicated or transferred.

- The *encoder* associates with each message an object that is suitable for transmission over the channel. In digital communications, the object is typically

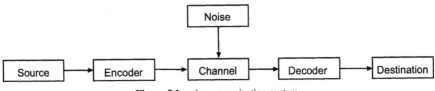

Figure 5.1 A communication system.

a sequence of bits. In analog communication, however, the object can be a signal represented by a continuous waveform.

- The *channel* is the medium over which the objects prepared by the encoder are actually communicated or transferred.

- The channel may be subjected to *noise*. This noise, in turn, may cause some objects to be modified or disturbed.

- The *decoder* operates on the output of the channel and attempts to associate a message with each object it receives from the channel.

- Similar to the source, the *destination* can be a person or machine. In either case, it receives the messages that are communicated or transferred.

Table 5.1
The Entities of a Communication System with Their Input and Output Parameters

Entity	Input	Output
Source		Message
Encoder	Message	(Input) object
Channel	(Input) object	(Output) object
Decoder	(Output) object	Message
Destination	Message	

The entities of a communication system with their input and output parameters are summarized in Table 5.1. Note that the objects mentioned earlier are divided into (input) objects that are input to the channel and (output) objects that are output to the channel.

The ultimate goal of information theory is to provide mathematically precise answers to many practically relevant questions in information processing, such as how you can optimally (i.e., most efficiently) compress and transmit information or information-encoding data. Against this background, information theory can only be applied if the question can be modeled by stochastic phenomena.

One of the major results of information theory is the so-called *fundamental theorem of information theory*. It basically says that it is possible to transmit information through a noisy channel at any rate less than channel capacity with an arbitrarily small error probability. There are many terms (e.g., "information," "noisy channel," "transmission rate," and "channel capacity") that need to be clarified before the theorem can be applied in some meaningful way. Nevertheless, an inital example may provide some preliminary ideas about the fundamental theorem of information theory.

Imagine a source of information that generates a sequence of bits at the rate of one bit per second. The bits 0 and 1 occur equally likely and are generated independently from each other. Suppose that the bits are communicated over a noisy channel. The nature of the noisy channel is unimportant, except that the probability that a particular bit is received in error is $1/4$ and that the channel acts on successive inputs independently. The statistical properties of the corresponding noisy channel are illustrated in Figure 5.2. We further assume that bits can be transmitted over the channel at a rate not to exceed one bit per second.

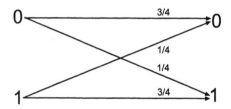

Figure 5.2   The statistical properties of a noisy channel.

If an error probability of $1/4$ is too high for a specific application, then one must find ways of improving the reliability of the channel. One way that immediately comes to mind is transmitting each source bit over the noisy channel more than once (typically an odd number of times). For example, if the source generated a zero, then one could transmit a sequence of three zeros, and if the source generated a one, then one could send a sequence of three ones. At the destination, one receives a sequence of three bits for each source bit (i.e., bit generated by the source). Consequently, one faces the problem of how to properly decode each sequence (i.e., make a decision, for each sequence received, as to the identity of the source bit). A reasonable way to decide is by means of a majority selector, meaning that there is a rule that if more ones than zeros are received, then the sequence is decoded as a one, and if more zeros than ones are received, then the sequence is decoded as a zero. For example, if the source generated a one, then a sequence of three ones would be transmitted over the noisy channel. If the first and third bits were received incorrectly, then the received sequence would be 010 and the decoder would incorrectly decide that a zero was transmitted.

In this example, one may calculate the probability that a given source bit is received in error. It is the probability that at least 2 of a sequence of 3 bits is received incorrectly, where the probability of a given bit being incorrect is $1/4$ and the bits are transmitted independently. The corresponding error probability $\Pr[error]$ (i.e., the probability of incorrectly receiving ≥ 2 bits) may be computed as follows:

$$\Pr[error] = \binom{3}{2} \left(\frac{1}{4}\right)^2 \frac{3}{4} + \left(\frac{1}{4}\right)^3 = \frac{10}{64}$$

Obviously, $10/64 < 1/4$, and the error probability is reduced considerably. There is, however, a price to pay for this reduction: the sequence to be transmitted is three times as long as the original one. This means that if one wants to synchronize the source with the channel, then one must slow down the rate of the source to $1/3$ bit per second (while keeping the channel rate fixed at 1 bit per second).

This procedure can be generalized. Let $\beta < 1/2$ be the error probability for each bit and each bit be represented by a sequence of $2n + 1$ bits.[1] Hence, the effective transmission rate of the source is reduced to $1/(2n + 1)$ bits per second. In either case, a majority selector is used at the receiving end. The probability $\Pr[error]$ of incorrectly decoding a given sequence of $2n + 1$ bits is equal to the probability of having $n + 1$ or more bits in error. This probability can be computed as follows:

$$\Pr[error] = \sum_{k=n+1}^{2n+1} \binom{2n+1}{k} \beta^k (1 - \beta)^{2n+1-k}$$

It can be shown that $\lim_{n\to\infty} \Pr[error] = 0$, meaning that the probability of incorrectly decoding a given sequence of $2n + 1$ bits can be made arbitrarily small for sufficiently large n. Put in other words: one can reduce the error probability to an arbitrarily small value at the expense of decreasing the effective transmission rate toward zero.

The essence of the fundamental theorem of information theory is that in order to achieve arbitrarily high reliability, it is not necessary to reduce the transmission rate to zero, but only to a number called the *channel capacity*. The means by which this is achieved is called *coding*, and the process of coding involves an *encoder*, as illustrated in Figure 5.1. The encoder assigns to each of a specified group of source signals (e.g., bits) a sequence of symbols called a *code word* suitable for transmission

1   This basically means that each source bit is represented by a bit sequence of odd length.

over the noisy channel. In the example given earlier, we have seen a very primitive form of coding (i.e., the source bit 0 is assigned a sequence of zeros, whereas the source bit 1 is assigned a sequence of ones). In either case, the code words are transmitted over the noisy channel and received by a decoder, which attempts to determine the original source signals. In general, to achieve reliability without sacrificing speed of transmission in digital communications, code words must not be assigned to single bits or bytes but instead to longer bit blocks. In other words, the encoder waits for the source to generate a block of bits of a specified length and then assigns a code word to the entire block. The decoder, in turn, examines the received sequence and makes a decision as to the identity of the original source bits. In practice, encoding and decoding are much more involved than this simple example may suggest.

In order to make these ideas more concrete, we need a mathematical measure for the information conveyed by a message, or—more generally—a measure of information. This is where the notion of entropy comes into play.

5.2 ENTROPY

Let $(\Omega, \Pr)$ be a discrete probability space (or random experiment, respectively) and $X : \Omega \to \mathcal{X}$ a random variable with range $\mathcal{X} = \{1, 2, \ldots, 5\}$ and uniformly distributed elements. If we have no prior knowledge about X and try to guess the correct value of X, then we have a probability of $1/|\Omega| = 1/5$ of being correct. If, however, we have some prior knowledge and know, for example, that $1 \leq X \leq 2$, then we have a higher probability of correctly guessing X (i.e., $1/2$ in this example). In other words, there is less uncertainty about the second situation, and knowing that $1 \leq X \leq 2$ has in fact reduced the uncertainty about the value of X. It thus appears that if we could pin down the notion of uncertainty, we would also be able to measure precisely the transfer of information.

Suppose that a discrete random experiment involves the observation of a random variable X, and let X take on a finite number of possible values $x_1, \ldots x_n$. The probability that X takes on x_i ($i = 1, \ldots, n$) is $\Pr[X = x_i] = P_X(x_i)$ and is abbreviated as p_i (note that all $p_i \geq 0$ and $\sum_{i=1}^{n} p_i = 1$). Our goal is to come up with a measure for the uncertainty associated with X. To achieve this goal, we construct the following two functions:

- First, we define the function h on the interval $[0, 1]$. The value $h(p)$ can be interpreted as the uncertainty associated with an event that occurs with probability p. If the event $(X = x_i)$ has probability p_i, then we say that $h(p_i)$ is the uncertainty associated with the event $(X = x_i)$ or the uncertainty removed (or information conveyed) by revealing that X has taken on value x_i.

- Second, we define the function H_n for $n \in \mathbb{N}$ probability values $p_1, \ldots, p_n$. The value $H_n([p_1, \ldots, p_n])$ represents the average uncertainty associated with the events $(X = x_i)$ for $i = 1, \ldots, n$ (or the average uncertainty removed by revealing X, respectively). More specifically, we require that

$$H_n([p_1, \ldots, p_n]) = \sum_{i=1}^{n} p_i h(p_i).$$

In this book, we write $H([p_1, \ldots p_n])$ instead of $H_n([p_1, \ldots, p_n])$ most of the time.

The function h is only used to introduce the function H. The function H is then used to measure the uncertainty of a probability distribution or a random variable. In fact, $H(X)$ is called the *entropy* of the random variable X, and it measures the average uncertainty of an observer about the value taken on by X. The entropy plays a central role in data compression. In fact, it can be shown that an optimal data compression technique can compress the output of an information source arbitrarily close to its entropy, but that error-free compression below this value is not possible.

In the literature, the function H is usually introduced by first setting up requirements (or axioms), and then showing that the only function satisfying these requirements is

$$H([p_1, \ldots, p_n]) = -C \sum_{i:1 \leq i \leq n; p_i > 0} p_i \log p_i$$

where C is an arbitrary positive number, and the logarithm base is any number greater than one. In this case, we have

$$h(p_i) = \log \frac{1}{p_i} = -\log p_i$$

and $h(p_i)$ measures the unexpectedness of an event with probability p_i. The units of H are usually called bits; thus the units are chosen so that there is one bit of uncertainty associated with the toss of an unbiased coin. Unless otherwise specified, we assume $C = 1$ and take logarithms to the base 2 for the rest of this book.

At this point it is important to note that the average uncertainty of a random variable X (i.e., $H(X)$) does not depend on the values the random variable assumes, or on anything else related to $\mathcal{X}$ except the probabilities associated with all values. That is why we said a few lines earlier that the entropy is defined for a random variable or a probability distribution. If we want to express the entropy of a random variable X, then we can use the following formula:

$$H(X) = - \sum_{x \in \mathcal{X}: P_X(x) \neq 0} P_X(x) \log_2 P_X(x) \qquad (5.1)$$

Alternatively speaking, $H(X) = E[-\log_2 P_X(X)] = E[g(X)]$ with $g(\cdot) = -\log_2 P_X(\cdot)$.

There are some intuitive properties of the entropy (as a measure of uncertainty). For example, if we add some values to a random variable that are impossible (i.e., their probability is zero), then the entropy does not change. This property can be formally expressed as follows:

$$H([p_1, \ldots, p_n]) = H([p_1, \ldots, p_n, 0])$$

Furthermore, a situation involving a number of alternatives is most uncertain if all possibilities are equally likely. This basically means that

$$0 \leq H([p_1, \ldots, p_n]) \leq \log_2 n$$

with equality on the left side if and only if one value occurs with probability one (and all other values occur with probability zero), and with equality on the right side if and only if all values are equally likely (i.e., $p_i = 1/n$). Similarly, we have

$$0 \leq H(X) \leq \log_2 |\mathcal{X}|$$

with the same conditions for equality on either side as mentioned earlier. In particular, if X is uniformly distributed, then we have $H(X) = \log_2 |\mathcal{X}|$, and this equation is often referred to as *Hartley's formula*.

If we increase the number of alternatives, then we also increase the entropy of the corresponding probability distribution. This property can be formally expressed as follows:

$$H\left(\left[\frac{1}{n}, \ldots, \frac{1}{n}\right]\right) < H\left(\left[\frac{1}{n+1}, \ldots, \frac{1}{n+1}\right]\right)$$

If $p = \sum_{i=1}^{k} p_i$ and $q = \sum_{i=1}^{l} q_i$, then the following equation holds and can be used:

$$H([p_1, \ldots, p_k, q_1, \ldots, q_l]) = H([p, q]) \;+\; pH\left(\left[\frac{p_1}{p}, \ldots, \frac{p_k}{p}\right]\right)$$
$$+\; qH\left(\left[\frac{q_1}{q}, \ldots, \frac{q_l}{q}\right]\right)$$

We now turn to the problem of characterizing the uncertainty associated with more than one random variable (associated with the same discrete probability space or random experiment). This is where the notion of a joint entropy comes into play.

5.2.1 Joint Entropy

First of all, it is important to note that a vector of random variables (associated with the same discrete probability space or random experiment) can always be viewed as a single random variable. If, for example, we have two random variables X and Y with n and m possible outcomes, then X and Y have joint probability $P_{XY}(x_i, y_j) = \Pr[X = x_i, Y = y_j] = p(x_i, y_j) = p_{ij}$ for $i = 1, \ldots, n$ and $j = 1, \ldots, m$. The resulting experiment has a total of nm possible outcomes, and the outcome $(X = x_i, Y = y_j)$ has probability $p_{ij} = p(x_i, y_j)$.

Against this background, the *joint entropy* (or joint uncertainty) of X and Y, denoted as $H(XY)$, is defined as follows:

$$H(XY) = -\sum_{i=1}^{n} \sum_{j=1}^{m} p(x_i, y_j) \log_2 p(x_i, y_j)$$

More formally, $H(XY)$ can be expressed as follows:

$$H(XY) = -\sum_{(x,y)} P_{XY}(x, y) \log_2 P_{XY}(x, y) \tag{5.2}$$

On the right side of (5.2), the index of the sum goes through all possible pairs (x, y) with $x \in \mathcal{X}$ and $y \in \mathcal{Y}$, or—equivalently—all (x_i, y_j) for $i = 1, \ldots, n$ and $j = 1, \ldots, m$.

Equation (5.2) can be generalized to the joint entropy of more than two random variables. In fact, the joint entropy of n random variables $X_1, X_2, \ldots, X_n$ can be expressed as follows:

$$H(X_1 \cdots X_n) = - \sum_{(x_1,\ldots,x_n)} P_{X_1 \cdots X_n}(x_1,\ldots,x_n) \log_2 P_{X_1 \cdots X_n}(x_1,\ldots,x_n)$$

In this equation, $P_{X_1 \cdots X_n}$ refers to the joint probability distribution of $X_1,\ldots,X_n$. Consequently, the joint entropy of $X_1,\ldots,X_n$ equals the entropy of the joint probability distribution $P_{X_1 \cdots X_n}$:

$$H(X_1 \cdots X_n) = H(P_{X_1 \cdots X_n})$$

There is a relation regarding the joint entropy of n random variables $X_1,\ldots,X_n$ and their individual entropies. In fact, it can be shown that

$$H(X_1 \cdots X_n) \leq H(X_1) + \ldots + H(X_n)$$

with equality if and only if $X_1,\ldots,X_n$ are mutually independent.

5.2.2 Conditional Entropy

Equation (5.1) also covers the case where the probability distribution is conditioned on an event $\mathcal{A}$ with $\Pr[\mathcal{A}] > 0$. Consequently,

$$
\begin{aligned}
H(X|\mathcal{A}) &= H(P_{X|\mathcal{A}}) \\
&= - \sum_{x \in \mathcal{X}: P_{X|\mathcal{A}}(x) \neq 0} P_{X|\mathcal{A}}(x) \log_2 P_{X|\mathcal{A}}(x)
\end{aligned}
$$

Remember from Section 4.2.3 that $P_{X|\mathcal{A}}$ is a regular probability distribution.
Let X and Y be two random variables. If we know the event $Y = y$, then we can replace $\mathcal{A}$ with $Y = y$ and rewrite the formula given above:

$$
\begin{aligned}
H(X|Y = y) &= H(P_{X|Y=y}) \\
&= - \sum_{x \in \mathcal{X}: P_{X|Y=y}(x) \neq 0} P_{X|Y=y}(x) \log_2 P_{X|Y=y}(x)
\end{aligned}
$$

Using the conditional entropy $H(X|Y = y)$, we can define the conditional entropy of the random variable X when given the random variable Y as the weighted average of the conditional uncertainties of X given that $Y = y$:

$$
\begin{aligned}
H(X|Y) &= \sum_y P_Y(y) H(X|Y = y) \\
&= -\sum_y P_Y(y) \sum_x P_{X|Y=y}(x) \log_2 P_{X|Y=y}(x) \\
&= -\sum_y \sum_x P_Y(y) \frac{P_{XY}(x,y)}{P_Y(y)} \log_2 P_{X|Y}(x,y) \\
&= -\sum_{(x,y)} P_{XY}(x,y) \log_2 P_{X|Y}(x,y)
\end{aligned}
$$

In this series of equations, the indices of the sums are written in a simplified way. In fact, x is standing for $x \in \mathcal{X}$: $P_{X|Y=y}(x) \neq 0$, y is standing for $y \in \mathcal{Y}$: $P_Y(y) \neq 0$, and—similar to (5.2)—(x,y) is standing for all possible pairs (x,y) with $x \in \mathcal{X}$ and $y \in \mathcal{Y}$ or all (x_i, y_j) for $i = 1, \ldots, n$ and $j = 1, \ldots, m$.

Note that in contrast to the previously introduced entropies, such as $H(X) = H(P_X)$, $H(XY) = H(P_{XY})$, or $H(X|Y = y) = H(P_{X|Y=y})$, the entropy $H(X|Y)$ is not the entropy of a specific probability distribution, but rather the expectation of the entropies $H(X|Y = y)$. It can be shown that

$$0 \leq H(X|Y) \leq H(X)$$

with equality on the left if and only if X is uniquely determined by Y and with equality on the right if and only if X and Y are (statistically) independent. More precisely, it can be shown that

$$H(XY) = H(X) + H(Y|X) = H(Y) + H(X|Y),$$

(i.e., the joint entropy of X and Y is equal to the entropy of X plus the entropy of Y given X, or the entropy of Y plus the entropy of X given Y). This equation is sometimes referred to as *chain rule* and can be used repeatedly to expand $H(X_1 \cdots X_n)$ as

$$H(X_1 \cdots X_n) = H(X_1) + H(X_2|X_1) + \ldots + H(X_n|X_1 \cdots X_{n-1})$$

$$= \sum_{i=1}^{n} H(X_i|X_1 \cdots X_{i-1}).$$

Note that the order in which variables are extracted is arbitrary. For example, if we have 3 random variables X, Y, and Z, we can compute their joint entropy as follows:

$$
\begin{aligned}
H(XYZ) &= H(X) + H(Y|X) + H(Z|XY) \\
&= H(X) + H(Z|X) + H(Y|XZ) \\
&= H(Y) + H(X|Y) + H(Z|XY) \\
&= H(Y) + H(Z|Y) + H(X|YZ) \\
&= H(Z) + H(X|Z) + H(Y|XZ) \\
&= H(Z) + H(Y|Z) + H(X|YZ)
\end{aligned}
$$

Similarly, we can compute the joint entropy of $X_1 \cdots X_n$ given Y as follows:

$$
\begin{aligned}
H(X_1 \cdots X_n|Y) &= H(X_1|Y) + H(X_2|X_1Y) + \ldots + H(X_n|X_1 \cdots X_{n-1}Y) \\
&= \sum_{i=1}^{n} H(X_i|X_1 \cdots X_{i-1}Y)
\end{aligned}
$$

5.2.3 Mutual Information

The *mutual information* $I(X;Y)$ between two random variables X and Y is defined as the amount of information by which the entropy (uncertainty) of X is reduced by learning Y. This can be formally expressed as follows:

$$I(X;Y) = H(X) - H(X|Y)$$

The mutual information is symmetric in the sense that $I(X;Y) = H(X) - H(X|Y) = H(Y) - H(Y|X) = I(Y;X)$.

The conditional mutual information between X and Y, given the random variable Z, is defined as follows:

$$I(X;Y|Z) = H(X|Z) - H(X|YZ)$$

We have $I(X; Y|Z) = 0$ if and only if X and Y are statistically independent when given Z. Furthermore, the conditional mutual information between X and Y is also symmetric, meaning that $I(X; Y|Z) = I(Y; X|Z)$.

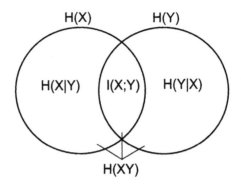

Figure 5.3   A Venn diagram graphically representing information-theoretic quantities related to two random variables.

Let X and Y be two random variables. Then the information-theoretic quantities $H(X)$, $H(Y)$, $H(XY)$, $H(X|Y)$, $H(Y|X)$, and $I(X; Y)$ can be graphically represented by a Venn diagram, as shown in Figure 5.3.

5.3 REDUNDANCY

If L is a natural language with alphabet Σ, then one may be interested in the entropy per letter, denoted by H_L. In the case of the English language, $\Sigma = \{A, B, \ldots, Z\}$ and $|\Sigma| = 26$. If every letter occured with the same probability and was independent from the other letters, then the entropy per letter would be

$$\log_2 26 \approx 4.70.$$

This value represents the *absolute rate* of the language L and is an upper bound for H_L (i.e., $H_L \leq 4.70$). The actual value of H_L, however, is smaller, because one must consider the fact that letters are typically not uniformly distributed, that they occur with frequencies (that depend on the language), and that they are also not independent from each other. If X is a random variable that refers to the letters of the English language (with their specific probabilities), then $H(X)$ is an upper bound for H_L:

$$H_L \leq H(X) \approx 4.14$$

Hence, instead of 4.7 bits of information per letter, we have around 4.14 bits of information per letter if we take into account the (statistical) letter frequencies of the English language. But this is still an overestimate, because the letters are not independent. For example, in the English language a Q is always followed by a U, and the bigram TH is likely to occur frequently. So one would suspect that a better statistic for the amount of entropy per letter could be obtained by looking at the distribution of bigrams (instead of letters). If X^2 denotes the random variable of bigrams in the English language, then we can refine the upper bound for H_L:

$$H_L \leq \frac{H(X^2)}{2} \approx 3.56$$

This can be continued with trigrams and—more generally—n-grams. In the most general case, the entropy of the language L is defined as follows:

$$H_L = \lim_{n \to \infty} \frac{H(X^n)}{n}$$

The exact value of H_L is hard to determine. All statistical investigations show that

$$1.0 \leq H_L \leq 1.5$$

for the English language (e.g., [6]). So each letter in an English text gives at most 1.5 bits of information. This implies that the English language (like all natural languages) contains a high degree of redundancy. The *redundancy* of language L, denoted by R_L, is defined as follows:

$$R_L = 1 - \frac{H_L}{|\Sigma|}$$

In the case of the English language, we have $H_L \approx 1.25$ and $|\Sigma| = \log_2 26 \approx 4.7$. So the redundancy of the English language is

$$R_L \approx 1 - \frac{1.25}{4.7} \approx 0.75.$$

This suggests that we are theoretically able to losslessly compress an English text to one fourth its size. This means that a 10-MB file can be compressed to 2.5 MB. Note that redundancy in a natural language occurs because there are known and frequently appearing letter sequences and that these letter sequences are the major starting point for cryptanalysis.

5.4 KEY EQUIVOCATION AND UNICITY DISTANCE

In addition to the notion of redundancy, Shannon introduced and formalized a couple of other concepts that can be used to analyze the security of deterministic (symmetric) encryption systems. Let M^n and C^n be random variables that denote the first n plaintext message and ciphertext bits, and K be a random variable that denotes the key that is in use. An interesting question one may ask is how much information about K is leaked as n increases. This brings us to the notion of the key equivocation formally introduced in Definition 5.1.

Definition 5.1 (Key equivocation) *The key equivocation is the function $H(K|C^n)$ (i.e., the entropy of the key as a function of the number of observed ciphertext bits).*

We generally assume that the plaintext and the key are statistically independent, meaning that $H(M|K) = H(M)$. We can show that

$$H(K|C^n) = H(K) + H(M^n) - H(C^n)$$

for a deterministic cipher. This is because

$$
\begin{aligned}
H(K) + H(M^n) &= H(KM^n) \\
&= H(KM^nC^n) \\
&= H(KC^n) \\
&= H(C^n) + H(K|C^n).
\end{aligned}
$$

In the first line, we exploit the fact that K and M^n are statistically independent. In the second and third line, we exploit the fact that $H(C^n|KM^n) = 0$ and $H(M^n|KC^n) = 0$.

We make the realistic assumption that the entropy of the plaintext grows approximately proportional to its length. That is,

$$H(M^n) \approx (1 - R_L)n,$$

where R_L is the redundancy of the plaintext language.

Against this background, it is interesting to analyze the key equivocation when n grows. For every n, there are possible keys (and it is hoped that the size of the set of possible keys decreases as n increases). More specifically, there is one correct key and a set of spurious keys (a spurious key is defined as a possible but not correct key). The most interesting question is how large n must be in order to be theoretically able to uniquely determine the key. This is where the notion of the unicity distance as introduced in Definition 5.2 comes into play.

Definition 5.2 (Unicity distance) *The unicity distance n_u is the approximate value of n for which the key is uniquely determined by the ciphertext (i.e., $H(K|C^n) \approx 0$).*

In other words, the unicity distance n_u is the minimum value for n so that the expected number of spurious keys equals zero. This is the average amount of ciphertext that is needed before an adversary can determine the correct key (again, assuming the adversary has infinite computing power). The unicity distance can be approximately determined as follows:

$$n_u \approx \frac{H(K)}{R_L}$$

If $n \geq n_u$ ciphertext bits are given, it is then theoretically possible to uniquely determine the key. For many practically relevant ciphers, n_u is surprisingly small.

5.5 FINAL REMARKS

In this chapter, we overviewed and briefly discussed the basic principles and results from information theory as far as they are relevant for contemporary cryptography. Most importantly, we introduced and put into perspective the entropy of a probability distribution or a random variable. The entropy is a fundamental measure of information, and almost all information-theoretic security proofs make use of it in one way or another. For example, in Section 10.4 we elaborate on perfectly secure encryption systems, and we use information-theoretic arguments to prove security properties.

Furthermore, we introduced the notion of redundancy of a (natural) language, as it is often exploited when cryptanalysts try to attack an encryption system. Furthermore, symmetric encryption systems are often analyzed using the key equivocation and the unicity distance. If the unicity distance of a cipher is small, then relatively few ciphertext bits are necessary to uniquely determine the key in use.

References

[1]   Shannon, C.E., "A Mathematical Theory of Communication," *Bell System Technical Journal*, Vol. 27, No. 3/4, July/October 1948, pp. 379–423/623–656.

[2]   Shannon, C.E., "Communication Theory of Secrecy Systems," *Bell System Technical Journal*, Vol. 28, No. 4, October 1949, pp. 656–715.

[3]   Ash, R.B., *Information Theory*. Dover Publications, Mineola, NY, 1990.

[4]   Cover, T.M., and J.A. Thomas, *Elements of Information Theory*. John Wiley & Sons, New York, 1991.

[5]   McEliece, R., *Theory of Information and Coding*, 2nd edition. Cambridge University Press, Cambridge, UK, 2002.

[6]   Shannon, C.E., "Prediction and Entropy of Printed English," *Bell System Technical Journal*, Vol. 30, January 1951, pp. 50–64.

Chapter 6

Complexity Theory

In Section 1.2.2, we introduced the notion of conditional or computational security, and we said that complexity theory (also known as computational complexity) is the mathematical theory behind this type of security. In this chapter, we overview and discuss the fundamentals and results from complexity theory as far as they are relevant for contemporary cryptography. More specifically, we start with some preliminary remarks in Section 6.1, introduce the topic in Section 6.2, briefly overview an asymptotic order notation in Section 6.3, elaborate on efficient computations in Section 6.4, address computational models in Section 6.5, focus on complexity classes in Section 6.6, and conclude with some final remarks in Section 6.7. More information about complexity theory and its applications is available in [1–3].

6.1 PRELIMINARY REMARKS

In theoretical computer science, one often uses a nonempty set of *characters* or *symbols* that is referred to as *alphabet* and denoted as Σ. For example, the following alphabet comprises all capital letters of the English language:

$$\Sigma = \{A, B, C, \ldots, Z\}$$

The length of the alphabet Σ corresponds to the number of elements (i.e., $|\Sigma|$). In the example given earlier, the length of the alphabet is $|\{A, B, C, \ldots, Z\}| = 26$.

Another alphabet frequently used in computer science is the American Standard Code for Information Interchange (ASCII) character set. As illustrated in Table 6.1, the ASCII character set assigns a value between 0 (i.e., 0x00) and 127 (i.e., 0x7F) to each character or symbol. Consequently, the length of the alphabet is

$2^7 = 128$ (i.e., it uses only 7 bits of each byte). There is also an extended ASCII character set with $2^8 = 256$ characters or symbols (i.e., it uses all 8 bits of each byte). For the purpose of this book, however, we don't distinguish between the two ASCII character sets.

Table 6.1
ASCII Character Set with Hexadecimal Values

	0x00	0x10	0x20	0x30	0x40	0x50	0x60	0x70
+0	NUL	DLE		0	@	P	`	p
+1	SOH	DC1	!	1	A	Q	a	q
+2	STX	DC2	"	2	B	R	b	r
+3	ETX	DC3	#	3	C	S	c	s
+4	EOT	DC4	$	4	D	T	d	t
+5	ENQ	NAK	%	5	E	U	e	u
+6	ACK	SYN	&	6	F	V	f	v
+7	BEL	ETB	'	7	G	W	g	w
+8	BS	CAN	(	8	H	X	h	x
+9	HT	EM	)	9	I	Y	i	y
+A	LF	SUB	*	:	J	Z	j	z
+B	VT	ESC	+	;	K	[	k	{
+C	FF	FS	,	<	L	\	l		
+D	CR	GS	−	=	M	]	m	}
+E	SO	RS	.	>	N	^	n	~
+F	SI	US	/	?	O	_	o	DEL

Instead of directly using letters or ASCII characters, computer systems normally operate on *binary digits* (or *bits*). Consequently, the alphabet most frequently used in computer science is $\Sigma = \{0, 1\}$ and its length is $|\{0, 1\}| = 2$.

If an alphabet Σ is finite (which is almost always the case), then its length is less than infinity (i.e., $|\Sigma| = n < \infty$). In this case, the n elements of Σ can also be associated with the n elements (residue classes) of $\mathbb{Z}_n = \{0, 1, \ldots, n - 1\}$. Consequently, it is possible to work in $\mathbb{Z}_n$ instead of any character set with n elements. This simplifies things considerably. In particular, it allows us to work with mathematical structures we know and with which we are familiar.

Let Σ be an alphabet. The term *word* (or *string*) over Σ refers to a finite sequence of characters or symbols from Σ, including, for example, the empty word ε. The length of a word w over Σ, denoted as $|w|$, corresponds to the number of characters. The empty word has length zero (i.e., $|\varepsilon| = 0$). The set of all words over Σ (again, including the empty word) is referred to as Σ^*. For every $n \in \mathbb{N}$, Σ^n refers to the set of all words of length n over Σ. For example, $\{0, 1\}^n$ denotes the set of all n-bit sequences, and $\{0, 1\}^*$ denotes the set of all binary words. This can be formally expressed as follows:

$$\{0,1\}^* = \bigcup_{n \in \mathbb{N}} \{0,1\}^n$$

Using the binary alphabet, a positive integer $n \in \mathbb{N}$ can always be encoded as a binary word $b_{l-1} \ldots b_1 b_0 \in \{0,1\}^l$ of length l:

$$n = \sum_{i=0}^{l-1} b_i 2^i$$

In complexity theory, a positive integer $n \in \mathbb{N}$ is frequently encoded using the *unary representation*:

$$n = 1^n = \underbrace{11 \cdots 1}_{n \text{ times}}$$

The relevant operation for words is the (string) concatenation, denoted as $\|$ or $\circ$ (in this book, we use $\|$ most of the time). If $v, w \in \Sigma^*$, then $v \parallel w$ results from concatenating v and w. The empty word ε is the neutral element of the concatenation operation, hence $v \parallel \varepsilon = \varepsilon \parallel v = v$ for every $v \in \Sigma^*$. It can be shown that $\langle \Sigma^*, \| \rangle$ represents a monoid, as formally introduced in Section 3.1.2.2.

6.2 INTRODUCTION

Complexity theory is a central field of study in theoretical computer science. According to [4], the

> main goal of complexity theory is to provide mechanisms for classifying computational problems according to the resources needed to solve them. The classification should not depend on a particular computational model, but rather should measure the intrinsic difficulty of the problem. The computational may include time, storage space, random bits, number of processors, etc., but typically the main focus is time, and sometimes space.

The important points are (a) that the computational problems should be classified according to the resources needed to solve them, and (b) that this classification should be independent from a particular computational model. Consequently, complexity theory has not much in common with benchmark testing as usually used in the trade press to compare the computational power of different computer systems, products, and models. Instead, complexity theory is used to determine the computational resources (e.g., time, space, and randomness) that are needed to compute a function or solve a problem. The computational resources, in turn, can be determined exactly or at approximately specifying lower and upper bounds.[1] Alternatively, one can consider the effects of limiting computational resources on the class of functions (problems) that can be computed (solved) in the first place.

In complexity theory, there are many functions and problems to look at. For example, for a positive integer $n \in \mathbb{N}$, one can always look at the problem of deciding whether n is prime (or composite). This problem is a decision problem and it is solved by providing a binary answer (i.e., yes or no).[2] An instance of this problem would be whether $n = 81$ is prime (which is arguably wrong, because $81 = 9 \cdot 9$). Consequently, a problem refers to a well-defined and compactly described large class of instances characterized by some input and output parameters. Examples include deciding primality (as mentioned earlier), factoring integers, or deciding graph isomorphisms. Against this background, it does not make a lot of sense to define the computational difficulty or complexity of a problem instance. There is always a trivial algorithm to solve the instance, namely the algorithm that simply outputs the correct solution. Consequently, the computational difficulty or complexity of a problem must always refer to a (potentially very) large class of instances. This fact is very important to understanding complexity theory and its results. Unfortunately, it also makes things considerably difficult to express and understand.

We said that results from complexity theory should be largely independent from a particular computational model (refer to Section 6.5 for an overview about the computational models in use today). Nevertheless, one must still have a model in mind when one works in theoretical computer science and complexity theory. As of this writing, the computational model of choice is the Turing machine.[3] Looking at Turing machines is sufficient, because there is a famous thesis in theoretical computer science—called *Church's thesis*[4]—that most results from complexity theory

---

1   To prove an upper bound is comparably simple. It suffices to give an algorithm together with an analysis of its computational complexity. To prove a lower bound is much more involved, because one must prove the nonexistence of an algorithm that is more efficient than the one one has in mind. Consequently, it does not come as a big surprise that no significant lower bound has been proven for the computational complexity of any practically relevant problem.

2   It was recently shown that there are deterministic polynomial-time algorithms to solve this problem (see Section 3.2.4.3). Consequently, this problem is known to be in $\mathcal{P}$ (the notion of the complexity class $\mathcal{P}$ is introduced later in this chapter).

3   Turing machines are named after Alan M. Turing, who lived from 1912 to 1954.

4   The thesis is named after Alonzo Church, who lived from 1903 to 1995.

hold regardless of the computational model in use (as long as it is "reasonable" in one way or another). More specifically, the thesis says that any physical computing device can be simulated by a Turing machine (in a number of steps polynomial in the resources used by the computing device).

For the rest of this chapter, we associate the Turing machine M with the function f_M it computes, and we sometimes write $M(x)$ instead of $f_M(x)$ for a given input x. As mentioned earlier, there are several things a Turing machine M can do, including, for example, computing a function, solving a search problem, or making a decision:

- A Turing machine M can *compute a function* $f : \{0,1\}^* \rightarrow \{0,1\}^*$. In this case, M is given input $x \in \{0,1\}^*$, and it computes and outputs $f_M(x) = y \in \{0,1\}^*$.

- A Turing machine M can *solve a search problem* $S \subseteq \{0,1\}^* \times \{0,1\}^*$. In this case, M is given input $x \in \{0,1\}^*$ that has a solution y (i.e., $(x,y) \in S$), and it computes and outputs a solution $f_M(x) = y' \in \{0,1\}^*$ with $(x,y') \in S$.

- A Turing machine M can *solve a decision problem* $D \subseteq \{0,1\}^*$. In this case, M is given input $x \in \{0,1\}^*$, and it determines and outputs a bit saying whether $x \in D$ (i.e., $f_M(x) = 1$ if and only if $x \in D$).

In theoretical computer science, a formal language L is usually defined as a subset of Σ^* with $\Sigma = \{0,1\}$:

$$L \subseteq \{0,1\}^*$$

Consequently, a decision problem can also be interpreted as a language membership problem when the problem instances are encoded as binary strings using an arbitrary but fixed encoding. For example, all binary encoded prime numbers represent a formal language, and the decision problem whether a number is prime or not can also be understood as a membership problem for this particular language.

For the sake of simplicity, complexity theorists usually focus on decision problems (i.e., problems that have either 1 (yes) or 0 (no) as an answer). This is not too restrictive, because all computational problems can be phrased as decision problems in such a way that an efficient algorithm for the decision problem yields an efficient algorithm for the computational problem, and vice versa.

6.3 ASYMPTOTIC ORDER NOTATION

In complexity theory, one is often interested in the asymptotic behavior of the complexity of a computation as a function of the input size[5] or some other parameter(s). This is where asymptotic analysis and asymptotic order notation come into play. In what follows, we only consider functions that are defined for positive integers and take on real values that are positive for some $n \geq n_0$. Let $f : \mathbb{N} \rightarrow \mathbb{R}^+$ and $g : \mathbb{N} \rightarrow \mathbb{R}^+$ be such functions. The following asymptotic bounds are frequently used in complexity theory.

Asymptotic upper bound: If there exist a positive constant c and a positive integer n_0 such that $0 \leq f(n) \leq cg(n)$ for all $n \geq n_0$, then we write

$$f(n) = O(g(n)).$$

If $g(n)$ is constant (and independent from n), then we write $f(n) = O(1)$, or $f = O(1)$ in short. Note that this applies even if the constant is very large, such as 2^{128}. Furthermore, if $0 \leq f(n) < cg(n)$ for all $n \geq n_0$, then we write

$$f(n) = o(g(n)).$$

Asymptotic lower bound: If there exist a positive constant c and a positive integer n_0 such that $0 \leq cg(n) \leq f(n)$ for all $n \geq n_0$, then we write

$$f(n) = \Omega(g(n)).$$

Asymptotic tight bound: If there exist positive constants c_1 and c_2, and a positive integer n_0 such that $c_1 g(n) \leq f(n) \leq c_2 g(n)$ for all $n \geq n_0$, then we write

$$f(n) = \Theta(g(n)).$$

5   The input size is the size or length of the (binary) word that is needed to represent the input (for a well-defined representation method).

Intuitively, $f(n) = O(g(n))$ means that $f(n)$ doesn't grow asymptotically faster than $g(n)$ within a constant multiple, whereas $f(n) = \Omega(g(n))$ means that $f(n)$ grows asymptotically at least as fast as $g(n)$ within a constant multiple. For example, if $f(n) = 2n^2 + n + 1$, then $2n^2 + n + 1 \le 4n^2$ for all $n \ge 1$, and hence $2n^2 + n + 1 = O(n^2)$. Similarly, $2n^2 + n + 1 \ge 2n^2$ for all $n \ge 1$, and hence $2n^2 + n + 1 = \Omega(n^2)$. Consequently, $2n^2 + n + 1 = \Theta(n^2)$. Furthermore, $f(n) = o(g(n))$ means that $g(n)$ is an upper bound for $f(n)$ that is not asymptotically tight, or in other words, the function $f(n)$ becomes insignificant relative to $g(n)$ as n gets larger. In practice, the expression $o(1)$ is often used to denote a function $f(n)$ whose limit is 0 as n approaches ∞. In practice, the asymptotic upper bound (i.e., the O-notation) is most frequently used.

In complexity-theoretic discussions and considerations, one often uses functions that are polynomials as suggested in Definition 3.30. Polynomials are useful because they have the property that they are closed under addition, multiplication, and composition. This basically means that one can add, multiply, and compose two (or even more) polynomials, and that one still gets a(nother) polynomial.

In addition to polynomials, one often uses functions that are negligible or nonnegligible as suggested in Definitions 6.1 and 6.2.

Definition 6.1 (Negligible function) *A function $f(n)$ is* negligible *if for every constant $c \ge 0$ there exists a positive integer n_0 such that $f(n) < n^{-c}$ for all $n \ge n_0$ (i.e., $f(n) = o(n^{-c})$ for every positive constant c).*

This basically means that $f(n)$ diminishes to zero faster than the reciprocal of any polynomial and hence that $f(n)$ gets arbitrarily small for sufficiently large n. For example, for any polynomial $p(n)$, the function $f(n) = p(n)/2^n$ is negligible.

Definition 6.2 (Nonnegligible function) *A function $f(n)$ is* nonnegligible *(or noticeable) if there exist a positive constant c and a positive integer n_0 such that $f(n) > n^{-c}$ for all $n > n_0$ (i.e., $f(n) = \Omega(n^{-c})$).*

Referring to Figure 6.1, there are functions that are neither negligible nor nonnegligible (noticeable). Examples include the sine and cosine functions.

6.4 EFFICIENT COMPUTATIONS

In practice, one is often interested in finding the most efficient (i.e., fastest) algorithm to compute a function or solve a problem. Consequently, the notion of efficiency is closely related to the running time of an algorithm. The *running time* of an algorithm on a particular input, in turn, can be defined as the number of primitive operations

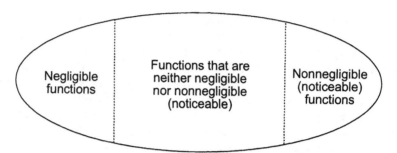

Figure 6.1   Negligible, nonnegligible (noticeable), and other functions.

or "steps" that must be executed. Often a step is taken to mean a bit operation. For some algorithms, however, it is more convenient to have a step mean something more comprehensive, such as a comparison, a machine instruction, a machine clock cycle, a modular multiplication, or anything else along these lines.

In either case, the running time of an algorithm can be measured in the worst or average case:

- The *worst-case running time* of an algorithm is an upper bound on the running time for any input, expressed as a function of the input size.

- The *average-case running time* of an algorithm is the average running time over all inputs of a fixed size, also expressed as a function of the input size.

In modern cryptography, it is common to call a computation efficient if it terminates within a worst-case running time that is polynomial in the input size. Polynomial functions and polynomial-time algorithms as formally introduced in Definitions 6.3 and 6.4 are defined along these lines.

Definition 6.3 (Polynomial function) *A function $f(n)$ is called* polynomial *if $f(n) = O(n^c)$ for some $c \in \mathbb{N}$. Otherwise, it is called* super-polynomial.

In some literature, a polynomial function is called *polynomially bounded*, and a super-polynomial function is called *nonpolynomially bounded*. In this book, however, we don't use these terms, and we say that a function is either polynomial or super-polynomial.

If ϵ and c are constants with $0 < \epsilon < 1 < c$, then the following functions are listed in increasing order of their asymptotic growth rates:

$$1 < \ln \ln n < \ln n < e^{\sqrt{\ln n \ln \ln n}} < n^{\epsilon} < n^{c} < n^{\ln n} < c^{n} < n^{n} < c^{c^{n}}$$

All function until n^c are polynomial, whereas all other functions (i.e., $n^{\ln n}$, c^n, n^n, and c^{c^n}) are super-polynomial.

Definition 6.4 (Polynomial-time algorithm) *An algorithm is called* polynomial-time *if its worst-case running time function is polynomial in the input size. Any algorithm whose running time cannot be bounded by a polynomial is called* super-polynomial-time.

Consequently, the worst-case running time of a polynomial-time algorithm is of the form $O(n^c)$, where n is the input size and c is a constant. The most important examples of super-polynomial-time algorithms are exponential-time algorithms (i.e., algorithms that run in time exponential in the input size). The worst-case running time of such an algorithm is of the form $O(c^n)$.

In complexity theory, one considers polynomial-time algorithms (be they deterministic or probabilistic) as being efficient and super-polynomial-time (e.g., exponential-time) algorithms as being inefficient. This is particularly true if the polynomials are of small degrees (e.g., $c \leq 10$). In practice, however, a super-polynomial-time algorithm may be quite practical for the input size of interest, and a polynomial-time algorithm may be completely impractical. Note, for example, that $n^{1000} \gg n^{\ln \ln \ln n}$ for all n that can ever be of relevance. Consequently, one has to be careful when one applies complexity-theoretic arguments.

Last but not least, it is important to note that there are algorithms that are super-polynomial-time but not exponential-time. Some of these algorithms are subexponential-time as specified in Definition 6.5.

Definition 6.5 (Subexponential-time algorithm) *An algorithm is* subexponential-time *if its worst-case running time function is of the form $e^{o(n)}$, where n is the input size.*

A subexponential-time algorithm runs asymptotically much slower than a polynomial-time algorithm, but it runs much faster than an exponential-time algorithm. There are subexponential-time algorithms for many computational problems that are relevant in cryptography, including, for example, integer factorization and computing discrete logarithms. To discuss the efficiency of these algorithms, one often uses the *running time function* $L_n[a, c]$ that is defined as follows:

$$L_n[a, c] = O(e^{(c+o(1))(\ln n)^a (\ln \ln n)^{1-a}})$$

The function has two parameters (i.e., a and c). In general, the smaller a and c are, the more efficient the corresponding algorithms are. The parameter $a \in [0, 1]$ is particularly important, because it controls whether the running time is exponential in $\ln n$ (if $a = 1$) or subexponential in $\ln n$ (if $a < 1$). The parameter $c \in \mathbb{R}$ is less important for our purposes.

In the running time analyses of integer factoring algorithms and algorithms to compute discrete logarithms, the following two cases occur frequently ($a = 1/2$ and $a = 1/3$):

$$
\begin{aligned}
L_n[1/2, c] &= O(e^{(c+o(1))\sqrt{\ln n}\sqrt{\ln \ln n}}) = O(e^{(c+o(1))\sqrt{\ln n \ln \ln n}}) \\
L_n[1/3, c] &= O(e^{(c+o(1))(\ln n)^{1/3}(\ln \ln n)^{2/3}})
\end{aligned}
$$

The second case occurs with the most efficient algorithm to factorize integers and compute discrete logarithms (see Chapter 7).

6.5 COMPUTATIONAL MODELS

In the theory of computation, the following computational models are usually considered:

- Boolean circuits;

- Turing machines;

- Random access machines.[6]

As mentioned earlier, Church's thesis says that all computational models itemized here are equivalent, meaning that if a function (problem) is computable (solvable) in one model, then it is also computable (solvable) in the other models. It also means that the computational complexities are equal (up to polynomial transformations). For example, simulating a random access machine by a Turing machine generally squares the number of steps. Consequently, from a theoretical point of view, it doesn't really matter which model is used. As mentioned earlier, the model that is most frequently used in theoretical computer science and complexity theory is the Turing machine.

A Turing machine is an imaginary computing device that yields a primitive but sufficiently general computational model. In fact, a Turing machine is more like a computer program (software) than a computer (hardware) and can be realized

---

6   A random access machine is similar to a Turing machine. The major distinguishing feature is that it provides access to arbitrary (i.e., randomly chosen) memory cells. As such, the random access machine even more closely represents contemporary computer systems.

or implemented on many different physical computing devices. In short, a Turing machine consists of a (finite-state) control unit and one (or several) tape(s), each of them equipped with a tapehead (i.e., a read/write head). Each tape is marked off into (memory) cells that can be filled with at most one symbol. The tapehead is able to read and/or write exactly one cell, namely the one that is located directly below it. Hence, the operations of the Turing machine are limited to reading and writing symbols on the tapes and moving along the tapes to the left or to the right. As such, the Turing machine represents a *finite state machine* (FSM). This basically means that the machine has a finite number of states (so-called functional states) and is in exactly one of these states at any given point in time.

The Turing machine solves a problem by having a tapehead scanning a string of a finite number of symbols that are placed sequentially in the leftmost cells of one tape (i.e., the input tape). Each symbol occupies one cell and the remaining cells to the right on that tape are blank. This string is called an *input* of a problem instance. The scanning starts from the leftmost cell of the tape that contains the input while the machine is in a designated *initial state*. At any time, only one tapehead of the Turing machine is accessing its tape. A step of access made by a tapehead on its tape is called a *move*. If the machine starts from an initial state, makes one move after another, completes scanning the input string, eventually causes a satisfaction of a terminating condition and thereby terminates, then the machine is said to recognize the input. Otherwise, the machine has no move to make at some point, and hence the machine halts without recognizing the input. An input that is recognized by a Turing machine is called an *instance* in a recognizable language.

Upon termination, the number of moves that a Turing machine M has taken to recognize an input is said to be the *running time* or *time complexity* of M and is denoted as T_M. It goes without saying that T_M can be expressed as a function $T_M(n) : \mathbb{N} \to \mathbb{N}$ where n is the length or size of the input (i.e., the number of symbols that represent the input string when M is in the initial state). It is always the case that $T_M(n) \geq n$, because the machine must at least read the input (typically encoded using the unary representation). In addition to the time requirement, M may also have a space requirement S_M that refers to the number of tape cells that the tapeheads of M have visited in writing access. The quantity S_M can also be expressed as a function $S_M(n) : \mathbb{N} \to \mathbb{N}$ and is said to be the *space complexity* of M.

In Definition 6.4 we introduced the notion of a polynomial-time algorithm. Such an algorithm can be implemented, for example, by a polynomial-time Turing machine. In fact, a Turing machine is called polynomial-time if its worst-case running time function is polynomial in the input size. For all practical purposes, polynomial-time Turing machines can perform computations that can also be carried out on contemporary computer systems within reasonable amounts of time.

Polynomial-time Turing machines work in a deterministic way, meaning that they repeatedly execute one (or several) deterministic step(s). This need not be the case, and there are at least two alternative types of Turing machines.

Nondeterministic Turing machine: This is a polynomial-time Turing machine that works in a nondeterministic way.

Probabilistic Turing machine: This is a polynomial-time Turing machine that works in a probabilistic way.

A nondeterministic Turing machine is arbitrary parallel, works in a nondeterministic way, and is able to solve a computational problem if such a solution exists. The existence of a nondeterministic Turing machine is a purely theoretical assumption, and it is generally not possible to build such a machine. Contrary to that, a probabilistic Turing machine can be built. It works in a probabilistic (and nondeterministic) way. Similar to a deterministic Turing machine, a probabilistic Turing machine may have a plural of tapes. One of these tapes is called *random tape* and contains uniformly distributed random symbols. During the scanning of an input instance, the machine interacts with the random tape, picks up a random string, and then proceeds like a deterministic Turing machine. The random string is called the *random input* to the probabilistic Turing machine (in practice, the random input is generated by a random or pseudorandom bit generator). With the involvement of the random input, the recognition of an instance by a probabilistic Turing machine is no longer a deterministic function of the instance, but is associated with a random variable (i.e., a function of the Turing machine's random input). This random variable typically assigns error probabilities to the event of recognizing the problem instance (this is explored further later). Remarkably, there are many problems for which probabilistic Turing machines can be constructed that are more efficient, both in terms of time and space, than the best known deterministic counterparts. Consequently, probabilistic Turing machines are an important field of study in complexity theory and have many cryptographic applications.

Last but not least, it is important to note that there are computational models that are not equivalent to the models itemized at the beginning of this section (in fact, they are more powerful). Examples include quantum computers and DNA computers.

- A *quantum computer* is a computational device that makes use of quantum mechanical principles to solve computational problems. A "conventional" computer operates on bits that represent either 0 or 1. In contrast, a quantum computer operates on *quantum bits* (qubits) that represent vectors in the two-dimensional Hilbert space. More specifically, a qubit is a linear combination or *superposition* of $|0\rangle$ and $|1\rangle$ (with $|0\rangle$ and $|1\rangle$ representing an orthonormal basis). A qubit can be written in terms of function $\psi = \alpha|0\rangle + \beta|1\rangle$ with $\alpha, \beta \in \mathbb{C}$ and $|\alpha|^2 + |\beta|^2 = 1$. It is a fundamental law of quantum mechanics that once we measure the state of a qubit ψ, we either get $|0\rangle$ or $|1\rangle$ as a result. More precisely, we measure $|0\rangle$ with probability $|\alpha|^2$ and $|1\rangle$ with probability $|\beta|^2$. The fundamental difference between bits and qubits is that qubits may be in states between $|0\rangle$ and $|1\rangle$. Only by measuring the state of a qubit, one can get one of the states $|0\rangle$ or $|1\rangle$. A quantum register of length n is built of n qubits $|q_k\rangle$ ($k = 1, \ldots, n$). Each $|q_k\rangle$ is of the form $\alpha_k|0\rangle + \beta_k|1\rangle$. Due to superposition, a quantum register may be in all of the 2^n possible states at the same time. A quantum computer may exploit this fact and make use of such a quantum register to solve a particular problem. In 1994, Peter W. Shor proposed randomized polynomial-time algorithms for computing discrete logarithms and factoring integers on a quantum computer [5, 6]. Although a group of researchers implemented Shor's algorithm to factor the integer 15 [7], it is not currently known whether a quantum computer of practical size will ever be put in practice. Furthermore, no polynomial-time algorithm for solving any $\mathcal{NP}$-complete problem[7] has been found so far. Further information about quantum computers can be found in [8].

- A *DNA computer* is a computational device that makes use of molecular biology to solve computational problems. More specifically, molecules of deoxyribonucleic acid (DNA) are used to encode problem instances, and standard protocols and enzymes are used to perform the steps of the corresponding computations. In 1994, Leonard M. Adleman[8] demonstrated the feasibility of using a small DNA computer to solve an (arguably small) instance of the directed Hamiltonian path problem, which is known to be $\mathcal{NP}$-complete [9]. Further information about the DNA computer can be found in [10, 11].

It is neither presently known how to build a quantum or DNA computer of a sufficiently large size, nor is it known to be possible at all (this is particularly true for DNA computers). Nevertheless, should either quantum computers or DNA computers ever become feasible and practical, they would have a tremendous impact on theoretical computer science in general, and cryptography in particular. In fact, many cryptographic systems that are computationally secure today would become completely insecure and worthless (this is not true for unconditionally secure systems).

---

7   Refer to Section 6.6.2.2 and Definition 6.11 for the notion of an $\mathcal{NP}$-complete problem.
8   Leonard M. Adleman is one of the inventors of the RSA public key cryptosystem.

6.6   COMPLEXITY CLASSES

In the previous section we introduced deterministic, nondeterministic, and probabilistic polynomial-time Turing machines. These machines can be used to define
complexity classes. In short, deterministic polynomial-time Turing machines can
be used to define the complexity class $\mathcal{P}$, nondeterministic polynomial-time Turing machines can be used to define the complexity class $\mathcal{NP}$ (and co$\mathcal{NP}$), and
probabilistic polynomial-time Turing machines can be used to define the complexity
class $\mathcal{PP}$ and its subclasses. All of these classes are overviewed, discussed, and put
into perspective next. For the sake of simplicity, we only focus on Turing machines
and decision problems. Note, however, that it is also possible to formally define
the previously mentioned complexity classes on the basis of algorithms (instead of
Turing machines) and for problems other than decision problems.

6.6.1   Complexity Class $\mathcal{P}$

As suggested in Definition 6.6, the complexity class $\mathcal{P}$ ("polynomial-time") assumes
the existence of deterministic polynomial-time Turing machines.

Definition 6.6 (Complexity class $\mathcal{P}$) *The complexity class $\mathcal{P}$ refers to the class
of decision problems $D \subseteq \{0,1\}^*$ that are solvable in polynomial time by a
deterministic Turing machine (i.e., there exists a deterministic polynomial-time
Turing machine M with $M(x) = 1$ if and only if $x \in D$).*

Consequently, the complexity class $\mathcal{P}$ comprises all problems that can be
solved deterministically in polynomial time. Similar to Definition 6.6, one can define
the complexity class $\mathcal{P}$ to comprise the class of functions or search problems that are
computable or solvable in polynomial time. This is not done in this book.

6.6.2   Complexity Classes $\mathcal{NP}$ and co$\mathcal{NP}$

As suggested in Definition 6.7, the complexity class $\mathcal{NP}$ ("nondeterministic
polynomial-time") assumes the existence of nondeterministic Turing machines.

Definition 6.7 (Complexity class $\mathcal{NP}$) *The complexity class $\mathcal{NP}$ refers to the
class of decision problems $D \subseteq \{0,1\}^*$ that are solvable in polynomial time by
a nondeterministic Turing machine (i.e., there exists a nondeterministic polynomial-
time Turing machine M with $M(x) = 1$ if and only if $x \in D$).*

As mentioned earlier, nondeterministic Turing machines are purely theoretical
constructs, and it is currently not known how to build such a machine. Consequently,

another possibility to define the complexity class $\mathcal{NP}$ is captured in Definition 6.8. It basically says that a decision problem is in $\mathcal{NP}$ if a yes answer can at least be verified efficiently.

Definition 6.8 (Complexity class $\mathcal{NP}$) *The complexity class $\mathcal{NP}$ refers to the class of decision problems $D \subseteq \{0,1\}^*$ for which a yes answer can be verified in polynomial time given some extra information, called a* certificate *or* witness.

It must be emphasized that if a decision problem is in $\mathcal{NP}$, then it may not be the case that a certificate for a yes answer can be obtained easily. What is asserted is only that such a certificate exists, and, if known, can be used to efficiently verify the yes answer. For example, the problem of deciding whether a positive integer n is composite (i.e., whether there exist integers $1 < p_1, p_2, \ldots, p_k \in \mathbb{N}$ such that $n = p_1 p_2 \ldots p_k$) belongs to $\mathcal{NP}$. This is because if n is composite, then this fact can be verified in polynomial time if one is given a divisor a of n (in this case, the certificate is a divisor p_i for $1 \leq i \leq k$).

It is not clear whether the existence of an efficient verification algorithm for yes answers also implies the existence of an efficient verification algorithm for no answers. Consequently, there is room for a complementary complexity class $\text{co}\mathcal{NP}$ as suggested in Definition 6.9.

Definition 6.9 (Complexity class $\text{co}\mathcal{NP}$) *The complexity class $\text{co}\mathcal{NP}$ refers to the class of decision problems $D \subseteq \{0,1\}^*$ for which a no answer can be verified in polynomial time given some extra information, called a* certificate *or* witness.

It is conjectured that $\text{co}\mathcal{NP} \neq \mathcal{NP}$. Note, however, that this is only a conjecture, and that nobody has been able to prove it (or the converse) so far.

$\mathcal{NP}$ ($\text{co}\mathcal{NP}$) refers to the class of decision problems for which a yes (no) answer can be verified in polynomial time given an appropriate certificate. Contrary to that, $\mathcal{P}$ consists of the class of decision problems for which an answer can be found in polynomial time. Consequently, we know that

$$\mathcal{P} \subseteq \mathcal{NP}$$

and

$$\mathcal{P} \subseteq \text{co}\mathcal{NP}.$$

We do not know, however, whether the existence of an efficient verification algorithm for decision problems (be it for yes or no answers) also implies the ability to efficiently provide an answer for such a problem. This question can be phrased in the single most important open question in theoretical computer science and complexity theory:

$$\text{Is } \mathcal{NP} = \mathcal{P} \text{ or } \mathcal{NP} \neq \mathcal{P}?$$

If this question is answered in the affirmative (i.e., $\mathcal{NP} = \mathcal{P}$), then every problem (function) in $\mathcal{NP}$ is theoretically solvable (computable) in polynomial time. It is, however, widely believed and conjectured that $\mathcal{P} \neq \mathcal{NP}$. The $\mathcal{P} \neq \mathcal{NP}$ conjecture is supported by our intuition that solving a problem is usually more involved than verifying a solution. Empirical evidence toward the conjectured inequality is given by the fact that literally thousands of problems in $\mathcal{NP}$, coming from a wide variety of mathematical and scientific disciplines, are not known to be solvable in polynomial time (in spite of extensive research attempts aimed at providing efficient algorithms to solve them).

If $\mathcal{P} = \mathcal{NP}$, then there is no computationally secure cryptographic system in a mathematically strong sense. Nevertheless, there may still exist cryptographic systems that are computationally secure for all practical purposes, provided that the complexity ratio between using the system and breaking it is a polynomial of sufficiently high degree. An example to illustrate this point is Merkle's Puzzles addressed in Section 16.2.1. Also, all unconditionally (i.e., information-theoretically) secure cryptographic systems remain unaffected and secure even if $\mathcal{P} = \mathcal{NP}$.

6.6.2.1 Polynomial Reducibility

It is sometimes useful to compare the relative difficulties of two (or more) computational problems. This is where the notion of polynomial reducibility comes into play. In short, a function f is *polynomially reducible* to a function g if there exists a(nother) function h that can be computed in polynomial time so that $f(x) = g(h(x))$ for every input x. Hence, we can compute f by first computing h (in polynomial time) and then computing g. If g is efficiently computable, then so is f (because we only require a polynomial number of invocations of g). If, however, g is not efficiently computable, then the notion of polynomial reducibility is not particularly useful. The notion of a polynomial-time reduction for decision problems can now be defined as suggested in Definition 6.10.

Definition 6.10 (Polynomial-time reduction) *Let $D_1, D_2 \subseteq \{0,1\}^*$ be two decision problems. D_1 is said to* polytime reduce *to D_2 (denoted as $D_1 \leq_P D_2$), if there is an algorithm that solves D_1 which uses, as a subroutine, an algorithm for solving D_2, and which runs in polynomial time if this algorithm does.*

In this case, the algorithm that solves D_2 serves as an oracle.[9] If $D_1 \leq_P D_2$, then D_2 is at least as difficult as D_1, or, equivalently, D_1 is no harder than D_2. If both $D_1 \leq_P D_2$ and $D_2 \leq_P D_1$, then D_1 and D_2 are *computationally equivalent*.

Polynomial-time reductions are transitive. This basically means that if $D_1 \leq_P D_2$ and $D_2 \leq_P D_3$, then $D_1 \leq_P D_3$. Furthermore, if $D_1 \leq_P D_2$ and $D_2 \in \mathcal{P}$, then $D_1 \in \mathcal{P}$. In either case, polynomial-time reductions are important when it comes to prove the $\mathcal{NP}$-completeness of a problem.

6.6.2.2 $\mathcal{NP}$-Completeness

Loosely speaking, a decision problem D is $\mathcal{NP}$-complete if it is in $\mathcal{NP}$ and every decision problem in $\mathcal{NP}$ polytime reduces to it. This idea is captured in Definition 6.11.

Definition 6.11 (NP-complete problem) *A decision problem* $D \subseteq \{0,1\}^*$ *is $\mathcal{NP}$-complete if* $D \in \mathcal{NP}$ *and* $D_1 \leq_P D$ *for every decision problem* $D_1 \in \mathcal{NP}$.

Note that this definition can't be used to show that a decision problem D is $\mathcal{NP}$-complete. This is because it is difficult to show the second condition for every $D_1 \in \mathcal{NP}$. If, however, we already know that a specific decision problem D_1 is $\mathcal{NP}$-complete, then we can prove the $\mathcal{NP}$-completeness of D by showing that it is in $\mathcal{NP}$ and that it polytime reduces to D_1. More specifically, the following three steps can be used to prove that a decision problem D is $\mathcal{NP}$-complete:

1. Prove that $D \in \mathcal{NP}$;

2. Select a decision problem D_1 that is known to be $\mathcal{NP}$-complete;

3. Prove that $D_1 \leq_P D$.

Consequently, $\mathcal{NP}$-complete (decision) problems are "universal" in the sense that providing a polynomial-time algorithm for solving one of them immediately implies polynomial-time algorithms for solving all of them. More specifically, if there exists a single $\mathcal{NP}$-complete decision problem that can be shown to be in $\mathcal{P}$, then $\mathcal{P} = \mathcal{NP}$ results immediately. Similarly, if there exists a single $\mathcal{NP}$-complete decision problem that can be shown in $co\mathcal{NP}$, then $co\mathcal{NP} = \mathcal{NP}$ results immediately. Such a result would be extremely surprising, and a proof that a problem is $\mathcal{NP}$-complete generally provides strong evidence for the computational intractability of it.

At first glance, it may be surprising that $\mathcal{NP}$-complete problems exist. There exist, however, many problems that are known to be $\mathcal{NP}$-complete (e.g., [1]). In

9   Note that the notion of an oracle has become very important in contemporary cryptography.

fact, there are thousands of $\mathcal{NP}$-complete problems, coming from a wide range of mathematical and scientific disciplines and fields of study. For example, deciding whether a Boolean formula is satisfiable and deciding whether a directed graph has a Hamiltonian cycle are both NP-complete decision problems. Furthermore, the subset sum problem is NP-complete and has been used as a basis for many public key cryptosystems in the past (i.e., knapsack-based cryptosystems). The subset sum problem is that given a set of positive integers $\{a_1, a_2, \ldots, a_n\}$ and a positive integer s, determine whether or not there is a subset of the a_i that sum to s.

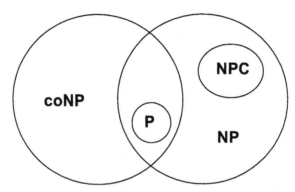

Figure 6.2   The conjectured relationship between $\mathcal{P}$, $\mathcal{NP}$, co$\mathcal{NP}$, and $\mathcal{NPC}$.

The class of all $\mathcal{NP}$-complete (decision) problems is sometimes also denoted by $\mathcal{NPC}$. Figure 6.2 illustrates the conjectured relationship between the complexity classes $\mathcal{P}$, $\mathcal{NP}$, co$\mathcal{NP}$, and $\mathcal{NPC}$. Again, we know that $\mathcal{P} \subseteq \mathcal{NP}$ and $\mathcal{P} \subseteq$ co$\mathcal{NP}$, as well as $\mathcal{NPC} \subseteq \mathcal{NP}$. We do not know, however, whether $\mathcal{P} = \mathcal{NP}$, $\mathcal{P} =$co$\mathcal{NP}$, or $\mathcal{P} = \mathcal{NP} \cap$ co$\mathcal{NP}$. Most experts believe that the answers to the last three questions is no (but nothing along these lines has been proven).

Last but not least, one sometimes attributes the term $\mathcal{NP}$-hard to a problem (not necessarily a decision problem). Referring to Definition 6.11, a problem is called $\mathcal{NP}$-hard if the second but not necessarily the first condition is satisfied, meaning that any decision problem in $\mathcal{NP}$ polytime reduces to it (or there is at least one $\mathcal{NP}$-complete problem that polytime reduces to it, respectively). For example, finding a satisfying assignment for a Boolean formula or finding a Hamiltonian cycle in a directed graph are NP-hard problems. We can also revisit the subset sum problem mentioned earlier. Given positive integers $\{a_1, a_2, \ldots, a_n\}$ and a positive integer s, a computational version of the subset sum problem would ask for a subset of the a_i that sum up to s, provided that such a subset exists. This problem can also be shown to be $\mathcal{NP}$-hard.

It is obvious to see that an $\mathcal{NP}$-complete problem must always be $\mathcal{NP}$-hard, whereas the converse may not be true (i.e., an $\mathcal{NP}$-hard problem may not be $\mathcal{NP}$-complete). In fact, there are (decision) problems that are $\mathcal{NP}$-hard but not $\mathcal{NP}$-complete. For example, the *halting problem* (i.e., the problem to decide whether a given program with a given input will halt or run forever) is $\mathcal{NP}$-hard but not $\mathcal{NP}$-complete. On one hand, one can show that there exists an $\mathcal{NP}$-complete problem (e.g., the satisfiability problem) that polytime reduces to the halting problem. On the other hand, one can show that the halting problem is not in $\mathcal{NP}$ (because all problems in $\mathcal{NP}$ must be decidable but the halting problem is not).

6.6.3 Complexity Class $\mathcal{PP}$ and Its Subclasses

As suggested in Definition 6.12, the complexity class $\mathcal{PP}$ ("probabilistic polynomial-time") comprises all decision problems that can be solved by probabilistic polynomial-time Turing machines.

Definition 6.12 (Complexity class $\mathcal{PP}$) *The complexity class $\mathcal{PP}$ refers to the class of decision problems $D \subseteq \{0,1\}^*$ that are solvable in polynomial time by a probabilistic Turing machine.*

Probabilistic Turing machines implement probabilistic algorithms, and there are basically three classes of such algorithms:

- A *Las Vegas algorithm* runs in expected polynomial time (related to the size of its input) and outputs a result that is always correct. The fact that it runs in expected polynomial time means that it may not provide a result at all.

- A *Monte Carlo algorithm* always runs in polynomial time but has only some probability of providing a correct result. In the case of a decision problem, a Monte Carlo algorithm is *yes-biased* if a yes answer is only correct with some probability, whereas a no answer is always correct. Contrary to that, a Monte Carlo algorithm is *no-biased* if a no answer is only correct with some probability, whereas a yes answer is always correct.

- Similar to a Monte Carlo algorithm, an *Atlantic City algorithm* always runs in polynomial time and has only some probability of providing correct results. Contrary to a Monte Carlo algorithm, however, an Atlantic City algorithm may err on either side, meaning that both possible answers (i.e., yes and no) are only correct with some probability.

In Section 6.5, we argued that the recognition of a problem instance by a probabilistic Turing machine is not a deterministic function of the problem instance but is associated with a random variable, and that this random variable typically assigns error probabilities to the event of recognizing the instance. Consequently, one has to consider the possibility that a probabilistic polynomial-time Turing machine may introduce errors and that the machine may recognize a problem instance only with certain error probabilities.

Let M be a probabilistic polynomial-time Turing machine, $D \subseteq \{0,1\}^*$ a decision problem, and $x \in \{0,1\}^*$ an input for M. The following two probability bounds are relevant for M:

$$\Pr[M \text{ outputs Yes } | \ x \in D] \ \geq \ \epsilon \in (\frac{1}{2}, 1]$$

$$\Pr[M \text{ outputs Yes } | \ x \notin D] \ \geq \ \delta \in [0, \frac{1}{2})$$

The first probability bound is for a correct answer and is sometimes called *completeness probability bound*. The need for bounding this probability from below is to limit the possibility to mistakenly output a no answer:

$$\Pr[M \text{ outputs No } | \ x \in D] \ < \ 1 - \epsilon$$

The second probability bound limits the probability that M mistakenly outputs yes. It is called the *soundness probability bound*, and the need for bounding it from above is quite obvious.

Note that we have expressed the probability bounds for M with two constants ϵ and δ taken from large intervals. This imprecision, however, does not cause any problem (if necessary, we can always run M multiple times to narrow down the intervals).

The complexity class $\mathcal{PP}$ has several subclasses which are defined by different (completeness and soundness) probability bounds, using different values for ϵ and δ, respectively.

6.6.3.1   Zero-Sided Errors

If we assume that a probabilistic polynomial-time Turing machine M does not make any error on either side, then we can formally introduce the complexity class $\mathcal{ZPP}$ as suggested in Definition 6.13.

Definition 6.13 (Complexity class $\mathcal{ZPP}$) $\mathcal{ZPP}$ *("zero-sided-error probabilistic polynomial time") is a subclass of $\mathcal{PP}$. It comprises all decision problems $D \subseteq$*

$\{0,1\}^*$ *for which there exists a probabilistic polynomial-time Turing machine M such that for every input $x \in \{0,1\}^*$*

$$\Pr[M \text{ outputs Yes} \mid x \in D] = 1$$

and

$$\Pr[M \text{ outputs Yes} \mid x \notin D] = 0.$$

This error-probability characterization means that the probabilistic polynomial-time Turing machine M does not make any error at all. This seems to imply that $\mathcal{ZPP}$ is equal to $\mathcal{P}$. Interestingly, this is not the case, and there are problems that can be solved with probabilistic Turing machines more efficiently than with deterministic Turing machines (both work in polynomial time).

In some literature, $\mathcal{ZPP}$ is defined as a subclass of decision problems which can be solved by a probabilistic polynomial-time Turing machine in an "always fast and always correct" fashion.

6.6.3.2 One-Sided Errors

There are basically two possibilities for a probabilistic polynomial-time Turing machine M to err on one side. The corresponding complexity classes $\mathcal{PP}$-Monte Carlo and $\mathcal{PP}$-Las Vegas are introduced in Definitions 6.14 and 6.15.

Definition 6.14 (Complexity class $\mathcal{PP}$-Monte Carlo) *$\mathcal{PP}$-Monte Carlo is a subclass of $\mathcal{PP}$ that comprises all decision problems $D \subseteq \{0,1\}^*$ for which a probabilistic polynomial-time Turing machine M exists such that for every input $x \in \{0,1\}^*$*

$$\Pr[M \text{ outputs Yes} \mid x \in D] = 1$$

and

$$\Pr[M \text{ outputs Yes} \mid x \notin D] \le \delta$$

with $\delta \in (0, \frac{1}{2})$.[10]

---

10 Note that in this case δ must be different from 0. Otherwise, the subclass $\mathcal{PP}$-Monte Carlo degenerates to the special case $\mathcal{ZPP}$.

Probabilistic polynomial-time Turing machines with this error-probability characterization have a one-sided error in the soundness side.

Definition 6.15 (Complexity class $\mathcal{PP}$-Las Vegas) $\mathcal{PP}$-*Las Vegas is a subclass of* $\mathcal{PP}$ *that comprises all decision problems* $D \subseteq \{0,1\}^*$ *for which a probabilistic polynomial-time Turing machine* M *exists such that for every input* $x \in \{0,1\}^*$

$$\Pr[M \text{ outputs Yes} \mid x \in D] \geq \epsilon$$

and

$$\Pr[M \text{ outputs Yes} \mid x \notin D] = 0$$

with $\epsilon \in \left(\frac{1}{2}, 1\right)$ *(or* $\epsilon \in (0,1)$*, respectively).*

Probabilistic polynomial-time Turing machines with this error-probability characterization have a one-sided error in the completeness side. In either case, the complexity classes $\mathcal{PP}$-Monte Carlo and $\mathcal{PP}$-Las Vegas are complementary in the sense that $\mathcal{ZPP} = \mathcal{PP}$-Monte Carlo $\cap$ $\mathcal{PP}$-Las Vegas.

6.6.3.3   Two-Sided Errors

If we assume that a probabilistic polynomial-time Turing machine M may err on either side, then we can formally introduce the complexity class $\mathcal{BPP}$ as suggested in Definition 6.16.

Definition 6.16 (Complexity class $\mathcal{BPP}$) $\mathcal{BPP}$ *("bounded-error probabilistic polynomial time") is a subclass of* $\mathcal{PP}$ *that comprises all decision problems* $D \subseteq \{0,1\}^*$ *for which a probabilistic polynomial-time Turing machine* M *exists such that for every input* $x \in \{0,1\}^*$

$$\Pr[M \text{ outputs Yes} \mid x \in D] \geq \epsilon$$

and

$$\Pr[M \text{ outputs Yes} \mid x \notin D] \leq \delta$$

with $\epsilon \in \left(\frac{1}{2}, 1\right)$ *and* $\delta \in \left(0, \frac{1}{2}\right)$.

Note that we must require that $\epsilon \neq 1$ and $\delta \neq 0$. Otherwise, the subclass $\mathcal{BPP}$ degenerates to $\mathcal{ZPP}$, $\mathcal{PP}$-Monte Carlo, or $\mathcal{PP}$-Las Vegas. The complexity class $\mathcal{P}$ and the various subclasses of $\mathcal{PP}$ can be ordered as follows:

$$\mathcal{P} \subseteq \mathcal{ZPP} \subseteq \begin{array}{c} \mathcal{PP} - \text{Monte Carlo} \\ \mathcal{PP} - \text{Las Vegas} \end{array} \subseteq \mathcal{BPP} \subseteq \mathcal{PP}$$

The challenging question is whether the inclusions are strict or not. In either case, algorithms that can solve problems in any of these complexity classes (not only $\mathcal{P}$) are called *efficient*, and the problems themselves are called *tractable*. Problems that are not tractable in this sense are called *intractable*. But keep in mind that polynomials can have vastly different degrees, and hence algorithms that solve tractable problems can still have vastly different time complexities. Therefore, an efficient algorithm for solving a tractable problem need not be efficient for all practical purposes. Against this background, people sometimes use the term *practically efficient* to refer to polynomial-time algorithms where the polynomials have considerably small degrees.

6.7 FINAL REMARKS

In this chapter, we overviewed and discussed the fundamentals and results from complexity theory as far as they are relevant for contemporary cryptography. It should have become clear that complexity theory provides a useful mathematical theory and tool to argue about the (computational) security of a cryptographic system. In fact, complexity theory is one of the foundations (and probably the most important foundation) for modern cryptography. The notion of an efficient (polynomial-time) computation is at the core of complexity-theoretic considerations. In fact, the complexity classes $\mathcal{P}$, $\mathcal{PP}$, and the subclasses of $\mathcal{PP}$ yield tractable problems (i.e., problems for which efficient deterministic or probabilistic algorithms are known). Contrary to that, the complexity classes $\mathcal{NP}$ and co$\mathcal{NP}$ comprise intractable problems (i.e., problems for which efficient algorithms are not known).[11] Against this background, the $\mathcal{P} \neq \mathcal{NP}$ conjecture plays a fundamental role in complexity-theoretic cryptography.

In spite of its usefulness, there are also a couple of shortcomings and limitations related to complexity theory that must be known and should be considered

---

11 Note that it is not known whether such algorithms are only not known or whether they do not exist in the first place.

with care (e.g., [12]). For example, it is impossible to elaborate on the computational complexity of a specific function (or algorithm that implements the function). Instead, one always has to consider an infinite class of functions (or algorithms). This is unfortunate and sometimes inappropriate, because many concrete cryptographic systems employ functions that are fixed and for which an asymptotic extension is not at all obvious. Furthermore, as mentioned earlier, the distinction between efficient (i.e., polynomial-time) algorithms and inefficient (i.e., super-polynomial-time) algorithms is vague. It sometimes leads to a situation in which a theoretically efficient algorithm is practically so inefficient that it is infeasible to execute it on any reasonably sized input. To make things worse, complexity theory deals with worst-case complexity. This concept is questionable in cryptography, where breaking a system must be hard for almost all problem instances, not just some of them. There are some results addressing the average-case complexity of problems (e.g., [13]). Note, however, that in cryptography even average-case complexity results are not good enough, because problems must be hard for almost all instances. Furthermore, instead of proving the hardness of finding an exact solution for a computational problem, one may want to reason that even approximating the exact solution is intractable (again, complexity theory is inappropriate for this kind of reasoning). As already mentioned at the beginning of Section 6.2, an inherent difficulty of complexity theory is related to the fact that the state of the art in lower bound proofs for the computational complexity of a problem is poor. From a cryptographic viewpoint, it would be nice to have (and prove) some nontrivial lower bounds (be they polynomial or super-polynomial) for the complexity of breaking a concrete cryptographic system. Unfortunately, we are far away from that. Finally, we noted that all computational models in use today are equivalent from a complexity-theoretic viewpoint. The discussion about the right model of computation, however, was reopened when Shor showed that certain problems can be solved in polynomial time on a quantum computer and Adleman showed that the same may be true for a DNA computer (see Section 6.5). A lot of research is currently being done (and large amounts of money are being spent) in quantum and DNA computing; hence, it will be interesting to see how these topics advance in the future.

References

[1] Garey, M.R., and D.S. Johnson, *Computers and Intractability: A Guide to the Theory of NP-Completeness.* W. H. Freeman & Co., New York, 1979.

[2] Papadimitriou, C.H., *Computational Complexity.* Addison-Wesley, Reading, MA, 1993.

[3] Hopcroft, J.E., R. Motwani, and J.D. Ullman, *Introduction to Automata Theory, Languages, and Computation,* 2nd edition. Addison-Wesley, Reading, MA, 2001.

[4] Menezes, A., P. van Oorschot, and S. Vanstone, *Handbook of Applied Cryptography.* CRC Press, Boca Raton, FL, 1996.

[5] Shor, P.W., "Algorithms for Quantum Computation: Discrete Logarithms and Factoring," *Proceedings of the IEEE 35th Annual Symposium on Foundations of Computer Science (FOCS)*, Santa Fe, NM, November 1994, pp. 124–134.

[6] Shor, P.W., "Polynomial-Time Algorithms for Prime Factorization and Discrete Logarithms on a Quantum Computer," *SIAM Journal of Computing*, October 1997, pp. 1484–1509.

[7] Vandersypen, L.M.K., et al., "Experimental Realization of Shor's Quantum Factoring Algorithm Using Nuclear Magnetic Resonance," *Nature*, Vol. 414, 2001, pp. 883–887.

[8] Nielsen, M., and I.L. Chuang, *Quantum Computation and Quantum Information.* Cambridge University Press, Cambridge, UK, 2000.

[9] Adleman, L.M., "Molecular Computation of Solutions to Combinatorial Problems," *Science*, Vol. 266, November 1994, pp. 1021–1024.

[10] Lipton, R.J., "DNA Solution of Hard Computational Problems," *Science*, Vol. 268, April 1995, pp. 542–545.

[11] Păun, G., G. Rozenberg, and A. Salomaa, *DNA Computing: New Computing Paradigms.* Springer-Verlag, New York, 1998.

[12] Maurer, U.M., *Cryptography 2000 ±10*, Springer-Verlag, New York, LNCS 2000, 2000, pp. 63–85.

[13] Ajtai, M., "Generating Hard Instances of Lattice Problems," *Proceedings of 28th ACM Symposium of the Theory of Computing (STOC)*, Philadelphia, PA, May 1996, pp. 99–108.

Part II

UNKEYED CRYPTOSYSTEMS

Chapter 7

One-Way Functions

As mentioned several times so far, one-way functions and trapdoor functions play a fundamental role in modern cryptography. In this chapter, we elaborate on these functions. More specifically, we introduce the topic in Section 7.1, overview and discuss some candidate one-way functions in Section 7.2, elaborate on integer factorization algorithms and algorithms to compute discrete logarithms in Sections 7.3 and 7.4, address hard-core predicates in Section 7.5, briefly introduce the notion of elliptic curve cryptography in Section 7.6, and conclude with final remarks in Section 7.7.

7.1 INTRODUCTION

In Section 2.1.1 and Definition 2.1, we introduced the notion of a one-way function. More specifically, we said that a function $f : X \rightarrow Y$ is one way if $f(x)$ can be computed efficiently for all $x \in X$, but $f^{-1}(y)$ cannot be computed efficiently for $y \in_R Y$ (see Figure 2.1). We also noted that this definition is not precise in a mathematically strong sense and that we must first introduce some complexity-theoretic basics (mainly to define more precisely what we mean by saying that we can or we cannot compute efficiently). Because we have done this in Chapter 6, we are now ready to better understand and more precisely define the notion of a one-way function. This is done in Definition 7.1.

Definition 7.1 (One-way function) *A function* $f : X \rightarrow Y$ *is* one way *if the following two conditions are fulfilled:*

- *The function f is easy to compute, meaning that $f(x)$ can be computed efficiently for all $x \in X$. Alternatively speaking, there is a probabilistic polynomial-time (PPT) algorithm A that outputs $A(x) = f(x)$ for all $x \in X$.*

- *The function f is hard to invert, meaning that it is not known how to efficiently compute $f^{-1}(f(x))$ for all $x \in X$ or $f^{-1}(y)$ for $y \in_R Y$. Alternatively speaking, there is no known PPT algorithm A that outputs $A(f(x)) = f^{-1}(f(x))$ for all $x \in X$ or $A(y) = f^{-1}(y)$ for $y \in_R Y$.*

X and Y are often set to $\{0, 1\}^*$. In either case, A is not required to find the correct x; it is only required to find some inverse of y (if the function f is injective, then the only inverse of y is x).

Another way to express the second condition in Definition 7.1 is to say that any PPT algorithm A attempting to invert the one-way function on an element in its range will succeed with no more than a negligible probability (i.e., smaller than any polynomial in the size of the input, where the probability is taken over the elements in the domain of the function and the internal coin tosses of A). The statement is probabilistic (i.e., A is not unable to invert the function, but it has a very low success probability). More formally,

$$\Pr[A(f(x), 1^n) \in f^{-1}(f(x))] \leq \frac{1}{p(n)}$$

for every PPT algorithm A, all $x \in X$, every polynomial p, and all sufficiently large n (with n representing the binary length of x). In this notation, the algorithm A is given $f(x)$ and the security parameter 1^n (expressed in unary representation). The only purpose of the second argument is to allow A to run in time polynomial in the length of x, even if $f(x)$ is much shorter than x. This rules out the possibility that a function is considered one way only because the inverting algorithm does not have enough time to print the output. Typically, f is a length-preserving function, and in this case the auxiliary argument 1^n is redundant.

Note that the notation given earlier is not standard, and that there are many notations used in the literature to express the same idea. For example, the following notion is also frequently used in the literature.

$$\Pr[(f(z) = y : x \stackrel{u}{\leftarrow} \{0, 1\}^n; y \leftarrow f(x); z \leftarrow A(y, 1^n)] \leq \frac{1}{p(n)}$$

It basically says the same thing: if x is selected uniformly from $\{0, 1\}^n$, y is assigned $f(x)$, and z is assigned $A(y, 1^n)$, then the probability that $f(z)$ equals y is negligible.

A few words concerning the notion of negligible probability are in place. We consider the success probability of a PPT algorithm A to be negligible if it is bound by a polynomial fraction. It follows that repeating A polynomially (in the input length) many times yields a new algorithm that also has a success probability that is negligible. Put in other words, events that occur with negligible probability remain negligible even if the experiment is repeated polynomially many times. This property is important for complexity-theoretic considerations.

In some literature, a distinction is made between strong one-way functions (as discussed earlier) and weak one-way functions, and it is then shown that the former can be constructed from the latter. The major difference is that whereas one only requires some nonnegligible fractions of the inputs on which it is hard to invert a weak one-way function, a strong one-way function must be hard to invert on all but a negligible fraction of the inputs. For the purpose of this book, we don't delve into the details of this distinction, and hence we don't distinguish between strong and weak one-way functions accordingly.

If X and Y are the same, then a one-way function $f : X \rightarrow X$ represents a *one-way permutation*. Hence, one-way permutations are just special cases of one-way functions, namely ones in which the domain and the range are the same.

Having in mind the notion of a one-way function, the notion of a *trapdoor function* (or *trapdoor one-way function*) is simple to explain and understand. According to Definition 2.2, a one-way function $f : X \rightarrow Y$ is a *trapdoor function* if there exist some extra information—called the *trapdoor*—with which f can be inverted efficiently—that is, there is a (deterministic or probabilistic) polynomial-time algorithm A that outputs $A(f(x)) = f^{-1}(f(x))$ for all $x \in X$ or $A(y) = f^{-1}(y)$ for $y \in_R Y$. Consequently, the notion of a trapdoor function can be defined by prepending the words "unless some extra information (i.e., the trapdoor) is known" in the second condition of Definition 7.1. More formally, a trapdoor function can be defined as suggested in Definition 7.2.

Definition 7.2 (Trapdoor function) *A one-way function $f : X \rightarrow Y$ is a* trapdoor *function if there is a trapdoor information t and a PPT algorithm I that can be used to efficiently compute $x' = I(f(x), t)$ with $f(x') = f(x)$.*

Many cryptographic functions required to be one way (or preimage resistant) output bitstrings of fixed size. For example, cryptographic hash functions are required to be one way and output strings of 128, 160, or more bits (see Chapter 8). Given such a function, one may be tempted to ask how expensive it is to invert it (i.e., one may ask for the computational complexity of inverting the hash function). Unfortunately, the (complexity-theoretic) answer to this question is not particularly useful. If the cryptographic hash function outputs n-bit values, then 2^n tries are always sufficient to invert the function or to find a preimage for a given hash value (2^{n-1} tries are sufficient on the average). Because 2^n is constant for any fixed $n \in \mathbb{N}$, the computational complexity to invert the hash function is $O(1)$, and hence one cannot say that inverting it is intractable. If we want to use complexity-theoretic arguments, then we cannot live with a constant n. Instead, we must make n variable, and it must be possible to let n grow arbitrarily large. Consquently, we must work with potentially infinite *families*[1] *of one-way functions* (i.e., at least one for each n). The notion of a family of one-way functions is formally captured in Definition 7.3.

Definition 7.3 (Family of one-way function) *A family of functions* $F = \{f_i : X_i \rightarrow Y_i\}_{i \in I}$ *is a family of one-way functions if the following three conditions are fulfilled:*

- *I is an infinite index set;*

- *Every $i \in I$ selects a function $f_i : X_i \rightarrow Y_i$ from the family;*

- *Every $f_i : X_i \rightarrow Y_i$ is a one-way function according to Definition 7.1.*

A family of one-way functions $\{f_i : X_i \rightarrow Y_i\}_{i \in I}$ is a *family of one-way permutations* if every f_i is a permutation over the domain X_i (i.e., $Y_i = X_i$). Furthermore, it is a *family of trapdoor functions* if every f_i is a trapdoor function with trapdoor information t_i.

In this book, we often talk about one-way functions and trapdoor functions when we should actually be talking about families of such functions. We make this simplification because we think that it is more appropriate and simpler to understand. In either case, we want to emphasize that there is no function—or family of functions—known to be one way (in a mathematically strong sense) and that the current state of knowledge in complexity theory does not allow us to prove the existence of one-way functions, even using more traditional assumptions as $\mathcal{P} \neq \mathcal{NP}$. Hence, only a few functions are conjectured to be one way. These candidate one-way functions are overviewed and discussed next.

7.2 CANDIDATE ONE-WAY FUNCTIONS

There are a couple of functions that are conjectured to be one way. For example, a symmetric encryption system that encrypts a fixed plaintext message yields such a function.[2] For example, the use of DES in this construction can be shown to be one way assuming that DES is a family of pseudorandom functions. Another simple example is the integer multiplication function $f : (x, y) \mapsto xy$ for $x, y \in \mathbb{Z}$. As discussed later in this chapter, no efficient algorithm is known to find the prime factors of a large integer.

---

1   In some literature, the terms "classes," "collections," or "ensembles" are used instead of "families."
2   For example, UNIX systems use such a function to store the user passwords in protected form.

The following three functions, which are conjectured to be one way, have many applications in (public key) cryptography:

- Discrete exponentiation function;

- RSA function;

- Modular square function.

The fact that these functions are conjectured to be one way means that we don't know how to efficiently invert them. The best algorithms we have at hand are super-polynomial—that is, they have an exponential or subexponential running time behavior (some of the algorithms are briefly overviewed in Sections 7.3 and 7.4). The three candidate one-way functions are addressed next.

7.2.1 Discrete Exponentiation Function

From the real numbers, we know that the exponentiation and logarithm functions are inverse to each other and that they can both be computed efficiently. This makes us believe that this must be the case in all algebraic structures. There are, however, algebraic structures in which we can compute the exponentiation function efficiently, but in which no known algorithm can be used to efficiently compute the logarithm function. For example, let p be a prime number and g be a generator (or primitive root) of $\mathbb{Z}_p^*$. The function

$$\mathrm{Exp}_{p,g} : \mathbb{Z}_{p-1} \longrightarrow \mathbb{Z}_p^*$$
$$x \longmapsto g^x$$

is then called *discrete exponentiation function* to the base g. It defines an isomorphism from the additive group $\langle \mathbb{Z}_{p-1}, + \rangle$ to the multiplicative group $\langle \mathbb{Z}_p^*, \cdot \rangle$—that is, $\mathrm{Exp}_{p,g}(x + y) = \mathrm{Exp}_{p,g}(x) \cdot \mathrm{Exp}_{p,g}(y)$. Because $\mathrm{Exp}_{p,g}$ is bijective, it has an inverse function that is defined as follows:

$$\mathrm{Log}_{p,g} : \mathbb{Z}_p^* \longrightarrow \mathbb{Z}_{p-1}$$
$$x \longmapsto \log_g x$$

It is called the *discrete logarithm function*. For any $x \in \mathbb{Z}_p^*$, the discrete logarithm function computes the *discrete logarithm* of x to the base g, denoted by

$\log_g x$. This value refers to the element of $\mathbb{Z}_{p-1}$ to which g must be set to the power of in order to get x.

$\text{Exp}_{p,g}$ is efficiently computable, for example, by using the square-and-multiply algorithm (i.e., Algorithm 3.3). Contrary to that (and contrary to the logarithm function in the real numbers), no efficient algorithm is known to exist for computing discrete logarithms for sufficiently large prime numbers p. All known algorithms have a super-polynomial running time, and it is widely believed that $\text{Log}_{p,g}$ is not efficiently computable.

Earlier in this chapter we said that—in order to use complexity-theoretic arguments—we must consider families of one-way functions. In the case of the discrete exponentiation function, we may use p and g as indexes for an index set I. In fact, I can be defined as follows:

$$I := \{(p,g) \mid p \in \mathbf{P}; \ g \text{ a generator of } \mathbb{Z}_p^*\}$$

Using this index set, we can formally define the Exp family (i.e., the family of discrete exponentiation functions)

$$\text{Exp} := \{\text{Exp}_{p,g} : \mathbb{Z}_{p-1} \longrightarrow \mathbb{Z}_p^*, \ x \longmapsto g^x\}_{(p,g) \in I}$$

and the Log family (i.e., the family of discrete logarithm functions)

$$\text{Log} := \{\text{Log}_{p,g} : \mathbb{Z}_p^* \longrightarrow \mathbb{Z}_{p-1}, \ x \longmapsto \log_g x\}_{(p,g) \in I}.$$

If we want to employ the Exp family as a family of one-way functions, then we must make sure that it is hard to invert, meaning that it is not known how to efficiently compute discrete logarithms. This is where the *discrete logarithm assumption* (DLA) as formally expressed in Definition 7.4 comes into play.

Definition 7.4 (Discrete logarithm assumption) *Let* $I_k := \{(p,g) \in I \mid |p| = k\}$ *for* $k \in \mathbb{N}$,[3] *$p(k)$ be a positive polynomial, and $A(p,g,y)$ be a PPT algorithm. Then the DLA says that there exists a $k_0 \in \mathbb{N}$, such that*

---

3   This means that the index set I consists of disjoint subsets I_k (i.e., $I = \bigcup_{k \in \mathbb{N}} I_k$). Consequently, k may be considered the security parameter of $i = (p,g) \in I_k$.

$$\Pr[A(p,g,y) = \mathrm{Log}_{p,g}(y) : (p,g) \overset{u}{\leftarrow} I_k; y \overset{u}{\leftarrow} \mathbb{Z}_p^*] \leq \frac{1}{p(k)}$$

for all $k \geq k_0$.

In this terminology, the PPT algorithm A models an adversary who tries to compute the discrete logarithm of y to the base g, or, equivalently, to invert the discrete exponentiation function $\mathrm{Exp}_{p,g}$. Furthermore, the term

$$y \overset{u}{\leftarrow} \mathbb{Z}_p^*$$

suggests that y is uniformly distributed, meaning that all $y \in \mathbb{Z}_p^*$ occur with the same probability (i.e., $\Pr[y] = 1/|\mathbb{Z}_p^*| = 1/(p-1)$). This is just another way of saying that $y \in_R \mathbb{Z}_p^*$. Similarly, the term

$$(p,g) \overset{u}{\leftarrow} I_k$$

suggests that the pair (p,g) is uniformly distributed, meaning that all $(p,g) \in I_k$ occur with the same probability. Consequently, the probability statement of Definition 7.4 can be read as follows: if we randomly select both the index $i = (p,g) \in I_k$ with security parameter k and $y = g^x$, then the probability that the PPT algorithm A successfully computes and outputs $\mathrm{Log}_{p,g}(y)$ is negligible (i.e., smaller than any polynomial bound). This means that $\mathrm{Exp}_{p,g}$ cannot be inverted by A for all but a negligible fraction of input values.

Even if the security parameter k is very large, there may be pairs (p,g) such that A can correctly compute $\mathrm{Log}_{p,g}(y)$ with a probability that is nonnegligible. For example, if $p - 1$ has only small prime factors, then there is an efficient algorithm due to Steve Pohlig and Martin E. Hellman that can be used to compute the discrete logarithm function [1]. In either case, the number of such special pairs (p,g) is negligibly small as compared to all keys with security parameter k. If (p,g) is randomly (and uniformly) chosen from I_k, then the probability of obtaining such a pair (i.e., a pair for which A can compute discrete logarithms) is negligibly small.

Under the DLA, the Exp family represents a family of one-way functions. It is used in many public key cryptosystems, including, for example, the ElGamal public key cryptosystem (see Sections 14.2.3 and 15.2.2) and the Diffie-Hellman key exchange protocol (see Section 16.3). Furthermore, several problems are centered around the DLA and the conjectured one-way property of the discrete exponential function. The most important problems are the *discrete logarithm problem* (DLP) captured in Definition 7.5, the (computational) *Diffie-Hellman problem* (DHP) captured in Definition 7.6, and the *Diffie-Hellman decision problem* (DHDP) captured in Definition 7.7. The problems can be specified in arbitrary cyclic groups.

Definition 7.5 (Discrete logarithm problem) *Let G be a cyclic group, g be a generator of G, and h be an arbitrary element in G. The DLP is to determine an integer x such that $g^x = h$.*

Definition 7.6 (Diffie-Hellman problem) *Let G be a cyclic group, g be a generator in G, and x and y be two integers smaller than the order of G (i.e., $x, y < |G|$). The terms g^x and g^y then represent two elements in G. The DHP is to determine g^{xy} from g^x and g^y.*

Definition 7.7 (Diffie-Hellman decision problem) *Let G be a cyclic group, g be a generator of G, and r, s, and t be three positive integers smaller than the order of G (i.e., $r, s, t < |G|$). The terms g^r, g^s, g^t, and g^{rs} then represent elements in G. The DHP is to determine whether g^{rs} or g^t solves the DHP for g^r and g^s. Alternatively speaking, the DHDP is to distinguish the triples $\langle g^r, g^s, g^{rs} \rangle$ and $\langle g^r, g^s, g^t \rangle$ when they are given in random order.*

When giving all of these problems, it may be interesting to know how they are related. This is done by giving complexity-theoretic reductions from one problem to another (see Definition 6.10 for the notion of a polynomial-time reduction). In fact, in can be shown that DHP $\leq_P$ DLP (i.e., the DHP polytime reduces to the DLP) and that DDHP $\leq_P$ DHP (i.e., the DDHP polytime reduces to the DHP) in an arbitrary finite Abelian group. So the DLP is the hardest among the problems (i.e., if one is able to solve the DLP, then one is trivially able to solve the DHP and the DDHP). The exact relationship and the complexity of the corresponding proof (if it is known in the first place) depend on the actual group in use. In many cyclic groups, the DLP and the DHP have been shown to be computationally equivalent [2, 3]. There are, however, groups in which one can solve the DDHP in polynomial time, but the fastest known algorithm to solve the DHP requires subexponential time. In order to better understand the DLP and the underlying DLA, it is worthwhile to have a look at the currently available algorithms to compute discrete logarithms. This is done in Section 7.4.

7.2.2 RSA Function

Let n be the product of two distinct primes p and q (i.e., $n = pq$), and e be relatively prime to $\phi(n)$. Then the function

$$\text{RSA}_{n,e} : \mathbb{Z}_n^* \longrightarrow \mathbb{Z}_n^*$$
$$x \longmapsto x^e$$

is called the *RSA function*. It computes the eth power for $x \in \mathbb{Z}_n^*$. To compute the inverse function, it is required to compute e^{th} roots. If the inverse d of e modulo $\phi(n)$ is known, then the following RSA function can be used to compute the inverse of $\text{RSA}_{n,e}$:

$$\text{RSA}_{n,d} : \mathbb{Z}_n^* \longrightarrow \mathbb{Z}_n^*$$
$$x \longmapsto x^d$$

$\text{RSA}_{n,e}$ can be efficiently computed by modular exponentiation. In order to compute $\text{RSA}_{n,d}$, however, one must know either d or the prime factors of n (i.e., p and q). As of this writing, no polynomial-time algorithm to compute $\text{RSA}_{n,d}$ is known if p, q, or d are not known. Hence, $\text{RSA}_{n,d}$ can only be computed if any of these values is known, and hence these values represent trapdoors for $\text{RSA}_{n,e}$.

If we want to turn the RSA function into a family of one-way functions, then we must define an index set I. This can be done as follows:

$$I := \{(n, e) \mid n = pq; p, q \in \mathbf{P}; p \neq q; 0 < e < \phi(n); (e, \phi(n)) = 1\}$$

Using this index set, the family of RSA functions can be defined as follows:

$$\text{RSA} := \{\text{RSA}_{n,e} : \mathbb{Z}_n^* \longrightarrow \mathbb{Z}_n^*, x \longmapsto x^e\}_{(n,e) \in I}$$

This family of RSA functions is called the *RSA family*. Because each RSA function $\text{RSA}_{n,e}$ represents a permutation over $\mathbb{Z}_n^*$, the RSA family represents a family of one-way (or trapdoor) permutations.

It is assumed and widely believed that the RSA family is a family of trapdoor permutations, meaning that $\text{RSA}_{n,e}$ is hard to invert (for sufficiently large and properly chosen n). The *RSA assumption* formally expressed in Definition 7.8 makes the one-way property of the RSA family explicit.

Definition 7.8 (RSA assumption) *Let* $I_k := \{(n,e) \in I \mid n = pq; |p| = |q| = k\}$
for $k \in \mathbb{N}$, $p(k) \in \mathbb{Z}[\mathbb{N}]$ *be a positive polynomial, and* $A(p,g,y)$ *be a PPT algorithm.*
Then the RSA assumption says that there exists a $k_0 \in \mathbb{N}$, *such that*

$$\Pr[A(n,e,y) = \mathrm{RSA}_{n,d}(y) : (n,e) \xleftarrow{u} I_k; y \xleftarrow{u} \mathbb{Z}_n^*] \leq \frac{1}{p(k)}$$

for all $k \geq k_0$.

Again, the PPT algorithm A models the adversary who tries to compute
$\mathrm{RSA}_{n,d}(y)$ without knowing the trapdoor information. The RSA assumption may
be interpreted in an analogous way to the DLA. The fraction of keys (n,e) in I_k, for
which A has a significant chance to succeed, must be negligibly small if the security
parameter k is sufficiently large.

There is also a stronger version of the RSA assumption known as the *strong
RSA assumption*. The strong RSA assumption differs from the RSA assumption
in that the adversary can select the public exponent e: given a modulus n and a
ciphertext c, the adversary must compute any plaintext m and public exponent e
such that $c = m^e \pmod{n}$. For the purpose of this book, we don't use the strong
RSA assumption anymore.

If we accept the RSA assumption, then the *RSA problem* (RSAP) captured in
Definition 7.9 is intractable.

Definition 7.9 (RSA problem) *Let* (n,e) *be a public key and* $c = m^e \pmod{n}$.
The RSAP is to determine m *(i.e., the* e^{th} *root of* c *modulo* n*) if the private key* (n,d)
and the factorization of n *(i.e.,* p *and* q*) are not known.*

The RSA assumption and the RSAP are at the core of many public key cryptosystems, including, for example, the RSA public key cryptosystem (see Sections
14.2.1 and 15.2.1). Because the prime factors of n (i.e., p and q) represent a(nother)
trapdoor for $\mathrm{RSA}_{n,d}$ (in addition to d), somebody who is able to factor n is also able
to compute $\mathrm{RSA}_{n,d}$ and to invert $\mathrm{RSA}_{n,e}$ accordingly. Consequently, one must make
the additional assumption that it is computationally infeasible (for the adversary one
has in mind) to factor n. This is where the *integer factoring assumption* (IFA) as
formally expressed in Definition 7.10 comes into play.

Definition 7.10 (Integer factoring assumption) *Let* $I_k := \{n \in I \mid n = pq; |p| =$
$|q| = k\}$ *for* $k \in \mathbb{N}$, $p(k)$ *be a positive polynomial, and* $A(n)$ *be a PPT algorithm.*
Then the IFA says that there exists a $k_0 \in \mathbb{N}$, *such that*

$$\Pr[A(n) = p : n \xleftarrow{u} I_k] \leq \frac{1}{p(k)}$$

for all $k \geq k_0$.

If we accept the IFA, then the *integer factoring problem* (IFP) captured in Definition 7.11 is intractable.

Definition 7.11 (Integer factoring problem) *Let n be a positive integer (i.e., $n \in \mathbb{N}$). The IFP is to determine the prime factors of n (i.e., to determine $p_1, \ldots, p_k \in \mathbf{P}$ and $e_1, \ldots, e_k \in \mathbb{N}$) such that*

$$n = p_1^{e_1} \cdots p_k^{e_k}.$$

The IFP is well defined, because every positive integer can be factored uniquely up to a permutation of its prime factors (see Theorem 3.5). Note that the IFP must not always be intractable, but that it must be possible to easily find an instance of the IFP that is intractable.

Again using complexity-theoretic arguments, one can show that RSAP $\leq_P$ IFP (i.e., the RSAP polytime reduces to the IFP). This means that one can invert the RSA function if one can solve the IFP. The converse, however, is not known to be true (i.e., it is not known whether there exists a simpler way to invert the RSA function than to solve the IFP). In order to better understand the RSAP and the underlying RSA assumption, it is worthwhile to have a look at the currently available integer factorization algorithms. This is done in Section 7.3.

7.2.3 Modular Square Function

Similar to the exponentiation function, the square function can be computed and inverted efficiently in the real numbers, but it is not known how to invert it efficiently in a cyclic group. If, for example, we consider $\mathbb{Z}_n^*$, then modular squares can be computed efficiently, but modular square roots can only be computed efficiently if the prime factorization of n is known. In fact, it can be shown that computing square roots in $\mathbb{Z}_n^*$ and factoring n are computationally equivalent. Consequently, the modular square function looks like a candidate one-way function. Unfortunately, the modular square function (in its general form) is neither injective nor surjective. It can, however, be made injective and surjective (and hence bijective) if the domain and range are both restricted to QR_n (i.e., the set of quadratic residues or squares modulo n), with n being a Blum integer (see Definition 3.33). The function

$$\text{Square}_n : QR_n \longrightarrow QR_n$$
$$x \longmapsto x^2$$

is then called *square function*. It is bijective, and hence the inverse function

$$\text{Sqrt}_n \; : \; QR_n \; \longrightarrow \; QR_n$$
$$x \; \longmapsto \; x^{1/2}$$

exists and is called the *square root function*. Either function maps an element of QR_n to another element of QR_n. The function represents a permutation.

To turn the square function into a one-way function (or one-way permutation, respectively), we must have an index set I. Taking into account that n must be a Blum integer, the index set can be defined as follows:

$$I := \{n \mid n = pq; p, q \in \mathbf{P}; p \neq q; |p| = |q|; p, q \equiv 3 \,(\text{mod}\,4)\}.$$

Using this index set, we can define the following family of square functions:

$$\text{Square} := \{\text{Square}_n \; : \; QR_n \longrightarrow QR_n, \; x \longmapsto x^2\}_{n \in I}.$$

This family is called the *Square family*, and the family of inverse functions can be defined as follows:

$$\text{Sqrt} := \{\text{Sqrt}_n \; : \; QR_n \longrightarrow QR_n, \; x \longmapsto x^{1/2}\}_{n \in I}.$$

It is called the *Sqrt family*. The Square family of trapdoor permutations is used by several public key cryptosystems, including, for example, the Rabin public key cryptosystem (see Section 14.2.2). For every $n \in I$, the prime factors p and q represent a trapdoor. Hence, if we can solve the IFP, then we can trivially invert the Square family. We look at algorithms to solve the IFP next.

7.3   INTEGER FACTORIZATION ALGORITHMS

Many algorithms can be used to solve the IFP.[4] They can be divided into two broad categories:

---

4   http://mathworld.wolfram.com/PrimeFactorizationAlgorithms.html.

- *Special-purpose algorithms* depend on and take advantage of special properties of the integer n to be factored, such as its size, the size of its smallest prime factor p, or the prime factorization of $p - 1$.

- Contrary to that, *general-purpose algorithms* depend on nothing (i.e., they work for all values of n).

In practice, algorithms of both categories are combined and used one after another. If one is given a large integer n with no clue about the size of its prime factors, then one usually employs special-purpose algorithms that are optimized to find small prime factors before one turns to the less efficient general-purpose algorithms.

7.3.1 Special-Purpose Algorithms

Examples of special-purpose algorithms include trial division, P±1, Pollard Rho, and the elliptic curve method (ECM).

7.3.1.1 Trial Division

If n is composite, then at least one prime factor is at most $\sqrt{n}$. Consequently, one can always factorize n by trying to divide it by all primes up to $\lfloor \sqrt{n} \rfloor$. This simple algorithm is called *trial division*. Its running time is $O(p)$, where p is the smallest prime factor of n (i.e., the one that is found first). In the worst case, this equals to

$$O(\sqrt{n}) = O(e^{\ln \sqrt{n}}) = O(e^{\ln(n^{1/2})})$$

if the smallest prime factor of n is about $\sqrt{n}$ (this occurs if n has two prime factors of about the same size). Consequently, the worst-case running time function of the trial division integer factorization algorithm is exponential in $\ln n$. If, for example, n is 1,024 bits long, then the algorithm requires

$$\sqrt{2^{1024}} = (2^{1024})^{1/2} = 2^{1024/2} = 2^{512}$$

trial divisions in the worst case. This is certainly beyond what is feasible today, and hence the trial division algorithm can only be used to factorize n if n is sufficiently small (e.g., smaller than 10^{12}) or smooth (i.e., it has only small prime factors). In either case, the space requirements of the trial division algorithm are negligible.

7.3.1.2   P±1

In the 1970s, John M. Pollard developed and proposed two special-purpose integer factorization algorithms that are optimized to find small prime factors. The first algorithm is known as P−1.

Let n be the integer to be factorized and p be some (yet unknown) prime factor of n, for which $p - 1$ is B-smooth—that is, $p - 1$ is the product of possibly many prime numbers that are smaller than or equal to B (see Definition 3.28). If k is the product of all prime numbers that are smaller than or equal to B, then k is a multiple of $p - 1$. Now consider what happens if we take a small integer (e.g. $a = 2$) and set it to the power of k. Fermat's Little Theorem (i.e., Theorem 3.7) tells us that

$$a^k \equiv 1 \ (\mathrm{mod} \ p),$$

and hence p divides $a^k - 1$. On the other hand, p must also divide n (remember that p is supposed to be a prime factor of n), and hence p divides the greatest common divisor of $a^k - 1$ and n (i.e., $p \mid gcd(a^k - 1, n)$). Note that k might be very large, but $a^k - 1$ can always be reduced modulo n.

Note that one knows neither the prime factorization of $p - 1$ nor the bound before one starts the algorithm. So one has to begin with an initially chosen bound B and perhaps increase it during the execution of the algorithm. Consequently, the algorithm is practical only if B is not too large. For the typical size of prime numbers in use today (e.g., for the RSA public key cryptosystem), the probability that one can factorize n using Pollard's P−1 algorithm is pretty small. Nevertheless, the mere existence of the algorithm is a reason that some cryptographic standards require RSA moduli to have prime factors p for which $p - 1$ has at least one large prime factor. In the literature, such primes are frequently called *strong*.

In either case, the running time of Pollard's P−1 algorithm is $O(|t|)$, where t is the largest prime power dividing $p-1$. Pollard's P−1 algorithm was later modified and a corresponding P+1 algorithm was proposed.

7.3.1.3   Pollard Rho

The second algorithm developed and proposed by Pollard in the 1970s is known as *Pollard Rho*. The basic idea is to have the algorithm successively draw random numbers less than n. If p is a (yet unknown) prime factor of n, then it follows from the birthday paradox (see Section 8.1) that after about $p^{1/2} = \sqrt{p}$ rounds one has drawn x_i and x_j with $x_i \neq x_j$ and $x_i \equiv x_j \ (\mathrm{mod} \ p)$. If this occurs, one knows that p divides the greatest common divisor of $x_i - x_j$ and n (i.e., $p \mid gcd(x_i - x_j, n)$).

The Pollard Rho algorithm has a running time of

$$O(\sqrt{p})$$

where p is the smallest prime factor of n, or

$$O(\sqrt[4]{n}) = O(n^{1/4}) = O(e^{\ln(n^{1/4})})$$

in the worst case. Consequently, the Pollard Rho algorithm is an algorithm that is exponential in $\ln n$, and as such it can only be used if p is small compared to n. For the size of the integers that are used today, the algorithm is still impractical. It was, however, used on the factorization of the eighth Fermat number

$$F_8 = 2^{2^8} + 1 = 2^{256} + 1,$$

which unexpectedly turned out to have a small prime factor. In either case, the space requirements of the Pollard Rho algorithm are small.

7.3.1.4 ECM

In the 1980s, Hendrik W. Lenstra developed and proposed the ECM [4]. It can be best thought of as a generalization or randomized version of Pollard's P−1 algorithm. The success of Pollard's P−1 algorithm depends on n having a divisor p such that $p − 1$ is smooth. If no such p exists, then the algorithm fails. The ECM randomizes the choice, replacing the group $\mathbb{Z}_p$ used in Pollard's P−1 algorithm by a random (or pseudorandom) elliptic curve over $GF(p)$.

The ECM has a subexponential running time. Its average-case (worst-case) running time is $L_p[\frac{1}{2}, \sqrt{2}]$ ($L_n[\frac{1}{2}, 1]$). The worst case occurs when p is roughly $\sqrt{n}$, which is often the case when one uses RSA or some other public key cryptosystem. So, although the ECM cannot be considered a threat against the standard RSA public key cryptosystem that uses two primes, it must nevertheless be taken into account when one implements the so-called multiprime RSA system, where the modulus may have more than two prime factors.

7.3.2 General-Purpose Algorithms

Examples of general-purpose integer factorization include continued fraction, the quadratic sieve (QS), and the number field sieve (NFS).

7.3.2.1   Continued Fraction

The continued fraction algorithm was developed and proposed in the 1970s [5]. It has a subexponential running time and was the the fastest integer factoring algorithm in use for quite a long time (i.e., until the QS was developed).

7.3.2.2   QS

In the 1980s, Carl Pomerance developed and proposed the QS [6]. Like many other general-purpose integer factorization algorithms, the QS is based on an idea that is due to Fermat. If we have two integers x and y with

$$x \neq \pm y \; (\text{mod } n)$$

and

$$x^2 \equiv y^2 \; (\text{mod } n), \tag{7.1}$$

then we can factorize n with a success probability of $1/2$. Let $n = pq$, and we want to use x and y to find p or q. First, we note that $x^2 \equiv y^2 \; (\text{mod } n)$ means that

$$x^2 - y^2 = (x - y)(x + y) = 0 \; (\text{mod } n).$$

Because $n = pq$, the four following cases are possible:

1. $p|x - y$ and $q|x + y$;
2. $p|x + y$ and $q|x - y$;
3. $p|x - y$ and $q|x - y$ (but neither p nor q divides $x + y$);
4. $p|x + y$ and $q|x + y$ (but neither p nor q divides $x - y$).

All of these cases are equally probable and occur with a probability of $1/4$. If we then compute

$$d = gcd(x - y, n),$$

then d refers to p in case 1, q in case 2, n in case 3, and 1 in case 4. Hence, in cases 1 and 2 we have indeed found a prime factor of n. So the success probability is in fact $1/2$ (as mentioned earlier).

So the question (most general-purpose integer factorization algorithms try to answer) is how to find two integers x and y that satisfy equivalence (7.1).

The general approach is to choose a set of t relatively small primes $S = \{p_1, p_2, \ldots, p_t\}$ (the so-called factor base) and to proceed with the following two steps:

- First, one computes $b_i \equiv a_i^2 \pmod{n}$ for arbitrary a_i, and this value is expressed as the product of powers of the primes in S. In this case, b_i can be represented as a vector in a t-dimensional vector space. This step is called the *relation collection stage*, and it is highly parallelizable.

- Second, if we have collected enough (e.g., $t + 1$) values for b_i, then a solution of equivalence (7.1) can be found by performing the Gaussian elimination on the matrix $B = [b_i]$. This step is called the *matrix step* and cannot be parallelized. It works on a huge (sparse) matrix and eventually comes up with a nontrivial factor of n.

Obviously, the choice of the number of primes of S is very important for the performance of the QS. If it is too small, then the relation collection stage may take very long (because a very small proportion of numbers factor over a small set of primes). If, however, it is too large (and too many primes are put into S), then the matrix may become too large to be reduced efficiently.

In either case, the QS has a subexponential running time of $L_n[\frac{1}{2}, c]$ for some constant c. As mentioned later, a variation of the QS was used in 1994 when RSA-129 was successfully factorized.

7.3.2.3 NFS

The NFS was developed and proposed in the 1990s (e.g., [7]). It is conceptually similar to the QS and is currently the fastest general-purpose integer factorization algorithm. It has a running time of $L_n[\frac{1}{3}, c]$ for $c = 1.923$ and was used in 1999 to factorize RSA-155 (see the following section). Furthermore, there are several variations of it, including, for example, the special number field sieve (SNFS) and the general number field sieve (GNFS).

7.3.3 State of the Art

When the RSA public key cryptosystem was published, a famous challenge was posted in the August 1977 issue of *Scientific American* [8]. In fact, US$100 were offered to anyone who could decrypt a message that was encrypted using a 129-digit integer acting as modulus. The number became known as RSA-129, and it was not factored until 1994 (with a distributed implementation of a variation of the QS algorithm [9]). Just to give an impression of the size of such an integer, RSA-129 and its prime factors are reprinted here:

$$
\begin{aligned}
RSA - 129 \ = \ & 1143816257578888676692357799761466120102182967212 \\
& 4236256256184293570693524573389783059712356395870 \\
& 5058989075147599290026879543541 \\[8pt]
= \ & 3490529510847650949147849619903898133417764638493 \\
& 387843990820577 \\
& * \\
& 32769132993266709549961988190834461413177642967 99 \\
& 2942539798288533
\end{aligned}
$$

Today, the RSA Factoring Challenge is sponsored by RSA Laboratories to learn more about the actual difficulty of factoring large integers of the type used in the RSA public key cryptosystem.[5] In 1999, a group of researchers completed the factorization of the 155-digit (512-bit) RSA Challenge Number, and in December 2003, researchers at the University of Bonn (Germany) completed the factorization of the 174-digit (576-bit) RSA Challenge Number. The next numbers to factor (in the RSA Factoring Challenge) are 640, 704, 768, 896, 1,024, 1,536, and 2,048 bits long.

In the past, a couple of proposals have been made to use specific hardware devices to speed up integer factoring algorithms. For example, TWINKLE is a device that can be used to speed up the first step in the QS algorithm—that is, find pairs (x, y) of distinct integers that satisfy equivalence (7.1) [10]. TWIRL is a more recent proposal [11].

7.4 ALGORITHMS FOR COMPUTING DISCRETE LOGARITHMS

There are basically two categories of algorithms to solve the DLP (and to compute discrete logarithms accordingly):

- Algorithms that attempt to exploit special characteristics of the group in which the DLP must be solved;

---

5   http://www.rsasecurity.com/rsalabs/challenges/factoring.

- Algorithms that do not attempt to exploit special characteristics of the group in which the DLP must be solved.

Algorithms of the first category are often called *special-purpose algorithms*, whereas algorithms of the second category are called *generic algorithms*. Let's start with the second category of algorithms.

7.4.1 Generic Algorithms

Let G be a cyclic group and g be a generator in this group. The difficulty of computing discrete logarithms to the base g in G then depends on whether we know the order of the group (i.e., $|G|$). If we don't know $|G|$, then the *Baby-step giant-step algorithm* is the best we can do. It has a running time of $O(\sqrt{|G|} \log |G|)$ and memory requirements of $O(\sqrt{|G|})$. If, however, we know $|G|$, then we can do better. In this case, we can use *Pollard's ρ-algorithm*, which is slightly more efficient than the Baby-step giant-step algorithm. In fact, Pollard's ρ-algorithm has a running-time complexity of $O(\sqrt{|G|})$ and requires almost no memory. It has been shown that this running time is a lower bound for any general-purpose algorithm to compute discrete logarithms in a cyclic group (if the factorization of the group order is not known) [12].

If, in addition to $|G|$, we also know the factorization of $|G|$, then we can use the *Pohlig-Hellman algorithm*, which has a running time of $O(\sqrt{q} \log q)$ (where q is the largest prime factor of $|G|$). This result implies, for example, that in DLP-based cryptosystems for $\mathbb{Z}_p^*$, $p - 1$ must have at least one large prime factor (as already mentioned in Section 7.2.1).

7.4.2 Special-Purpose Algorithms

If we are talking about special-purpose algorithms, then we are talking about specific groups. If, for example, we are talking about $\mathbb{Z}_p^*$, then there are basically two algorithms to solve the DLP in a subexponential running time.

- The *index calculus algorithm* has a running time of $L_p[\frac{1}{2}, c]$ for some small constant c;

- The NFS algorithm can also be used to compute discrete logarithms. Remember that it has a running time of $L_p[\frac{1}{3}, 1.923]$.

Consequently, the NFS algorithm is the algorithm of choice to solve the DLP in $\mathbb{Z}_p^*$.

7.4.3   State of the Art

Given that the NFS algorithm can be used to factor integers and compute discrete logarithms in $\mathbb{Z}_p^*$, we note that the state of the art in computing discrete logarithms in $\mathbb{Z}_p^*$ is comparable to the state of the art in factoring integers. This suggests that we must also work with 1,024-bit prime numbers p. Special care must be taken that $p-1$ does not have only small prime factors. Otherwise, the Pohlig-Hellman algorithm [1] can be used to efficiently compute discrete logarithms.

If we are not working in $\mathbb{Z}_p^*$, then the special-purpose algorithms mentioned earlier do not work, and the state of the art in computing discrete logarithms is worse than the state of the art in factoring integers. In this case, we have to use general-purpose algorithms (that do not have subexponential running times). This fact is, for example, exploited by elliptic curve cryptography.

7.5   HARD-CORE PREDICATES

The fact that f is a one-way function does not mean that $f(x)$ necessarily hides all information about x. Nevertheless, it seems likely that there is at least some information (e.g., one bit) about x that is hard to guess from $f(x)$, given that x in its entirety is hard to compute. One may ask if it is possible to point to specific bits of x that are hard to compute and how hard to compute they are. These questions can be answered in the affirmative. A number of results are known that give a particular bit of x, which is hard to guess given $f(x)$ for some particular one-way functions.

A *hard-core predicate* for f is a predicate about x that cannot be computed from $f(x)$. More formally, a hard-core predicate B can be defined as suggested in Definition 7.12 and illustrated in Figure 7.1.

Definition 7.12 (Hard-core predicate) *Let $f : X \rightarrow Y$ be a one-way function. A hard-core predicate of f is a Boolean predicate $B : X \rightarrow \{0,1\}$, such that the following two conditions hold:*

- *$B(x)$ can be computed efficiently for all $x \in X$. Alternatively speaking, there is a PPT algorithm A that on input x outputs $B(x)$ for all $x \in X$.*

- *It is not known how to efficiently compute $B(x)$ for all $y = f(x) \in Y$. Alternatively speaking, there is no known PPT algorithm A that on input $f(x)$ outputs $B(x)$ for all $x \in X$.*

Again, there are many possibilities to express the same properties. For example, the second condition can also be expressed as follows: for every PPT A and for all constants c, there exists a k_0 such that

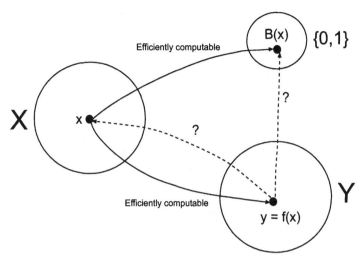

Figure 7.1   A hard-core predicate of a one-way function.

$$\Pr[A(f(x)) = B(x)] < \frac{1}{2} + \frac{1}{k^c}$$

for all $k > k_0$, where the probability is taken over over the random coin tosses of A and random choices of x of length k (i.e., the success probability of A is only negligibly smaller than $1/2$). It is simple and straightforward to extend the notion of a hard-core predicate for a family of one-way functions.

Historically, the notion of a hard-core predicate was first captured by Manuel Blum and Silvio Micali in a paper on pseudorandom number generation [13]. In fact, they showed that the *most significant bit* (MSB) is a hard-core predicate for the Exp family. This is in contrast to the RSA family, for which the *least significant bit* (LSB) represents a hard-core predicate [14]. In the context of probabilistic encryption, Oded Goldwasser and Micali showed that Square has a hard-core predicate, as well [15]. Andrew C. Yao[6] generalized the notion of a hard-core predicate and showed that given any one-way function f, there is a predicate $B(x)$ that is as hard to guess from $f(x)$ as to invert f [16].

---

6   In 2000, Andrew Chi-Chih Yao won the Turing Award for his seminal work on the theory of computation in general, and pseudorandom number generation, cryptography, and communication complexity in particular.

7.6 ELLIPTIC CURVE CRYPTOGRAPHY

Most public key cryptosystems get their security from the assumed intractability of inverting a one-way function (as discussed earlier). Against this background, it is important to note that inverting a one-way function is not necessarily equally difficult in all algebraic structures one may think of. If we look at inverting the discrete exponentiation function in $\mathbb{Z}_p^*$, then there are known algorithms that are subexponential. This need not be the case in all possible groups (in which the function is assumed to be one way). In fact, ECC has become popular (and important) mainly because groups have been found in which subexponential algorithms to invert the discrete exponentiation function (i.e., compute discrete logarithms) are not known to exist.[7] This basically means that one has to use a general-purpose (and exponential-time) algorithm to compute discrete logarithms and break the security of the corresponding public key cryptosystem accordingly. Note, however, that it is not known whether subexponential algorithms in these groups exist; we simply don't know them.

The fact that subexponential algorithms are not known to exist has the positive side effect (from the cryptographer's viewpoint) that the resulting elliptic curve cryptosystems are equally secure with smaller key sizes than their conventional counterparts. This is important for implementations in which key sizes and performance are important issues (e.g., smartcards). For example, to reach the security level of 1,024 (2,048) bits in a conventional public key cryptosystem (e.g., RSA), it is estimated that 163 (224) bits are sufficient for an elliptic curve cryptosystem (e.g., [17]). This is a nonnegligible factor that can speed up implementations considerably.

Most elliptic curve cryptosystems are based on the *elliptic curve discrete logarithm problem* (ECDLP) in such a group. Similar to the DLP, the ECDLP can be defined as suggested in Definition 7.13. Again, the ECDLP is assumed to be computationally intractable.

Definition 7.13 (Elliptic Curve Discrete Logarithm Problem) *Let $E(\mathbb{F}_q)$ be an elliptic curve over $\mathbb{F}_q$, P be a point on $E(\mathbb{F}_q)$ of order n, and Q be another point on $E(\mathbb{F}_q)$. The ECDLP is to determine an integer x (with $0 \leq x < n$), such that $Q = xP$.*

Based on the intractability assumption of the ECDLP, Neal Koblitz [18] and Victor Miller [19] independently proposed using elliptic curves to implement public key cryptosystems based on the DLP. This proposal dates back to the mid 1980s, and since then many public key cryptosystems have been reformulated in an elliptic

---

7   An interesting online tutorial about elliptic curves in general, and ECC in particular, is available at
     http://www.certicom.com/resources/ecc_tutorial/ecc_tutorial.html.

curve setting. Examples include Diffie-Hellman, ElGamal, and DSA. Today, many books address ECC and elliptic curve cryptosystems in detail (e.g., [20–23]). You may refer to any of these books if you want to get more involved in elliptic curves and ECC.

Since 1985, the ECDLP has received considerable attention from leading mathematicians around the world. It is currently believed that the ECDLP is much harder than integer factorization or DLP. More specifically, there is no algorithm known that has a subexponential running time in the worst case. A few vulnerabilities and potential attacks should be considered with care and kept in mind when elliptic curves are used. For example, it was shown that the ECDLP can be reduced to the DLP in extension fields of F_q, where the index-calculus methods can be applied [24]. However, this reduction algorithm is only efficient for a special class of elliptic curves known as *supersingular curves*. Moreover, there is a simple test to ensure that an elliptic curve is not supersingular and hence not vulnerable to this attack. Consequently, it is possible to avoid them in the first place. Some other vulnerabilities and potential attacks can be found in the literature.

A distinguishing feature of ECC is that each user may select a different elliptic curve $E(F_q)$—even if all users use the same underlying finite field F_q. From a security viewpoint, this flexibility is advantageous (because the elliptic curve can be changed periodically). From a practical viewpoint, however, this flexibility is also disadvantageous (because it makes interoperability much more difficult and because it has led to a situation in which the field of ECC is tied up in patents). Note that there is (more or less) only one way to implement a conventional public key cryptosystem, such as RSA, but usually many ways to implement an elliptic curve cryptosystem. In fact, one can work with different finite fields, different elliptic curves over these fields, and a wide variety of representations of the elements on these curves. Each choice has advantages and disadvantages, and one can construct an efficient curve for each application. Consequently, the relevant standardization bodies, such as the Institute of Electrical and Electronics Engineers (IEEE),[8] ISO/IEC JTC1, the American National Standards Institute (ANSI), and the National Institute of Standards and Technology (NIST), are working hard to come up with ECC standards and recommendations that are commonly accepted and widely deployed.[9]

7.7 FINAL REMARKS

In this chapter, we elaborated on one-way functions and trapdoor functions. More specifically, we defined the notion of a family of one-way functions or trapdoor

---

8   http://grouper.ieee.org/groups/1363.
9   http://www.certicom.com/resources/standards/eccstandards.html.

functions, and we overviewed and discussed some functions that are conjectured to be one way or trapdoor. More specifically, we looked at the discrete exponentiation function, the RSA function, and the modular square function. We further looked at hard-core predicates and algorithms for factoring integers or computing discrete logarithms. Curiously, factoring integers and computing discrete logarithms seem to have essentially the same difficulty (and computational complexity), at least as indicated by the current state-of-the-art algorithms.

Most public key cryptosystems in use today are based on one (or several) of the conjectured one-way functions mentioned earlier. This is also true for ECC, which works in cyclic groups in which known special-purpose algorithms to compute discrete logarithms do not work. From a practical viewpoint, ECC is interesting because it allows us to use smaller keys (compared to other public key cryptosystems). This is advantageous especially when it comes to implementing cryptographic systems and applications in environments that are restricted in terms of computational resources (e.g., smartcards). For the purpose of this book, however, we don't make a major distinction between public key cryptosystems that are based on the DLP and public key cryptosystems that are based on the ECDLP.

In either case, it is sometimes recommended to use cryptosystems that combine different candidate one-way functions in one way or another. If one of these functions then turns out not to be one way, then the other functions still remain and keep on securing the cryptosystem. Obviously, this strategy becomes useless if all functions turn out not to be one way.

References

[1] Pohlig, S., and M.E. Hellman, "An Improved Algorithm for Computing Logarithms over GF(p)," *IEEE Transactions on Information Theory*, Vol. 24, January 1978, pp. 106–110.

[2] Maurer, U.M., "Towards the Equivalence of Breaking the Diffie-Hellman Protocol and Computing Discrete Logarithms," *Proceedings of CRYPTO '94*, Springer-Verlag, LNCS 839, 1994, 271–281.

[3] Maurer, U.M., and S. Wolf, "The Diffie-Hellman Protocol," *Designs, Codes, and Cryptography*, Special Issue on Public Key Cryptography, Vol. 19, No. 2-3, 2000, pp. 147–171.

[4] Lenstra, H.W., "Factoring Integers with Elliptic Curves," *Annals of Mathematics*, Vol. 126, 1987, pp. 649–673.

[5] Morrison, M.A., and J. Brillhart, "Method of Factoring and the Factorization of F_7," *Mathematics of Computation*, Vol. 29, 1975, pp. 183–205.

[6] Pomerance, C., "The Quadratic Sieve Factoring Algorithm," *Proceedings of EUROCRYPT '84*, Springer-Verlag, 1984, pp. 169–182.

[7] Lenstra, A.K., and H.W. Lenstra, *The Development of the Number Field Sieve*. Springer-Verlag, LNCS 1554, New York, 1993.

[8] Gardner, M., "A New Kind of Cipher That Would Take Millions of Years to Break," *Scientific American*, Vol. 237, pp. 120–124.

[9] Atkins, D., "The Magic Words Are Squeamish Ossifrage," *Proceedings of ASIACRYPT '94*, Springer-Verlag, LNCS 917, 1995, pp. 263–277.

[10] Shamir, A., "Factoring Large Numbers with the TWINKLE Device," *Proceedings of CHES '99*, Springer-Verlag, LNCS 1717, 1999, pp. 2–12.

[11] Shamir, A., and E. Tromer, "Factoring Large Numbers with the TWIRL Device," *Proceedings of CRYPTO 2003*, Springer-Verlag, LNCS 2729, 2003, pp. 1–26.

[12] Shoup, V., "Lower Bounds for Discrete Logarithms and Related Problems," *Proceedings of EUROCRYPT '97*, Springer-Verlag, LNCS 1233, 1997, pp. 256–266.

[13] Blum, M., and S. Micali, "How to Generate Cryptographically Strong Sequences of Pseudo-Random Bits," *SIAM Journal of Computing*, Vol. 13, No. 4, November 1984, pp. 850–863.

[14] Alexi, W.B., et al., "RSA/Rabin Functions: Certain Parts Are as Hard as the Whole," *SIAM Journal of Computing*, Vol. 17, No. 2, April 1988, pp. 194–209.

[15] Goldwasser, S., and S. Micali, "Probabilistic Encryption," *Journal of Computer and System Sciences*, Vol. 28, No. 2, April 1984, pp. 270–299.

[16] Yao, A.C., "Theory and Application of Trapdoor Functions," *Proceedings of 23rd IEEE Symposium on Foundations of Computer Science*, IEEE Press, Chicago, 1982, pp. 80–91.

[17] Lenstra, A.K., and E.R. Verheul, "Selecting Cryptographic Key Sizes," *Journal of Cryptology*, Vol. 14, No. 4, 2001, pp. 255–293.

[18] Koblitz, N., "Elliptic Curve Cryptosystems," *Mathematics of Computation*, Vol. 48, No. 177, 1987, pp. 203–209.

[19] Miller, V., "Use of Elliptic Curves in Cryptography," *Proceedings of CRYPTO '85*, LNCS 218, Springer-Verlag, 1986, pp. 417–426.

[20] Koblitz, N.I., *A Course in Number Theory and Cryptography*, 2nd edition. Springer-Verlag, New York, 1994.

[21] Blake, I., G. Seroussi, and N. Smart, *Elliptic Curves in Cryptography*, Cambridge University Press, Cambridge, UK, 2000.

[22] Washington, L.C., *Elliptic Curves: Number Theory and Cryptography.* Chapman & Hall/CRC, Boca Raton, FL, 2003.

[23] Hankerson, D., A. Menezes, and S.A. Vanstone, *Guide to Elliptic Curve Cryptography.* Springer-Verlag, New York, NY, 2004.

[24] Menezes, A., T. Okamoto, and S.A. Vanstone, "Reducing Elliptic Curve Logarithms to Logarithms in a Finite Field," *IEEE Transactions on Information Theory*, Vol. 39, 1993, pp. 1639–1646.

Chapter 8

Cryptographic Hash Functions

In this chapter, we elaborate on cryptographic hash functions. More specifically, we introduce the basic principles and properties of such functions in Section 8.1, address a basic construction (i.e., the Merkle-Damgård construction) in Section 8.2, overview exemplary cryptographic hash functions in Section 8.3, and conclude with some final remarks in Section 8.4.

8.1 INTRODUCTION

As mentioned in Section 2.1.2 and formally expressed in Defintion 2.3, a *hash function* is an efficiently computable function $h : \Sigma_{in}^* \rightarrow \Sigma_{out}^n$ that takes an arbitrarily sized[1] input word $x \in \Sigma_{in}^*$ (with Σ_{in} representing the input alphabet) and generates an output word $y \in \Sigma_{out}^n$ (with Σ_{out} representing the output alphabet) of size n. Furthermore, a *cryptographic hash function* is a hash function that has specific properties. There are basically three properties that are relevant from a cryptographic viewpoint.

- A hash function h is *preimage resistant* if it is computationally infeasible to find an input word $x \in \Sigma_{in}^*$ with $h(x) = y$ for a given (and randomly chosen) output word $y \in_R \Sigma_{out}^n$.

- A hash function h is *second-preimage resistant* or *weak collision resistant* if it is computationally infeasible to find a second input word $x' \in \Sigma_{in}^*$ with $x' \neq x$ and $h(x') = h(x)$ for a given (and randomly chosen) input word $x \in_R \Sigma_{in}^*$.

---

1 Remember from Section 2.1.2 that one usually has to assume a maximum length n_{max} for input words. In this case, the hash function is formally expressed as $h : \Sigma_{in}^{n_{max}} \rightarrow \Sigma_{out}^n$.

195

- A hash function h is *collision resistant* or *strong collision resistant* if it is computationally infeasible to find two input words $x, x' \in \Sigma_{in}^*$ with $x' \neq x$ and $h(x') = h(x)$.

There are some comments to make at this point:

- In some literature, collision resistant hash functions are also called *collision free*. This term is inappropriate, because collisions always occur if one uses hash functions (i.e., functions that hash arbitrarily sized arguments to a fixed size). Consequently, the term collision free is not used as an attribute to cryptographic hash functions in this book.

- In a complexity-theoretic setting, one cannot say that finding a collision for a given hash function is a difficult problem. In fact, finding a collision (for a given hash function) is a problem instance rather than a problem (refer to Section 6.2 for a discussion about the difference between a problem and a problem instance). This is because there is always an efficient algorithm that finds a collision, namely one that simply outputs two input words that hash to the same value. Thus, the concept of collision resistance only makes sense if one considers a sufficiently large class (or family) of hash functions from which one is chosen at random. An algorithm to find collisions must then work for all hash functions of the class, including the one that is chosen at random.

- A collision resistant hash function must be second-preimage resistant. Otherwise it is possible to find a second preimage for an arbitrarily chosen input word, and this second preimage then yields a collision. The converse, however, is not true—that is, a second-preimage resistant hash function must not be collision resistant (that's why we used the terms *weak collision resistant* and *strong collision resistant* in the first place). Consequently, collision resistance implies second-preimage resistance, but not vice versa.

- A (strong or weak) collision resistant hash function must not be preimage resistant. For example, let g be a collision resistant hash function with an n-bit output and h a pathological $(n + 1)$-bit hash function that is defined as follows:[2]

$$h(x) = \begin{cases} 1 \,\|\, x & \text{if } |\,x\,| = n \\ 0 \,\|\, g(x) & \text{otherwise} \end{cases}$$

2   This example is taken from Ueli Maurer's seminar entitled "Cryptography—Fundamentals and Applications."

On the one hand, h is collision resistant. If $h(x)$ begins with a one, then there is no collision at all. If $h(x)$ begins with a zero, then finding a collision means finding a collision for g (which is assumed to be computationally infeasible). On the other hand, h is not preimage resistant. For all $h(x)$ that begin with a one, it is trivial to find a preimage (just drop the leading one) and to invert h accordingly. Consequently, h is a hash function that is collision resistant but not preimage resistant, and we conclude that preimage resistance and collision resistance are inherently different properties that must be distinguished accordingly.

In practice, Σ_{in} and Σ_{out} are often set to $\{0, 1\}$, and a hash function then represents a map from $\{0, 1\}^*$ to $\{0, 1\}^n$. A question that occurs immediately is how large to choose the parameter n. A lower bound for n is obtained by the *birthday attack*. This attack is based on the *birthday paradox* that is well known in probability theory. It says that the probability of two persons in a group sharing the same birthday is greater than $1/2$ if the group is chosen at random and has more than 23 members. To obtain this result, we employ a sample space Σ that consists off all n-tuples over the 365 days of the year (i.e., $\mid \Sigma \mid = 365^n$). Let $\Pr[\mathcal{A}]$ be the probability that at least two out of n persons have the same birthday. This value is difficult to compute directly. It is much simpler to compute $\Pr[\overline{\mathcal{A}}]$ (i.e., the probability that all persons have different birthdays) and to derive $\Pr[\mathcal{A}]$ from this value. In fact, $\Pr[\mathcal{A}]$ can be computed as follows (for $0 \le n \le 365$):

$$
\begin{aligned}
\Pr[\mathcal{A}] &= 1 - \Pr[\overline{\mathcal{A}}] \\
&= 1 - \frac{\mid \overline{\mathcal{A}} \mid}{\mid \Sigma \mid} \\
&= 1 - 365 \cdot 364 \cdot \ldots \cdot (365 - n) \cdot \frac{1}{365^n} \\
&= 1 - \frac{365!}{(365 - n)!} \cdot \frac{1}{365^n} \\
&= 1 - \frac{365!}{(365 - n)! 365^n}
\end{aligned}
$$

$\Pr[\mathcal{A}]$ is equal to 1 for $n > 365$ (in this case, it is not possible that all n persons have different birthdays). In either case, $\Pr[\mathcal{A}]$ grows surprisingly fast and n must only be 23 to reach a probability greater or equal to $1/2$. If $n = 23$, then

$$
\Pr[\mathcal{A}] = 1 - \frac{365!}{(365 - 23)! 365^{23}}
$$

$$= 1 - \frac{365!}{(342)!365^{23}}$$

$$= 1 - \frac{365 \cdot 364 \cdots 343}{365^{23}} \approx 0.508$$

This result is somehow paradoxical. If we fix a date and ask for the number of persons that are required to make the probability that at least one person has this date as his or her birthday, then n must be much larger. In fact, in this case n has to be $\lceil 362/2 \rceil = 183$.

Applying this argument to hash functions means that finding two persons with the same birthday reveals a collision, whereas finding a person with a given birthday reveals a second preimage. Hence, due to the birthday paradox, one can argue that collision resistance is much more difficult to achieve than second-preimage resistance. More specifically, one can show that for any collision resistant hash function with an n-bit output, no attack finding a collision betters a birthday attack with a worst-case running time of

$$O(\sqrt{2^n}) = O(2^{n/2})$$

That's why the birthday attack is sometimes also referred to as *square root attack*. This result implies that a collision resistant hash function must produce outputs that are twice as long as one would usually suggest to make an exhaustive search computationally infeasible. For example, if we assume that searching a key space of 2^{64} is computationally infeasible, then we must use a hash function that outputs at least $2 \cdot 64 = 128$ bits.

In addition to preimage, second-preimage, and collision resistance, there are also some other properties of hash functions mentioned (and sometimes discussed) in the literature.

- A hash function h is *noncorrelated* if its input bits and output bits are not correlated in one way or another.

- A hash function h is *generalized collision resistant* if it is computationally infeasible to find two input words x and x' with $x' \neq x$ such that $h(x)$ and $h(x')$ are similar in some specific sense (e.g., they are equal in some bits).

- A hash function h is *weakened collision resistant* if it is computationally infeasible to find two input words x and x' with $x' \neq x$ and $h(x) = h(x')$ such that x and x' are similar in some specified sense (e.g., they are equal in some bits).

These properties are just mentioned for completeness; they are not further used in this book.

Having the previously mentioned properties (i.e., preimage, second-preimage, and collision resistance) in mind, one can define *one-way hash functions* (OWHFs), *collision resistant hash functions* (CRHFs), and *cryptographic hash functions* as suggested in Definitions 8.1 and 8.2.

Definition 8.1 (One-way hash function) *An OWHF is a hash function* $h : \Sigma_{in}^* \rightarrow \Sigma_{out}^n$ *that is preimage resistant and second-preimage resistant.*

Definition 8.2 (Collision resistant hash function) *A CRHF is a hash function* $h : \Sigma_{in}^* \rightarrow \Sigma_{out}^n$ *that is preimage resistant and collision resistant.*

Note that a CRHF is always an OWHF (whereas the converse may not be true). Also note that alternative terms sometimes used in the literature are *weak one-way hash functions* for OWHFs and *strong one-way hash functions* for CRHFs. As suggested in Definition 2.4, we use the term *cryptographic hash function* to refer to either of them.

8.2 MERKLE-DAMGÅRD CONSTRUCTION

Most cryptographic hash functions in use today follow a construction that was independently proposed by Ralph C. Merkle and Ivan B. Damgård in the late 1980s [1, 2].[3] According to their construction, an *iterated hash function* h is computed by repeated application of a collision resistant compression function $f : \Sigma^m \longrightarrow \Sigma^n$ with $m, n \in \mathbb{N}$ and $m > n$ to successive blocks $x_1, \ldots, x_n$ of a message x.[4]

As illustrated in Figure 8.1, the compression function f takes two input arguments:

1. A b-bit message block;

2. An l-bit chaining value (sometimes referred to as H_i for $i = 0, \ldots, n$).

In a typical setting, l is 128 or 160 bits and b is 512 bits. The output of the compression function can be used as a new l-bit chaining value, which is input to the next iteration of the compression function. Referring to the notation introduced earlier, $m = b + l$ and $n = l$.

---

3 Both papers were presented at CRYPTO '89.
4 Note that the input alphabet Σ_{in} and the output alphabet Σ_{out} are assumed to be the same (denoted as Σ).

b bits

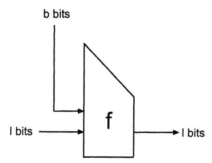

Figure 8.1   A compression function f.

Against this background, an iterated hash function h can then be constructed, as illustrated in Figure 8.2. In this figure, f represents the compression function and g represents an output function.[5] The message x is padded to a multiple of b bits and divided into a sequence of n b-bit message blocks $x_1, \ldots, x_n$. The compression function f is then repeatedly applied, starting with an initial value ($IV = H_0$) and the first message block x_1, and continuing with each new chaining value H_i and successive message block x_{i+1} for $i = 1, \ldots, n - 1$. After the last message block x_n has been processed, the final chaining value H_n is subject to the output function g, and the output of this function is the output of the iterated hash function h for x (i.e., $h(x)$).

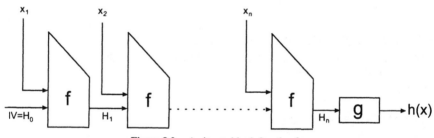

Figure 8.2   An iterated hash function h.

Hence, an iterative hash function h for $x = x_1 x_2 \ldots x_n$ can be recursively computed according to the following set of equations:

$$H_0 \;=\; IV$$

$$H_i = f(H_{i-1}, x_i) \text{ for } i = 1, \ldots, n$$
$$h(x) = g(H_n)$$

As mentioned earlier, the message to be hashed must be padded to a multiple of b bits. One possibility is to pad x with zeros. Padding with zeros, however, may also introduce ambiguity about x. For example, the message 101110 padded to 8 bits would be 10111000 and it is then unclear how many trailing zeros were present in the original message. Several methods are available to resolve this problem. Merkle proposed to append the bit length of x at the end of x. To make the additional length field easy to find, it is right-justified in the final block. Following this proposal, the padding method of choice in currently deployed hash functions is to append a one, a variable number of zeros, and the binary encoding of the length of the original message to the end of the message.

Merkle and Damgård showed that in their construction, finding a collision for h (i.e., finding two input words x and x' with $x \neq x'$ and $h(x) = h(x')$) is at least as hard as finding a collision for the underlying compression function f. This also means that if f is a collision resistant compression function, and h is an iterated hash function making use of f, then h is a cryptographic hash function that is also collision resistant. Put in other words, the iterated hash function inherits the collision resistance property from the underlying compression function.

In the literature, there are many proposals for collision resistant compression functions that can be turned into collision resistant cryptographic hash functions according to the Merkle-Damgård construction. Some examples can, for example, be found in [1, 2].

8.3 EXEMPLARY CRYPTOGRAPHIC HASH FUNCTIONS

The driving force for cryptographic hash functions was public key cryptography in general, and digital signature systems in particular. Consequently, the company RSA Security, Inc., played a crucial role in the development and deployment of many practically relevant cryptographic hash functions. The first cryptographic hash function developed by RSA Security, Inc., was acronymed MD (standing for *message digest*). It was proprietary and never published. MD2 specified in RFC 1319 [3] was the first published cryptographic hash function in widespread use (it was, for example, used in the secure messaging products of RSA Security, Inc.). When Merkle proposed a cryptographic hash function called SNEFRU that was several times faster than MD2,[6] RSA Security, Inc., responded to the challenge with MD4[7] specified in RFC 1320 [4] (see Section 8.3.1). MD4 took advantage of the fact that newer processors could do 32-bit operations, and it was therefore able to be faster than SNEFRU. In 1991, SNEFRU and some other cryptographic hash functions were successfully attacked[8] using differential cryptanalysis [5]. Furthermore, some weaknesses were found in a version of MD4 with two rounds instead of three [6]. This did not officially break MD4, but it made RSA Security, Inc., sufficiently nervous that it was decided to strengthen MD4. MD5 was designed and specified in RFC 1320 [7] (see Section 8.3.2). MD5 is assumed to be more secure than MD4, but it is also a little bit slower. Due to some recent results, MD4 must be considered to be insecure [8], and MD5 must be considered to be partially broken [9].[9] In 2004, a group of Chinese researchers found and published collisions for MD4, MD5, and some other cryptographic hash functions.[10] Nevertheless, MD4 and MD5 are still useful study objects for the design principles of cryptographic hash functions.

Table 8.1
Secure Hash Algorithms as Specified in FIPS 180-2

Algorithm	Message Size	Block Size	Word Size	Hash Value Size
SHA-1	$< 2^{64}$ bits	512 bits	32 bits	160 bits
SHA-224	$< 2^{64}$ bits	512 bits	32 bits	224 bits
SHA-256	$< 2^{64}$ bits	512 bits	32 bits	256 bits
SHA-384	$< 2^{128}$ bits	1,024 bits	64 bits	384 bits
SHA-512	$< 2^{128}$ bits	1,024 bits	64 bits	512 bits

In 1993, the U.S. NIST proposed the *Secure Hash Algorithm* (SHA), which is similar to MD5, but even more strengthened and also a little bit slower. Probably after discovering a never-published weakness in the orginal SHA proposal,[11] the NIST revised it and called the revised version SHA-1. As such, SHA-1 is specified in the Federal Information Processing Standards Publication (FIPS PUB) 180-1 [12],[12] also known as *Secure Hash Standard* (SHS). In 2002, FIPS PUB 180 was revised

---

6   The function was proposed in 1990 in a Xerox PARC technical report entitled *A Software One Way Function*.
7   There was an MD3 cryptographic hash function, but it was superseded by MD4 before it was ever published or used.
8   The attack was considered successful because it was shown how to systematically find a collision (i.e., two messages with the same hash value).
9   One problem with MD5 is that the compression function is known to have collisions (e.g., [10]).
10 http://eprint.iacr.org/2004/199.pdf.
11 At CRYPTO '98, Florent Chabaud and Antoine Joux published a weakness of SHA-0 [11]. This weakness was fixed by SHA-1, so it is reasonable to assume that they found the original weakness.
12 SHA-1 is also specified in informational RFC 3174 [13].

Table 8.2
Truth Table of the Logical Functions Employed by MD4

X	Y	Z	f	g	h
0	0	0	0	0	0
0	0	1	1	0	1
0	1	0	0	0	1
0	1	1	1	1	0
1	0	0	0	0	1
1	0	1	0	1	0
1	1	0	1	1	0
1	1	1	1	1	1

a second time and the resulting FIPS PUB 180-2[13] superseded FIPS PUB 180-1 beginning February 1, 2003. In addition to superseding FIPS 180-1, FIPS 180-2 also added three new algorithms that produce and output larger hash values (see Table 8.1). The SHA-1 algorithm specified in FIPS 180-2 is the same algorithm as specified in FIPS 180-1, although some of the notation has been modified to be consistent with the notation used in SHA-256, SHA-384, and SHA-512. As summarized in Table 8.1, SHA-1, SHA-256, SHA-384, and SHA-512 produce and output hash values of different sizes (160, 256, 384, and 512 bits), and their maximal message sizes, block sizes, and word sizes also vary considerably. In February 2004, the NIST published a change notice for FIPS 180-2 to include SHA-224.[14] SHA-224 is identical to SHA-256, but uses different initial hash values and truncates the final hash value to its leftmost 224 bits. It is also included in Table 8.1.

In addition to the cryptographic hash functions proposed by RSA Security, Inc., and the NIST, there are at least two competing proposals developed entirely in Europe (i.e., RIPEMD-128 and RIPEMD-160 [15, 16]). These cryptographic hash functions are not further addressed in this book.

MD4, MD5, and RIPEMD-128 produce hash values of 128 bits, whereas RIPEMD-160 and SHA-1 produce hash values of 160 bits. The newer versions of SHA produce hash values that are even longer. From a security viewpoint, long hash values are preferred (because they reduce the likelihood of collisions in the first place). Consequently, it is recommended to replace MD5 with SHA-1 (or any other hash function from the SHA family) where possible and appropriate. MD4, MD5, and SHA-1 are overviewed and discussed next.

---

13 http://csrc.nist.gov/publications/fips/fips180-2/fips180-2.pdf.
14 SHA-224 is also specified in informational RFC 3874 [14].

Algorithm 8.1   The MD4 hash function (overview).

$(m = m_0 m_1 \ldots m_{s-1})$

Construct $M = M[0]M[1] \ldots M[N-1]$
$A \leftarrow \texttt{0x67452301}$
$B \leftarrow \texttt{0xEFCDAB89}$
$C \leftarrow \texttt{0x98BADCFE}$
$D \leftarrow \texttt{0x10325476}$
for $i = 0$ to $N/16 - 1$ do
 for $j = 0$ to 15 do $X[j] = M[i \cdot 16 + j]$
 $A' \leftarrow A$
 $B' \leftarrow B$
 $C' \leftarrow C$
 $D' \leftarrow D$
 Round 1 (Algorithm 8.2)
 Round 2 (Algorithm 8.3)
 Round 3 (Algorithm 8.4)
 $A \leftarrow A + A'$
 $B \leftarrow B + B'$
 $C \leftarrow C + C'$
 $D \leftarrow D + D'$

$(h(m) = A \parallel B \parallel C \parallel D)$

8.3.1   MD4

As mentioned earlier, MD4 was proposed in 1990 and is specified in RFC 1320 [4].[15] It represents a Merkle-Damgård construction that hashes a message in 512-bit blocks (i.e., $b = 512$) and that produces an output of 128 bits (i.e., $l = 128$). As also mentioned earlier, MD4 was designed to be efficiently implementable on 32-bit processors. It assumes a little-endian architecture, meaning that a 4-byte word $a_1 a_2 a_3 a_4$ represents the following integer:

$$a_4 2^{24} + a_3 2^{16} + a_2 2^8 + a_1$$

In a big-endian architecture, the same 4-byte word $a_1 a_2 a_3 a_4$ would represent the integer

$$a_1 2^{24} + a_2 2^{16} + a_3 2^8 + a_4.$$

---

15   The original version of MD4 was published in October 1990 in RFC 1196. A slightly revised version of it was published in April 1992 (at the same time as MD5) in RFC 1320.

Algorithm 8.2 Round 1 of the MD4 hash function.

1. $A \leftarrow (A + f(B, C, D) + X[0]) \hookleftarrow 3$
2. $D \leftarrow (D + f(A, B, C) + X[1]) \hookleftarrow 7$
3. $C \leftarrow (C + f(D, A, B) + X[2]) \hookleftarrow 11$
4. $B \leftarrow (B + f(C, D, A) + X[3]) \hookleftarrow 19$
5. $A \leftarrow (A + f(B, C, D) + X[4]) \hookleftarrow 3$
6. $D \leftarrow (D + f(A, B, C) + X[5]) \hookleftarrow 7$
7. $C \leftarrow (C + f(D, A, B) + X[6]) \hookleftarrow 11$
8. $B \leftarrow (B + f(C, D, A) + X[7]) \hookleftarrow 19$
9. $A \leftarrow (A + f(B, C, D) + X[8]) \hookleftarrow 3$
10. $D \leftarrow (D + f(A, B, C) + X[9]) \hookleftarrow 7$
11. $C \leftarrow (C + f(D, A, B) + X[10]) \hookleftarrow 11$
12. $B \leftarrow (B + f(C, D, A) + X[11]) \hookleftarrow 19$
13. $A \leftarrow (A + f(B, C, D) + X[12]) \hookleftarrow 3$
14. $D \leftarrow (D + f(A, B, C) + X[13]) \hookleftarrow 7$
15. $C \leftarrow (C + f(D, A, B) + X[14]) \hookleftarrow 11$
16. $B \leftarrow (B + f(C, D, A) + X[15]) \hookleftarrow 19$

Let $m = m_0 m_1 \ldots m_{s-1}$ be an s-bit message that is to be hashed with MD4. In a first step, an array

$$M = M[0]M[1] \ldots M[N-1]$$

is constructed, where each $M[i]$ represents a 32-bit word and $N \equiv 0 \bmod 16$. Consequently, the length of M equals a multiple of $32 \cdot 16 = 512$ bits. It is constructed in two steps:

- First, the message m is padded so that its bit length is congruent to 448 modulo 512. Therefore, a single one is appended, and then zero bits are appended so that the bit length of the padded message becomes congruent to 448 modulo 512 (i.e., at least one bit and at most 512 bits must be appended). Note that padding is always performed, even if the length of the message is already congruent to 448 modulo 512. Also note that the padded message is 64 bits short of being a multiple of 512 bits.

- Second, a 64-bit binary representation of s (i.e., the length of the original message before the padding bits were added) is appended to the result of the first step. In the unlikely case that s is greater than 2^{64}, then only the low-order 64 bits of s are used (i.e., s is computed modulo 2^{64}). In either case, the 64 bits fill up the last message block from 448 to 512 bits.

Algorithm 8.3 Round 2 of the MD4 hash function.

1. $A \leftarrow (A + g(B, C, D) + X[0] + c_1) \hookleftarrow 3$
2. $D \leftarrow (D + g(A, B, C) + X[4] + c_1) \hookleftarrow 5$
3. $C \leftarrow (C + g(D, A, B) + X[8] + c_1) \hookleftarrow 9$
4. $B \leftarrow (B + g(C, D, A) + X[12] + c_1) \hookleftarrow 13$
5. $A \leftarrow (A + g(B, C, D) + X[1] + c_1) \hookleftarrow 3$
6. $D \leftarrow (D + g(A, B, C) + X[5] + c_1) \hookleftarrow 5$
7. $C \leftarrow (C + g(D, A, B) + X[9] + c_1) \hookleftarrow 9$
8. $B \leftarrow (B + g(C, D, A) + X[13] + c_1) \hookleftarrow 13$
9. $A \leftarrow (A + g(B, C, D) + X[2] + c_1) \hookleftarrow 3$
10. $D \leftarrow (D + g(A, B, C) + X[6] + c_1) \hookleftarrow 5$
11. $C \leftarrow (C + g(D, A, B) + X[10] + c_1) \hookleftarrow 9$
12. $B \leftarrow (B + g(C, D, A) + X[14] + c_1) \hookleftarrow 13$
13. $A \leftarrow (A + g(B, C, D) + X[3] + c_1) \hookleftarrow 3$
14. $D \leftarrow (D + g(A, B, C) + X[7] + c_1) \hookleftarrow 5$
15. $C \leftarrow (C + g(D, A, B) + X[11] + c_1) \hookleftarrow 9$
16. $B \leftarrow (B + g(C, D, A) + X[15] + c_1) \hookleftarrow 13$

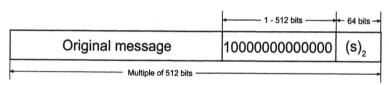

Figure 8.3   The structure of a message preprocessed to be hashed using MD4.

At this point, the resulting message has a structure as illustrated in Figure 8.3. It has a length that is an exact multiple of 512 bits. Consequently, it can be broken up into 32-bit words, and the resulting number of words (i.e., N) is still divisible by 16.

A 128-bit MD4 hash value can be constructed using Algorithm 8.1. In short, the hash value is constructed as the concatenation of four words (or registers) A, B, C, and D. First, the array M is constructed as discussed earlier, and the four registers are initialized with constant values. The array M is then processed iteratively. In each iteration, 16 words of M are taken and stored in an array X. The values of the four registers are stored for later reuse. In the main part of the algorithm, three rounds of hashing are performed (i.e., Round 1, Round 2, and Round 3). Each round consists of one operation on each of the 16 words in X (described later). The operations done in the three rounds produce new values for the four registers. Finally, the four registers are updated by adding back the values that were stored previously (the addition is always performed modulo 2^{32}).

Algorithm 8.4 Round 3 of the MD4 hash function.

1. $A \leftarrow (A + h(B, C, D) + X[0] + c_2) \hookleftarrow 3$
2. $D \leftarrow (D + h(A, B, C) + X[8] + c_2) \hookleftarrow 9$
3. $C \leftarrow (C + h(D, A, B) + X[4] + c_2) \hookleftarrow 11$
4. $B \leftarrow (B + h(C, D, A) + X[12] + c_2) \hookleftarrow 15$
5. $A \leftarrow (A + h(B, C, D) + X[2] + c_2) \hookleftarrow 3$
6. $D \leftarrow (D + h(A, B, C) + X[10] + c_2) \hookleftarrow 9$
7. $C \leftarrow (C + h(D, A, B) + X[6] + c_2) \hookleftarrow 11$
8. $B \leftarrow (B + h(C, D, A) + X[14] + c_2) \hookleftarrow 15$
9. $A \leftarrow (A + h(B, C, D) + X[1] + c_2) \hookleftarrow 3$
10. $D \leftarrow (D + h(A, B, C) + X[9] + c_2) \hookleftarrow 9$
11. $C \leftarrow (C + h(D, A, B) + X[5] + c_2) \hookleftarrow 11$
12. $B \leftarrow (B + h(C, D, A) + X[13] + c_2) \hookleftarrow 15$
13. $A \leftarrow (A + h(B, C, D) + X[3] + c_2) \hookleftarrow 3$
14. $D \leftarrow (D + h(A, B, C) + X[11] + c_2) \hookleftarrow 9$
15. $C \leftarrow (C + h(D, A, B) + X[7] + c_2) \hookleftarrow 11$
16. $B \leftarrow (B + h(C, D, A) + X[15] + c_2) \hookleftarrow 15$

The three rounds used in the MD4 hash function are different. The following operations are employed in the three rounds (X and Y denote input words, and each operation produces an output word):

$X \wedge Y$ Bitwise and of X and Y (AND)

$X \vee Y$ Bitwise or of X and Y (OR)

$X \oplus Y$ Bitwise exclusive or of X and Y (XOR)

$\neg X$ Bitwise complement of X (NOT)

$X + Y$ Integer addition of X and Y modulo 2^{32}

$X \hookleftarrow s$ Circular left shift of X by s positions ($0 \leq s \leq 31$)

Note that all of these operations are very fast and that the only arithmetic operation is addition modulo 2^{32}. As mentioned earlier, MD4 assumes a little-endian architecture.[16] Consequently, if an MD4 hash value must be computed on a big-endian machine, then the addition operation is a little bit more involved and must be implemented accordingly.

Rounds 1, 2, and 3 of the MD4 hash algorithm use the following three auxiliary functions f, g, and h:

$$f(X, Y, Z) = (X \wedge Y) \vee ((\neg X) \wedge Z)$$

16   Rivest chose to assume a little-endian architecture mainly because he observed that big-endian architectures are generally faster and can therefore better afford the processing penalty (of reversing each word for processing).

$$g(X, Y, Z) = (X \wedge Y) \vee (X \wedge Z) \vee (Y \wedge Z)$$
$$h(X, Y, Z) = X \oplus Y \oplus Z$$

Each function takes as input three 32-bit words and produces as output a 32-bit word. The truth table is illustrated in Table 8.2 on page 203. The function f is sometimes known as the *selection function*, because if the nth bit of X is 1, then it selects the nth bit of Y for the nth bit of the output. Otherwise (i.e., if the nth bit of X is 0), it selects the nth bit of Z for the nth bit of the output. The function g is sometimes known as the *majority function*, because the nth bit of the output is 1 if and only if at least two of the three input words' n^{th} bits are 1. Last but not least, the function h simply adds all input words modulo 2.

Algorithm 8.5 The MD5 hash function (overview).

$(m = m_0 m_1 \ldots m_{s-1})$

Construct $M = M[0]M[1] \ldots M[N-1]$

$A \leftarrow 0\text{x}67452301$
$B \leftarrow 0\text{xEFCDAB89}$
$C \leftarrow 0\text{x}98\text{BADCFE}$
$D \leftarrow 0\text{x}10325476$
for $i = o$ to $N/16 - 1$ do
    for $j = 0$ to 15 do $X[j] = M[i \cdot 16 + j]$
    $A' \leftarrow A$
    $B' \leftarrow B$
    $C' \leftarrow C$
    $D' \leftarrow D$
    Round 1 (Algorithm 8.6)
    Round 2 (Algorithm 8.7)
    Round 3 (Algorithm 8.8)
    Round 4 (Algorithm 8.9)
    $A \leftarrow A + A'$
    $B \leftarrow B + B'$
    $C \leftarrow C + C'$
    $D \leftarrow D + D'$

$(h(m) = A \parallel B \parallel C \parallel D)$

The complete descriptions of rounds 1, 2, and 3 of the MD4 hash algorithm are given in Algorithms 8.2–8.4. The constants c_1 and c_2 employed in rounds 2 and 3 refer to $c_1 = \lfloor 2^{30}\sqrt{2} \rfloor = 0\text{x}5\text{A}827999$ and $c_2 = \lfloor 2^{30}\sqrt{3} \rfloor = 0\text{x}6\text{ED}9\text{EBA1}$.

A reference implementation of the MD4 hash algorithm (in the C programming language) is provided in Appendix A of RFC 1320 [4].

Algorithm 8.6 Round 1 of the MD5 hash function.

1. $A \leftarrow (A + f(B, C, D) + X[0] + T[1]) \hookleftarrow 7$
2. $D \leftarrow (D + f(A, B, C) + X[1] + T[2]) \hookleftarrow 12$
3. $C \leftarrow (C + f(D, A, B) + X[2] + T[3]) \hookleftarrow 17$
4. $B \leftarrow (B + f(C, D, A) + X[3] + T[4]) \hookleftarrow 22$
5. $A \leftarrow (A + f(B, C, D) + X[4] + T[5]) \hookleftarrow 7$
6. $D \leftarrow (D + f(A, B, C) + X[5] + T[6]) \hookleftarrow 12$
7. $C \leftarrow (C + f(D, A, B) + X[6] + T[7]) \hookleftarrow 17$
8. $B \leftarrow (B + f(C, D, A) + X[7] + T[8]) \hookleftarrow 22$
9. $A \leftarrow (A + f(B, C, D) + X[8] + T[9]) \hookleftarrow 7$
10. $D \leftarrow (D + f(A, B, C) + X[9] + T[10]) \hookleftarrow 12$
11. $C \leftarrow (C + f(D, A, B) + X[10] + T[11]) \hookleftarrow 17$
12. $B \leftarrow (B + f(C, D, A) + X[11] + T[12]) \hookleftarrow 22$
13. $A \leftarrow (A + f(B, C, D) + X[12] + T[13]) \hookleftarrow 7$
14. $D \leftarrow (D + f(A, B, C) + X[13] + T[14]) \hookleftarrow 12$
15. $C \leftarrow (C + f(D, A, B) + X[14] + T[15]) \hookleftarrow 17$
16. $B \leftarrow (B + f(C, D, A) + X[15] + T[16]) \hookleftarrow 22$

8.3.2 MD5

As mentioned earlier, MD5 is a strengthened version of MD4. It was proposed in 1991 and is specified in RFC 1321 [7]. There are only a few differences between MD4 and MD5, the most obvious being that MD5 uses four rounds (instead of three). This is advantageous from a security viewpoint. It is, however, also disadvantageous from a performance viewpoint. In fact, the additional round decreases the performance of the hash function about 30% (as compared to MD4).

The MD5 hash function is conceptually and structurally similar to MD4. In fact, the padding of the message m works exactly the same way. Again, there are some auxiliary functions. The selection function f and the function h are defined the same way as for MD4. The majority function g has changed from

$$g(X, Y, Z) = (X \wedge Y) \vee (X \wedge Z) \vee (Y \wedge Z)$$

to

$$g(X, Y, Z) = ((X \wedge Z) \vee (Y \wedge (\neg Z)))$$

to make it less symmetric. In addition, there is a new function i that is defined as follows:

Algorithm 8.7   Round 2 of the MD5 hash function.

1. $A \leftarrow (A + g(B, C, D) + X[1] + T[17]) \hookleftarrow 5$
2. $D \leftarrow (D + g(A, B, C) + X[6] + T[18]) \hookleftarrow 9$
3. $C \leftarrow (C + g(D, A, B) + X[11] + T[19]) \hookleftarrow 14$
4. $B \leftarrow (B + g(C, D, A) + X[0] + T[20]) \hookleftarrow 20$
5. $A \leftarrow (A + g(B, C, D) + X[5] + T[21]) \hookleftarrow 5$
6. $D \leftarrow (D + g(A, B, C) + X[10] + T[22]) \hookleftarrow 9$
7. $C \leftarrow (C + g(D, A, B) + X[15] + T[23]) \hookleftarrow 14$
8. $B \leftarrow (B + g(C, D, A) + X[4] + T[24]) \hookleftarrow 20$
9. $A \leftarrow (A + g(B, C, D) + X[9] + T[25]) \hookleftarrow 5$
10. $D \leftarrow (D + g(A, B, C) + X[14] + T[26]) \hookleftarrow 9$
11. $C \leftarrow (C + g(D, A, B) + X[3] + T[27]) \hookleftarrow 14$
12. $B \leftarrow (B + g(C, D, A) + X[8] + T[28]) \hookleftarrow 20$
13. $A \leftarrow (A + g(B, C, D) + X[13] + T[29]) \hookleftarrow 5$
14. $D \leftarrow (D + g(A, B, C) + X[2] + T[30]) \hookleftarrow 9$
15. $C \leftarrow (C + g(D, A, B) + X[7] + T[31]) \hookleftarrow 14$
16. $B \leftarrow (B + g(C, D, A) + X[12] + T[32]) \hookleftarrow 20$

$$i(X, Y, Z) \;=\; Y \oplus (X \vee (\neg Z))$$

The truth table of the logical functions f, g, h, i is illustrated in Table 8.3. Furthermore, the MD5 hash function uses a 64-element table T constructed from the sine function. Let $T[i]$ be the ith element of the table, then

$$T[i] = \lfloor 4,294,967,296 \cdot |\sin(i)| \rfloor$$

where i is in radians. Because $4,294,967,296$ is equal to 2^{32} and $|\sin(i)|$ is a number between 0 and 1, each element of T is an integer that can be represented in 32 bits. Consequently, the table T provides a "randomized" set of 32-bit patterns, which should eliminate any regularities in the input data. The elements of T as employed by the MD5 hash function are listed in Table 8.4.

The MD5 hash function is overviewed in Algorithm 8.5. It is structurally similar to the MD4 hash function. The four rounds of MD5 are specified in Algorithms 8.6–8.9.

Again, a reference implementation of the MD5 hash function (in the C programming language) is provided in Appendix A of the relevant RFC 1321 [7].

Algorithm 8.8 Round 3 of the MD5 hash function.

1. $A \leftarrow (A + h(B, C, D) + X[5] + T[33]) \hookleftarrow 4$
2. $D \leftarrow (D + h(A, B, C) + X[8] + T[34]) \hookleftarrow 11$
3. $C \leftarrow (C + h(D, A, B) + X[11] + T[35]) \hookleftarrow 16$
4. $B \leftarrow (B + h(C, D, A) + X[14] + T[36]) \hookleftarrow 23$
5. $A \leftarrow (A + h(B, C, D) + X[1] + T[37]) \hookleftarrow 4$
6. $D \leftarrow (D + h(A, B, C) + X[4] + T[38]) \hookleftarrow 11$
7. $C \leftarrow (C + h(D, A, B) + X[7] + T[39]) \hookleftarrow 16$
8. $B \leftarrow (B + h(C, D, A) + X[10] + T[40]) \hookleftarrow 23$
9. $A \leftarrow (A + h(B, C, D) + X[13] + T[41]) \hookleftarrow 4$
10. $D \leftarrow (D + h(A, B, C) + X[0] + T[42]) \hookleftarrow 11$
11. $C \leftarrow (C + h(D, A, B) + X[3] + T[43]) \hookleftarrow 16$
12. $B \leftarrow (B + h(C, D, A) + X[6] + T[44]) \hookleftarrow 23$
13. $A \leftarrow (A + h(B, C, D) + X[9] + T[45]) \hookleftarrow 4$
14. $D \leftarrow (D + h(A, B, C) + X[12] + T[46]) \hookleftarrow 11$
15. $C \leftarrow (C + h(D, A, B) + X[15] + T[47]) \hookleftarrow 16$
16. $B \leftarrow (B + h(C, D, A) + X[2] + T[48]) \hookleftarrow 23$

8.3.3 SHA-1

The SHA-1 hash function is conceptually and structurally similar to MD4 and MD5. The two most important differences are that SHA-1 was designed to run optimally on computer systems with a big-endian architecture (rather than a little-endian architecture) and that it employs five registers (instead of four) and hence outputs hash values of 160 bits.

The SHA-1 hash function uses a sequence of functions $f_0, f_1, \ldots, f_{79}$ that are defined as follows:

$$f_t(X, Y, Z) = \begin{cases} Ch(X, Y, Z) = (X \wedge Y) \oplus ((\neg X) \wedge Z) & 0 \leq t \leq 19 \\ Parity(X, Y, Z) = X \oplus Y \oplus Z & 20 \leq t \leq 39 \\ Maj(X, Y, Z) = (X \wedge Y) \oplus (X \wedge Z) \oplus (Y \wedge Z) & 40 \leq t \leq 59 \\ Parity(X, Y, Z) = X \oplus Y \oplus Z & 60 \leq t \leq 79 \end{cases}$$

The truth table of the logical functions employed by SHA-1 is illustrated in Table 8.5.

Furthermore, the function uses a sequence of 80 constant 32-bit words K_0, $K_1, \ldots, K_{79}$ that are defined as follows:

Algorithm 8.9   Round 4 of the MD5 hash function.

1. $A \leftarrow (A + i(B,C,D) + X[0] + T[49]) \hookleftarrow 6$
2. $D \leftarrow (D + i(A,B,C) + X[7] + T[50]) \hookleftarrow 10$
3. $C \leftarrow (C + i(D,A,B) + X[14] + T[51]) \hookleftarrow 15$
4. $B \leftarrow (B + i(C,D,A) + X[5] + T[52]) \hookleftarrow 21$
5. $A \leftarrow (A + i(B,C,D) + X[12] + T[53]) \hookleftarrow 6$
6. $D \leftarrow (D + i(A,B,C) + X[3] + T[54]) \hookleftarrow 10$
7. $C \leftarrow (C + i(D,A,B) + X[10] + T[55]) \hookleftarrow 15$
8. $B \leftarrow (B + i(C,D,A) + X[1] + T[56]) \hookleftarrow 21$
9. $A \leftarrow (A + i(B,C,D) + X[8] + T[57]) \hookleftarrow 6$
10. $D \leftarrow (D + i(A,B,C) + X[15] + T[58]) \hookleftarrow 10$
11. $C \leftarrow (C + i(D,A,B) + X[6] + T[59]) \hookleftarrow 15$
12. $B \leftarrow (B + i(C,D,A) + X[13] + T[60]) \hookleftarrow 21$
13. $A \leftarrow (A + i(B,C,D) + X[4] + T[61]) \hookleftarrow 6$
14. $D \leftarrow (D + i(A,B,C) + X[11] + T[62]) \hookleftarrow 10$
15. $C \leftarrow (C + i(D,A,B) + X[2] + T[63]) \hookleftarrow 15$
16. $B \leftarrow (B + i(C,D,A) + X[9] + T[64]) \hookleftarrow 21$

Table 8.3
Truth Table of the Logical Functions Employed by MD5

X	Y	Z	f	g	h	i
0	0	0	0	0	0	1
0	0	1	1	0	1	0
0	1	0	0	1	1	0
0	1	1	1	0	0	1
1	0	0	0	0	1	1
1	0	1	0	1	0	1
1	1	0	1	1	0	0
1	1	1	1	1	1	0

$$
K_t = \begin{cases}
\lfloor 2^{30}\sqrt{2} \rfloor = \text{0x5A827999} & 0 \le t \le 19 \\
\lfloor 2^{30}\sqrt{3} \rfloor = \text{0x6ED9EBA1} & 20 \le t \le 39 \\
\lfloor 2^{30}\sqrt{5} \rfloor = \text{0x8F1BBCDC} & 40 \le t \le 59 \\
\lfloor 2^{30}\sqrt{10} \rfloor = \text{0xCA62C1D6} & 60 \le t \le 79
\end{cases}
$$

Note that the first two values correspond to c_1 and c_2 employed by MD4.

The preprocessing of the message to be hashed is identical to the one employed by MD4 and MD5. Because the SHA-1 hash function was designed to run on a big-endian architecture, the final two 32-bit words specifying the bit length s is appended with the most significant word preceding the least significant word.

Table 8.4
The Elements of Table T Employed by the MD5 Hash Function

$T[1]$=0xD76AA478	$T[17]$=0xF61E2562	$T[33]$=0xFFFA3942	$T[49]$=0xF4292244
$T[2]$=0xE8C7B756	$T[18]$=0xC040B340	$T[34]$=0x8771F681	$T[50]$=0x432AFF97
$T[3]$=0x242070DB	$T[19]$=0x265E5A51	$T[35]$=0x6D9D6122	$T[51]$=0xAB9423A7
$T[4]$=0xC1BDCEEE	$T[20]$=0xE9B6C7AA	$T[36]$=0xFDE5380C	$T[52]$=0xFC93A039
$T[5]$=0xF57C0FAF	$T[21]$=0xD62F105D	$T[37]$=0xA4BEEA44	$T[53]$=0x655B59C3
$T[6]$=0x4787C62A	$T[22]$=0x02441453	$T[38]$=0x4BDECFA9	$T[54]$=0x8F0CCC92
$T[7]$=0xA8304613	$T[23]$=0xD8A1E681	$T[39]$=0xF6BB4B60	$T[55]$=0xFFEFF47D
$T[8]$=0xFD469501	$T[24]$=0xE7D3FBC8	$T[40]$=0xBEBFBC70	$T[56]$=0x85845DD1
$T[9]$=0x698098D8	$T[25]$=0x21E1CDE6	$T[41]$=0x289B7EC6	$T[57]$=0x6FA87E4F
$T[10]$=0x8B44F7AF	$T[26]$=0xC33707D6	$T[42]$=0xEAA127FA	$T[58]$=0xFE2CE6E0
$T[11]$=0xFFFF5BB1	$T[27]$=0xF4D50D87	$T[43]$=0xD4EF3085	$T[59]$=0xA3014314
$T[12]$=0x895CD7BE	$T[28]$=0x455A14ED	$T[44]$=0x04881D05	$T[60]$=0x4E0811A1
$T[13]$=0x6B901122	$T[29]$=0xA9E3E905	$T[45]$=0xD9D4D039	$T[61]$=0xF7537E82
$T[14]$=0xFD987193	$T[30]$=0xFCEFA3F8	$T[46]$=0xE6DB99E5	$T[62]$=0xBD3AF235
$T[15]$=0xA679438E	$T[31]$=0x676F02D9	$T[47]$=0x1FA27CF8	$T[63]$=0x2AD7D2BB
$T[16]$=0x49B40821	$T[32]$=0x8D2A4C8A	$T[48]$=0xC4AC5665	$T[64]$=0xEB86D391

In addition to f_t and K_t, there is a message schedule W that comprises eighty 32-bit words. The schedule is initialized as follows:

$$W_t = \begin{cases} M[t] & 0 \le t \le 15 \\ (W_{t-3} \oplus W_{t-8} \oplus W_{t-14} \oplus W_{t-16}) \hookleftarrow 1 & 16 \le t \le 79 \end{cases}$$

After preprocessing is completed, the message is hashed iteratively using Algorithm 8.10. First, the five registers are initialized (the first four registers are indentically initialized as in the case of MD4, and the fifth register is initialized with 0xC3D2E1F0). Afterwards, each message block $M[1]$, $M[1]$, ..., $M[N]$ is processed iteratively, where the result of each iteration is used in the next iteration. Finally, the result is the concatenation of the values of the five registers. It is a 160-bit hash value that may serve as message digest for message m.

From a security viewpoint, there are two remarks to make at this point:

- First, a SHA-1 hash value is 32 bits longer than an MD5 hash value. This is advantageous, because it means that SHA-1 is potentially more resistant against brute-force attacks. This is even more true for the SHA variants itemized in Table 8.1.

Table 8.5
Truth Table of the Logical Functions Employed by SHA-1

X	Y	Z	$Ch = f_{0...19}$	$Parity = f_{20...39}$	$Maj = f_{40...59}$	$Parity = f_{60...79}$
0	0	0	0	0	0	0
0	0	1	1	1	0	1
0	1	0	0	1	0	1
0	1	1	1	0	1	0
1	0	0	0	1	0	1
1	0	1	0	0	1	0
1	1	0	1	0	1	0
1	1	1	1	1	1	1

- Second, SHA-1 appears not to be vulnerable to the attacks against MD4 and MD5. However, little is publicly known about the design criteria for SHA-1, so its strength is somehow difficult to evaluate.

On the other hand, SHA-1 involves more steps (80 as compared to 64) and must process a 160-bit register compared to the 128-bit register of MD4 and MD5. Consequently, SHA-1 executes a little bit more slowly.

8.4 FINAL REMARKS

In this chapter, we elaborated on cryptographic hash functions. Most of these functions that are practically relevant (e.g., MD5 and SHA-1) follow the Merkle-Damgård construction. This also applies to some more recent alternatives, such as Whirlpool.[17] The fact that cryptographic hash function follows the Merkle-Damgård construction basically means that a collision resistant compression function is iterated multiple times (one iteration for each block of the message). Each iteration can only start if the preceding iteration has finished. This suggests that the resulting cryptographic hash function may become a performance bottleneck. For example, Joe Touch showed that the currently achievable hash rates of MD5 are insufficient to keep up with high-speed networks [17]. The problem is the iterative nature of MD5 and its block chaining structure, which prevent parallelism. As also shown in [17], it is possible to modify the MD5 algorithm to accommodate a slightly higher throughput. Alternatively, it is possible to design and come up with cryptographic hash functions that are inherently more qualified to provide support for parallelism.

Although most cryptographic hash functions in use today follow the Merkle-Damgård construction, the design of the underlying compression functions still

17 http://planeta.terra.com.br/informatica/paulobarreto/WhirlpoolPage.html

Algorithm 8.10 The SHA-1 hash function (overview).

$$\frac{(m = m_0 m_1 \dots m_{s-1})}{}$$

Construct $M = M[0] M[1] \dots M[N-1]$
$A \leftarrow \text{0x67452301}$
$B \leftarrow \text{0xEFCDAB89}$
$C \leftarrow \text{0x98BADCFE}$
$D \leftarrow \text{0x10325476}$
$E \leftarrow \text{0xC3D2E1F0}$
for $i = 0$ to N do
    Prepare the message schedule W
    $A' \leftarrow A$
    $B' \leftarrow B$
    $C' \leftarrow C$
    $D' \leftarrow D$
    $E' \leftarrow E$
    for $t = 0$ to 79 do
        $T \leftarrow (A \hookleftarrow 5) + f_t(B, C, D) + E + K_t + W_t$
        $E \leftarrow D$
        $D \leftarrow C$
        $C \leftarrow B \hookleftarrow 30$
        $B \leftarrow A$
        $A \leftarrow T$
    $A \leftarrow A + A'$
    $B \leftarrow B + B'$
    $C \leftarrow C + C'$
    $D \leftarrow D + D'$
    $E \leftarrow E + E'$

$(h(m) = A \parallel B \parallel C \parallel D \parallel E)$

looks more like an art than a science. For example, finding collisions in such functions has recently become a very active area of research (e.g., [18]). Remember from Section 8.3 that collisions were recently found for MD4, MD5, and some other cryptographic hash functions. Also, as this book went to press, a group of Chinese researchers claimed to have found an attack that requires only 2^{69} (instead of 2^{80}) hash operations to find a collision in SHA-1.[18]

As of this writing, there are hardly any design criteria that can be used to design and come up with new compression functions (for cryptographic hash functions that follow the Merkle-Damgård construction) or entirely new cryptographic hash functions. This lack of design criteria is somehow in contrast to the relative importance of cryptographic hash functions in almost all cryptographic systems and applications. Consequently, an interesting and challenging area of research and

18 http://theory.csail.mit.edu/~yiqun/shanote.pdf.

development would try to specify design criteria for compression functions (if the Merkle-Damgård construction is used) or entirely new cryptographic hash functions (if the Merkle-Damgård construction is not used). For example, *universal hashing* as originally proposed in the late 1970s by Larry Carter and Mark Wegman [19, 20] provides an interesting design paradigm for new cryptographic hash functions. Instead of using a single hash function, universal hashing considers families of hash functions. The hash function in use is then chosen randomly from the family. We briefly revisit the topic when we address MACs using families of universal hash functions in Section 11.2.4.

References

[1] Merkle, R.C., "One Way Hash Functions and DES," *Proceedings of CRYPTO '89*, Springer-Verlag, LNCS 435, 1989, pp. 428–446.

[2] Damgård, I.B., "A Design Principle for Hash Functions," *Proceedings of CRYPTO '89*, Springer-Verlag, LNCS 435, 1989, pp. 416–427.

[3] Kaliski, B., *The MD2 Message-Digest Algorithm*, Request for Comments 1319, April 1992.

[4] Rivest, R.L., *The MD4 Message-Digest Algorithm*, Request for Comments 1320, April 1992.

[5] Biham, E., and A. Shamir, "Differential Cryptanalysis of Snefru, Khafre, REDOC-II, LOKI, and Lucifer," *Proceedings of CRYPTO '91*, Springer-Verlag, LNCS 576, 1991, pp. 156–171.

[6] den Boer, B., and A. Bosselaers, "An Attack on the Last Two Rounds of MD4," *Proceedings of CRYPTO '91*, Springer-Verlag, LNCS 576, 1991, pp. 194–203.

[7] Rivest, R.L., *The MD5 Message-Digest Algorithm*, Request for Comments 1321, April 1992.

[8] Dobbertin, H., "Cryptanalysis of MD4," *Journal of Cryptology*, Vol. 11, No. 4, 1998, pp. 253–271.

[9] Dobbertin, H., "The Status of MD5 After a Recent Attack," *CryptoBytes*, Vol. 2, No. 2, Summer 1996.

[10] den Boer, B., and A. Bosselaers, "Collisions for the Compression Function of MD5," *Proceedings of EUROCRYPT '93*, Springer-Verlag, LNCS 765, 1993, pp. 293–304.

[11] Chabaud, F., and A. Joux, "Differential Collisions in SHA-0," *Proceedings of CRYPTO '98*, Springer-Verlag, LNCS 1462, 1998, pp. 56–71.

[12] U.S. Department of Commerce, National Institute of Standards and Technology, *Secure Hash Standard*, FIPS PUB 180-1, April 1995.

[13] Eastlake, D., and P. Jones, *US Secure Hash Algorithm 1 (SHA1)*, Request for Comments 3174, September 2001.

[14] Housley, R., *A 224-Bit One-Way Hash Function: SHA-224*, Request for Comments 3874, September 2004.

[15] Dobbertin, H., A. Bosselaers, and B. Preneel, "RIPEMD-160: A Strengthened Version of RIPEMD," *Proceedings of the 3rd International Workshop on Fast Software Encryption*, Springer-Verlag, LNCS 1039, 1996, pp. 71–82.

[16] Preneel, B., A. Bosselaers, and H. Dobbertin, "The Cryptographic Hash Function RIPEMD-160," *CryptoBytes*, Vol. 3, No. 2, 1997, pp. 9–14.

[17] Touch, J., *Report on MD5 Performance*, Request for Comments 1810, June 1995.

[18] Biham, E., and R. Chen, "Near-Collisions of SHA-0," *Proceedings of CRYPTO 2004*, Springer-Verlag, LNCS 3152, 2004.

[19] Carter, J.L., and M.N. Wegman, "Universal Classes of Hash Functions," *Journal of Computer and System Sciences*, Vol. 18, 1979, pp. 143–154.

[20] Carter, J.L., and M.N. Wegman, "New Hash Functions and Their Use in Authentication and Set Equality," *Journal of Computer and System Sciences*, Vol. 22, 1981, pp. 265–279.

Chapter 9

Random Bit Generators

Random numbers should not be generated with a method chosen at random.

— Donald E. Knuth

In this chapter, we elaborate on random bit generators. More specifically, we introduce the topic in Section 9.1, overview and discuss some possible realizations and implementations of random bit generators in Section 9.2, address statistical randomness testing in Section 9.3, and conclude with final remarks in Section 9.4.

9.1 INTRODUCTION

The term randomness is commonly used to refer to nondeterminism. If we say that something is random, then we mean that we cannot determine its outcome, or—equivalently—that its outcome is nondeterministic. Whether randomness really exists or not is primarily a philosophical question. Somebody who believed that everything is determined or behaves in a deterministic way would typically argue that randomness does not exist in the first place. According to the present knowledge in physics, however, randomness exists inherently in physical processes. For example, randomness is a prerequisite and plays a crucial role in quantum physics. For the purpose of this book, we don't address the philosophical question and simply assume that randomness exists.

If we assume the existence of randomness, then we may ask whether it is possible to measure it in one way or another. For example, we may ask for a given value whether it is random. Is 13 random? Is 27 random? Is 13 more random than 27?

219

Unfortunately, these questions don't make a lot of sense unless they are considered in a specific context.

In theory, there exists a measure of randomness for a finite sequence of values. In fact, the *Kolmogorov complexity* measures the minimal length of a program for a Turing machine[1] that is able to generate the sequence. Unfortunately, the Kolmogorov complexity is inherently noncomputable (i.e., it is not known how to compute the Kolmogorov complexity for a given sequence of values), and hence it is not particularly useful. If we know that a (pseudorandom) bit sequence was generated with a *linear feedback shift register* (LFSR), then we could use the *linear complexity* to measure its randomness. In fact, the linear complexity measures the size (i.e., number of bits) of the shortest LFSR that can produce the sequence. The measure therefore speaks to the difficulty of generating—and perhaps analyzing— the bit sequence. There is an algorithm due to Berlekamp and Massey [1] that can be used to compute the linear complexity. Note, however, that the linear complexity (and hence also the Berlekamp-Massey algorithm) assumes that the (pseudorandom) bit sequence is generated with an LFSR. Consequently, it is possible that a bit sequence has a large linear complexity but can still be generated easily with some other means.

Without arguing about the existence of randomness and without trying to measure the randomness of a given sequence of values (e.g., bits or numbers), we elaborate on the question of how random bits can be generated in the rest of this chapter. According to Definition 2.5, a random bit generator is a device or algorithm that outputs a sequence of statistically independent and unbiased bits. This basically means that the bits occur with the same probability (i.e., $\Pr[0] = \Pr[1] = 1/2$), and that all 2^k possible k-tuples occur approximately equally often (i.e., with probability $1/2^k$ for all $k \in \mathbb{N}$).

If we can generate random bits, then we can also generate (uniformly distributed) random numbers of any size. If, for example, we want to construct an n-bit random number a, then we set $b_1 = 1$, use the random bit generator to generate $n - 1$ random bits $b_2, \ldots, b_n$, and set

$$a = \sum_{i=1}^{n} b_i 2^{n-i}. \tag{9.1}$$

Similarly, if we want to construct a number that is randomly selected from the interval $[0, m]$ for $m \in \mathbb{N}$, then we set n to the length of m (i.e., $n = \lfloor \log m \rfloor + 1$) and use the random bit generator to generate n random bits $b_1, \ldots, b_n$. If a constructed according to (9.1) is smaller or equal to m, then we use it. If, however, a is bigger

1   Refer to Section 6.5 for an introduction to Turing machines.

than m, then we don't use it and generate another number instead. Consequently, in what follows we only elaborate on the generation of random bits, and we consider the construction of random numbers from random bits to be simple and straightforward.

According to the leading quote of this chapter, random numbers (and random bits) should not be generated with a method chosen at random, and hence the question of how to actually generate random bits arises immediately. This question is addressed next.

9.2 REALIZATIONS AND IMPLEMENTATIONS

In informational RFC 1750 [2], it is recommended that special hardware is used to generate truly random bits. There are, however, also some situations in which special hardware is not available, and software must be used to generate random bits instead. Consequently, there is room for both hardware-based and software-based random bit generators. Some general ideas about how to realize and implement such generators are overviewed next. Afterwards, the notion of deskewing techniques is introduced and very briefly explained.

9.2.1 Hardware-Based Random Bit Generators

Hardware-based random bit generators exploit the randomness that occurs in physical processes and phenomena. According to [3], examples of such processes and phenomena include:

- The elapsed time between emission of particles during radioactive decay;

- The thermal noise from a semiconductor diode or resistor;

- The frequency instability of a free-running oscillator (e.g., [4]);

- The amount a metal insulator semiconductor capacitor is charged during a fixed period of time (e.g., [5]);

- The air turbulence within a sealed disk drive that causes random fluctuations in disk drive sector read latency times (e.g., [6, 7]);

- The sound from a microphone or video input from a camera.

It goes without saying that other physical processes and phenomena may be employed by hardware-based random bit generators.

Hardware-based random bit generators could be easily integrated into contemporary computer systems. This is not yet the case, and hardware-based random bit generators are neither readily available nor widely deployed. There are, however, some existing hardware devices that may be used to serve as sources of randomness. The last two examples itemized earlier illustrate this possibility.

9.2.2 Software-Based Random Bit Generators

First of all, it is important to note that designing a random bit generator in software is even more difficult than doing so in hardware. According to [3], processes upon which software-based random bit generators may be based include:

- The system clock (e.g., [8]);

- The elapsed time between keystrokes or mouse movements;

- The content of input/output buffers;

- The input provided by the user;

- The values of operating system variables, such as system load or network statistics.

Again, this list is not exclusive, and many other processes may also be used by software-based random bit generators.

In either case, the behavior of the processes may vary considerably depending on various factors, such as the computer platform, the operating system, and the actual software release in use. It may also be difficult to prevent an adversary from observing or manipulating these processes. For example, if an adversary has a rough idea of when a random bit sequence was generated, he or she can guess the content of the system clock at that time with a high degree of accuracy. Consequently, care must be taken when the system clock and the identification numbers of running processes are used to generate random bit sequences. This type of problem first gained publicity in 1995, when it was found that the encryption in Netscape browsers could be broken in around a minute due to the limited range of values provided by such a random bit generator. Because the values used to generate session keys could be established without too much difficulty, even U.S. domestic browsers with 128-bit session keys carried only 47 bits of entropy in their session keys at most [9]. Shortly afterwards, it was found that the Massachusetts Institute of Technology (MIT) implementations of Kerberos version 4 (e.g., [10]) and the magic cookie key generation mechanism of the X windows system suffered from similar weaknesses.

Sometimes, it is possible to use external (i.e., external to the computer system that needs the randomness) sources of randomness. For example, a potential source of randomness is the unpredictable behavior of the stock market. This source, however, has some disadvantages of its own. For example, it is sometimes predictable (e.g., during a crash), it can be manipulated (e.g., by spreading rumors or by placing a large stock transaction), and it is never secret.

In [2], it is argued that the best overall strategy for meeting the requirement for unguessable random bits in the absence of a single reliable source is to obtain random input from a large number of uncorrelated sources and to mix them with a strong mixing function. A strong mixing function, in turn, is one that combines two or more inputs and produces an output where each output bit is a different complex nonlinear function of all input bits. On average, changing an input bit will change about half of the output bits. But because the relationship is complex and nonlinear, no particular output bit is guaranteed to change when any particular input bit is changed. A trivial example for such a function is addition modulo 2^{32}. More general strong mixing functions (for more than two inputs) can be constructed using other cryptographic systems, such as cryptographic hash functions or symmetric encryption systems.

9.2.3 Deskewing Techniques

Any source of random bits may be defective in that the output bits may be biased (i.e., the probability of the source emitting a one is not equal to $1/2$) or correlated (i.e., the probability of the source emitting a one depends on previously emitted bits). There are many *deskewing techniques* for generating truly random bit sequences from the output bits of such a defective random bit generator. For example, if a random bit generator outputs biased but uncorrelated bits, then one can group the output sequence into pairs of bits, with a 10 pair transformed to a 1, a 01 pair transformed to a 0, and 00 and 11 pairs discarded. The resulting binary sequence is both unbiased and uncorrelated. This simple technique is due to John von Neumann [11]. It was later generalized to achieve an output rate near the source entropy [12]. Handling a correlated bit source is more involved. Manuel Blum showed how to produce unbiased uncorrelated bits from a biased correlated source [13].[2] These results were later generalized in many respects.

9.3 STATISTICAL RANDOMNESS TESTING

While it is impossible to give a mathematical proof that a generator is indeed a random bit generator, statistical randomness tests may help detect certain kinds of weaknesses in the generator. This is accomplished by taking a sample output sequence of the random bit generator and subjecting it to various (statistical randomness) tests.

---

2   Note, however, that this does not imply that the resulting bits have good randomness properties; it only means that they are unbiased and uncorrelated.

Each test determines whether the sequence possesses a certain attribute that a truly random sequence would be likely to exhibit. An example of such an attribute is that the sequence has roughly the same number of zeros as ones. The conclusion of each test is not definite, but rather probabilistic. If the sequence is deemed to have failed any one of the statistical tests, then the generator may be rejected as being non-random. Otherwise, the generator may be subjected to further testing. On the other hand, if the sequence passes all statistical randomness tests, then the generator is accepted as being random.[3]

Many statistical randomness tests are described in the literature, and we are not going to delve into this topic for the purpose of this book. Nevertheless, we want to note that Ueli Maurer proposed a *universal statistical test* that can be used instead of many statistical randomness tests [14]. The basic idea behind Maurer's universal statistical test is that it should not be possible to significantly compress (without loss of information) the output sequence of a random bit generator. Alternatively speaking, if a sample output sequence of a bit generator can be significantly compressed, then the generator should be rejected as being defective. Instead of actually compressing the sequence, Maurer's universal statistical test can be used to compute a quantity that is related to the length of the compressed sequence. The universality of Maurer's universal statistical test arises because it is able to detect any one of a very general class of possible defects a bit generator may have. A drawback is that it requires a much longer sample output sequence in order to be effective. Provided that the required output sequence can be generated efficiently, however, this drawback is not particularly worrisome.

9.4   FINAL REMARKS

Random bit generators are at the core of most systems that employ cryptographic techniques in one way or another. If, for example, a secret key cryptosystem is used, then a random bit generator should be used to generate and establish a shared secret between the communicating peer entities. If a public key cryptosystem is used, then a random bit generator should be used to generate a public key pair. Furthermore, if the cryptosystem is probabilistic, then a random bit generator should be used for each and every encryption or digital signature generation.

In this chapter, we elaborated on random bit generators and overviewed and discussed some possible realizations and implementations thereof. There are

---

3   More precisely, the term *accepted* should be replaced by *not rejected*, because passing the tests merely provides probabilistic evidence that the generator produces sequences that have specific properties of random sequences.

hardware-based and software-based random bit generators. In either case, deskewing techniques may be used to improve the defectiveness of a specific random bit generator, and statistical randomness testing (e.g., Maurer's universal statistical test) may be used to evaluate the quality of its output. In practice, it is often required that a random bit generator conforms to a security level specified in FIPS PUB 140-2 [15].[4]

From an application viewpoint, it is important to be able to generate some truly random bits (using a random bit generator) and use them to seed a PRBG as introduced in Section 2.2.3. The PRBG is then used to generate a potentially infinite sequence of pseudorandom bits. It depends on a secret key (i.e., a seed), and hence it represents a secret key cryptosystem. PRBGs are further addressed in Chapter 12.

References

[1] Massey, J., "Shift-Register Synthesis and BCH Decoding," *IEEE Transactions on Information Theory*, IT-15(1), 1969, pp. 122–127.

[2] Eastlake, D., S. Crocker, and J. Schiller, "Randomness Recommendations for Security," Request for Comments 1750, December 1994.

[3] Menezes, A., P. van Oorschot, and S. Vanstone, *Handbook of Applied Cryptography*. CRC Press, Boca Raton, FL, 1996.

[4] Fairfield, R.C., R.L. Mortenson, and K.B. Koulhart, "An LSI Random Number Generator (RNG)," *Proceedings of CRYPTO '84*, 1984, pp. 203–230.

[5] Agnew, G.B., "Random Sources for Cryptographic Systems," *Proceedings of EUROCRYPT '87*, Springer-Verlag, LNCS 304, 1988, pp. 77–81.

[6] Davis, D., R. Ihaka, and P. Fenstermacher, "Cryptographic Randomness from Air Turbulance in Disk Drives," *Proceedings of CRYPTO '94*, Springer-Verlag, LNCS 839, 1994, pp. 114–120.

[7] Jakobsson, M., et al., "A Practical Secure Physical Random Bit Generator," *Proceedings of the ACM Conference on Computer and Communications Security*, 1998, pp. 103–111.

[8] Lacy, J.B., D.P. Mitchell, and W.M. Schell, "CryptoLib: Cryptography in Software," *Proceedings of the USENIX Security Symposium IV*, USENIX Association, October 1993, pp. 1–17.

[9] Goldberg, I., and D. Wagner, "Randomness and the Netscape Browser—How Secure Is the World Wide Web?" *Dr. Dobb's Journal*, January 1996.

[10] Dole, B., S. Lodin, and E.H. Spafford, "Misplaced Trust: Kerberos 4 Session Keys," *Proceedings of the ISOC Network and Distributed System Security Symposium*, 1997, pp. 60–70.

[11] von Neumann, J., "Various Techniques for Use in Connection with Random Digits," In *von Neumann's Collected Works*, Vol. 5, Pergamon Press, New York, NY, 1963, pp. 768–770.

4   http://csrc.nist.gov/publications/fips/fips140-2/fips1402.pdf.

[12] Elias, P., "The Efficient Construction of an Unbiased Random Sequence," *Annals of Mathematical Statistics*, Vol. 43, No. 3, 1972, pp. 865–870.

[13] Blum, M., "Independent Unbiased Coin Flips from a Correlated Biased Source: A Finite State Markov Chain," *Proceedings of the 25th IEEE Symposium on Foundations of Computer Science*, IEEE, 1984, Singer Island, FL, pp. 425–433.

[14] Maurer, U.M., "A Universal Statistical Test for Random Bit Generators," *Journal of Cryptology*, Vol. 5, 1992, pp. 89–105.

[15] U.S. Department of Commerce, National Institute of Standards and Technology, *Security Requirements for Cryptographic Modules*, FIPS PUB 140-2, May 2001.

Part III

SECRET KEY CRYPTOSYSTEMS

Chapter 10

Symmetric Encryption Systems

In this chapter, we elaborate on symmetric encryption systems. More specifically, we introduce the topic in Section 10.1, address block ciphers, stream ciphers, and perfectly (i.e., information-theoretically) secure encryption systems in Sections 10.2–10.4, and conclude with some final remarks in Section 10.5. Note that symmetric encryption systems are the most widely deployed cryptographic systems in use today and that many books on cryptography elaborate only on these systems. Consequently, this chapter is important and rather long.

10.1 INTRODUCTION

According to Definition 2.6, a *symmetric encryption system* (or *cipher*) consists of the following five components:

- A plaintext message space $\mathcal{M}$;
- A ciphertext space $\mathcal{C}$;
- A key space $\mathcal{K}$;
- A family $E = \{E_k : k \in \mathcal{K}\}$ of encryption functions $E_k : \mathcal{M} \longrightarrow \mathcal{C}$;
- A family $D = \{D_k : K \in \mathcal{K}\}$ of decryption functions $D_k : \mathcal{C} \longrightarrow \mathcal{M}$.

In every practically relevant symmetric encryption system

$$D_k(E_k(m)) = m$$

229

must hold for every plaintext message $m \in \mathcal{M}$ and every key $k \in \mathcal{K}$ (otherwise, a ciphertext may not be decryptable, and hence the symmetric encryption system may not be useful in the first place).[1] In addition to this definition, a symmetric encryption system may be randomized in the sense that the encryption function takes additional random input. In fact, it turns out that randomized symmetric encryption systems are advantageous from a security viewpoint (as discussed later in this chapter).

10.1.1 Examples

Many symmetric encryption systems use specific alphabets and corresponding plaintext message, ciphertext, and key spaces. If, for example, the alphabet is $\Sigma = \{A, \ldots, Z\}$, then the spaces consist of all words that can be constructed with the capital letters from A to Z. These letters can be associated with the 26 elements of $\mathbb{Z}_{26} = \{0, 1, \ldots, 25\}$. In fact, there is a bijective map from $\{A, \ldots, Z\}$ into $\mathbb{Z}_{26}$, and hence we can work either with $\Sigma = \{A, \ldots, Z\}$ or $\mathbb{Z}_{26} = \{0, \ldots, 25\}$.

Let $\Sigma \cong \mathbb{Z}_{26} = \{0, \ldots, 25\}$ and $\mathcal{M} = \mathcal{C} = \mathcal{K} = \mathbb{Z}_{26}$. The encryption function of an *additive cipher* is defined as follows:

$$E_k \ : \ \mathcal{M} \longrightarrow \mathcal{C}$$
$$m \longmapsto m + k \ (\mathrm{mod}\ 26) = c$$

Similarly, the decryption function is defined as follows:

$$D_k \ : \ \mathcal{C} \longrightarrow \mathcal{M}$$
$$c \longmapsto c - k \ (\mathrm{mod}\ 26) = m$$

In the additive cipher, the decryption key is the additive inverse of the encryption key. Consequently, it is simple for anybody knowing the encryption key to determine the decryption key (that's why the encryption system is called symmetric in the first place). In Section 1.3, we briefly mentioned the Caesar cipher. This is an example of an additive cipher with a fixed key $k = 3$.

Similar to the additive cipher, one can define a *multiplicative cipher* or combine an additive and a multiplicative cipher in an *affine cipher*.[2] In the second case,

---

1   This condition is specific for symmetric encryption systems. In asymmetric encryption systems, the keys that select an encryption function and a decryption function from the corresponding families are not equal and may not be efficiently computable from one another. This point is further addressed in Chapter 14.

2   The multiplicative cipher works similar to the additive cipher. It uses multiplication instead of addition. Also, to make sure that one can decrypt all the time, one must work with $\{1, 2, \ldots, 26\}$ instead of $\{0, 1, \ldots, 25\}$.

the key space $\mathcal{K}$ consists of all pairs $(a, b) \in \mathbb{Z}_{26}^2$ with $gcd(a, 26) = 1$. As such, the key space has $\phi(26) \cdot 26 = 312$ elements and is far too small for practical use. It can, however, be used for demonstrational purposes. In fact, the encryption function of an affine cipher is defined as follows:

$$E_{(a,b)} \quad : \quad \mathcal{M} \longrightarrow \mathcal{C}$$
$$m \longmapsto am + b \,(\text{mod } 26) = c$$

Similarly, the decryption function is defined as follows:

$$D_{(a,b)} \quad : \quad \mathcal{C} \longrightarrow \mathcal{M}$$
$$c \longmapsto a^{-1}(c - b) \,(\text{mod } 26) = m$$

Obviously, the multiplicative inverse of a (i.e., a^{-1}) in $\mathbb{Z}_{26}$ is needed to decrypt c. Remember from Chapter 3 that the extended Euclid algorithm (i.e., Algorithm 3.2) can be used to efficiently compute this element.

An affine cipher can be broken with two known plaintext-ciphertext pairs. If, for example, the adversary knows $(F, Q) = (5, 16)$ and $(T, G) = (19, 6)$,[3] then he or she can set up the following system of two equivalences:

$$a5 + b \quad \equiv \quad 16 \,(\text{mod } 26)$$
$$a19 + b \quad \equiv \quad 6 \,(\text{mod } 26)$$

The first equivalence can be rewritten as $b \equiv 16 - 5a \,(\text{mod } 26)$ and used in the second equivalence: $19a + b \equiv 19a + 16 - 5a \equiv 14a + 16 \equiv 6 \,(\text{mod } 26)$. Consequently, $14a \equiv -10 \equiv 16 \,(\text{mod } 26)$, or $7a \equiv 8 \,(\text{mod } 13)$, respectively. By multiplying either side with the multiplicative inverse element of 7 modulo 26 (which is 2), one gets $a \equiv 16 \equiv 3 \,(\text{mod } 13)$, and hence $a = 3$ and $b = 1$. The adversary can now efficiently compute $D_{(a,b)}$ similar to the legitimate recipient of the encrypted message.

$\Sigma = \{A, \ldots, Z\} \cong \mathbb{Z}_{26}$ is a good choice for human beings. If, however, computer systems are used for encryption and decryption, then it is advantageous and more appropriate to use $\Sigma = \mathbb{Z}_2 = \{0, 1\} \cong \mathbb{F}_2$ and to set the plaintext message,

---

3   This means that the letter "F" is mapped to the letter "Q" and the letter "T" is mapped to the letter "G."

ciphertext, and key spaces to $\{0, 1\}^*$. More often than not, the key space is set to $\{0, 1\}^l$ (instead of $\{0, 1\}^*$) for a reasonably sized key length l.

Additive, multiplicative, and affine ciphers are the the simplest examples of *monoalphabetic substitution ciphers*. In a monoalphabetic substitution cipher, each letter of the plaintext alphabet is replaced by another letter of the ciphertext alphabet. The replacement is fixed, meaning that a plaintext letter is always replaced by the same ciphertext letter. Consequently, monoalphabetic substitution ciphers can easily be attacked using frequency analysis. An early attempt to increase the difficulty of frequency analysis attacks on substitution ciphers was to disguise plaintext letter frequencies by homophony. In a *homophonic substitution cipher*, plaintext letters can be replaced by more than one ciphertext letter. Usually, the highest frequency plaintext letters are given more equivalents than lower frequency letters. In this way, the frequency distribution is flattened, making analysis more difficult. Alternatively, *polyalphabetic substitution ciphers* flatten the frequency distribution of ciphertext letters by using multiple ciphertext alphabets. All of these substitution ciphers are overviewed and discussed in the literature. Most of them, including, for example, the *Vigenère cipher*,[4] are quite easy to break. You may refer to any book about (classical) cryptography if you want to get into these historically relevant ciphers and the cryptanalysis thereof (some books are mentioned in the Preface and Chapter 1). For the purpose of this book, we don't look into these ciphers. Instead, we focus on ciphers that are considered to be secure and hence are practically relevant. We begin with a classification of such symmetric encryption systems.

10.1.2 Classes of Symmetric Encryption Systems

Every practically relevant symmetric encryption system processes plaintext messages unit by unit. A unit, in turn, may be either a bit or a block of bits (e.g., one or several bytes). Furthermore, the symmetric encryption system may be implemented as an FSM, meaning that the ith ciphertext unit depends on the ith plaintext unit, the secret key, and some internal state. Depending on the existence and use of internal state, block ciphers and stream ciphers are usually distinguished.

Block ciphers: In a *block cipher*, the encrypting and decrypting devices have no internal state (i.e., the ith ciphertext unit only depends on the ith plaintext unit and the secret key). There is no memory involved, except for the internal memory that is used by the implementation of the cipher. Block ciphers are further addressed in Section 10.2.

---

4   The Vigenère cipher is a polyalphabetic substitution cipher that was published in 1585 (and considered unbreakable until 1863) and was widely deployed in previous centuries.

Stream ciphers: In a *stream cipher*, the encrypting and decrypting devices have internal state (i.e., the ith ciphertext unit depends on the ith plaintext unit, the secret key, and the internal state). Consequently, stream ciphers represent theoretically more advanced and more powerful symmetric encryption systems than block ciphers (in practice, things are more involved and the question of whether block ciphers or stream ciphers are more advanced is discussed controversially). There are two major classes of stream ciphers that differ in their state transition function (i.e., in the way they manipulate the internal state and compute the next state). In a *synchronous* stream cipher, the next state does not depend on the previously generated ciphertext units, whereas in a *nonsynchronous* stream cipher, the next state also depends on some (or all) of the previously generated ciphertext units. Synchronous stream ciphers are also called *additive stream ciphers*, and nonsynchronous stream ciphers are also called *self-synchronizing stream ciphers*. In this book, we use these terms synonymously and interchangeably. Stream ciphers are further addressed in Section 10.3.

The distinction between block ciphers and stream ciphers is less precise than one might expect. In fact, there are modes of operation that turn a block cipher into a stream cipher (be it synchronous or nonsynchronous). Some of these modes are overviewed and briefly discussed in Section 10.2.3.

10.1.3 Secure Symmetric Encryption Systems

In Section 1.2.2, we said that we must formally define the term *security* before we can make precise statements about the security of a cryptographic system, such as a symmetric encryption system. More specifically, we must specify and nail down the adversary's capabilities and the task he or she is required to solve in order to be successful (i.e., to break the security of the system). This brings us to the following list of attacks that are usually distinguished in the literature.

Ciphertext-only attacks: In a *ciphertext-only attack*, the adversary knows one or several ciphertext units and tries to determine the corresponding plaintext message units or the key(s) that has (have) been used for encryption. In the second case, the adversary is able to decrypt any ciphertext unit that is encrypted with the key(s). An encryption system that is (known to be) vulnerable to a ciphertext-only attack is totally insecure and should not be used.

Known-plaintext attacks: In a *known-plaintext attack*, the adversary knows one or several ciphertext and plaintext pairs, and tries either to determine the key(s) that has (have) been used for encryption or to decrypt a ciphertext for which he or she does not yet know the corresponding plaintext.

Chosen-plaintext attacks: In a *chosen-plaintext attack*, the adversary has access to the encryption function (or the device that implements the function, respectively) and can encrypt any plaintext message unit of his or her choice. He or she tries either to determine the key(s) that has (have) been used for encryption or to decrypt ciphertext units for which he or she does not yet know the corresponding plaintext message units. In a typical setting, the adversary has to choose the plaintext units in advance (i.e., before the attack begins). In an *adaptive chosen-plaintext attack*, however, the adversary can dynamically choose plaintext message units while the attack is going on. Needless to say, adaptive chosen-plaintext attacks are generally at least as powerful as their (nonadaptive) counterparts.

Chosen-ciphertext attacks: In a *chosen-ciphertext attack*, the adversary has access to the decryption function (or the device that implements the function, respectively) and can decrypt any ciphertext unit of his or her choice. He or she tries either to determine the key(s) that has (have) been used for decryption or to encrypt plaintext message units for which he or she does not yet know the corresponding ciphertext units. Again, in a typical setting, the adversary has to choose the ciphertext units in advance, whereas in an *adaptive chosen-ciphertext attack*, the adversary can dynamically choose ciphertext units while the attack is going on. An adaptive chosen-ciphertext attack is again more powerful than its (nonadaptive) counterpart.

In general, there are many possibilities to implement these attacks. For example, if an adversary knows the symmetric encryption system that is in use, he or she can implement a ciphertext-only attack simply by trying every possible key to decrypt a given ciphertext unit. This attack can even be parallelized (if many processors participate in the key search). Let $|\mathcal{K}|$ be the size of the key space (i.e., the number of possible keys), t be the time it takes to test a candidate key, and p be the number of processors performing the key search. Then each processor is responsible for approximately $|\mathcal{K}|/p$ keys, and hence it takes time $|\mathcal{K}|t/p$ to test them all. On the average, one can expect to find the correct key about halfway through the search, making the expected time approximately

$$\frac{|\mathcal{K}|t}{2p}. \tag{10.1}$$

This attack is known as *brute-force attack* or *exhaustive key search*. The attack is possible whenever the adversary is able to decide whether he or she has found a correct plaintext message unit (or a correct key, respectively). For example, it may be the case that the plaintext message is text written in a specific language or that it otherwise contains enough redundancy to tell it apart from illegitimate plaintext messages. Suppose, for example, that the adversary does not know the plaintext message (for a given ciphertext), but that he or she knows that the plaintext message is coded with one ASCII character per byte. This means that each byte has a leading zero bit. This is usually enough redundancy to tell legitimate plaintext messages apart from illegitimate ones.

If the adversary knows a plaintext mesage (that is encrypted), then he or she can implement a known-plaintext attack. In the realm of affine ciphers, we already introduced an exemplary known-plaintext attack. Such attacks are generally simpler and more likely to occur than one might expect. Note, for example, that many communication protocols have specific fields whose values are either known or can be easily guessed (for example, if they are padded with zero bytes).

In practice, (adaptive) chosen-plaintext and (adaptive) chosen-ciphertext attacks are considerably more difficult to implement (than ciphertext-only and known-plaintext attacks), mainly because they seem to require access to the encryption or decryption function (or the device that implements the function, respectively). Nevertheless, they must still be considered and kept in mind when one discusses the security of an encryption system (chosen-ciphertext attacks have in fact become important for asymmetric encryption systems, as addressed in Section 14.1). This is also true for side-channel attacks, mentioned in Section 1.2.2 but not further addressed in this book.

10.1.4 Evaluation Criteria

In order to evaluate the goodness of a symmetric encryption system, it is necessary to have a set of well-defined evaluation criteria. Referring to Shannon,[5] the following five criteria may be used.

Amount of secrecy: The ultimate goal of a symmetric encryption system is to keep plaintext messages secret. Consequently, the amount of secrecy provided by a symmetric encryption system is an important criterion. It is particularly interesting to be able to measure (and quantify in one way or another) the amount of secrecy a symmetric encryption system is able to provide. Unfortunately, we are far away from having or being able to develop such a measure.

---

5 Refer to Section 1.3 for references to Shannon's original work.

Size of key: Symmetric encryption systems employ secret keys that must be securely generated, distributed, managed, and memorized. It is therefore desirable (from an implementation and performance viewpoint) to have keys that are as small as possible.

Complexity of enciphering and deciphering operations: To allow an efficient implementation, the enciphering and deciphering operations should not be too complex (again, they should be as simple as possible).

Propagation of errors: Different symmetric encryption systems and different modes of operation have different characteristics with regard to the propagation of errors. Sometimes propagation of errors is desirable, and sometimes it is not. Consequently, the nature and the characteristics of the application determines the requirements with regard to error propagation. In many situations, it is desirable to have small error propagation.

Expansion of messages: In some symmetric encryption systems, the size of a message is increased by the encryption, meaning that the ciphertext is larger than the corresponding plaintext message. This is not always desirable, and sometimes symmetric encryption systems are designed to minimize message expansion. If, for example, encrypted data must be fed into a fixed-length field of a communication protocol, then the symmetric encryption system must not expand the plaintext message.

This list is not comprehensive, and many other and complementary evaluation criteria may be important in a specific environment or application setting. Furthermore, not all criteria introduced by Shannon are still equally important today. For example, the "size of key" and the "complexity of enciphering and deciphering operations" criteria are not so important anymore (because there are computer systems that manage keys and run the enciphering and deciphering operations).

10.2 BLOCK CIPHERS

As mentioned before, every practical symmetric encryption system processes plaintext messages unit by unit, and in the case of a block cipher a unit is called a block. Consequently, a block cipher maps plaintext message blocks of a specific length into ciphertext blocks of the same length, and hence $\mathcal{M} = \mathcal{C} = \Sigma^n$ (for a specific alphabet Σ and a specific block length n). For example, the additive, multiplicative, and affine ciphers mentioned earlier are block ciphers with alphabet $\Sigma = \mathbb{Z}_{26}$ and block length 1.

In Section 3.1.4 (and Definition 3.23), we introduced the notion of a permutation. In short, we said that a permutation on set S is a bijective function $f : S \rightarrow S$. In the case of block ciphers, the set is Σ^n, and $E = \{E_k : k \in \mathcal{K}\}$ is a family of bijective encryption functions $E_k : \Sigma^n \rightarrow \Sigma^n$. This means that the encryption functions of a block cipher actually represent permutations of Σ^n (or that a block cipher is a family of permutations, respectively). If we fix the block length n and work with the plaintext message and ciphertext spaces $\mathcal{M} = \mathcal{C} = \Sigma^n$, then the key space potentially comprises all permutations over Σ^n (i.e., $\mathcal{K} = P(\Sigma^n)$). For every key $\pi \in P(\Sigma^n)$, the encryption and decryption functions are defined as follows:

$$E_\pi : \Sigma^n \longrightarrow \Sigma^n$$
$$w \longmapsto \pi(w)$$

$$D_\pi : \Sigma^n \longrightarrow \Sigma^n$$
$$w \longmapsto \pi^{-1}(w)$$

There are $|P(\Sigma^n)| = (\Sigma^n)!$ possible permutations that can be used as block ciphers with block length n. If, for example, $\Sigma = \{0, 1\}$, then there are $(2^n)!$ possible permutations. The function $f(n) = (2^n)!$ grows tremendously (see Table 10.1 for the first 10 values). For a typical block length n of 64 bits, $f(n)$ returns

$$2^{64}! = 18,446,744,073,709,551,616!$$

This number is so huge that it requires more than 2^{69} bits only to encode it. Consequently, if we wanted to specify a particular permutation, then we would have to introduce a numbering and use an index number that is approximately of that size. This 2^{69}-bit number would then serve as a secret key for the communicating entities. It is, however, doubtful whether the entities would be able to manage such a long key. Instead, symmetric encryption systems are usually designed to take a reasonably long key[6] and generate a one-to-one mapping that looks random to someone who does not know the secret key. So it is reasonable to use only some possible permutations of Σ^n (out of $P(\Sigma^n)$) as encryption and decryption functions and to use comparably small keys to refer to them. To analyze the security of such a block cipher, one has to study the algebraic properties of the underlying permutations. If, for example, the order of such a permutation is small, then one can easily decrypt a ciphertext by encrypting it multiple times.

6   A reasonably long key has more like 69 bits than 2^{69} bits.

Table 10.1
The Growth Rate of $f(n) = (2^n)!$ for $n = 1, \ldots, 10$

n	$(2^n)!$
1	$2^1! = 2! = 2$
2	$2^2! = 4! = 24$
3	$2^3! = 8! = 40'320$
4	$2^4! = 16! = 20'922'789'888'000$
5	$2^5! = 32! \approx 2.63 \cdot 10^{35}$
6	$2^6! = 64! \approx 1.27 \cdot 10^{89}$
7	$2^7! = 128! \approx 3.86 \cdot 10^{215}$
8	$2^8! = 256! \approx 8.58 \cdot 10^{506}$
9	$2^9! = 512! \approx 3.48 \cdot 10^{1166}$
10	$2^{10}! = 1024! \approx 5.42 \cdot 10^{2639}$

In the design of symmetric encryption systems, permutations and substitutions are usually used and combined to provide confusion and diffusion.

- The purpose of *confusion* is to make the relation between the key and the ciphertext as complex as possible.

- The purpose of *diffusion* is to spread the influence of a single plaintext bit over many ciphertext bits. In a block cipher, diffusion propagates bit changes from one part of a block to other parts of the block.

Symmetric encryption systems that combine permutations and substitutions in multiple rounds (to provide a maximum level of confusion and diffusion) are sometimes also referred to as *substitution-permutation ciphers*. Many practically relevant symmetric encryption systems, including, for example, the DES overviewed and discussed next, are substitution-permutation ciphers. When we describe DES and a few other symmetric encryption systems in this chapter, we are not as formal and formally correct as one could possibly be. Instead, we adopt some terminology and notation used in the original descriptions and specifications of the encryption systems (mainly to make it simpler for the reader to get into these documents).

10.2.1 DES

The DES was developed by IBM in the 1970s[7] and was adopted by the National Bureau of Standards (NBS) as FIPS PUB 46 in 1977. Nowadays, the FIPS PUBS are developed and maintained by the NIST. The standard was reaffirmed in 1983, 1988,

---

7   The symmetric encryption system was called *Lucifer* internally at IBM.

1993, and 1999, and it was officially withdrawn in July 2004.[8] The DES specification that was reaffirmed in 1999 (i.e., FIPS PUB 46-3 [1]) is publicly and freely available on the Internet.[9] It specifies both the DES and the *Triple Data Encryption Algorithm* (TDEA), which may be used to protect highly sensitive data (see Section 10.2.1.6). From a security viewpoint, the TDEA is certainly the preferred choice. In either case, cryptographic modules that implement FIPS 46-3 should also conform to the requirements specified in FIPS 140-1 [2]. As of this writing, there is an increasingly large number of DES implementations (both in hardware and software) that conform to the various levels specified in this standard.

DES is the major representative of a *Feistel cipher*.[10] These ciphers are overviewed first. Afterwards, the DES encryption and decryption algorithms are described, and the security of the DES is briefly analyzed. Finally, a variant of DES (named DESX) and TDEA are overviewed, discussed, and put into perspective.

10.2.1.1 Feistel Ciphers

A Feistel cipher is a block cipher with a particular structure (known as *Feistel network*). The alphabet is $\Sigma = \mathbb{Z}_2 = \{0, 1\}$, and the block length is $2t$ (for a reasonably sized $t \in \mathbb{N}^+$). The Feistel cipher runs in $r \in \mathbb{N}^+$ rounds. For every $k \in \mathcal{K}$, r round keys $k_1, \ldots, k_r$ must be generated and used on a per-round basis.

The encryption function E_k starts by splitting the plaintext message block m into two halves of t bits each. Let L_0 be the left half, and R_0 be the right half (i.e., $m = (L_0, R_0)$). A sequence of pairs (L_i, R_i) for $i = 1, \ldots, r$ is then recursively computed as follows:

$$(L_i, R_i) = (R_{i-1}, L_{i-1} \oplus f_{k_i}(R_{i-1})) \tag{10.2}$$

This means that $L_i = R_{i-1}$ and $R_i = L_{i-1} \oplus f_{k_i}(R_{i-1})$. For example, if $i = 1$, then L_1 and R_1 are computed as follows:

$$L_1 = R_0$$
$$R_1 = L_0 \oplus f_{k_1}(R_0)$$

---

8   http://csrc.nist.gov/Federal-register/July26-2004-FR-DES-Notice.pdf.
9   http://csrc.nist.gov/publications/fips/fips46-3/fips46-3.pdf.
10 Feistel ciphers are named after the IBM researcher Horst Feistel who was involved in the original design of Lucifer and DES. Feistel lived from 1915 to 1990 and was one of the first nongovernment cryptographers.

Similarly, if $i = 2$, then L_2 and R_2 are computed as follows:

$$
\begin{aligned}
L_2 &= R_1 \\
R_2 &= L_1 \oplus f_{k_2}(R_1)
\end{aligned}
$$

This continues until, in the last round, L_r and R_r are computed as follows:

$$
\begin{aligned}
L_r &= R_{r-1} \\
R_r &= L_{r-1} \oplus f_{k_r}(R_{r-1})
\end{aligned}
$$

The pair (L_r, R_r) in reverse order then represents the ciphertext block. Hence, the encryption of plaintext message m using key k can formally be expressed as follows:

$$
E_k(m) = E_k(L_0, R_0) = (R_r, L_r)
$$

The recursive formula (10.2) can also be written as follows:

$$
(L_{i-1}, R_{i-1}) = (R_i \oplus f_{k_i}(L_i), L_i)
$$

This means that it is possible to recursively compute L_{i-1} and R_{i-1} from L_i, R_i, and k_i and to determine (L_0, R_0) from (R_r, L_r) using the round keys in reverse order (i.e., $k_r, \ldots, k_1$) accordingly. Consequently, a Feistel cipher can always be decrypted using the same (encryption) algorithm and applying the round keys in reverse order. This property simplifies the implementation of the decryption function considerably (in fact, the encryption and decryption functions are the same). Note that it is possible to design and come up with iterative block ciphers that are not Feistel ciphers, yet whose encryption and decryption (after a certain reordering or recalculation of variables) are structurally the same. One example is the *International Data Encryption Algorithm* (IDEA) employed by many security products, including, for example, former versions of Pretty Good Privacy (PGP). Also, Feistel ciphers have important applications in public key cryptography as well. For example, the optimal asymmetric encryption padding scheme addressed in Section 14.3.2 is basically a two-round Feistel cipher. It is difficult to make statements about the security of a Feistel cipher, unless one considers a particular round function f. Let's elaborate on the DES encryption and decryption functions or algorithms next.

10.2.1.2 Encryption Algorithm

DES is a Feistel cipher with $t = 32$ and $r = 16$. This means that the block length of DES is 64 bits, and hence $\mathcal{M} = \mathcal{C} = \{0,1\}^{64}$, and that the DES encryption and decryption algorithms operate in 16 rounds. Furthermore, DES keys are 64-bit strings with the additional property that the last bit of each byte is set to odd parity. This means that the sum modulo 2 of all bits in a byte must be odd and that the parity bit is set accordingly. This can be formally expressed as follows:

$$\mathcal{K} = \{(k_1, \ldots, k_{64}) \in \{0,1\}^{64} \mid \sum_{i=1}^{8} k_{8j+i} \equiv 1 \ (\mathrm{mod} \ 2) \ \text{for} \ j = 0, \ldots, 7\}$$

For example, F1DFBC9B79573413 is a valid DES key. Its odd parity can be verified using the following table:

F1	1	1	1	1	0	0	0	1
DF	1	1	0	1	1	1	1	1
BC	1	0	1	1	1	1	0	0
9B	1	0	0	1	1	0	1	1
79	0	1	1	1	1	0	0	1
57	0	1	0	1	0	1	1	1
34	0	0	1	1	0	1	0	0
13	0	0	0	1	0	0	1	1

Consequently, the first seven bits of a DES key byte determine the last bit, and the size of the resulting key space is 2^{56} (instead of 2^{64}). As mentioned earlier, the round keys derived from the DES key are the same for encryption and decryption; they are only used in reverse order.

The DES encryption algorithm is specified in Algorithm 10.1 and illustrated in Figure 10.1. To encrypt plaintext message block m using key k, the algorithm operates in three steps:

1. The initial permutation (IP) as illustrated in Table 10.2 is applied to m. If $m = m_1 m_2 m_3 \ldots m_{64} \in \mathcal{M} = \{0,1\}^{64}$, then $IP(m) = m_{58} m_{50} m_{42} \ldots m_7 \in \mathcal{M}$.

Algorithm 10.1   The DES encryption algorithm.

$$\frac{(m,k)}{\begin{array}{l} m \leftarrow IP(m) \\ L_0 \leftarrow \text{leftmost 32 bits of } m \\ R_0 \leftarrow \text{rightmost 32 bits of } m \\ \text{for } i = 1 \text{ to } 16 \text{ do} \\ \quad L_i \leftarrow R_{i-1} \\ \quad R_i \leftarrow L_{i-1} \oplus f_{k_i}(R_{i-1}) \\ c \leftarrow IP^{-1}(R_{16}, L_{16}) \end{array}}$$

$$\overline{(c)}$$

2. A 16-round Feistel cipher is applied to $IP(m)$. The corresponding round function f is addressed later.

3. The inverse initial permutation (IP^{-1}) as illustrated in Table 10.3 is applied. If (L_{16}, R_{16}) is the output of step 2, then $c = IP^{-1}(R_{16}, L_{16})$.

Table 10.2
The Initial Permutation IP of the DES

58	50	42	34	26	18	10	2
60	52	44	36	28	20	12	4
62	54	46	38	30	22	14	6
64	56	48	40	32	24	16	8
57	49	41	33	25	17	9	1
59	51	43	35	27	19	11	3
61	53	45	37	29	21	13	5
63	55	47	39	31	23	15	7

The DES round function f operates on blocks of 32 bits and uses a 48-bit key k_i in each round (i.e., $f_{k_i} : \{0,1\}^{32} \to \{0,1\}^{32}$ for every $k_i \in \{0,1\}^{48}$). The working principle of the DES round function f is illustrated in Figure 10.2. First, the 32-bit argument R is expanded to 48 bits using the expansion function $E : \{0,1\}^{32} \to \{0,1\}^{48}$. As shown in Table 10.4, the expansion function basically works by doubling some bits. If $R = r_1 r_2 \ldots r_{31} r_{32}$, then $E(R) = r_{32} r_1 \ldots r_{32} r_1$. Afterward, the string $E(R)$ is added modulo 2 to the 48-bit key k. The result is split into 8 blocks $B_1, \ldots, B_8$ of 6 bits each (i.e., $E(R) \oplus k = B_1 B_2 B_3 B_4 B_5 B_6 B_7 B_8$ and $B_i \in \{0,1\}^6$ for $i = 1, \ldots, 8$). Next, each 6-bit block B_i is transformed into a 4-bit block C_i for $i = 1, \ldots, 8$ using a function $S_i : \{0,1\}^6 \longrightarrow \{0,1\}^4$ (this function is called *S-box* and explained later). For $i = 1, \ldots, 8$, we have $C_i = S_i(B_i)$, and hence $C = C_1 C_2 \ldots C_8$. Each C_i $(i = 1, \ldots, 8)$ is 4 bits long, so the total length

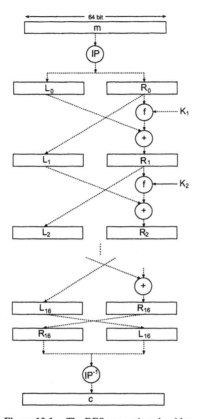

Figure 10.1 The DES encryption algorithm.

of C is 32 bits. It is subject to the permutation P, as specified in Table 10.5. If $C = c_1c_2\ldots c_{32}$, then $P(C) = c_{16}c_7\ldots c_{25}$. The result is $f_k(R)$, and it is the output of the round function f.

The S-boxes $S_1, \ldots, S_8$ of the DES are illustrated in Table 10.6. Each S-box can be represented by a table that consists of 4 rows and 16 columns. If $B = b_1b_2b_3b_4b_5b_6$ is input to S_i, then the binary string $b_1b_6 \in \{0,1\}^2$ represents a number between 0 and 3 (this number is the row index for the table), whereas the binary string $b_2b_3b_4b_5 \in \{0,1\}^4$ represents a number between 0 and 15 (this number is the column index for the table). The output of $S_i(B)$ is the number found in the table (on the row that corresponds to the row index and the column that corresponds to the column index), written in binary notation. For example, if $B = 011001$, then the row index is $b_1b_6 = 01 = 1$ and the column index is $b_2b_3b_4b_5 = 1100 = 12$.

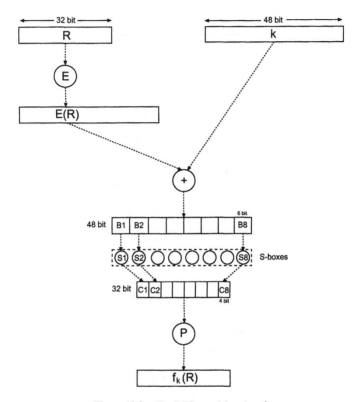

Figure 10.2   The DES round function f.

Consequently, $S_5(011001)$ refers to the decimal number 3 that can be written as a sequence of bits (i.e., 0011). This sequence is the output of the S-box.

Last but not least, we must explain how the 16 round keys $k_1, \ldots, k_{16} \in \{0, 1\}^{48}$ are derived from the DES key $k \in \{0, 1\}^{64}$. We therefore define v_i for $i = 1, \ldots, 16$:

$$v_i = \begin{cases} 1 & \text{if } i \in \{1, 2, 9, 16\} \\ 2 & \text{otherwise (i.e., if } i \in \{3, 4, 5, 6, 7, 8, 10, 11, 12, 13, 14, 15\}) \end{cases}$$

We also use two functions called $PC1$ and $PC2$.[11] $PC1$ maps a 64-bit string (i.e., a DES key k) to two 28-bit strings C and D (i.e., $PC1 : \{0, 1\}^{64} \rightarrow$

11   The acronym PC stands for *permuted choice*.

Table 10.3

The Inverse Initial Permutation IP^{-1} of the DES

40	8	48	16	56	24	64	32
39	7	47	15	55	23	63	31
38	6	46	14	54	22	62	30
37	5	45	13	53	21	61	29
36	4	44	12	52	20	60	28
35	3	43	11	51	19	59	27
34	2	42	10	50	18	58	26
33	1	41	9	49	17	57	25

Table 10.4

The Expansion Function E of the DES

32	1	2	3	4	5	4	5	6	7	8	9
8	9	10	11	12	13	12	13	14	15	16	17
16	17	18	19	20	21	20	21	22	23	24	25
24	25	26	27	28	29	28	29	30	31	32	1

$\{0,1\}^{28} \times \{0,1\}^{28}$), and $PC2$ maps two 28-bit strings to a 48-bit string (i.e., $PC2 : \{0,1\}^{28} \times \{0,1\}^{28} \to \{0,1\}^{48}$).

- The function $PC1$ is illustrated in Table 10.7. The upper half of the table specifies the bits that are taken from k to construct C, and the lower half of the table specifies the bits that are taken from k to construct D. If $k = k_1 k_2 \ldots k_{64}$, then $C = k_{57} k_{49} \ldots k_{36}$ and $D = k_{63} k_{55} \ldots k_4$. Note that the 8 parity bits $k_8, k_{16}, \ldots, k_{64}$ are not considered and occur neither in C nor in D.

- The function $PC2$ is illustrated in Table 10.8. The two 28-bit strings that are input to the function are concatenated to form a 56-bit string. If this string is $b_1 b_2 \ldots b_{56}$, then the function $PC2$ turns this string into $b_{14} b_{17} \ldots b_{32}$. Note

Table 10.5

The Permutation P of the DES

16	7	10	21	29	12	28	17
1	15	23	26	5	18	31	20
2	8	24	14	32	27	3	9
19	13	30	6	22	11	4	25

Table 10.6
The S-Boxes S_1 to S_8 of the DES

		0	1	2	3	4	5	6	7	8	9	10	11	12	13	14	15
S_1	0	14	4	13	1	2	15	11	8	3	10	6	12	5	9	0	7
	1	0	15	7	4	14	2	13	1	10	6	12	11	9	5	3	8
	2	4	1	14	8	13	6	2	11	15	12	9	7	3	10	5	0
	3	15	12	8	2	4	9	1	7	5	11	3	14	10	0	6	13
S_2	0	15	1	8	14	6	11	3	4	9	7	2	13	12	0	5	10
	1	3	13	4	7	15	2	8	14	12	0	1	10	6	9	11	5
	2	0	14	7	11	10	4	13	1	5	8	12	6	9	3	2	15
	3	13	8	10	1	3	15	4	2	11	6	7	12	0	5	14	9
S_3	0	10	0	9	14	6	3	15	5	1	13	12	7	11	4	2	8
	1	13	7	0	9	3	4	6	10	2	8	5	14	12	11	15	1
	2	13	6	4	9	8	15	3	0	11	1	2	12	5	10	14	7
	3	1	10	13	0	6	9	8	7	4	15	14	3	11	5	2	12
S_4	0	7	13	14	3	0	6	9	10	1	2	8	5	11	12	4	15
	1	13	8	11	5	6	15	0	3	4	7	2	12	1	10	14	9
	2	10	6	9	0	12	11	7	13	15	1	3	14	5	2	8	4
	3	3	15	0	6	10	1	13	8	9	4	5	11	12	7	2	14
S_5	0	2	12	4	1	7	10	11	6	8	5	3	15	13	0	14	9
	1	14	11	2	12	4	7	13	1	5	0	15	10	3	9	8	6
	2	4	2	1	11	10	13	7	8	15	9	12	5	6	3	0	14
	3	11	8	12	7	1	14	2	13	6	15	0	9	10	4	5	3
S_6	0	12	1	10	15	9	2	6	8	0	13	3	4	14	7	5	11
	1	10	15	4	2	7	12	9	5	6	1	13	14	0	11	3	8
	2	9	14	15	5	2	8	12	3	7	0	4	10	1	13	11	6
	3	4	3	2	12	9	5	15	10	11	14	1	7	6	0	8	13
S_7	0	4	11	2	14	15	0	8	13	3	12	9	7	5	10	6	1
	1	13	0	11	7	4	9	1	10	14	3	5	12	2	15	8	6
	2	1	4	11	13	12	3	7	14	10	15	6	8	0	5	9	2
	3	6	11	13	8	1	4	10	7	9	5	0	15	14	2	3	12
S_8	0	13	2	8	4	6	15	11	1	10	9	3	14	5	0	12	7
	1	1	15	13	8	10	3	7	4	12	5	6	11	0	14	9	2
	2	7	11	4	1	9	12	14	2	0	6	10	13	15	3	5	8
	3	2	1	14	7	4	10	8	13	15	12	9	0	3	5	6	11

that only 48 bits are taken into account and that b_9, b_{18}, b_{22}, b_{25}, b_{35}, b_{38}, b_{43}, and b_{54} are discarded.

To derive the 16 round keys $k_1, \ldots, k_{16}$ from the DES key k, (C_0, D_0) are first initialized with $PC1(k)$ according to the construction given earlier. For $i = 1, \ldots 16$, C_i is then set to the string that results from a cyclic shift left of C_{i-1} for v_i positions, and D_i is set to the string that results from a cyclic shift left of D_{i-1} for v_i positions. Finally, the round key k_i is the result of concatenating C_i and D_i, and applying the function $PC2$ to the result (i.e., $k_i = PC2(C_i \parallel D_i)$. The resulting key schedule calculation is illustrated in Figure 10.3.

In the literature, many numeric examples can be found to illustrate the working principles of the DES encryption algorithm or to verify the correct input-output behavior of a specific DES implementation, respectively.

10.2.1.3 Decryption Algorithm

As mentioned earlier, the DES is a Feistel cipher and as such the decryption algorithm is the same as the encryption algorithm. This means that Algorithm 3.1 can also be used for decryption. The only difference is that the key schedule must

Table 10.7
The Function $PC1$ of the DES

57	49	41	33	25	17	9
1	58	50	42	34	26	18
10	2	59	51	43	35	27
19	11	3	60	52	44	36
63	55	47	39	31	23	15
7	62	54	46	38	30	22
14	6	61	53	45	37	29
21	13	5	28	20	12	4

Table 10.8
The Function $PC2$ of the DES

14	17	11	24	1	5
3	28	15	6	21	10
23	19	12	4	26	8
16	7	27	20	13	2
41	52	31	37	47	55
30	40	51	45	33	48
44	49	39	56	34	53
46	42	50	36	29	32

be reversed, meaning that the DES round keys must be used in reverse order (i.e., $k_{16}, \ldots, k_1$) to decrypt a given ciphertext.[12]

10.2.1.4 Security Considerations

Since its standardization in the 1970s, the DES has been subject to a lot of public scrutiny. For example, people found that there are 4 weak keys and 12 semiweak keys.

- A DES key k is *weak* if $DES_k(DES_k(m)) = m$ for all $m \in \mathcal{M} = \{0,1\}^{64}$, meaning that the DES encryption with k is inverse to itself (i.e., if m is encrypted twice with a weak key, then the result is again m).

- The DES keys K_1 and K_2 are *semiweak* if $DES_{k_1}(DES_{k_2}(m)) = m$ for all $m \in \mathcal{M} = \{0,1\}^{64}$, meaning that the DES encryptions with k_1 and k_2 are inverse to each other.

---

12 Test vectors for DES encryption and decryption can be found, for example, in a NIST document available at http://csrc.nist.gov/publications/nistpubs/800-17/800-17.pdf.

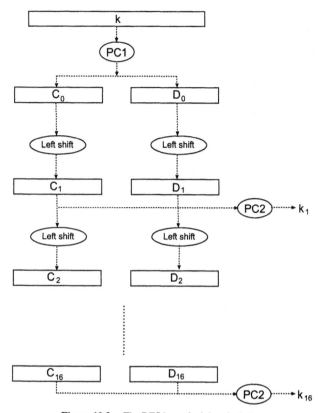

Figure 10.3　The DES key schedule calculation.

Because of their strange properties, weak and semiweak DES keys should not be used in practice. Because there are only $16 = 2^4$ such keys, the probability of randomly generating one is only

$$\frac{2^4}{2^{56}} = 2^{-52} \approx 2.22 \cdot 10^{-16}.$$

This probability is not particularly worrisome. It's certainly equally insecure to use a very small (large) key, as an adversary is likely to start searching for keys from the bottom (top). Consequently, there is no need to worry much about weak and semiweak keys in a specific application setting.

More interestingly, several cryptanalytical attacks have been developed in an attempt to break the security of DES. Examples include *differential cryptanalysis* [3] and *linear cryptanalysis* [4]. Using differential cryptanalysis to break DES requires 2^{47} chosen plaintexts, whereas linear cryptanalysis requires 2^{43} known plaintexts.[13] In either case, the amount of chosen or known plaintext is far too large to be practically relevant. The results, however, are theoretically interesting and have provided principles and criteria for the design of secure block ciphers (people have since admitted that defending against differential cryptanalysis was one of the design goals for DES [5]).

From a practical viewpoint, the major vulnerability and security problem of DES is its relatively small key length (and key space). Note that a DES key is effectively 56 bits long, and hence the key space comprises only 2^{56} elements. Consequently, a key search is successful after 2^{56} trials in the worst case and $2^{56}/2 = 2^{55}$ trials on the average. Furthermore, the DES encryption has the following property:

$$DES_k(m) = \overline{DES_{\overline{k}}(\overline{m})} \tag{10.3}$$

This property can be used in a known-plaintext attack to narrow down the key space with another factor of two. If the adversary knows two plaintext-ciphertext pairs (m, c_1) with $c_1 = DES_k(m)$ and $(\overline{m}, c_2)$ with $c_2 = DES_k(\overline{m})$, then he or she can compute for every key candidate k' the value $c = DES_{k'}(m)$ and verify whether this value matches c_1 or $\overline{c_2}$.

- If $c = c_1$, then k' is the correct key. In fact, $k = k'$ follows from $c = DES_{k'}(m)$ and $c_1 = DES_k(m)$.

- If $c = \overline{c_2}$, then $\overline{k'}$ is the correct key. In fact, $k = \overline{k'}$ follows from $c = DES_{k'}(m)$, $c_2 = \overline{DES_k(\overline{m})}$, and (10.3).

So in every trial with key candidate k', the adversary can also verify the complementary key candidate $\overline{k'}$. As mentioned earlier, this narrows down the key space with a factor of two. Against this background, it can be concluded that an exhaustive key search is successful after 2^{54} trials on the average.

The feasibility of an exhaustive key search was first publicly discussed in 1977 [6]. Note that an exhaustive key search needs a lot of time but almost no memory. On the other hand, if one has a lot of memory and is willing to precompute the ciphertext c for any given plaintext message m and all possible keys k, then one can store the pairs (c, k) and quickly find the correct key in a known-plaintext attack. Consequently, there is a lot of room for time-memory tradeoffs (e.g.,[7]).

---

13 Both cryptanalytical attacks require less plaintexts if one reduces the number of rounds.

In either case, many people have discussed the possibility to design and actually build dedicated machines to do an exhaustive key search for DES. For example, Michael J. Wiener proposed such a design in 1993 [8]. He came to the conclusion that a US$1,000,000 version of such a machine would be capable of finding a DES key in 3.5 hours on the average. In 1997, he modified his estimates with a factor of 6 (i.e., a US$1,000,000 version of the machine would be capable of finding a DES key in 35 minutes on the average and a US$10,000 version of the machine would be capable of finding a DES key in 2.5 days on the average [9]). These numbers are worrisome (for the security of DES against an exhaustive key search).

It was not until 1998 that a hardware-based search machine named *Deep Crack* was built by the Electronic Frontier Foundation (EFF) [10].[14] Deep Crack costs US$200,000 to build and consists of 1,536 processors, each capable of searching through 60 million keys per second. Referring to (10.1), the time to do an exhaustive key search is then

$$\frac{|\mathcal{K}|t}{2p} = \frac{2^{56}}{60,000,000 \cdot 2 \cdot 1,536} = \frac{2^{55}}{60,000,000 \cdot 1,536} \approx 390,937 \text{ seconds.}$$

Consequently, Deep Crack is able to recover a DES key in approximately 6,516 minutes, 109 hours, or 4.5 days.

More interestingly, one can also spend the idle time of networked computer systems to look for DES keys and run an exhaustive key search. If enough computer systems participate in the search, then a DES key can be found without having to build a dedicated machine such as Deep Crack. For example, in January 1999, the participants of the *Distributed.Net project*[15] broke a DES key in only 23 hours. More than 100,000 computer systems participated, received, and did a little part of the work. This allowed a rate of 250 billion keys being checked every second.

Against this background, it is obvious that the relatively small key length and the corresponding feasibility of an exhaustive key search is the most serious vulnerability and security problem of the DES. There are only a few possibilities to protect a block cipher with a small key length, such as DES, against this type of attack. For example, one can frequently change keys, eliminate known plaintext, or use a complex key setup procedure. An interesting idea to slow down an exhaustive key search attack is due to Rivest and is known as *all-or-nothing encryption* [11]. It yields an encryption mode for block ciphers that makes sure that one must decrypt the entire ciphertext before one can determine even one plaintext message block.

14 http://www.eff.org/descracker.html.
15 http://www.distributed.net.

This means that an exhaustive key search attack against an all-or-nothing encryption is slowed down by a factor equal to the number of ciphertext blocks.

The simplest method to protect a block cipher against exhaustive key search attacks is to work with sufficiently long keys. It goes without saying that modern ciphers with key lengths of 128 bits and more are resistant to exhaustive key search attacks with current technology. In a 1996 paper[16] written by a group of well-known and highly respected cryptographers, it was argued that keys should be at least 75 bits long and that they should be at least 90 bits long if data must be protected adequately for the next 20 years (i.e., until 2016). Note that these numbers only provide a lower bound for the key length; there is no reason not to work with longer keys in the first place.[17]

In practice, there are three possibilities to address (and possibly solve) the problem of the small key length of DES:

1. The DES may be modified in a way that compensates for its relatively small key length;

2. The DES may be iterated multiple times;

3. An alternative symmetric encryption system with a larger key length may be used.

The first possibility leads us to a modification of DES that is known as DESX (addressed later). The second possibility leads us to the TDEA addressed in Section 10.2.1.6. Last but not least, the third possibility leads us to the AES as addressed in Section 10.2.2 (the AES has a key length of 128, 192, or even 256 bits).

10.2.1.5 DESX

In order to come up with a modification of DES that compensates for its relatively small key length, Rivest developed and proposed a simple technique called *DESX*. DESX is practically relevant, because it was the first symmetric encryption system employed by the Encrypted File System (EFS) in the Microsoft Windows 2000 operating system.

The DESX construction is illustrated in Figure 10.4. In addition to the DES key k, the DESX construction employs two additional 64-bit keys, k_1 and k_2.[18] They

---

16 http://www.schneier.com/paper-keylength.html.

17 It is sometimes argued that long keys slow down the encryption and decryption algorithms considerably. This argument is wrong. In most symmetric encryption systems, the secret key is expanded by a highly efficient key schedule algorithm, and this algorithm is largely independent from how many key bits are provided in the first place.

18 Note that k_1 and k_2 must be different. Otherwise, the binary additions modulo 2 (i.e., XOR operations) would cancel themselves out.

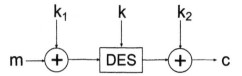

Figure 10.4   The DESX construction.

are added modulo 2 to the plaintext message m before and after the DES encryption takes place. Consequently, the DESX encryption of a plaintext message m using keys k, k_1, and k_2 can be formally expressed as follows:

$$c = k_2 \oplus DES_k(m \oplus k_1)$$

DESX requires a total of $56 + 64 + 64 = 184$ bits of keying material. As such, it improves resistance against exhaustive key search considerably (e.g., [12]). It does not, however, improve resistance against other cryptanalytical attacks, such as differential or linear cryptanalysis (protection against such attacks has not been a design goal of DESX).

10.2.1.6   TDEA

As mentioned earlier, a possibility to address (or solve) the small key length problem is to iterate DES multiple times. There are two points to make:

- First, multiple iterations with the same key are not much more secure than a single encryption. This is because an adversary can also iterate the encryption functions multiple times. If, for example, DES is iterated twice (with the same key), then each step of testing a key is also twice as much work (because the adversary has to do a double encryption). A factor of two for the adversary is not considered much added security, especially because the legitimate users have their work doubled, as well. Consequently, multiple iterations must always be done with different keys to improve security.

- Second, it was shown that the DES encryption functions are not closed with regard to concatenation (i.e., they do not provide a group) [13]. If the DES encryption functions provided a group, then there would exist a DES key k_3 for all pairs (k_1, k_2) of DES keys, such that $DES_{k_3} = DES_{k_1} \circ DES_{k_2}$. This would be unfortunate, and the iterated use of the DES would not provide any security advantage.

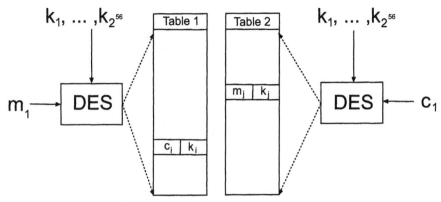

Figure 10.5   The meet-in-the-middle attack against double DES.

Against this background, the first (meaningful) possibility to iterate the DES is the double encryption with two independent keys. However, it was first shown by Diffie and Hellman that double encryption is not particularly useful due to the existence of a *meet-in-the-middle attack*. Assume an adversary has a few plaintext-ciphertext pairs (m_i, c_i), where c_i is derived from a double encryption of m_i with k_1 and k_2, and he or she wants to find k_1 and k_2. The meet-in-the-middle attack is illustrated in Figure 10.5; it operates in the following four steps:

1. The adversary computes a first table (i.e., Table 1) with 2^{56} entries. Each entry consists of a possible DES key k_i and the result of applying that key to encrypt the plaintext message m_1. Table 1 is sorted in numerical order by the resulting ciphertexts. Hence, the entry (c_i, k_i) refers to the ciphertext that results from encrypting m_1 with k_i for $i = 1, \ldots, 2^{56}$.

2. The adversary computes a second table (i.e., Table 2) with 2^{56} entries. Each entry consists of a possible DES key k_j and the result of applying that key to decrypt the ciphertext c_1. Table 2 is sorted in numerical order by the resulting plaintexts. Hence, the entry (m_j, k_j) refers to the plaintext that results from decrypting c_1 with k_j for $j = 1, \ldots, 2^{56}$.

3. The adversary searches through the sorted tables to find matching entries. Each matching entry $c_i = p_j$ yields k_i as a key candidate for k_1 and k_j as a key candidate for k_2 (because k_i encrypts m_1 to a value to which k_j decrypts c_1).

4. If there are multiple matching pairs (which there almost certainly will be),[19] the adversary tests the candidate pairs (k_1, k_2) against m_2 and c_2. If multiple candidate pairs still work for m_2 and c_2, then the same test procedure is repeated for m_3 and c_3. This continues until a single candidate pair remains. Note that the correct candidate pair always works, whereas an incorrect candidate pair will almost certainly fail to work on any particular (m_i, c_i) pair.

The meet-in-the-middle attack is not particularly worrisome, because it requires two tables with 2^{56} entries each (there are some improvements not addressed in this book). The mere existence of the attack, however, is enough reason to iterate DES three times, and to do *triple DES* (3DES) accordingly. It may be that double DES would be good enough, but because triple DES is not much harder, it is usually done in the first place. As mentioned earlier, FIPS PUB 46-3 specifies the TDEA, and this specification also conforms to ANSI X9.52.

A TDEA key consists of three keys that are collectively referred to as a key bundle (i.e., $k = (k_1, k_2, k_3)$. The TDEA encryption function works as follows:

$$c = E_{k_3}(D_{k_2}(E_{k_1}(m)))$$

Consequently, a TDEA or 3DES encryption is sometimes also referred to as EDE (standing for "encrypt-decrypt-encrypt"). The reason for the second iteration of DES being a decryption (instead of an encryption) is that a 3DES implementation can then easily be turned into a single-key DES implementation by feeding all three iterations with the same key k. If we then compute $c = E_{k_3}(D_{k_2}(E_{k_1}(m)))$, we actually compute $c = E_k(D_k(E_k(m))) = E_k(m)$.

Similarly, the TDEA decryption function works as follows:

$$m = D_{k_1}(E_{k_2}(D_{k_3}(c)))$$

FIPS PUB 46-3 specifies the following three options for the key bundle $k = (k_1, k_2, k_3)$:

- Keying option 1: k_1, k_2, and k_3 are independent keys;
- Keying option 2: k_1 and k_2 are independent keys and $k_3 = k_1$;

---

19 There are 2^{64} possible plaintext and ciphertext blocks, but only 2^{56} entries in each table. Consequently, each 64-bit block appears with a probability of $1/256$ in each of the tables, and of the 2^{56} blocks that appear in the first table, only $1/256$ of them also appear in the second table. That means that there should be 2^{48} entries that appear in both tables.

- Keying option 3: All keys are equal (i.e., $k_1 = k_2 = k_3$). As mentioned earlier, the 3DES implementation then represents a single-key DES implementation.

Note that iterating a block cipher multiple times can be done with any block cipher and that there is nothing DES-specific about this construction. It is, however, less frequently used with other symmetric encryption systems (mainly because many other systems have been designed to use longer keys in the first place).

10.2.2 AES

In the time between 1997 and 2000, the NIST carried out an open competition with the aim to standardize the AES as a successor for the DES. Contrary to the DES standardization effort in the 1970s, many parties from industry and academia participated in the AES competition. In fact, there were 15 submissions qualifying as serious AES candidates, and among these submissions, NIST selected five finalists: MARS,[20] RC6, Rijndael,[21] Serpent,[22] and Twofish.[23] On October 2, 2000, the NIST decided to propose Rijndael as the AES.[24] According to [15], the NIST could not distinguish between the security of the finalist algorithms, and Rijndael was selected mainly because of its ease of implementation in hardware and its strong performance on nearly all platforms. The AES is officially specified in FIPS PUB 197 [16].[25]

Table 10.9
The Three Official Versions of the AES

	N_b	N_k	N_r
AES-128	4	4	10
AES-192	4	6	12
AES-256	4	8	14

According to the requirements specified by the NIST, the AES is a block cipher with a block length of 128 bits and a variable key length of 128, 192, or 256 bits.[26]

20 http://www.research.ibm.com/security/mars.html
21 The Rijndael algorithm was developed and proposed by the two Belgium cryptographers Joan Daemen and Vincent Rijmen. Its design and some background information is described in [14]. More recent information is available at http://www.iaik.tu-graz.ac.at/research/krypto/AES. A nice animation of the AES encryption algorithm is made available at the book's home page.
22 http://www.cl.cam.ac.uk/~rja14/serpent.html
23 http://www.schneier.com/twofish.html
24 Refer to the NIST *Report on the Development of the Advanced Encryption Standard (AES)* available at http://csrc.nist.gov/CryptoToolkit/aes/round2/r2report.pdf.
25 http://csrc.nist.gov/publications/fips/fips197/fips-197.pdf
26 Rijndael was originally designed to handle additional block sizes and key lengths (that are, however, not adopted in the current AES specification).

The corresponding AES versions are referred to as AES-128, AES-192, and AES-256. The number of rounds depends on the key length (i.e., 10, 12, or 14 rounds). Table 10.9 summarizes the three official versions of the AES. N_b refers to the block length (in number of 32-bit words), N_k to the key length (in number of 32-bit words), and N_r to the number of rounds. Note that the official versions of the AES all work with a block size of $N_b \cdot 32 = 4 \cdot 32 = 128$ bits.

While FIPS PUB 197 explicitly defines the allowed values for N_b, N_k, and N_r, future reaffirmations may include changes or additions to these values. Implementors of the AES should therefore make their implementations as flexible as possible (this is a general recommendation that does not only apply for the AES).

10.2.2.1 Preliminary Remarks

Similar to most other symmetric encryption systems, the AES is byte oriented, meaning that the basic unit for processing is a byte (i.e., a sequence of 8 bits). Each byte may be written in binary or hexadecimal notation.

- In binary notation, a byte is written as $\{b_7 b_6 b_5 b_4 b_3 b_2 b_1 b_0\}$ with $b_i \in \{0, 1\} = \mathbb{Z}_2 \cong \mathbb{F}_2$ for $i = 0, \ldots, 7$. Hence, a byte also represents an element of $\mathbb{F}_{2^8}$.

- In hexadecimal notation, a byte is written as 0xXY with X, Y $\in \{0, \ldots, 9,$ A, $\ldots,$ F $\}$. In this case, X refers to $\{b_7 b_6 b_5 b_4\}$ and Y refers to $\{b_3 b_2 b_1 b_0\}$.

Alternatively, the 8 bits can be interpreted as coefficients of a polynomial:

$$b_7 x^7 + b_6 x^6 + b_5 x^5 + b_4 x^4 + b_3 x^3 + b_2 x^2 + b_1 x + b_0 = \sum_{i=0}^{7} b_i x^i \qquad (10.4)$$

Consequently, the byte $\{10100011\} = $ 0xA3 can be written as polynomial $x^7 + x^5 + x + 1$ (for every bit equal to one, the corresponding coefficient in the polynomial is set to one). This means that we can add and multiply either bytes or polynomials. Let's have a closer look at addition and multiplication.

Addition: If we consider bytes, then the addition is achieved by adding modulo 2 the bits in the bytes representing the two elements of $\mathbb{F}_{2^8}$ (e.g., $\{01010111\} \oplus \{10000011\} = \{11010100\}$). If we consider polynomials, then the addition is achieved by adding modulo 2 the coefficients for the corresponding powers in the polynomials representing the two elements (e.g., $(x^6 + x^4 + x^2 + x + 1) + (x^7 + x + 1) = x^7 + x^6 + x^4 + x^2$).

Multiplication: If we consider bytes, then there is no simple operation that represents the multiplication. If, however, we consider polynomials, then the multiplication is achieved by multiplying polynomials over $\mathbb{Z}_2$ modulo an irreducible polynomial of degree 8. In the case of the AES, the irreducible polynomial is

$$f(x) = x^8 + x^4 + x^3 + x + 1.$$

The modular reduction by $f(x)$ ensures that the result is a binary polynomial of degree less than 8 and—according to (10.4)—that it can hence be represented in a single byte. Note that the multiplication is associative and that the polynomial 1 (i.e., $\{00000001\}$ or $0x01$ in the byte representation) is the multiplicative identity element for the multiplication operation.

Remember from Section 3.3.6 that $\mathbb{Z}_2[x]_f$ is a field if $f(x)$ is an irreducible polynomial over $\mathbb{Z}_2$. In the case of the AES, the degree of f is 8, and hence $\mathbb{Z}_2[x]_f$ is isomorph to $\mathbb{F}_{2^8}$. In the sequel, we use the term *AES field* to refer to this field. The fact that the AES field is a field means that every onzero element $b(x)$ (i.e., every nonzero polynomial over $\mathbb{Z}_2$ with degree less than 8) has a multiplicative inverse $b^{-1}(x)$ and that this element can be found using the extended Euclid algorithm.

Multiplying the polynomial defined in (10.4) with the polynomial x (or $\{00000010\}$ or $0x02$ in the byte representation) results in the following polynomial:

$$b_7x^8 + b_6x^7 + b_5x^6 + b_4x^5 + b_3x^4 + b_2x^3 + b_1x^2 + b_0x = \sum_{i=0}^{7} b_ix^{i+1}$$

Again, this polynomial must be reduced modulo $f(x)$. If $b_7 = 0$, then the result is already in reduced form. Otherwise, if $b_7 = 1$, then the reduction is accomplished by subtracting (i.e., adding modulo 2) the polynomial $f(x)$. It follows that multiplication by x can be implemented efficiently at the byte level as a shift left and a subsequent conditional addition modulo 2 with $f(x)$.

10.2.2.2 State

Internally, the AES operates on a two-dimensional array s of bytes, called the *State*. The State consists of 4 rows and N_b columns (where N_b is the block length divided by 32). In the current AES specification, N_b is always 4 (for all official versions of the AES). Note, however, that this need not be the case and that there may be future versions of the AES that work with larger values for N_b.

Each entry in the State refers to a byte $s_{r,c}$ or $s[r, c]$ (where $0 \leq r < 4$ refers to the row number and $0 \leq c < 4$ refers to the column number). Note that the four bytes $s_{r,0}, s_{r,1}, s_{r,2},$ and $s_{r,3}$ ($s_{0,c}, s_{1,c}, s_{2,c},$ and $s_{3,c}$) in row r (column c) of the State form a 32-bit word. Consequently, the State can also be viewed as a one-dimensional array of four 32-bit words (be it rows or columns).

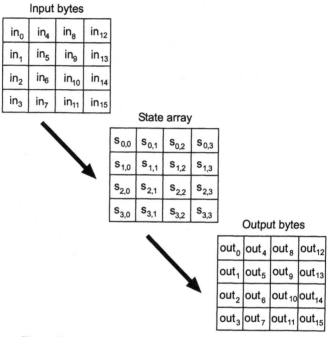

Figure 10.6   Input bytes, State array, and output bytes of the AES.

As illustrated in Figure 10.6, the 16 input bytes $in_0, \ldots, in_{15}$ are copied into the State at the beginning of the AES encryption or decryption process. The encryption or decryption process is then conducted on the State, and the State's final bytes are copied back to the output bytes $out_0, \ldots, out_{15}$. More formally speaking, the input array in is copied into the State according to

$$s_{r,c} = in_{r+4c}$$

for $0 \leq r < 4$ and $0 \leq c < 4$ at the beginning of the encryption (or decryption) process. Similarly, the State is copied back into the output array out according to

$$out_{r+4c} = s_{r,c}$$

for $0 \le r < 4$ and $0 \le c < 4$ at the end of the encryption (or decryption). The AES encryption, key expansion, and decryption algorithms are overviewed next.

10.2.2.3 Encryption Algorithm

The AES specification uses the term *cipher* to refer to the encryption algorithm. This term, however, is not used in this book (note that we use the term *cipher* to refer to a full-fledged symmetric encryption system and not only to an encryption algorithm or function).

As mentioned earlier, the 16 input bytes $in_0, \ldots, in_{15}$ are copied into the State s at the beginning of the AES encryption algorithm. After an initial application of the AddRoundKey() transformation, the State is transformed by implementing a *round function* $N_r = 10$, 12, or 14 times (depending on the key length in use), with a final round that slightly differs from the previous $N_r - 1$ rounds (i.e., the final round does not include a MixColumns() transformation). The content of the State is finally taken to represent the output of the AES encryption algorithm.

The round function, in turn, consists of the following four transformations:

1. The bytes of the State are substituted according to a given substitution table (this transformation is called SubBytes() in the AES specification);

2. The rows of the State are shifted left by different offsets (this transformation is called ShiftRows() in the AES specification);

3. The data within each column of the State are mixed (this transformation is called MixColumns() in the AES specification);

4. A round key is added to the State (this transformation is called AddRound-Key() in the AES specification). This is where the secret key and the key schedule derived from it come into play.

The AES encryption algorithm is illustrated in Algorithm 10.2. Note that the SubBytes() and ShiftRows() transformations commute—that is, a SubBytes() transformation immediately followed by a ShiftRows() transformation is equivalent to a ShiftRows() transformation immediately followed by a SubBytes() transformation. Also note that $w[i]$ refers to the ith word in the key schedule and that $w[i, j]$ refers to the $j - i + 1$ words between w_i and w_j in the key schedule.

Algorithm 10.2   The AES encryption algorithm.

(in)
$s \leftarrow in$
$s \leftarrow \text{AddRoundKey}(s, w[0, N_b - 1])$
for $r = 1$ to $(N_r - 1)$ do
$\quad s \leftarrow \text{SubBytes}(s)$
$\quad s \leftarrow \text{ShiftRows}(s)$
$\quad s \leftarrow \text{MixColumns}(s)$
$\quad s \leftarrow \text{AddRoundKey}(s, w[rN_b, (r+1)N_b - 1])$
$s \leftarrow \text{SubBytes}(s)$
$s \leftarrow \text{ShiftRows}(s)$
$s \leftarrow \text{AddRoundKey}(s, w[N_r N_b, (N_r + 1)N_b - 1])$
$out \leftarrow s$
(out)

Table 10.10
The S-Box of the AES Encryption Algorithm

	0	1	2	3	4	5	6	7	8	9	A	B	C	D	E	F
0	63	7C	77	7B	F2	6B	6F	C5	30	01	67	2B	FE	D7	AB	76
1	CA	82	C9	7D	FA	59	47	F0	AD	D4	A2	AF	9C	A4	72	C0
2	B7	FD	93	26	36	3F	F7	CC	34	A5	E5	F1	71	D8	31	15
3	04	C7	23	C3	18	96	05	9A	07	12	80	E2	EB	27	B2	75
4	09	83	2C	1A	1B	6E	5A	A0	52	3B	D6	B3	29	E3	2F	84
5	53	D1	00	ED	20	FC	B1	5B	6A	CB	BE	39	4A	4C	58	CF
6	D0	EF	AA	FB	43	4D	33	85	45	F9	02	7F	50	3C	9F	A8
7	51	A3	40	8F	92	9D	38	F5	BC	B6	DA	21	10	FF	F3	D2
8	CD	0C	13	EC	5F	97	44	17	C4	A7	7E	3D	64	5D	19	73
9	60	81	4F	DC	22	2A	90	88	46	EE	B8	14	DE	5E	0B	DB
A	E0	32	3A	0A	49	06	24	5C	C2	D3	AC	62	91	95	E4	79
B	E7	C8	37	6D	8D	D5	4E	A9	6C	56	F4	EA	65	7A	AE	08
C	BA	78	25	2E	1C	A6	B4	C6	E8	DD	74	1F	4B	BD	8B	8A
D	70	3E	B5	66	48	03	F6	0E	61	35	57	B9	86	C1	1D	9E
E	E1	F8	98	11	69	D9	8E	94	9B	1E	87	E9	CE	55	28	DF
F	8C	A1	89	0D	BF	E6	42	68	41	99	2D	0F	B0	54	BB	16

SubBytes() Transformation

The SubBytes() transformation implements a nonlinear substitution cipher. Each byte $s_{r,c}$ of the State is substituted with another byte $s'_{r,c}$ according to the substitution table (called S-box) illustrated in Table 10.10. For input byte 0xXY, the high-order byte (i.e., 0xX) refers to the vertical axis, and the low-order byte (i.e., 0xY) refers to the horizontal axis. The output byte is the one found in the S-box in row 0xX and column 0xY. For example, the input byte 0x52 (i.e., 01010010) is mapped to the output byte 0x00 (i.e., 00000000).

Contrary to many other symmetric encryption systems (inlcuding, for example, the DES), the S-box of the AES has a well-documented design. It is constructed by composing the following two transformations:

1. The input byte $s_{r,c}$ is mapped to the multiplicative inverse in the AES field (the element `0x00` is mapped to itself). The resulting byte is referred to as b.

2. The following affine transformation modulo 2 is applied for all bits b_i ($0 \leq i < 8$) of b:

$$b_i' = b_i \oplus b_{(i+4) \bmod 8} \oplus b_{(i+5) \bmod 8} \oplus$$
$$b_{(i+6) \bmod 8} \oplus b_{(i+7) \bmod 8} \oplus c_i$$

In this formula, c_i refers to the ith bit of a byte c with the hexadecimal value 63 (i.e., `01100011`). This transformation can be expressed in matrix form as follows:

$$
\begin{bmatrix} b_0' \\ b_1' \\ b_2' \\ b_3' \\ b_4' \\ b_5' \\ b_6' \\ b_7' \end{bmatrix}
=
\begin{bmatrix}
1 & 0 & 0 & 0 & 1 & 1 & 1 & 1 \\
1 & 1 & 0 & 0 & 0 & 1 & 1 & 1 \\
1 & 1 & 1 & 0 & 0 & 0 & 1 & 1 \\
1 & 1 & 1 & 1 & 0 & 0 & 0 & 1 \\
1 & 1 & 1 & 1 & 1 & 0 & 0 & 0 \\
0 & 1 & 1 & 1 & 1 & 1 & 0 & 0 \\
0 & 0 & 1 & 1 & 1 & 1 & 1 & 0 \\
0 & 0 & 0 & 1 & 1 & 1 & 1 & 1
\end{bmatrix}
\cdot
\begin{bmatrix} b_0 \\ b_1 \\ b_2 \\ b_3 \\ b_4 \\ b_5 \\ b_6 \\ b_7 \end{bmatrix}
+
\begin{bmatrix} 1 \\ 1 \\ 0 \\ 0 \\ 0 \\ 1 \\ 1 \\ 0 \end{bmatrix}
$$

The resulting byte b' is the output byte $s_{r,c}'$ of the transformation.

In summary, the SubBytes() transformation can be written as

$$s_{r,c}' = A \cdot s_{r,c}^{-1} + c$$

where A and c represent the matrix and the vector of bytes specified earlier. Note that the nonlinerarity of the SubBytes() transformation comes from the inversion $s_{r,c}^{-1}$ only (if the transformation were applied on $s_{r,c}$ directly, then the corresponding SubBytes() transformation would be linear). Also note that the invertibility of the SubBytes() transformation requires that A is an invertible matrix (i.e., its rows and columns must be linearly independent in the AES field). This is obviously the case, and hence the SubBytes() transformation is invertible (the corresponding InvSubBytes() transformation is addressed later).

ShiftRows() Transformation

The ShiftRows() transformation cyclically shifts left the bytes in row r ($0 \le r \le 3$) for r bytes. This means that the bytes in the first row (i.e., $r = 0$) are not shifted at all, the bytes in the second row (i.e., $r = 1$) are cyclically shifted left one byte, the bytes in the third row (i.e., $r = 2$) are cyclically shifted left two bytes, and the bytes in the fourth row (i.e., $r = 3$) are cyclically shifted left three bytes. Consequently, for $0 \le r < 4$ and $0 \le c < N_b = 4$, the ShiftRows() transformation can be formally expressed as follows:

$$s'_{r,c} = s_{r,c+shift(r,N_b) \bmod N_b} \qquad (10.5)$$

In this formula, the shift value $shift(r, N_b)$ depends only on the row number r (remember that N_b is always equal to 4):

$$shift(1,4) = 1$$
$$shift(2,4) = 2$$
$$shift(3,4) = 3$$

For example, $s'_{2,1} = s_{2,1+shift(2,4) \bmod 4} = s_{2,1+2 \bmod 4} = s_{2,3}$. The ShiftRows() transformation is illustrated in Figure 10.7. Note that the elements of s' are the same as the elements of s, and that only their ordering changes when the State is being tranformed.

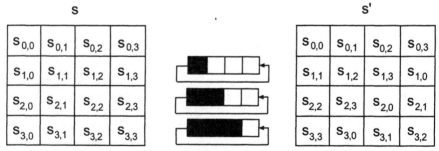

Figure 10.7   The ShiftRows() transformation of the AES encryption algorithm.

MixColumns() Transformation

The MixColumns() transformation operates on each column of the State individually. This means that the transformation is repeated four times (once for each column of the State). More specifically, we consider the four bytes $s_{0,c}, s_{1,c}, s_{2,c}$, and $s_{3,c}$ of column c ($0 \leq c < 4$) of the State, denoted by s_0, s_1, s_2, and s_3 (the column number is omitted for clarity in exposition), and we use these bytes to represent the coefficients of a four-term polynomial

$$s(x) = s_3 x^3 + s_2 x^2 + s_1 x + s_0$$

over $\mathbb{F}_{2^8}$. In a short representation, $s(x)$ can also be written as $[s_0, s_1, s_2, s_3]$. Because the coefficients of $s(x)$ are bytes (i.e., elements of $\mathbb{F}_{2^8}$), the polynomial $s(x)$ is over $\mathbb{F}_{2^8}$, and hence it is not an element of the AES field.

Against this background, the MixColumns() transformation on a column is defined by multiplying the corresponding column polynomial $s(x)$ with a fixed polynomial $c(x)$ of degree 3. Again, a polynomial is used to reduce the product and to make sure that the resulting polynomial is of degree 3. The fixed polynomial $c(x)$ is

$$c(x) = c_3 x^3 + c_2 x^2 + c_1 x + c_0$$

with $c_3 = $ 0x03 (i.e., $\{00000011\}$), $c_2 = $ 0x01 (i.e., $\{00000001\}$), $c_1 = $ 0x01 (i.e., $\{00000001\}$), and $c_0 = $ 0x02 (i.e., $\{00000010\}$), and the polynomial to reduce the product is $x^4 + 1$. Note that this polynomial is reducible in $\mathbb{F}_2$ (i.e., $x^4 + 1 = (x+1)^4$) and that the only reason for the multiplication being performed modulo $x^4 + 1$ is to make sure that the operation outputs a polynomial of degree 3 at most (i.e., to achieve a transformation from a value that matches into a column to another value that also matches into a column).

In essence, the MixColumns() transformation maps $s(x)$ to the following polynomial:

$$c(x) \cdot s(x) \ (\mathrm{mod}\ x^4 + 1)$$

Alternatively speaking, the MixColumns() transformation can also be achieved by implementing the following linear algebraic transformation for each column c ($0 \leq c < 4$):

$$
\begin{bmatrix} s'_{0,c} \\ s'_{1,c} \\ s'_{2,c} \\ s'_{3,c} \end{bmatrix} = \begin{bmatrix} 0\text{x}02 & 0\text{x}03 & 0\text{x}01 & 0\text{x}01 \\ 0\text{x}01 & 0\text{x}02 & 0\text{x}03 & 0\text{x}01 \\ 0\text{x}01 & 0\text{x}01 & 0\text{x}02 & 0\text{x}03 \\ 0\text{x}03 & 0\text{x}01 & 0\text{x}01 & 0\text{x}02 \end{bmatrix} \cdot \begin{bmatrix} s_{0,c} \\ s_{1,c} \\ s_{2,c} \\ s_{3,c} \end{bmatrix}
$$

This can also be expressed as follows:

$$
\begin{aligned}
s'_{0,c} &= (0\text{x}02 \cdot s_{0,c}) \oplus (0\text{x}03 \cdot s_{1,c}) \oplus s_{2,c} \oplus s_{3,c} \\
s'_{1,c} &= s_{0,c} \oplus (0\text{x}02 \cdot s_{1,c}) \oplus (0\text{x}03 \cdot s_{2,c}) \oplus s_{3,c} \\
s'_{2,c} &= s_{0,c} \oplus s_{1,c} \oplus (0\text{x}02 \cdot s_{2,c}) \oplus (0\text{x}03 \cdot s_{3,c}) \\
s'_{3,c} &= (0\text{x}03 \cdot s_{0,c}) \oplus s_{1,c} \oplus s_{2,c} \oplus (0\text{x}02 \cdot s_{3,c})
\end{aligned}
$$

Because the polynomial $c(x)$ is relatively prime to $x^4 + 1$ in $\mathbb{F}_2[x]$, an inverse polynomial $c(x)^{-1}$ (mod $x^4 + 1$) exists, and hence the MixColumns() transformation is invertible.

AddRoundKey() Transformation

In the AddRoundKey() transformation, a word of the key schedule w is added modulo 2 to each column of the State. This means that

$$
[s'_{0,c}, s'_{1,c}, s'_{2,c}, s'_{3,c}] = [s_{0,c}, s_{1,c}, s_{2,c}, s_{3,c}] \oplus w[rN_b + c]
$$

for $0 \leq c < N_b$ and $0 \leq r \leq N_r$. Because the AddRoundKey() transformation only consists of a bitwise addition modulo 2, it is its own inverse.

10.2.2.4   Key Expansion Algorithm

The AES key expansion algorithm takes a secret key k and generates a key schedule w that is employed by the AddRoundKey() transformation. The key k comprises $4N_k$ bytes or $32N_k$ bits. In the byte-wise representation, k_i refers to the ith byte of k ($0 \leq i < 4N_k$). The key schedule w is $N_b(N_r + 1)$ words long (the algorithm requires an initial set of N_b words, and each of the N_r rounds requires N_b additional words of key data). This means that w consists of a linear array of 4-byte words. Again, we use $w[i]$ for $0 \leq i < N_b(N_r + 1)$ to refer to the ith word in this array.

Algorithm 10.3 The AES key expansion algorithm.

(k)

RCon[1] ← 0x01000000
RCon[2] ← 0x02000000
RCon[3] ← 0x04000000
RCon[4] ← 0x08000000
RCon[5] ← 0x10000000
RCon[6] ← 0x20000000
RCon[7] ← 0x40000000
RCon[8] ← 0x80000000
RCon[9] ← 0x1B000000
RCon[10] ← 0x36000000
for $i = 0$ to $(N_k - 1)$ do
    $w[i] \leftarrow [k_{4i}, k_{4i+1}, k_{4i+2}, k_{4i+3}]$
for $i = N_k$ to $(N_b(N_r + 1) - 1)$ do
    $t \leftarrow w[i-1]$
    if $(i \mod N_k = 0)$
        then $t \leftarrow$ SubWord(RotWord(t)) $\oplus$ RCon[i/N_k]
        else if $(N_k > 6$ and $i \mod N_k = 4)$
        then $t \leftarrow$ SubWord(t)
    $w[i] \leftarrow w[i - N_k] \oplus t$

(w)

The AES key expansion algorithm is summarized in Algorithm 10.3. We assume that N_k is included in k, so we don't have to consider N_k as additional parameter. The algorithm employs a round constant word array, RCon[i] for $0 < i \leq N_r$. The array contains the values given by $[x^{i-1}, 0\text{x}00, 0\text{x}00, 0\text{x}00]$, with x^{i-1} being powers of x (x is 0x02) in the field $\mathbb{F}_{2^8}$.[27] In addition to RCon, the algorithm employs two auxiliary functions:

- SubWord() takes a 4-byte input word and applies the S-box of the SubBytes() transformation to each of the 4 bytes to produce an output word.

- RotWord() takes a 4-byte input word and performs a cyclic shift left (i.e., if the input word is $[a_0, a_1, a_2, a_3]$, then the output word is $[a_1, a_2, a_3, a_0]$).

The AES key expansion algorithm works as follows: First, the round constant word array RCon is initialized as described before. Then the first N_k words of the key schedule are filled with the bytes of the original key. The rest of the key schedule is filled in a second for-loop. In this loop, every word $w[i]$ is set to the sum modulo 2 of the previous word $w[i - 1]$ and the word that is located N_k positions earlier

---

27 Note that the index i starts at 1 (not 0).

(i.e., $w[i - N_k]$). For words in positions that are a multiple of N_k, a transformation is applied to $[w_{i-1}]$ prior to the addition modulo 2, followed by an addition modulo 2 with the round constant word RCon$[i]$. This transformation basically consists of a cyclic shift of the bytes in a word (i.e., RotWord()), followed by the application of a table lookup to all 4 bytes of the word (i.e., SubWord()). It is important to note that the AES key expansion algorithm for $N_k = 8$ is different than for $N_k = 6$ (i.e., AES-192) and $N_k = 4$ (i.e., AES-128). If $N_k = 8$ and $i - 4$ is a multiple of N_k, then SubWord() is applied to $w[i - 1]$ prior to the addition modulo 2.

10.2.2.5 Decryption Algorithm

The transformations used by the AES encryption algorithm can be inverted and implemented in reverse order to produce a straightforward AES decryption algorithm. The individual transformations used in the AES decryption algorithm are called InvShiftRows(), InvSubBytes(), InvMixColumns(), and AddRoundKey(). As mentioned earlier, the AddRoundKey() transformation is its own inverse, as it only involves a bitwise addition modulo 2. Also, note that the SubBytes() and ShiftRows() transformations commute, and that this is also true for their inverse InvSubBytes() and InvShiftRows() transformations. The AES decryption algorithm is formally expressed in Algorithm 10.4, and the three inverse transformations are addressed next.

Algorithm 10.4 The AES decryption algorithm.

(in)

$s \leftarrow in$
$s \leftarrow$ AddRoundKey$(s, w[N_r N_b, (N_r + 1)N_b - 1])$
for $r = N_r - 1$ downto 1 do
    $s \leftarrow$ InvShiftRows(s)
    $s \leftarrow$ InvSubBytes(s)
    $s \leftarrow$ AddRoundKey$(s, w[rN_b, (r + 1)N_b - 1])$
    $s \leftarrow$ InvMixColumns(s)
$s \leftarrow$ InvShiftRows(s)
$s \leftarrow$ InvSubBytes(s)
$s \leftarrow$ AddRoundKey$(s, w[0, N_b - 1])$
$out \leftarrow s$

(out)

InvShiftRows() Transformation

The InvShiftRows() transformation is the inverse of the ShiftRows() transformation. As such, the bytes in the last three rows of the State are cyclically shifted right over

$shift(r, N_b)$ bytes (note that the $shift$ function is the same for both the encryption and decryption algorithms). Similar to (10.5), the InvShiftRows() transformation can be specified as

$$s'_{r,(c+shift(r,N_b)) \bmod N_b} = s_{r,c}$$

for $0 \le r < 4$ and $0 \le c < N_b = 4$. It is illustrated in Figure 10.8.

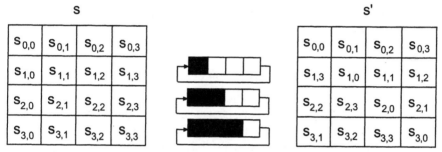

Figure 10.8   The InvShiftRows() transformation of the AES decryption algorithm.

Table 10.11
The Inverse S-Box of the AES Decryption Algorithm

	0	1	2	3	4	5	6	7	8	9	A	B	C	D	E	F
0	52	09	6A	D5	30	36	A5	38	BF	40	A3	9E	81	F3	D7	FB
1	7C	E3	39	82	9B	2F	FF	87	34	8E	43	44	C4	DE	E9	CB
2	54	7B	94	32	A6	C2	23	3D	EE	4C	95	0B	42	FA	C3	4E
3	08	2E	A1	66	28	D9	24	B2	76	5B	A2	49	6D	8B	D1	25
4	72	F8	F6	64	86	68	98	16	D4	A4	5C	CC	5D	65	B6	92
5	6C	70	48	50	FD	ED	B9	DA	5E	15	46	57	A7	8D	9D	84
6	90	D8	AB	00	8C	BC	D3	0A	F7	E4	58	05	B8	B3	45	06
7	D0	2C	1E	8F	CA	3F	0F	02	C1	AF	BD	03	01	13	8A	6B
8	3A	91	11	41	4F	67	DC	EA	97	F2	CF	CE	F0	B4	E6	73
9	96	AC	74	22	E7	AD	35	85	E2	F9	37	E8	1C	75	DF	6E
A	47	F1	1A	71	1D	29	C5	89	6F	B7	62	0E	AA	18	BE	1B
b	FC	56	3E	4B	C6	D2	79	20	9A	DB	C0	FE	78	CD	5A	F4
C	1F	DD	A8	33	88	07	C7	31	B1	12	10	59	27	80	EC	5F
D	60	51	7F	A9	19	B5	4A	0D	2D	E5	7A	9F	93	C9	9C	EF
E	A0	E0	3B	4D	AE	2A	F5	B0	C8	EB	BB	3C	83	53	99	61
F	17	2B	04	7E	BA	77	D6	26	E1	69	14	63	55	21	.0C	7D

InvSubBytes() Transformation

The InvSubBytes() transformation is the inverse of the SubBytes() transformation. It is obtained by applying the inverse of the affine transformation specified in 10.2.2.3, followed by taking the multiplicative inverse in $\mathbb{F}_{2^8}$. The corresponding inverse S-box is illustrated in Table 10.11. It is simple to verify that the S-boxes specified in Tables 10.10 and 10.11 are inverse to each other. For example, the S-box maps $\mathtt{0xA3}$ to $\mathtt{0x0A}$, whereas the inverse S-box maps $\mathtt{0x0A}$ back to $\mathtt{0xA3}$.

InvMixColumns() Transformation

The InvMixColumns() transformation is the inverse of the MixColumns() transformation. Similar to the MixColumns() transformation, it operates on the State column by column, treating each column as a 4-term polynomial $s(x)$ over $\mathbb{F}_{2^8}$. More specifically, the polynomial $s(x)$ is multiplied modulo $x^4 + 1$ with polynomial

$$c^{-1}(x) = c'_3 x^3 + c'_2 x^2 + c'_1 x + c'_0,$$

where $c'_3 = \mathtt{0x0B}$ (i.e., $\{00001011\}$), $c'_2 = \mathtt{0x0D}$ (i.e., $\{00001101\}$), $c'_1 = \mathtt{0x09}$ (i.e., $\{00001001\}$), and $c'_0 = \mathtt{0x0E}$ (i.e., $\{00001110\}$). Consequently, the InvMix-Columns() transformation maps $s(x)$ to the following polynomial:

$$c^{-1}(x) \cdot s(x) \; (\mathrm{mod} \; x^4 + 1)$$

Alternatively, this can be expressed as

$$\begin{bmatrix} s'_{0,c} \\ s'_{1,c} \\ s'_{2,c} \\ s'_{3,c} \end{bmatrix} = \begin{bmatrix} \mathtt{0x0E} & \mathtt{0x0B} & \mathtt{0x0D} & \mathtt{0x09} \\ \mathtt{0x09} & \mathtt{0x0E} & \mathtt{0x0B} & \mathtt{0x0D} \\ \mathtt{0x0D} & \mathtt{0x09} & \mathtt{0x0E} & \mathtt{0x0B} \\ \mathtt{0x0B} & \mathtt{0x0D} & \mathtt{0x09} & \mathtt{0x0E} \end{bmatrix} \cdot \begin{bmatrix} s_{0,c} \\ s_{1,c} \\ s_{2,c} \\ s_{3,c} \end{bmatrix}$$

or

$$\begin{aligned} s'_{0,c} &= (\mathtt{0x0E} \cdot s_{0,c}) \oplus (\mathtt{0x0B} \cdot s_{1,c}) \oplus (\mathtt{0x0D} \cdot s_{2,c}) \oplus (\mathtt{0x09} \cdot s_{3,c}) \\ s'_{1,c} &= (\mathtt{0x09} \cdot s_{0,c}) \oplus (\mathtt{0x0E} \cdot s_{1,c}) \oplus (\mathtt{0x0B} \cdot s_{2,c}) \oplus (\mathtt{0x0D} \cdot s_{3,c}) \\ s'_{2,c} &= (\mathtt{0x0D} \cdot s_{0,c}) \oplus (\mathtt{0x09} \cdot s_{1,c}) \oplus (\mathtt{0x0E} \cdot s_{2,c}) \oplus (\mathtt{0x0B} \cdot s_{3,c}) \\ s'_{3,c} &= (\mathtt{0x0B} \cdot s_{0,c}) \oplus (\mathtt{0x0D} \cdot s_{1,c}) \oplus (\mathtt{0x09} \cdot s_{2,c}) \oplus (\mathtt{0x0E} \cdot s_{3,c}) \end{aligned}$$

10.2.2.6 Security Analysis

Since its submission to the AES competition, and especially since its standardization in FIPS PUB 197 [16], the AES has been subject to a lot of public scrutiny. There is good and bad news. The good news is that the encryption system is designed in a way that lower bounds for the complexity of differential cryptanalysis, linear cryptanalysis, and some related attacks can be provided (e.g., [14]). Consequently, the AES encryption system is resistant against these attacks. The bad news, however, is that many new cryptanalytical techniques have been developed (and will probably continue to be developed) to eventually break the AES symmetric encryption system. In fact, cryptanalyzing AES is an active field of study, and it will be interesting to learn about future results.[28] From a cryptanalyst's viewpoint, the AES is attractive, because it is supposed to become widely deployed in the future and because the symmetric encryption system has a rather simple mathematical structure.

10.2.3 Modes of Operation

There are several modes of operation for a block cipher with block length n. In FIPS PUB 81 [17], a couple of such modes are specified for DES.[29] The standard was published in 1980 and is electronically available on the Internet.[30] Note that some of the modes specified in FIPS PUB 81 turn a block cipher into a stream cipher.

10.2.3.1 Electronic Code Book Mode

The simplest and most straightforward mode of operation is the *electronic code book* (ECB) mode (see Figure 10.9). In this mode, an arbitrarily long plaintext message $m \in \mathcal{M}$ is split into t n-bit blocks (n representing the block length). If the total length of the plaintext message is not a multiple of n bits, then it must be padded with some random bits. The plaintext message block m_i $(1 \leq i \leq t)$ is encrypted with the secret key k by the sending device (on the left side). The resulting ciphertext block c_i is transmitted to the decrypting device, where it is decrypted with the same key k (on the right side). Consequently, the ECB mode is defined as

$$
\begin{aligned}
c_i &= E_k(m_i) \\
m_i &= D_k(c_i)
\end{aligned}
$$

---

28 http://www.cryptosystem.net/aes.

29 Note that the specification of the modes of operation are not specific for DES; instead, they work for any block cipher with block length n.

30 http://csrc.nist.gov/publications/fips/fips81/fips81.htm.

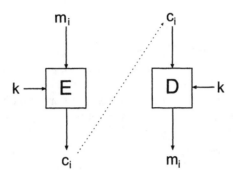

Figure 10.9   The working principle of the ECB mode.

for $1 \leq i \leq t$. The major advantages of the ECB mode are simplicity and the lack of message expansion and error propagation. There are, however, also some important disadvantages that should be kept in mind and considered with care when one intends to use a symmetric encryption system in ECB mode:

- In ECB mode, identical plaintext message blocks are mapped to identical ciphertext blocks (if the key is the same). This is disadvantageous, because a multiple-block ciphertext can then reveal statistical information about the corresponding plaintext message, even if it is not possible to decrypt the entire ciphertext. In fact, this type of statistical information is what cryptanalysts are usually looking for and what they try to exploit in one way or another.

- The ECB mode does not protect a sequence of ciphertext blocks. This means that an adversary can modify a long message simply by deleting or reordering single blocks in it. If an adversary has ciphertext blocks that are encrypted with the same key, then he or she can also insert them into the ciphertext. Note that in neither of these cases does the adversary need to be able to decrypt any of the ciphertext blocks used in the attack.

The disadvantages are severe (compared to the advantages), and hence the ECB mode should not be used to encrypt multiple-block plaintext messages.

10.2.3.2   Cipherblock Chaining Mode

The *cipherblock chaining* (CBC) mode of operation was designed to remove some of the disadvantages of the ECB mode. In CBC mode, the encryption of the plaintext message block m_i depends not only on m_i and the key k, but also on all previous message blocks $m_1, \ldots, m_{i-1}$, as well as an *initialization vector* (IV) that must not be kept secret. The resulting encryption function is context sensitive, meaning that identical plaintext message blocks are usually mapped to different ciphertext blocks.

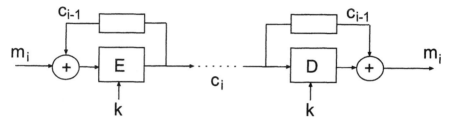

Figure 10.10 The working principle of the CBC mode.

Again, let $m \in \mathcal{M}$ be an arbitrarily long plaintext message that is split into t n-bit blocks $m_1, m_2, \ldots, m_t$. The working principle of the CBC mode is illustrated in Figure 10.10. In a first step, c_0 is initialized with the IV (this step is not illustrated in the figure). For $i = 1, \ldots, t$, the plaintext message block m_i is then added modulo 2 to c_{i-1} (i.e., the ciphertext block from the previous round) and the sum is encrypted with key k to produce the ciphertext block c_i (on the left side). Consequently, the encryption function can be recursively defined as follows:

$$\begin{aligned} c_0 &= IV \\ c_i &= E_k(m_i \oplus c_{i-1}) \text{ for } 1 \leq i \leq t \end{aligned}$$

Due to the use of an IV, the ciphertext is one block longer than the plaintext message. Consequently, the CBC mode is not length preserving and leads to a message expansion of one block (i.e., the actual message expansion depends on the block length of the encryption system in use). In either case, the resulting ciphertext blocks c_i $(i = 0, \ldots, t)$[31] are transmitted to the decrypting device and put in a queue (used for decryption). Again, the queue is initialized with $c_0 = IV$. To decrypt c_i $(i = 1, \ldots, t)$, the decrypting device decrypts c_i with key k and adds the result modulo 2 to c_{i-1} (on the right side). The result yields the plaintext message block m_i. Hence, the decryption function can be recursively defined as follows:

$$c_0 = IV$$

---

31 The ciphertext block c_0 must not be transmitted if the decrypting device is initialized with the same IV.

$$m_i = D_k(c_i) \oplus c_{i-1} \text{ for } 1 \leq i \leq t$$

As can be verified easily, this recursive definition yields a correct plaintext message block m_i:

$$
\begin{aligned}
m_i &= D_k(c_i) \oplus c_{i-1} \\
&= D_k(E_k(m_i \oplus c_{i-1})) \oplus c_{i-1} \\
&= m_i \oplus c_{i-1} \oplus c_{i-1} \\
&= m_i
\end{aligned}
$$

The major advantage of the CBC mode is that it removes the previously mentioned disadvantages of the ECB mode. There are, however, also a few disadvantages that must be kept in mind when one uses a symmetric encryption system in CBC mode. For example, the CBC mode comes along with a message expansion of one block. Furthermore, the fact that ciphertext blocks are chained also means that errors are propagated, and that one has to deal with error propagation and the consequences of incorrectly transmitted ciphertext blocks (i.e., transmisson errors). If, for example, ciphertext block c_i is transmitted with an error, then c_i and the subsequent block (i.e., c_{i+1}) decrypt incorrectly. All other ciphertext blocks (i.e., $c_1, \ldots, c_{i-1}, c_{i+2}, \ldots, c_t$) decrypt correctly, unless there are other transmission errors. Note that the fact that an incorrectly transmitted ciphertext block only affects two blocks suggests that communicating entities can start with different IVs, and that the difference only affects the first ciphertext block (this property is important if two entities don't share a common IV).

Having the advantages and disadvantages of the ECB and CBC modes in mind, it is obvious that the CBC mode is usually the preferred choice in block cipher encryption.[32]

10.2.3.3   Cipher Feedback Mode

As mentioned earlier, there are modes of operation that turn a block cipher into a stream cipher. One of these modes is the *cipher feedback* (CFB) mode. It basically uses the block cipher to generate a sequence of pseudorandom bits, and these bits are then added modulo 2 to the plaintext bits to produce the ciphertext bits.

Let n be the block length of the block cipher, $IV \in \{0,1\}^n$ be an n-bit initialization vector, and $1 \leq r \leq n$ be the number of bits that are simultaneously

---

[32]   It should always be made sure that a block cipher with block length n is rekeyed after the encryption of at most $2^{n/2}$ blocks.

encrypted in each round (typically $r = 1$ for one bit or $r = 8$ for one byte). The plaintext message $m \in \mathcal{M}$ is then split into t blocks of r bits each, and hence the plaintext block sequence $m_1, \ldots, m_t$ is the one that is actually encrypted in CFB mode.

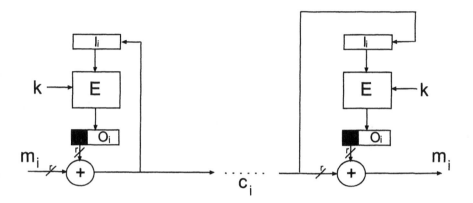

Figure 10.11   The working principle of the CFB mode.

As illustrated in Figure 10.11, the encrypting and decrypting devices use two registers each (i.e., an input register I and an output register O). The input registers are both initialized with the IV (i.e., $I_0 = IV$ on either side of the communication channel). In step i ($1 \leq i \leq t$), the encrypting device encrypts the input register I_i with the key k (using the underlying block cipher), and the result is written into the output register O_i. The r leftmost and most significant bits of O_i are then added modulo 2 to the plaintext message block m_i (optionally, it is possible to use the remaining $n - r$ bits of O_i to encrypt subsequent plaintext blocks). The resulting r-bit ciphertext block c_i is sent to the decrypting device and fed back into the input register from the right. The decrypting device reverses the process. This means that ciphertext block c_i is decrypted by adding it modulo 2 to the leftmost and most significant r bits of O_i. O_i, in turn, results from an encryption of the contents of the input register.

The major advantage of the CFB mode is that it turns a block cipher into a stream cipher. Consequently, it is possible to encrypt blocks that are smaller than the block length of the block cipher (i.e., $r < n$). This is important for applications that normally don't require the transmission of large messages. Examples include applications that are character oriented, such as terminal access protocols (e.g., Telnet or rlogin). In this case, r is typically set to 8 bits.

There are also a couple disadvantages that should be kept in mind when using a symmetric encryption system in CFB mode:

- The major disadvantage is performance. Note that a full encryption of n bits is required to encrypt only r bits. The impact of this disadvantage depends on the symmetric encryption system in use and the size of r as compared to the block length n. For example, if DES is used in CFB mode and r is 8 bits (meaning that the encryption is character oriented), then the performance is $n/r = 64/8 = 8$ times slower than "normal" DES (whether it is operated in the ECB or CBC mode). Consequently, there is a tradeoff to make to choose an optimal value for r (and this tradeoff may depend on the application one has in mind). Note that it is at least possible to use the $n - r$ bits of the output register to encrypt subsequent plaintext blocks or bits.

- The size of r also influences the error propagation properties of the encryption. Note that an incorrectly transmitted ciphertext block disturbs the decryption process until it "falls out" of the input register. Consequently, the larger r is, the fewer errors are propagated.

- As mentioned earlier, the encryption is a simple addition modulo 2, and the block cipher is only used to generate the key stream. This generation, however, also depends on the ciphertext bits that are fed back into the input register (that's why the mode is called cipher feedback in the first place). Consequently, it is not possible to precompute the key stream.

The last point (i.e., the impossibility to precompute the key stream) is the major difference between the CFB and the mode addressed next.

10.2.3.4   Output Feedback Mode

The *output feedback* (OFB) mode is conceptually similar to the CFB mode. As illustrated in Figure 10.12 (and contrary to the CFB mode), the key stream is generated independently from the ciphertext blocks in the OFB mode. This suggests that the OFB mode has no error propagation. In some application settings, this is advantageous, and only the OFB mode is used for this purpose. In other application settings, the lack of error propagation is disadvantageous, and the CFB mode is used instead. From a performance viewpoint, the OFB mode is advantageous because the key stream can be computed independently from the plaintext or ciphertext. This means that the key stream can be precomputed and that the encryption throughput can be made very large.

In OFB mode, it is important to change the IV regularly (e.g., [18]). This is particularly true if two plaintext messages are encrypted with the same key k.

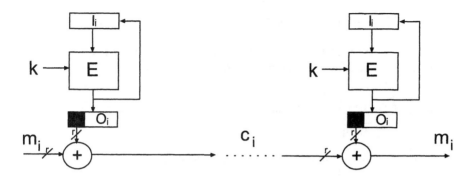

Figure 10.12 The working principle of the OFB mode.

Otherwise, the same key stream is generated, and this fact can be exploited by an adversary. If, for example, two plaintext message blocks m_i and m_i' are encrypted with the same r-bit key k, then the resulting ciphertext blocks are $c_i = m_i \oplus k$ and $c_i' = m_i' \oplus k$. Consequently, it is possible to add the two ciphertext blocks modulo 2 and remove the effect of the encryption accordingly:

$$\begin{aligned}
c_i \oplus c_i' &= (m_i \oplus k) \oplus (m_i' \oplus k) \\
&= m_i \oplus m_i' \oplus k \oplus k \\
&= m_i \oplus m_i' \oplus 0 \\
&= m_i \oplus m_i'
\end{aligned}$$

If m_i is known, then m_i' can be computed immediately (and vice versa). Even if m_i is not known, the statistical properties of the plaintext language in use can eventually be exploited to illegitimately determine m_i' or parts thereof.

Finally, note that—contrary to the ECB and CBC modes—in the CFB and OFB modes, both the sending and receiving devices use only the encryption function of the underlying encryption system. This means that these modes of operation can also be used if the encryption function is replaced with a one-way function (this may be important if symmetric encryption systems are not available or if their use is restricted in one way or another, respectively).

10.2.3.5   Other Modes of Operation

In addition to FIPS PUB 81, ANSI X9.52-1998 entitled *Triple Data Encryption Algorithm Modes of Operation* specifies the following seven different modes of operation for the TDEA:

- The TDEA ECB (TECB) mode;

- The TDEA CBC (TCBC) mode;

- The TDEA CBC Interleaved (TCBC-I) mode;

- The TDEA CFB (TCFB) mode;

- The TDEA CFB Pipelined (TCFB-P) mode;

- The TDEA OFB (TOFB) mode;

- The TDEA OFB Interleaved (TOFB-I) mode.

As their names suggest, the TECB, TCBC, TCFB, and TOFB modes are based upon the ECB, CBC, CFB, and OFB modes (obtained by substituting the DES encryption and decryption operations with the TDEA encryption and decryption operations).

To accommodate the AES and to add a parallelizable mode, NIST Special Publication 800-38A[33] introduced a new mode of operation (in addition to ECB, CBC, CFB, and OFB). This new mode of operation is called *counter* (CTR) mode. Similar to the CFB and OFB modes, the CTR mode yields a stream cipher. In essence, a key stream is generated and added modulo 2 (i.e., XORed) to the plaintext to produce the ciphertext. The key stream, in turn, is generated by encrypting a counter that is incremented by one after each encryption. Consequently, the major property of CTR mode is that there is no feedback or chaining; therefore, one can perform several encryptions in parallel.

In addition to the standardized modes of operation, researchers have proposed many new modes to NIST.[34] Among the more interesting are the modes that can be parallelized and the ones that combine encryption, authentication, and integrity protection for little more than the cost of encryption (e.g., the mode proposed in [19]). Working on modes of operation is maybe less glamorous, but it is certainly more fundamental than the work on the underlying block ciphers. Unfortunately, the current patent licensing status of most of these modes is unclear, as different parties are claiming patent coverage of various modes. As of this writing, using one of these modes should be considered with care (or discussed with a patent attorney).

33   http://csrc.nist.gov/publications/nistpubs/800-38a/sp800-38a.pdf.
34   http://csrc.nist.gov/CryptoToolkit/modes/proposedmodes.

10.3 STREAM CIPHERS

Stream ciphers have played and continue to play an important role in cryptography. In fact, many (proprietary) symmetric encryption systems used in military are stream ciphers.[35] Remember from Section 10.1 that stream ciphers use internal state and that the ith ciphertext unit depends on the ith plaintext unit, the secret key, and some state. Also remember that it is common to distinguish between synchronous (or additive) stream ciphers and nonsynchronous (or self-synchronizing) stream ciphers. Having the modes of operation for block ciphers in mind, it is obvious that operating a block cipher in CFB mode yields a nonsynchronous (self-synchronizing) stream cipher (i.e., the next state depends on previously generated ciphertext units), whereas operating a block cipher in OFB mode yields a synchronous (additive) stream cipher (i.e., the next state does not depend on previously generated ciphertext units). Due to their lack of error propagation, most stream ciphers in use today are synchronous (or additive). They try to copy Vernam's one-time pad (see Section 10.4), adding modulo 2 the plaintext message bitwise to a key stream.

Let $\Sigma = \mathbb{Z}_2 = \{0, 1\}$, $\mathcal{M} = \mathcal{C} = \Sigma^*$, and $\mathcal{K} = \Sigma^n$ for some reasonably sized key length n. To encrypt an l-bit plaintext message $m = m_1 \ldots m_l \in \mathcal{M}$ using an additive stream cipher, a secret key $k \in \mathcal{K}$ must be expanded into a stream of l key bits $k_1, \ldots, k_l$. The encryption function is then defined as follows:

$$E_k(m) = m_1 \oplus k_1, \ldots, m_l \oplus k_l = c_1, \ldots, c_l$$

Similarly, the decryption function is defined as follows:

$$D_k(c) = c_1 \oplus k_1, \ldots, c_l \oplus k_l = m_1, \ldots, m_l$$

The main question in the design of an additive stream cipher is how to expand k into a potentially infinite key stream $(k_i)_{i \geq 1}$. This is where the notion of a *feedback shift register* (FSR) comes into play.

As illustrated in Figure 10.13, an FSR consists of a register, a feedback function, and an internal clock. At every clock signal, the feedback function computes a new value from the register cells, and this new value is fed into the register from the left. Consequently, the contents of all register cells are shifted to the right, and the

---

35 The popularity of stream ciphers, however, is also controversial (to say the least). At the Cryptographer's Panel of the RSA Conference 2004, for example, Adi Shamir gave a short but very interesting talk entitled "The Death of the Stream Cipher." In this talk, Shamir noticed and tried to explain why stream ciphers are losing popularity against block ciphers. Nevertheless, stream ciphers have been, and continue to be, important for military and commercial encryption systems.

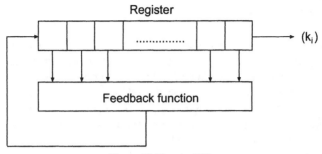

Figure 10.13   An FSR.

content of the rightmost register cell is the output of the FSR (for this clock cycle). This procedure is repeated for every clock cycle. Consequently, the FSR may be used to generate a sequence of (pseudorandom) output values. Because the length of the register and the alphabet in use are finite, the FSR represents an FSM and can be illustrated with a State diagram. If the register has n cells and the alphabet comprises q characters or symbols, then the FSR represents an FSM with q^n states at most. This also means that the FSR has a maximal period of q^n (needless to say that a large period is preferred from a security viewpoint). The mathematical or graph-theoretical instrument of choice to investigate on FSRs is the *Good-deBruijn graph*. This is not further addressed in this book.

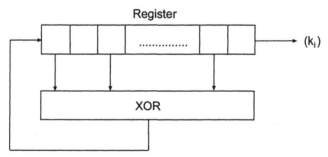

Figure 10.14   An exemplary LFSR.

In practice, LFSRs are most widely deployed. An FSR is linear if it operates in a field and the feedback function is linear over this field. Note that a function $f : X \rightarrow Y$ is *linear* if $f(x_1 + x_2) = f(x_1) + f(x_2)$ for all $x_1, x_2 \in X$ and $f(\alpha x) = \alpha f(x)$ for all $x \in X$ and $\alpha \in \mathbb{R}$. If we consider an FSR in $\mathbb{Z}_2 \cong \mathbb{F}_2$, then the feedback function is linear if and only if it represents the modulo 2 sum of a subset of the register cells (i.e., if any only if it can be realized by XOR gates). An exemplary LFSR is illustrated in Figure 10.14. In this example, three register cells are added modulo 2 and fed from the left into the register.

LFSRs have the advantage that they are mathematically structured and can be studied and formally analyzed accordingly. To study and formally analyze an n-cell LFSR, one usually expresses its state as a polynomial

$$a(x) = a_{n-1}x^{n-1} + \ldots + a_1 x^1 + a_0$$

of degree $n - 1$ in $\mathbb{F}_2[x]$, and its feedback coefficients as another polynomial

$$c(x) = c_n x^n + c_{n-1}x^{n-1} + \ldots + c_1 x^1 + c_0$$

of degree n in $\mathbb{F}_2[x]$. One then looks at $\mathbb{F}_2[x]_c$—that is, the ring of polynomials with degree less than or equal to $n - 1$ and the two operations addition and multiplication modulo $c(x)$. This ring has 2^n elements and is a (finite) field if and only if $c(x)$ is irreducible over $\mathbb{F}_2$ (see Section 3.3.6). In this case, $\mathbb{F}_2[x]_c^*$ is the multiplicative group of $\mathbb{F}_2[x]_c$ and has $2^n - 1$ elements. This is the algebraic structure of choice to study and formally analyze LFSRs (e.g., [20]). Note, however, that the output of an LFSR should never be directly used as a key stream. Otherwise, one can use the Berlekamp-Massey algorithm (see Section 9.1) to reconstruct the entire key stream using only very few known key stream bits.

In 1987, Rivest proposed an additive stream cipher that is based on an entirely different design paradigm (than LFSRs) and that has been widely deployed in many commercial applications, including, for example, Microsoft Windows and Oracle SQL. More importantly, the stream cipher is used in the *Wired Equivalent Privacy* (WEP) protocol used in many wireless networks, as well as the SSL and TLS protocols used on the Web (see, for example, Chapter 6 of [21] for an overview and discussion of the SSL/TLS protocol). The stream cipher was named *RC4*[36] and is currently one of the most widely deployed stream ciphers. The design of RC4 was kept (and is still being kept) as a trade secret of RSA Security, Inc.[37] In 1994, however, the source code of an RC4 implementation was anonymously posted to the Cypherpunks mailing list. The correctness of this unofficial posting was later confirmed by comparing its outputs to those produced by licensed implementations. Because the RC4 stream cipher is treated as a trade secret, the algorithm that was

---

36 The acronym RC stands for "Ron's Code." Note that RC2, RC5, and RC6 are block ciphers that are not closely related to RC4.

37 http://www.rsasecurity.com

anonymously posted is commonly referred to as *ARCFOUR*. It is the term we use in this book.

ARCFOUR is a synchronous (additive) stream cipher—that is, a sequence of pseudorandom bytes (i.e., a key stream) is generated independently from the plaintext message or ciphertext, and this sequence is added modulo 2 to the plaintext message byte sequence. The cipher takes a variable-length key that may range from 1 to 256 bytes (i.e., 2,048 bits). To generate the key stream, ARCFOUR employs an array S of 256 bytes of State information (called S-box). The elements of S are labeled $S[0], \ldots, S[255]$. They are initialized as follows: three steps:

1. All elements of S are initialized with their index:

$$
\begin{aligned}
S[0] &= 0 \\
S[1] &= 1 \\
&\cdots \\
S[255] &= 255
\end{aligned}
$$

2. Another array S_2 of 256 bytes is allocated and filled with the key, repeating bytes as necessary.

3. The S-box is then initialized as suggested in Algorithm 10.5. Note that this algorithm only operates on S (i.e., there is no other input or output parameter than S). Also note that $S[i] \leftrightarrow S[j]$ means that the S-box entries $S[i]$ and $S[j]$ are swapped.

Algorithm 10.5   The S-Box initialization algorithm of ARCFOUR.

(S)

---
for $i = 0$ to 255 do
     $j \leftarrow (j + S[i] + S_2[i]) \bmod 256$
     $S[i] \leftrightarrow S[j]$

(S)

After S is initialized (according to Algorithm 10.2), i and j are set to zero (all entries of S_2 are also set to zero). Algorithm 10.6 is then used to generate a potentially infinite sequence of key bytes. The algorithm takes S as input parameter and outputs a key byte k. If a plaintext message (ciphertext) of l bytes must be encrypted (decrypted), then the algorithm must be iterated l times, and each key byte k_i ($i = 1, \ldots, l$) must be added modulo 2 to the corresponding plaintext message (ciphertext) byte.

Algorithm 10.6 The key generation algorithm of ARCFOUR.

$$\frac{(S, i, j)}{\begin{array}{l} i \leftarrow (i + 1) \bmod 256 \\ j \leftarrow (j + S[i]) \bmod 256 \\ S[i] \leftrightarrow S[j] \\ t \leftarrow (S[i] + S[j]) \bmod 256 \\ k \leftarrow S[t] \end{array}}$$
$$(k)$$

In spite of its simplicity, ARCFOUR had turned out to be quite resistant to many cryptanalytical attacks. In 2001, however, it was discovered that the randomness properties of the first bytes in the key stream generated by ARCFOUR are poor and that this fact can be exploited in an attack against the WEP protocol [22, 23]. Since then, people are worried about the security of ARCFOUR (at least in some specific environments).

10.4 PERFECTLY SECURE ENCRYPTION

As mentioned several times so far, the field of information-theoretically secure encryption was pioneered by Shannon in the late 1940s [24, 25].[38] The aim was to come up with an encryption system that is perfectly secure in the sense that it is impossible for an adversary to derive any information about a plaintext message from a given ciphertext.[39] This must be true even if the adversary has the best available computer technology at hand and even if he or she is not limited in computational resources (e.g., time and memory). Having such an absolute notion of security in mind, it is not at all obvious that perfect security exists at all. There is good and bad news. The good news is that perfect secrecy is possible and technically feasible. The bad news is that perfect secrecy is usually too expensive for almost all practical applications.

As illustrated in Figure 10.15, Shannon introduced a model of a symmetric encryption system. In this model, a source (left side) wants to transmit a plaintext message m to the destination (right side) over an unsecure communications channel (dotted line). To secure the message during its transmission, the source has an encryption device and the destination has a decryption device. The devices implement

---

38 Refer to Chapter 5 for a brief introduction to information theory.
39 This means that one has a ciphertext-only attack in mind when one talks about perfect secrecy and information-theoretically secure encryption.

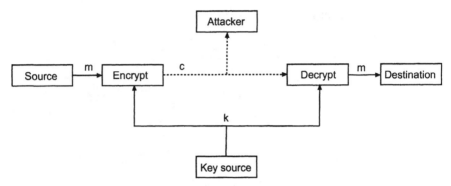

Figure 10.15   Shannon's model of a symmetric encryption system.

an encryption and decryption algorithm[40] and are both fed with the same secret key k generated by a key source. It is assumed that there exists a secure channel between the key source and the encryption and decryption devices. The encryption device turns the plaintext message m into a ciphertext c, and the decryption device does the opposite. It is assumed that the adversary has only access to the ciphertext c and that he or she has no information about the secret key other than that obtained by observing c. In this situation, the adversary tries to obtain useful information about the plaintext message m or the secret key k.

A cryptographic technique not covered by Shannon's model is probabilistic or randomized encryption. Figure 10.16 shows a model of a randomized symmetric encryption system. In addition to the components of the original Shannon model, this model includes a random source that generates a random input s for the encryption process. The random input may either be used as an additional nonsecret "key" that is transmitted to the destination, and multiplexed with the ciphertext, or it may be used to randomize the plaintext, in which case the adversary does not obtain the randomizer in the clear. In either case, it is important to note that the decryption process cannot be randomized and hence that the decryption process need not be fed with s.

An encryption (process) that takes place in a symmetric encryption system $(\mathcal{M}, \mathcal{C}, \mathcal{K}, \mathcal{E}, \mathcal{D})$ can also be viewed as a discrete random experiment. In this case, M and K represent real-valued random variables that are distributed according to $P_M : \mathcal{M} \rightarrow \mathbb{R}^+$ and $P_K : \mathcal{K} \rightarrow \mathbb{R}^+$ (see Definition 4.2 for the notion of a random variable). Note that P_M typically depends on the plaintext language in use, whereas P_K is often uniformly distributed over all possible keys (i.e., all

---

40   More specifically, they implement the families $\mathcal{E}$ and $\mathcal{D}$ of encryption and decryption functions.

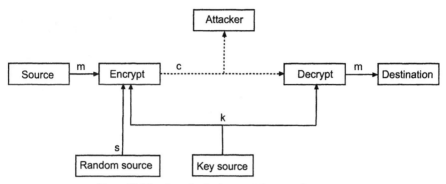

Figure 10.16   A randomized symmetric encryption system.

keys are equiprobable). In either case, it is reasonable to assume that M and K are independent (random variables). In addition to M and K, there is a third random variable C that is distributed according to $P_C : C \rightarrow \mathbb{R}^+$. This random variable models the ciphertext, and hence its probability distribution is completely determined by P_M and P_K. The random variable C is the one that a passive attacker will recognize, and—based on its analysis—he or she will try to derive information about M or K. More specifically, he or she will try to find plaintext messages (or keys) that are more likely than others.

If an adversary is able to eavesdrop on a communications line and analyze the ciphertexts transmitted on it, he or she is also able, in principle at least, to determine the *a posteriori* probabilities of the various plaintext messages. If these probabilities are equal to the *a priori* probabilities of the plaintext messages, then the symmetric encryption system is said to provide perfect secrecy. In this case, intercepting the ciphertext(s) has given the adversary no information about the plaintext message(s) actually transmitted. This means that the a posteriori probability of a plaintext message, given that a ciphertext is observed, is identical to the a priori probability of the message (i.e., observing the ciphertext does not help the adversary). This idea (to formally define a perfectly secure symmetric encryption system) is captured in Definition 10.1.

Definition 10.1 (Perfectly secure symmetric encryption system) *A symmetric encryption system* $(\mathcal{P}, \mathcal{C}, \mathcal{K}, \mathcal{E}, \mathcal{D})$ *is perfectly secure if* $H(M|C) = H(M)$ *for every probability distribution* P_M.

For example, let $\mathcal{M} = \{0, 1\}$ with $P_M(0) = 1/4$ and $P_M(1) = 3/4$, $\mathcal{K} = \{A, B\}$ with $P_K(A) = 1/4$ and $P_K(B) = 3/4$, and $\mathcal{C} = \{a, b\}$. Then the probability that the plaintext 0 is encrypted with key A is $P_{MK}(0, A) =$

$P_M(0) \cdot P_K(A) = 1/4 \cdot 1/4 = 1/16$. Furthermore, the encryption function works as follows

$$
\begin{aligned}
E_A(0) &= a \\
E_A(1) &= b \\
E_B(0) &= b \\
E_B(1) &= a
\end{aligned}
$$

In this example, the probability that ciphertext a occurs is $P_C(a) = \Pr[0, A] + \Pr[1, B] = 1/4 \cdot 1/4 + 3/4 \cdot 3/4 = 1/16 + 9/16 = 10/16 = 5/8$, and the probability that ciphertext b occurs is $P_C(b) = \Pr[1, A] + \Pr[0, B] = 3/4 \cdot 1/4 + 1/4 \cdot 3/4 = 3/16 + 3/16 = 6/16 = 3/8$. Furthermore, the following conditional probabilities can be computed for all $m \in \mathcal{M}$ and $c \in \mathcal{C}$:

$$
\begin{aligned}
\Pr[0|a] &= 1/10 \\
\Pr[1|a] &= 9/10 \\
\Pr[0|b] &= 1/2 \\
\Pr[1|b] &= 1/2
\end{aligned}
$$

These numbers show that the encryption is not perfectly secure. For example, if the adversary observes the ciphertext a, he or she can be pretty sure (with a probability of $9/10$) that the corresponding plaintext is 1 (he or she cannot be similarly sure if the ciphertext b is observed). The encryption system can be made perfectly secure if $P_K(A) = P_K(B) = 1/2$.

In his seminal work, Shannon showed for nonrandomized symmetric encryption systems that a necessary (but usually not sufficient) condition for such a system to be perfectly secure is that the entropy of K is at least as large as the entropy of M (this means that the secret key must be at least as long as the total amount of plaintext that must be transmitted). This important result is formally expressed in Theorem 10.1.

Theorem 10.1 (Shannon's Theorem) *In a perfectly secure symmetric encryption system $H(K) \geq H(M)$.*

Proof.

$$
H(M) = H(M|C) \leq H(MK|C)
$$

$$\begin{aligned}
&= \ H(K|C) + H(M|CK) \\
&= \ H(K|C) \\
&\leq \ H(K)
\end{aligned}$$

In the first line, we employ the definition of perfect secrecy, namely that $H(M) = H(M|C)$ and the fact that $H(MK|C)$ is at least $H(M|C)$. In the second line, we use the basic expansion rule for uncertainties (generalized to conditional uncertainties). In the third line, we use the fact that $H(M|CK) = 0$ for any symmetric encryption system (i.e., it is required that a plaintext can be uniquely decrypted if a ciphertext and a key are known). The inequality stated in the theorem then follows immediately.

$\square$

A practical encryption scheme that can be proven information-theoretically secure (using, for example, Shannon's Theorem) was proposed by Gilbert Vernam in 1917 [26]. *Vernam's one-time pad* consists of a randomly generated and potentially infinite stream of key bits $k = k_1, k_2, k_3, \ldots$ that is shared between the sender and the recipient. To encrypt the plaintext message $m = m_1, m_2, \ldots, m_n$, the sender adds each bit m_i ($1 \leq i \leq n$) modulo 2 with a key bit k_i:

$$c_i = m_i \oplus k_i \text{ for } i = 1, \ldots, n$$

The ciphertext $c = c_1, c_2, c_3, \ldots, c_n$ is sent from the sender to the recipient. It is then up to the recipient to recover the plaintext by adding each ciphertext bit c_i modulo 2 with the corresponding key bit k_i:

$$p_i = c_i \oplus k_i = (p_i \oplus k_i) \oplus k_i = p_i \oplus (k_i \oplus k_i) = p_i \oplus 0 = p_i \text{ for } i = 1, \ldots, n$$

Consequently, the plaintext is recovered by adding each ciphertext bit with the corresponding key bit. Vernam's one-time pad is *perfect* when the key is truly random and used only once. In this case, the ciphertext gives no information about the plaintext.

In addition to perfect security as expressed in Definition 10.1, Shannon also introduced the notion of ideal security. The idea of ideal security is that an adversary does not get any information about a key from a ciphertext of arbitrary length. Alternatively speaking, no matter how much ciphertext an adversary knows, the entropy of K is not decreased. This idea is captured and formally expressed in Definition 10.2.

Definition 10.2 (Ideal security) *An encryption system* $(\mathcal{P}, \mathcal{C}, \mathcal{K}, \mathcal{E}, \mathcal{D})$ *is* ideally secure *if* $H(K|C^n) = H(K)$ *for all* $n \in \mathbb{N}$.

Ideally secure encryption systems are not further addressed in this book.

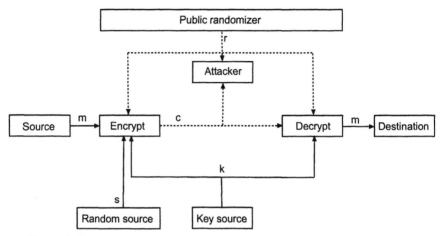

Figure 10.17　A randomized symmetric encryption system that employs a public randomizer.

In summary, Shannon's Theorem says that unless two entities initially share a secret key that is at least as long as the plaintext message to be transmitted, the adversary will always obtain some information about the message. This result has caused many cryptographers to believe that perfect security (or secrecy) is impractical. This pessimism can be relativized by pointing out that Shannon's analysis assumes that, except for the secret key, the adversary has access to exactly the same information as the communicating entities and that this apparently innocent assumption is much more restrictive than is generally realized. For example, Ueli Maurer showed that it is possible to develop randomized symmetric encryption systems that employ public randomizers as illustrated in Figure 10.17 to provide perfect security (even if the secret keys are much smaller than the plaintext messages that are encrypted) [27]. The output of a public randomizer is assumed to be publicly accessible (also to the adversary) but impossible to modify. It can be modeled as a random variable R. There are basically two different ways of implementing a public randomizer: broadcasting and storing. A source (e.g., a satellite) could broadcast random data or storage devices that contain the same random data could be distributed. In the first case, it is possible to come up with a randomized symmetric encryption system that employs a public randomizer and that is perfectly secure under the sole assumption that the noise on the main channel (i.e., the channel from the source to the destination) is at least to some extent independent of the noise on the channel from the sender to the adversary. This system demonstrates that a mere difference in the signals received by the legitimate receiver and by the adversary, but not necessarily with an advantage to the legitimate receiver, is sufficient for achieving security. From Maurer's results, one may also conclude that, for cryptographic purposes, a given communication channel that is noisy is not necessarily bad. In addition, such a channel should not be turned into an error-free channel by means of error-correcting codes, but rather that cryptographic coding and error-control coding should be combined.

10.5 FINAL REMARKS

In this chapter, we elaborated on symmetric encryption systems and had a closer look at some exemplary systems (i.e., the block ciphers DES and AES, and the stream cipher ARCFOUR). These systems are arbitrarily chosen and only reflect their wide deployment. In fact, the DES has been widely deployed for financial applications, whereas the AES is slowly but steadily replacing DES. RC4 is widely deployed because it is built into many commercial off-the-shelf (COTS) products (e.g., Web browsers and mail clients). There are many other symmetric encryption systems developed and proposed in the literature that are not addressed in this book. Examples include the other AES finalists (i.e., the competitors of Rijndael), MISTY1 [28, 29], Camellia [30], and SHACAL-2 from the New European Schemes for Signatures, Integrity and Encryption (NESSIE) project, as well as some more recent proposals (e.g., [31]). It goes without saying that all of these systems represent good alternatives.

All symmetric encryption systems in use today look somehow similar in the sense that they all employ a mixture of more or less complex functions that are iterated multiple times (i.e., in multiple rounds) to come up with something that is inherently hard to understand and analyze. There are also many details in a cryptographic design that may look mysterious or arbitrary to some extent. For example, the S-boxes of DES look arbitrary, but they are not and are well chosen to protect against differential cryptanalysis (which was published almost two decades after the DES specification). Against this background, one may get the impression that it is simple to design and come up with a new symmetric encryption system. Unfortunately, this is not the case, and the design of a symmetric encryption system that is secure and efficient is still a very tricky business. Legions of systems had been proposed, implemented, and deployed before a formerly unknown successful attack was discovered and applied to break them. Such a discovery then often brings the end to several symmetric encryption systems. For example, the discovery of differential cryptanalysis in the public brought the end to many symmetric encryption systems (and other cryptosystems), including, for example, the fast data encipherment algorithm and some variations thereof.

Unless one enters the field of information-theoretically secure encryption systems, the level of security (and assurance) a symmetric encryption system may provide is inherently difficult to determine and quantify. How resistant is a symmetric encryption system against known and yet-to-be-discovered cryptanalytical attacks? This question is difficult to answer mainly because it is not possible to say what cryptanalytical attacks are known and what cryptanalytical attacks will be discovered in the future. In this situation, it is simple to put in place and distribute rumors about possible weaknesses and vulnerabilities of encryption systems. Many of these rumors are placed for marketing reasons (rather than for security reasons). For example, there are people not selling AES encryption devices who argue that the very fact that the NIST has standardized the AES suggests that it contains trapdoors. There are other people (typically the ones selling AES encryption devices) who argue that the fact that the AES has been subject to public scrutiny suggests that it does not contain any trapdoor. Who is right? Who is able to say who is right? Why would you trust this somebody? The point we want to make at the end of this chapter is that fairly little is known about the real security of symmetric encryption systems (except for information-theoretically secure encryption systems). After many decades of research and development, the design of symmetric encryption systems is still more an art than a science. This is in contrast, for example, to the design of asymmetric encryption systems and many other public key cryptosystems (where it is often possible to prove security properties in a mathematically rigorous sense).

References

[1] U.S. Department of Commerce, National Institute of Standards and Technology, *Data Encryption Standard (DES)*, FIPS PUB 46-3, October 1999.

[2] U.S. Department of Commerce, National Institute of Standards and Technology, *Security Requirements for Cryptographic Modules*, FIPS PUB 140-1, January 1994.

[3] Biham, E., and A. Shamir, *Differential Cryptanalysis of DES*. Springer-Verlag, 1993.

[4] Matsui, M., "Linear Cryptanalysis of DES Cipher," *Proceedings of EUROCRYPTO '93*, Springer-Verlag, New York, NY, 1994, pp. 386–397.

[5] Coppersmith, D., "The Data Encryption Standard (DES) and Its Strength Against Attacks," *IBM Journal of Research and Development*, Vol. 38, No. 3, 1994, pp. 243–250.

[6] Diffie, W., and M.E. Hellman, "Exhaustive Cryptanalysis of the NBS Data Encryption Standard," *IEEE Computer*, Vol. 10, No. 6, 1977, pp. 74–84.

[7] Hellman, M.E., "A Cryptanalytic Time-Memory Tradeoff," *IEEE Transactions on Information Theory*, Vol. 26, No. 4, July 1980, pp. 401–406.

[8] Wiener, M.J., "Efficient DES Key Search," presented at the rump session of the CRYPTO '93 conference and reprinted in Stallings, W. (Ed.), *Practical Cryptography for Data Internetworks*, IEEE Computer Society Press, 1996, pp. 31–79.

[9] Wiener, M.J., "Efficient DES Key Search—An Update," *CryptoBytes*, Vol. 3, No. 2, Autumn 1997, pp. 6–8.

[10] Electronic Frontier Foundation (EFF), *Cracking DES: Secrets of Encryption Research, Wiretap Politics & Chip Design*. O'Reilly & Associates, Sebastopol, CA, 1998.

[11] Rivest, R.L., "All-or-Nothing Encryption and the Package Transform," *Proceedings of 4th International Workshop on Fast Software Encryption*, Springer-Verlag, LNCS 1267, 1997, pp. 210–218.

[12] Kilian, J., and P. Rogaway, "How to Protect DES Against Exhaustive Key Search," *Proceedings of CRYPTO '96*, Springer-Verlag, 1996, pp. 252–267.

[13] Campbell, K.W., and M.J. Wiener, "DES Is Not a Group," *Proceedings of CRYPTO '92*, Springer-Verlag, 1993, pp. 512–520.

[14] Daemen, J., and V. Rijmen, *The Design of Rijndael*. Springer-Verlag, New York, 2002.

[15] Burr, W.E., "Selecting the Advanced Encryption Standard," *IEEE Security & Privacy*, Vol. 1, No. 2, March/April 2003, pp. 43–52.

[16] U.S. Department of Commerce, National Institute of Standards and Technology, *Specification for the Advanced Encryption Standard (AES)*, FIPS PUB 197, November 2001.

[17] U.S. Department of Commerce, National Institute of Standards and Technology, *DES Modes of Operation*, FIPS PUB 81, December 1980.

[18] Dawson, E., and L. Nielsen, "Automated Cryptanalysis of XOR Plaintext Strings," *Cryptologia*, Vol. XX, No. 2, April 1996, pp. 165–181.

[19] Rogaway, P., et al., "OCB: A Block-Cipher Mode of Operation for Efficient Authenticated Encryption," *Proceedings of the ACM Conference on Computer and Communications Security*, ACM Press, 2001, pp. 196–205.

[20] Rueppel, R.A., *Analysis and Design of Stream Ciphers*. Springer-Verlag, New York, 1986.

[21] Oppliger, R., *Security Technologies for the World Wide Web*, 2nd edition. Artech House Publishers, Norwood, MA, 2003.

[22] Fluhrer, S., I. Mantin, and A. Shamir, "Weaknesses in the Key Scheduling Algorithm of RC4," *Proceedings of the Eighth Annual Workshop on Selected Areas in Cryptography*, Springer-Verlag, LNCS 2259, August 2001, pp. 1–24.

[23] Stubblefield, A., J. Ioannidis, and A.D. Rubin,"Using the Fluhrer, Mantin, and Shamir Attack to Break WEP," Technical Report TD-4ZCPZZ, AT&T Labs, August 2001.

[24] Shannon, C.E., "A Mathematical Theory of Communication," *Bell System Technical Journal*, Vol. 27, No. 3/4, July/October 1948, pp. 379–423/623–656.

[25] Shannon, C.E., "Communication Theory of Secrecy Systems," *Bell System Technical Journal*, Vol. 28, No. 4, October 1949, pp. 656–715.

[26] Vernam, G.S., "Cipher Printing Telegraph Systems for Secret Wire and Radio Telegraphic Communications," *Journal of the American Institute for Electrical Engineers*, Vol. 55, 1926, pp. 109–115.

[27] Maurer, U.M., "Secret Key Agreement by Public Discussion," *IEEE Transaction on Information Theory*, Vol. 39, No. 3, 1993, pp. 733–742.

[28] Matsui, M., "New Block Encryption Algorithm MISTY," *Proceedings of the Fourth International Fast Software Encryption Workshop (FSE '97)*, Springer-Verlag, LNCS 1267, 1997, pp. 54–68.

[29] Otha, H., and M. Matsui, *A Description of the MISTY1 Encryption Algorithm*, Request for Comments 2994, November 2000.

[30] Aoki, K., et al., "Camellia: A 128-Bit Block Cipher Suitable for Multiple Platforms—Design and Analysis," *Proceedings of the Seventh Annual Workshop on Selected Areas in Cryptography (SAC 2000)*, Springer-Verlag, LNCS 2012, August 2000, pp. 39–56.

[31] Junod, P., and S. Vaudenay, "FOX: a new family of block ciphers," *Proceedings of the Eleventh Annual Workshop on Selected Areas in Cryptography (SAC 2004)*, Springer-Verlag, LNCS 3357, 2004, pp. 114–129.

Chapter 11

Message Authentication Codes

In this chapter, we elaborate on MACs and systems to compute and verify MACs. More specifically, we introduce the topic in Section 11.1, overview, discuss, and put into perspective computationally secure and information-theoretically secure MACs in Sections 11.2 and 11.3, and conclude with some final remarks in Section 11.4.

11.1 INTRODUCTION

There are basically two technologies that can be used to authenticate messages:

- Public key cryptography and digital signatures;
- Secret key cryptography and MACs.

Digital signatures are further addressed in Chapter 15. In this chapter, we focus only on MACs. As introduced in Section 2.2.2, a MAC is an authentication tag that is computed and verified with a secret key. This means that the sender and the recipient(s) must share a secret key and that this key must be used to compute and verify a MAC for a message. Consequently, a MAC depends on both the message it authenticates and the secret key that only the legitimate sender and the legitimate recipient(s) are assumed to know.

Note that there is a fundamental difference between message authentication using MACs and message authentication using digital signatures. If one uses MACs, then the same secret key that is used to compute the MAC must also be used to verify it. This is different with digital signatures. If one uses digital signatures, then the key to generate a digital signature and the key to verify it are different (the former represents the private key and the latter represents the public key). There are two implications we want to emphasize at this point:

- Digital signatures can be used to provide nonrepudiation services, whereas MACs cannot be used for this purpose;

- A digital signature can typically be verified by everybody,[1] whereas a MAC can be verified only by somebody who knows the secret key (or can perform specific attacks).

These differences are fundamental, and it must be decided for a specific application whether digital signatures or MACs better meet the security requirements.

In Definition 2.8, we said that a message authentication system consists of the following five components:

- A message space $\mathcal{M}$;

- An authentication tag space $\mathcal{T}$;

- A key space $\mathcal{K}$;

- A family $\mathcal{A} = \{A_k : k \in \mathcal{K}\}$ of authentication functions $A_k : \mathcal{M} \longrightarrow \mathcal{T}$;

- A family $\mathcal{V} = \{V_k : k \in \mathcal{K}\}$ of verification functions $V_k : \mathcal{M} \times \mathcal{T} \longrightarrow \{valid, invalid\}$. $V_k(m, t)$ must return $valid$ if and only if t is a valid authentication tag for message $m \in \mathcal{M}$ and key $k \in \mathcal{K}$ (i.e., $t = A_k(m)$).

Furthermore, we noted that in a typical setting $\mathcal{M} = \{0,1\}^*$, $\mathcal{T} = \{0,1\}^{l_{tag}}$ for some fixed tag length l_{tag}, and $\mathcal{K} = \{0,1\}^{l_{key}}$ for some fixed key length l_{key}, and that $l_{tag} = l_{key} = 128$ bits is frequently used in practice.

Informally speaking, a message authentication system is secure if an adversary has no better possibility to generate a valid MAC than to guess. To more specifically define the notion of a secure message authentication system, we must first say what types of attacks are feasible and what an adversary is required to perform in order to be successful (i.e., to break the security of the system). The following types of attacks must be distinguished:

- In a *known-message attack*, the adversary knows one (or several) message(s) and corresponding MAC(s);

- In a *chosen-message attack*, the adversary not only knows certain message-MAC pairs, but he or she is also able to obtain such pairs in one way or another. In fact, he or she is able to obtain the MAC(s) of one (or several) message(s) of his or her choice. Again, one must distinguish whether the adversary can adaptively choose the message(s) for which he or she is able

---

1   Note that there are also digital signature systems that limit the verifiability of the signatures to specific entities. The corresponding signatures are sometimes also referred to as *undeniable signatures*.

to obtain the MAC(s). In this case, the attack represents an *adaptive chosen-message attack.*

It goes without saying that chosen-message attacks are more powerful than known-message attacks and that adaptive chosen-message attack are more powerful than their nonadaptive counterparts.

Furthermore, an adversary may be required to perform different tasks in order to be successful (i.e., to break the security of the system). The tasks lead to different notions of security.

- If the adversary is able to determine the secret key in use, then he or she *totally breaks* the system. The result is a *total break.*

- If the adversary is able to determine a MAC for a (typically meaningful) message selected by him or her, then he or she *selectively forges* a MAC. The result is a *selective forgery.*

- If the adversary is able to determine a MAC for any (not necessarily meaningful) message, then he or she *existentially forges* a MAC. The result is an *existential forgery.*

Obviously, a message authentication system is absolutely worthless if it does not provide protection against a total break, and a message authentication system that provides protection against an existential forgery is inherently more secure than one that provides protection against a selective forgery.

Note that it is always possible to guess a MAC. If, for example, an authentication tag space has n elements, then a MAC can be guessed with a probability of $1/n$ (this probability is always greater than 0 for all $n \in \mathbb{N}$). More specifically, if a MAC is n bits long, then it can be guessed with a probability of $2^{-n} = 1/2^n$. This probability can be made arbitrarily small by increasing the tag length. From an adversary's viewpoint, the major question is whether he or she is able to verify his or her guesses.

- If the adversary is able to verify a guess, we are in the realm of *verifiable MACs*. In this case, the adversary can always try all 2^n possible n-bit MACs and find a correct MAC after 2^{n-1} guesses on the average.

- If the adversary is not able to verify a guess, we are in the realm of *non-verifiable MACs*. In this case, the adversary can only guess and hope that he or she has found a correct MAC.

Whether a MAC is verifiable largely depends on whether the message it authenticates is known to the adversary. If the adversary does not know the message, then it is impossible for him or her to decide whether a specific MAC is correct.

Note that nonverifiable MACs are inherently more secure than their verifiable counterparts (because it is not possible to find a correct MAC with a brute-force attack). Also note that there is evidence that nonverifiable MACs really exist (even if one assumes that the adversary knows the message to which a MAC is referring) because, in principle, the verification of a MAC requires knowledge of the secret key. From an adversary's viewpoint, however, it is sometimes possible to use an entity that knows the key as an oracle. Consider, for example, an entity that knows the key and provides an online service only if a request message is authenticated with a MAC. In this case, the adversary can send (adaptively) chosen messages to the server and look whether the server responds (in this case, the MAC is valid) or not (in this case, the MAC is invalid). This type of chosen-message attack is often considered when one analyzes the security of cryptographic protocols.

As mentioned earlier, a message authentication system is secure if an adversary has no better possibility to forge a MAC than to guess. More specifically, even if we assume that an adversary is able to perform an adaptive chosen-message attack, we want to be sure that it is impossible or computationally infeasible for him or her to (existentially or selectively) forge a MAC. In the first case (i.e., if it is impossible for him or her to forge a MAC), then the message authentication system (or the MACs, respectively) is (are) called *information-theoretically secure*. In the second case (i.e., if it is computationally infeasible for him or her to forge a MAC), then the message authentication system (or the MACs, respectively) is (are) called *computationally secure*. Because computationally secure MACs are more widely deployed in practice, we begin with them.

11.2 COMPUTATIONALLY SECURE MACS

There are many possibilities to design and come up with MACs that are computationally secure. Examples include:

• MACs that use symmetric encryption systems;

• MACs that use keyed hash functions;

• MACs that use pseudorandom functions (PRFs);

• MACs that use universal hash functions.

In addition to these four classes that are overviewed and briefly discussed next, some outdated proposals are standardized but not widely deployed. For example, the *message authenticator algorithm* (MAA) as specified in ISO 8731-2 [1] was published in 1984. Until today, no significant structural weakness has been found in the MAA. Its major problem is that it generates MACs of only 32 bits length. This is unacceptable for most applications in use today. Consequently, we don't address this MAC construction in this book.

11.2.1 MACs Using Symmetric Encryption Systems

A standard method for message authentication is to use a symmetric encryption system (e.g., DES), encrypt the plaintext message in CBC mode (see Section 10.2.3.2), use the last ciphertext block as MAC, and send it along with the (plaintext) message to the recipient(s). In this case, the last ciphertext block is sometimes also called *CBC residue* or *CBC MAC*. The use of CBC MACs is, for example, standardized in ANSI X9.9 [2], FIPS PUB 113 [3], and ISO/IEC 9797 [4]. Unfortunately, the terminology is not used consistently. For example, the algorithm to compute a CBC MAC is sometimes called *data authentication algorithm* (DAA) and the MAC itself is sometimes called *data authentication code* (DAC). These terms are not used in this book.

In order to compute and verify a CBC MAC, one must know the secret key k. If somebody not knowing the key (e.g., an adversary) modified the message, then the CBC MAC would no longer be valid, and he or she would have to adapt the CBC MAC accordingly (otherwise, the message modification could easily be detected). If the CBC MAC is generated using a block cipher with block length n, then he or she has a success probability of $1/2^n$. This probability is sufficiently small for large block lengths. A more fomal analysis of the CBC MAC construction is provided in [5]. Furthermore, a general birthday attack against iterated MACs, including, for example, MAA and CBC MAC, is described in [6].

Sometimes, people argue that the encryption of a message also protects its authenticity and integrity, and hence that one must not authenticate a message that is encrypted (using, for example, an additive stream cipher). This line of argumentation is inherently flawed, and it is generally recommended and good practice to authenticate a message even if it is encrypted. If one uses a block cipher in CBC mode, this means that one has to encrypt the message twice with two independent keys (in one step the message is CBC encrypted to generate the ciphertext, and in the other step the message is CBC encrypted to generate the CBC MAC). Alternatively, one may also use two keys that are not independent (e.g., derived from a master key or derived from each other). There are no known weaknesses or vulnerabilities in this approach, but few advantages either. It is generally neither much more difficult to distribute and manage a pair of keys than a single key, nor is it computationally more efficient. A more efficient approach is to replace the CBC MAC with a MAC that uses a keyed hash function. In this case, one uses a cryptographic hash function to compute a hash value from the message, appends the hash value to the message, and encrypts the result with the block cipher in CBC mode. In this case, two passes are still required, but only one pass comprises the computation of a hash value. Some alternative constructions that don't require an encryption in CBC mode are addressed next.

11.2.2 MACs Using Keyed Hash Functions

The idea to use cryptographic hash functions to protect the authenticity and integrity of data and program files dates back to the late 1980s [7]. In the early 1990s, people started to think more seriously about the possibility of using cryptographic hash functions (instead of symmetric encryption systems) to efficiently authenticate messages. In fact, there are a couple of arguments in favor of using cryptographic hash functions:

- There are a number of cryptographic hash functions in widespread use (refer to Chapter 8 for an overview);

- Cryptographic hash functions can be implemented efficiently in hardware and/or software;

- Many implementations of cryptographic hash functions are publicly and freely available;

- Cryptographic hash functions are free to use (meaning, for example, that they are not subject to patent claims and/or export controls);

- Cryptographic hash functions have well-defined security properties, such as preimage resistance, second-preimage resistance, and collision resistance.

Some of these arguments have become obsolete (e.g., export restrictions), whereas others still apply (e.g., widespread availability and use) and will likely apply in the forseeable future (e.g., efficiency).

Against this background, Li Gong and Gene Tsudik first proposed an encryption-free message authentication based on keyed one-way hash functions instead of a symmetric encryption system [8, 9].[2] More specifically, Tsudik proposed and discussed the following three methods to authenticate a message $m \in \mathcal{M}$ using a one-way hash function h and a secret key $k \in \mathcal{K}$:

- In the *secret prefix* method, k is a prefix to m and h is applied to the composite message (i.e., $MAC_k(m) = h(k \parallel m)$);

2   An earlier version of [9] was presented at IEEE INFOCOM '92.

- In the *secret suffix* method, k is a suffix to m and h is applied to the composite message (i.e., $MAC_k(m) = h(m \parallel k)$);

- In the *envelope* method, there are two keys k_1 and k_2 that are a prefix and a suffix to m. Again, h is applied to the composite message (i.e., $MAC_{k_1,k_2}(m) = h(k_1 \parallel m \parallel k_2)$).

The three methods and some variations thereof are overviewed and briefly discussed next. The first two methods are insecure. They were, however, still used in version 2 of the simple network management protocol (SNMP).

If one uses an iterated hash function (e.g., MD5 or SHA-1), then another method to key the hash function is to use the IV, meaning that the otherwise fixed IV is replaced by k. If the IV (and hence the key k) is l bits long (according to the notation introduced in Section 8.2), then this method is bascially the same as the secret prefix method addressed first.

11.2.2.1 Secret Prefix Method

As mentioned earlier, the secret prefix method consists of prepending a secret key $k \in \mathcal{K}$ to the message $m \in \mathcal{M}$ before it is hashed with the cryptographic hash function h. The construction is as follows:

$$MAC_k(m) = h(k \parallel m)$$

If h is an iterated hash function, then the secret prefix method is insecure. Anybody who knows a single message-MAC pair can selectively forge a MAC for a message that has the known message as a prefix. If one considers Figure 8.2 and the way an iterated hash function h is constructed (using a compression function f), then one easily notices that $t_{i+1} = h(k \parallel m_1 \parallel m_2 \parallel \ldots \parallel m_{i+1})$ can be computed from $t_i = h(k \parallel m_1 \parallel m_2 \parallel \ldots \parallel m_i)$ as follows:

$$t_{i+1} = h(t_i \parallel m_{i+1})$$

Consequently, if one knows t_i and m_{i+1}, then one can compute t_{i+1} without knowing k. Consequently, the messages for which a MAC can be selectively forged are restricted to those having a message with a known MAC as a prefix. This restriction is not very strong.

Tsudik was aware of this type of *message extension* or *padding attack*, and he suggested three possibilities to protect against it:

- Only part of the hash value is taken as output (e.g., only 64 bits);
- The messages are always of fixed length;
- An explicit length field is included at the beginning of a message.

Neither of these possibilities is very comfortable, and hence the secret prefix method is seldom used in practice.

11.2.2.2   Secret Suffix Method

Because of the message extension attack against the secret prefix method, the secret suffix method seems to be the preferred choice. As mentioned earlier, the secret suffix method consists of appending the key k to the message m before it is hashed with the cryptographic hash function h. The construction is as follows:

$$MAC_k(m) = h(m \parallel k)$$

If h is an iterated hash function, then the secret suffix method has a structural problem.[3] Whether this problem is serious or not depends on the compression function (of the hash function in use). The structural problem is due to the fact that the MAC is a function of some known values[4] and the key, assuming the key is passed entirely to the last iteration of the compression function. Consequently, an adversary may see the result of applying the compression function to many different known values and the same key. This means that he or she may perform a known-message attack against the compression function. While it is unlikely that currently used compression functions reveal information about the key, other cryptographic hash functions may not fare as well, and one may go for a more secure design in the first place.

11.2.2.3   Envelope Method

The envelope method combines the prefix and suffix methods. As mentioned earlier, the envelope method consists of prepending a key k_1 and appending another key k_2 to the message m before it is hashed with the cryptographic hash function h. The construction is as follows:

---

3   The secret prefix method has the same problem, but only when the message is very short (i.e., if there is only one iteration of the compression function).

4   The known values are (1) the next-to-last chaining value, which by assumption depends only on the message, (2) the last part of the message, and (3) some padding.

$$MAC_{k_1,k_2}(m) = h(k_1 \parallel m \parallel k_2)$$

Until the middle of the 1990s, people thought that this method would be secure and that breaking it would require a simultaneous exhaustive key search for k_1 and k_2 (see, for example, [9] for a corresponding line of argumentation). In 1995, however, it was shown that this is not the case and that there are more efficient attacks against the envelope method than to do a simultaneous exhaustive key search for k_1 and k_2 [6]. Since then, the envelope method is slowly being replaced by some alternative methods, as addressed next.

11.2.2.4 Alternative Methods

After Tsudik had published his results, many cryptographers turned their interest to the problem of using keyed one-way hash functions for message authentication and finding proofs for their security claims (e.g., [6, 10, 11]). Most importantly, Mihir Bellare, Ran Canetti, and Hugo Krawczyk developed a pair of message authentication schemes—the *nested MAC* (NMAC) and the *hashed MAC* (HMAC)—that can be proven to be secure as long as the underlying hash function is reasonably strong (in a cryptographic sense) [12]. From a practical point of view, the HMAC construction has become particularly important [13]. In a slightly modified form, it was, for example, specified in informational RFC 2104 [14] and has been adopted by many standardization bodies working in the field.

The HMAC construction uses the following pair of 64-byte strings:

- The string *ipad* (standing for "inner pad") consists of the byte 0x36 (i.e., 00110110) repeated 64 times;

- The string *opad* (standing for "outer pad") consists of the byte 0x5C (i.e., 01011100) repeated 64 times.

Consequently, *ipad* and *opad* are $64 \cdot 8 = 512$ bits long. Let h be a cryptographic hash function, k be the secret key,[5] and m be the message to be authenticated. The HMAC construction is as follows:

$$HMAC_k(m) \quad = \quad h(k \oplus opad \parallel h(k \oplus ipad \parallel m))$$

---

5 The recommended minimal length of the key is l bits.

This construction looks more involved than it actually is. It begins by appending zero bytes (i.e., $0x00$) to the end of k to create a 64-byte or 512-bit string.[6] If, for example, k is 128 bits long, then 48 zero bytes are appended. The resulting $48 \cdot 8 = 384$ bits and the 128 key bits sum up to a total of 512 bits. This key is then added modulo 2 to $ipad$, and the message m is appended to this value. At this point in time, the cryptographic hash function h is applied a first time to the entire data stream generated so far. The key (again, appended with zero bytes) is next added modulo 2 to $opad$, and the result of the first application of h is appended to this value. To compute the final hash value, h is applied a second time (note that this time the argument for the hash function is comparably short). Last but not least, the output of the HMAC construction may be truncated to a value that is shorter than l (e.g., 80 or 96 bits). In fact, it was shown that some analytical advantages result from truncating the output [6]. In either case, $k \oplus ipad$ and $k \oplus opad$ are intermediate results of the HMAC construction that can be precomputed at the time of generation of the key k, or before its first use. This precomputation allows the HMAC construction to be implemented very efficiently.

The appeal of the HMAC construction is that its designers have been able to prove a mathematical relationship between the strength of the construction and the strength of the underlying hash function. In fact, it has been shown that a passive attacker can break the HMAC construction only if he or she is able to successfully attack the underlying hash function in a certain way and that the probability of such an attack can be made sufficiently small.

11.2.3 MACs Using PRFs

In 1995, Mihir Bellare, Roch Guérin, and Phillip Rogaway proposed a method for message authentication using families of finite PRFs [15]. The notion of a PRF was introduced in Section 2.2.4 and is further addressed in Chapter 13. In short, a function $f : X \rightarrow Y$ is pseudorandom if it is randomly chosen from the set of all mappings from domain X to range Y. A family of PRFs can, for example, be constructed with a block cipher (e.g., DES) or a compression function of an iterated hash function. In the first case, $DES_k(m)$ yields a family of finite PRF (k represents the seed and m represents the argument) with $n = 64$.

The MAC constructions developed and proposed by Bellare, Guérin, and Rogaway are collectively called $XOR\ MACs$ (because they make use of many parallel XOR operations). In [15], it was argued that XOR MACs have many efficiency and security advantages (compared to the MAC constructions addressed so far). Roughly speaking, an XOR MAC is computed in three steps:

---

6   If the key is longer than 64 bytes, then it must be truncated to the appropriate length.

1. The message m is block encoded, meaning that it is encoded as a collection of n message blocks (i.e., $m = m_1 \parallel m_2 \parallel \ldots \parallel m_n$);

2. A finite PRF is applied to each message block, creating a set of PRF images;

3. The PRF images are added modulo 2, building the XOR MAC.

Note that there are different choices for a block encoding in step 1 and a finite PRF in step 2, and that each of these choices yields a different XOR MAC construction. In fact, a randomized (and stateless) XOR MAC construction $XMACR_{F,b}$ and a deterministic (and stateful)[7] XOR MAC construction $XMACC_{F,b}$ can be defined for every family F of finite PRFs and every block size b. Both constructions can be shown to be secure if the underlying family F of finite PRFs is secure.[8]

As mentioned earlier, the two MAC constructions can be instantiated using the DES. For any 56-bit DES key k and l-bit message block m_i ($i = 1, \ldots, n$), let $f_k(m_i)$ be the first 48 bits of $DES_k(m_i)$.[9] Consequently, f_k specifies a pseudorandom function that is keyed with k, and this key is shared between the sender and recipient of the message m to be authenticated. We assume the length of M (i.e., $\mid m \mid$) is a multiple of 32 bits.[10] The message m can then be viewed as a sequence of n 32-bit blocks, $m = m_1 \parallel m_2 \parallel \ldots \parallel M[n]$ with $\mid m_i \mid = 32$. Furthermore, let $\langle i \rangle$ denote the binary representation of the message block index i for $i = 1, \ldots, n$.

11.2.3.1 Randomized XOR MAC

The *randomized XOR MAC* (XMACR) to authenticate message m is computed as follows:

1. A random 63-bit string r is selected as a seed;

2. The value z is computed as follows:

$$
\begin{aligned}
z \;=\; & f_k(0 \parallel r) \oplus \\
& f_k(1 \parallel \langle 1 \rangle \parallel m_1) \oplus \\
& f_k(1 \parallel \langle 2 \rangle \parallel m_2) \oplus \\
& \ldots \\
& f_k(1 \parallel \langle n \rangle \parallel m_n)
\end{aligned}
$$

---

7   In a stateful MAC the sender maintains information, such as a counter, which he or she updates each time a message is authenticated.

8   In formalizing this, security of a family of finite PRFs means that it is indistinguishable from a family of random functions in the sense of [16].

9   Note that f_k outputs only 48 bits and not the full 64-bit ciphertext block. The output is truncated because DES is a pseudorandom permutation, while what we want is a pseudorandom function.

10 This can easily be achieved by a suitable padding.

3. The XMACR of m using k is the pair (r, z).

The sender transmits both m and the XMACR of m (i.e., (r, z)) to the recipient, and the recipient receives m' and (r', z'). The recipient then computes

$$
\begin{aligned}
z \ = \ & f_k(0 \parallel r') \oplus \\
& f_k(1 \parallel \langle 1 \rangle \parallel m'_1) \oplus \\
& f_k(1 \parallel \langle 2 \rangle \parallel m'_2) \oplus \\
& \cdots \\
& f_k(1 \parallel \langle n \rangle \parallel m'_n)
\end{aligned}
$$

and accepts the XMACR if and only if $z = z'$.

11.2.3.2 Counter-Based XOR MAC

The *counter-based XOR MAC* (XMACC) construction uses a 63-bit counter c (instead of a random string r). The counter is initially set to zero and is incremented for each message. The XMACC for message m is computed as follows:

1. The counter c is incremented by 1;

2. The value z is computed as follows:

$$
\begin{aligned}
z \ = \ & f_k(0 \parallel c) \oplus \\
& f_k(1 \parallel \langle 1 \rangle \parallel m_1) \oplus \\
& f_k(1 \parallel \langle 2 \rangle \parallel m_2) \oplus \\
& \cdots \\
& f_k(1 \parallel \langle n \rangle \parallel m_n)
\end{aligned}
$$

3. The XMACC of m using k is the pair (c, z).

Again, the sender transmits both m and (c, z) to the recipient, and the recipient receives m' and (c', z'). The recipient then computes

$$
\begin{aligned}
z \ = \ & f_k(0 \parallel c') \oplus \\
& f_k(1 \parallel \langle 1 \rangle \parallel m'_1) \oplus \\
& f_k(1 \parallel \langle 2 \rangle \parallel m'_2) \oplus \\
& \cdots \\
& f_k(1 \parallel \langle n \rangle \parallel m'_n)
\end{aligned}
$$

and accepts the XMACC if and only if $z = z'$.

11.2.3.3 Discussion

Similar to other MAC constructions, such as HMAC, the security of XOR MACs can be formally analyzed and quantified. In fact, an adversary's inability to forge an XOR MAC can be expressed in terms of his or her (presumed) inability to break the underlying PRF.

The major advantage of XOR MACs (compared to other MAC constructions) is parallelizability, meaning that all n invocations of the PRF (to generate or verify an XOR MAC) can be done in parallel. As mentioned later, this fact is important and may be a prerequisite for message authentication in high-speed networks. Similarly, message authentication can proceed even if the message blocks arrive out of order. It is only required that each message block m_i comes along with its index i. Out-of-order MAC verification is in fact a very useful property in contemporary networks, such as the Internet (because of packet losses and retransmission delays). Furthermore, an XOR MAC is incremental in the sense of [17]. Suppose, for example, that the message block m_i is modified to a new 32-bit value m_i'. Then, for a long message m, one can update the XOR MAC much faster than it would take to recompute it. For example, let (r, z) be an XMACR for message m and let m' be m with message block i replaced by m_i'. To compute an XMACR for m', one can randomly select r' and compute

$$z' = z \oplus f_k(0 \parallel r) \oplus f_k(0 \parallel r') \oplus f_k(1 \parallel \langle i \rangle \parallel m_i) \oplus f_k(1 \parallel \langle i \rangle \parallel m_i').$$

The pair (r', z') then represents the XMACR for m'. Note that this works because adding a value twice modulo 2 entirely removes its impact.

One disadvantage of XOR MACs is performance. This disadvantage, however, largely depends on the family of finite PRFs in use. In the case of DES (as discussed earlier), the number of DES computations for an XOR MAC is twice that of a CBC MAC (because XOR MACs operate on 32-bit blocks instead of 64-bit blocks). So an XOR MAC may be twice as slow as a CBC MAC.

In summary, XOR MACs have many properties that make them an appropriate choice in many situations, especially if one considers high-speed networks that do not guarantee an absolutely reliable data transmission. If the computer systems communicating over the network are powerful, then the performance degradation with a factor of two (as in the case of DES) is not particularly worrisome.

11.2.4   MACs Using Families of Universal Hash Functions

At the end of Chapter 8, we mentioned that universal hashing as originally proposed in [18] provides an interesting design paradigm for cryptographic hash functions in general, and message authentication in particular [19]. After the initial work of Larry Carter and Mark Wegman, the use of universal hashing for message authentication was further explored by Gilles Brassard [20] and many other researchers (see, for example, [21]). Most of these constructions use two-universal families of hash functions. In short, a family H of hash functions $h : X \rightarrow Y$ is two-universal if for every $x, y \in X$ with $x \neq y$

$$\Pr_{h \in H}[h(x) = h(y)] \leq \frac{1}{|Y|}.$$

As of this writing, the most important MAC that uses families of universal hash functions is known as *universal MAC* (UMAC) [22]. The output of the UMAC construction is a 32-, 64- or 96-bit authentication tag (depending on the user's preference). A 64-bit authentication tag is recommended for most applications.

Let H be a two-universal family of hash functions and F be a PRF family (see Chapter 13) that generates outputs of the same length. A secret key k is used to select a hash function h_k from H and a PRF f_k from F. The hash function h_k is then used to hash a given message into a short string, and the short string is encrypted by adding it modulo 2 to a string that is generated with the PRF f_k and a random value (i.e., nonce) r. Consequently, the authentication tag $UMAC_k(m)$ is constructed as follows:

$$UMAC_k(m) = f_k(r) \oplus h_k(m)$$

In this notation, r refers to the nonce that must change with every authentication tag. The recipient needs to know which nonce was used by the sender, so some method of synchronizing nonces needs to be used. This can be done by explicitly sending the nonce along with the message and the tag (in this case, r and $UMAC_k(m)$ must be sent together) or agreeing upon the use of some other nonrepeating value such as message number. The nonce need not be kept secret, but care needs to be taken to ensure that, over the lifetime of the shared secret key k, a different nonce is used with each message m.

11.3 INFORMATION-THEORETICALLY SECURE MACS

As mentioned before, a MAC is information-theoretically secure if it is impossible to forge a MAC. Let us begin with a simple and pathological example. We consider the situation in which we want to authenticate the outcome of a random coin flipping experiment. The outcome of the experiment is a single bit saying either H (standing for "head") or T (standing for "tail"). The secret key is assumed to consist of two randomly chosen bits (i.e., 00, 01, 10, or 11) and the MAC consists of one single bit. An exemplary message authentication system scheme is illustrated in Table 11.1. The rows in the table refer to the four possible keys. If, for example, the secret key shared between the sender and the recipient is 01 (i.e., the key found in the second row) and the outcome of the experiment is a head, then H0 is transmitted. Similarly, if the outcome of the experiment is a tail, then we transmit T1 (for the same secret key 01).

Table 11.1
An Exemplary Message Authentication System

	H0	H1	T0	T1
00	H	-	T	-
01	H	-	-	T
10	-	H	T	-
11	-	H	-	T

If we talk about information-theoretically secure message authentication systems and MACs, then we must be sure that every key can be used only once (this is similar to the one-time pad in the case of information-theoretically secure symmetric encryption systems). In the example given earlier, this means that we need $2n$ bits of keying material to authenticate n outcomes of the random experiment in an information-theoretically secure way. If, for example, we wanted to authenticate the sequence TTHTH using the five keys 00, 10, 11, 11, and 01, then we would actually transmit T0, T0, H1, T1, and H0. We hence need a 10-bit key to authenticate a 5-bit message.

In this example, the bit length of the MAC is one. Consequently, an adversary can guess a MAC with a probability of $2^{-1} = 1/2^1 = 1/2$. To show that the message authentication system is secure, we must show that an adversary has no better possibility to forge a MAC (for a message of his or her choice) than to guess. We consider the case in which the adversary wants to forge a MAC for the message H (for the message T, the line of argumentation is similar). Assuming all four keys occur with equal probability (i.e., probability $1/4$), the MAC is 0 for two out of four possibilities (i.e., 00 and 01) and 1 for the other two possibilities (i.e., 10 and

11). Consequently, the adversary has a $2/4 = 1/2$ chance of correctly guessing the MAC, and there is nothing else he or she can do to increase his or her odds.

Note that this line of argumentation (about the security of a message authentication system or MAC) also applies if the sender provides a message with a correct MAC and the adversary wants to modify the message (and its MAC). Going back to our example, let us assume that the adversary has received H0, that he or she wants to change the message from H to T, and that he or she wants to generate a valid MAC for the new message (without actually knowing the secret key). If the adversary has received H0, then the only possible keys are 00 and 01 (according to Table 11.1):

- If 00 is the proper key, then the message T must be authenticated with 0, and the adversary must change the message to T0.

- Similarly, if 01 is the proper key, then the message T must be authenticated with 1, and the adversary must change the message to T1.

In either case, the adversary has a probability of $1/2$ to correctly guess the proper key and to correctly change the message accordingly. Again, there is nothing the adversary can do to increase the probability.

In lossy and unreliable networks, one may be concerned about the error probability of a message authentication system. In this case, it is always possible to reduce the error probability of a message authentication system simply by appending s MACs instead of just one. Consequently, the message m is accompanied by s MACs. If each of these MACs requires n key bits, then the total amount of key bits sums up to $s \cdot n$. Also, if each MAC has an error probability of ϵ, then the total error probability of n MACs is ϵ^s. In the example given earlier, $\epsilon = 1/2$ and the total error probability is $(1/2)^s$.

Similar to information-theoretically secure encryption systems, information-theoretically secure message authentication systems and corresponding MACs require keys of a specific size. It has been shown that it is possible to construct information-theoretically secure message authentication systems and corresponding MACs that require relatively short keys. The disadvantage of all of these schemes is that a different key must be used for every message. If this is not acceptable, then one can also generate the keys using a cryptographically strong PRBG (see Chapter 12). In this case, however, the resulting scheme is at most computationally secure. This is similar to the approximation of a one-time pad using a PRBG in the case of symmetric encryption systems.

11.4 FINAL REMARKS

In this chapter, we elaborated on possibilities to authenticate messages and to compute and verify MACs. We focused on the notion of security (in the context of message authentication), and we overviewed and discussed several message authentication systems that are computationally or information-theoretically secure. From a practical viewpoint, computationally secure message authentication systems and MACs are important. More specifically, most applications and standards that require message authentication in one way or another employ MACs that use keyed hash function (this is because cryptographic hash functions are assumed to be more efficient than symmetric or asymmetric systems). Most importantly, the HMAC construction is part of most Internet security protocols in use today, including, for example, the IPsec and SSL/TLS protocols (e.g., [23]). In a typical implementation, the HMAC construction is based on an iterated cryptographic hash function, such as MD5 or SHA-1. As already mentioned in Section 8.4, these functions have the problem that they operate strongly sequential, and hence that they are not parallelizable. This may lead to performance problems in high-speed networks.

Against this background, there is a strong incentive to go for message authentication systems and MAC constructions that can be parallelized. The XOR MACs were historically the first proposal that went into this direction. Today, the UMAC construction is the one that looks most promising for the future. Another possibility that may be worthwhile to consider is probabilistic message authentication. The basic idea is that not all bits of a message are input to the authentication function. The more efficient an authentication function must be, the more bits are considered. Consequently, there is a tradeoff to make between the security requirements of a MAC and its efficiency.

References

[1] ISO 8731-2, *Banking—Approved Algorithms for Message Authentication—Part 2: Message Authenticator Algorithm*, 1992.

[2] American National Standards Institute, *American National Standard for Financial Message Authentication*, ANSI X9.9, April 1982.

[3] U.S. Department of Commerce, National Institute of Standards and Technology, *Computer Data Authentication*, FIPS PUB 113, May 1985.

[4] ISO/IEC 9797, *Information Technology—Security Techniques—Data Integrity Mechanism Using a Cryptographic Check Function Employing a Block Cipher Algorithm*, 1994.

[5] Bellare, M., J. Kilian, and P. Rogaway, "The Security of Cipher Block Chaining," *Proceedings of CRYPTO '94*, Springer-Verlag, LNCS 839, 1994, pp. 341–358.

[6] Preneel, B., and P. van Oorschot, "MDx-MAC and Building Fast MACs from Hash Functions," *Proceedings of CRYPTO '95*, Springer-Verlag, LNCS 963, 1995, pp. 1–14.

[7] Cohen, F., "A Cryptographic Checksum for Integrity Protection," *Computers & Security*, Vol. 6, No. 5, 1987, pp. 505–510.

[8] Gong, L., "Using One-Way Functions for Authentication," *ACM SIGCOMM Computer Communication Review*, Vol. 19, No. 5, October 1989, pp. 8–11.

[9] Tsudik, G., "Message Authentication with One-Way Hash Functions," *ACM SIGCOMM Computer Communication Review*, Vol. 22, No. 5, October 1992, pp. 29–38.

[10] Kaliski, B., and M. Robshaw, "Message Authentication with MD5," *CryptoBytes*, Vol. 1, No. 1, Spring 1995, pp. 5–8.

[11] Preneel, B., and P. van Oorschot, "On the Security of Two MAC Algorithms," *Proceedings of EUROCRYPT '96*, Springer-Verlag, 1996.

[12] Bellare, M., R. Canetti, and H. Krawczyk, "Keying Hash Functions for Message Authentication," *Proceedings of CRYPTO '96*, Springer-Verlag, LNCS 1109, 1996, pp. 1–15.

[13] Bellare, M., R. Canetti, and H. Krawczyk, "The HMAC Construction," *CryptoBytes*, Vol. 2, No. 1, Spring 1996, pp. 12–15.

[14] Krawczyk, H., M. Bellare, and R. Canetti, *HMAC: Keyed-Hashing for Message Authentication*, Request for Comments 2104, February 1997.

[15] Bellare, M., R. Guerin, and P. Rogaway, "XOR MACs: New Methods for Message Authentication Using Block Ciphers," *Proceedings of CRYPTO '95*, Springer-Verlag, 1995.

[16] Goldreich, O., S. Goldwasser, and S. Micali, "How to Construct Random Functions," *Journal of the ACM*, Vol. 33, No. 4, 1986, pp. 210–217.

[17] Bellare, M., O. Goldreich, and S. Goldwasser, "Incremental Cryptography: The Case of Hashing and Signing," *Proceedings of CRYPTO '94*, Springer-Verlag, 1994.

[18] Carter, J.L., and M.N. Wegman, "Universal Classes of Hash Functions," *Journal of Computer and System Sciences*, Vol. 18, 1979, pp. 143–154.

[19] Wegman, M.N., and J.L. Carter, "New Hash Functions and Their Use in Authentication and Set Equality," *Journal of Computer and System Sciences*, Vol. 22, 1981, pp. 265–279.

[20] Brassard, G., "On Computationally Secure Authentication Tags Requiring Short Secret Shared Keys," *Proceedings of CRYPTO '82*, 1982, pp. 79–86.

[21] Shoup, V., "On Fast and Provably Secure Message Authentication Based on Universal Hashing," *Proceedings of CRYPTO '96*, Springer-Verlag, LNCS 1109, 1996, pp. 313–328.

[22] Black, J. et al., "UMAC: Fast and Secure Message Authentication," *Proceedings of CRYPTO '99*, Springer-Verlag, LNCS 1666, 1999, pp. 216–233.

[23] Oppliger, R., *Internet and Intranet Security*, 2nd edition. Artech House Publishers, Norwood, MA, 2002.

Chapter 12

Pseudorandom Bit Generators

Anyone who considers arithmetical methods of producing random digits is, of course, in a state of sin.

— John von Neumann[1]

In Chapter 9, we concluded that it is often important to be able to generate truly random bits (using, for example, a random bit generator), to use these bits to seed a PRBG, and to use the PRBG to generate a potentially infinite pseudorandom bit sequence. Consequently, PRBGs have many applications in practice. In this chapter, we elaborate on PRBGs. More specifically, we introduce the topic in Section 12.1, address cryptographically secure PRBGs in Section 12.2, and conclude with some final remarks in Section 12.3.

12.1 INTRODUCTION

According to Section 2.2.3 and Definition 2.9, a PRBG is an efficient deterministic algorithm that, given as input a truly random binary sequence of length k (i.e., the seed), generates and outputs a binary sequence of length $l \gg k$ (i.e., the pseudorandom bit sequence) that appears to be random. Note that we require the algorithm that represents the PRBG to be deterministic, and hence the existence of PRBGs seems to contradict the quote of John von Neumann given above. If, however, one understands von Neumann's quote to refer to the seed of a PRBG (and hence to a random bit generator), it still applies. The seed for a PRBG must be generated non-deterministically, and hence the existence and use of a PRBG does not eliminate the

---

1   In: Des MacHale, *Comic Sections: The Book of Mathematical Jokes, Humour, Wit, and Wisdom*, Boole Press, Dublin, Ireland, 1993.

need for a natural source of randomness. It is rather a "randomness expander" that must still be given a truly random seed to begin with.

In practice, many additive stream ciphers are based on a PRBG. For example, the practically relevant and widely deployed additive stream cipher ARCFOUR (RC4) addressed in Section 10.3 basically represents a PRBG.

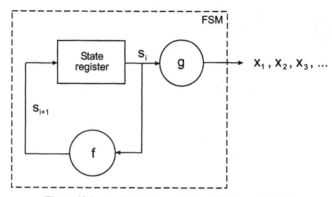

Figure 12.1   An idealized model of an FSM-based PRBG.

Due to its deterministic nature, a PRBG must be implemented as an FSM, and this FSM generates a binary sequence that is cyclic (with a potentially very large cycle). Figure 12.1 illustrates an idealized model of an FSM-based PRBG. The model comprises

- A state register;

- A next-state function f;

- An output function g.

The state register is initialized with a seed s_0, and the next-state function f computes s_{i+1} from s_i for $i \geq 0$. For each s_i, the function g computes an output value x_i for the PRBG (typically a bit or a series of bits). Consequently, the PRBG generates and outputs a sequence

$$(x_i)_{i \geq 1} = x_1, x_2, x_3, \ldots$$

In this idealized model, the function f operates recursively on the state register, and there is no other input to the PRBG than the seed. Some PRBGs used in practice slightly deviate from this idealized model by allowing the state to be reseeded periodically. This may be modeled by having a function f that takes into account additional sources of randomness (this possibility is not illustrated in Figure 12.1). In this case, however, the distinction between a random bit generator and a PRBG gets fuzzy.

There are many security requirements for PRBGs. For example, an obvious (minimal) security requirement is that the length of the seed (i.e., $|s_0|$) must be sufficiently large so that a search over all $2^{|s_0|}$ elements of the space of all possible seeds is computationally infeasible for the adversary. Furthermore, the bit sequence generated by a PRBG must pass all relevant statistical randomness tests (as mentioned in Section 9.3). Note, however, that passing statistical randomness tests is only a necessary but usually not sufficient condition for a PRBG to be secure in a cryptographically strong sense. For example, the following PRBGs pass most statistical randomness tests but are still not sufficiently secure for cryptographic purposes:

1. PRBGs that employ LFSRs as introduced and briefly discussed in Section 10.3;

2. PRBGs that employ the binary expansion of algebraic numbers, such as $\sqrt{3}$ or $\sqrt{5}$;

3. Linear congruential generators that take as input a seed $x_0 = s_0$ and three integer parameters a, b, and n, and that use the linear recurrence

$$x_i = ax_{i-1} + b \ (\text{mod} \ n)$$

to recursively generate an output sequence $(x_i)_{i \geq 1}$.

LFSRs have well-known shortcomings and weaknesses when used as PRBGs. The same is true for the binary expansion of algebraic numbers. Last but not least, linear congruential generators are frequently used for simulation purposes and probabilistic algorithms (see, for example, Chapter 3 of [1]), but they are predictable—that is, it is possible to infer the parameters a, b, and n given just a few output values x_i (e.g., [2, 3]). This makes them particularly useless for cryptographic applications.

Contrary to these examples, there are PRBGs that can be used for cryptographic purposes. For example, if we have a one-way function f, then we can always construct a conceptually simple PRBG by selecting a seed s_0 and applying f to the sequence of values

$$s_1 = s_0 + 1$$

$$s_2 = s_0 + 2$$
$$s_3 = s_0 + 3$$
$$\ldots$$

Talking in terms of an FSM, the state register is initialized with the seed s_0, the next-state function is the function that increments s by one (i.e., $s_{i+1} = s_i + 1$ for $i \geq 0$), and the output function is the one-way function. The output sequence of such a PRBG is as follows:

$$f(s_0), f(s_0 + 1), f(s_0 + 2), f(s_0 + 3), \ldots$$

Depending on the properties of the one-way function f, it may be necessary to keep only a few bits of the $(i + 1)^{th}$ output value $f(s + i)$ for $i \geq 0$ (mainly to destroy possible correlations between successive values). Examples of suitable one-way functions include block ciphers, such as DES or AES (see Chapter 10), with a secret key, or cryptographic hash functions, such as MD5 or SHA-1 (see Chapter 8).

Algorithm 12.1   ANSI X9.17 PRBG.

$$\frac{(s, k, n)}{\begin{array}{l} I \leftarrow E_k(D) \\ \text{for } i = 1 \text{ to } n \text{ do} \\ \quad x_i \leftarrow E_k(I \oplus s) \\ \quad s \leftarrow E_k(x_i \oplus I) \\ \quad \text{output } x_i \end{array}}$$
$$(x_1, x_2, \ldots, x_n)$$

A practically relevant PRBG is specified in ANSI X9.17 [4] and illustrated in Algorithm 12.1. It defines a way to pseudorandomly generate encryption keys and initialization vectors for use with DES. In the specification of Algorithm 12.1, E_k denotes a TDEA or 3DES encryption with keying option 2, according to Section 10.2.1.6 (in this option, only two DES keys are used, and in Algorithm 12.1 k refers to both of them). The algorithm takes as input a random (and secret) seed value s, a 3DES key k, and an integer n. It then produces and outputs a sequence of n pseudorandom 64-bit strings $x_1, x_2, \ldots, x_n$. D is an internally used 64-bit representation of the date and time (in a resolution that is as fine as possible), and I is an intermediate value that is determined in an initialization step at the beginning of the algorithm.

Other practically relevant PRBGs are, for example, specified in FIPS PUB 186 [5]. Although such ad hoc methods to generate pseudorandom bit sequences have not proven to be secure in a cryptographical sense, they appear sufficiently secure for most (cryptographic) applications. Unfortunately, only a few publications elaborate on the exact cryptographical strength of such a PRBG (e.g., [6]). For example, some PRBGs (including the ANSI X9.17 PRBG) have the property that once the internal state has been compromised, an adversary is forever after able to predict the output bit sequence of the PRBG. From a theoretical point of view, this is a minor concern and does not disturb the overall security of the PRBG (because one assumes that the adversary is not able to read out the internal state of the PRBG). From a practical point of view, however, this is a major concern and may require reseeding the PRBG periodically.

One branch of research tries to find PRBG constructions that are resistant against all known attacks. The resulting PRBGs are relevant and called *practically strong*. Note, however, that a practically strong PRBG is not necessarily secure in a cryptographical sense and that it is only assumed to be secure against a specific set of attacks that is known at some point in time. On the positive side, practically strong PRBGs are usually very efficient and can be implemented entirely in software. Possible constructions for practically strong PRBGs are given in [7] and [8]. For the purpose of this book, we don't further address practically strong PRBGs. Instead, we elaborate on PRBGs that are secure in a cryptographically strong sense; they are called cryptographically secure.[2]

12.2 CRYPTOGRAPHICALLY SECURE PRBG

From a theoretical point of view, there are many possibilities to formally define what "secure in a cryptographically strong sense" or "cryptographically secure" means with respect to PRBGs. Historically, the first possibility was formalized by Manuel Blum and Silvio Micali in the early 1980s [9]. They called a PRBG cryptographically secure if an adversary cannot guess the next bit in a sequence from the prefix of the sequence better than guessing at random, and they also proposed the first method for designing such a cryptographically secure PRBG based on the DLA (see Definition 7.4). Leonore Blum, Manuel Blum, and Michael Shub proposed another PRBG, called the *BBS PRBG* or *squaring generator*, which is simpler to implement and provably secure assuming that the QRP (see Definition 3.32) is hard [10]. Later it was shown that the assumption that the QRP is hard can be replaced by the weaker assumption that the IFP is hard [11]. A related PRBG is obtained by using the RSA function. All three PRBGs are addressed later.

---

2   Cryptographically secure PRBGs are sometimes also called *cryptographically strong*.

In addition to these constructions of cryptographically secure PRBGs, Andrew C. Yao showed that they are all perfect in the sense that no PPT algorithm can guess with a probability significantly greater than $1/2$ whether an input string of length k was randomly selected from $\{0,1\}^k$ or generated by such a PRBG [12]. Note that this notion of a perfect PRBG is conceptually similar to the Turing Test[3] used in artificial intelligence [13]. One can rephrase Yao's result by saying that a PRBG that passes the Blum-Micali next-bit test is perfect in the sense that it passes all polynomial-time statistical tests.

The Blum-Micali and BBS PRBGs, together with the proof of Yao, represent a major achievement in the development of cryptographically secure PRBGs. More recently, it was shown that the existence of a one-way function is equivalent to the existence of a cryptographically secure PRBG (i.e., a PRBG that passes all polynomial-time statistical tests) [14].

On a high level of abstraction, one can say that a PRBG is called cryptographically secure if the (pseudorandom) bit sequence it generates and outputs cannot be distinguished (by any PPT algorithm) from a true random bit sequence of the same length. In analogy, one may not care if a pseudorandom bit sequence is random or not; all one may care about is whether a difference can be observed between the pseudorandomly generated bit sequence and a true random bit sequence (of the same length). Consequently, the notion of *effective similarity* (as, for example, used in [12, 15]) or *computational indistinguishability* are fundamental for the definition of cryptographically secure PRBGs. To make these ideas more precise, let

$$X = \{X_n\} = \{X_n\}_{n \in \mathbb{N}} = \{X_1, X_2, X_3, \ldots\}$$

and

$$Y = \{Y_n\} = \{Y_n\}_{n \in \mathbb{N}} = \{Y_1, Y_2, Y_3, \ldots\}$$

3   The Turing Test is meant to determine if a computer program has intelligence. According to Alan M. Turing, the test can be devised in terms of a game (a so-called imitation game). It is played with three people, a man (A), a woman (B), and an interrogator (C) who may be of either sex. The interrogator stays in a room apart from the other two. The object of the game for the interrogator is to determine which of the other two is the man and which is the woman. He knows them by labels X and Y, and at the end of the game he says either "X is A and Y is B" or "X is B and Y is A." The interrogator is allowed to put questions to A and B. When talking about the Turing Test today, what is generally understood is the following: the interrogator is connected to one person and one machine via a terminal, and therefore can't see her counterparts. Her task is to find out which of the two candidates is the machine and which is the human only by asking them questions. If the machine can "fool" the interrogator, it is intelligent.

be two probability ensembles. For every $n \in \mathbb{N}^+$, X_n and Y_n refer to probability distributions on $\{0,1\}^n$. By saying $t \in X_n$ ($t \in Y_n$), we mean that $t \in \{0,1\}^n$, and t is selected according to the probability distribution X_n (Y_n). We then say that X is *poly-time indistinguishable* from Y if for every PPT algorithm D and every polynomial p, there exists a $n_0 \in \mathbb{N}^+$ such that for all $n > n_0$

$$|\mathrm{Pr}_{t \in X_n}[D(t) = 1] - \mathrm{Pr}_{t \in Y_n}[D(t) = 1]| \leq \frac{1}{p(n)}.$$

This means that for sufficiently large t, no PPT algorithm D can tell whether it was sampled according to X_n or Y_n. In some literature, the PPT algorithm D is also called *polynomial-time statistical test* or *distinguisher* (the letter "D" is chosen to refer to a distinguisher). In either case, it is important to note that such a definition cannot make sense for a single string t (as it can be drawn from either distribution).

In computational complexity theory, it is assumed and widely believed that computationally indistinguishable probability ensembles exist. This assumption is sometimes referred to as the general indistinguishability assumption.

Having the general indistinguishability assumption in mind, we say that $\{X_n\}$ is *pseudorandom* if it is poly-time indistinguishable from $\{U_n\}$, where U_n denotes the uniform probability distribution on $\{0,1\}^n$. More specifically, this means that for every PPT algorithm D and every polynomial p, there exists a $n_0 \in \mathbb{N}^+$ such that for all $n > n_0$

$$|\mathrm{Pr}_{t \in X_n}[D(t) = 1] - \mathrm{Pr}_{t \in U_n}[D(t) = 1]| \leq \frac{1}{p(n)}.$$

We are now ready to formally define the notion of a cryptographically secure PRBG. This is done in Definition 12.1.

Definition 12.1 (Cryptographically secure PRBG) *Let G be a PRBG with stretch function $l : \mathbb{N} \to \mathbb{N}$ (i.e., $l(n) > n$ for all $n \in \mathbb{N}$). G is cryptographically secure if it satisfies the following two conditions:*

- $|G(s)| = l(|s|)$ *for every $s \in \{0,1\}^*$;*

- $\{G(U_n)\}$ *is pseudorandom (i.e., it is poly-time indistinguishable from $\{U_{l(n)}\}$).*

The first condition captures the stretching property of the PRBG (i.e., the fact that the output of the PRBG is larger than its input), and the second condition captures the property that the generated pseudorandom bit sequence is computationally indistinguishable from (and hence practically the same as) a true random bit sequence. Combining the two conditions yields a PRBG that is secure and can be used for cryptographic purposes. Referring to the fundamental results of Blum, Micali, and Yao (mentioned earlier), a PRBG is cryptographically secure if it passes the next-bit test (and hence all polynomial-time statistical tests) possibly under some intractability assumption.

If one has a one-way function f with hard-core predicate B, then a cryptographically secure PRBG G with seed s_0 can be constructed as follows:

$$G(s_0) = B(s_0), B(f(s_0)), B(f^2(s_0)), \ldots, B(f^{l(|s_0|)-1}(s_0))$$

Talking in terms of an FSM-based PRBG, the state register is initialized with s_0, the next-state function f is the one-way function, and the output function g computes the hard-core predicate B. This idea is employed by many cryptographically secure PRBGs. The three most important examples—the Blum-Micali, RSA, and BBS PRBGs—are overviewed and briefly discussed next.

12.2.1 Blum-Micali PRBG

The Blum-Micali PRBG [9] as specified in Algorithm 12.2 employs the fact that the discrete exponentiation function is a (conjectured) one-way function (see Section 7.2.1) and that the MSB is a hard-core predicate of it. The PRBG takes as input a large prime p and a generator g of $\mathbb{Z}_p^*$. It is initialized by randomly selecting a seed $x_0 = s_0$ from $\mathbb{Z}_p^*$. The PRBG then generates an output bit b_i by computing $x_i = g^{x_{i-1}} \pmod{p}$ and setting $b_i = msb(x_i)$ for $i \geq 1$. A potentially infinite bit sequence $(b_i)_{i \geq 1}$ can be generated along this way. It is the output of the Blum-Micali PRBG.

Algorithm 12.2 The Blum-Micali PRBG.

$$(p, g)$$

$x_0 \in_R \mathbb{Z}_p^*$
for $i = 1$ to ∞ do
$\quad x_i \leftarrow g^{x_{i-1}} \pmod{p}$
$\quad b_i \leftarrow msb(x_i)$
$\quad$ output b_i

$(b_i)_{i \geq 1}$

The security of the Blum-Micali PRBG is based on the DLA (see Definition 7.4). This means that anybody who is able to compute discrete logarithms can also break the security of the Blum-Micali PRBG.

12.2.2 RSA PRBG

The RSA PRBG as specified in Algorithm 12.3 employs the fact that the RSA function is a (conjectured) one-way function (see Section 7.2.2) and that the LSB is a hard-core predicate of it. Similar to the RSA public key cryptosystem, the RSA PRBG takes as input a large integer n (that is the product of two large primes p and q) and e (that is a randomly chosen integer between 2 and $\phi(n)-1$ with $gcd(e, \phi(n)) = 1$). The PRBG is then initialized by randomly selecting a seed $x_0 = s_0$ from $\mathbb{Z}_n^*$. It then generates an output bit b_i by computing $x_i = x_{i-1}^e \pmod{n}$ and setting $b_i = lsb(x_i)$ for $i \geq 1$. Again, a potentially infinite bit sequence $(b_i)_{i \geq 1}$ can be generated along this way. It is the output of the RSA PRBG.

Algorithm 12.3 The RSA PRBG.

$$
\begin{array}{l}
\underline{(n, e)} \\
x_0 \in_R \mathbb{Z}_n^* \\
\text{for } i = 1 \text{ to } \infty \text{ do} \\
\quad x_i \leftarrow x_{i-1}^e \pmod{n} \\
\quad b_i \leftarrow lsb(x_i) \\
\quad \text{output } b_i \\
\hline
(b_i)_{i \geq 1}
\end{array}
$$

If, for example, $e = 3$, then generating an output bit requires only one modular multiplication and one modular squaring. This is efficient. The efficiency of the RSA PRBG can be further improved by extracting the j least significant bits of x_i (instead of only the LSB), where $j = c \log \log n$ for a constant c.

In either case, the security of the RSA PRBG is based on the IFA (see Definition 7.10). This means that anybody who is able to factorize large integers can also break the security of the RSA PRBG.

12.2.3 BBS PRBG

The BBS PRBG [10] as specified in Algorithm 12.4 employs the fact that the modular square function restricted to Blum integers is a (conjectured) one-way function (see Section 7.2.2), and that—similar to the RSA function—the LSB is a hard-core predicate of it. The BBS PRBG takes as input a Blum integer n (i.e., an integer n that is the product of two primes p and q, each of them congruent to 3 modulo 4). Similar to the RSA PRBG, the BBS PRBG is initialized by randomly selecting a seed $x_0 = s_0$ from $\mathbb{Z}_n^*$. It then generates an output bit b_i by computing $x_i = x_{i-1}^2 \pmod{n}$ and setting $b_i = lsb(x_i)$ for $i \geq 1$. A potentially infinite bit sequence $(b_i)_{i \geq 1}$ is the output of the BBS PRBG.

Algorithm 12.4   The BBS PRBG.

$$\frac{(n)}{\begin{array}{l} x_0 \in_R \mathbb{Z}_n^* \\ \text{for } i = 1 \text{ to } \infty \text{ do} \\ \quad x_i \leftarrow x_{i-1}^2 \ (\text{mod } n) \\ \quad b_i \leftarrow lsb(x_i) \\ \quad \text{output } b_i \end{array}}{(b_i)_{i \geq 1}}$$

Alternatively speaking, the BBS PRBG takes as input a large Blum integer n and generates the following binary output sequence (using a randomly chosen seed x_0):

$$G(x_0) = lsb(x_0), lsb(x_0^2 \bmod n), \ldots, lsb(x_0^{2^{l(|x_0|)-1}} \bmod n)$$

From a practical viewpoint, the BBS PRBG is the cryptographically secure PRBG of choice used in many applications. There are basically two reasons:

- First, the BBS PRBG is efficient. It requires only one modular squaring for the generation of an output bit. Furthermore, the efficiency of the PRBG can be improved by extracting the $j = c \log \log n$ least significant bits of x_i (instead of only the LSB).

- Second, the BBS PRBG has the practically relevant property that x_i can be computed directly for $i \geq 1$ if one knows the prime factors p and q of n:

$$x_i = x_0^{(2^i) \bmod ((p-1)(q-1))}$$

In either case (and similar to the RSA PRBG), the security of the BBS PRBG is based on the IFA (see Definition 7.10 on page 178).

12.3   FINAL REMARKS

In this chapter, we introduced the notion of a PRBG and elaborated on the requirements for a PRBG to be cryptographically secure. In short, a cryptographically secure PRBG is an efficient deterministic algorithm that is able to stretch a binary input sequence into a longer output sequence, and for which no PPT algorithm can be specified that is able to distinguish the output of the PRBG from the output of a true random bit generator with a success probability that is nonnegligibly larger than 1/2. Put in other words, there is no PPT algorithm that can distinguish the output of a PRBG and the output of a random bit generator (of the same length) considerably better than guessing.

In practice, PRBGs are important because they are used in many applications to replace true random bit generators. This is advantageous because PRBGs use much less randomness than true random bit generators (they still need randomness and hence the quote of von Neumann still applies). Also, in an interactive setting, it is possible to eliminate all random steps from the online computation and replace them with the generation of pseudorandom bits based on a seed selected and fixed offline (or at set-up time). The underlying assumption is that a cryptographic system that is secure when the parties use a true random bit generator remains secure when they use (only) a PRBG. For cryptographically secure PRBGs, we can have a "good feeling" about this assumption; for practically relevant (or strong) PRBGs, we can at least hope that the assumption holds. As soon as there is evidence that the assumption may not hold, there is a strong incentive to replace these PRBGs with cryptographically secure ones. In either case, if one has the choice, then there is good reason to go for PRBGs that are cryptographically secure. In either case, it is a good idea to periodically reseed the PRBG (even if it is a cryptographically secure one).

References

[1] Knuth, D.E., *The Art of Computer Programming—Volume 2: Seminumerical Algorithms*, 3rd edition. Addison-Wesley, Reading, MA, 1997.

[2] Plumstead, J., "Inferring a Sequence Generated by a Linear Congruence," *Proceedings of the 23rd IEEE Symposium on Foundations of Computer Science*, IEEE, Chicago, 1982, pp. 153–159.

[3] Krawczyk, H., "How to Predict Congruential Generators," *Journal of Algorithms*, Vol. 13, No. 4, 1992, pp. 527–545.

[4] American National Standards Institute, *American National Standard X9.17: Financial Institution Key Management*, Washington, DC, 1985.

[5] U.S. National Institute of Standards and Technology (NIST), *Digital Signature Standard (DSS)*, FIPS PUB 186, May 1994.

[6] Kelsey, J., et al., "Cryptanalytic Attacks on Pseudorandom Number Generators," *Proceedings of the Fifth International Workshop on Fast Software Encryption*, Springer-Verlag, March 1998, pp. 168–188.

[7] Gutmann, P., "Software Generation of Practically Strong Random Numbers," *Proceedings of the Seventh USENIX Security Symposium*, June 1998, pp. 243–255.

[8] Kelsey, J., B. Schneier, and N. Ferguson, "Yarrow-160: Notes on the Design and Analysis of the Yarrow Cryptographic Pseudorandom Number Generator," *Proceedings of the 6th Annual Workshop on Selected Areas in Cryptography*, Springer-Verlag, August 1999.

[9] Blum, M., and S. Micali, "How to Generate Cryptographically Strong Sequences of Pseudo-Random Bits," *SIAM Journal of Computing*, Vol. 13, No. 4, November 1984, pp. 850–863.

[10] Blum, L., M. Blum, and M. Shub, "A Simple Unpredictable Pseudo-Random Number Generator," *SIAM Journal of Computing*, Vol. 15, May 1986, pp. 364–383.

[11] Alexi, W., et al., "RSA/Rabin Functions: Certain Parts Are as Hard as the Whole," *SIAM Journal of Computing*, Vol. 17, No. 2, April 1988, pp. 194–209.

[12] Yao, A.C., "Theory and Application of Trapdoor Functions," *Proceedings of the 23rd IEEE Symposium on Foundations of Computer Science*, 1982, pp. 80–91.

[13] Turing, A.M., "Computing Machinery and Intelligence," *Mind*, Vol. 59, No. 236, 1950, pp. 433–460.

[14] Hastad, J., et al., "A Pseudorandom Generator from Any One-Way Function," *SIAM Journal of Computing*, Vol. 28, No. 4, 1999, pp. 1364–1396.

[15] Goldwasser, S., and S. Micali, "Probabilistic Encryption," *Journal of Computer and System Sciences*, Vol. 28, No. 2, 1984, pp. 270–299.

Chapter 13

Pseudorandom Functions

After having looked at PRBGs in the previous chapter, we now elaborate on PRFs in this chapter. PRBGs and PRFs are somehow related but still conceptually different. While a PRBG is an algorithm that generates and outputs a bit sequence that is computationally indistinguishable from the output of a random bit generator, a PRF is a function that is computationally indistinguishable from a random function (i.e., a function that is randomly chosen from the set of all functions with a specific domain and range). Consequently, we are interested in the output of a PRBG, whereas we are interested in the way a PRF was chosen in the first place. Interestingly, a PRF family can be used to construct a PRBG, and a PRBG can be used to construct a PRF family (this fact was already mentioned in Section 2.2.4). In this chapter, we thoroughly introduce the topic in Section 13.1, overview and discuss the contructions mentioned earlier in Section 13.2, elaborate on the random oracle model in Section 13.3, and conclude with some final remarks in Section 13.4.

13.1 INTRODUCTION

To properly understand the statement that a PRF is computationally indistinguishable from a random function, we must first introduce the notion of a random function. Roughly speaking, a *random function* (also known as *random oracle*) f is an arbitrary mapping from X to Y (i.e., $f : X \rightarrow Y$), meaning that it maps an input value $x \in X$ to an arbitrary output value $f(x) \in Y$. The only requirement is that the same input value x must always be mapped to the same output value $f(x)$.

As illustrated in Figure 13.1, a random function is best thought of as a black box that implements a function with a specific input-output behavior. This behavior can be observed by everybody, meaning that anybody can feed input values $x \in X$ into the box and observe the output values $f(x) \in Y$ that are sent out. Again, the

Figure 13.1   A random function f.

only requirement is that if a specific input value x is fed multiple times into the box, then the output value $f(x)$ must always be the same.

Another way to think about a random function f is as a large random table T with entries of the form $T[x] = (x, f(x))$ for all $x \in X$. The table can either be statically determined or dynamically generated:

- If T is statically determined, then somebody must have flipped coins (or used another source of random bits) to determine $f(x)$ for all $x \in X$ and put these values into the table.

- If T is dynamically generated, then there must be a program that initializes the table with empty entries and that proceeds as follows for every input value x: it checks whether $T[x]$ is empty. If it is empty, then it randomly chooses $f(x)$ from Y, writes this value into $T[x]$, and returns it as a result. If $T[x]$ is not empty, then it returns the corresponding value as a result.

Note that a random function is neither something useful in practice nor something that is intended to be implemented in the first place. It is only a conceptual and theoretical construct. Also note that the term *random function* is somehow misleading. In fact, it may lead one to believe that some functions are more random than others or—more generally—that randomness is a property that can be attributed to a function or the output it eventually provides. This is not the case. The attribute *random* in the term random function refers only to the way it was chosen. In fact, a random function $f : X \to Y$ is a function that is randomly chosen from $Rand^{X \to Y}$ (i.e., the set of all functions of X to Y). Consequently, even a constant function can occur as a random function (even though one would intuitively think that a constant function is not random at all).

Similarly, we use the term *random permutation* to refer to a function $f : X \to X$ that is randomly chosen from $Perm^{X \to X}$, and hence the identity function can also occur as random permutation. Most of the things we say in this chapter about PRFs also apply to *pseudorandom permutations* (PRPs) in an analog way.

The fact that a PRF is computationally indistinguishable from a random function means that somebody who has only black box access to a function (in the sense that he or she can only observe the input-output behavior of a box that implements the function) is not able to tell whether it is a random function or a PRF. To make this idea more precise (in a mathematically strong sense), we consider an experiment. Let $F : K \times X \to Y$ be a PRF family that is publicly known. Imagine an adversary who is locked up in a room with a computer system connected to another computer system located somewhere outside the room (and out of sight). The outside computer system implements a function $g : X \to Y$ that is either a random function or an instance of F (and hence a PRF).

- If g is a random function, then it is drawn at random from $Rand^{X \to Y}$ (i.e., $g \xleftarrow{r} Rand^{X \to Y}$).

- If g is a PRF, then it is drawn at random from the PRF family F, namely $g \xleftarrow{r} F$. More specifically, a key k is chosen according to $k \xleftarrow{r} K$ and g is then set to the instance f_k of the PRF family F.

In this setting, the adversary's job is to decide whether g is a random function or an instance of the PRF family F. He or she can adaptively choose input values $x \in X$ and observe the corresponding output values $f(x) \in Y$. If the PRF family F is good (bad), then the probability that the adversary can make a correct decision is only negligibly (nonnegligibly) better than $1/2$. Hence, the quality of a PRF family can be measured by the difficulty of telling its instances apart from true random functions.

To further formalize this idea, we must again make use of a *distinguisher*. This time, however, the distinguisher is a PPT algorithm that has oracle access to some function and that makes a decision whether this function is random or pseudo-random. In the rest of this chapter, we use the term D^g to refer to a distinguisher D with oracle access to function g (be it a random function or an instance of a PRF family). In either case, the output of D^g is one bit. We then consider the following two experiments:

1) Experiment $\mathrm{Exp}_{Rand,D}$
$f \xleftarrow{r} Rand^{X \to Y}$
$b \leftarrow D^f$
output b

2) Experiment $\mathrm{Exp}_{F,D}$
$k \xleftarrow{r} K$
$b \leftarrow D^{f_k}$
output b

In $\mathrm{Exp}_{Rand,D}$, a (random) function f is randomly chosen from $Rand^{X \to Y}$ and the distinguisher D with oracle access to f returns bit b. This bit, in turn, is D's decision whether f is random or pseudorandom. In $\text{Exp}_{F,D}$, a key k is randomly chosen from K to fix a function $f_k \in F$, and the distinguisher D with oracle access to f_k returns bit b. Again, this bit is D's decision whether f_k is random or pseudorandom. Each experiment has a certain probability of returning 1. The probabilities are taken over all random choices made in the experiments (i.e., in the first experiment, the probability is taken over all choices of f and all internal random choices of D^f, whereas in the second experiment, the probability is taken over all choices of k and all internal random choices of D^{f_k}). To qualify a distinguisher D (with regard to its ability to distinguish between a random function and a PRF), one looks at the difference between the two probabilities. Note that if D is a good distinguisher, then it returns 1 more often in one experiment than in the other. Consequently, the *prf-advantage* of D for F can be defined as followed:

$$\text{Adv}_{F,D}^{prf} = \Pr[\text{Exp}_{F,D} = 1] - \Pr[\text{Exp}_{Rand,D} = 1]$$

It goes without saying that different distinguishers may have different prf-advantages. For example, one distinguisher may achieve a greater prf-advantage than another simply by asking more or more intelligent questions or by using a better strategy to process the replies. Also, it is reasonable to assume that the more input-output examples that can be observed, the better the ability to tell the two types of functions apart. Consequently, the quality of a function family F must also be measured as a function of the resources allowed to a distinguisher. For any given resource limitation, we may be interested in the prf-advantage achieved by the best (i.e., most intelligent) distinguisher (among all distinguishers that are restricted to the given resource limitations). We associate to F a prf-advantage that on input of any values of the resource parameters returns the maximum prf-advantage that an adversary restricted to these resources is able to obtain. Consequently, for any given t, q, and μ, we define the *prf-advantage* of F as

$$\text{Adv}_{F}^{prf}(t, q, \mu) = \max_D \{\text{Adv}_{F,D}^{prf}\}$$

where the maximum is taken over all D having time complexity t and making at most q oracle queries, the sum of the lengths of these queries being at most μ bits. The main reason for using the prf-advantage of F as a measure for the quality of F is that it does not specify anything about the kinds of strategies that can be used by a distinguisher. In fact, it can do anything as long as it stays within the specified resource bounds.

So far, we have only assigned a prf-advantage to a function family F. We have neither specified the requirements for F to be a PRF family, nor have we said what we mean by saying that F is secure. Intuitively, we would say that F is a secure PRF family if its prf-advantage is negligible for all practically relevant input parameters, and we would then say that input parameters are practically relevant if they refer to resources that are polynomially bound. The notion of a secure PRF can be defined along these lines. In fact, this definitional framework is frequently used in modern cryptography. It basically consists of the following steps:

- First, one defines experiments that involve an adversary.

- Second, one specifies an advantage function associated to an adversary. For a specific adversary, the advantage function returns the probability that he or she "breaks" the scheme (i.e., provides a correct answer).

- Third, one specifies an advantage function associated to the cryptographic system in question. This function takes input resource parameters and returns the maximum probability of "breaking" the system if the adversary is restricted to the specified resource parameters.

If the advantage function returns a sufficiently small maximum probability for all reasonable resource parameters, then one considers the cryptographic system to be secure for practical purposes.

13.2 CONSTRUCTIONS

As mentioned earlier, a PRF family can be used to construct a PRBG, and a PRBG can be used to construct a PRF family. Let us overview and briefly discuss these constructions.

13.2.1 PRF-Based PRBG

If we ask whether it is possible to construct a PRBG using a PRF family, then we can answer in the affirmative. In fact, the corresponding construction is fairly trivial. Let F be a PRF family with key space K. If we randomly choose $k \in_R K$, fix the PRF f_k, iteratively apply f_k to a counter value (starting, for example, with zero), then we generate the following sequence of values:

$$f_k(0)$$
$$f_k(1)$$
$$f_k(2)$$

$$f_k(3)$$

$$\ldots$$

If we take these values as the output values of a PRBG (seeded with k), then the resulting PRF-based PRBG can be specified as follows:

$$G(k) = f_k(0), f_k(1), f_k(2), f_k(3), \ldots = (f_k(i))_{i \geq 0}$$

If we assume the PRF family F to be secure (in the sense mentioned earlier), then the corresponding PRF-based PRBG $G(k)$ can also be shown to be cryptographically secure. The efficiency of this PRBG mainly depends on the efficiency of the underlying PRF family (i.e., the PRF-based PRBG is efficient if the instances of the underlying PRF family can be implemented efficiently).

13.2.2   PRBG-Based PRF

More suprisingly, if we ask whether it is possible to construct a PRF family using a PRBG, then we can also answer in the affirmative. The first construction was proposed by Oded Goldreich, Shafi Goldwasser, and Silvio Micali in the 1980s [1].

Let $G(s)$ be a PRBG with stretching function $l(n) = 2n$, $G_0(s)$ ($G_1(s)$) be the first (last) n bits of $G(s)$ for $s \in \{0,1\}^n$, $X = Y = \{0,1\}^n$, and $x = \sigma_n \cdots \sigma_2 \sigma_1$ the bitwise representation of x. A simple PRBG-based PRF $f_s : X \to Y$ can then be constructed as follows:

$$f_s(x) = f_s(\sigma_n \cdots \sigma_2 \sigma_1) = G_{\sigma_n}(\cdots G_{\sigma_2}(G_{\sigma_1}(s)) \cdots)$$

Let's consider a toy example. For $n = 2$, we can use the following PRBG $G(s)$:

$$
\begin{aligned}
G(00) &= 1001 \\
G(01) &= 0011 \\
G(10) &= 1110 \\
G(11) &= 0100
\end{aligned}
$$

For $s = 10$ and $x = 01$, we have

$$f_s(\sigma_2\sigma_1) = f_{10}(01) = G_0(G_1(10)) = 11.$$

To compute this value, we must first compute $G_1(10) = 10$ (i.e., the last two bits of $G(10) = 1110$) and then $G_0(10) = 11$ (i.e., the first two bits of $G(10) = 1110$). Hence, the output of the PRF is 11.

If the PRBG $G(s)$ is cryptographically secure, then the function f_s as defined earlier can be shown to be a PRF. Considering the fact that s is an element $\{0,1\}^n$, the set of all functions f_s yields a PRF family. The efficiency of this PRF family mainly depends on the efficiency of the underlying PRBG (i.e., the PRBG-based PRFs are efficient if the underlying PRBG can be implemented efficiently).

13.3 RANDOM ORACLE MODEL

In Section 1.2.2, we introduced the notion of provable security and mentioned that the random oracle methodology is frequently used to design cryptographic systems (typically security protocols) that are provably secure in the so-called random oracle model. The methodology was proposed by Mihir Bellare and Philip Rogaway in the early 1990s to provide "a bridge between cryptographic theory and cryptographic practice" [2]. In fact, they formalized a heuristic argument that was already expressed in [1, 3, 4]. The random oracle methodology consists of the following steps:[1]

- First, an ideal system is designed in which all parties (including the adversary) have access to a random function (or a random oracle, respectively).

- Second, one proves the security of this ideal system.

- Third, one replaces the random function with a PRF (e.g., a cryptographic hash function) and provides all parties (again, including the adversary) with a specification of this function.

As a result, one obtains an implementation of the ideal system in the real world. Bellare and Rogaway showed the usefulness of this methodology to design and analyze the security properties of asymmetric encryption, digital signature, and zero-knowledge proof systems. Meanwhile, many researchers have used the random oracle model to analyze the security properties of various cryptographic systems used in practice. Note, however, that a formal analysis in the random oracle model is not a security proof (because of the underlying ideal assumption) but that it still

---

1   In some literature, steps 1 and 2 are collectively referred to step one.

provides some useful evidence for the security of a cryptographic system. In fact, Bellare and Rogaway claimed that the random oracle model can serve as the basis for efficient cryptographic systems with security properties that can at least be analyzed to some extent. Because people do not often want to pay more than a negligible price for security, such an argument for practical systems seems to be more useful than formal security proofs for inefficient systems.

There are basically two problems when it comes to an implementation of an ideal system (in step three of the random oracle methodology).

- First, it is impossible to implement a random function by a (single) cryptographic hash function. In a random function f, the preimages and images are not related to each other, meaning that x does not reveal any information about $f(x)$ and $f(x)$ does not reveal any information about x. If the random function were implemented by a (single) cryptographic hash function h, then the preimage x would leak a lot of information about the image $h(x)$. In fact, $h(x)$ would be completely determined by x. This problem can easily be solved by using a (large) family of cryptographic hash functions and choosing one at random [5].

- Second, it was shown that random oracles cannot be implemented cryptographically. More specifically, it was shown in [6] that there exists a(n artificially designed) DSS that is secure in the random oracle model but that gets insecure when the random oracle is implemented by a family of cryptographic hash functions.

The second problem is particularly worrisome, and since the publication of [6] many researchers have started to think controversially about the usefulness of the random oracle methodology in general, and the random oracle model in particular. Following a line of argumentation that is due to Doug Stinson,[2] the

correct way to interpret a proof of security for a protocol P in the random oracle model is to view it as a proof of security against certain types of attacks on the protocol P. More precisely, the proof shows that the protocol P is secure against what might be termed "hash-generic" attacks. This means that any attack which treats the hash function as a random function will not be successful (regardless of whether the hash function is actually a random function). In other words, it is better to think of a proof in the random oracle model as a proof in which we make an assumption about the attacking algorithm rather than an assumption about the hash function.

2   http://www.cacr.math.uwaterloo.ca/~dstinson/CO_685/randomoracle.html

Consequently, a security proof in the random oracle model makes sure that the protocol is secure against hash-generic attacks. It is of course possible that an adversary can break the protocol for some particular cryptographic hash functions (or even for the entire family of cryptographic hash functions) by somehow taking advantage of how the hash function(s) is (are) computed. Nevertheless, a proof in the random oracle model can still be regarded as evidence of security when the random oracle is replaced by a particular cryptographic hash function (this was the original claim of Bellare and Rogaway). It should be stressed at this point that no practical protocol proven secure in the random oracle model has been broken when used with a cryptographic hash function, such as SHA-1. The protocol used in [6] was not a natural protocol for a "reasonable" cryptographic application (i.e., it was designed explicitly for the purposes of the proof).

13.4 FINAL REMARKS

In this chapter, we elaborated on PRFs and their close relationship to PRBGs. In particular, we showed that it is possible to construct a PRBG if one has a PRF family and that it is possible to contruct a PRF family if one has a PRBG. The constructions we gave are conceptually simple and straightforward. To be used in practice, one would certainly go for constructions that are more efficient.

Having introduced the notion of a PRF family, we then introduced, overviewed, and put into perspective the random oracle methodology that is frequently used in modern cryptography to design cryptographic systems and to analyze their security properties in the so-called random oracle model. Mainly due to a negative result [6], people have started to think controversially about the random oracle model and to look for alternative approaches to analyze the security properties of cryptographic systems. In fact, security proofs avoiding the random oracle model are popular and have appeared in many recent cryptographic publications.

References

[1] Goldreich, O., S. Goldwasser, and S. Micali, "How to Construct Random Functions," *Journal of the ACM*, Vol. 33, No. 4, October 1986, pp. 792–807.

[2] Bellare, M., and P. Rogaway, "Random Oracles Are Practical: A Paradigm for Designing Efficient Protocols," *Proceedings of First Annual Conference on Computer and Communications Security*, ACM Press, New York, 1993, pp. 62–73.

[3] Fiat, A., and A. Shamir, "How To Prove Yourself: Practical Solutions to Identification and Signature Problems," *Proceedings of CRYPTO '86*, Springer-Verlag, LNCS 263, 1987, pp. 186–194.

[4] Goldreich, O., S. Goldwasser, and S. Micali, "On the Cryptographic Applications of Random Functions," *Proceedings of CRYPTO '84*, Springer-Verlag, LNCS 196, 1984, pp. 276–288.

[5] Canetti, R., "Towards Realizing Random Oracles: Hash Functions That Hide All Partial Information," *Proceedings of CRYPTO '97*, Springer-Verlag, LNCS 1294, 1997, pp. 455–469.

[6] Canetti, R., O. Goldreich, and S. Halevi, "The Random Oracles Methodology, Revisited," *Proceedings of 30th STOC*, ACM Press, New York, 1998, pp. 209–218.

Part IV

PUBLIC KEY
CRYPTOSYSTEMS

Chapter 14

Asymmetric Encryption Systems

In this chapter, we elaborate on asymmetric encryption systems. More specifically, we introduce the topic in Section 14.1, overview and discuss some basic and secure systems in Sections 14.2 and 14.3, address identity-based encryption in Section 14.4, and conclude with final remarks in Section 14.5.

14.1 INTRODUCTION

In Section 2.3.1, we introduced the idea of using a family of trapdoor functions to come up with an encryption system that is asymmetric in nature (because the encryption and decryption algorithms use different keys). Furthermore, we defined an asymmetric encryption system to consist of three efficiently computable algorithms (i.e., Generate, Encrypt, and Decrypt) with Encrypt and Decrypt being inverse to each other (see Definition 2.10).

The working principle of an asymmetric encryption system is illustrated in Figure 2.7. If the sender wants to encrypt a plaintext message m that is longer than the maximum message length, then m must be split into a sequence of message blocks $m_1, m_2, \ldots, m_n$ (each block must be shorter than or equal to the maximal message length), and each message block must be encrypted and decrypted individually (or sequentially in a specific mode of operation, respectively). In this chapter, we only consider the situation in which we must encrypt a single message block m. But keep in mind that this message block may only be part of a potentially very long message.

Similar to a symmetric encryption system, one may wonder whether a given asymmetric encryption system is secure. Information-theoretic or perfect security does not make a lot of sense in the realm of an asymmetric encryption system, because we assume the Encrypt algorithm to work with a fixed key of finite length.

Consequently, an adversary who is given a ciphertext can always use the recipient's public key (which is publicly known) and perform a brute-force attack to find the plaintext message. If we assume a computationally unbound adversary, then this attack is always successful (at least if we assume the plaintext message to represent some reasonable or meaningful message).

Referring to Section 1.2.2, we must specify the adversary's capabilities and the task he or she is required to solve in order to be successful before we can meaningfully discuss the security properties of an asymmetric encryption system.

- With regard to the first point (i.e., the adversary's capabilities), one usually assumes an adversary who is polynomially bound with respect to his or her computing power (or some other resources, such as available memory or time).

- With regard to the second point (i.e., the task he or she is required to solve in order to be successful), there are several possibilities, and these possibilities lead to different notions of security (as addressed later).

In Section 10.1, we introduced and distinguished between ciphertext-only, known-plaintext, (adaptive) chosen-plaintext, and (adaptive) chosen-ciphertext attacks. Again, ciphertext-only and known-plaintext attacks are very important and certainly the types of attacks one wants to protect against. Because the encryption key is public in an asymmetric encryption system, (adaptive) chosen-plaintext attacks are always possible and trivial to perform (just take the public key and encrypt arbitrary plaintext messages with it). This is not the case with (adaptive) chosen-ciphertext attacks. Because the private key is kept secret, it may not be possible for an adversary to decrypt a ciphertext of his or her choice (unless he or she has access to a decryption device or oracle).[1] Consequently, protection against (adaptive) chosen-ciphertext attacks is important for asymmetric encryption systems, and the design of systems that are resistant against these types of attacks is an important and timely research area.

Taking all of these considerations into account, there are several notions of security for an asymmetric encryption system. The most commonly used notion can be described as "semantic security against adaptive chosen-ciphertext attacks." We already know what an adaptive chosen-ciphertext attack is (the term was originally introduced in [1]), so it remains to be seen what "semantic security" means. The term *semantic security* was introduced and formalized in the context of probabilistic encryption in [2] (see Section 14.3.1 for a brief overview and discussion of

---

1   Remember that an oracle is an efficient (i.e., PPT) algorithm that takes an arbitrary input and that is able to generate a correct output. The algorithm itself is not known, and hence the oracle must be considered a black box.

probabilistic encryption). It is sometimes also described as *indistinguishability of ciphertexts*. It basically means that ciphertexts can't be distinguished in the sense that they can be attributed to plaintext messages that are more likely than others. Semantic security (or indistinguishability of ciphertexts) is particularly useful when one considers message spaces that are sparse (i.e., message spaces that contain only a few possible messages, such as "yes" and "no" or "buy" and "sell"). This situation is not unlikely for many practical applications of asymmetric encryption.

In order to better understand the notion of semantic security against adaptive chosen-ciphertext attacks, let us consider the following experiment: somebody has specified two plaintext messages m_0 and m_1 (e.g., $m_0 = 0$ and $m_1 = 1$) and encrypted both messages (using, of course, the same key). The resulting ciphertexts are published in random order. Furthermore, we assume a polynomially bound adversary who has access to a decryption oracle. This means that he or she can adaptively choose ciphertexts and have them decrypted by the oracle at will (needless to say that the adversary is not allowed to ask for the decryption of any of the encrypted messages m_0 and m_1). The adversary's job is to decide which ciphertext belongs to which plaintext message. If the adversary has no significantly better chance than guessing (to do the job), even if he or she can ask the oracle polynomially often, then we say that the encryption system in use is *semantically secure*. Alternatively speaking, the success probability of the adversary in the experiment only negligibly deviates from $1/2$.

Note that semantic security against adaptive chosen-ciphertext attacks only makes sense for probabilistic (asymmetric) encryption systems (i.e., encryption systems that don't employ a deterministic encryption algorithm). Otherwise, an adversary can always compute himself or herself the ciphertexts of m_0 and m_1. Consequently, many practically relevant asymmetric encryption systems (that are deterministic in nature) cannot be semantically secure. Examples include the RSA and Rabin asymmetric encryption systems discussed in the next section. These systems, however, can still be made semantically secure by applying an appropriate padding scheme prior to encryption. We revisit this possibility when we elaborate on the *optimal asymmetric encryption padding* (OAEP) scheme in Section 14.3.2.

Semantic security against adaptive chosen-ciphertext attacks is the commonly accepted notion of security for (asymmetric) encryption systems. There are, however, also some other notions of security one may think of and come up with. For example, a more intricate notion of security is *nonmalleability* [3]. Roughly speaking, an asymmetric encryption system is *nonmalleable* if it is computationally infeasible to modify a ciphertext so that it has a predictable effect on the plaintext message. For example, when given the ciphertext of a bid in an auction, it must be computationally infeasible for a polynomially bound adversary to come up with a ciphertext of a smaller bid (at least not with a success probability that is greater than without being given the ciphertext). It has been shown that the notion of non-malleability is equivalent to the notion of semantic security against adaptive chosen-ciphertext attacks [4]. This means that an asymmetric encryption system that is non-malleable is also semantically secure against adaptive chosen-ciphertext attacks, and vice versa. Consequently, the two notions of security are often used synonymously and interchangeably in the literature. For the purpose of this book, however, we use the term semantic security against adaptive chosen-ciphertext attacks most of the times.

14.2 BASIC SYSTEMS

A couple of asymmetric encryption systems were developed and proposed in the late 1970s and early 1980s (when public key cryptography was discovered and started to take off). We overview and briefly discuss the RSA, Rabin, and ElGamal asymmetric encryption systems. For all of these systems, we address the key generation, encryption, and decryption algorithms, and we provide a brief security analysis.

For the sake of simplicity, we assume that public keys are always published in certified form (we discuss the implications of this assumption at the end of this chapter and in Section 19.5).

14.2.1 RSA

The RSA public key cryptosystem was jointly invented by Ronald L. Rivest, Adi Shamir, and Leonard M. Adleman at MIT in 1977. A U.S. patent application was filed on December 14, 1977, and a corresponding article was published in the *Communications of the ACM* in February 1978 [5].[2] On September 20, 1983, the U.S. patent 4,405,829 entitled "Cryptographic Communications System and Method" was assigned to MIT. It was one of the most important patents ever granted for an invention related to cryptography.[3] After 17 years, the patent expired in September 2000. Recognizing the relevance of their work, Rivest, Shamir, and Adleman were granted the prestigious ACM Turing Award in 2002.

---

2   The RSA public key cryptosystem was first described in Martin Gardner's column in the August 1977 issue of the *Scientific American*. In this article, a 129-digit (i.e., 426-bit) number was introduced to illustrate the computational intractability of the IFP, and the security of the RSA public key cryptosystem accordingly. This number was referred to as RSA-129. In 1991, RSA Security, Inc., used it to launch an RSA Factoring Challenge. RSA-129 was successfully factored in March 1994 (see Section 7.3).

3   Note that the RSA patent was a U.S. patent, and that the RSA public key cryptosystem was not patented outside the U.S.

The RSA public key cryptosystem is based on the RSA family of trapdoor permutations as overviewed and discussed in Section 7.2.2. Contrary to many other public key cryptosystems, RSA yields both an asymmetric encryption system and a DSS. This means that basically the same set of algorithms can be used to encrypt and decrypt messages, as well as to digitally sign messages and verify digital signatures accordingly. The function provided actually depends on the cryptographic key in use.

• If the recipient's public key is used to encrypt a plaintext message, then the RSA public key cryptosystem yields an asymmetric encryption system. In this case, the recipient's private key must be used to decrypt the ciphertext.

• If the sender's private key is used to encrypt a plaintext message (or a hash value thereof), then the RSA key cryptosystem yields a DSS. In this case, the sender's public key must be used to verify the digital signature.

In this chapter, we only look at the RSA asymmetric encryption system. The RSA DSS is addressed in Section 15.2.1.

14.2.1.1   Key Generation Algorithm

Before the RSA asymmetric encryption system can be employed, the Generate algorithm must be used to generate a public key pair. The algorithm is probabilistic in nature. It takes as input a security parameter (that represents the bit length of the RSA modulus), and it generates as output a public key pair. It consists of two steps:

• First, the algorithm randomly selects[4] two prime numbers p and q of roughly the same size and computes the RSA modulus $n = pq$. Given the current state of the art in integer factorization, a modulus size of 1,024 or 2,024 bits is appropriate and recommended. This means that both primes must be about 512 or 1,024 bits long.

• Second, the algorithm randomly selects an integer $1 < e < \phi(n)$ with $gcd(e, \phi(n)) = 1$,[5] and computes another integer $1 < d < \phi(n)$ with

---

4   It is not possible to randomly select large primes (from the set of all prime numbers P). Instead, large integers are randomly chosen and probabilistic primality testing algorithms are then used to decide whether these integers are prime (see Section 3.2.4.3).

5   Note that e must be odd and greater than 2 (it is not possible to set $e = 2$, because $\phi(n) = (p-1)(q-1)$ is even and $gcd(e, \phi(n)) = 1$ must hold) and that the smallest possible value for e is 3. The use of $e = 3$ should be considered with care, because a corresponding implementation may be subject to a low exponent attack, as mentioned in Section 14.2.1.4.

$$de \equiv 1 \ (\text{mod} \ \phi(n))$$

using, for example, the extended Euclid algorithm (i.e., Algorithm 3.2).[6]

The output of the Generate algorithm is a public key pair that consists of a public key (n, e) and a corresponding private key (n, d).[7] The public key is mainly used for encryption, whereas the private key is mainly used for decryption. Consequently, e is sometimes also referred to as *public* or *encryption exponent*, whereas d is referred to as *private* or *decryption exponent*.

Let us consider a toy example to illustrate what is going on in the RSA Generate algorithm (and the other algorithms of the RSA asymmetric encryption system). In the first step, the RSA Generate algorithm selects $p = 11$ and $q = 23$, and then computes $n = 11 \cdot 23 = 253$ and $\phi(253) = 10 \cdot 22 = 220$. In the second step, the RSA Generate algorithm selects $e = 3$ and uses the extended Euclid algorithm to compute $d = 147$ modulo 220 (note that $3 \cdot 147 = 441 \equiv 1 \ (\text{mod} \ 220)$, and hence $d = 147$ really represents the multiplicative inverse element of $e = 3$ modulo 220). Then $(253, 3)$ represents the public key, and $(253, 147)$ represents the private key.

14.2.1.2 Encryption Algorithm

In its basic form, the RSA Encrypt algorithm is deterministic. It takes as input a public key (n, e) and a plaintext message $m \in \mathbb{Z}_n$, and it generates as output the ciphertext

$$c = \text{RSA}_{n,e}(m) \equiv m^e \ (\text{mod} \ n).$$

To compute c, the RSA Encrypt algorithm must employ a modular exponentiation algorithm, such as, for example, the square-and-multiply algorithm (i.e., Algorithm 3.3). In either case, the computation can be done efficiently.

If we want to encrypt the plaintext message $m = 26$ in our toy example, then we compute

$$c \equiv m^e \ (\text{mod} \ n) \equiv 26^3 \ (\text{mod} \ 253) = 119.$$

---

6 Note that $gcd(e, \phi(n)) = 1$ suggests that an integer d with $de \equiv 1 \ (\text{mod} \phi(n))$ exists.
7 Note that the modulus n need not be a part of the private key. It is, however, often useful and convenient to include it in the private key.

Then 119 represents the ciphertext for the plaintext message 26. As such, it is transmitted to the recipient(s).

In either case, it is important to note that the public key (n, e) is publicly available, and hence anybody can use it to compute $\text{RSA}_{n,e}(m)$ and to encrypt an arbitrary plaintext message m. Consequently, RSA encryption provides neither data origin authentication nor data integrity. Complementary mechanisms must be employed to provide these types of security services.

14.2.1.3 Decryption Algorithm

The RSA Decrypt algorithm is deterministic. It takes as input a private key (n, d) and a ciphertext c, and it generates as output the corresponding plaintext message

$$m = \text{RSA}_{n,d}(c) \equiv c^d \ (\text{mod } n).$$

Again, a modular exponentiation algorithm must be used to compute m, and this computation can be done efficiently.

The correctness of the decryption algorithm results from Fermat's Little Theorem (i.e., Theorem 3.7) and Euler's Theorem (i.e., Theorem 3.8). In fact, Fermat's Little Theorem says that for every $m \in \mathbb{Z}_n$ with $gcd(m, p) = 1$

$$m^{k\phi(p)} \equiv m^{\phi(p)} \equiv m^{p-1} \equiv 1 \ (\text{mod } p).$$

If we multiply either side with m, then we get

$$m^{k\phi(p)+1} \equiv m \ (\text{mod } p).$$

This equivalence holds for all $m \in \mathbb{Z}_n$ (it trivially holds for all $m \equiv 0 \ (\text{mod } p)$). The same arguments apply for q, and hence we have

$$m^{k\phi(p)+1} \equiv m \ (\text{mod } q)$$

for all $m \in \mathbb{Z}_n$. Putting the last two equivalences together, it follows that

$$m^{k\phi(n)+1} \equiv m^{ed} \equiv m \ (\text{mod } n),$$

and hence $c^d \pmod{n}$ properly decrypts to m.

In our toy example, the ciphertext $c = 119$ is decrypted as follows:

$$m \equiv c^d \pmod{n} = 119^{147} \pmod{253} = 26$$

Consequently, we have properly decrypted our originally encrypted plaintext message $m = 26$.

If the RSA Decrypt algorithm has access to the prime factors p and q (in addition to d), then the CRT (i.e., Theorem 3.6) can be used to speed up the decryption process considerably. Instead of directly computing $m \equiv c^d \pmod{n}$, one can compute

$$m_p \equiv c^d \pmod{p}$$

and

$$m_q \equiv c^d \pmod{q},$$

and then use the CRT to compute $m \in \mathbb{Z}_n$, which satisfies $m \equiv m_p \pmod{p}$ and $m \equiv m_q \pmod{q}$. In our toy example, we have

$$m_p \equiv c^d \pmod{p} \equiv 119^{147} \pmod{11} = 4$$

and

$$m_q \equiv c^d \pmod{q} \equiv 119^{147} \pmod{23} = 3.$$

We can then use the CRT to compute $m \in \mathbb{Z}_{253}$, which satisfies $m \equiv 4 \pmod{11}$ and $m \equiv 3 \pmod{11}$, and the resulting plaintext message is again $m = 26$.

In addition to the CRT, there are several other possibilities and techniques to speed up the RSA decryption (and signature generation) algorithm. Examples include batch RSA, multifactor RSA, and rebalanced RSA as overviewed and discussed in [6]. These possibilities and techniques are important when it comes to an implementation of the RSA asymmetric encryption system, especially if one uses low-power computational devices. They are, however, beyond the scope of this book.

14.2.1.4 Security Analysis

Since its invention in 1977, the security of the RSA public key cryptosystem has been subject to a lot of public scrutiny. Many people have challenged and analyzed the security of RSA (e.g., [7]). While no devastating vulnerability or weakness has been found so far, almost three decades of cryptanalytical research have still given us a broad insight into its security properties and have provided us with valuable guidelines for the proper implementation and usage of RSA. In this section, we give a brief security analysis of the RSA asymmetric encryption system. We start with some general remarks before we turn to specific attacks and provide some conclusions and recommendations for the practical use of RSA.

General Remarks

If we ask whether the RSA asymmetric encryption system is secure, we must first define what we mean with the term *secure*. Because an adversary can always mount a chosen plaintext attack against an asymmetric encryption system, we must require that the RSA asymmetric encryption system is secure under such an attack, meaning that an adversary who is able to mount a chosen plaintext attack is not able to decrypt a given ciphertext, or, equivalently, that it is computationally infeasible for him or her to invert an RSA trapdoor permutation (without knowledge of the private key that represents the trapdoor). This is known as the RSAP (see Definition 7.9), and it is assumed to be intractable (if the modulus n is sufficiently large and the plaintext message m is an integer between 0 and $n-1$). Note that the two conditions mentioned in parentheses are very important from a security point of view:

- If n were small, then an adversary could try all elements of $\mathbb{Z}_n$ until the correct m was found.[8]

- Similarly, if the plaintext message m was known to be from a small subset of $[0, n-1]$, then an adversary could also try all elements from this subset until the correct m was found.

But even if n is sufficiently large and m is between 0 and $n-1$, then the adversary can still try to find the correct m (by a brute-force attack). In this case, however, the adversary must employ a search algorithm that has a running time of n, which is exponential in the input length $\log n$. Consequently, such a brute-force

8   This basically means that he or she can compute $m'^e \pmod{n}$ for every possible plaintext message $m' \in \mathbb{Z}_n$. If the resulting value matches c, then he or she has found the correct plaintext message.

attack is prohibitively expensive in terms of computational power even for a very strong adversary.

Next, it is important to note that the security of the RSA asymmetric encryption system is intimately related to the IFA (see Definition 7.10) and the intractability assumption of the IFP (see Definition 7.11). Clearly, the RSAP is not harder to solve than the IFP, because an adversary who can factorize n (using, for example, a brute-force attack) can also compute the private exponent d from the public key (n, e).[9] However, it is not known whether the converse is also true (i.e., whether an algorithm to solve the IFP can be efficiently constructed from an algorithm to solve the RSAP). There is some evidence that such a construction may not exist if the public exponent is very small, such as $e = 3$ or $e = 17$ [8]. This result suggests that—for very small public exponents—the RSAP may be easier to solve than the IFP. For arbitrary public exponents, however, the question of computational equivalence between the RSAP and the IFP remains unanswered.

Having in mind the notion of polynomial-time reductions (see Definition 6.10), we can say that the RSAP polytime reduces to the IFP (i.e., RSAP $\leq_P$ IFP), but that the converse is not known to be true. This suggests that the RSAP and the IFP are not computationally equivalent, or at least that we cannot prove such a relationship (this is why we don't prove a theorem about a computational equivalence relationship between the RSAP and some other problem assumed to be intractable, as we do for the other basic systems). The best we can do is to prove that the following problems or tasks are computationally equivalent:

- Factorize n;

- Compute $\phi(n)$ from n;

- Determine d from (n, e).

This means that an adversary who knows $\phi(n)$ or d can also factorize n. It also means that there is no point in hiding the factorization of n (i.e., the prime factors p and q) from an entity that already knows d. In either case, we conclude that if an efficient algorithm to factorize n, compute $\phi(n)$, or determine d existed, then the RSA asymmetric encryption system would be insecure.

Even if the RSA asymmetric encryption system were secure in the sense discussed earlier (i.e., that the RSAP is computationally equivalent to the IFP), then it could still be true that it "leaks" partial information about the plaintext messages that are encrypted. For example, it may be the case that certain plaintext message bits are easy to predict from a given ciphertext. Consequently, one may ask whether the RSA asymmetric encryption system provides security to every individual bit of

9   Refer to Section 7.3 for an overview about the current state of the art of integer factorization algorithms.

a plaintext message. This question can be answered in the affirmative. In fact, it has been shown that all plaintext message bits are protected by the RSA function in the sense that having a nontrivial advantage for predicting a single message bit would enable an adversary to invert the RSA function entirely. This result about the bit security of the RSA asymmetric encryption system can be proven by a reduction technique. More specifically, one must show that an efficient algorithm for solving the RSAP can be constructed from an algorithm for predicting one (or more) plaintext message bit(s). Note, however, that the bit-security proof of the RSA asymmetric encryption system is a double-edged sword, because the security reduction used in the proof also provides a possibility to attack a "leaky" implementation. In fact, if an implementation of the RSA Decrypt algorithm leaked some bits of a plaintext message, then this leakage could be (mis)used to solve the RSAP and to decrypt a ciphertext without knowing the private key.

Specific Attacks

Several attacks are known and must be considered with care when it comes to an implementation of the RSA asymmetric encryption system. In addition to the attacks mentioned next, there is always the risk of having side-channel attacks against a specific implementation. Refer to Section 1.2.2 for a corresponding overview and discussion. Side-channel attacks are not further addressed in this book.

Common modulus attacks: To avoid generating a different modulus $n = pq$ for every user, it is tempting to work with a common modulus n for all (or at least several) users. In this case, a trusted authority must generate the public key pairs and provide user i with a public key (n, e_i) and a corresponding private key (n, d_i). At first sight, this seems to work, because a ciphertext $c \equiv m^{e_i} \pmod{n}$ encrypted for user i cannot be decrypted by user j (as user j does not know the private exponent d_i). Unfortunately, this argument is incorrect, and the use of a common modulus is completely insecure. There are common modulus attacks that can be mounted from both an insider and an outsider:

- Remember from the previous discussion that knowing the private key d_j is computationally equivalent to knowing the prime factors of n (or knowing $\phi(n)$, respectively). Consequently, insider j can use d_j to factorize n, and the prime factors of n can then be used to efficiently compute d_i from e_i.

- Even more worrisome, an outsider can also mount a common modulus attack against a message m that is encrypted with the public keys of two users having the same modulus n. Let (n, e_1) be the public key of the first user and (n, e_2) be the public key of the second user. The message m is then encrypted as

$$c_1 \equiv m^{e_1} \pmod{n}$$

for the first user and

$$c_2 \equiv m^{e_2} \pmod{n}$$

for the second user. The outside adversary sees c_1 and c_2, and can compute the following pair of values:

$$
\begin{aligned}
t_1 &\equiv e_1^{-1} \pmod{e_2} \\
t_2 &= (t_1 e_1 - 1)/e_2
\end{aligned}
$$

Equipped with t_1 and t_2, the adversary can then recover the message m as $c_1^{t_1} c_2^{-t_2}$. This is because

$$
\begin{aligned}
c_1^{t_1} c_2^{-t_2} &= m^{e_1 t_1} m^{-e_2 t_2} \\
&= m^{1 + e_2 t_2} m^{-e_2 t_2} \\
&= m^{1 + e_2 t_2 - e_2 t_2} \\
&= m^1 = m.
\end{aligned}
$$

Due to the common modulus attacks, it is important that a modulus n is never used by more than one entity. This also means that the prime numbers used to generate the moduli must be unique for all users.

Attacks that exploit the multiplicative structure of the RSA function: There are several attacks against the RSA public key cryptosystem that exploit the multiplicative structure (or homomorphic property) of the RSA function. If, for example, two plaintext messages m_1 and m_2 are encrypted with the same public key (n, e), then one gets $c_1 \equiv m_1^e \pmod{n}$ and $c_2 \equiv m_2^e \pmod{n}$. In this case, one can construct the following ciphertext:

$$c = c_1 c_2 \equiv (m_1 m_2)^e \pmod{n}$$

This means that anybody who knows two ciphertexts c_1 and c_2 can easily construct (by a single modular multiplication) the ciphertext for the plaintext message

$m = m_1 m_2$ without knowing it. More interestingly, consider the situation in which an adversary wants to decrypt $c \equiv m^e \pmod{n}$ with a chosen-ciphertext attack. He or she therefore computes $c' \equiv cr^e \pmod{n}$, has c' (which is different from c) be decrypted by the decryption oracle, and deduces m from $rm \pmod{n}$ returned by the decryption oracle (by a modular division). The multiplicative structure of the RSA function is even more worrisome when the RSA DSS is used. Consequently, good practices in security engineering must take care of the multiplicative structure of the RSA function and protect against corresponding exploits. One possibility is to require plaintext messages to have a certain (nonmultiplicative) structure. This means that the product of two valid plaintext messages no longer yields a valid plaintext message. Another possibility is to randomly pad the plaintext message prior to encryption. This randomizes the ciphertext and eliminates the homomorphic property accordingly. Again, we revisit this possibility in Section 14.3.2 when we elaborate on OAEP.

Low exponent attacks: To improve the performance of the RSA asymmetric encryption system, one may consider the use of small (public or private) exponents. The line of argumentation goes as follows: if one employed a small public exponent e, then the encryption (or signature verification) process would be fast, and if one employed a small private exponent d, then the decryption (or signature generation) would be fast. Unfortunately, this line of argumentation must be considered with care, and there are a couple of low exponent attacks that are possible.

On one hand, Michael Wiener showed in 1990 that the choice of a small private exponent d can lead to a total break of the RSA asymmetric encryption system [9]. This result was later improved by various authors (e.g., [10]). Given the current state of the art, the private exponent d should be at least 300 bits long for a typical 1,024-bit RSA modulus n. In practice, people frequently use a public exponent e that is 3, 17, or $2^{16} + 1 = 65,537$. In these cases, it is guaranteed that the corresponding private exponent d is nearly as long as n and hence that the attacks that exploit small private exponents do not work.

On the other hand, it was already mentioned earlier that using small public exponents (e.g., $e = 3$ or $e = 17$) may lead to the problem that the RSAP eventually becomes simpler to solve than the IFP [8]. Consequently, one may not want to work with public exponents that are too small. Furthermore, there is a very specific problem if one uses a small public exponent e to encrypt a small message m. In fact, if $m < \sqrt[e]{n}$, then $c = m^e$, and hence m can be decrypted as follows (note that there is no modular arithmetic involved in this computation):

$$m = \sqrt[e]{c}$$

Last but not least, there is another low exponent attack if a plaintext message m is encrypted for multiple recipients that share a common public exponent e (with different moduli). More specifically, let m be a plaintext message that is encrypted $r \geq 2$ times and all r recipients have the same public exponent e (but different moduli n_i for $i = 1, \ldots, r$). Then an adversary who knows the ciphertexts $c_i \equiv m^e \pmod{n_i}$ for $i = 1, \ldots, r$ can use the CRT to compute c with $c \equiv c_i \pmod{n_i}$ for $i = 1, \ldots, r$ and $0 \leq c < \prod_{i=1}^{r} n_i$. Obviously, c is equal to m^e, so m can be efficiently determined by computing the eth root of c. The low exponent attack is relevant only for small values of e. If, for example, $e = 3$, $n_1 = 143$, $n_2 = 391$, $n_3 = 899$, and $m = 135$, then the adversary can solve the following system of three equivalences:

$$c_1 \equiv m^e \pmod{n_1} = 135^3 \pmod{143} = 60$$
$$c_2 \equiv m^e \pmod{n_2} = 135^3 \pmod{391} = 203$$
$$c_3 \equiv m^e \pmod{n_3} = 135^3 \pmod{899} = 711$$

Using the CRT, he or she can compute $c = 2,460,375$, and hence $m = \sqrt[3]{2,460,375} = 135$. There are several generalizations of this attack.

Conclusions and Recommendations

The question that is most frequently asked when it comes to an implementation or use of the RSA asymmetric encryption system is related to the size of the modulus n. Obviously, n must be at least as large as to make it impossible to use an existing algorithm to factorize n. As of this writing, there is general consensus that at least 1,024-bit moduli should be used (this recommendation is also supported by the NIST). Note, however, that the value of the data must be taken into account when one recommends specific security parameters. So it is not uncommon to recommend 2,048-bit moduli for the asymmetric encryption of more valuable data. If one has fixed the size of the modulus, then one has implicitly also fixed the size of the prime factors p and q (because they should be of roughly similar size). If, for example, one wants to work with a 1,024-bit modulus n, then p and q must be about 512 bits long each. Unless one uses short moduli (where Pollard's P-1 algorithm can be applied), there is no urgent need to work only with strong primes.

The question that is less frequently asked (but is also important from a security viewpoint) is related to the size of the public and private exponents. As discussed earlier, working with small private exponents is dangerous. So d should not be smaller than a certain threshold (i.e., $d < N^{0.292}$ according to [10]). If, for example, n is 1,024 bits long, then d should not be smaller than 300 bits. On the other hand, it is not clear how much the RSA asymmetric encryption system is weakened (in the sense that there may be simpler ways to break the RSA problem than to solve the IFP) if a very small public exponent e is used. Consequently, one should be cautious with very small public exponents and use them only if necessary. For all practical purposes, the use of $e = 2^{16} + 1 = 65,537$ seems to be appropriate.

In either case, the RSA asymmetric encryption system should not be used natively (i.e., in raw form). Instead, messages should be preprocessed and encoded prior to applying the RSA function. The use of OAEP (see Section 14.3.2) is highly recommended for this purpose.

14.2.2 Rabin

As mentioned earlier, the RSAP is not known to be computationally equivalent to the IFP. This means that it is theoretically possible to break the security of the RSA public key cryptosystem without solving the IFP. This possibility is worrisome, and—since the beginning of public key cryptography—people have been looking for public key cryptosystems that can be shown to be computationally equivalent to a hard problem, such as the IFP. As mentioned in Section 1.2.2, Michael O. Rabin was the first person who found and proposed such a system in 1979 [11].[10] The *Rabin asymmetric encryption system* is based on the Square family of trapdoor permutations overviewed and discussed in Section 7.2.3. As addressed later, the security of the Rabin system can be proven to be computationally equivalent to the IFP, meaning that there is provably no easier way to break the Rabin system than to solve the IFP.

14.2.2.1 Key Generation Algorithm

The Rabin Generate algorithm takes as input a security parameter, and it generates as output a Blum integer of about this size. More specifically, it randomly selects two primes p and q that are both equivalent to 3 modulo 4 and that are each about half of the size specified by the security parameter. It then computes $n = pq$, and outputs the modulus n to represent the public key and the prime factors (p, q) of n to represent the private key.

Let us consider a toy example to illustrate what is going on (in this and in the other algorithms of the Rabin asymmetric encryption system). The Rabin Generate algorithm randomly selects $p = 11$ and $q = 23$ (note that 11 and 23 are both equivalent to 3 modulo 4), computes the Blum integer $n = pq = 11 \cdot 23 = 253$, and outputs the public key 253 and the private key $(11, 23)$.

---

10 At this time, Rabin was also working at MIT (like Rivest, Shamir, and Adleman).

14.2.2.2   Encryption Algorithm

Similar to the RSA asymmetric encryption system, the Rabin system can be used to encrypt and decrypt plaintext messages that represent numbers and elements of $\mathbb{Z}_n = \{0, \ldots, n-1\}$.

The Rabin Encrypt algorithm is deterministic. It takes as input a public key n and a plaintext message $m \in \mathbb{Z}_n$, and it generates as output the ciphertext

$$c = \text{Square}_n(m) \equiv m^2 \pmod{n}.$$

The ciphertext c is then transmitted to the recipient. Note that the Rabin Encrypt algorithm takes only one modular squaring,[11] and hence it is extremely efficient.

If, in our toy example, the plaintext message is $m = 158$, then the Rabin Encrypt algorithm computes $c = m^2 \pmod{n} = 158^2 \pmod{253} = 170$, and the resulting ciphertext $c = 170$ is sent to the recipient.

14.2.2.3   Decryption Algorithm

The Rabin Decrypt algorithm is also deterministic. It takes as input a private key (p, q) and a ciphertext c, and it generates as output the square root of c representing the plaintext message m. Note that the recipient can find a square root of c modulo n only if he or she knows the prime factors p and q of n (this property is proven later). Also note that there is no single square root of c modulo n, but that there are four of them. Let m_1, m_2, m_3, and m_4 be the four square roots of c modulo n. The recipient must then decide which m_i ($1 \leq i \leq 4$) to go with (i.e., which square root represents the correct plaintext message). This ambiguity is a major disadvantage of the Rabin asymmetric encryption system (both from a practical and theoretical viewpoint).

Computing square roots modulo n is simple if n is a Blum integer (this is why we have required that n is a Blum integer in the first place). In this case, one usually first computes the square roots of c modulo p and q. Let m_p be the square roots of c modulo p and m_q be the square roots of c modulo q . According to (3.6), m_p and m_q can be computed as follows:

$$m_p = c^{\frac{p+1}{4}} \pmod{p}$$

---

11 By comparison, the RSA Encrypt algorithm with $e = 3$ takes one modular multiplication and one modular squaring, and for larger e many more modular operations (i.e., multiplication or squaring) must be performed.

$$m_q \;=\; c^{\frac{q+1}{4}} \pmod{q}$$

It can easily be verified that

$$m_p^2 \equiv c^{(p+1)/2} \equiv m^{p+1} \equiv m^{\phi(n)}m^2 \equiv m^2 \equiv c \pmod{p}$$

and

$$m_q^2 \equiv c^{(q+1)/2} \equiv m^{q+1} \equiv m^{\phi(n)}m^2 \equiv m^2 \equiv c \pmod{q}.$$

Consequently, $\pm m_p$ are the two square roots of c in $\mathbb{Z}_p$, and $\pm m_q$ are the two square roots of c in $\mathbb{Z}_q$. There is a total of four possibilities to combine $\pm m_p$ and $\pm m_q$, and these possibilities result in four different systems with two congruence relations each. The systems are as follows:

$$
\begin{aligned}
1)\quad m_1 &\equiv +m_p \pmod{p}\\
m_1 &\equiv +m_q \pmod{q}
\end{aligned}
$$

$$
\begin{aligned}
2)\quad m_2 &\equiv -m_p \pmod{p}\\
m_2 &\equiv -m_q \pmod{q}
\end{aligned}
$$

$$
\begin{aligned}
3)\quad m_3 &\equiv +m_p \pmod{p}\\
m_3 &\equiv -m_q \pmod{q}
\end{aligned}
$$

$$
\begin{aligned}
4)\quad m_4 &\equiv -m_p \pmod{p}\\
m_4 &\equiv +m_q \pmod{q}
\end{aligned}
$$

Each system yields a possible square root of c modulo n, and we use m_1, m_2, m_3, and m_4 to refer to them. Note that only one solution m_i ($i = 1, 2, 3$, or 4) represents the original plaintext message m. To determine this message, it is necessary to solve the four congruence relation systems and to select one of the corresponding solutions (i.e., m_1, m_2, m_3, or m_4).

The simplest way to find the four solutions is to use the CRA as introduced in Section 3.3.3. First, one uses the extended Euclid algorithm to compute $y_p \equiv p^{-1} \pmod{q}$ and $y_q \equiv q^{-1} \pmod{p}$. These computations do not depend on the plaintext message or ciphertext. They only depend on the prime factorization of n, and hence they can be done once and for all during the key generation process. Using y_p and y_q, one can then compute the following values r and s:

$$
\begin{aligned}
r &= y_p p m_q + y_q q m_p \pmod{n} \\
s &= y_p p m_q - y_q q m_p \pmod{n}
\end{aligned}
$$

The four square roots of c in $\mathbb{Z}_n$ are $\pm r$ and $\pm s$. They represent the four possible solutions m_1, m_2, m_3, and m_4. It is now up to the recipient to decide which solution is the correct one (i.e., which solution represents the correct plaintext message).

In our toy example, the recipient gets the ciphertext $c = 170$ and wants to decrypt it with the public key $(p, q) = (11, 23)$. He or she therefore computes $y_p = -2$ and $y_q = 1$, and computes the square roots m_p and m_q as follows:

$$
\begin{aligned}
m_p &= c^{(p+1)/4} \pmod{p} = c^3 \pmod{11} = 4 \\
m_q &= c^{(q+1)/4} \pmod{q} = c^6 \pmod{23} = 3
\end{aligned}
$$

Using these values, the recipient can determine r and s:

$$
\begin{aligned}
r &= y_p p m_q + y_q q m_p \pmod{n} = -2 \cdot 11 \cdot 3 + 1 \cdot 23 \cdot 4 \pmod{n} = 26 \\
s &= y_p p m_q - y_q q m_p \pmod{n} = -2 \cdot 11 \cdot 3 - 1 \cdot 23 \cdot 4 \pmod{n} = 95
\end{aligned}
$$

Consequently, the square roots of $c = 170$ modulo 253 are 26, 95, 158, and 227, and one of these values must be the correct plaintext message (in this example it is 158).

An obvious drawback of the Rabin asymmetric encryption system is that the recipient must select the correct plaintext message m from four possible values. This ambiguity in decryption can be overcome by adding redundancy to the original plaintext message prior to encryption. Then, with high probability, exactly one of the four square roots of c modulo n possesses this redundancy, and the recipient can easily (and automatically) select this value to represent the original plaintext message.

14.2.2.4 Security Analysis

A major advantage of the Rabin asymmetric encryption system is that it is based on the Square family and that the problem of inverting a trapdoor permutation from this family can be shown to be computationally equivalent to solving the IFP. This is expressed in Theorem 14.1.

Theorem 14.1 *Breaking the Rabin asymmetric encryption system is computationally equivalent to solving the IFP.*

Proof. To prove the theorem, one must show (a) that somebody who can solve the IFP can also break the Rabin asymmetric encryption system (by inverting a trapdoor permutation), and (b) that somebody who can break the Rabin system can also solve the IFP.

Direction (a) is obvious—that is, somebody who can solve the IFP for n can easily break the Rabin system by factorizing n and (mis)using the private key (p, q) to find square roots for a given ciphertext $c \in \mathbb{Z}_n$.

Direction (b) is less obvious. For this directon, we must show that somebody who can break the Rabin system by inverting the trapdoor permutation (i.e., computing square roots) can also factorize n and solve the IFP, accordingly. We assume an adversary who has a Rabin oracle O^{Rabin} that takes as input a ciphertext c and that returns as output a possible plaintext m (that represents a square root of c modulo n). The adversary can use this oracle to solve the IFP, and to factorize n. He or she therefore selects $x \in_R \mathbb{Z}_n$. If $gcd(x, n) \neq 1$, then the adversary has already found a prime factor of n and is done. Otherwise (if $gcd(x, n) = 1$), then the adversary computes

$$c \equiv x^2 \pmod{n}$$

and

$$m = O^{Rabin}(c).$$

Note that m must be one of the four square roots of c. Also note that m and x may be different, but that they must at least fulfill one of the following pairs of congruences:

1. $m \equiv x \pmod{p}$ and $m \equiv x \pmod{q}$: In this case, $m = x$ and $gcd(m - x, n) = gcd(0, n) = n$, and this is not useful to find a prime factor of n.

2. $m \equiv -x \pmod{p}$ and $m \equiv -x \pmod{q}$: In this case, $m = n - x$ and $gcd(m - x, n) = 1$, and this is not useful to find a prime factor of n.

3. $m \equiv x \pmod{p}$ and $m \equiv -x \pmod{q}$: In this case, p divides $m - x$ but q does not divide $m - x$. This is useful to find a prime factor of n. In fact, $p = gcd(m - x, n)$.

4. $m \equiv -x \pmod{p}$ and $m \equiv x \pmod{q}$: In this case, p does not divide $m - x$ but q divides $m - x$. Again, this is useful to find a prime factor of n. In fact, $q = gcd(m - x, n) = q$.

In summary, we have two cases that are useful to find a prime factor of n (i.e., cases 3 and 4) and two cases that are not (i.e., cases 1 and 2). Consequently, the adversary can find a prime factor of n in each iteration of the algorithm with a probability of $1/2$. In k iterations, the prime factors of n can be found with a probability of $1 - (1/2)^k$, so we conclude that the adversary can can solve the IFP.

□

The outline of the proof may be better understood if one looks at a simple example. Let $n = 253$ and O^{Rabin} the Rabin oracle that finds square roots modulo 253. The adversary randomly selects $x = 17$ and verifies that $gcd(17, 253) = 1$. He or she then computes

$$c \equiv x^2 \pmod{n} \equiv 17^2 \pmod{253} = 36$$

and

$$m = O^{Rabin}(36).$$

The oracle returns one of the four square roots of 36 modulo 253 (i.e., 6, 17, 236, or 247). In two of the four cases, the adversary can determine a prime factor of 253. For 6 and 247, he or she gets $gcd(6 - 17, 253) = 11$ and $gcd(247 - 17, 253) = 23$. These are the prime factors of 253.

We mentioned earlier that one can add redundancy to the original plaintext message prior to encryption for easy identification among the four possible square roots and to simplify (or automate) the decryption process accordingly. Suppose that the Rabin asymmetric encryption system is modified this way. If the adversary has access to a Rabin oracle O^{Rabin} that takes advantage of redundancy to always select the correct plaintext message from the four square roots of a given ciphertext, then he or she can no longer use O^{Rabin} to factorize n. This is because the oracle always returns the square root that really represents the original plaintext message. This means that for $c \equiv x^2 \pmod{n}$ and $m = O^{Rabin}(c)$, the only solution is $m = x$. In this case, however, one cannot find p or q. Consequently, if the plaintext message has to be of a special form, then Theorem 14.1 does no longer apply, meaning that breaking this modified Rabin asymmetric encryption system is no longer computationally equivalent to solving the IFP.

Theorem 14.1 is important from a security point of view. It suggests that breaking the Rabin asymmetric encryption system is computationally equivalent to solving the IFP, and hence that the Rabin system can be broken if and only if the corresponding modulus n can be factorized. Unfortunately, the theorem and its proof also suggest that the Rabin system is vulnerable to chosen-ciphertext attacks. An adversary who can perform a chosen-ciphertext attack has access to a Rabin oracle O^{Rabin}—that is, he or she can select $x \in_R \mathbb{Z}_n$, compute $c \equiv x^2 \pmod{n}$, and ask the oracle for $m = O^{Rabin}(c)$. According to the proof of Theorem 14.1, the adversary can then use c and m to factorize n with a success probability of $1/2$. So the construction used in the proof of Theorem 14.1 can also be employed by an adversary to break the Rabin system with a chosen-ciphertext attack. On the other hand, if one employs redundancy to protect the Rabin system against chosen-ciphertext attacks, then one can no longer prove that breaking the Rabin system is computationally equivalent to solving the IFP. So the user of the Rabin asymmetric encryption system has the choice:

- Either he or she goes for a system that is provably as difficult to break as it is to solve the IFP, but that is vulnerable to chosen-ciphertext attacks;

- Or he or she goes for a system that is not provably as difficult to break as it is to solve the IFP, but that is also not vulnerable to chosen-ciphertext attacks (at least not the one described earlier).

This choice is not an easy one. From a practical point of view, however, the use of redundancy to automate the decryption process is often preferred.

14.2.3 ElGamal

As already mentioned in Section 1.3, Diffie and Hellman introduced public key cryptography in 1976 [12]. In Section 16.3, we overview and discuss the protocol they proposed to have two entities agree on a secret key over a public channel. In its native form, the Diffie-Hellman key exchange protocol can be used neither to encrypt and decrypt data nor to digitally sign messages and verify digital signatures. It was not until 1984 that Taher ElGamal[12] found a way to turn the Diffie-Hellman

---

12   Taher ElGamal was a Ph.D. student of Hellman at Stanford University.

key exchange protocol into a full-fledged public key cryptosystem (i.e., a public key cryptosystem that can be used to encrypt and decrypt messages as well as to digitally sign messages and verify digital signatures) [13].[13]

In this section, we overview and discuss the ElGamal asymmetric encryption system. The ElGamal DSS is addressed in Section 15.2.2.

14.2.3.1   Key Generation Algorithm

The ElGamal Generate algorithm is the same as the one employed by the Diffie-Hellman key exchange protocol (see Section 16.3). One needs a cyclic group in which the DLP is (assumed to be) intractable. In this section, we use the multiplicative group of a finite field of prime order (i.e., $\mathbb{Z}_p^*$) to describe the ElGamal asymmetric encryption system. Note, however, that there are many other cyclic groups that can be used instead.

To make use of the ElGamal asymmetric encryption system, every user must have a large prime p and a generator g of $\mathbb{Z}_p^*$. The ElGamal Generate algorithm then works in two steps:

- First, a private exponent x is randomly selected from $\mathbb{Z}_p^*$;
- Second, a public exponent $y \equiv g^x \pmod{p}$ is computed.

It is up to the user to make y publicly available (in addition to p and g). The triple (p, g, y) then represents the public ElGamal key, whereas x represents the private ElGamal key.

Note that the parameters p and g can be the same for all users. In this case, they represent system parameters. The advantage of this approach is that the sum of the lengths of all public keys can be effectively minimized. The disadvantage, however, is that weak or vulnerable parameters affect all users. In either case, the private and public ElGamal keys are assumed to be used for a comparably long period of time (this is in contrast to the keys used in the Diffie-Hellman key exchange protocol).

Again, we consider a toy example that we revisit for each algorithm to illustrate the ElGamal asymmetric encryption system. Let $p = 27$ and $g = 7$ be system parameters. The ElGamal Generate algorithm randomly selects the private key $x = 6$ and computes the public key $y \equiv 7^6 \pmod{27} = 10$.

14.2.3.2   Encryption Algorithm

We assume that a user wants to use the ElGamal asymmetric encryption system to send an encrypted message $m \in \mathbb{Z}_p$ to another user and that the recipient's

13   A preliminary version of [13] was presented at the CRYPTO '84 conference.

public key (p, g, y) is available to the sender. The ElGamal Encryt algorithm is probabilistic. It consists of three steps:

- First, an integer k is randomly selected from $\mathbb{Z}_p^*$.[14]

- Second, the recipient's public key y and k are used to compute $K \equiv y^k \pmod{p}$.[15]

- Third, k and K are used to compute the following pair of values:

$$
\begin{aligned}
c_1 &\equiv g^k \pmod{p} \\
c_2 &\equiv Km \pmod{p}
\end{aligned}
$$

(c_1, c_2) then represents the ciphertext for message m.

It is important not to reuse k multiple times. If k were used more than once, then knowledge of one plaintext message m_1 would enable an adversary to compute another plaintext message m_2. Let

$$(c_1^{(1)}, c_2^{(1)}) = (g^k \pmod{p}, Km_1 \pmod{p})$$

and

$$(c_1^{(2)}, c_2^{(2)}) = (g^k \pmod{p}, Km_2 \pmod{p})$$

be the ciphertexts of m_1 and m_2 (that are both encrypted with the same key k). It then follows that

$$m_1/m_2 \equiv c_2^{(1)}/c_2^{(2)} \pmod{p},$$

and hence that m_2 can be computed if m_1 is known. Consequently, we need a fresh and unique $k \in_R \mathbb{Z}_p^*$ for the encryption of every plaintext message (this requirement also applies if the ElGamal public key cryptosystem is used as a DSS).

---

14 This value plays the role of the sender's private exponent in the Diffie-Hellman key exchange protocol.
15 This value basically plays the role of the outcome of the Diffie-Hellman key exchange protocol. In the ElGamal asymmetric encryption system, however, it is used to mask (i.e., hide) the message (using the multiplication modulo p operation).

The ElGamal Encryt algorithm requires only two modular exponentiations to encrypt a plaintext message, and hence it is efficient. The efficiency can be further improved by making use of precomputation. Note that k and K are independent from the plaintext message that is encrypted and that they can be precomputed and securely stored before they are used. This is also true for c_1. If k, K, and c_1 are precomputed, then it takes only one modular multiplication to encrypt a plaintext message. This is arguably much more efficient than the modular exponentiation it takes to encrypt a plaintext message using the RSA asymmetric encryption system.

In either case, the size of the ciphertext is double the size of the plaintext message (i.e., there is a message expansion with a factor two). This is disadvantageous from a practical viewpoint. From a theoretical (and security) viewpoint, the fact that the ElGamal Encryt algorithm is probabilistic means that the same plaintext message is encrypted differently in every encryption process. This is advantageous, because it protects against a probable plaintext attack. In such an attack, the adversary suspects that the plaintext message is m and then tries to encrypt m and checks whether the resulting ciphertext c matches a specific ciphertext.

If, in our toy example, the plaintext message to be encrypted is $m = 7$, then the ElGamal Encryt randomly selects $k = 3$ (in step 1), computes $K = 10^3 \pmod{27} = 1$ (in step 2), and concludes with $c_1 \equiv 7^3 \pmod{27} = 19$ and $c_2 \equiv 1 \cdot 7 \pmod{27} = 7$ (in step 3). Consequently, $(19, 7)$ is the ciphertext transmitted to the recipient.

14.2.3.3   Decryption Algorithm

Upon reception of (c_1, c_2), the recipient must use the ElGamal Decryt algorithm to recover the plaintext message m. The algorithm consists of two steps:

- First, K is retrieved by computing $K \equiv c_1^x \pmod{p}$. This works, because

$$c_1^x \equiv (g^k)^x \equiv (g^x)^k \equiv y^k \equiv K \pmod{p}.$$

- Second, K is used to unmask the plaintext message m:

$$m \equiv c_2/K \pmod{p}$$

Note that it is also possible to decrypt (c_1, c_2) by first retrieving

$$x' = p - 1 - x$$

and then computing

$$
\begin{aligned}
c_1^{x'} c_2 &\equiv g^{kx'} K m \pmod{p} \\
&\equiv g^{k(p-1-x)} K m \pmod{p} \\
&\equiv g^{k(p-1-x)} y^k m \pmod{p} \\
&\equiv (g^{p-1})^k (g^x)^{-k} y^k m \pmod{p} \\
&\equiv y^{-k} y^k m \pmod{p} \\
&\equiv m \pmod{p}.
\end{aligned}
$$

Similar to the RSA asymmetric encryption system, the ElGamal system requires a modular exponentiation to decrypt a ciphertext. In the case of the ElGamal asymmetric encryption system, however, there is no possibility to use the CRT to speed up the decryption algorithm.

In our toy example, the recipient receives $(19, 7)$ and wants to recover the plaintext message m. The ElGamal Decrypt algorithm therefore computes $K \equiv 19^6 \pmod{27} = 1$ and $m \equiv 7/1 \equiv 7 \pmod{27} = 7$.

14.2.3.4 Security Analysis

The security of the ElGamal asymmetric encryption system is based on the DLA (see Definition 7.4)—that is, the assumed intractability of computing discrete logarithms. In fact (and as suggested in Theorem 14.2), one can prove that breaking the ElGamal asymmetric encryption system (by computing a discrete logarithm) is computationally equivalent to solving the DHP (see Definition 7.6). One cannot, however, prove that breaking the ElGamal asymmetric encryption system is computationally equivalent to solving the DLP (remember from Section 7.2.1 that the intractability assumption for the DHP is stronger than the intractability assumption for the DLP).

Theorem 14.2 *Breaking the ElGamal asymmetric encryption system is computationally equivalent to solving the DHP.*

Proof. To prove the theorem, one must show (a) that somebody who can solve the DHP can also break the ElGamal asymmetric encryption system, and (b) that somebody who can break the ElGamal system can also solve the DHP. To simplify the notation, we use an arbitrary cyclic group G with order p and generator g for the purpose of this proof.

For direction (a) we must show that somebody who can solve the DHP can also break the ElGamal system. We therefore assume an adversary who has access to a DHP oracle O^{DHP}. The DHP oracle, in turn, takes as input g^a and g^b, and returns as output g^{ab} for all $a, b \in G$:

$$O^{DHP}(g^a, g^b) = g^{ab}$$

The adversary can use this oracle to break the ElGamal system—that is, to decrypt a given ciphertext (c_1, c_2) that is encrypted for user A. Therefore, the adversary must invoke the DHP oracle with $y_A = g^{x_A}$ and $c_1 = g^k$, and wait for the oracle to respond with $g^{x_A k}$ (i.e., $O^{DHP}(g^{x_A}, g^k) = g^{x_A k}$). Then he or she must compute the inverse element of this result and use $g^{-x_A k}$ to recover message m according to the following formula:

$$m = g^{-x_A k} c_2$$

Consequently, the adversary can decrypt a given ciphertext if he or she is given access to a DHP oracle. This means that one can break the ElGamal system if one can solve the DHP.

For direction (b) we must show that somebody who can break the ElGamal system can also solve the DHP. We therefore assume an adversary who has an ElGamal oracle $O^{ElGamal}$ that takes as input g^a, g^b, and $g^{ab}m$, and that returns as output m:

$$O^{ElGamal}(g^a, g^b, g^{ab}m) = m$$

The adversary can use this oracle to solve the DHP (i.e., to compute g^{ab} from g^a and g^b). He or she must therefore invoke the ElGamal oracle with $y_A = g^{x_A}$, $c_1 = g^k$, and $c_2 = g^{x_A k}m$, and wait for the oracle to respond with m (i.e., $O^{ElGamal}(y_A, c_1, c_2) = m$). The adversary now knows m and can compute m^{-1} modulo p. Because $c_2 = g^{x_A k}m$, he or she can finally determine $g^{x_A k}$ according to the following formula:

$$g^{x_A k} = c_2 m^{-1}$$

Consequently, the adversary can solve the DHP if he or she is given access to an ElGamal oracle.

□

Because breaking the ElGamal asymmetric encryption system is computationally equivalent to solving the DHP, we know from Section 7.4.3 that we must work with moduli that are at least 1,024 bits long. Furthermore, special care must be taken not to use primes with special properties (i.e., properties for which discrete logarithms are known to be efficiently computable in the corresponding cyclic groups).

14.3 SECURE SYSTEMS

In Section 14.1, we looked at different notions of security for asymmetric encryption systems, and we introduced and briefly discussed the notion of semantic security. In this section, we elaborate on two asymmetric encryption systems that can be shown to be semantically secure: probabilistic encryption and OAEP (as already mentioned in Section 14.2.1.4).

14.3.1 Probabilistic Encryption

The notion of *probabilistic encryption* was developed and proposed in the early 1980s by Shafi Goldwasser and Silvio Micali at MIT [2]. The implementation they suggested is based on the QRP (see Definition 3.32). It is widely believed that the QRP is computationally equivalent to the IFP and hence that solving the QRP is computationally intractable for sufficiently large integers n.

In Section 3.3.7, we said that

$$x \in QR_p \Leftrightarrow \left(\frac{x}{p}\right) = 1$$

for every prime number p. So if we work with a prime number p, then the Legendre symbol of x modulo p is 1 if and only if x is a quadratic residue modulo p. We also said that the Legendre symbol of x modulo p can be efficiently computed using, for example, Euler's criterion (see Theorem 3.9).

Things are more involved if one does not work with prime numbers. In fact, if we work with a composite integer n, then

$$x \in QR_n \Rightarrow \left(\frac{x}{n}\right) = 1$$

but

$$x \in QR_n \nLeftarrow \left(\frac{x}{n}\right) = 1.$$

This means that if x is a quadratic residue modulo n, then the Jacobi symbol of x modulo n must be 1, but the converse is not true (i.e., even if the Jacobi symbol of x modulo n is 1, x must not be a quadratic residue modulo n). If, however, the Jacobi symbol of x modulo n is -1, then we know that x is a quadratic nonresidue modulo n:

$$x \in QNR_n \Leftarrow \left(\frac{x}{n}\right) = -1$$

Again referring to Section 3.3.7, $\widetilde{QR_n} = J_n \setminus QR_n$ refers to the set of all pseudosquares modulo n. If $n = pq$, then

$$|QR_n| = |\widetilde{QR_n}| = (p-1)(q-1)/4.$$

This means that half of the elements in J_n are quadratic residues and the other half are pseudosquares modulo n. So if an arbitrary element of J_n is given, it is computationally difficult to decide whether it is a square or a pseudosquare modulo n. Probabilistic encryption as proposed by Goldwasser and Micali takes advantage of this computational difficulty.

14.3.1.1   Key Generation Algorithm

Similar to the RSA public key cryptosystem, the Generate algorithm employed by probabilistic encryption takes as input a security parameter and generates as output two primes p and q and a modulus $n = pq$ of about the security parameter's size. Furthermore, the algorithm selects a pseudosquare $y \in \widetilde{QR_n}$. The pair (n, y) then represents the public key, and (p, q) represents the private key. So each user holds as secret the factorization of his or her modulus n.

14.3.1.2   Encryption Algorithm

The Encrypt algorithm employed by probabilistic encryption must specify how a k-bit plaintext message $m = m_1 m_2 \ldots m_k$ is encrypted so that only the recipient (or somebody holding the recipient's private key) is able to decrypt it. As its name suggests, the Encrypt algorithm is probabilistic. It takes as input a public key (n, y) and a message m, and it generates as output the ciphertext c.

For every message bit m_i $(i = 1, \ldots, k)$, the Encrypt algorithm chooses $x_i \in_R \mathbb{Z}_n^*$ and computes c_i as follows:

$$c_i \equiv \begin{cases} x_i^2 \ (\mathrm{mod} \ n) & \text{if } m_i = 0 \\ yx_i^2 \ (\mathrm{mod} \ n) & \text{if } m_i = 1 \end{cases}$$

If $m_i = 0$, then $c_i \equiv x_i^2$ (mod n) represents a quadratic residue modulo n. If, however, $m_i = 1$, then $c_i \equiv yx_i^2$ (mod n) represents a pseudosquare modulo n.

In either case, each message bit m_i ($i = 1, \ldots, k$) is encrypted with an element of $\mathbb{Z}_n^*$, and the resulting ciphertext c is the k-tuple $c = (c_1, \ldots, c_k)$.

14.3.1.3 Decryption Algorithm

The Decrypt algorithm employed by probabilistic encryption takes as input the k-tuple $c = (c_1, \ldots, c_k)$ with elements of $\mathbb{Z}_n^*$ and a private key (p, q), and it generates as output the k-bit plaintext message m. Again, it proceeds sequentially on every ciphertext bit c_i ($i = 1, \ldots, k$). For c_i, the Decrypt algorithm evaluates the Legendre symbol

$$e_i = \left(\frac{c_i}{p} \right)$$

and computes

$$m_i = \begin{cases} 0 & \text{if } e_i = 1 \\ 1 & \text{otherwise} \end{cases}$$

This means that m_i is set to 0 if $c_i \in QR_n$ (remember from the Encrypt algorithm that c_i is set to a quadratic residue if $m_i = 0$). Otherwise, m_i is set to 1. Finally, the plaintext message m is set to $m = m_1 m_2 \ldots m_k$.

14.3.1.4 Security Analysis

As mentioned earlier, probabilistic encryption as proposed by Goldwasser and Micali can be shown to semantically secure [2]. Because this is the best notion of security we currently have at hand for (asymmetric) encryption systems, there is not much to add from a theoretical point of view.

From a practical point of view, the fact that every plaintext message bit m_i ($i = 1, \ldots, k$) is encrypted with an element of $\mathbb{Z}_n^*$ results in a considerable message expansion. Consequently, probabilistic encryption has been improved to minimize message expansion (e..g, [14]). In fact, message expansion can be reduced to a constant number of bits, and hence these improved probabilistic encryption systems are comparable to RSA, both in terms of performance and message expansion. They are not addressed in this book.

14.3.2 Optimal Asymmetric Encryption Padding

As mentioned in Section 14.2.1.4, the multiplicative structure (or homomorphic property) of the RSA function leads to a vulnerability of the RSA asymmetric encryption system that can be exploited with an adaptive chosen-ciphertext attack. One possibility to eliminate this vulnerability is to randomly pad the plaintext message prior to encryption. The public key cryptography standard (PKCS) #1 is a standardized and widely deployed padding scheme for RSA.

In 1998, Daniel Bleichenbacher found a chosen-ciphertext attack against PKCS #1 version 1.5 that also applied to Web servers implementing the SSL v3.0 protocol [15]. The Bleichenbacher attack basically refers to a failure analysis, as introduced in Section 1.2.3. In short, the adversary sends adaptively chosen ciphertexts to an SSL server, and the server responds for every ciphertext with one bit saying whether the decrypted data structure conforms to PKCS #1 version 1.5. So the Web server basically acts as a one-bit oracle for PKCS #1 conformance. If the adversary can query the oracle a sufficiently large number of times, then he or she can illegitimately perform one operation with the private key of the server (e.g., an RSA decryption or digital signature generation). This operation can then be used, for example, to decrypt a session key that was previously transmitted from a client to the server in encrypted form. The Bleichenbacher attack is theoretically interesting and has had a deep impact on the way people think about formal security arguments in general, and encryption systems that can be shown to be secure against chosen-ciphertext attacks in particular.

Before Bleichenbacher published his attack, Mihir Bellare and Philip Rogaway had developed and proposed a padding scheme that protects against chosen-ciphertext attacks [16]. As already mentioned in Section 14.1, this scheme is acronymed OAEP. It is illustrated in Figure 14.1. In this figure, h and g represent cryptographic hash functions, m represents the plaintext message, and r represents a random(ly chosen) binary string that is used to mask the message. The output of the OAEP padding scheme are two binary strings—s and t—that are concatenated to form the output of the OAEP padding scheme. So the OAEP padding scheme can be formally expressed as follows:

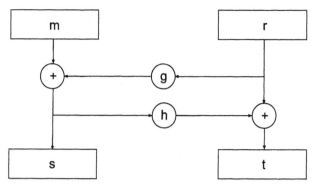

Figure 14.1 OAEP padding scheme.

$$\text{OAEP}(m) = (s,t) = \underbrace{m \oplus g(r)}_{s} \parallel \underbrace{r \oplus h(m \oplus g(r))}_{t}$$

This value can then be taken as input for an asymmetric encryption system, such as the RSA asymmetric encryption system. The resulting system is sometimes referred to as RSA-OAEP.

Bellare and Rogaway argued that OAEP provides semantic security against chosen-ciphertext attacks in the random oracle model. Hence, quite naturally, OAEP was adopted in PKCS #1 version 2.0. In 2001, however, Victor Shoup showed that the security arguments provided by Bellare and Rogaway are formally incorrect [17]. A formal and complete proof of the semantic security against adaptive chosen-ciphertext attacks provided by RSA-OAEP was given in [18]. Unfortunately, this security proof does not guarantee security for key sizes used in practice (due to the inefficiency of the security reduction). Consequently, a few alternative padding schemes have been proposed in the literature that admit more efficient proofs and provide adequate security for key sizes used in practice (see, for example, [19]). The development and formal treatment of padding schemes for asymmetric encryption is still a hot research topic in contemporary cryptography.

14.4 IDENTITY-BASED ENCRYPTION

In an asymmetric encryption system, every user has a public key pair, and the keys the pair consist of look somehow arbitrary and random. Consequently, one usually faces the problem that one cannot easily attribute a specific public key to a specific entity (i.e., user) and that one has to work with public key certificates. A public key certificate, in turn, is a data structure that is issued by a trusted (or trustworthy) certification authority (CA), that states that a specific public key really belongs to a specific entity, and that itself is digitally signed by the certificate-issuing CA. If there are multiple CAs in place, then one frequently talks about public key infrastructures (PKIs). In general, public key certificates, CAs, and PKIs are very complex topics, and we are just at the beginning of understanding all issues involved.[16]

In the early 1980s, Shamir came up with the idea that if one chose a public key to uniquely identify the entity that holds the key, then one would no longer have to care about public key certification in the first place. Instead, a public key would then be self evident in the sense that it automatically becomes clear to whom it belongs (or at least to whom it was issued in the first place). Shamir coined the term *identity-based encryption* for this idea. The major advantage of identity-based encryption is that neither public key certificates nor directory services are needed (because messages are encrypted with keys that are directly derivable from information characterizing the recipients). The disadvantage, however, is related to the fact that a trusted authority is needed to generate public key pairs and to distribute them to the appropriate entities. Note that in a conventional asymmetric encryption system, all entities can generate their own public key pairs using the Generate algorithm. In an identity-based encryption system, this cannot be the case because the public keys must have specific values and it must not be possible for anybody (except the trusted authority) to determine the private key that belongs to a specific public key (otherwise, this person could determine the private keys of everybody). Consequently, in an identity-based encryption system, all entities must provide their identities to the trusted authority, and the trusted authority must provide them with their appropriate public key pair.

In [21], Shamir introduced the idea of identity-based encryption and also proposed an identity-based digital signature system. Almost two decades later, Dan Boneh and Matthew K. Franklin developed and proposed an *identity-based encryption* (IBE) system [22]. They suggested using the IBE system as an alternative to commonly used secure messaging technologies and solutions that are based on public key certificates.[17]

---

16 See, for example, Chapter 7 of [20].
17 In fact, Boneh co-founded Voltage Security, Inc., (http://www.voltage.com) to market the IBE system.

14.5 FINAL REMARKS

In this chapter, we elaborated on asymmetric encryption systems. More specifically, we overviewed and discussed basic systems (i.e., RSA, Rabin, and ElGamal), and secure systems (i.e., probabilistic encryption and OAEP), and we addressed the notion of IBE.

In addition to the asymmetric encryption systems addressed so far, there are other systems that have been developed and proposed in the literature. Some of these systems have been broken and become obsolete. For example, we mentioned in Section 6.6.2.2 that the $\mathcal{NP}$-complete subset sum problem has served as a basis for many public key cryptosystems. All of these knapsack-based public key cryptosystems proposed in the past have been broken. In fact, knapsack-based cryptosystems are good candidates to illustrate the fact that it is a necessary but usually not sufficient condition that a public key cryptosystem is based on a mathematical problem that is assumed to be intractable. Breaking a knapsack-based public key cryptosystem is generally possible without solving the underlying subset sum problem.

Nevertheless, there are still a few asymmetric encryption systems that have turned out to be resistant against various types of cryptanalytical attacks. An example is the McEliece public key cryptosystem developed and published in the late 1970s [23]. In spite of their resistance against cryptanalytical attacks, these asymmetric encryption systems are not further addressed in this book.

Early in Section 14.2, we said that we assume verification keys to be published in some certified form. This simple and innocent assumption has huge implications on the practical side. How does one make sure that all entities have public keys? How does one publish them, and how does one certify them? Finally, how does one make sure that public keys can be revoked and that status information about a public key is publicly available in a timely fashion? All of these questions related to digital certificates are typically addressed (and solved) by a PKI. Unfortunately, the establishment and operation of a PKI is more involved than it looks at first sight (see, for example, Chapter 7 of [20]). We revisit and more specifically address the notion of a PKI in Section 19.5.

References

[1] Rackoff, C., and D.R. Simon, "Non-Interactive Zero-Knowledge Proof of Knowledge and Chosen Ciphertext Attack," *Proceedings of CRYPTO '91*, Springer-Verlag, LNCS 576, 1992, pp. 433–444.

[2] Goldwasser, S., and S. Micali, "Probabilistic Encryption," *Journal of Computer and System Sciences*, Vol. 28, No. 2, April 1984, pp. 270–299.

[3] Dolev, D., C. Dwork, and M. Naor, "Non-Malleable Cryptography," *SIAM Journal on Computing*, Vol. 30, No. 2, 2000, pp. 391–437.

[4] Bellare, M., et al., "Relations Among Notions of Security for Public-Key Encryption Schemes," *Proceedings of CRYPTO '98*, Springer-Verlag, LNCS 1462, 1998, pp. 26–45.

[5] Rivest, R.L., A. Shamir, and L. Adleman, "A Method for Obtaining Digital Signatures and Public-Key Cryptosystems," *Communications of the ACM*, 21(2), February 1978, pp. 120–126.

[6] Boneh, D., and H. Shacham, "Fast Variants of RSA," *CryptoBytes*, Vol. 5, No. 1, 2002, pp. 1–9.

[7] Boneh, D., "Twenty Years of Attacks on the RSA Cryptosystem," *Notices of the American Mathematical Society (AMS)*, Vol. 46, No. 2, 1999, pp. 203–213.

[8] Boneh, D., and R. Venkatesan, "Breaking RSA May Not Be Equivalent to Factoring," *Proceedings of EUROCRYPT '98*, Springer-Verlag, LNCS 1403, 1998, pp. 59–71.

[9] Wiener, M., "Cryptanalysis of Short RSA Secret Exponents," *IEEE Transaction on Information Theory*, Vol. 36, No. 3, 1990, pp. 553–558.

[10] Boneh, D., and G. Durfee, "Cryptanalysis of RSA with Private Exponent $d < N^{0.292}$," *Proceedings of EUROCRYPT '99*, Springer-Verlag, LNCS 1592, 1999, pp. 1–11.

[11] Rabin, M.O., "Digitalized Signatures and Public-Key Functions as Intractable as Factorization," MIT Laboratory for Computer Science, MIT/LCS/TR-212, 1979.

[12] Diffie, W., and M.E. Hellman, "New Directions in Cryptography," *IEEE Transactions on Information Theory*, IT-22(6), 1976, pp. 644–654.

[13] ElGamal, T., "A Public Key Cryptosystem and a Signature Scheme Based on Discrete Logarithm," *IEEE Transactions on Information Theory*, IT-31(4), 1985, pp. 469–472.

[14] Blum, M., and S. Goldwasser "An Efficient Probabilistic Public Key Encryption Scheme Which Hides All Partial Information," *Proceedings of CRYPTO '84*, Springer-Verlag, 1985, pp. 289–299.

[15] Bleichenbacher, D., "Chosen Ciphertext Attacks Against Protocols Based on the RSA Encryption Standard PKCS #1," *Proceedings of CRYPTO '98*, Springer-Verlag, LNCS 1462, 1998, pp. 1–12.

[16] Bellare, M., and P. Rogaway, "Optimal Asymmetric Encryption," *Proceedings of EUROCRYPT '94*, Springer-Verlag, LNCS 950, 1994, pp. 92–111.

[17] Shoup, V., "OAEP Reconsidered," *Proceedings of CRYPTO '01*, Springer-Verlag, LNCS 2139, 2001, pp. 239–259.

[18] Fujisaki, E., et al., "RSA-OAEP Is Secure Under the RSA Assumption ," *Journal of Cryptology*, Vol. 17, No. 2, Spring 2004, pp. 81–104.

[19] Pointcheval, D., "How to Encrypt Properly with RSA," *CryptoBytes*, Vol. 5, No. 1, 2002, pp. 10–19.

[20] Oppliger, R., *Security Technologies for the World Wide Web*, 2nd edition. Artech House Publishers, Norwood, MA, 2003.

[21] Shamir, A., "Identity-Based Cryptosystems and Signatures," *Proceedings of CRYPTO '84*, Springer-Verlag, 1984, pp. 47–53.

[22] Boneh, D., and M. Franklin, "Identity Based Encryption from the Weil Pairing," *SIAM Journal of Computing*, Vol. 32, No. 3, 2003, pp. 586–615.

[23] McEliece, R.J., "A Public-Key Cryptosystem Based on Algebraic Coding Theory," Deep Space Network Progress Report 42-44, Jet Propulsion Lab., California Institute of Technology, 1978, pp. 114–116.

Chapter 15

Digital Signature Systems

In this chapter, we elaborate on digital signatures and DSSs. More specifically, we introduce the topic in Section 15.1, elaborate on basic and secure systems in Sections 15.2 and 15.3, overview and discuss one-time signature systems, digital signatures for streams, and variations of "normal" DSSs in Sections 15.4–15.6, and conclude with some final remarks in Section 15.7. Note that all books on cryptography (including the ones itemized in the Preface) address digital signatures and DSSs and that there are even a few books that focus entirely on this topic (e.g., [1, 2]).

15.1 INTRODUCTION

In Section 2.3.2, we introduced, briefly discussed, and put into perspective digital signatures and corresponding DSSs with appendix or message recovery. According to Definitions 2.11 and 2.12, a DSS consists of three efficiently computable algorithms (i.e., Generate, Sign, and Verify or Recover). In short, the Generate algorithm is used to generate public key pairs (that consist of a signing key and a corresponding verification key), the Sign algorithm is used to generate digital signatures, and the Verify or Recover algorithm is used to verify the digital signatures in one way or another. In either case, a DSS must be correct and secure to be useful in practice.

- *Correctness* means that valid signatures must be accepted. For DSSs with appendix, this means that $\mathsf{Verify}(k, m, \mathsf{Sign}(k^{-1}, m))$ must return $valid$ for all public key pairs (k, k^{-1}) and all messages m. Similarly, for DSSs with message recovery, this means that $\mathsf{Recover}(k, \mathsf{Sign}(k^{-1}, m))$ must return m for all public key pairs (k, k^{-1}) and all messages m.

- *Security* means that it must be impossible or computationally infeasible (for an adversary) to forge a signature (i.e., to compute, without knowledge of the signing key k^{-1}, a valid signature for a given verification key k and message m).

The correctness requirement is simple and straightforward, and it does not lend itself to multiple interpretations. This is not true for the security requirement. In fact, there are many ways to read and interpret the security requirement. For example, it is possible to say that a DSS is secure if it is computationally infeasible for an adversary to compute, without knowledge of the signing key, a digital signature for a specific message m. This is certainly something one would require from a DSS. In fact, all systems overviewed and discussed in this chapter are secure in this sense. Another way to read and interpret the security requirement is that it must be computationally infeasible for an adversary to compute a valid signature for any (random-looking and not necessarily meaningful) message. This is obviously much more difficult to achieve, and not all systems overviewed and discussed in this chapter are secure in this sense. There are even more ways to read and interpret the security requirement.

To be a little bit more specific about the security requirement, we remember from Section 1.2.2 that every security definition must specify both the adversary's capabilities and the task the adversary is required to solve in order to be successful (i.e., to break the security of the system). The terminology most frequently used in this area was originally developed and introduced by Shafi Goldwasser, Silvio Micali, and Ron Rivest in the 1980s [3]. It is still in use today, and we adopt it in this book.

With respect to the *adversary's capabilities*, it is first of all important to note that we are in the realm of public key cryptography, where unconditional security does not exist. Consequently, we have to make assumptions about the computing power of the adversary we have in mind against whom we want to protect. The assumption most frequently made in modern cryptography is that the adversary has computing power at his or her disposal that is polynomially bound (with respect to the length of the input for the underlying mathematical problem). Furthermore, we have to specify what type of attack the adversary is able to mount. There are two major classes of such attacks.

- In a *key-only attack*, the adversary knows only the signatory's verification key. In particular, he or she has no information about the message(s) that is (are) signed.

- In a *message attack*, the adversary knows the signatory's verification key and has some information about the message(s) that is (are) signed or is at least able to retrieve this information in some way or another.

For all practical purposes, it is reasonable to assume that the adversary can mount message attacks. In fact, there are a couple of subclasses of message attacks that are distinguished in the literature.

- In a *known message attack*, the adversary knows $t \geq 1$ messages $m_1, m_2, \ldots,$ m_t and their digital signatures $s_1, s_2, \ldots, s_t$. The messages are known to the adversary, but they are not chosen by him or her.

- In a *generic chosen message attack*, the adversary is able to obtain digital signatures $s_1, s_2, \ldots, s_t$ for a chosen list of $t \geq 1$ messages $m_1, m_2, \ldots, m_t$. In such an attack, the list of messages must be fixed and independent from the signatory and his or her signing key. Furthermore, it must be chosen before the attack is mounted. This is why the chosen message attack is called *generic* (it is generic in the sense that it is not directed against a particular signatory's signing key).

- The *directed chosen message attack* is similar to the generic chosen message attack, except that the list of $t \geq 1$ messages $m_1, m_2, \ldots, m_t$ to be signed is chosen with respect to the signatory's verification key k. Consequently, the attack is directed against a particular signatory's signing key. It is, however, still a nonadaptive attack.

- In an *adaptive chosen message attack*, the adversary is able to obtain digital signatures $s_1, s_2, \ldots, s_t$ for a chosen list of $t \geq 1$ messages $m_1, m_2, \ldots, m_t$. In such an attack, the list of messages depends on the signatory's signing key and can be adaptively chosen while the attack is going on. Alternatively speaking, one can say that the adversary has access to a signature generation oracle. For every message m he or she provides, the oracle returns a valid digial signature s for m.

The message attacks are itemized in order of increasing severity, with the adaptive chosen message attack being the strongest and most severe attack an adversary can mount. While an adaptive chosen message attack may be impossible to mount in practice, a well-designed DSS should nonetheless be designed to protect against it.

With respect to the *task the adversary is required to solve*, there are at least four possibilities one may discover.

- In a *total break*, the adversary must be able to determine the signatory's signing key k^{-1}. This is a total break, because the adversary can then use the signing key to generate valid signatures for all messages of his or her choice. A DSS that does not provide protection against a total break is sometimes also called *totally breakable*.

- In a *universal forgery*, the adversary must be able to find an efficient algorithm that is functionally equivalent to the signatory's Generate algorithm (but does not require the signatory's signing key).[1] A DSS that does not protect against a universal forgery is sometimes also called *universally breakable*.

- In a *selective forgery*, the adversary is able to forge a digital signature for a particular message (that is chosen before the attack is mounted). A DSS that does not protect against a selective forgery is sometimes also called *selectively breakable*.

- In an *existential forgery*, the adversary is able to forge a digital signature for at least one (possibly random-looking and not necessarily meaningful) message. A DSS that does not protect against an existential forgery is sometimes also called *existentially breakable*.

The types of security breaks are itemized in order of decreasing severity, meaning that a total break is the most severe break and an existential forgery is the least severe break. Many DSSs used in practice are existentially breakable. If, for example, a DSS is built from a family of trapdoor permutations (e.g., the RSA or Rabin DSS), then every possible value represents a valid signature for a (probably random-looking and not very meaningful) message. This problem and ways to solve it are discussed later in this chapter.

The adversary's capabilities (i.e., types of attack) and the task an adversary is required to solve can be combined to come up with different notions of security for DSSs. For example, we can say that a DSS is totally breakable even if we allow only key-only attacks. Such a DSS is not very useful in practice. When people talk about (provably) secure DSSs, then they usually refer to DSSs that protect against existential forgery, even if one assumes an adversary who is able to mount adaptive chosen message attacks. This notion of security is further addressed in Section 15.3. We first begin with some basic DSSs (that are not secure in this strong sense).

15.2 BASIC SYSTEMS

In this section, we overview and discuss some basic DSSs that are practically relevant. More specifically, we elaborate on RSA, ElGamal, and the DSA. RSA and ElGamal are fundamentally different DSSs, whereas the DSA can also be understood as a variation of ElGamal. For each of these DSSs, we describe the

---

1 Note that the distinction between a total break and a universal forgery is somehow vague. It would also be possible to say that a total break occurs if an adversary is either able to compute the signatory's private (signing) key or find an efficient signature generation algorithm that is functionally equivalent to the signatory's true signature generation algorithm.

key generation, signature generation, and signature verification algorithms, and we provide a brief security analysis. Again, we assume that all verification keys are published in certified form (we already made this assumption in Section 14.2).

15.2.1 RSA

As already pointed out by Diffie and Hellman in their seminal paper [4], a family of trapdoor functions can also be used to digitally sign messages and verify digital signatures accordingly. As mentioned in Section 14.2.1, the RSA family represents a family of trapdoor permutations, and hence the RSA public key cryptosystem as proposed in [5] also yields a DSS (with appendix or message recovery).

15.2.1.1 Key Generation Algorithm

The RSA Generate algorithm as described in Section 14.2.1.1 is the same for the RSA asymmetric encryption system and the RSA DSS. It takes as input a security parameter, and it generates as output a public key pair that consists of a public key (n, e) and a corresponding private key (n, d) of appropriate size. In the case of the RSA DSS, the public key represents the verification key and the private key represents the signing key.

Let us consider a toy example to illustrate the working principle of the RSA DSS. We use the same numbers as in Section 14.2.1. Consequently, $p = 11$, $q = 23$, $n = 253$, $\phi(n) = 10 \cdot 22 = 220$, the (private) signing key is $(n, d) = (253, 147)$, and the (public) verification key is $(n, e) = (253, 3)$.

15.2.1.2 Signature Generation Algorithm

The RSA Sign algorithm is deterministic and can be used to digitally sign a message m. If RSA is used as a DSS with message recovery, then m must be sufficiently small (i.e., smaller than n if interpreted as integer). If RSA is used as a DSS with appendix, then m must either be sufficiently small or hashed to a bit sequence of fixed size. In practice, it is highly recommended to use RSA only to digitally sign hash values. The cryptographic hash functions that can be used are overviewed and discussed in Chapter 8.

In its basic form, the RSA Sign algorithm takes as input a signing key (n, d) and a message $m \in \mathbb{Z}_n$, and it generates as output the digital signature

$$s = \text{RSA}_{n,d}(m) \equiv m^d \pmod{n}.$$

The algorithm is simple and efficient. In fact, it requires only one modular exponentiation that can be done, for example, using the square-and-multiply algorithm (see Algoritm 3.3).

As mentioned above, the RSA DSS is most frequently used in conjunction with a cryptographic hash function (it then yields a DSS with appendix). In this case, the RSA Sign algorithm consists of the following two steps:

- First, the cryptographic hash function h is used to compute $h(m)$—that is, the hash value of the message.

- Second, the digital signature s for $h(m)$ is computed as follows:

$$s = \text{RSA}_{n,d}(h(m)) \equiv h(m)^d \pmod{n}.$$

In this case, it is necessary to expand $h(m)$ to the size of the modulus n. This can be done implicitly, by prepending zeros to $h(m)$, or explicitly, by using a message expansion function. In practice, the second approach is preferred, and there are many message expansion functions that can be used. For example, a message expansion function that is frequently used in practice is specified in PKCS #1 (currently in version 2.1).[2] According to this standard, $h_{PKCS\#1}(m)$ is constructed as follows:

$$h_{PKCS\#1}(m) = \text{0x 00 01 FF FF} \ldots \text{FF FF 00} \| h(m)$$

Consequently, $h(m)$ is padded by prepending a zero byte, a byte representing one, a series of bytes representing 255, and another zero byte. In fact, there are so many bytes representing 255 inserted that the total bit length of $h_{PKCS\#1}(m)$ equals the bit length of the modulus n. Other standards use other ad hoc expansion functions. In [6], Mihir Bellare and Phillip Rogaway proposed the *probabilistic signature scheme* (PSS) that uses random values to expand $h(m)$. Furthermore, they specified a *probabilistic signature scheme with message recovery* (PSS-R). PSS and PSS-R can be shown to be secure in the random oracle model (see Section 15.3).

After the RSA Sign algorithm has generated a digital signature s, it must be transmitted to the verifier. If RSA is used as a DSS with message recovery, then it is sufficient to transmit s. If, however, RSA is used as a DSS with appendix, then s must be transmitted together with the message m.

Let us assume that the signatory wants to digitally sign the message $m = 26$ (or $h(m) = 26$, respectively) in our toy example. In this case, the RSA Sign algorithm computes

---

2　　ftp://ftp.rsasecurity.com/pub/pkcs/pkcs-1/pkcs-1v2-1.pdf.

$$d \equiv m^d \ (\text{mod } n) \equiv 26^{147} \ (\text{mod } 253) = 104.$$

Then 104 represents the digital signature for 26, and 26 may be either the message or the hash value thereof.

15.2.1.3 Signature Verification Algorithm

For the purpose of signature verification, one must distinguish whether the RSA DSS is used with appendix or with message recovery. In either case, the corresponding algorithm (i.e., Verify or Recover) is deterministic and efficient (i.e., it requires only a modular exponentiation and optionally the invocation of a cryptographic hash function).

DSS with Appendix

If RSA is used as a DSS with appendix, then the Verify algorithm must be employed to verify the digital signature s that is transmitted together with the message m. The algorithm takes as input a verification key (n, e), a message m, and a digital signature s, and it generates as output one bit that indicates whether s is a valid signature for m with respect to (n, e). The RSA Verify algorithm operates in two steps:

- First, it computes

$$m' = \text{RSA}_{n,e}(s) \equiv s^e \ (\text{mod } n).$$

- Second, it compares m' either with m or $h(m)$. The signature is valid if and only if equality holds (i.e., $m' = m$ or $m' = h(m)$).

In our toy example, the RSA Verify algorithm computes

$$m' = \text{RSA}_{253,3}(104) \equiv 104^3 \ (\text{mod } 253) = 26$$

and returns *valid* (because $m' = 26$ matches the message $m = 26$ that is originally transmitted together with the signature s).

DSS with Message Recovery

If RSA is used as a DSS with message recovery, then the Recover algorithm takes as input a verification key (n, e) and a digital signature s, and it generates as output either the message m or a notification indicating that s is not a valid signature for m with respect to (n, e). The RSA Recover algorithm operates in two steps:

- First, it computes

$$m = \text{RSA}_{n,e}(s) \equiv s^e \ (\text{mod } n).$$

- Second, it decides whether m is a valid message. In the positive case, it returns m, and in the negative case, it returns a notification that indicates that s is not a valid signature for m with respect to (n, e).

The second step is important. If every message represented a valid message, then an adversary could trivially find an existential forgery by selecting $s \in \mathbb{Z}_n$ and claiming that it is an RSA signature (if somebody verifies the signature, he or she computes $m \equiv s^e \ (\text{mod } n)$, and hence s is indeed a valid signature for m). If m represented a meaningful message, then the signatory would be in trouble (i.e., he or she may be held accountable for the message and cannot repudiate having signed it). Consequently, it is important that random messages are unlikely to be meaningful, or—alternatively speaking—that the probability that a randomly chosen message is meaningful is negligible. There are basically two possibilities to achieve this.

- One can use a natural language to construct messages to be signed. Natural languages have generally enough redundancy so that a randomly chosen string (over the alphabet in use) is not likely to be meaningful.

- One can use a specific (redundancy) structure for messages to be signed. If, for example, one digitally signs $m \parallel m$ instead of m, then one can easily verify the structure of the message after its recovery (i.e., it must then consist of two equal halves). It goes without saying that more efficient redundancy structures are used in practice.

In our toy example, the RSA Recover algorithm computes

$$m = \text{RSA}_{253,3}(104) \equiv 104^3 \ (\text{mod } 253) = 26$$

and decides whether m is a valid message. If, for example, valid messages must be congruent to 6 modulo 20, then $m = 26$ is a valid message and is returned as a result.

15.2.1.4   Security Analysis

In Section 14.2.1.4, we analyzed the security of the RSA asymmetric encryption system. Most things we said there also apply for the RSA DSS. This is particularly true for the properties of the RSA family of trapdoor permutations. If, for example, somebody is able to factorize the modulus n, then he or she is also able to determine the signing key and to generate digital signatures at will. Consequently, the modulus n must be so large that its factorization is computationally infeasible for the (polynomially bound) adversary one has in mind and against which one wants to protect.

Also, the multiplicative property of the RSA function is particularly dangerous when RSA is used as a DSS. If m_1 and m_2 are two messages with signatures s_1 and s_2, then

$$s = s_1 s_2 \equiv (m_1 m_2)^d \pmod{n}$$

is a valid signature for $m = m_1 m_2 \pmod{n}$. Consequently, we reemphasize that good practices in security engineering must take care of the multiplicative structure of the RSA function and protect against corresponding attacks. Remember from our previous discussion that one can either require that messages have a certain (nonmultiplicative) structure or randomly pad the messages prior to the generation of the digital signatures.

In many applications, RSA is used as an asymmetric encryption system and as a DSS. Consequently, it may be necessary to apply both the RSA Encrypt algorithm and the RSA Sign algorithm to a particular message m. The question that arises immediately is whether the order of the operations matters. More specifically, does one have to encrypt m before it is digitally signed, or does one have to digitally sign it prior to encryption? In the general case, the answer is not clear, and it matters what the purpose of the cryptographic protection really is. In many practically relevant situations, however, the second possibility is the preferred choice. Consequently, it is often recommended to use the RSA DSS to digitally sign a message and then use the RSA asymmetric encryption system to encrypt the result. In this case, one must be concerned about the relative sizes of the moduli in use.

Assume that user A wants to digitally sign and then encrypt message m for user B. Also assume that (n_A, d_A) is A's private RSA signing key and (n_B, e_B) is B's public RSA encryption key. If $n_A \leq n_B$, then the application of the two algorithms is simple and straightforward (i.e., the output of the RSA Sign algorithm is smaller than or equal to the modulus n_A, and this value can then be used as input for the RSA Encrypt algorithm). If, however, $n_A > n_B$, then the output of the RSA Sign algorithm may be larger than what is allowed as input for the RSA

Encrypt algorithm. Obviously, one can split the output of the RSA Sign algorithm into two input blocks for the RSA Encrypt algorithm and then encrypt each block individually. Unfortunately, there are situations where this type of reblocking is not feasible. In these situations, one may consider one of the following three possibilities to avoid the reblocking problem in the first place:

- One can prescribe the form of the moduli to make sure that the reblocking problem does not occur.

- One can enforce that the operation using the smaller modulus is applied first. In this case, however, it may happen that a message is first encrypted and then digitally signed.

- One can equip each user with two public key pairs. One pair has a "small" modulus and is used by the RSA Sign algorithm, and the other pair has a "large" modulus and is used by the RSA Encrypt algorithm.

The first possibility is not recommended, because it is difficult to prescribe the form of the moduli in some binding way. The second possibility is not recommended either, because conditional reordering can change the meaning of the cryptographic protection one wants to implement. So the third possibility is often the preferred choice. Unfortunately, using two public key pairs per user also increases the key management overhead.

In summary, the RSA DSS can be considered reasonably secure. This is particularly true if the modulus n is sufficiently large. In fact, n must be at least large enough to make it computationally infeasible to factorize it with any known integer factorization algorithm. As we said before (in the context of the RSA asymmetric encryption system), this means that n should be at least 1,024 bits long. Because digital signatures are often valuable (digital) goods, it is often recommended to use longer moduli, such as 2,048 bits. Also, for all practical purposes, it is recommended to use RSA as a DSS with appendix and to use a cryptographic hash function accordingly. It is obvious that one then has to select a cryptographic hash function (e.g., MD5 or SHA-1). It is less obvious that one also has to select an expansion function, such as $h_{PKCS\#1}(m)$ or the one employed by the PSS and the PSS-R. The choice of an appropriate expansion function is particularly important if one wants to prove or show security claims for the resulting DSS. We revisit this topic in Section 15.3.

15.2.2 ElGamal

In Section 14.2.3, we introduced the ElGamal asymmetric encryption system and mentioned that the ElGamal public key cryptosystem as suggested in [7] also yields a DSS. Contrary to the RSA public key cryptosystem, the ElGamal public key cryptosystem uses different algorithms to encrypt and decrypt messages, or to digitally sign messages and verify digital signatures, respectively. This is disadvantageous from the developer's point of view (because he or she must implement more algorithms). Furthermore, ElGamal signatures are typically twice as long as RSA signatures (see Section 15.2.2.2). For both reasons, the ElGamal DSS is not as widely deployed in practice as the RSA DSS.

In its basic form, the ElGamal DSS is with appendix. This is also true for the many generalizations and variations of the ElGamal DSS that have been developed and proposed in the literature (e.g., [8]). There is, however, also an ElGamal variation that yields a DSS with message recovery [9]. Due to the names of their developers, this DSS is sometimes also referred to as the Nyberg-Rueppel DSS.

Similar to the ElGamal asymmetric encryption system, the security of the ElGamal DSS is based on the DLA and the intractability assumption of the DLP. Consequently, one needs a cyclic group in which the DLP is (assumed to be) intractable. For example, ElGamal introduced and originally proposed the DSS in the multiplicative group $\mathbb{Z}_p^*$ (for a sufficiently large prime number p). We also use this group to overview and discuss the ElGamal DSS next. Note, however, that there are many other cyclic groups that can be used instead of $\mathbb{Z}_p^*$. In ECC, for example, one uses $E(\mathbb{F}_q)$ as introduced in Section 7.6.

15.2.2.1 Key Generation Algorithm

The ElGamal Generate algorithm is the same as the one employed by the ElGamal asymmetric encryption system (see Section 14.2.3.1). For every user, it generates a public ElGamal verification key (p, g, y) and a corresponding private ElGamal signing key x. The modulus p and the generator g may be system parameters (i.e., they may be the same for all users and not be part of the verification key).

We consider a toy example to illustrate the ElGamal DSS. Let $p = 17$ and $g = 2$ be system parameters. For a particular user, the ElGamal Generate algorithm randomly selects $x = 4$ and computes $y \equiv 2^4 \pmod{17} = 16$. So the private ElGamal signing key is 4 and the corresponding public ElGamal verification key is 16.

15.2.2.2 Signature Generation Algorithm

Contrary to the RSA Sign algorithm, the ElGamal Sign algorithm is probabilistic and requires a cryptographic hash function. The cryptographic hash function, in turn, is used to turn a message into a hash value that is then digitally signed.

Algorithm 15.1　The ElGamal Sign algorithm.

$$\frac{(p, g, x, m)}{\begin{array}{l} k \in_R \mathbb{Z}_p^* \\ r \equiv g^k \pmod{p} \\ s \equiv (k^{-1}(h(m) - xr)) \pmod{(p-1)} \end{array}}$$
$$(r, s)$$

The ElGamal Sign algorithm is specified in Algorithm 15.1. It takes as input a private ElGamal signing key x (together with the system parameters p and g) and a message m, and it generates as output the digital signature for m. The digital signature, in turn, consists of two numbers—r and s—that are both elements of $\mathbb{Z}_p^*$. The algorithm consists of three steps:

- First, a number k must be randomly selected from $\mathbb{Z}_p^*$ such that $gcd(k, p-1) = 1$.[3] This suggests that k has an inverse element k^{-1} in $\mathbb{Z}_p^*$ (i.e., $kk^{-1} \equiv 1 \pmod{p-1}$), and hence that k^{-1} modulo $p-1$ can be determined using the extended Euclid algorithm (i.e., Algorithm 3.2).

- Second, k must be used to compute $r \equiv g^k \pmod{p}$.

- Third, the message m must be hashed with h, and the result $h(m)$ must be used to compute $s \equiv (k^{-1}(h(m) - xr)) \pmod{(p-1)}$.

Note that the algorithm can be sped up considerably by using precomputation. In fact, it is possible to select $k \in_R \mathbb{Z}_p^*$ and precompute

$$r \equiv g^k \pmod{p}$$

and

$$k^{-1} \pmod{p-1}.$$

Both values do not depend on a particular message m. If one has precomputed k, r, and k^{-1}, then one can digitally sign a message m by hashing it and computing $s \equiv (k^{-1}(h(m) - xr)) \pmod{(p-1)}$. This can be done very efficiently.

In either case, the ElGamal digital signature for m consists of the pair (r, s). Because m, r, and s are all numbers smaller than p, an ElGamal digital signature

---

3　As already mentioned in Section 14.2.3.4 and further explained in Section 15.2.2.4, a value k must never be used more than once (otherwise, the system is insecure).

is at most twice as long as the message that is signed (or the hash value thereof, respectively). As mentioned earlier, the basic ElGamal DSS is a DSS with appendix, meaning that the signatory must transmit both the message m and the signature (r, s) to the verifier.

In our toy example, we assume that the signatory wants to digitally sign a message m with a hash value $h(m) = 6$. The ElGamal Sign algorithm randomly selects $k = 3$ and computes $r \equiv 2^3 \pmod{17} = 8$, $k^{-1} \equiv 3^{-1} \pmod{16} = 11$, and $s \equiv 11(6 - 4 \cdot 8) \pmod{16} \equiv -14 \pmod{16} = 2$. Consequently, the ElGamal signature for $h(m) = 6$ is $(8, 2)$, and the numbers that are actually transmitted are 6, 8, and 2.

15.2.2.3 Signature Verification Algorithm

Like all signature verification algorithms, the ElGamal Verify algorithm is deterministic. It takes as input a verification key (p, g, y), a message m, and an ElGamal signature (r, s), and it generates as output one bit saying whether (r, s) is a valid ElGamal signature for m with respect to (p, g, y). The algorithm verifies the relation

$$1 \leq r \leq p - 1$$

and the equivalence

$$g^{h(m)} \equiv y^r r^s \pmod{p}. \tag{15.1}$$

The signature is valid if and only if both verification checks are positive. Otherwise, the signature is rejected and considered to be invalid. Note that the verification equivalence (15.1) works, because

$$
\begin{aligned}
y^r r^s &\equiv g^{xr} g^{kk^{-1}(h(m)-xr)} \pmod{p} \\
&\equiv g^{xr} g^{(h(m)-xr)} \pmod{p} \\
&\equiv g^{xr} g^{-xr} g^{h(m)} \pmod{p} \\
&\equiv g^{h(m)} \pmod{p}.
\end{aligned}
$$

Also note that it is mandatory to verify $1 \leq r \leq p-1$. Otherwise, it is possible to construct a new signature from a known signature [10]. Let, for example, (r, s) be the ElGamal signature of a message m and m' be another message for which an adversary wants to generate a valid signature. In this case, the adversary first generates[4]

$$u \equiv h(m')h(m)^{-1} \pmod{(p-1)}$$

and then computes

$$s' \equiv su \pmod{(p-1)}$$

and r' that satisfies the following system of two equivalences:

$$
\begin{aligned}
r' &\equiv ru \pmod{(p-1)} \\
r' &\equiv r \pmod{p}
\end{aligned}
$$

Obviously, the CRT and the CRA can be used to compute r' (see Section 3.3.3). The pair (r', s') then represents the ElGamal signature for m' (or $h(m')$, respectively). In fact, one can show that

$$
\begin{aligned}
y^{r'}(r')^{s'} &\equiv y^{ru}r^{su} \pmod{p} \\
&\equiv g^{u(xr+ks)} \pmod{p} \\
&\equiv g^{h(m')} \pmod{p}.
\end{aligned}
$$

On the other hand, one can show that then $r' \geq p$, and hence $1 \leq r \leq p-1$ does not apply.

In either case, it is necessary to use a cryptographic hash function h and not to directly sign a message m. If m were signed directly (i.e., without first hashing it), then it would be possible to existentially forge a digital signature. In fact, if m is signed directly, then the signature verification equivalence is $g^m \equiv y^r r^s \pmod{p}$. In this case, it is possible to select r, s, and m in a way that the equivalence is satisfied. More specifically, one can randomly select two integers u and v with $gcd(v, p-1) = 1$, and compute r, s, and m as follows:

$$
\begin{aligned}
r &\equiv g^u y^v \pmod{p} \\
s &\equiv -rv^{-1} \pmod{(p-1)} \\
m &\equiv su \pmod{(p-1)}
\end{aligned}
$$

4   Note that it is required that there exists a multiplicative inverse of $h(m)$ modulo $p - 1$.

With these values, one has

$$
\begin{aligned}
y^r r^s &\equiv y^r g^{su} y^{sv} \pmod{p} \\
&\equiv y^r g^{su} y^{-r} \pmod{p} \\
&\equiv g^m \pmod{p},
\end{aligned}
$$

and hence the verification equivalence (15.1) is satisfied. If one uses a cryptographic hash function h (i.e., one digitally signs $h(m)$ instead of m), then one can still generate signatures for hash values. Due to the one-way property of cryptographic hash functions, however, it is not possible to compute m from $h(m)$. Similar to the multiplicative property of the RSA function, one can also solve this problem with the use of redundancy.

In our toy example, the ElGamal Verify algorithm verifies that $8 \leq 16$ and $2^6 \equiv 16^8 \cdot 8^2 \pmod{17}$. Both verification checks are positive, and hence $(8, 2)$ represents a valid ElGamal signature for a message m with $h(m) = 6$.

15.2.2.4 Security Analysis

In Section 14.2.3.4, we analyzed the security of the ElGamal asymmetric encryption system. Some parts of this analysis also apply for the ElGamal DSS. More specifically, we showed in Theorem 14.2 that breaking the ElGamal system is computationally equivalent to solving the DHP. Consequently, one must select the cyclic group and the system parameters so that the DHP is computationally intractable. If, for exmaple, $\mathbb{Z}_p^*$ is used as a cyclic group (as done earlier), then p should be at least 1,024 bits long. Furthermore, one should select p so that efficient algorithms to compute discrete logarithms do not work. For example, it is necessary to select p so that $p - 1$ does not have only small prime factors (otherwise the Pohlig-Hellman algorithm [11] can be applied to efficiently compute discrete logarithms). There are other constraints that should be kept in mind when properly implementing the ElGamal DSS. The constraints can be found in the relevant literature (they are not repeated in this book).

Last but not least, we elaborate on the requirement that the ElGamal Sign algorithm must use a fresh and unique $k \in \mathbb{Z}_p^*$ for every digital signature it generates (this requirement is analog to the one used in the ElGamal asymmetric encryption system). If this requirement was not made, then it would be possible to retrieve the signing key from only two valid digital signatures. Let s_1 and s_2 be two ElGamal signatures for messages m_1 and m_2 that are generated with the same k:

$$
s_1 = (k^{-1}(h(m_1) - xr)) \pmod{(p-1)}
$$

$$s_2 = \left(k^{-1}(h(m_2) - xr)\right)(\bmod(p-1))$$

If k is the same, then $r \equiv g^k \pmod{p}$ is also the same for both signatures. Consequently, one has

$$
\begin{aligned}
s_1 - s_2 &\equiv \left(k^{-1}(h(m_1) - xr) - k^{-1}(h(m_2) - xr)\right)(\bmod(p-1)) \\
&\equiv \left(k^{-1}h(m_1) - k^{-1}xr - k^{-1}h(m_2) + k^{-1}xr\right)(\bmod(p-1)) \\
&\equiv \left(k^{-1}h(m_1) - k^{-1}h(m_2)\right)(\bmod(p-1)) \\
&\equiv \left(k^{-1}(h(m_1) - h(m_2))\right)(\bmod(p-1)).
\end{aligned}
$$

If $h(m_1) - h(m_2)$ is invertible modulo $p - 1$, then one can compute k. Furthermore, given k, s_1, r, and $h(m_1)$, one can retrieve the private key x. Note that $s_1 \equiv (k^{-1}(h(m_1) - xr)) \pmod{(p-1)}$, and hence

$$x \equiv \left(r^{-1}(h(m_1) - ks_1)\right) \pmod{(p-1)}.$$

This is unfortunate, and we stress the requirement that a fresh and unique k is randomly chosen from $\mathbb{Z}_p^*$ for every ElGamal signature that is generated.

15.2.3 DSA

In the early 1990s, Claus-Peter Schnorr proposed a modification of the basic El-Gamal DSS that can be used to optimize the signature generation and signature verification algorithms considerably [12]. The idea is to do the modular arithmetic not in a group of order $p-1$ (e.g., $\mathbb{Z}_p^*$), but in a much smaller subgroup of prime order q with $q \mid p - 1$. As a consequence, the computations can be done more efficiently and the resulting digital signatures can be made much shorter (as compared to the basic ElGamal DSS).

Based on the ElGamal DSS and the proposed modification of Schnorr, the NIST developed the *digital signature algorithm* (DSA) and specified a corresponding *digital signature standard* in FIPS PUB 186 [13]. Since its publication in 1994, FIPS PUB 186 has been revised twice.[5] The acronym ECDSA refers to the elliptic curve analog of the DSA. That is, instead of working in a subgroup of $\mathbb{Z}_p^*$, one works in a group of points on an elliptic curve over a finite field (see Section 7.6).

---

5   The first revision was made in December 1998 and led to the publication of FIPS PUB 186-1. The second and latest revision was made in January 2000 and led to the publication of FIPS PUB 186-2. It is electronically available at http://csrc.nist.gov/publications/fips/fips186-2/fips186-2-change1.pdf.

The ECDSA is being standardized within the ANSI X9F1 and IEEE P1363. Also, in the latest revision of FIPS PUB 186, a couple of elliptic curves are recommended for governmental use.

15.2.3.1 Key Generation Algorithm

The DSA Generate algorithm takes as input a security parameter and generates as output a private DSA signing key and a corresponding public DSA verification key. In a first step, the algorithm determines two prime moduli:

- A prime modulus p that is $512 + 64t$ bits long (for $t \in \{0, \ldots, 8\}$);
- A prime modulus q that divides $p - 1$ and that is 160 bits long (i.e., $2^{159} < q < 2^{160}$).

Note that the requirement that q divides $p - 1$ implies that $\mathbb{Z}_p^*$ has a subgroup of order q (i.e., the subgroup has approximately 2^{160} elements). Such a subgroup of $\mathbb{Z}_p^*$ can be determined by using a positive integer h with $1 < h < p - 1$ and $h^{(p-1)/q} \pmod{p} > 1$, and computing a generator g of a subgroup of order q as follows:

$$g \equiv h^{(p-1)/q} \pmod{p}$$

The numbers p, q, and g can then be considered as system parameters that are shared and can be the same for all users (or at least a specific subset of all users). For every user, the DSA Generate algorithm must then randomly select a private DSA signing key $x \in \mathbb{Z}_q$ and compute the corresponding public DSA verification key $y \equiv g^x \pmod{p}$. If they are not system parameters, then p, q, and g are also part of the verification key.

We consider a toy example to illustrate the DSA. Let $p = 23$, $q = 11$, and $g = 2$ be system parameters. Note that $q = 11$ is prime and divides $p - 1 = 22$. For a particular user, the DSA Generate algorithm randomly selects $x = 3$ and computes $y \equiv 2^3 \pmod{23} = 8$. So the private DSA signing key is 3 and the corresponding public DSA verification key is 8.

15.2.3.2 Signature Generation Algorithm

The DSA Sign algorithm is illustrated in Algorithm 15.2. It requires and makes use of a cryptographic hash function h. In the current version of the DSA, it is intended to use SHA-1 (see Section 8.3.3) as h. The algorithm consists of three steps:

Algorithm 15.2 The DSA Sign algorithm.

$$
\begin{array}{l}
(p,q,g,x,m) \\
\hline
k \in_R \mathbb{Z}_q^* \\
r \equiv (g^k \,(\mathrm{mod}\ p))\,(\mathrm{mod}\ q) \\
s \equiv (k^{-1}(h(m) + xr))\,(\mathrm{mod}\ q) \\
\hline
(r,s)
\end{array}
$$

- First, a number k must be randomly selected from $\mathbb{Z}_q^*$.

- Second, k must be used to compute $r \equiv (g^k \,(\mathrm{mod}\ p))\,(\mathrm{mod}\ q)$.

- Third, the message m must be hashed with h, and the result $h(m)$ must be used to compute $s \equiv (k^{-1}(h(m) + xr))\,(\mathrm{mod}\ q)$. In this case, k^{-1} is the inverse of k modulo q.

The pair (r, s) with r and s elements of $\mathbb{Z}_q$ represents the digital signature for m (or $h(m)$, respectively). Note that r and s are both 160-bit numbers. This is in contrast to an ElGamal signature, in which r and s are both of the size of p and m (e.g., 1,024 bits). Consequently, a DSA signature is about 320 bits long, which is more than six times shorter than a corresponding ElGamal signature.

In our toy example, we assume that the signatory wants to digitally sign a message m with a hash value $h(m) = 6$. The DSA Sign algorithm then randomly selects $k = 7$, computes $r \equiv (2^7 \,(\mathrm{mod}\ 23))\,(\mathrm{mod}\ 11) = 2$, determines $7^{-1} \,(\mathrm{mod}\ 11) = 8$, and computes $s \equiv (8(6 + 3 \cdot 2))\,(\mathrm{mod}\ 11) = 8$. Consequently, the DSA signature for $h(m) = 6$ is $(2, 8)$.

15.2.3.3 Signature Verification Algorithm

The DSA Verify algorithm is deterministic and can be used to verify DSA signatures. It takes as input a verification key (p, q, g, y), a message m, and a DSA signature (r, s), and it generates as output one bit saying whether (r, s) is a valid DSA signature for m with respect to (p, q, g, y). The algorithm first verfies that $r, s \in \mathbb{Z}_q$ (i.e., $0 < r' < q$ and $0 < s' < q$). If r or s is not in $\mathbb{Z}_q$, then the signature is considered to be invalid and must be rejected accordingly. If, however, the two conditions are satisfied, then the algorithm must compute the following values:

$$
\begin{aligned}
w &\equiv s^{-1} \,(\mathrm{mod}\ q) \\
u_1 &\equiv h(m)w \,(\mathrm{mod}\ q) \\
u_2 &\equiv rw \,(\mathrm{mod}\ q)
\end{aligned}
$$

$$v \equiv (g^{u_1} y^{u_2} \,(\mathrm{mod}\ p))\,(\mathrm{mod}\ q)$$

The signature is valid if and only if v equals r. To see why this signature verification equation works, we start with $s \equiv (k^{-1}(h(m) + xr))\,(\mathrm{mod}\ q)$, and hence $h(m) \equiv (ks - xr)\,(\mathrm{mod}\ q)$. If we multiply both sides by w and rearrange the congruence, then we get $wh(m) + xrw \equiv k\,(\mathrm{mod}\ q)$. This congruence is the same as $u_1 + xu_2 \equiv k\,(\mathrm{mod}\ q)$. Raising g to both sides of this congruence yields $(g^{u_1} y^{u_2}\,(\mathrm{mod}\ p))\,(\mathrm{mod}\ q) = (g^k\,(\mathrm{mod}\ p))\,(\mathrm{mod}\ q)$, and hence, $v = r$.

Obviously, it is also possible to represent the verification check in one line. In this case, the algorithm must verify that the following equation holds:

$$r = (g^{h(m)s^{-1}\,(\bmod\ q)} y^{rs^{-1}\,(\bmod\ q)}\,(\mathrm{mod}\ p))\,(\mathrm{mod}\ q)$$

In our toy example, the DSA Verify algorithm must first verify $0 < 2 < 11$ and $0 < 8 < 11$, and then compute

$$w \equiv 8^{-1}\,(\mathrm{mod}\ 11) = 7$$
$$u_1 \equiv 6 \cdot 7\,(\mathrm{mod}\ 11) \equiv 42\,(\mathrm{mod}\ 11) = 9$$
$$u_2 \equiv 2 \cdot 7\,(\mathrm{mod}\ 11) \equiv 14\,(\mathrm{mod}\ 11) = 3$$
$$v \equiv 2^9 8^3\,(\mathrm{mod}\ 23)\,(\mathrm{mod}\ 11) \equiv 512 \cdot 512\,(\mathrm{mod}\ 23)\,(\mathrm{mod}\ 11) = 2$$

Consequently, this value of v equals r, and hence the signature is considered to be valid.

15.2.3.4 Security Analysis

Because the DSA is a modified version of the ElGamal DSS, most things we said in Section 15.2.2.4 also apply for the DSA. Similar to the ElGamal DSS, the security of the DSA relies on the DLA and the DLP in a cyclic group. Contrary to the ElGamal DSS, however, the DSA relies on the DLP in a cyclic subgroup of $\mathbb{Z}_p^*$ with prime order q. This problem can only be solved by using a generic algorithm. As mentioned in Section 7.4, the best we can expect from such a generic algorithm is a running time that is of the order of the square root of the order of the subgroup. If, for example, the subgroup has the order 2^{160} (as in the case of the DSA), then the best we can expect from an algorithm to compute discrete logarithms is a running time that is of the order of

$$\sqrt{2^{160}} = 2^{160/2} = 2^{80}.$$

This is certainly beyond the computational power of the adversary one has in mind. Consequently, it is not possible to solve the DLP in the cyclic subgroup of $\mathbb{Z}_p^*$ with prime order q (for sufficiently large values of q).

15.3 SECURE SYSTEMS

As mentioned in the Introduction of this chapter, the security requirement of a DSS is somehow difficult to interpret and even more difficult to define in a mathematically precise way. In [3], Goldwasser, Micali, and Rivest proposed a definition for a secure DSS that is still in widespread use today. They modeled an adversary as a PPT algorithm that can mount adaptive chosen-message attacks. They then argued that a DSS is *secure* if all possible adversaries can existentially forge a digital signature only with a success probability that is negligible. If such a statement can be mathematically proven (under some standard intractability assumption), then the DSS is called *provably secure*.

Historically, the first provably secure DSS was the one proposed by Goldwasser, Micali, and Rivest. Due to the initials of its developers, this DSS is sometimes also referred to as GMR DSS. It is basically a one-time signature system (see Section 15.4) that is based on the existence of a "claw-free" pair of permutations (this assumption is potentially weaker than the IFA). Unfortunately, the efficiency of the GMR DSS and its derivates is too poor to be considered for practical use. In 1994, however, Cynthia Dwork and Moni Naor proposed a provably secure DSS— the so-called Dwork-Naor DSS—that is quite efficient [14].[6] Both the GMR DSS and the Dwork-Naor DSS can be proven secure without assuming a cryptographic hash function to behave like a random oracle (i.e., the security proofs are not in the random oracle model).

For all practical purposes, we now have very efficient DSSs that can be shown secure in the random oracle model. In fact, Mihir Bellare and Philip Rogaway introduced the random oracle model and a DSS that can be shown secure in it around the same time when Dwork and Naor developed their DSS [15]. Bellare and Rogaway originally argued that a hash-then-decrypt DSS that uses, for example, MD5, PKCS #1, and RSA has the problem that the set of points

$$\{h_{PKCS\#1}(m) \mid m \in \{0,1\}^*\}$$

has a size at most 2^{128} and hence is a very sparse and structured subset of $\mathbb{Z}_n^*$. This may be disadvantageous and may lend itself to cryptanalytical attacks (note

---

6   The DSS was originally proposed at CRYPTO '94.

that such attacks are not yet known, but that they may exist and be found at some point in time in the future). Consequently, they suggested hashing a message m onto the full domain $\mathbb{Z}_n^*$ (of the RSA function) before signing, and they constructed and proposed a corresponding *full-domain-hash* (FDH) function

$$h_{FDH} : \{0,1\}^* \to \mathbb{Z}_n^*.$$

The function is understood to hash arbitrarily sized strings "uniformly" into $\mathbb{Z}_n^*$. In either case, the FDH signature of m is the digital signature for h_{FDH}. Assuming that h_{FDH} is ideal (i.e., it behaves like a random function) and RSA is a trapdoor permutation, the security of the FDH DSS can then be shown in the random oracle model. In [6], Bellare and Rogaway improved the FDH DSS and proposed the PSS and the PSS-R. These are the secure DSSs that are addressed next. We elaborate on the PSS and the PSS-R constructions for the RSA DSS. Similar constructions for the Rabin DSS can be found in [6]. In either case, standardization efforts related to the PSS and PSS-R are underway in several forums, including, for example, ANSI X9F1, IEEE P1363, ISO/IEC JTC1 SC27, and PKCS.

15.3.1 PSS

The PSS is a DSS with appendix. In its RSA version, the PSS Generate algorithm is the same as the RSA key generation algorithm. On input of a security parameter, it outputs a signing key (n, d) and a corresponding verification key (n, e). The PSS is further parametrized by k_0 and k_1, which are both numbers between 1 and $k = \log n - 1$ (typically, $k = 1,024$ and $k_0 = k_1 = 128$). In addition, the PSS Sign and Verify algorithms make use of two hash functions h and g.

- The hash function $h : \{0,1\}^* \to \{0,1\}^{k_1}$ is called the *compressor*. It hashes arbitrarily long bit sequences to sequences of k_1 bits.

- The hash function $g : \{0,1\}^{k_1} \to \{0,1\}^{k-k_1-1}$ is called the *generator*. Let g_1 be the function that on input $w \in \{0,1\}^{k_1}$ returns the first k_0 bits of $g(w)$, and let g_2 be the function that on input $w \in \{0,1\}^{k_1}$ returns the remaining $k - k_0 - k_1 - 1$ bits of $g(w)$.

For the security analyis in the random oracle model, we must make the assumption that h and g are ideal, meaning that they behave like random functions. For all practical purposes, however, h and g must be implemented with cryptographic hash functions.

The PSS Sign algorithm is specified in Algorithm 15.3 and illustrated in Figure 15.1 (note that the figure only illustrates how the message is prepared for the RSA

Algorithm 15.3   The PSS Sign algorithm.

$$(n, d, m)$$

$r \in_R \{0,1\}^{k_0}$
$w \leftarrow h(m \parallel r)$
$r^* \leftarrow g_1(w) \oplus r$
$y \leftarrow 0 \parallel w \parallel r^* \parallel g_2(w)$
$s \leftarrow y^d \pmod{n}$

$$(s)$$

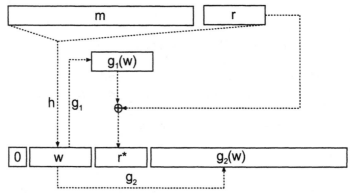

Figure 15.1   The PSS Sign algorithm.

signature generation). It takes as input a signing key (n, d) and a message m, and it generates as output a signature s. As its name suggests, the PSS is probabilistic (i.e., a k_0-bit random value r is used to digitally sign m).

The PSS Verify algorithm is deterministic, and it is specified in Algorithm 15.4. It takes as input a verification key (n, e), a message m, and a signature s, and it generates as output one bit b saying whether s is a valid signature for message m with respect to (n, e). Note that in step 2, y can be broken up into the four components b, w, r^*, and γ, because every component has a fixed and known length (i.e., b is one bit long, w is k_1 bits long, r^* is k_0 bits long, and γ is $k - k_0 - k_1 - 1$ bits long). Also note that b is set to true (or valid) if and only if all three conditions (i.e., $b = 0$, $h(m \parallel r) = w$, and $g_2(w) = \gamma$) are true.

As mentioned earlier, the PSS is very efficient. In fact, the PSS Sign and Verify algorithms both take only one application of h, one application of g, and one application of the RSA function. This is only slightly more expensive than the basic RSA DSS.

Algorithm 15.4 The PSS Verify algorithm.

$$
\begin{array}{l}
\underline{(n, e, m, s)} \\
y \leftarrow s^e \ (\mathrm{mod}\ n) \\
\text{break up } y \text{ as } b \parallel w \parallel r^* \parallel \gamma \\
r \leftarrow r^* \oplus g_1(w) \\
b \leftarrow (b = 0 \ \text{and} \ h(m \parallel r) = w \ \text{and} \ g_2(w) = \gamma) \\
\hline
(b)
\end{array}
$$

15.3.2 PSS-R

PSS-R is a DSS with message recovery. This means that the Sign algorithm must fold the message m into the signature s in such a way that it can be recovered by the Recover algorithm. When the length of the message is sufficiently small, then one can in fact fold the entire message into the signature. In PSS-R, if the security parameter is $k = 1,024$, then one can fold up to 767 message bits into a single signature.

Similar to the PSS, the PSS-R is parametrized by k_0 and k_1. The PSS-R Generate algorithm is the same as before. Also, the PSS-R Sign and Recover algorithms make use of the compressor h, generator g, g_1, and g_2 as defined earlier. We assume that the messages to be signed have length $l = k - k_0 - k_1 - 1$. Suggested choices are $k = 1,024$, $k_0 = k_1 = 128$, and $l = 767$. In this case, we produce a k-bit enhanced signature from which the verifier can recover the l-bit message and simultaneously check its authenticity.

Algorithm 15.5 The PSS-R Sign algorithm.

$$
\begin{array}{l}
\underline{(n, d, m)} \\
r \in_R \{0, 1\}^{k_0} \\
w \leftarrow h(m \parallel r) \\
r^* \leftarrow g_1(w) \oplus r \\
m^* \leftarrow g_2(w) \oplus m \\
y \leftarrow 0 \parallel w \parallel r^* \parallel m^* \\
s \leftarrow y^d \ (\mathrm{mod}\ n) \\
\hline
(s)
\end{array}
$$

The PSS-R Sign algorithm is specified in Algorithm 15.5 and illustrated in Figure 15.2 (again, the figure illustrates how the message is prepared for the RSA signature generation). The input and output parameters of the PSS-R Sign algorithm are the same as of the PSS Sign algorithm. In the PSS-R Sign algorithm, however,

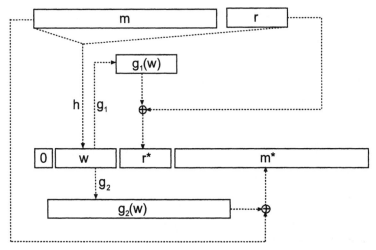

Figure 15.2   The PSS-R Sign algorithm.

the last part of y is $g_2(w) \oplus m$ (instead of only $g_2(w)$). This means that $g_2(w)$ is used to mask the message.

Algorithm 15.6   The PSS-R Recover algorithm.

$$(n, e, s)$$

$y \leftarrow s^e \pmod{n}$
break up y as $b \parallel w \parallel r^* \parallel m^*$
$r \leftarrow r^* \oplus g_1(w)$
$m \leftarrow m^* \oplus g_2(w)$
if $(b = 0$ and $h(m \parallel r) = w)$
  then output m
  else output $invalid$

$(m \mid invalid)$

The PSS-R Recover algorithm is specified in Algorithm 15.6. Again, this algorithm is similar to the PSS Recover algorithm. The major difference is that in the PSS-R Recover algorithm the message m must be recovered from m^*. This can be done by adding modulo 2 $g_2(w)$ to m^*. Also, the output of the algorithm depends on a condition. If $b = 0$ and $h(m \parallel r) = w$, then the PSS-R Recover algorithm outputs m. Otherwise, it outputs one bit saying that the signature s is invalid. In this case, the message is not recovered by the algorithm.

Again, the PSS-R is very efficient and only slightly more expensive than the basic RSA DSS. So for all practical purposes, there is no reason not to use the PSS or PSS-R instead of the basic RSA DSS.

15.4 ONE-TIME SIGNATURE SYSTEMS

A *one-time signature system* is a DSS that can be used to digitally sign single messages. This means that a new verification key is typically required for every message that is signed (otherwise, it is often the case that digital signatures can be forged). On one hand, the advantages of one-time signature systems are simplicity and efficiency (consequently, they are useful in application environments, where low computational complexity is required). On the other hand, the disadvantages of one-time signature systems are related to the size of the verification key(s) and the corresponding key management overhead. If, however, one-time signatures are combined with techniques to authenticate verification keys, then it is possible to sign multiple messages with one verification key, and hence the resulting one-time signature systems become practical.

In 1978, Michael O. Rabin was the first person who proposed a one-time signature system. The system employs a symmetric encryption system and is far too inefficient to be used in practice. In 1979, Leslie Lamport proposed a one-time signature system that is efficient, because it employs a one-way function instead of a symmetric encryption system and can be used in practice [16].

Let f be a one-way function and m be a message to be signed. The length of m is assumed to be bound by n. For example, n may be 128 or 160 bits, and any message longer than this must first be hashed using a cryptographic hash function. To digitally sign m using the Lamport one-time signature system, the signatory must have a private key that consists of n pairs of randomly chosen preimages for f:

$$[u_{10}, u_{11}], [u_{20}, u_{21}], \ldots, [u_{n0}, u_{n1}]$$

Each preimage u_{ij} ($i = 1, \ldots, n; j = 0, 1$) may, for example, be a string of 64 bits. In an efficient implementation, the $2n$ arguments are typically generated using a PRBG with an appropriate seed. The public key then consists of the $2n$ images $f(u_{ij})$:

$$[f(u_{10}), f(u_{11})], [f(u_{20}), f(u_{21})], \ldots, [f(u_{n0}), f(u_{n1})]$$

Furthermore, in an efficient implementation, the $2n$ images $f(u_{ij})$ are hashed to a single value p representing a new (master) public key:

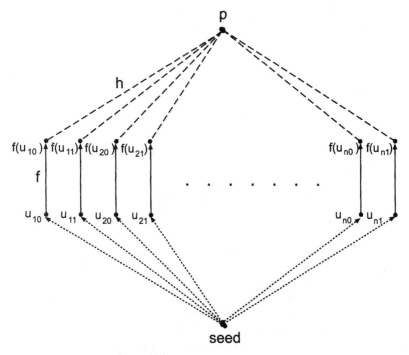

Figure 15.3   Lamport's one-time signature system.

$$p = h(f(u_{10}), f(u_{11}), f(u_{20}), f(u_{21}), \ldots, f(u_{n0}), f(u_{n1}))$$

In this notation, h represents a cryptographic hash function. To digitally sign message m, each bit m_i is signed individually using $[u_{i0}, u_{i1}]$. The index i runs from 1 to n. More specifically, the signature for m_i is the pair $[u_{im_i}, f(u_{i\overline{m_i}})]$, where $\overline{m_i}$ represents the complement of m_i. So if $m_i = 0$, then this bit is signed with $[u_{i0}, f(u_{i1})]$, and if $m_i = 1$, then it is signed with $[u_{i1}, f(u_{i0})]$. The resulting signature s consists of $[u_{im_i}, f(u_{i\overline{m_i}})]$ for all n bits of the message:

$$s = [u_{1m_1}, f(u_{1\overline{m_1}})], [u_{2m_2}, f(u_{2\overline{m_2}})], \ldots, [u_{nm_n}, f(u_{n\overline{m_n}})]$$

The signature s can be verified by computing all images $f(u_{ij})$, hashing all of these values to p', and comparing p' with the public key p. The signature is valid if and only if $p' = p$.

The Lamport one-time signature system is illustrated in Figure 15.3. As mentioned earlier, a PRBG and a seed are typically used to generate the $2n$ values $u_{10}, u_{11}, u_{20}, u_{21}, \ldots, u_{n0}, u_{n1}$, and a cryptographic hash function h is typically used to compute the public key p.

There are several possibilities to generalize and improve the efficiency of the Lamport one-time signature system. These generalizations and improvements, however, are beyond the scope of this book. Neverthelss, it is important to note that the Lamport one-time signature system and variations thereof are used in many cryptographic applications. For example, it can be used to protect against the double-spending problem in anonymous offline digital cash systems (e.g., [17]).

15.5 DIGITAL SIGNATURES FOR STREAMS

Most DSSs in use today are message oriented, meaning that they are used to sign messages or message blocks and to verify the signatures that are attached to them accordingly. A problem first addressed by Rosario Gennaro and Pamkaj Rohatgi in 1997 is how one can digitally sign streams[7] [18]. There are several approaches and corresponding solutions one can find.

- The simplest approach is to split the digital stream into a sequence of blocks, to digitally sign each block individually, and to have the recipient verify the digital signature of each block before he or she consumes it. This approach works for every stream (even if it is infinitely long). However, it has the disadvantage that it forces the sender to generate a digital signature and the recipient to verify a signature for every block in the stream. This is computationally expensive (for both the sender and the verifier).

- A less expensive approach can be used if the digital stream that must be signed is finite and known in advance to the sender. In this case, the sender can split the stream into a sequence of blocks, create a table that contains a cryptographic hash value for every block in the stream, and digitally sign the table. The digital stream is then transmitted with the prepended table to the recipient. The recipient, in turn, can verify the digital signature for the table, temporarily store the table in the positive case, and verify the hash value for every block in the stream with the entry in the table. This apporach has the

---

7 A *digital stream* (or *stream* in short) is a potentially very long (or even infinite) message or sequence of bits that a sender sends to one (or multiple) recipient(s) and the recipient(s) is (are) required to consume at more or less the input rate (i.e., without excessive delays). Examples of digital streams include digitized audio or video files, data feeds, and software modules that are dynamically downloaded if needed (e.g., Java applets).

disadvantage (in addition to the fact that it only works for streams that are finite and known in advance to the sender) that it requires potentially very large tables to be managed.

- One can address the table management problem of the previous approach by using a hybrid scheme, in which the digital stream to be signed is split into consecutive pieces and each piece is treated individually, meaning that it is preceded by a small digitally signed table.

- Another approach is to use a Merkle authentication tree [19] to even more efficiently authenticate the blocks of a digital stream.

When Gennaro and Rohatgi first addressed the problem of digitally signing streams [18], they followed a chaining strategy, meaning that the digital stream is divided into blocks and each block carries some authentication information for the next block of the stream (i.e., the authentication information of block i is used to authenticate block $i + 1$). This way the sender only needs to digitally sign the first block, and the properties of this signature propagate to the rest of the stream through the authentication information. Of course, the key problem is then to perform the authentication of all blocks in a way that is as efficient as possible. Gennaro and Rohatgi distinguished the following two cases:

- The digital stream is finitely long, and the sender knows the entire stream in advance. In this case, Gennaro and Rohatgi proposed a solution that is known as offline solution.

- The digital stream is (potentially) infinitely long, and the sender does not know the entire stream in advance. In this case, Gennaro and Rohatgi proposed a solution that is known as online solution.

Because digital streams can also be seen as messages (with specific properties), we use m to refer to such a stream. In the descriptions that follow, m refers to the digital stream that must be signed, and m' refers to the signed stream (i.e., m' is the stream that is actually transmitted to the recipient). Note that m and m' may be infinitely long, that the blocks of m and m' may not be equally long (the blocks of m' are typically longer than the blocks of m, because they comprise authentication information), and that an initial block m'_0 must usually be prepended to m' (such a block is not present in m). Let us overview and briefly discuss the offline and online solutions of Gennaro and Rohatgi next.

- In the *offline solution*, the digital stream m is assumed to be finitely long and the entire stream is known to the sender in advance—that is, m comprises k blocks (i.e., $m = m_1, m_2, \ldots, m_k$) and m' comprises $k + 1$ blocks (i.e.,

$m' = m'_0, m'_1, \ldots, m'_k$. The basic idea is to include in every block m'_i the hash value of the subsequent block m'_{i+1} (in addition to m_i) and to prepend a block m'_0 that includes a digital signature for the hash value of m'_1. The sender then computes m' as follows:

$$m'_k = [m_k]$$
$$m'_i = [m_i, h(m'_{i+1})] \text{ for } i = k - 1, \ldots, 1$$
$$m'_0 = [h(m'_1), s]$$

Consequently, m'_k contains m_k, m'_i contains m_i and the hash value of the subsequent block m'_{i+1} for $i = k - 1, \ldots, 1$, and m'_0 contains the hash value of $h(m'_1)$ and a digital signature s for this hash value. If k^{-1} refers to the sender's signing key, then s refers to $\text{Sign}(k^{-1}, h(m'_1))$. Note that all blocks of m' may be padded to meet a specific block length of m' (this is particularly true for m'_0 and m'_k). Also note that digitally signing a stream with the off-line solution requires a backward pass on the stream (this is why we must make the assumption that the stream is finitely long and known in advance to the sender). The structure of a signed digital stream is illustrated in Figure 15.4. In either case, the digital stream m' is the one that is transmitted to the recipient.

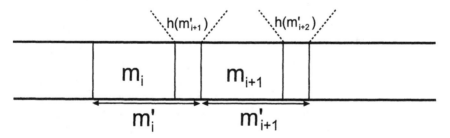

Figure 15.4   A signed digital stream according to the offline solution of Gennaro and Rohatgi.

On receiving m'_0, the recipient must verify that s is a valid signature for $h(m'_1)$ with respect to the verification key k of the sender—that is, he or she must verify that $\text{Verify}(k, h(m'_1), s)$ retuns *valid*. Afterwards, on receiving $m'_i = [m_i, h(m'_{i+1})]$ for $i = 1, \ldots, k - 1$, the recipient must accept block m'_i as valid if and only if it hashes to the same value that was transmitted in the preceding block m'_{i-1} (note that m'_{i-1} includes

$h(m'_{i-1+1}) = h(m'_i)$. Consequently, the recipient must verify a digital signature only at the beginning of the stream and a hash value for every subsequent block. The resulting offline solution is efficient for both the sender and the recipient.

- In the online solution, the digital stream m is assumed to be (potentially) infinitely long and the sender does not know the entire stream in advance— that is, m comprises a sequence of blocks (i.e., $m = m_1, m_2, m_3, \ldots$) and m' comprises another sequence of blocks (i.e., $m' = m'_0, m'_1, m'_2, \ldots$). The basic idea of the online solution is to use a "normal" DSS only to digitally sign the first block of the stream and to use a fast one-time signature system to digitally sign all subsequent blocks. More specifically, let (k, k^{-1}) be the sender's public key pair of a "normal" DSS and (k_i, k_i^{-1}) be the ith public key pair of a one-time signature system. The sender then computes the following sequence of blocks:

$$m'_0 = [k_0, s]$$
$$m'_i = [m_i, k_i, s_i] \text{ for } i \geq 1$$

The first block m'_0 contains only a verification key k_0 of a one-time signature system and a digital signature $s = \text{Sign}(k^{-1}, k_0)$ for k_0. All subsequent blocks m'_i ($i \geq 1$) contain m_i, k_i, and a one-time signature $s_i = \text{Sign}(k_{i-1}^{-1}, h(m_i \parallel k_i))$. The resulting stream m' is sent to the recipient. On receiving $m'_0 = [k_0, s]$, the recipient verifies that s is a valid signature for k_0 with respect to the verification key k of the sender—that is, he or she must verify that $\text{Verify}(k, k_0, s)$ returns $valid$. Afterward, on receiving $m'_i = [m_i, k_i, s_i]$, the recipient must verify that s_i is a valid one-time signature for $h(m_i \parallel k_i)$ with respect to the verification key of the previous block (i.e., k_{i-1}). Consequently, the recipient has to verify a single digital signature at the beginning of the stream and then one one-time signature for every subsequent block of the stream. Again, the resulting online solution is efficient for both the sender and the recipient. The major disadvantage of the solution is message expansion, meaning that m' is considerably larger than m (this disadvantage also applies for the offline solution).

Since the late 1990s, the problem of digitally signing streams has been more seriously addressed in the research community. The use of streams and stream-oriented network communication protocols is certainly the driving force behind this development. It is assumed that digital signatures for streams are becoming more and more important in the future.

15.6 VARIATIONS

Several variations of "normal" DSSs can be used in practice. In this section, we briefly overview and put into perspective blind signatures, undeniable signatures, and fail-stop signatures. More variations are proposed and discussed in the relevant literature.[8]

15.6.1 Blind Signatures

The idea of blind signatures was developed and originally proposed by David Chaum in the early 1980s [20, 21]. In short, a *blind signature* is a digital signature with the additional property that the signatory does not obtain any information about the message it signs or the signature it actually generates. The message is blinded in a way that can be reversed by the recipient of the blind signature.

Protocol 15.1 Protocol to issue blind RSA signatures.

$$\begin{array}{cc} \textbf{B} & \textbf{A} \end{array}$$

$$\begin{array}{cc} (n, e, m) & (n, d) \\ r \in_R \mathbb{Z}_n^* & \\ t \equiv mr^e \pmod{n} & \end{array}$$

$$\xrightarrow{\quad t \quad}$$

$$u \equiv t^d \equiv t^{1/e} \equiv m^d r \pmod{n}$$

$$\xleftarrow{\quad u \quad}$$

$$\frac{s \equiv u/r \equiv m^d r/r \equiv m^d \pmod{n}}{(s)}$$

For example, the RSA DSS as introduced in Section 15.2.1 can be turned into a blind RSA DSS. Let A be a signatory with public RSA verification key (n, e) and B be a recipient of a blind signature from A. Protocol 15.1 can then be used to have A issue a blind RSA signature s for a message m chosen by B. On B's side, the protocol takes as input the verification key of A and the message m to be signed, and it generates as output the RSA digital signature s for m. On A's side, the protocol only takes the signing key of A as input. B first randomly chooses an r from $\mathbb{Z}_n^*$ and uses this random value to blind the message m. Blinding is performed by multiplying the message with r to the power of e modulo n. The resulting blinded message t is transmitted to A and digitally signed there. Digital signing is performed by setting t to the power of d modulo n. The resulting message u is sent back to B,

---

8 A good and comprehensive bibliography on digital signatures and corresponding DSS is maintained by Guilin Wang. It is available at http://www.i2r.a-star.edu.sg/icsd/staff/guilin/bible.htm.

and B is now able to unblind the message. Unblinding is performed by dividing u by r or multiplying u with the multiplicative inverse of r modulo n. This inverse, in turn, can be found because r is a unit (and hence invertible) in $\mathbb{Z}_n$.

To prove the blindness property of the blind RSA DSS, one has to show that the pair (t, u) is statistically independent of the pair (m, s). Because $r^e \pmod{n}$ is a random group element of $\mathbb{Z}_n^*$, t and m are statistically independent. Furthermore, because u is determined by t and s is determined by m, (t, u) and (m, s) are statistically independent as well.

At first sight, one would argue that blind signatures are not particularly useful, because a signatory always wants to know what it signs. Surprisingly, this is not always the case, and there are many applications for blind signatures and corresponding DSSs. Examples include anonymous digital cash and electronic voting. After Chaum published his results in the early 1980s, almost all DSS have been extended in one way or another to also provide the possibility to issue blind signatures.

15.6.2 Undeniable Signatures

The notion of an *undeniable signature* was developed and originally proposed by David Chaum and Hans van Antwerpen at the end of the 1980s [22]. In short, undeniable signatures are digital signatures that cannot be verified with a public key. Instead, they must be verified interactively, meaning that an undeniable signature can only be verified with the aid of the signatory and that the Verify algorithm is therefore replaced with a signature verification protocol that is executed between the verifier and the signatory. Because a dishonest signatory can always refuse participation in a signature verification protocol, an undeniable signature system must come along with a disavowal protocol that can be used to prove that a given signature is a forgery.

15.6.3 Fail-Stop Signatures

The notion of a *fail-stop signature* was developed and originally proposed by Birgit Pfitzmann in the early 1990s [23] (see [24] for a more formal treatment). Fail-stop signatures can be briefly characterized as digital signatures that allow the signatory to prove that a signature purportedly (but not actually) signed by itself is a forgery. This is done by showing that the underlying assumption on which the DSS is based has been compromised. After such a proof has been published, the system can be stopped (that's why the signatures are called fail-stop in the first place). Fail-stop signatures are theoretically interesting, but they are practically not very important. Note that it is much more likely that a signing key is compromised than the underlying assumption is broken.

15.7 FINAL REMARKS

In this chapter, we elaborated on digital signatures and DSSs, and we overviewed and discussed some exemplary systems (i.e., RSA, ElGamal, DSA, PSS, and PSS-R). Note that many other DSSs—with or without specific properties—are described and discussed in the literature. There are even a few DSSs that can be constructed from zero-knowledge authentication protocols (see Section 17.3).

In either case, it is hoped that digital signatures and DSSs provide the digital counterpart to handwritten signatures and that they can be used to provide non-repudiation services (i.e., services that make it impossible or useless for communicating peers to repudiate their participation). Against this background, many countries and communities have put forth new legislation regarding the use of digital signatures. Examples include the Directive 1999/93/EC of the European Parliament and of the Council of December 13, 1999, on a Community Framework for Electronic Signatures and the Electronic Signatures in Global and National Commerce Act in the United States (commonly known as E-SIGN). But although many countries have digital signature laws, it is important to note that these laws have not been seriously challenged in court and that it is not clear what the legal status of digital signatures really is. The fact that digital signatures are based on mathematical formulas intuitively makes us believe that the evidence they provide is particularly strong. This belief is seductive and often wrong (e.g., [25–27]).

References

[1] Pfitzmann, B., *Digital Signature Schemes: General Framework and Fail-Stop Signatures*. Springer-Verlag, LNCS 1100, 1996.

[2] Hammond, B., et al., *Digital Signatures*. RSA Press, Osborne/McGraw-Hill, Emeryville, CA, 2002.

[3] Goldwasser, S., S. Micali, and R.L. Rivest, "A Digital Signature Scheme Secure Against Adaptive Chosen-Message Attacks," *SIAM Journal of Computing*, Vol. 17, No. 2, April 1988, pp. 281–308.

[4] Diffie, W., and M.E. Hellman, "New Directions in Cryptography," *IEEE Transactions on Information Theory*, IT-22(6), 1976, pp. 644–654.

[5] Rivest, R.L., A. Shamir, and L. Adleman, "A Method for Obtaining Digital Signatures and Public-Key Cryptosystems," *Communications of the ACM*, 21(2), February 1978, pp. 120–126.

[6] Bellare, M., and P. Rogaway, "The Exact Security of Digital Signatures—How to Sign with RSA and Rabin," *Proceedings of EUROCRYPT '96*, Springer-Verlag, LNCS 1070, 1996, pp. 399–414.

[7] ElGamal, T., "A Public Key Cryptosystem and a Signature Scheme Based on Discrete Logarithm," *IEEE Transactions on Information Theory*, IT-31(4), 1985, pp. 469–472.

[8] Horster, P., M. Michels, and H. Petersen, "Meta-ElGamal Signature Schemes," *Proceedings of 2nd ACM Conference on Computer and Communications Security*, ACM Press, New York, 1994, pp. 96–107.

[9] Nyberg, K., and R.A. Rueppel, "Message Recovery for Signature Schemes Based on the Discrete Logarithm Problem," *Designs, Codes and Cryptography*, Vol. 7, 1996, pp. 61–81.

[10] Bleichenbacher, D., "Generating ElGamal Signatures Without Knowing the Secret Key," *Proceedings of EUROCRYPT '96*, Springer-Verlag, LNCS 1070, 1996, pp. 10–18.

[11] Pohlig, S., and M.E. Hellman, "An Improved Algorithm for Computing Logarithms over $GF(p)$ and its Cryptographic Significance," *IEEE Transactions on Information Theory*, IT-24, 1978, pp. 108–110.

[12] Schnorr, C.P., "Efficient Signature Generation by Smart Cards," *Journal of Cryptology*, Vol. 4, 1991, pp. 161–174.

[13] U.S. National Institute of Standards and Technology (NIST), *Digital Signature Standard (DSS)*, FIPS PUB 186, May 1994.

[14] Dwork, C., and M. Naor, "An Efficient Existentially Unforgeable Signature Scheme and Its Applications," *Journal of Cryptology*, Vol. 11, No. 3, 1998, pp. 187–208.

[15] Bellare, M., and P. Rogaway, "Random Oracles Are Practical: A Paradigm for Designing Efficient Protocols," *Proceedings of 1st ACM Conference on Computer and Communications Security*, ACM Press, New York, 1993, pp. 62–73.

[16] Lamport, L. , *Constructing Digital Signatures from a One-Way Function*, Technical Report CSL-98, SRI International, October 1979.

[17] Chaum, D., A. Fiat, and M. Naor, "Untraceable Electronic Cash," *Proceedings of CRYPTO '88*, Springer-Verlag, LNCS 403, 1988, pp. 319–327.

[18] Gennaro, R., and P. Rohatgi, "How to Sign Digital Streams," *Proceedings of CRYPTO '97*, Springer-Verlag, LNCS 1294, pp. 180–197.

[19] Merkle, R., "Protocols for Public Key Cryptosystems," *Proceedings of the IEEE Symposium on Security and Privacy*, Oakland, CA, April 1980, pp. 122–134.

[20] Chaum, D., "Blind Signatures for Untraceable Payments," *Proceedings of CRYPTO '82*, Plenum Press, New York, 1983, pp. 199–203.

[21] Chaum, D., "Blind Signature System," *Proceedings of CRYPTO '83*, Plenum Press, New York, 1984, p. 153.

[22] Chaum, D., and H. van Antwerpen, "Undeniable Signatures," *Proceedings of CRYPTO '89*, Springer-Verlag, LNCS 435, 1990, pp. 212–216.

[23] Pfitzmann, B., "Fail-Stop Signatures: Principles and Applications," *Proceedings of the 8th World Conference on Computer Security, Audit and Control (COMPSEC '91)*, 1991, pp. 125-134.

[24] Pedersen, T.P., and B. Pfitzmann, "Fail-Stop Signatures," *SIAM Journal on Computing*, Vol. 26, No. 2, 1997, pp. 291–330.

[25] Oppliger, R., and R. Rytz, "Digital Evidence: Dream and Reality," *IEEE Security & Privacy*, Vol. 1, No. 5, September/October 2003, pp. 44–48.

[26] Maurer, U.M., "Intrinsic Limitations of Digital Signatures and How to Cope with Them," *Proceedings of the 6th Information Security Conference (ISC '03)*, Springer-Verlag, LNCS 2851, pp. 180–192.

[27] Maurer, U.M., "New Approaches to Digital Evidence," *Proceedings of the IEEE*, Vol. 92, No. 6, June 2004, pp. 933–947.

Chapter 16

Key Establishment

In this chapter, we elaborate on some cryptographic protocols that two entities can use to establish a shared secret key. More specifically, we introduce the topic in Section 16.1, elaborate on key distribution and key agreement protocols in Sections 16.2 and 16.3, address quantum cryptography in Section 16.4, and conclude with some final remarks in Section 16.5. Note that this chapter is not complete in the sense that there are many key establishment protocols that are not addressed. A comprehensive overview is given in [1]. Also note that the problem of key establishment can also be considered if more than two entities are involved. In this case, however, the corresponding cryptographic key establishment protocols are much more involved (see, for example, [2]). Again, these protocols are not addressed in this book.

16.1 INTRODUCTION

In Section 2.3.3, we argued that the establishment of secret keys is a major problem and the Achilles' heel for the large-scale deployment of secret key cryptography, and that there are basically two approaches to address the key establishment problem:

1. The use of a KDC, such as Kerberos [3];

2. The use of a key establishment protocol.

We further made a distinction between a key distribution protocol and a key agreement protocol (both of them representing key establishment protocols).

- A *key distribution protocol* can be used to securely transmit a secret key (that is generated locally or otherwise obtained) from one entity to another.

- A *key agreement protocol* can be used by two entities to establish and mutually agree on a secret key. Alternatively speaking, the key is derived from information provided by both entities.

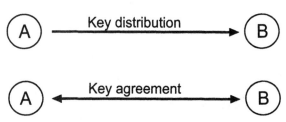

Figure 16.1   Key distribution versus key agreement.

Figure 16.1 illustrates the notion of a key distribution as compared to a key agreement. In the first case, a secret key is distributed from entity A to entity B, whereas in the second case, A and B establish and mutually agree on a secret key. So in the first case, the relationship between A and B is unidirectional, whereas the relationship is bidirectional in the second case.

As already mentioned in Section 2.3.3, key agreement protocols are advantageous from a security viewpoint, and hence they should be the preferred choice. Unfortunately, key agreement protocols also tend to be more involved than key distribution protocols. In either case, the most important key distribution and key agreement protocols are overviewed and briefly discussed next.

16.2   KEY DISTRIBUTION PROTOCOLS

Only a few key distribution protocols are in use today. In this section, we elaborate on Merkle's Puzzles, Shamir's three-pass protocol, and an asymmetric encryption-based key distribution protocol. The former two protocols are only theoretically (or historically) relevant, whereas the asymmetric encryption-based key distribution protocol is the key distribution protocol of choice for practical use. In fact, it is employed in almost all network security protocols in use today in one way or another.

16.2.1   Merkle's Puzzles

In 1975, Ralph C. Merkle developed and proposed an idea that is conceptually similar and very closely related to public key cryptography and asymmetric encryption as we know it today [4].[1] The idea is simple and has become known as *Merkle's Puzzles*.

Protocol 16.1 Merkle's Puzzles.

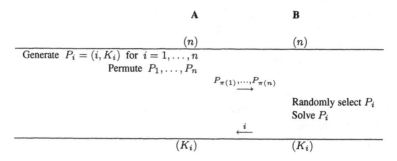

Let A and B be two entities that can communicate with each other over a public but authentic channel. A and B can then use Protocol 16.1 to establish a shared secret key K. The protocol takes a security parameter n on either side and then proceeds with the following three steps:

- First, A generates n puzzles $P_1, \ldots, P_n$, randomly permutes the puzzles (using permutation π), and sends $P_{\pi(1)}, \ldots, P_{\pi(n)}$ to B. Each puzzle P_i consists of an index i and a randomly chosen secret key K_i (i.e., $P_i = (i, K_i)$). Solving a puzzle is technically feasible but requires a nonnegligible computational effort (as explained later).

- Second, B randomly selects a puzzle P_i from $P_{\pi(1)}, \ldots, P_{\pi(n)}$ and solves it. The solution is (i, K_i), and B sends back to A the index i (the transmission is in the clear).

- Third, A can use i to extract the secret key K_i, and this key can then be used as a shared secret key between A and B.

Having a closer look at the protocol, one realizes that B gets K_i after having solved one single puzzle (i.e., P_i), whereas an adversary gets K_i only after having solved all n puzzles and having found the puzzle with the appropriate index i (on the average, the adversary has to solve half of the puzzles). For sufficiently large n, this is computationally infeasible for the adversary, and hence Merkle's Puzzles provide a theoretically interesting possibility to have two entities establish a secret key between them.

---

1   Note that this article appeared in the *Communications of the ACM* in 1978 (i.e., three years after it was submitted to the magazine).

One possibility to generate a puzzle P_i is to symmetrically encrypt (i, K_i) with a key that has a fixed part and a variable part. If, for example, the variable part is 30 bits, then solving a puzzle requires 2^{30} tries in the worst case (or 2^{29} tries on the average). This is the computational effort of B. If an adversary wants to compromise the key, then the computational effort is $n \cdot 2^{30}$ in the worst case (or $n/2 \cdot 2^{29} = n \cdot 2^{28}$ on the average). The computational security of Merkle's Puzzles is based on the difference between 2^{30} (for B) and $n \cdot 2^{30}$ (for an adversary). Again, for a sufficiently large n, this difference can be made significant.

As mentioned earlier, Merkle's Puzzles are theoretically (or historically) relevant. From a more practical point of view, however, Merkle's Puzzles have the problem that the amount of data that must be transmitted from A to B is proportional to the security parameter n. This is prohibitively expensive for a reasonably sized security parameter n.

16.2.2 Shamir's Three-Pass Protocol

Another theoretically and historically relevant key distribution protocol proposal is due to Adi Shamir. Let A and B be two entities that share no secret key initially but have a way to encrypt and decrypt messages using a specific encryption system (i.e., they can use different encryption systems). If the two encryption systems commute, then A and B can use *Shamir's three-pass protocol* illustrated in Protocol 16.2 to securely send a secret message (e.g., a secret key) from A to B.

Protocol 16.2 Shamir's three-pass protocol.

$$
\begin{array}{ccc}
\text{A} & & \text{B} \\
\hline
(K_A) & & (K_B) \\
\hline
K \in_R \mathcal{K} & & \\
K_1 = E_{K_A}(K) & \xrightarrow{K_1} & \\
 & \xleftarrow{K_2} & K_2 = E_{K_B}(K_1) \\
K_3 = D_{K_A}(K_2) & \xrightarrow{K_3} & \\
 & & K = D_{K_B}(K_3) \\
\hline
(K) & & (K)
\end{array}
$$

A first randomly selects a key K from the key space $\mathcal{K}$ and encrypts this key with his or her encryption system and his or her key K_A. The resulting value

$$K_1 = E_{K_A}(K)$$

is transmitted to B. B, in turn, uses his or her encryption system and his or her key K_B to compute

$$K_2 = E_{K_B}(K_1)$$
$$= E_{K_B}(E_{K_A}(K)).$$

This double encrypted value is returned to A. A then uses K_A to decrypt K_2, and compute

$$K_3 = D_{K_A}(K_2)$$
$$= D_{K_A}(E_{K_B}(E_{K_A}(K)))$$
$$= D_{K_A}(E_{K_A}(E_{K_B}(K)))$$
$$= E_{K_B}(K)$$

accordingly. This value is sent to B, and B uses K_B to decrypt K_3:

$$K = D_{K_B}(K_3) = D_{K_B}(E_{K_B}(K))$$

Both entities can now output the key K and use it for a symmetric encryption system.

Unfortunately, it is currently not known how to instantiate Shamir's three-pass protocol efficiently (i.e., using only symmetric encryption systems). Because one needs symmetric encryption systems that commute, an obvious choice would be additive binary stream ciphers, such as the one-time pad introduced in Section 10.4. In this case, however, one faces the problem that all encryptions cancel themselves out and that the protocol becomes completely insecure. Let r_A be the sequence of random bits that A uses to compute K_1 and K_3, and r_B be the sequence of random bits that B uses to compute K_2. K_1, K_2, and K_3 can then be expressed as follows:

$$K_1 = r_A \oplus K$$
$$K_2 = r_B \oplus K_1 = r_B \oplus r_A \oplus K$$
$$K_3 = r_A \oplus K_2 = r_A \oplus r_B \oplus r_A \oplus K = r_B \oplus K$$

K_1, K_2, and K_3 are the values an adversary can observe when he or she mounts a passive wiretapping attack. In this case, the adversary can add K_1 and K_2 modulo 2 to retrieve r_B:

$$\begin{aligned} K_1 \oplus K_2 &= r_A \oplus K \oplus r_B \oplus r_A \oplus K \\ &= r_A \oplus r_A \oplus K \oplus K \oplus r_B \\ &= r_B \end{aligned}$$

This value can then be added to K_3 modulo 2 to determine K:

$$r_B \oplus K_3 = r_B \oplus r_B \oplus K = K$$

Consequently, although we use a perfectly secure symmetric encryption system (i.e., the one-time pad), the resulting key distribution protocol is completely insecure.

Shamir's three-pass protocol can be instantiated using modular exponentiation in $\mathbb{Z}_p^*$. This idea is due to James L. Massey and Jim K. Omura, and hence the resulting key distribution protocol is sometimes also referred to as the *Massey-Omura protocol*. Let A and B be two entities that want to run the Massey-Omura protocol. A has an encryption exponent e_A and a corresponding decryption exponent $d_A \equiv (e_A)^{-1} \pmod{p-1}$, and B has an encryption exponent e_B and a corresponding decryption exponent d_B that is the multiplicative inverse modulo $p-1$ (i.e., $d_B \equiv (e_B)^{-1} \pmod{p-1}$). Shamir's three-pass protocol can then be instantiated with the following values for K_1, K_2, and K_3:

$$\begin{aligned} K_1 &\equiv K^{e_A} \pmod{p} \\ K_2 &\equiv (K^{e_A})^{e_B} \equiv K^{e_A e_B} \pmod{p} \\ K_3 &\equiv ((K^{e_A})^{e_B})^{d_A} \\ &\equiv ((K^{e_A})^{d_A})^{e_B} \\ &\equiv (K^{e_A d_A})^{e_B} \\ &\equiv K^{e_B} \pmod{p} \end{aligned}$$

Finally, B can use d_B to retrieve K:

$$K \equiv (K^{e_B})^{d_B} \equiv K^{e_B d_B} \equiv K \pmod{p}$$

Unfortunately, this instantiation of Shamir's three-pass protocol employs modular exponentiation, and hence there is no immediate advantage related to the use of an asymmetric encryption system in the first place.

16.2.3 Asymmetric Encryption-Based Key Distribution Protocol

Asymmetric encryption-based key distribution and corresponding protocols are simple and straightforward. As illustrated in Protocol 16.3, such a protocol can be used by two entities—A and B—that share no secret key initially. B is assumed to have a public key pair of an asymmetric encryption system (E_B refers to the encryption function that is keyed with k_B, and D_B refers to the corresponding decryption function that is keyed with k_B^{-1}). A randomly selects a secret key K from an appropriate key space $\mathcal{K}$, encrypts it with E_B, and transmits $E_B(K)$ to B. B, in turn, uses D_B to decrypt K. A and B now both share the secret key K.

Protocol 16.3 An asymmetric encryption-based key distribution protocol.

$$
\begin{array}{cc}
\text{A} & \text{B} \\
(k_B) & (k_B^{-1}) \\
\hline
K \in_R \mathcal{K} & \\
& \xrightarrow{\;E_B(K)\;} \\
& K = D_B(E_B(K)) \\
\hline
(K) & (K)
\end{array}
$$

Many cryptographic security protocols for the Internet make use of asymmetric encryption-based key distribution in one way or another. We already mentioned in Section 2.3.3 that the SSL/TLS protocol works this way (see, for example, Chapter 6 of [5]). Another example is some keying option in the Internet key exchange (IKE) protocol used in the IPsec protocol suite (see, for example, [6]).

16.3 KEY AGREEMENT PROTOCOLS

As mentioned in Sections 1.3 and 14.2.3, Whitfield Diffie and Martin E. Hellman published their landmark paper entitled "New Directions in Cryptography" in 1976 [7]. The paper introduced the basic idea of public key cryptography and provided some evidence for its feasibility by proposing a key agreement protocol. In fact, the *Diffie-Hellman key exchange protocol* can be used by two entities that have no prior relationship to agree on a secret key by communicating over a public but authentic channel. As such, the mere existence of the Diffie-Hellman key exchange protocol sounds like a paradox.

The Diffie-Hellman key exchange protocol can be implemented in any group in which the DLP (see Definition 7.5) is intractable, such as the multiplicative group of a finite field $\mathbb{Z}_p$ (i.e., $\mathbb{Z}_p^*$). The Diffie-Hellman key exchange protocol

Protocol 16.4 The Diffie-Hellman key exchange protocol using $\mathbb{Z}_p^*$.

A	B
(p, g)	(p, g)
$x_a \in_R \{0, \ldots, p-2\}$	$x_b \in_R \{0, \ldots, p-2\}$
$y_a \equiv g^{x_a} \pmod p$	$y_b \equiv g^{x_b} \pmod p$
$\xrightarrow{\quad y_a \quad}$	
$\xleftarrow{\quad y_b \quad}$	
$K_{ab} \equiv y_b^{x_a} \pmod p$	$K_{ba} \equiv y_a^{x_b} \pmod p$
(K_{ab})	(K_{ba})

using this group is illustrated in Protocol 16.4. Let p be a large prime and g be a generator of $\mathbb{Z}_p^*$. A and B know p and q, and want to use the Diffie-Hellman key exchange protocol to agree on a shared secret key K. A randomly selects a private exponent $x_a \in \{0, \ldots, p-2\}$, computes the corresponding public exponent $y_a \equiv g^{x_a} \pmod p$, and sends y_a to B. B, in turn, randomly selects a private exponent $x_b \in \{0, \ldots, p-2\}$, computes the corresponding public exponent $y_b \equiv g^{x_b} \pmod p$, and sends y_b to A. A then computes

$$K_{ab} \equiv y_b^{x_a} \equiv g^{x_b x_a} \pmod p$$

and B computes

$$K_{ba} \equiv y_a^{x_b} \equiv g^{x_a x_b} \pmod p.$$

Because the exponents commute, K_{ab} is equal to K_{ba}. It is the output of the Diffie-Hellman key exchange protocol and can be used as a secret key K.

Let us consider two toy examples to illustrate the working principle of the Diffie-Hellman key exchange protocol:

- Let $p = 17$ and $g = 3$ (i.e., $g = 3$ generates $\mathbb{Z}_{17}^*$). A randomly selects $x_a = 7$, computes $y_a \equiv 3^7 \pmod{17} = 11$, and sends the resulting value 11 to B. B, in turn, randomly selects $x_b = 4$, computes $y_b \equiv 3^4 \pmod{17} = 13$, and sends the resulting value 13 to A. A now computes $y_b^{x_a} \equiv 13^7 \pmod{17} = 4$, and B computes $y_a^{x_b} \equiv 11^4 \pmod{17} = 4$. Consequently, $K = 4$ is the shared secret that can be used as a session key.

- Let $p = 347$ and $g = 11$ (i.e., $g = 11$ generates $\mathbb{Z}_{347}^*$). A randomly selects $x_a = 240$, computes $y_a \equiv 11^{240} \pmod{347} = 49$, and sends the resulting value 49 to B. B, in turn, randomly selects $x_b = 39$, computes $y_b \equiv 11^{39} \pmod{347} = 285$, and sends the resulting value 285 to A. A now computes $y_b^{x_a} \equiv 285^{240} \pmod{347} = 268$, and B computes $y_a^{x_b} \equiv 49^{39} \pmod{347} = 268$. Consequently, $K = 268$ is the shared secret that can be used as a session key.

Note that an adversary eavesdropping on the communication channel between A and B knows p, g, y_a, and y_b, but does not know x_a and x_b. The problem of determining $K \equiv g^{x_a x_b} \pmod{p}$ from y_a and y_b (without knowing x_a or x_b) is known as the DHP (see Definition 7.6). As already explained in Section 7.2.1, the DHP is as difficult to solve as the DLP, but it is still an open question whether it is always (i.e., in every group) necessary to compute a discrete logarithm to solve an instance of the DHP.

Also note that the Diffie-Hellman key exchange protocol can be transformed into a (probabilistic) asymmetric encryption system. For a plaintext message m (that represents an element of the cyclic group), A randomly selects an x_a, computes the common key K_{ab} (using B's public exponent and following the Diffie-Hellman key exchange protocol), and combines m with K_{ab} to obtain the ciphertext c. The special case where $c = mK_{ab}$ refers to the ElGamal asymmetric encryption system addressed in Section 14.2.3.

Like any other protocol that employs public key cryptography, the Diffie-Hellman key exchange protocol is vulnerable to the *man-in-the-middle attack*. Note what happens if an adversary C is able to place himself or herself between A and B and provide both with messages of his or her choice. In this case, C can provide A and B with faked public exponents. More specifically, C can provide A with y_b' (of which he or she knows the private exponent x_b') and B with y_a' (of which he or she knows the private exponent x_a'). In this case, A computes $K_{ab'} \equiv y_b'^{x_a} \pmod{p}$ and thinks that he or she shares this key with B, and B computes $K_{b'a} \equiv y_a'^{x_b} \pmod{p}$ and thinks that he or she shares this key with A. In reality, they both don't share any key with each other, but they both share a key with C. If, for example, A wanted to send a secret message to B, A would use the key he or she thinks is being shared with B to encrypt the message, and send it to B accordingly. C would be sitting in the line and grab the message. Equipped with $K_{ab'}$, C would be able to decrypt the message, eventually modify it, reencrypt it with $K_{b'a}$, and forward it to B. B, in turn, would successfully decrypt the message using $K_{b'a}$ and think that the message is authentically coming from A. The only way to protect the communicating entities against this type of attack is to make sure that the public exponents are authentic. So, in practice, the native Diffie-Hellman key exchange protocol is usually combined with a mutual authentication protocol to come up with an authenticated key exchange protocol. Examples include the station-to-station (STS) protocol [8] and—more importantly—the IKE protocol mentioned earlier. In these protocols, the public exponents used in the Diffie-Hellman key exchange are authenticated using RSA signatures. Consequently, digital certificates and PKIs must be used to securely deploy authenticated key exchange protocols.

As mentioned earlier, the Diffie-Hellman key exchange protocol can be used in any group (other than $\mathbb{Z}_p^*$) in which the DLP is intractable. There are basically two reasons for using other groups.

Performance: There may be groups in which the Diffie-Hellman key exchange protocol (or the modular exponentiation function) can be implemented more efficiently in hardware or software.

Security: There may be groups in which the DLP is more difficult to solve.

The two reasons are not independent from each other. If, for example, one has a group in which the DLP is more difficult to solve, then one can work with much smaller keys (for a similar level of security). This is the major advantage of ECC as addressed in Section 7.6. The ECDLP is more difficult to solve (than the DLP in $\mathbb{Z}_p^*$), and hence one can work with smaller keys.

16.4 QUANTUM CRYPTOGRAPHY

In this section, we provide a brief overview about quantum cryptography. We introduce the basic principles and elaborate on the quantum key exchange protocol that may provide an alternative for the establishment of secret keys.

16.4.1 Basic Principles

In cryptography, it is usually taken for granted that a communication channel can be eavesdropped and that data transmitted on this channel can be attacked passively. In Section 10.4, we saw that unconditional security (in an information-theoretic sense) can only be achieved if the entropy of the secret key is greater than or equal to the entropy of the plaintext message (i.e., if the key is at least as long as the plaintext message). This is usually too expensive for all practical purposes, and hence essentially all practically relevant symmetric encryption systems are "only" computationally secure.

Against this background, it is sometimes argued that *quantum cryptography* yields an alternative way to provide unconditional security. In short, quantum cryptography uses the basic laws of quantum physics to make sure that eavesdropping cannot go undetected. Consequently, quantum cryptography takes its security from quantum physics (instead of information theory). More specifically, quantum cryptography makes use and takes advantage of the *Heisenberg uncertainty principle* of quantum physics to provide a secure quantum channel. Roughly speaking, the Heisenberg uncertainty principle states that certain pairs of physical properties are related in such a way that measuring one property prevents an adversary from simultaneously knowing the value of the other. In particular, when measuring the polarization of a photon, the choice of what direction to measure affects all measurements. For example, suppose you measure the polarization of a photon using a vertical filter. Classically, you would assume that if the photon passes through, it is vertically polarized, and therefore if you placed in front of the photon another filter with some angle t to the vertical, then the photon would not pass through. However, quantum mechanics states that, in fact, there is a certain probability that the photon passes through the second filter as well, and this probability depends on the angle t. As t increases, the probability of the photon passing through the second filter decreases until it reaches 0 at $t = 90$ deg (i.e., the second filter is horizontal). When $t = 45$ deg, the chance of the photon passing through the second filter is exactly $1/2$. In measuring the polarization of photons, we refer to a pair of orthogonal polarization states, such as 0 deg and 90 deg or 45 deg and 135 deg, as a (polarization) *basis*. A pair of bases is said to be *conjugate* if the measurement of the polarization in the first basis completely randomizes the measurement in the second basis (as in the previous example above with $t = 45$ deg). Consequently, the 0/90-deg and 45/135-deg bases are conjugate. Note that if someone else gives the photon an initial polarization (either horizontal or vertical, but you don't know which) and you use a filter in the 45/135-deg basis to measure the photon, you cannot determine any information about the initial polarization of the photon.

As further explained later, these principles can be used to establish a quantum channel that cannot be attacked passively without detection, meaning that the fact that someone is trying to eavesdrop on the channel can be detected by the communicating entities. In fact, the adversary cannot gain even partial information about the data being transmitted without altering it in a random and uncontrollable way that is likely to be detected. As such, the quantum channel can be used to transmit secret information or to agree on a secret key. It cannot be used, however, to implement digital signatures and to provide nonrepudiation services accordingly. Anyway, the quantum channel is provably secure even against an opponent with superior technology and unlimited computational power (and even if $\mathcal{P} = \mathcal{NP}$).

The field of quantum cryptography was pioneered by Stephen Wiesner in the early 1970s [9]. Wiesner had two applications in mind:

- Making money that is impossible to counterfeit;

- Multiplexing two or three messages in such a way that reading one destroys the other(s).

The first feasible quantum cryptosystems were designed in the early 1980s by Charles H. Bennett and Gilles Brassard [10]. The most important quantum cryptosystem is the quantum key exchange (see Section 16.4.2). Their first apparatus that implemented a quantum key exchange was capable of transmitting a secret key over a distance of approximately 30 cm. Note that a major disadvantage of quantum cryptography in practice is the fact that quantum transmissions are necessarily weak and cannot be amplified in transit (an amplifier is like an adversary from a quantum system's perspective). This severely limits the distance that can be overcome with a quantum channel. Since the early work of Bennett and Brassard, many researchers have turned towards quantum cryptography[2] and many improvements have been made. In 1993, for example, a 10 km quantum channel was built, and today it is possible to overcome a distances of 67 km.[3] Furthermore, many other quantum cryptographic protocols have been developed and proposed, such as quantum protocols for oblivious transfer and bit commitment (again, refer to the bibliography of quantum cryptography referenced in footnote 2).

16.4.2 Quantum Key Exchange Protocol

Let A be the sender and B the receiver on a quantum channel. A may send out photons in one of four polarizations: 0, 45, 90, or 135 deg (we use the symbols $\longrightarrow$, $\nearrow$, $\uparrow$, and $\nwarrow$ to refer to these polarizations). At the other end of the quantum channel, B is to measure the polarizations of the received photons. According to the laws of quantum mechanics, the receiving device can distinguish between rectilinear polarizations (i.e., 0 and 90 deg), or it can quickly be reconfigured to discriminate between diagonal polarizations (i.e., 45 and 135 deg); it cannot, however, distinguish both types of polarization simultaneously (this is because the rectilinear and diagonal polarizations' bases are conjugate, meaning that the measurement of the polarization in the first basis completely randomizes the measurement in the second basis).

In this setting, A and B can use the quantum key exchange protocol proposed by Bennett and Brassard to agree on a shared secret key. In a first step, A chooses a random bitstring and a random sequence of polarization bases (i.e., rectilinear or diagonal). A sends B a sequence of photons, each representing one bit of the bitstring in the polarization basis chosen for that bit position. For example, a horizontal or 45-deg photon can be used to represent a zero, whereas a vertical or 135-deg photon

---

2   Refer to http://www.cs.mcgill.ca/~crepeau/CRYPTO/Biblio-QC.html for a bibliography of quantum cryptography.

3   The company id Quantique SA (http://www.idquantique.com) is selling corresponding devices.

can be used to represent a one. Note at this point that an adversary who wants to measure the polarization of the photons sent from A to B does not know the bases in which they must be measured. If the measurement is made with the correct bases, the measurement yields a correct result. If, however, the measurement is made with the wrong bases, the measurement will randomly change the polarization of the measured photons (by the laws of quantum mechanics). Consequently, without knowing the polarization bases originally chosen by A, the adversary has only a negligible chance of correctly guessing them and correctly measuring the polarization of the photons accordingly. More likely, he or she is going to cause errors that can be detected in the aftermath. Also note at this point that B does not know either which bases to use for the measurements (from the quantum channel's perspective, there is no difference between B and an adversary). As B receives the photons, he or she decides, randomly for each photon and independently of A, whether to measure the photon's rectilinear or diagonal polarization. B then interprets each result as a zero or one, depending on the outcome of the measurement. Following this strategy, B obtains meaningful data from only about half the photons he or she detects (those for which he or she guesses the correct polarization base). Unfortunately, B does not know which ones are correctly measured and which ones are measured with the wrong polarization base. B's information is further degraded by the fact that, in practice, some of the photons will be lost in transit or would fail to be counted by B's imperfect detectors. In either case, B records the results of his or her measurements and keeps them secret.

Subsequent steps of the quantum key exchange protocol may take place over a public channel. Let us assume that this channel is only susceptible to passive attacks (e.g., eavesdropping), and that it is not susceptible to active attacks (e.g., injection, alteration, or deletion of messages). This basically means that we assume a public channel that is authentic. This assumption can be made obsolete by having A and B share a secret key that can be used for message origin authentication. In this case, the quantum key exchange protocol will still work as a method of "key expansion" rather than key generation.

A and B can now use the public channel to determine, by exchange of messages, which photons were successfully received and of these which were measured by B in the correct polarization base. B therefore publicly announces the type of measurements (but not the results), and A tells B which measurements were of the correct type. All of these announcements occur on the public channel. A and B keep all cases in which B's measurements were of the correct type. These cases are then translated into ones and zeros, representing the agreed secret key. If the quantum transmission has been undisturbed, A and B should now agree on the bits encoded by these photons, even though this fact has never been discussed over the public channel.

Last but not least, it remains to be seen how A and B can decide whether their resulting bitstrings are identical (indicating with high probability that no eavesdropping has occured on the quantum channel) or different (indicating that the quantum channel has been subject to eavesdropping). A simple and straightforward solution is for A and B to publicly compare some of the bits on which they think they should agree. The position of these bits must be chosen randomly after the quantum transmission has been completed. Obviously, this process sacrifices the secrecy of these bits. Because the bit positions used in this comparison are only a random subset of the correctly received bits, eavesdropping on more than a few photons is likely to be detected. If all comparisons agree, A and B can conclude that the quantum channel has been free of significant eavesdropping. Therefore, most of the remaining bits can safely be used as a one-time pad for subsequent communication over the public channel. When this one-time pad is used up, the protocol can be repeated arbitrarily often.

Table 16.1 illustrates an exemplary execution of the quantum key exchange protocol. Lines 1 and 2 illustrate the bits and the polarization bases that are randomly chosen by A (+ refers to a rectilinear basis and x refers to a diagonal basis). Line 3 illustrates the polarization of the photons that are actually sent from A to B. Again, the polarization can be 0 (i.e., $\longrightarrow$), 45 (i.e., $\nearrow$), 90 (i.e., $\uparrow$), or 135 (i.e., $\diagdown$) deg. If A has chosen a rectilinear basis, a zero is encoded as $\longrightarrow$ and a one is encoded as $\uparrow$. If, however, A has chosen a diagonal basis, a zero is encoded as $\nearrow$ and a one is encoded as $\diagdown$. The photons as polarized in line 3 are sent from A to B and are expected to reach B. Line 4 illustrates the polarization bases that are randomly chosen by B, and line 5 illustrates the binary values that are measured and decoded by B. Note that not all of these values must be correct (only the ones that are measured with the correct polarization basis). In line 5, the values that are not necessarily correct are written in italics. Also, B may miss the reception of specific photons. In line 5, for example, B has missed measuring the polarization of the second photon. Anyway, the bitstring that is received by B is 010000110, and A and B must now find out which bits they can use. In line 6, B publicly announces the bases in which he or she measured the received photons, and in line 7 A says which bases were correctly guessed by B. In the example, five bases were correctly guessed by B. This information is presumably shared. Line 8 illustrates the corresponding bitstring (i.e., 01001). In line 9, B reveals some bits chosen at random, and in line 10, A confirms these bits (if they are correct). In line 11, the remaining bits are illustrated; they may now serve as shared secret bits.

The eavesdropping-detection subprotocol as described earlier is rather wasteful because a significant proportion of the bits (2/5 in the example given here) are sacrificed to obtain a good probability that eavesdropping is detected even if attempted on only a few photons. Moreover, the probability that the resulting strings

Table 16.1
An Exemplary Execution of the Quantum Key Exchange Protocol

1)	0	0	1	0	1	1	0	1	1	0
2)	+	x	x	+	x	+	+	x	x	+
3)	→	↗	↘	→	↘	↑	→	↘	↘	→
4)	+	+	x	+	+	x	+	+	x	x
5)	0		1	0	0	0	0	*1*	1	0
6)	+		x	+	+	x	+	+	x	x
7)	OK		OK	OK			OK		OK	
8)	0		1	0			0		1	
9)			1				0			
10)			OK				OK			
11)	0			0					1	

of A and B agree completely cannot be made arbitrarily close to one, unless most of the bits are sacrificed. Both of these difficulties can be resolved by a protocol that is commonly referred to serve the need of privacy amplification. This topic is not further addressed (it is beyond the scope of this book).

Last but not least, we note that the quantum key exchange protocol as discussed so far is also subject to the man-in-the-middle attack. An adversary can claim to be B and use the quantum key exchange protocol to establish a key with A. Thus, there must be out-of-band authentication mechanisms that A can use to properly authenticate B.

16.5 FINAL REMARKS

In this chapter, we elaborated on some cryptographic protocols that two entities can execute to establish a secret key. Among these protocols, key agreement protocols are particularly useful, because they allow both entities to participate in the generation of the secret key. If this is not the case (such as in the case of a key distribution protocol), then the quality of the secret key is bound by the quality of the entity that actually generates the key. If this entity employs a cryptographically weak PRBG, then the resulting secret keys may be weak. This happened, for example, when the first implementations of the SSL protocol were found vulnerable because the Netscape browser implemented such a cryptographically weak PRBG (see Section 9.2 and the reference given therein). Contrary to that, all PRBGs of all entities involved in a key agreement must be cryptographically weak, so that the resulting secret key is weak.

The Diffie-Hellman key exchange protocol is omnipresent in security applications. Whenever two entities must establish a secret key, the Diffie-Hellman key exchange protocol can be used and provides an elegant solution. In the future, it is possible and likely that alternative key agreement protocols are developed and deployed. This is particularly true if more than two entities are involved.

In the second part of the chapter, we introduced the basic principles of quantum cryptography and elaborated on the quantum key exchange protocol. This protocol is interesting, because it is unconditionally secure and does not depend on a computational intractability assumption. Instead, it depends on the laws of quantum physics. As such, the security of the quantum key exchange protocol is independent from any progress that is made in solving mathematical problems (e.g., the IFP or the DLP). Quantum cryptography is currently not practical for actual applications. It may, however, be used in the future, especially because public key cryptography and corresponding cryptosystems may be attacked by quantum computers (see Section 6.5). In fact, this is the principle benefit of quantum cryptography. In either case, quantum cryptography is a timely and very active area of research and development (see, for example, [11]).

References

[1] Boyd, C., and A. Mathuria, *Protocols for Key Establishment and Authentication.* Springer-Verlag, New York, 2003.

[2] Hardjono, T., and L.R. Dondeti, *Multicast and Group Security.* Artech House Publishers, Norwood, MA, 2003.

[3] Oppliger, R., *Authentication Systems for Secure Networks.* Artech House Publishers, Norwood, MA, 1996.

[4] Merkle, R., "Secure Communication over Insecure Channels," *Communications of the ACM,* 21(4), April 1978, pp. 294–299.

[5] Oppliger, R., *Security Technologies for the World Wide Web,* 2nd edition. Artech House Publishers, Norwood, MA, 2003.

[6] Frankel, S., *Demystifying the IPsec Puzzle.* Artech House Publishers, Norwoord, MA, 2001.

[7] Diffie, W., and M.E. Hellman, "New Directions in Cryptography," *IEEE Transactions on Information Theory,* IT-22(6), 1976, pp. 644–654.

[8] Diffie, W., P. van Oorshot, and M.J. Wiener, "Authentication and Authenticated Key Exchanges," *Designs, Codes and Cryptography,* Vol. 2, No. 2, 1992, pp. 107–125.

[9] Wiesner, S., "Conjugate Coding," *SIGACT News,* Vol. 15, No. 1, 1983, pp. 78–88, original manuscript written in 1970.

[10] Bennett, C.H., and G. Brassard, "Quantum Cryptography: Public Key Distribution and Coin Tossing," *Proceedings of the International Conference on Computers, Systems and Signal Processing*, Bangalore, India, 1984, pp. 175–179.

[11] Bouwmeester, D., A. Ekert, and A. Zeilinger, *The Physics of Quantum Information: Quantum Cryptography, Quantum Teleportation, Quantum Computation.* Springer-Verlag, New York, 2000.

Chapter 17

Entity Authentication

In this chapter, we elaborate on entity authentication in general, and (cryptographic) authentication protocols that implement a proof by knowledge in particular. More specifically, we introduce the topic in Section 17.1, overview and discuss authentication technologies in Section 17.2, elaborate on zero-knowledge authentication protocols in Section 17.3, and conclude with some final remarks in Section 17.4.

17.1 INTRODUCTION

Generally speaking, an entity identifies itself if it claims to have a specific identity, and it authenticates itself if it proves in one way or another that the claimed identity really belongs to it. Consequently, *identification* refers to the process by which an entity—let's call it the *claimant* or *prover*—claims to have a specific identity, whereas *entity authentication* refers to the process by which the claimant proves to another entity—let's call it the *verifier*—that the claimed identity really belongs to it. At the end, the verifier is assured of the claimed identity of the prover. Note that in some literature, the terms identification and entity authentication are used synonymously and interchangeably. In this book, however, we make a clear distinction between the two terms (and the corresponding processes). Anybody can identify himself or herself as anybody (and claim to have a particular identity). Contrary to that, it may not be feasible to authenticate as anybody else (if the authentication mechanisms are strong enough).

Entity authentication can be *unilateral* (if only one entity authenticates itself to another) or *mutual* (if the entities authenticate to each other). In either case, the verifier must know an authentic reference parameter (e.g., a shared secret key, a public key certificate, or some biometric information) relative to which the entity authentication is performed.

Many entity authentication protocols can also be used to establish a secret key to be shared between the claimant and the verifier, and this key can then serve as a session key. The resulting protocols are called *authentication and key distribution protocols* or *authenticated key distribution protocols*. These protocols are very important in practice. A comprehensive overview and analysis of authentication and key distribution protocols is beyond the scope of this book. You may refer to [1].

The major security objective of an entity authentication protocol is to make it impossible (or at least computationally infeasible) for an adversary to impersonate a claimant, even if he or she has witnessed or has been involved in a large number of protocol executions with both the claimant and the verifier. An impersonation attack must always take place online, but it may be possible to prepare some parts of it offline. Consequently, it is common to distinguish between offline and online attacks.

- In an *offline attack*, the adversary must not directly communicate with the verifier to prepare the attack. Instead, he or she can analyze information acquired from previous protocol executions and retrieve information that he or she can (mis)use to impersonate the claimant at some later point in time.

- In an *online attack*, the adversary must directly communicate with the verifier to prepare the attack. Consequently, every preparation step for the attack must be carried out with the verifier.

Obviously, offline attacks are much more powerful and hence are much more difficult to protect against (than online attacks). In fact, it is possible to protect against online attacks by limiting and setting an upper bound for the number of attempts an entity can try to authenticate itself, introducing a time delay between the individual attempts, or, if the attacker must be physically present to mount the attack, by threatening to apply some physical measures (e.g., exit locks). In the following section, we look at some technologies that can be used for entity authentication. More information is available, for example, in [2].

17.2 AUTHENTICATION TECHNOLOGIES

It is common to divide the technologies that can be used for (entity) authentication into four categories, depending on whether it is based on:

- Something the claimant possesses (proof by possession);

- Something the claimant knows (proof by knowledge);

- Some biometric characteristics of the claimant (proof by property);

- Somewhere the claimant is located (proof by location).

The last category of authentication technologies is nonstandard. It is, however, assumed that the use of information about the current location of a communicating entity will become more and more important in the future, and it is therefore considered as a category of its own for the purpose of this book.

Some exemplary authentication techniques are overviewed and briefly discussed next. Note that the techniques are not mutually exclusive, and that they complement each other quite nicely. So, in practice, two or more techniques (of different categories) are usually combined in some way or another.

17.2.1 Proof by Possession

In a *proof by possession*, the claimant proves to the verifier his or her identity by showing possession of a physical token. On the verifier side, the proof can be verified manually or automatically. In the second case, a corresponding detecting device (hardware or software) is required. Examples of physical tokens include:

- Physical keys;
- Identification cards;
- Magnetic stripe cards;
- Smart cards;
- Universal serial bus (USB) tokens.

Physical keys have been in use for many centuries (in varying forms). Contrary to this, all other examples itemized above are relatively new. For example, the use of smart cards to store and make use of cryptographic keys has evolved in the last two decades (e.g., [3]). USB tokens are even more recent possibilities to store and make use of cryptographic keys.

The major advantage of a proof by possession is that it is relatively simple and straightforward to use by human beings, whereas the major disadvantage is related to the difficult production, distribution, and management of the physical tokens and the corresponding detecting devices (if the proofs must be verified automatically). As a result of this disadvantage, large-scale deployment is often prohibitively complex and expensive.

17.2.2   Proof by Knowledge

In a *proof by knowledge*, the claimant proves to the verifier his or her identity by showing knowledge of some secret information, such as a password, a personal identification number (PIN), or a cryptographic key. This information, in turn, may either be static or dynamically changing. Roughly speaking, static information can be used to implement weak authentication, whereas dynamically changing information can be used to implement strong authentication. Note that in either case, the secret information may be too large or include too much entropy to be memorized by human users. Consequently, the use of some auxiliary technology to store and make available the secret information is widely deployed. Examples include magnetic-stripe cards, smart cards, USB tokens, and personal digital assistants (PDAs) that store secret information (in possibly encrypted form). Note, however, that in contrast to the use of these technologies in a proof by possession, these technologies are only used to extend the capacities of the human users (or their memories) in a proof by knowledge. The existence of the physical device by itself need not be verified.

It is possible and makes a lot of sense to combine a proof by possession with a proof by knowledge. For example, if we want to withdraw money from an automatic teller machine (ATM), then we routinely insert our ATM card and enter a PIN into the terminal associated with the ATM. In this case, the insertion of the ATM card represents a proof by possession, whereas the fact that the user enters his or her PIN represents a proof by knowledge. An adversary who wants to illegitimately withdraw money from an ATM must have both the ATM card and the user's PIN.

17.2.2.1   Static Information

As mentiond earlier, examples of static information that may be used in a proof by knowledge include passwords, passphrases, PINs, and cryptographic keys. As of this writing, passwords are by far the most widely deployed authentication technology used in computer networks and distributed systems. This is because they are simple to implement and use. Unfortunately, however, passwords and the way they are managed have the following two major security problems:

1. Users tend to select passwords that are easy to remember. Consequently, such passwords are not uniformly distributed and are often simple to guess [4, 5]. Password guessing is the process of correctly guessing the password of a legitimate user. Dan Klein analyzed the feasibility of password-guessing attacks for approximately 15,000 user accounts in 1990. As a result, he found that he could guess 2.7% of the passwords in the first 15 minutes and 21%

within the first week [6]. It is assumed that these numbers have not changed much since their publication. To make things worse, there are many tools available on the Internet that can be used to automate password guessing (e.g., L0phtCrack or @stake LC 5).[1]

2. The transmission of passwords (which may be well chosen or not) is exposed to passive eavesdropping and subsequent replay attacks. This is because the passwords are often transmitted in the clear. Also, if passwords are not transmitted in the clear but "encrypted" using a well-known one-way function, it is still possible to launch a password-guessing attack by simply "encrypting" password candidates with the one-way function and checking whether the result matches the string that has been transmitted in the first place. So if passwords are encrypted for transmission, then it must be made sure that a password is encrypted differently each time it is encrypted and transmitted. This is, for example, usually the case if a cryptographic security protocol, such as the SSL/TLS protocol, is used.

Obviously, these security problems do not only apply to passwords and are equally true for any other static information that may be employed in a proof by knowledge (e.g., PINs or passphrases). Consequently, the use of static information in a proof by knowledge is not recommended for contemporary computer networks and distributed systems. In fact, the information is too easy to intercept and reuse. While this vulnerability has been known for a very long time, it was not until 1994 that it was demonstrated on a large scale with the discovery of planted password collecting routines at some critical points on the Internet.[2] To improve the level of security of a proof by knowledge, one must use information that is dynamically changing over time.

17.2.2.2 Dynamically Changing Information

The basic idea of using dynamically changing information in a proof by knowledge is that each authentication process requires a unique piece of (authentication) information and that this piece of information cannot be (mis)used at some later point in time. Consequently, if an attacker is able to eavesdrop on an authentication protocol execution and grab the relevant authentication information, he or she will not be able to (mis)use this information in a replay attack (i.e., the information will not be valid a second time).

The use of dynamically changing information is not new. In fact, we have been using transaction authentication numbers (TANs) for quite a long time. In

---

1 http://www.atstake.com/products/lc.
2 CERT Advisory CA-94:01, "Ongoing Network Monitoring Attacks," 1994.

short, a TAN is a piece of authentication information that can be used for one single authentication process or transaction. It is randomly chosen by the verifier and provided to the claimant using some secure channel (i.e., a trusted courier). The use of TANs is simple and straightforward, and as such there are many applications for them. For example, banks have been using TANs (together with passwords) to authenticate users and account owners for years. Similarly, many e-government applications can provide client authentication using TANs (e.g., code voting for remote Internet voting [7]). If the number of authentication processes or transactions increases beyond a certain threshold, the generation, distribution, and management of TANs becomes difficult (i.e., the use of TANs does not scale well). In this case, it is generally a good idea to use cryptographic techniques to come up with authentication schemes that make use of secure channels or dynamically changing information [8]. For example, on the Internet it is common practice today to use the SSL/TLS protocol [9, 10] to securely transmit a password from a claimant (typically a browser) to a verifier (typically a Web server). There are some theoretical attacks against passwords transmitted over SSL/TLS channels if specific symmetric encryption systems are used in specific modes of operation (e.g., [11, 12]), but for all practical puposes passwords transmitted over SSL/TLS channels can be made sufficiently secure.

One-Time Password Schemes

As its name suggests, a one-time password is a password that can be used only once, meaning that it can be used for only one single authentication process. As such, a one-time password is conceptually similar to a TAN. The major difference is that TANs are generated randomly by the verifier and distributed to the claimant using some secure channel, whereas one-time passwords are typically generated dynamically and deterministically on either side (i.e., by the claimant and verifier). As such, a one-time password scheme is an authentication scheme that uses one-time passwords. There are many one-time password schemes and corresponding systems available today.

- SecurID tokens marketed by RSA Security, Inc., are the most important and most widely deployed one-time password systems in use today. The design and algorithms of the SecurID tokens are not published. It is known, however, that every SecurID token contains a cryptographic processor that implements a symmetric encryption system, a secret key, a local clock that is synchronized with the verifier (i.e., an ACE/server), and a small display. The one-time passwords are generated by the token reading out the time from the local clock and encrypting the corresponding value with the secret key. At each time interval (e.g., each minute), the SecurID token generates a new one-time password and displays it. If the holder of the SecurID token (i.e., the user) wants to authenticate himself or herself, he or she reads from the token's display the currently valid one-time password and types it in at the login prompt (typically together with a static password). Due to the proprietary nature, there are only a few security analyses related to the SecurID tokens and the cryptographic algorithms they implement (e.g., [13]).

- An alternative one-time password scheme that does not require the implementation of a cryptosystem was originally proposed by Leslie Lamport in the early 1980s [14]. In this scheme, the claimant (i.e., the user) begins with a secret password pw. A one-way function h is then used to generate a sequence of t one-time passwords:

$$pw, h(pw), h(h(pw)), \ldots, h^t(pw)$$

This sequence is then used by the claimant in the reverse order, meaning that $h^t(pw)$ is used first and that $h^{t-1}(pw)$, $h^{t-2}(pw)$, ... , $h(h(pw))$, and $h(pw)$ are then used afterwards. In fact, the (one-time) password for the ith authentication process (for $1 \leq i \leq t$) is $h^{t-i}(pw)$. This password is used by the claimant to authenticate himself or herself to the verifier. Lamport's one-time password scheme was implemented at Bell Communications Research (Bellcore) in a one-time password system called S/Key [15]. S/Key employed the one-time function MD4. More recently, the use of MD4 was replaced with MD5 in a similar system called one-time passwords in everything (OPIE) developed at the U.S. Naval Research Laboratory (NRL). S/Key and OPIE both conform to the one-time password system specified in [16].

In addition to SecurID tokens, S/Key, and OPIE, many other one-time password systems are commercially or freely available on the Internet. Many of them are proprietary, and hence they are not addressed in this book.

Challenge-Response Mechanisms

One-time password schemes and corresponding systems are simple and straightforward. The major advantage is that they do not require an interaction between the claimant and the verifier. The claimant simply provides a piece of authentication information to the verifier, and the verifier can verify the validity of it (without interacting with the claimant). The major disadvantage, however, is that the claimant and verifier must be synchronized in some way or another.

Like one-time password schemes, challenge-response mechanisms are authentication schemes that make use of dynamically changing information. Unlike one-time password schemes, however, challenge-response mechanisms require the claimant and verifier to interact but generally do not require them to be synchronized. In a challenge-response mechanism, the verifier provides the claimant with a *challenge* (e.g., a randomly chosen number that is sometimes also called a nonce), and the claimant must compute and provide a valid *response*. This can be repeated multiple times (if necessary). In either case, there must be some cryptographic key material on either side of the protocol execution (i.e., to compute and verify the claimant's response).

For example, a DSS can be used to implement a simple challenge-response mechanism. If the claimant holds a private key and the verifier holds the corresponding public key (or public key certificate), then the verifier can challenge the claimant with a randomly chosen number and the claimant can respond with the digital signature for that number. Because the verifier holds the public key (certificate), he or she can easily verify the validity of the claimant's response. Note, however, that this exemplary challenge-response mechanism is far too simple to be used for real applications. It would be too dangerous for a claimant to digitally sign arbitrary values that claim to be legitimate challenges. What would happen, for example, if the claimant were challenged with a cryptographic hash value computed from the message string "I owe you $1,000"? In this case, the claimant would respond with the digital signature for a message he or she would not have signed in the first place. Consequently, the design and analysis of challenge-response mechanisms are tricky and must be considered with care.

There is a special class of challenge-response mechanisms and authentication protocols that have a property called zero knowledge. Using such a protocol, a claimant can prove knowledge of a secret (e.g., a cryptographic key) while revealing no information whatsover about the secret [17]. It is possible and very likely that zero-knowledge authentication protocols will become important and more widely deployed in the future. They are further addressed in Section 17.3.

17.2.3 Proof by Property

In a *proof by property*, the claimant proves his or her identity by proving some biometric characteristics. The biometric characteristics, in turn, are measured and compared with a reference pattern by the verifier. Historically, the first biometric characteristics that were used for authentication were fingerprints. Today, it is possible to use other characteristics, such as facial images, retinal images, and voice patterns (e.g., [18, 19]). In the recent past, biometric authentication technologies have been well received on the security market. In either case, they are appropriate to authenticate local users; they are less appropriate to authenticate remote users for at least three reasons:

- First and foremost, all terminals and end systems must be equipped with devices that are able to read biometric characteristics from users.

- Second, all communication lines between the readers and the verifier must be made secure (i.e., physically or cryptographically protected).

- Third, the use of biometric characteristics requires some form of liveness testing, and this type of testing is usually difficult and expensive.

In either case, biometric authentication is a high-end technology (that is difficult and expensive if done properly). Also, there are some privacy concerns related to the widespread use of biometric authentication technologies and techniques.

17.2.4 Proof by Location

In a *proof by location*, the claimant proves his or her identity by proving his or her current location. If, for example, an entity is assumed to be local but is physically located somewhere remote, then something is likely to be wrong. There are various possibilities to implement a proof by location.

- For example, a dial-back system implements a proof by location, because the claimant is called back by the verifier using some predefined number (i.e., a number that is bound to a specific network access point).

- An address-based authentication scheme also implements a proof by location (if one considers the fact that a network address specifies a network access point, and that this network access point is geographically located somewhere). Address-based authentication is, for example, implemented by the Berkeley r-tools (i.e., `rlogin`, `rsh`, and `rcp`). It is also implemented by systems that match the source address of incoming IP packets with huge databases (of ISPs and corresponding IP address ranges) to decide whether the packets are legitimate or not.

- In a more sophisticated location-based authentication scheme, the verifier can also check the information provided by the global positioning system (GPS) on the claimant's side.

Dial-back systems and simple address-based authentication schemes are in widespread use today. More sophisticated address-based authentication schemes and GPS-based authentication schemes are not (yet) widely deployed. It is, however, possible and very likely that such schemes will become important in the future (to complement other authentication technologies and mechanisms). More recently, for example, people have started to think about the possibility to use and take advantage of the information that is available in cellular phone networks to complement user authentication. Needless to say that there are some nontrivial privacy concerns that must be addressed before such a technology may become feasible.

17.3 ZERO-KNOWLEDGE AUTHENTICATION PROTOCOLS

Most entity authentication protocols in use today implement a proof by knowledge, but leak some (partial) information about the secret information known and used by the claimant. If, for example, a DSS is used to digitally sign randomly chosen challenges, then the corresponding authentication protocol leaks digital signatures for the values that serve as challenges. Whether this poses a problem depends on the application context. If, for example, the claimant uses the same signing key to digitally sign challenges and electronic documents, then the verifier can challenge the claimant with the hash value of a document he or she wants the claimant to sign. The claimant then thinks to digitally sign a challenge, whereas in reality he or she digitally signs the document.[3]

If one wants to make sure that an authentication protocol does not leak any information, then one must consider the use of *zero-knowledge proofs* and corresponding *zero-knowledge authentication protocols*. This field of study was pioneered by Shafi Goldwasser, Silvio Micali, and Charles Rackoff in the 1980s [20]. After the discovery of public key cryptography in the 1970s, the development of zero-knowledge proofs and zero-knowledge authentication protocols was the next fundamental step in modern cryptography. Loosely speaking, a zero-knowledge proof is a proof that yields nothing but the validity of the assertion. That is, a verifier obtaining such a proof only gains conviction in the validity of the assertion. This can be formulated by saying that anything that is feasibly computable from a zero-knowledge proof is also feasibly computable from the valid assertion alone. This formulation automatically leads to the simulation paradigm discussed later. Let's begin with some preliminary remarks about proofs and proof systems.

17.3.1 Preliminary Remarks

Formally speaking, a statement is a finite sequence of symbols (i.e., a string) taken from a finite alphabet. There are syntactic rules that specify how statements can be formed, and there are semantic rules that specify whether a given statement is true.

---

3   Obviously, this problem can be addressed by using separate public key pairs for authentication and digital signatures. Sometimes, it is even recommended to use a third public key pair for encryption.

If a statement is true (false), then there may be a *proof* that further explains why (i.e., according to which semantic rules) the statement is true (false). If such a proof exists, then it can typically also be represented and expressed as a string.

A conventional (i.e., noninteractive) *proof system* is a system in which statements and proofs can be expressed and efficiently verified. This means that part of the system is an efficient (proof verification) algorithm that takes as input a statement and a proof and that generates as output a binary decision (i.e., the statement is true or false). If the output is true, then the proof is valid for the statement. If, however, the output is false, then the proof is not valid for the statement. In addition to the efficiency requirement for the proof verification algorithm, one usually requires that a particular proof system is also complete and sound.

Completeness: A proof system is *complete* if for every valid proof the proof verification algorithm outputs true (i.e., the proof is accepted).

Soundness: A proof system is *sound* if for every invalid proof the proof verification algorithm outputs false (i.e., the proof is rejected).

We mention but do not further address the results of Kurt Gödel,[4] who showed in the early 1930s that there are theories for which there is no proof system that is complete and consistent, meaning that there are theories in which some statements may not have a proof [21].

Contrary to a conventional proof, an *interactive proof* is a(n interactive) protocol that can be used by a prover to prove a statement to a verifier. Formally speaking, the prover and the verifier are probabilistic algorithms or probabilistic Turing machines. The verifier is assumed to be polynomially bound, whereas one usually doesn't make such an assumption on the prover's side. Needless to say, an interactive proof that is efficient for the prover is practically more useful than an interactive proof that is inefficient. If the soundness requirement assumes a polynomially bound prover (in addition to the polynomially bound verifier), then the protocol is called an *interactive argument* (instead of an interactive proof). In either case, the prover and the verifier must exchange messages during the execution of the protocol, and at the end the verifier must decide whether the proof is valid (i.e., accepted) or not (i.e., rejected).

Again, we require that an interactive proof and a corresponding *interactive proof system* is complete and sound. Because we are now in a probabilistic world, we must say that the interactive proof system is complete if the verifier accepts every true statement with an overwhelmingly large probability, and that the interactive proof system is sound if the verifier rejects every false statement (i.e., if the verifier accepts a false statement only with a probability that is negligibly small).

4   Kurt Gödel was a German mathematician who lived from 1906 to 1978.

The soundness requirement, in turn, must hold for every possible prover strategy. Consequently, an interactive proof system should allow a prover to convince a verifier of the validity of a true statement (completeness requirement), whereas no prover strategy should be able to fool the verifier to accept a false statement (soundness requirement).

It is obvious that interactive proofs are usually more powerful than conventional ones (i.e., they sometimes allow the proof of statements that cannot be proven conventionally). More specifically, it has been shown that when both randomization and interaction are allowed, then the proofs that can be verified in polynomial time are exactly those that can be generated with polynomial space [22].

Remember from Section 12.2 that two probability ensembles are poly-time indistinguishable if no PPT algorithm (acting as a polynomial-time statistical test or distinguisher) can tell them apart. Having this notion of computational indistinguishability in mind, one can say that an interactive proof between prover P and a verifier V is *computationally zero knowledge* if for every PPT algorithm V', representing a dishonest verifier, there exists an efficient program S, called the *simulator*, whose output T' is computationally indistinguishable from the communication T taking place between P and V' in a real protocol execution.

Zero knowledge implies the highest possible security for the prover P. Anything a verifier can compute after performing the protocol with P, he or she can also compute by himself or herself, in a way that is identical or at least statistically indistinguishable from what would happen if the actual protocol has been performed. More importantly, anybody can simulate transcripts of protocol executions that are statistically indistinguishable from a real execution of the protocol. We overview and discuss three exemplary zero-knowledge authentication protocols next.

17.3.2 Fiat-Shamir

Soon after Goldwasser, Micali, and Rackoff had introduced the notion of a zero-knowledge proof, Amos Fiat and Adi Shamir[5] found a way to implement a zero-knowledge protocol for authentication and/or digital signature generation and verification [23]. The Fiat-Shamir authentication protocol takes its security from the fact that computing square roots and factoring a modulus are computationally equivalent—that is, a square root modulo n can be efficiently computed if and only if the factorization of n is known (see Section 3.3.7).[6]

Similar to the RSA public key cryptosystem, let p and q be two primes and n be their product (i.e., $n = pq$). Let the prover hold a private key $x \in \mathbb{Z}_n^*$ and a corresponding public key $y_A \equiv x_A^2 \pmod{n}$. The Fiat-Shamir authentication

---

5   Adi Shamir is a co-inventor of the RSA public key cryptosystem.
6   The Rabin asymmetric encryption system is based on the same principle.

protocol then works in rounds, where each round can be formally expressed as illustrated in Protocol 17.1. In this setting, A is the prover and B is the verifier.

Protocol 17.1 A round in the Fiat-Shamir authentication protocol.

$$
\begin{array}{ll}
\text{A} & \text{B} \\
\hline
(n, x) & (n, y) \\
\hline
r \in_R \mathbb{Z}_n^* & \\
t = r^2 \ (\text{mod } n) \quad \xrightarrow{\ t\ } & \\
\quad \xleftarrow{\ c\ } & c \in_R \{0, 1\} \\
s \equiv rx^c \ (\text{mod } n) \quad \xrightarrow{\ s\ } & \\
& s^2 \stackrel{?}{\equiv} ty^c \ (\text{mod } n) \\
\hline
& (accept \text{ or } reject)
\end{array}
$$

In every round, A randomly selects $r \in_R \mathbb{Z}_n^*$ and computes $t = r^2 \ (\text{mod } n)$. This value is sent to B. B, in turn, randomly selects a bit $c \in_R \{0, 1\}$ and uses it to challenge A. If $c = 0$, then A must respond with $s = r$ and B must verify that $s^2 \equiv t \ (\text{mod } n)$. If, however, $c = 1$, then A must respond with $s = rx \ (\text{mod } n)$ and B must verify that $s^2 \equiv ty \ (\text{mod } n)$. In either case, the authentication is accepted or rejected (depending on the outcome of the corresponding verification step). The protocol is complete, because

$$
s^2 \equiv r^2(x^c)^2 \equiv t(x^2)^c \equiv ty^c \ (\text{mod } n).
$$

To show that it is also sound, one must look at the adversary and ask what he or she can do in every single round. Obviously, the adversary can randomly select a $t \in_R \mathbb{Z}_n^*$, wait for B to provide a challenge $c \in_R \{0, 1\}$, and guess an appropriate value for s. Fortunately (from A's viewpoint), the success probability of this attack is negligibly small (for any reasonably sized n). There are, however, also more subtle attacks one may think of. If, for example, an adversary were able to properly predict the challenge c, then he or she could prepare himself or herself to provide the correct response.

- If $c = 0$, then the protocol can be executed as normal (i.e., he or she can randomly select r and send $t = r^2 \ (\text{mod } n)$ and $s = r$ to the verifier);

- If $c = 1$, then the adversary can randomly select $s \in_R \mathbb{Z}_n^*$ and compute $t = s^2/y \ (\text{mod } n)$. These values are then sent to the verifier in the appropriate protocol steps.

In either case, it is not possible for the adversary to prepare himself or herself for both cases (otherwise, he or she could extract the private key x). If, for example, the adversary were able to prepare s_0 for $c = 0$ (i.e., $s_0 = r$) and s_1 for $c = 1$ (i.e., $s_1 = rx$), then he or she could easily compute $x = s_1/s_0$.

Consequently, the attacker has a probability of $1/2$ to cheat in every protocol round. This suggests that the protocol must be executed in multiple rounds (until an acceptable cheating probability is reached). If, for example, the protocol is repeated k times (where k is a security parameter), then the cheating probability is $1/2^k$.

The Fiat-Shamir authentication protocol has the zero-knowledge property, because it is possible to efficiently simulate the protocol execution transcripts and to compute t, c, and s (with the same probability distributions) without interacting with the prover. Furthermore, there are several variations of the basic Fiat-Shamir authentication protocol:

- The k rounds can be performed in parallel to reduce the number of rounds. In this case, the values t, c, and s are replaced with vectors of k values each. This variation was actually the one proposed by Fiat and Shamir in their original paper [23]. It is not zero knowledge, because the simulation cannot be done efficiently.

- Another parallel version is for A to have z different private keys $x_1, \ldots, x_z$ (and hence public keys $y_1, \ldots, y_z$) [24]. As before, the first message is $t = r^2 \pmod{n}$, but now the challenge consists of z bits $c_1, \ldots, c_z$ and the prover must respond with $s = r \sum_{i=1}^{z} x_i^{c_i} \pmod{n}$. In this case, the cheating probability is at most 2^{-z}.

Other variations are described and discussed in the literature. For example, the basic Fiat-Shamir authentication protocol can be generalized in a way that e^{th} powers (where e is a prime) are used (instead of squares), and the challenge c is a value between 0 and $e - 1$ (instead of 0 or 1). The resulting protocol is due to Louis C. Guillou and Jean-Jacques Quisquater [25]. Similar to RSA, it is assumed that extracting e^{th} roots requires factoring a large integer, and hence it is assumed to be computationally infeasible.

17.3.3 Guillou-Quisquater

Similar to the Fiat-Shamir authentication protocol, the Guillou-Quisquater authentication protocol works in rounds. A round is illustrated in Protocol 17.2. Again, A is the prover and B is the verifier.

In every round, A proves that he or she knows the private key x that refers to the public key $y \equiv x^e \pmod{n}$. A randomly selects an $r \in_R \mathbb{Z}_n^*$ and computes

Protocol 17.2 A round in the Guillou-Quisquater authentication protocol.

A	B
(n, x)	(n, y)

$$r \in_R \mathbb{Z}_n^*$$

$t = r^e \pmod{n} \quad \xrightarrow{t}$

$\xleftarrow{c} \quad c \in_R \{0, \dots, e-1\}$

$s \equiv rx^c \pmod{n} \quad \xrightarrow{s}$

$$s^e \stackrel{?}{\equiv} ty^c \pmod{n}$$

(*accept* or *reject*)

$t = r^e \pmod{n}$. This value is sent to B. B, in turn, randomly selects a number between 0 and $e - 1$ and challenges A with it. A computes $s \equiv rx^c \pmod{n}$ and sends s to B. B must now verify that $s^e \equiv ty^c \pmod{n}$. Based on this verification, he or she either accepts or rejects the proof of knowledge.

The protocol is complete, because

$$s^e \equiv (rx^c)^e \equiv r^e(x^e)^c \equiv ty^c \pmod{n}.$$

The protocol is sound, because an attacker can either guess s or prepare himself or herself for one challenge c (before he or she sends out commitment t). In the first case, the success probability (i.e., the probability to correctly guess s) is negligible for any reasonably sized n. In the second case, the attacker guesses c, randomly selects s, computes $t \equiv s^e y^{-c} \pmod{n}$, and uses this value as commitment. If B really used c as a challenge, then the attacker could respond with s. B, in turn, could compute $ty^c \equiv s^e y^{-c} y^c \equiv s^e \pmod{n}$ and accept the proof. Of course, if the guess was wrong and B provides a different challenge, then the attacker can only guess s.

One may wonder whether an attacker can prepare himself or herself for different challenges to improve his or her odds. Let us assume that an attacker can prepare himself or herself for two challenges c_1 and c_2 and sends a corresponding t to B. In this case, the following pair of equivalences must hold:

$$s_1^e \equiv ty^{c_1} \pmod{n}$$
$$s_2^e \equiv ty^{c_2} \pmod{n}$$

Dividing the two equivalences yields $(s_1/s_2)^e \equiv y^{c_1-c_2} \equiv (x^{c_1-c_2})^e \pmod{n}$, and hence $s_1/s_2 \equiv x^{c_1-c_2} \pmod{n}$. Because $gcd(e, c_1 - c_2) = 1$ (note that e is prime), the attacker can use the Euclid extended algorithm to compute u and v with $u(c_1 - c_2) + ve = 1$. He or she can then compute A's private key x as follows:

$$(s_1/s_2)^u y^v \equiv x^{u(c_1-c_2)} x^{ve} \equiv x \pmod{n}$$

Consequently, if an attacker knew to prepare himself or herself for at least two challenges, he or she could extract e^{th} roots without knowing the group order $\phi(n)$. Against this background, it is reasonable to assume that the attacker can prepare himself or herself for one challenge at most, and hence the success probability is $1/e$. If e is sufficiently large, this probability can be made sufficiently small.

17.3.4 Schnorr

The Fiat-Shamir and Guillou-Quisquater protocols are based on the difficulty of computing e^{th} roots in a finite group of unknown order ($e = 2$ in the case of Fiat-Shamir). There are other protocols that are based on the discrete logarithm problem (e.g., [26, 27]). In such a protocol, the prover shows that he or she knows the discrete logarithm of his or her public key.

In this section, we briefly look at Claus P. Schnorr's proposal [27]. Unfortunately, the Schnorr protocol cannot be shown to have the zero-knowledge property in a mathematically strong sense (i.e., it is currently not known how to build a simulator that can generate (t, c, s)).

Protocol 17.3   A round in the Schnorr authentication protocol.

A		B
(p, g, x)		(p, g, y)
$r \in_R \mathbb{Z}_p^*$		
$t = g^r \pmod{p}$	$\xrightarrow{t}$	
	$\xleftarrow{c}$	$c \in_R \{0, \dots, 2^k - 1\}$
$s \equiv r + cx \pmod{p-1}$	$\xrightarrow{s}$	
		$g^s \stackrel{?}{\equiv} ty^c \pmod{p}$
		(*accept* or *reject*)

In the Schnorr authentication protocol, it is assumed that there is a trusted party that acts as key authentication center (KAC). The KAC publishes a large prime p that represents the modulus and a generator g of $\mathbb{Z}_p^*$. The prover A receives a private key x, the public key $y \equiv g^x \pmod{p}$, and a public key certificate from the KAC. He or she can use the Schnorr protocol to authenticate to the verifier B in multiple rounds. A round of the Schnorr authentication protocol is illustrated in Protocol 17.3. A randomly selects $r \in_R \mathbb{Z}_p^*$, computes $t = g^r \pmod{p}$, and sends this value to B. B, in turn, randomly selects c between 0 and $2^k - 1$ (k representing the security parameter) and uses this value to challenge A. A must respond with $s \equiv r + cx \pmod{p - 1}$, and B must verify that $g^s \equiv ty^c \pmod{p}$.

The protocol is complete, because

$$g^s \equiv g^r g^{cx} \equiv ty^c \pmod{p}.$$

The protocol is sound, because the adversary can either guess or prepare himself or herself for one particular challenge. If the adversary were able to prepare himself or herself for two challenges c_1 and c_2, then he or she could also determine the A's private key x. From $g^{s_1} \equiv ty^{c_1} \pmod{p}$ and $g^{s_2} \equiv ty^{c_2} \pmod{p}$, it follows that $g^{s_1 - s_2} \equiv y^{c_1 - c_2} \equiv g^{x \cdot (c_1 - c_2)} \pmod{p}$, and hence $x \equiv (s_1 - s_2) \cdot (c_1 - c_2)^{-1} \pmod{p - 1}$. The success probability is 2^{-k}. For any reasonably sized k (e.g., 20 to 70 bits), this probability is sufficiently small.

The efficiency of the Schnorr authentication protocol doesn't look impressive at first sight. Note that computation of the commitment t is similar to the computation of an RSA digital signature (if p and n are equally sized). The major advantage of the Schnorr authentication protocol, however, is related to the fact that the computation of the commitment can be preprocessed, meaning that A can use offline computing power to precompute many values for t that he or she can use later on. The computation he or she has to do during the interaction with B is restricted to a modular addition and a modular multiplication (both of them being efficient). This is particularly advantageous for smart card implementations.

17.3.5 Turning Interactive Proofs of Knowledge into DSSs

Any (zero-knowledge) interactive proof of knowledge can be turned into a digital signature system. In this case, there is no possibility for the verifier to challenge the signatory. Instead, the challenge must be computed from the message m to be signed. It must, however, be ensured that only c can be computed, once the signer has committed to a specific value t. Consequently, $c = h(m, t)$ with h being a cryptographic hash function. In this setting, m is digitally signed with a pair (t, s), and the digital signature can be verified similar to the protocol that implements the interactive proof of knowledge. The resulting DSS is quite efficient.

17.4 FINAL REMARKS

In this chapter, we elaborated on entity authentication in general, and (cryptographic) authentication protocols that implement a proof by knowledge in particular. Among these protocols, the ones that employ static (authentication) information on the claimant's side are the preferred choice from a security viewpoint (because they are not vulnerable against eavesdropping and replay attacks). For example, one-time password schemes and challenge-response mechanisms are perfectly fine in many applications and application settings. Some of these authentication protocols even have the zero-knowledge property. As such, they are able to optimally protect the prover's secret authentication information. Unfortunately, the possibility to efficiently simulate a zero-knowledge authentication protocol execution transcript also makes it infeasible to provide nonrepudiation services with respect to authentication. In either case, it is reasonable to expect that zero-knowledge authentication protocols will play an increasingly large role in future entity authentication technologies and systems.

References

[1] Boyd, C., and A. Mathuria, *Protocols for Key Establishment and Authentication.* Springer-Verlag, New York, 2003.

[2] Smith, R.E., *Authentication: From Passwords to Public Keys.* Addison-Wesley Professional, Reading, MA, 2001.

[3] Jurgensen, T.M., and S.B. Guthery, *Smart Cards: The Developer's Toolkit.* Prentice Hall PTR, Upper Saddle River, NJ, 2002.

[4] Morris, R., and K. Thompson, "Password Security: A Case History," *Communications of the ACM,* Vol. 22, 1979, pp. 594–597.

[5] Feldmeier, D.C., and P.R. Karn, "UNIX Password Security—Ten Years Later," *Proceedings of CRYPTO '89,* 1990, pp. 44–63.

[6] Klein, D.V., "Foiling the Cracker: A Survey of, and Improvements to, Password Security," *Proceedings of USENIX UNIX Security Symposium,* August 1990, pp. 5–14.

[7] Oppliger, R., "How to Address the Secure Platform Problem for Remote Internet Voting," *Proceedings of 5th Conference on "Sicherheit in Informationssystemen" (SIS 2002),* October 2002, pp. 153–173.

[8] Haller, N., and R. Atkinson, *On Internet Authentication,* Request for Comments 1704, October 1994.

[9] Dierks, T., and C. Allen, *The TLS Protocol Version 1.0,* Request for Comments 2246, January 1999.

[10] Oppliger, R., *Security Technologies for the World Wide Web*, 2nd edition. Artech House Publishers, Norwood, MA, 2003.

[11] Vaudenay, S., "Security Flaws Induced by CBC Padding—Applications to SSL, IPSEC, WTLS …," *Proceedings of EUROCRYPT '02*, Springer-Verlag, LNCS 2332, 2002, pp. 534–545.

[12] Canvel, B., et al., "Password Interception in a SSL/TLS Channel," *Proceedings of CRYPTO '03*, Springer-Verlag, LNCS 2729, 2003, pp. 583–599.

[13] Biryukov, A., J. Lano, and B. Preneel, "Cryptanalysis of the Alleged SecurID Hash Function," *Proceedings of 10th Annual Workshop on Selected Areas in Cryptography (SAC '03)*, August 2003, Ontario, CA, Springer-Verlag, LNCS 3006, 2004, pp. 130–144.

[14] Lamport, L., "Password Authentication with Insecure Communication," *Communications of the ACM*, Vol. 24, 1981, pp. 770–772.

[15] Haller, N., *The S/KEY One-Time Password System*, Request for Comments 1760, February 1995.

[16] Haller, N., and C. Metz, *A One-Time Password System*, Request for Comments 1938, May 1996.

[17] Quisquater, J.J., and L. Guillou, "How to Explain Zero-Knowledge Protocols to Your Children," *Proceedings of CRYPTO '89*, 1990, pp. 628–631.

[18] Ashbourn, J.D.M., *Biometrics—Advanced Identify Verification: The Complete Guide*. Springer-Verlag, New York, 2000.

[19] Woodward Jr., J.D., N.M. Orlans, and P.T. Higgins, *Biometrics*. Osborne/McGraw-Hill, Emeryville, CA, 2002.

[20] Goldwasser, S., S. Micali, and C. Rackoff, "The Knowledge Complexity of Interactive Proof Systems," *SIAM Journal of Computing*, Vol. 18, No. 1, 1989, pp. 186–208.

[21] Gödel, K., "Über formal unentscheidbare Sätze der Principia Mathematica und verwandter Systeme I," *Monatshefte der Mathematischen Physik*, Vol. 38, 1931, pp. 173–198.

[22] Shamir, A., "IP = PSPACE," *Journal of the ACM*, Vol. 39, Issue 4, October 1992, pp. 869–877.

[23] Fiat, A., and A. Shamir, "How To Prove Yourself: Practical Solutions to Identification and Signature Problems," *Proceedings of CRYPTO '86*, Springer, LNCS 263, 1987, pp. 186–194.

[24] Feige, U., and A. Shamir, "Zero Knowledge Proofs of Knowledge in Two Rounds," *Proceedings of CRYPTO '89*, Springer-Verlag, LNCS 435, 1989, pp. 526–544.

[25] Guillou, L.C., and J.J. Quisquater, "A Practical Zero-Knowledge Protocol Fitted to Security Microprocessor Minimizing both Transmission and Memory," *Proceedings of EUROCRYPT '88*, Springer-Verlag, LNCS 330, 1988, pp. 123–128.

[26] Beth, T., "Efficient Zero-Knowledge Identification Schemes for Smart Cards," *Proceedings of EUROCRYPT '88*, Springer-Verlag, LNCS 330, 1988, pp. 77–84.

[27] Schnorr, C.P., "Efficient Identification and Signatures for Smart Cards," *Proceedings of CRYPTO '89*, Springer-Verlag, 1989, pp. 239–251.

Chapter 18

Secure Multiparty Computation

In this chapter, we address secure multiparty computation (MPC) (i.e., the problem of how mutually distrusting parties can compute a function without revealing their individual input values to each other). We introduce the topic in Section 18.1, summarize the major results in Section 18.2, and conclude with some final remarks in Section 18.3. This chapter is intentionally kept short. Oded Goldreich has written a primer entitled *Secure Multi-Party Computation*[1] that is comprehensive and recommended reading for anybody interested or working in this area of research (the material is also included in Chapter 7 of [1]).

18.1 INTRODUCTION

From a very high level of abstraction, almost all (cryptographic) problems can be solved by specifying and actually implementing a random process that maps n inputs to n outputs. The inputs to the process can be thought of as local inputs of n parties, whereas the n outputs can be thought of as their local outputs. In either case, it has to be distinguished whether there is a(n inside or outside) party that is trusted by all parties.

- If such a (trusted) party exists, then it can be used to implement the process. In this case, the n parties can send their local inputs to the trusted party, and the trusted party can then compute the outcome of the process and send each party its local output. It goes without saying that all communications between the n parties and the trusted party must take place over secure channels.

---

1   http://www.wisdom.weizmann.ac.il/~oded/pp.html.

- If, however, such a (trusted) party does not exist, then the situation is more involved. The question that arises immediately is whether and to what extent the trusted party can be simulated by the n (mutually distrusting) parties. This is what *secure function evaluation* as originally introduced by Andrew C. Yao[2] in the early 1980s [2] and MPC are all about: finding cryptographic protocols that can be used to simulate (and hence replace) trusted parties.

For the sake of simplicity, we consider only the case where the specified random process is deterministic (e.g., computing a function) and the n local outputs (for the n parties) are essentially the same. In this case, we consider an arbitrary n-ary function and n parties that wish to obtain the evaluation of the function on their private inputs. More specifically, we allow a set

$$P = \{P_1, P_2, \ldots, P_n\}$$

of n players to compute an arbitrary agreed function of their private inputs, even if an adversary may corrupt and control some of the players in various ways (see the following). Two communication models must be distinguished:

- In a *synchronous* communication model, any pair of players can communicate synchronously over a secure channel. Sometimes, it is assumed that a broadcast channel is available that guarantees the consistency of the received values if a player sends a value to several players. In practice, however, such a broadcast channel seldom exists. If one is needed, then it must be simulated by a quite inefficient Byzantine agreement protocol (e.g., [3]).

- In the *asynchronous* communication model, any pair of players can only communicate asynchronously. This suggests that one does not have guarantees about the arrival times of sent messages. This complicates things considerably.

Security in MPC means that the players' inputs remain secret during the evaluation of the function and that the results of the computation (i.e., function evaluation) are guaranteed to be correct. More specifically, security in MPC is defined relative to an ideal-world specification involving a trusted party. If anything an adversary can achieve in the real world (i.e., the world in which the MPC protocol is executed) can also be achieved in the ideal world (i.e., the world in which there exists a trusted party), then we are talking about a *secure multiparty computation*. A secure multiparty computation does not, for example, protect against the possibility of having players provide wrong inputs. Such a manipulation is possible in either world (i.e., in the real world and in the ideal world). There is nothing a cryptographic

2   Andrew C. Yao received the ACM Turing Award in 2000.

protocol can do against it.[3] In either case, we must say a few more things about the adversary and his or her capabilities. First and foremost, we must specify whether his or her computing power is restricted:

- If the adversary has unrestricted computing power and can still not cheat or violate the security of an MPC, then we are in the realm of *information-theoretic security*.

- If, however, the adversary has restricted computing power and the security of the MPC relies on (unproven) intractability assumptions, then we are in the realm of *cryptographic security*.

Similar to other cryptographic systems, there are MPC protocols that provide information-theoretic security and protocols that provide cryptographic security.

Furthermore, the potential misbehavior of some of the players is typically modeled by considering a central adversary with an overall cheating strategy who can corrupt some of the players. There are basically three types of corruption:

- In a *passive corruption*, the adversary learns the entire information of the corrupted player but the player continues to perform the protocol correctly (such players are sometimes called *semihonest*).

- In an *active corruption*, the adversary learns the entire information of the corrupted player and takes full control of the corrupted player. This also means that the adversary can make the corrupted player deviate arbitrarily from the protocol.

- In a *fail corruption*, the adversary can let the player stop the protocol execution but does not learn its information. This allows the adversary to model denial-of-service attacks against one (or several) player(s).

It is only recently that people have started to look at fail corruption as a type of corruption of its own. Many theoretical results that were achieved in the late 1980s only distinguish between passive and active corruptions (see Section 18.2). It goes without saying that if no active corruptions are considered, then the only security issue is the secrecy of the players' inputs. In most papers on secure MPC, the adversary's corruption capability is specified by a threshold t—that is, the adversary is assumed to be able to corrupt up to t players (but not more). In this setting, a distinction can be made between passive, active, and fail corruptions. For each of these types of corruption, one can work with a different threshold.

---

3 This fact must be kept in mind and considered with care when one discusses the use of protocols for secure MPC for applications like electronic voting.

18.2   MAJOR RESULTS

In the late 1980s, a couple of fundamental results about secure MPC were found and published. Most importantly, Oded Goldreich, Silvio Micali, and Avi Wigderson proved that cryptographically secure MPC is possible if and only if $t < n/2$ ($t < n$) players are corrupted actively (passively) [4]. Similarly, Michael Ben-Or, Goldreich, and Wigderson, as well as David Chaum, Claude Crépeau, and Ivan B. Damgård, proved that information-theoretic secure MPC is possible in the synchronous communication model if and only if $t < n/3$ ($t < n/2$) players are corrupted actively (passively) [5, 6]. If a physical broadcast channel is available, then the last result regarding active corruption can be improved to $t < n/2$ [7, 8].

These fundamental results were published at a time in which intensive electronic multiparty interactions seemed only a remote possibility. This may explain the impression that, while generating considerable interest within the community that deals with the theory of computation, the results went almost unnoticed in the community that deals with applied cryptography. This situation has changed fundamentally, and intensive electronic multiparty interactions are possible today using the Internet. Against this background, many cryptographers have started to reactivate the field and to work again on secure MPC. For example, the previously mentioned results for the information-theoretic setting were improved in the late 1990s by considering a mixed model in which an adversary can corrupt up to t_a players actively, up to t_p players passively, and up to t_f players using a fail corruption (see, for example, [9, 10] for specific results). As of this writing, secure MPC has become a very active area of cryptographic research, and many results and findings are published in the relevant literature.

18.3   FINAL REMARKS

In this chapter, we briefly touched on secure MPC and summarized the major results that have been achieved. The results suggest that unless a substantial perecentage of the players are corrupted, secure MPC is possible (in either an information-theoretic or cryptographic sense).

There are many applications for MPC. If, for example, n parties want to compute a function without revealing their individual input values, then a protocol for secure MPC can be employed. The following problems are often mentioned for two parties:

Millionaires' problem: Two millionaires want to determine who is richer without involving a trusted person and without revealing any information about each other's wealth (except who is richer).

Software protection problem: A software vendor wants to let a user use the functionality of a software without sending the software to the user and without having the user send his or her data to the software vendor for processing.

More specifically, many cryptographic protocols can be seen as special cases of a secure MPC. This is particularly true if more than two players are involved (in the two-player scenario, the major results are not particularly useful). For specific tasks like collective contract signing, online auctions, or electronic voting, there exist efficient protocols. These protocols, however, are beyond the scope of this book. We conclude with the remark that MPC in general, and secure MPC in particular, provides a very powerful paradigm to reduce the level of trust one must put into a particular party.

References

[1] Goldreich, O., *Foundations of Cryptography: Volume 2, Basic Applications.* Cambridge University Press, Cambridge, UK, 2004.

[2] Yao, A.C., "Protocols for Secure Computations," *Proceedings of the 23rd IEEE Symposium on the Foundations of Computer Science (FOCS)*, IEEE Press, 1982, pp. 160–164.

[3] Lamport, L., R. Shostak, and M. Pease, "The Byzantine Generals Problem," *ACM Transactions on Programming Languages and Systems*, Vol. 4, 1982, pp. 382–401.

[4] Goldreich, O., S. Micali, and A. Wigderson, "How to Play Any Mental Game or a Completeness Theorem for Protocols with Honest Majority," *Proceedings of the 19th ACM Symposium on the Theory of Computing (STOC)*, ACM Press, 1987, pp. 218–229.

[5] Ben-Or, M., O. Goldwasser, and A. Wigderson, "Completeness Theorems for Non-Cryptographic Fault-Tolerant Distributed Computation," *Proceedings of the 20th ACM Symposium on the Theory of Computing (STOC)*, ACM Press, 1988, pp. 1–10.

[6] Chaum, D., C. Crépeau, and I.B. Damgård, "Multiparty Unconditionally Secure Protocols," *Proceedings of the 20th ACM Symposium on the Theory of Computing (STOC)*, ACM Press, 1988, pp. 11–19.

[7] Rabin, T., and M. Ben-Or, "Verifiable Secret Sharing and Multiparty Protocols with Honest Majority," *Proceedings of the 21st ACM Symposium on the Theory of Computing (STOC)*, ACM Press, 1989, pp. 73–85.

[8] Beaver, D., "Secure Multi-Party Protocols and Zero-Knowledge Proof Systems Tolerating a Faulty Minority," *Journal of Cryptology*, Vol. 4, No. 2, 1991, pp. 75–122.

[9] Fitzi, M., M. Hirt, and U.M. Maurer, "Trading Correctness for Privacy in Unconditional Multi-Party Computation," *Proceedings of CRYPTO '98*, Springer-Verlag, LNCS 1462, 1998.

[10] Hirt, M., and U.M. Maurer, "Player Simulation and General Adversary Structures in Perfect Multi-Party Computation," *Journal of Cryptology*, Vol. 13, No. 1, 2000, pp. 31–60.

Part V

EPILOGUE

Chapter 19

Key Management

In this chapter, we elaborate on the key management process. More specifically, we introduce the topic in Section 19.1, overview and discuss the major phases of a key life cycle in Section 19.2, address secret sharing, key recovery, and PKIs in Sections 19.3–19.5, and conclude with some final remarks in Section 19.6. Consequently, this chapter touches on all important questions related to key management. A more thorough and comprehensive treatment of the questions is beyond the scope of this book. It would deserve a book of its own.[1]

19.1 INTRODUCTION

According to RFC 2828, the term *key management* refers to "the process of handling and controlling cryptographic keys and related material (such as initialization values) during their life cycle in a cryptographic system, including ordering, generating, distributing, storing, loading, escrowing, archiving, auditing, and destroying the material" [1]. This definition is fairly broad. The important things to remember are

- That key management is a process;

- That the key management process is about the handling and controlling of cryptographic keys and related material (e.g., IVs);

- That there is a life cycle for the cryptographic keys;

- That there are many activities and tasks that must be addressed in such a key life cycle.

---

1   Unfortunately, such a book is not (yet) available, and there is no reference to be made at this point.

In the definition given earlier, the life cycle for cryptographic keys comprises many activities and tasks. For the purpose of this book, we use a slightly simplified key life cycle that is illustrated in Figure 19.1. In this cycle, we distinguish between key generation, key distribution, key storage, and key destruction. Key generation, key distribution, and key destruction refer to discrete points in time, whereas key storage refers to an entire period of time (between the key generation and key destruction). The four activities and tasks are further addressed in the following section.

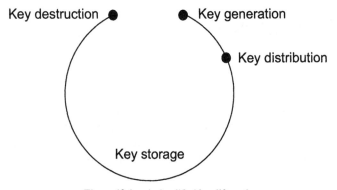

Figure 19.1 A simplified key life cycle.

In almost every security system that employs cryptography and cryptographic techniques, the key management process represents the Achilles' heel (we already made this point in Section 2.3.3). There are at least two conclusions one may draw from this fact:

- First, if one is in charge of designing a security system, then one is well advised to start with the key management process first. A properly designed key management process must be at the core of every security system.

- Second, if one is in charge of breaking a security system, then one is also well advised to start with the key management process first. Most attacks against cryptographic security systems that have been published in the past are basically attacks that exploit vulnerabilities or weaknesses in the underlying key management processes.

Consequently, the key management process is the most important part of a security system that employs cryptography and cryptographic techniques. This is true for the security professional who designs the security system as well as the adversary who tries to break it.

Because the key management process is so comprehensive and complex, there is usually no single standard to which one can refer. Instead, there are many standards that address specific questions and problems related to the key management process. Some of the standards are overviewed, discussed, and put into perspective in [2]; they are not repeated in this book.

19.2 KEY LIFE CYCLE

Every cryptographic key has a life cycle. As mentioned earlier, in a simplified key life cycle, one can distinguish between key generation, distribution, storage, and destruction. These activities and tasks are overviewed and briefly discussed next.

19.2.1 Key Generation

Unless one is in the realm of unkeyed cryptosystems, the use of a cryptographic system always requires the generation of cryptographic keys and related material (e.g., IVs) in one way or another. The generation of this material, in turn, requires the use of a random bit generator as addressed in Chapter 9. Either the random bit generator is used directly to generate the cryptographic keys or the random bit generator is used indirectly to seed a PRBG (that then generates the cryptographic keys that are needed for the cryptographic system in use). In either case, it is mandatory to know and properly understand the possible realizations and implementations for hardware-based or software-based random bit generators (see Section 9.2), as well as the ways to test the statistical randomness properties of the output of these generators (see Section 9.3).

19.2.2 Key Distribution

In an ideal world, the cryptographic keys are used where they are generated. In this case, the distribution of the cryptographic keys is not a problem. In all other cases, however, the distribution of the cryptographic keys must be considered carefully. In fact, it must be ensured that cryptographic keys cannot be attacked passively or actively during their distribution. This is an important and challenging engineering task. In fact, many key distribution protocols and systems have been developed, proposed, implemented, and deployed in the past (see, for example, [3]). There are many subtle details that must be considered and addressed with care.

19.2.3 Key Storage

Almost all cryptographic keys must be used for a comparably long period of time (i.e., between the generation of the key and its destruction). In this case, the keys must be securely stored, meaning that they must be stored in a way that they cannot be attacked passively or actively. Again, this is an important and challenging engineering task. Compared to the key distribution problem, the key storage problem is theoretically and practically even more involved. One reason is that the storage of a cryptographic key can only be considered in the context of a specific operating system. So the key storage problem and the operating system security problem are not independent from each other, and the first problem depends on the second (unfortunately, we all know that the security of contemporary operating systems is not in particularly good shape). Consequently, there are many low-level details that must be considered when one wants to provide a (secure) solution for the key storage problem.

If there is no single place to store a key, then one may use a secret sharing scheme as addressed in the following section to store the key in a decentralized and distributed way. As of this writing, these schemes are not as widely deployed as one would expect considering their theoretical practicality and usefulness. It is possible and likely that this will change in the future.

19.2.4 Key Destruction

If a cryptographic key is stored in electronic form, then it is possible and very likely that it must be destroyed at some point in time. Unfortunately, the key destruction problem is not as simple to solve as one would expect at first sight. There are basically two reasons:

- First, it is technically difficult to delete data that has been stored electronically. In practice, it is usually required to overwrite the memory locations (where the keys have been stored) with randomly chosen bit patterns multiple times.

- Second, there may be (many) temporary copies of the cryptographic keys in use that are held somewhere in the available memory.

Again, the question whether the key destruction problem can be solved mainly depends on the operating system in use. There is no general answer that applies for all operating systems.

19.3 SECRET SHARING

As already mentioned above, there are situations in which it may be useful to split a secret value (e.g., a cryptographic key) into multiple parts and to have different parties hold and manage these parts. If, for example, one wants to have n parties share a secret value s, then one can randomly choose $n - 1$ keys $s_1, \ldots, s_{n-1}$, compute

$$s_n = s \oplus s_1 \oplus \ldots \oplus s_{n-1},$$

and distribute $s_1, \ldots, s_n$ to the n parties. The secret value s can then only be reconstructed if all n parties provide their parts. Consequently, such a *secret splitting system* requires that all parties are available and reliable, and that they all behave honestly in one way or another. If only one party is not available, loses its part, or refuses to provide it, then the secret value s can no longer be reconstructed. Needless to say, this is a major drawback and shortcoming of a secret splitting scheme and its practicality.

In a *secret sharing system*, it is generally not required that all parties are available and reliable, and that they all behave honestly. Instead, the reconstruction of the secret value s requires only the parts of a well-defined subset of all parts (in this case, the parts are called shares). More specifically, a secret sharing system allows an entity, called the dealer, to share a secret value s among a set of n players, $P = \{P_1, \ldots, P_n\}$, such that only a qualified subset of the players can reconstruct s from their shares. It is usually required that all nonqualified subsets of the players get absolutely no information about s (as mentioned later, the secret sharing system is then called perfect). The secret and the shares are usually elements of the same domain, most often a finite field.

Formally, the set of qualified subsets is a subset of the power set 2^P and is called the *access structure* Γ of the secret sharing system. If, for example, $\Gamma = \{\{P_1, \ldots, P_n\}\}$ (i.e., only all players are qualified), then the secret sharing system is a secret splitting system as described earlier. More generally, a *k-out-of-n secret sharing scheme* can be defined as suggested in Definition 19.1.

Definition 19.1 (*K*-**out-of-**n **secret sharing system**) *A k-out-of-n secret sharing scheme is a secret sharing system in which the access structure is*

$$\Gamma = \{M \subseteq 2^P : |M| \geq k\}.$$

Furthermore, a k-out-of-n secret sharing scheme is *perfect* if $k - 1$ players who collaborate (and pool their shares) are not able to reconstruct s (or retrieve any information about s).

In 1979, Adi Shamir developed and proposed a perfect k-out-of-n secret sharing system based on polynomial interpolation [4]. The scheme employs the fact that that a polynomial $f(x)$ of degree $k-1$ (over a field) can be uniquely interpolated from k points. This means that a polynomial of degree 1 can be interpolated from 2 points, a polynomial of degree 2 can be interpolated from 3 points, and so on. The corresponding interpolation algorithm has been around for a long time. It is usually attributed to Lagrange. Let

$$f(x) = r_0 + r_1 x + \ldots + r_{k-1} x^{k-1} = \sum_{i=0}^{k-1} r_i x^i \tag{19.1}$$

be a polynomial of degree $k-1$ that passes through the k points

$$(x_1, f(x_1) = y_1)$$
$$(x_2, f(x_2) = y_2)$$
$$\cdots$$
$$(x_k, f(x_k) = y_k).$$

The Lagrange interpolating polynomial $P(x)$ is then given by

$$P(x) = \sum_{i=1}^{k} P_i(x),$$

where

$$P_i(x) = y_i \prod_{j=1; j \neq i}^{k} \frac{x - x_j}{x_i - x_j}.$$

Written explicitly,

$$
\begin{aligned}
P(x) &= P_1(x) + P_2(x) + \ldots + P_k(x) \\
&= y_1 \frac{(x - x_2)(x - x_3) \cdots (x - x_k)}{(x_1 - x_2)(x_1 - x_3) \cdots (x_1 - x_k)}
\end{aligned}
$$

$$+y_2 \frac{(x - x_1)(x - x_3) \cdots (x - x_k)}{(x_2 - x_1)(x_2 - x_3) \cdots (x_2 - x_k)}$$
$$+ \ldots$$
$$+y_k \frac{(x - x_1)(x - x_2) \cdots (x - x_{k-1})}{(x_k - x_1)(x_k - x_2) \cdots (x_k - x_{k-1})}.$$

In Shamir's k-out-of-n secret sharing system, the secret (to be shared) represents the coefficient r_0. The dealer randomly selects $k - 1$ coefficients $r_1, \ldots, r_{k-1}$ to define a polynomial according to formula (19.1). For every player P_i, the dealer then assigns a fixed nonzero field element x_i and computes $y_i = f(x_i)$. The pair $(x_i, f(x_i))$ is then taken for P_i's share.

Anybody who is given k shares can compute the secret r_0 by evaluating the Lagrange interpolating polynomial at point zero (i.e., $s = r_0 = P(0)$). Anybody who is given fewer than k shares cannot compute the secret. More precisely, anybody who is given fewer than k shares does not obtain any (partial) information about the secret. This means that Shamir's k-out-of-n secret sharing system is perfect.

K-out-of-n secret sharing systems are interesting from a theoretical viewpoint. This is particularly true if the systems are perfect. From a more practical viewpoint, however, there are at least two problems that must be addressed and considered with care:

- If a malicious player is not honest and provides a wrong share, then the secret that is reconstructed is also wrong.

- If the dealer is malicious or untrusted, then the players may want to have a guarantee that they can in fact put together the correct secret.

A *verifiable secret sharing system* can be used to overcome these problems. For example, Shamir's k-out-of-n secret sharing system can be made verifiable by having the dealer make commitments to the coefficients of the polynomial $f(x)$ and providing the players with help-shares they can use to verify shares. We don't delve deeper into secret sharing systems and verifiable secret sharing systems in this book. Note, however, that (verifiable) secret sharing systems play a central role in many cryptographic systems and applications, such as electronic cash or electronic voting. Most importantly, verifiable secret sharing systems are at the core of many protocols to implement secure MPC (see Chapter 18).

19.4 KEY RECOVERY

If one uses cryptographic techniques for data encryption, then one may also be concerned about the fact that (encryption and decryption) keys get lost. What happens, for example, if all data of a company are securely encrypted and the decryption key is lost? How can the company recover its data? The same questions occur if only the data of a specific employee are encrypted. What happens if the corresponding decryption key gets lost? What happens if the employee himself or herself gets lost? It is obvious that a professional use of cryptography and cryptographic techniques for data encryption must take into account a way to recover keys.

According to RFC 2828, the term *key recovery* refers to "a process for learning the value of a cryptographic key that was previously used to perform some cryptographic operation" [1]. Alternatively, one may also use the term to refer to "techniques that provide an intentional, alternate (i.e., secondary) means to access the key used for data confidentiality service" [1]. There are basically two classes of key recovery techniques:

Key escrow: According to RFC 2828, *key escrow* is "a key recovery technique for storing knowledge of a cryptographic key or parts thereof in the custody of one or more third parties called escrow agents, so that the key can be recovered and used in specified circumstances" [1]. In this context, escrow agents are also frequently called trusted third parties (TTPs).

Key encapsulation: According to RFC 2828, *key encapsulation* is "a key recovery technique for storing knowledge of a cryptographic key by encrypting it with another key and ensuring that only certain third parties called *recovery agents* can perform the decryption operation to retrieve the stored key. Key encapsulation typically allows direct retrieval of the secret key used to provide data confidentiality" [1]. Key encapsulation is used in many communication security protocols that do not have key recovery as their primary goal. Examples include swIPe [5] and simple key-management for Internet protocols (SKIP) [6] (see, for example, Chapter 14 of [7]).

The basic principles of key escrow and key encapsulation are illustrated in Figure 19.2. In key escrow, the cryptographically protected data is sent from A to B, whereas the key recovery data is sent to a TTP. In key encapsulation, either data is sent directly from A to B. Another way to look at things is to say that key escrow refers to out-band key recovery, whereas key encapsulation refers to in-band key recovery. These terms, however, are less frequently used in the literature.

Key recovery in general, and key escrow in particular, became hotly debated research topics in the mid 1990s (see, for example, [8] for a taxonomy referring to and taking into account all of the proposals that were made). The discussion was even intensified when the U.S. government published the *escrowed encryption standard* (EES) [9] and released a corresponding implementation in the Clipper chip.

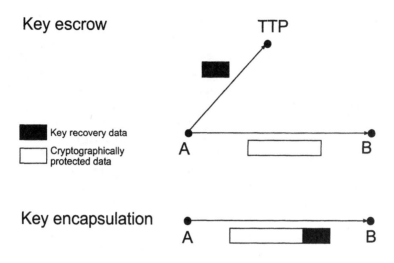

Key escrow

TTP

Key recovery data

Cryptographically
protected data

A   B

Key encapsulation

A   B

Figure 19.2 Key escrow and key encapsulation.

The EES was basically a secret splitting scheme with two governmental bodies acting as escrow agents. This was the major problem of the EES. People were concerned about the possibility of having the government illegitimitely decrypting their communications (without any restriction in time). Also, it was argued that key escrow on transmitted data is neither necessary nor particularly useful (because either end of the communication can always provide the data in unencrypted form).

The controversy about the EES and the Clipper chip suddenly came to an end when it was shown that the original design of the EES was deeply flawed [10] (you may also refer to [11] for the entire story about the EES, the Clipper chip, and the crypto debate). The flaw was an authentication field that was too short to provide protection against a brute-force attack.

In 1997, a group of recognized cryptographers wrote and published an influential paper entitled *The Risks of Key Recovery, Key Escrow, and Trusted Third-Party Encryption* [12]. This paper provides a good summary about all relevant arguments against key recovery that is controlled by external TTPs, such as governmental agencies. As a result of the relaxation of the U.S. export controls on cryptography (as briefly addressed in the Preface), the situation is more relaxed today, and many commercial products implement key recovery mechanisms and services for voluntary use.

19.5 PUBLIC KEY INFRASTRUCTURE

According to RFC 2828, the term *certificate* refers to "a document that attests to the truth of something or the ownership of something" [1]. Historically, the term certificate was coined and first used by Loren M. Kohnfelder to refer to a digitally signed record holding a name and a public key [13]. As such, the certificate attests to the legitimate ownership of a public key and attributes a public key to a particular entity, such as a person, a hardware device, or anything else. The resulting certificates are frequently called *public key certificates.* According to RFC 2828, a public key certificate is a special case of a digital certificate, namely one "that binds a system entity's identity to a public key value, and possibly to additional data items" [1]. As such, it is a digitally signed data structure that attests to the ownership of a public key.

More generally and in accordance with RFC 2828, a certificate can not only be used to attest to the legitimate ownership of a public key (in the case of a public key certificate), but also to attest to the truth of any property attributable to a certificate owner. This more general class of certificates is commonly referred to as attribute certificates. In short, the major difference between a public key certificate and an attribute certificate is that the former includes a public key (i.e., the public key that is certified), whereas the latter includes a list of attributes (i.e., the attributes that are certified). In either case, the certificates are issued (and possibly revoked) by authorities that are recognized and trusted by some community of users. In the case of public key certificates, these authorities are called *certification authorities* (CAs).[2] In the case of attribute certificates, however, these authorities are called *attribute authorities* (AAs).

In short, a PKI consists of one (or several) CA(s). According to RFC 2828, a PKI is "a system of CAs that perform some set of certificate management, archive management, key management, and token management functions for a community of users" [1] that employ public key cryptography.[3] Another way to look at a PKI is as an infrastructure that can be used to issue, validate, and revoke public keys and public key certificates. As such, a PKI comprises a set of agreed-upon standards, CAs, structures among multiple CAs, methods to discover and validate certification paths, operational and management protocols, interoperable tools, and supporting legislation. In the last couple of years, PKIs have experienced a hype, and many companies and organizations have announced plans to provide certification

---

2   In the past, CAs were often called TTPs. This is particularly true for CAs that are operated by government bodies.
3   The last part of the sentence is particularly important, because in the past many people felt they had to enter the field of PKIs without having a legitimate reason (if, for example, they are not using public key cryptography in the first place).

services to the general public. Unfortunately, only a few of these companies and organizations have succeeded and actually provide such services that can be taken seriously.

Many standardization bodies are working in the field of public key certificates and PKIs. Most importantly, the Telecommunication Standardization Sector of the International Telecommunication Union (ITU-T) has released and is periodically updating a recommendation that is commonly referred to as ITU-T X.509 [14], or X.509 in short. The current version of ITU-T X.509 is version 3. Meanwhile, the ITU-T X.509 has also been adopted by many other standardization bodies, including, for example, the ISO/IEC JTC1 [15].

The format of an X.509v3 certificate is specified in the abstract syntax notation one (ASN.1),[4] and the resulting certificates are encoded according to specific encoding rules[5] to produce a series of bits and bytes suitable for transmission. Anyway, an X.509 public-key certificate contains the following data items:

1. A version number (identifying version 1, version 2, or version 3);

2. A serial number (i.e., a unique integer value assigned by the issuer);

3. An object identifier (OID) that specifies the signature algorithm that is used to sign the public key certificate;

4. The distinguished name (DN)[6] of the issuer (i.e., the name of the CA that actually signed the certificate);

5. A validity period that specifies an interval in which the certificate is valid;

6. The DN of the subject (i.e., the owner of the certificate);

7. Information related to the public key of the subject (i.e., the key and the OID of the algorithm);

8. Some optional information related to the issuer (defined for versions 2 and 3 only);

9. Some optional information related to the subject (defined for versions 2 and 3 only);

10. Some optional extensions (defined for version 3 only).

---

4   ASN.1 is officially specified in ITU-T X.680 and ISO/IEC 8824.

5   There are three standardized encoding rules, namely the basic encoding rules (BER), the distinguished encoding rules (DER), and the packet encoding rules (PER). Obviously, anybody can specify and use their own set of encoding rules.

6   The DN is assumed to uniquely identify an entity (i.e., a public key certificate owner or a CA) in a globally unique namespace.

All three versions of X.509 certificates contain the items 1 through 7 listed. Only version 2 and version 3 certificates may additionally contain items 8 and 9, whereas only version 3 may contain item 10.

The trust model employed by ITU-T X.509 is hierarchical.[7] This basically means that a user must define a number of root CAs and corresponding root certificates (i.e., certificates that are trusted by default) from which trust may extend. Typically, a root certificate is self-signed, meaning that the root CA has issued its own certificate (i.e., the subject and issuer are identical). Note that from a theoretical point of view, self-signed certificates are not particularly useful. Anybody can claim something and issue a certificate for this claim. Consequently, a self-signed certificate basically says: "Here is my public key, trust me."

Having established a number of root CAs and corresponding root certificates, a user can try to find a *certification path* (or *certification chain*) that leads from a root certificate to a leaf certificate (i.e., a certificate that is issued for a user or system). Formally speaking, a certification path or chain is defined in a tree or wood of CAs (root CAs and intermediate CAs) and refers to a sequence of one or more certificates that lead from a root certificate to a leaf certificate. Each certificate certifies the public key of its successor. Finally, the leaf certificate is typically issued for a person or a system. Let's assume that CA_{root} is a root certificate and B is an entity for which a certificate must be verified. In this case, a certification path or chain with n intermediate CAs (i.e., $CA_1, CA_2, \ldots, CA_n$) would look as follows:

$$CA_{root} \ll CA_1 \gg$$
$$CA_1 \ll CA_2 \gg$$
$$CA_2 \ll CA_3 \gg$$
$$\ldots$$
$$CA_{n-1} \ll CA_n \gg$$
$$CA_n \ll B \gg$$

The simplest model one may think of is a certification hierarchy representing a tree with a single root CA. However, more general structures and graphs (including mutually certifying CAs, cross-certificates, and multiple root CAs) are possible, as well. A PKI structure or graph among multiple CAs generally provides one or more certification paths between two entities.

---

7   Note, however, that ITU-T X.509 does *not* embody a hierarchic trust model. The existence of cross-certificates, as well as forward and reverse certificates, makes the X.509 model a mesh, analogous in some ways to PGP's web of trust. The X.509 model is often erroneously characterized as a hierarchic trust model because it is usually mapped to the directory information tree (DIT), which is hierarchic, more like name schemes.

ITU-T X.509 can be used in many ways. Consequently, every nontrivial group of users who want to work with X.509 certificates has to produce a profile that nails down the features left undefined in X.509. The difference between a specification (i.e., ITU-T X.509) and a profile is that a specification does not generally set any limitations on what combinations can and cannot appear in various certificate types, whereas a profile sets various limitations, for example, by requiring that signing and confidentiality keys be different. Many standardization bodies work in the field of "profiling" ITU-T X.509 for specific application environments.[8] For example, the Internet Engineering Task Force (IETF) has chartered the PKI X.509 (PKIX)[9] working group (WG) to profile the use of ITU-T X.509 on the Internet. The IETF PKIX WG is a dynamic and very active WG that has published many documents.

19.6 FINAL REMARKS

In this chapter, we elaborated on key management (i.e., the process of handling and controlling cryptographic keys and related material during their life cycle in a cryptographic system). Key management is a very complex process, and it does not come as a surprise that it is the Achilles' heel of almost every system that employs cryptography and cryptographic techniques. The key life cycle includes many important phases, and we had a closer look at key generation, distribution, storage, and destruction.

If there are keys that are so valuable that there is no single entity that is trustworthy enough to serve as a key repository, then one may look into secret splitting schemes or—more importantly—secret sharing systems. In fact, secret sharing systems are likely to be widely deployed in future systems that employ cryptography and cryptographic techniques. The same is true for key recovery. If data encryption techniques are implemented and widely deployed, then mechanisms and services for key recovery are valuable and in many situations unavoidable. Following this line of argumentation, the first products that implement and make use of key recovery features already appeared on the marketplace a few years ago. For example, the commercial versions of PGP have support key recovery on a voluntary basis. This trend is likely to continue in the future. Last but not least, we briefly elaborated on digital certificates and PKIs. This is a very difficult topic, both from a theoretical and practical point of view. In this book, we only scratched the surface.

---

8   To "profile" ITU-T X.509—or any general standard or recommendation—basically means to fix the details with regard to a specific application environment. The result is a profile that elaborates on how to use and deploy ITU-T X.509 in the environment.

9   http://www.ietf.org/html.charters/pkix-charter.html.

More information about digital certificates and PKIs is available, for example, in Chapter 7 of [16] and [17–20].

References

[1] Shirey, R., *Internet Security Glossary*, Request for Comments 2828, May 2000.

[2] Dent, A.W., and C.J. Mitchell, *User's Guide to Cryptography and Standards*. Artech House Publishers, Norwood, MA, 2004.

[3] Boyd, C., and A. Mathuria, *Protocols for Key Establishment and Authentication*. Springer-Verlag, New York, 2003.

[4] Shamir, A., "How to Share a Secret," *Communications of the ACM*, Vol. 22, 1979, pp. 612–613.

[5] Ioannidis, J., and M. Blaze, "The Architecture and Implementation of Network-Layer Security Under UNIX," *Proceedings of USENIX UNIX Security Symposium IV*, October 1993, pp. 29–39.

[6] Caronni, G., et al., "SKIP—Securing the Internet," *Proceedings of WET ICE '96*, Workshops on Enabling Technologies: Infrastructure for Collaborative Enterprises, June 1996, pp. 62–67.

[7] Oppliger, R., *Internet and Intranet Security*, 2nd edition. Artech House Publishers, Norwood, MA, 2002.

[8] Denning, D.E., and D.K. Branstad, "A Taxonomy for Key Escrow Encryption Systems," *Communications of the ACM*, Vol. 39, No. 3, March 1996, pp. 34–40.

[9] U.S. Department of Commerce, National Institute of Standards and Technology, *Escrowed Encryption Standard*, FIPS PUB 185, February 1994.

[10] Blaze, M., "Protocol Failure in the Escrowed Encryption Standard," *Proceedings of the 2nd ACM Conference on Computer and Communications Security*, Fairfax, VA, November 1994, pp. 59–67.

[11] Hoffman, L.J. (Ed.), *Building in Big Brother: The Cryptographic Policy Debate*. Springer-Verlag, New York, 1995.

[12] Abelson, H., et al., "The Risks of Key Recovery, Key Escrow, and Trusted Third-Party Encryption," May 1997, available at http://www.cdt.org/crypto/risks98.

[13] Kohnfelder, L.M., "Towards a Practical Public-Key Cryptosystem," Bachelor's thesis, Massachusetts Institute of Technology, Cambridge, MA, May 1978.

[14] ITU-T, Recommendation X.509: The Directory—Authentication Framework, 1988.

[15] ISO/IEC 9594-8, *Information Technology—Open Systems Interconnection—The Directory—Part 8: Authentication Framework*, 1990.

[16] Oppliger, R., *Security Technologies for the World Wide Web*, 2nd edition. Artech House Publishers, Norwood, MA, 2003.

[17] Feghhi, J., J. Feghhi, and P. Williams, *Digital Certificates: Applied Internet Security*. Addison-Wesley Longman, Reading, MA, 1999.

[18] Ford, W., and M.S. Baum, *Secure Electronic Commerce: Building the Infrastructure for Digital Signatures & Encryption*, 2nd edition. Prentice Hall PTR, Upper Saddle River, NJ, 2000.

[19] Adams, C., and S. Lloyd, *Understanding PKI: Concepts, Standards, and Deployment Considerations*, 2nd edition. New Riders Publishing, Indianapolis, IN, 2002.

[20] Choudhury, S., *Public Key Infrastructure: Implementation and Design.* John Wiley & Sons, New York, 2002.

Chapter 20

Conclusions

In this book, we overviewed, discussed, and put into perspective many cryptographic systems in use today. In doing so, we made a distinction between the following three classes of cryptosystems:

- Unkeyed cryptosystems (see Definition 1.5);
- Secret key cryptosystems (see Definition 1.6);
- Public key cryptosystem (see Definition 1.7).

We also noted that this distinction is somehow arbitrary and that other classification schemes may be used instead. Nevertheless, we think that the classification scheme is still useful and appropriate (especially for educational purposes). We reuse it in this chapter to provide some conclusions.

20.1 UNKEYED CRYPTOSYSTEMS

Unkeyed cryptosystems play a fundamental role in contemporary cryptography and are used in many higher level cryptographic systems and applications. In Part II of the book, we had a closer look at one-way functions, cryptographic hash functions, and random bit generators.

- One-way functions (and trapdoor functions) are at the core of modern cryptography. This may come as a surprise, especially if one considers the fact that no function has been shown to be one way in a mathematically strong sense and that even the existence of one-way functions has not been proven so far. In fact, there are only a few candidate one-way functions (i.e., functions that are conjectured to be one way) in widespread use: the discrete exponentiation function, the RSA function, and the modular square function. All of these functions are overviewed and discussed in Section 7.2. The fact that it is currently not known how to efficiently invert these functions gives us a good feeling when we use these functions in higher level cryptographic systems and applications. Unfortunately, we don't know how justified this feeling really is. If somebody found an algorithm to efficiently invert a candidate one-way function, then many deployed cryptographic systems and applications would become totally useless.

- In many cryptographic systems and applications, cryptographic hash functions (i.e., hash functions that are one way and weak or strong collision resistant) are used and play a fundamental role. This is particularly true for digital signatures with appendix and corresponding DSSs. If one can make the idealized assumption that a cryptographic hash function behaves like a random function, then one is often able to prove security properties for cryptographic systems that one is not able to prove without making this assumption (the corresponding proofs are then valid in the so-called random oracle model). In spite of their fundamental role in cryptography, there are not many practically relevant cryptographic hash functions to choose from (see Section 8.3 for a corresponding overview). In fact, most cryptographic hash functions in use today follow the Merkle-Damgård construction (i.e., they iteratively apply a compression function to the blocks of a message). There are only a few alternative proposals to design cryptographic hash functions. One possibility that is being looked into more seriously for message authentication is universal hashing. It is possible and likely that more alternatives for the design of cryptographic hash functions will be developed and proposed in the future.

- Most cryptographic systems in use today employ random bits (or random numbers, respectively) in one way or another. Consequently, random bit generators have many applications and play a fundamental role in contemporary cryptography. There are various types of hardware-based and software-based random bit generators that are used in practice (see Section 9.2 for a corresponding overview). In either case, it is important to test the statistical randomness properties of the output of a random bit generator before it is actually used. Many random bit generators have statistical deficiencies that are surprisingly simple to find and exploit.

20.2 SECRET KEY CRYPTOSYSTEMS

Secret key cryptosystems are the cryptographic systems one usually thinks of first when one talks about cryptography. This is particularly true for symmetric encryption systems. These systems have been in use for ages to protect the secrecy of messages. In Part III of the book, we had a closer look at symmetric encryption systems, MACs, PRBGs, and PRFs.

- Symmetric encryption systems have a long and thrilling history. The level of security they provide varies considerably. As was shown by Shannon in the late 1940s, a symmetric encryption system can only be unconditionally secure and provide perfect secrecy if the key is at least as long as the plaintext message (see Theorem 10.1). The one-time pad is an example of an unconditionally secure symmetric encryption system. Unfortunately, the key length requirement of an unconditionally secure symmetric encryption system restricts its practicality and usefulness considerably. There are, however, a couple of modifications of the basic Shannon model that can be used to provide unconditionally secure symmetric encryption that is efficient (these modifications are only briefly touched on in Section 10.4). But for all practical purposes, the symmetric encryption systems in use today are "only" conditionally secure. As such, they can be broken theoretically by mounting an exhaustive key search. Consequently, it is important to make the key space so large that an exhaustive key search is not feasible. This is certainly the case if the key has a size of 100 bits or more (in this case, the key space is 2^{100}). Examples of conditionally secure symmetric encryption systems are the DES and the AES (see Section 10.2). There are several modes of operations in which these systems (and others) can be operated.

- Contrary to symmetric encryption systems, MACs can be used to protect the authenticity and integrity of messages. As compared to digital signatures, MACs can usually be generated and verified more efficiently. On the negative side, however, MACs cannot be used to provide nonrepudiation services (this is because both the sender and the recipient hold a secret key that is needed to generate the MAC).[1] There are constructions for computationally secure or information-theoretically secure MACs. For all practical purposes, computationally secure MACs are the preferred choice. More specifically, the HMAC construction is employed in almost every Internet security protocol in use today, whereas the UMAC construction is a possible successor that is very efficient.

---

1   Note, however, that it is sometimes required that nonrepudiation services cannot be provided.

- PRBGs can be used to stretch a relatively short seed value into a potentially very long pseudorandom bit sequence. Whenever random bits are needed, it is usually efficient to use a random bit generator to generate a seed for a PRBG and to then use the PRBG to generate a sequence of pseudorandom bits. The PRBG is secure if its output is computationally indistinguishable from the output of a true random bit generator. In fact, the notion of computational indistinguishability has turned out to be very useful in theoretical considerations (and proofs) of other cryptographic systems.

- Contrary to PRBGs, PRFs do not generate an output that meets specific (randomness) requirements. Instead, PRFs try to model the input-output behavior of random functions. PRBGs and (families of) PRFs are closely related to each other in the sense that a PRF family can be used to construct a PRBG, and a PRBG can be used to construct a PRF family (see Section 13.2).

20.3 PUBLIC KEY CRYPTOSYSTEMS

Public key cryptosystems have been developed since the late 1970s and are typically associated with modern cryptography. In fact, DSSs and key establishment protocols were the two major driving forces behind the invention and development of public key cryptography in general, and public key cryptosystems in particular. In Part IV of the book, we had a closer look at asymmetric encryption systems, DSSs, and cryptographic protocols for key establishment, entity authentication, and secure MPC.

- Asymmetric encryption systems are typically used to protect the secrecy of only small messages. If, for example, an entity has to transmit a secret key (i.e., a key from a symmetric encryption system) to another entity, then the use of an asymmetric encryption system is efficient: the sender simply encrypts the key with the public key of the recipient. Asymmetric encryption systems have the inherent problem that chosen-plaintext attacks are trivial to mount (because the public keys are by definition publicly known), and that many practical applications require security against chosen-ciphertext attacks. Furthermore, unless one employs an IBE system (see Section 14.4), the use of an asymmetric encryption system always requires digital certificates and PKIs. We briefly touched on this requirement in Section 19.5.

- Many public key cryptosystems can be used as an asymmetric encryption system or a DSS. In fact, the possibility to digitally sign electronic documents and verify digital signatures is very powerful, and it is often argued that it is a prerequisite for the successful deployment of electronic commerce. This line of argumentation may be a little bit exaggerated, but digital signatures and DSSs certainly play a crucial role in the provision of nonrepudiation services. Consequently, digital signatures, DSSs, and digital signature legislation are very important and timely topics from a practical point of view.

- Many cryptographic protocols have been developed, proposed, implemented, and partly deployed. Among these protocols, the Diffie-Hellman key exchange protocol is by far the most important protocol in use today. This is quite astonishing if one considers the fact that the Diffie-Hellman key exchange protocol (see Section 16.3) was actually the first public key cryptosystem ever published in the open literature. In addition, many other cryptographic protocols can be used for entity authentication, secure MPC, and many other tasks and problems. In fact, several problems that seem to be impossible to solve at first sight have quite elegant solutions if one considers the use of public key cryptography. These solutions, in turn, are part of the fascination many people have with cryptography.

20.4 FINAL REMARKS

In practice, unkeyed, secret key, and public key cryptosystems are often combined to complement each other. For example, we saw that a random bit generator can be used to seed a PRBG and that symmetric and asymmetric encryption can be combined in hybrid encryption systems. In fact, public key cryptosystems are often used for authentication and key distribution, whereas secret key cryptosystems are often used for bulk data encryption and message authentication (if performance is a major issue). Consequently, real applications often combine all types of cryptosystems (including unkeyed cryptosystems) to come up with a mix that can be implemented in an efficient and secure way.

Last but not least, we note that it is sometimes argued that public key cryptography is inherently more secure than secret key cryptography. This argument is fundamentally flawed, and there are secure and insecure public key and secret key cryptosystems. If one has to decide what cryptosystem to use, then one has to look at the requirements from an application point of view. If, for example, it is required that data can be authenticated efficiently, then a MAC is usually a good choice. If, however, it is required that the sender cannot later repudiate having sent a particular message, then a DSS is usually more appropriate. Consequently, there is no single best cryptosystem to be used for all applications. Instead, it is important to understand the working principles, advantages, and disadvantages, as well as the shortcomings and limitations of all practically relevant and deployed cryptosystems, and to design and implement a security architecture that is appropriate for the application one has in mind. This is not an easy task, and it should be dealt with professionally by security architects.

Chapter 21

Outlook

It would appear that we have reached the limits of what is possible to achieve with computer technology, although one should be careful with such statements, as they tend to sound pretty silly in 5 years.

— John von Neumann[1]

After having overviewed, discussed, and put into perspective the state of the art in cryptography, it may be worthwhile to elaborate a little bit on possible or likely trends and developments in the future. In spite of John von Neumann's quote given above, we try to provide an outlook that goes beyond the next five years. Note, however, that the outlook is subjective and based on the author's own assessment. Other people working in the field may have a different perception and may come to different conclusions (especially if they work for companies that market specific security technologies, mechanisms, services, or products).

We have both a theoretical and a practical viewpoint to offer. Before we begin, however, we want to note that cryptography as a field of study and area of research has become mature and is establishing itself as an independent science. An increasing number of universities provide courses and diplomas on cryptography and information security. As a consequence of this development, we have experienced and will continue to see a significant level of diversification and specialization in cryptographic research. In the past, we have seen cryptographers who were able to talk about every topic that is directly or indirectly related to cryptography. This is more and more seldom the case. Today, there are cryptographers who are only able to talk about integer factorization algorithms and algorithms to solve the DLP,

---

1   John von Neumann lived from 1903 to 1957.

cryptographers who are only able to talk about stream ciphers, cryptographers who are only able to talk about block ciphers, cryptographers who are only able to talk about modes of operation for these block ciphers, cryptographers who only work on RSA, cryptographers who only work on ECC, and so on. There are plenty of cryptographical fields of study that are populated with small research communities. This development goes hand in hand with the maturity level of a particular science. If somebody wants to get into cryptographic research, then he or she must first select a particular problem on which to work. Sometimes these problems are so specific that it is difficult to see the forest for the trees.

21.1 THEORETICAL VIEWPOINT

From a theoretical viewpoint, a central theme in cryptographic research is provability. How can one define security, and how can one prove that a given cryptographic system is secure in exactly this sense? Shannon introduced information theory to precisely define the notion of perfect secrecy (see Definition 10.1). Other researchers have done similar things for PRBGs, asymmetric encryption systems, DSSs, and many other cryptographic systems.

In modern cryptography, one often assumes that a particular (mathematical) problem is intractable, and one then shows that a cryptographic system is secure as long as this intractability assumption holds. For example, assuming that the DHP is intractable, we showed that the ElGamal public key cryptosystem is secure (see Theorem 14.2). Furthermore, it is sometimes assumed that a cryptographic hash function behaves like a random function (in addition to the intractability assumption of the underlying mathematical problem), and one is then able to show that a cryptographic system is secure in the random oracle model (see Section 13.3 for a corresponding overview). There are other ideas to define the notion of security with respect to a particular cryptographic system or class of such systems (e.g., computational indistinguishability). Furthermore, formal methods play a central role when one elaborates on the security of complex cryptographic protocols. In many areas, we are only at the beginning of understanding and defining the notion of security in a mathematically precise sense. But this is what modern cryptography is all about: finding definitions for security and proving that certain cryptographic systems meet these definitions.

Against this background, it is important to note that it has not been possible to provide an absolute proof for the security of a cryptographic system. We are only able to prove the security (properties) of a cryptographic system if we make assumptions. Some of these assumptions are implicit (and appear too trivial to be mentioned in the first place). For example, when we talk about encryption systems, we often make the implicit assumption that telepathy does not exist or does not work (otherwise, encrypting data does not make a lot of sense). Similarly, we assume that randomness exists (otherwise, secret keys cannot exist in principle). Other assumptions are less obvious. As mentioned earlier, we often work with intractability assumptions when we prove the security of a cryptographic system. These intractability assumptions are often related to a specific adversary and assumptions about his or her capabilities and computational power. For example, if we assume that an adversary is an illiterate (i.e., he or she cannot read and write), then it is fairly trivial to come up with a secure encryption system.[2] More realistic assumptions are related to the computing power, available time, and available memory. Last but not least, we often make assumptions about the correct behavior of system entities and human users. These assumptions are particularly difficult to make, and many cryptographic security protocols can be broken if an adversary does not play by the rules. These considerations must also be taken into account when one tries to work with formal methods.

According to [1], all assumptions that are made implicitly and explicitly must be taken into account and considered with care when one considers cryptography and security proofs. It is particularly important to note

- That every security proof for a cryptographic system is only relative to certain assumptions;

- That assumptions should be made explicit;

- That assumptions should always be as weak as possible.

A major future goal for cryptographic research is to reduce the necessary assumptions to a set of realistic assumptions, while preserving the practicality of the systems. This is particularly true for computational intractability assumptions.

After a talk I gave on Internet security,[3] I was asked whether the fact that almost nothing in cryptography can be proven in a mathematically strong and absolute sense wasn't potentially dangerous and worrisome. I had to answer in the affirmative and confess that the current types of reasoning about the security of cryptographic systems are not satisfactory but simply the best we currently have at hand. We would like to see absolute proofs for the security of cryptographic systems (instead of proofs that are relative to specific computational intractability assumptions). Similarly, we would like to have functions that can be shown to be

---

2   This is why the Caesar cipher mentioned in Sections 1.3 and 10.1.1 was secure. It was used in a time when most people were illiterate.

3   The talk was entitled "Sicherheit im Internet" and was held on November 21, 1996, at the Swiss Association for the Security of Information Services (CLUSIS) meeting on "Sicherheit und Gefahren des Internet" in Zürich (Switzerland).

one way and proofs that one-way functions really exist. Furthermore, we would like to get rid of the random oracle model and be able to prove security properties of cryptographic systems without having to make the idealized assumption that cryptographic hash functions behave like random functions. Unfortunately, we are not there (yet), and it is questionable whether we will ever be there. In either case, it will be interesting to see where the cryptographic research community is heading to in the future.

21.2   PRACTICAL VIEWPOINT

From a practical viewpoint, it is unavoidable that standardization and profiling activities will become more and more important in the future. There are simply too many and too complex cryptographic systems (i.e., cryptographic algorithms and protocols) and modes of operation from which to choose. Anybody not actively working in the field is likely to be overtaxed. The DES is a success story mainly because its promoters (i.e., the U.S. NIST) realized the need for a standardized symmetric encryption system in the 1970s. In the late 1990s, the NIST wanted to repeat (and improve) the success story by standardizing the AES. In a couple of years from now, people will use products that implement the AES (similar to how they use products that implement the DES or 3DES today).

There are many complementary standards for cryptographic systems and their use. Examples include:

- HMAC for message authentication (see Section 11.2.2);

- OAEP for asymmetric encryption (see Section 14.3.2);

- PSS and PSS-R for digital signatures (see Section 15.3).

The more we can prove about the security properties of these standardized cryptographic systems, the better the odds that they are successful and get widely deployed. The most we can hope is that the complexity of the cryptographic systems will be hidden in the reference implementation and programming libraries that provide some cryptographic application programming interface (API). Examples include the CryptoAPI and the Base Cryptographic Provider of Microsoft Corporation, and the Java Cryptography Extension of Sun Microsystems, Inc.[4]

In addition to the U.S. NIST, several other (national and international) standardization bodies, forces, and groups work on cryptography. Examples include the ANSI, the IEEE, the IETF, and the W3C. Unfortunately, many of these bodies have

4   http://java.sun.com/products/jce.

problems of their own, and hence the current state in international standardization is not particularly good. This is worrisome but must be addressed elsewhere. In the meantime, industry-sponsored standardization activities, like the specification of the PKCS, are important to fill the gap. Again, a comprehensive overview about the standards that are relevant in applied and practical cryptography is provided in [2].

References

[1] Maurer, U.M., *Cryptography 2000 ±10*, Springer-Verlag, New York, LNCS 2000, 2000, pp. 63–85.

[2] Dent, A.W., and C.J. Mitchell, *User's Guide to Cryptography and Standards*. Artech House Publishers, Norwood, MA, 2004.

Appendix A

Abbreviations and Acronyms

AA	attribute authority
ACM	Association for Computing Machinery
AES	advanced encryption standard
ANSI	American National Standards Institute
API	application programming interface
ASCII	American Standard Code for Information Interchange
ASN.1	abstract syntax notation one
ATM	automatic teller machine
BBS	Blum, Blum, Shub
B.C.	Before Christ
Bellcore	Bell Communications Research
BER	basic encoding rules
BIS	Bureau of Industry and Security
bit	binary digit
BXA	Bureau of Export Administration
CA	certification authority
CBC	cipherblock chaining
CFB	cipher feedback
CLUSIS	Association for the Security of Information Services
cm	centimeter
COCOM	Coordinating Committee for Multilateral Export Controls
COTS	commercial off-the-shelf
CRA	Chinese remainder algorithm
CRHF	collision resistant hash function

CRT	Chinese remainder theorem
	cathode-ray tube
CTR	counter
DAA	data authentication algorithm
DAC	data authentication code
DEA	data encryption algorithm
DER	distinguished encoding rules
DES	data encryption standard
DHDP	Diffie-Hellman decision problem
DHP	Diffie-Hellman problem
DIT	directory information tree
DLA	discrete logarithm assumption
DLP	discrete logarithm problem
DN	distinguished name
DNA	deoxyribonucleic acid
DoC	Department of Commerce
DSA	digital signature algorithm
DSS	digital signature system
EAR	Export Administration Regulations
ECB	electronic code book
ECC	elliptic curve cryptography
ECDLP	elliptic curve DLP
ECDSA	elliptic curve digital signature algorithm
ECM	elliptic curve method
EES	escrowed encryption standard
EFF	Electronic Frontier Foundation
EFS	encrypted file system
FDH	full-domain-hash
FIPS	federal information processing standards
FSM	finite state machine
FSR	feedback shift register
FSUIT	Federal Strategy Unit for Information Technology
GCHQ	Government Communications Headquarters
GMR	Goldwasser, Micali, Rivest
GNFS	general NFS
GPS	global positioning system

GSM   Groupe Speciale Mobile

HMAC   hashed MAC

IACR	International Association for Cryptologic Research
IBE	identity-based encryption
IBM	International Business Machines
ICSI	International Computer Science Institute
IDEA	international data encryption algorithm
IEC	International Electrotechnical Committee
IEEE	Institute of Electrical and Electronics Engineers
IETF	Internet Engineering Task Force
IFA	integer factoring assumption
IFIP	International Federation for Information Processing
IFP	integer factoring problem
IKE	Internet key exchange
IP	Internet Protocol
	initial permutation
IPsec	IP security
ISO	International Organization for Standardization
ISOC	Internet Society
ISP	Internet service provider
IT	information technology
ITU	International Telecommunication Union
ITU-T	ITU Telecommunication Standardization Sector
IV	initialization vector

JTC1   Joint Technical Committee 1

KAC	key authentication center
KDC	key distribution center
km	kilometer

LFSR	linear feedback shift register
LNCS	Lecture Notes in Computer Science
LSB	least significant bit

MAA	message authenticator algorithm
MAC	message authentication code
MD	message digest

MIC	message integrity code
MIT	Massachusetts Institute of Technology
MPC	multiparty computation
MSB	most significant bit
NBS	National Bureau of Standards
NESSIE	new European schemes for signatures, integrity and encryption
NFS	number field sieve
NIST	National Institute of Standards and Technology
NMAC	nested MAC
NRL	Naval Research Laboratory
NSE	non-secret encryption
OAEP	optimal asymmetric encryption padding
OFB	output feedback
OID	object identifier
OPIE	one-time passwords in everything
OWHF	one-way hash function
PC	permuted choice
	personal computer
PD	Privatdozent
PDA	personal digital assistant
PER	packet encoding rules
PGP	Pretty Good Privacy
PIN	personal identification number
PKCS	public key cryptography standard
PKI	public key infrastructure
PKIX	PKI X.509
PPT	probabilistic polynomial-time
PRBG	pseudorandom bit generator
PRF	pseudorandom function
PRP	pseudorandom permutation
PSS	probabilistic signature scheme
PSS-R	probabilistic signature scheme with message recovery
QRP	quadratic residuosity problem
QS	quadratic sieve
qubit	quantum bit

RA	registration authority
RC	Ron's Code
RFC	request for comments
RSA	Rivest, Shamir, Adleman
RSAP	RSA problem

SHA	secure hash algorithm
SHS	secure hash standard
SKIP	simple key-management for Internet protocols
SNFS	special NFS
SNMP	simple network management protocol
SSL	secure sockets layer
STS	station-to-station

TAN	transaction authentication number
TCBC	TDEA CBC
TCBC-I	TDEA CBC interleaved
TCFB	TDEA CFB
TCFB-P	TDEA CFB pipelined
TDEA	triple data encryption algorithm
TECB	TDEA ECB
TLS	transport layer security
TOFB	TDEA OFB
TOFB-I	TDEA OFB interleaved
TTP	trusted third party

UMAC	universal MAC
URL	uniform resource locator
U.S.	United States
USB	universal serial bus

W3C	World Wide Web Consortium
WEP	wired equivalent privacy
WG	working group
WWW	World Wide Web

XMACC	counter-based XOR MAC
XMACR	randomized XOR MAC

Appendix B

Mathematical Notation

$\forall$	quantifier "for all"
$\exists$	quantifier "there exists"
$\equiv$	congruence relation
$:=$	definition
$\sum$	sum
$\prod$	product
$\square$	end of proof
∞	infinity
$\mathcal{O}$	point at infinity
S	set
$|S|$	cardinality of S (i.e., number of elements)
2^S	power set of S (i.e., set of all subsets of S)
$\emptyset$	empty set (i.e., $|\emptyset| = 0$)
$P(S)$	set of all permutations on S (i.e., $Perm^{S \to S}$)
$x \in S$	x is an element of S
$x \notin S$	x is not an element of S
$x \in_R S$	x is a random (i.e., randomly chosen) element of S
$x \in (a,b)$	x is an element from the open interval (a,b)
$x \in [a,b]$	x is an element from the closed interval $[a,b]$
$A \cup B$	union of sets A and B
$A \cap B$	intersection of sets A and B
$A \setminus B$	difference of sets A and B
$A \subseteq B$	set A is a subset of set B (or B is a superset of A)
$\mathbb{N}$	natural numbers
$\mathbb{N}^+$	positive natural numbers (i.e., $\mathbb{N}^+ := \mathbb{N} \setminus \{0\}$
$\mathbb{Z}$	integer numbers (i.e., integers)

$\mathbb{Z}^+$	positive integers
$\mathbb{Z}^-$	negative integers
$\mathbb{Z}_n$	integers modulo n
$\mathbb{Z}_n^*$	multiplicative group of integers modulo n
$(x\|p)$	Legendre symbol of x modulo p
$(x\|n)$	Jacobi symbol of x modulo p
J_n	elements of $\mathbb{Z}_n^*$ with Jacobi symbol 1
QR_n	set of quadratic residues modulo n
QNR_n	set of quadratic nonresidues modulo n
$\widetilde{QR_n}$	set of pseudosquares modulo n
$\mathbb{Q}$	rational numbers
$\mathbb{R}$	real numbers
$\mathbb{R}^+$	positive real numbers
$\mathbb{R}^-$	negative real numbers
π	transcendental number that expresses the ratio of the circumference of a perfect circle to its diameter ($\pi = 3.14159\ldots$)
e	transcendental number that represents the base of the natural logarithm ($e = 2.71828\ldots$)
$\mathbb{C}$	complex numbers
i	$\sqrt{-1}$
$\mathbb{F}$	finite field
$\mathbb{F}_q$	finite field with q elements (i.e., $\|\mathbb{F}_q\| = q$)
$E(\mathbb{F}_q)$	elliptic curve over $\mathbb{F}_q$
$\mathbf{P}$	set of all primes
$*$	binary operation
$+$	addition
$-$	subtraction
$\cdot$	multiplication
$/$	division
$x \leftarrow X$	value assignment (i.e., x is assigned a value from X)
$x \overset{u}{\leftarrow} X$	value assignment according to the uniform distribution
$\neg X$	bitwise negation of the Boolean variable X (NOT)
$X \wedge Y$	bitwise and of the Boolean variables X and Y (AND)
$X \vee Y$	bitwise or of the Boolean variables X and Y (OR)
$X \oplus Y$	bitwise exclusive of the Boolean variables X and Y (XOR)
$X \hookleftarrow s$	circular left shift of Boolean variable X by s positions
$X \hookrightarrow s$	circular right shift of Boolean variable X by s positions
$a = b$	a is equal to b
$a < b$	a is smaller than b
$a \ll b$	a is much smaller than b

$a > b$	a is greater than b
$a \gg b$	a is much greater than b
$\lfloor x \rfloor$	greatest integer less than or equal to x (i.e., floor of x)
$\lceil x \rceil$	smallest integer greater than or equal to x (i.e., ceiling of x)
div	integer division
mod	modulo operator
$a \mid b$	integer a divides integer b
$a \nmid b$	integer a does not divide integer b
$gcd(a_1, \ldots, a_k)$	greatest common divisor of integers $a_1, \ldots, a_k$
$lcm(a_1, \ldots, a_k)$	least common multiple of integers $a_1, \ldots, a_k$
$n!$	factorial of integer n (with $0! = 1$)
$\pi(n)$	prime counting function of integer n
$\phi(n)$	Euler's totient function of integer n
L	formal language
Σ	alphabet
Σ_{in}	input alphabet
Σ_{out}	output alphabet
$\{0, 1\}$	binary alphabet
w	word (i.e., string over an alphabet)
$|w|$	length of w
ε	empty word
Σ^n	set of all words of length n over alphabet Σ
Σ^*	set of all words over alphabet Σ
$\circ$ or $\parallel$	string concatenation
f	function
$X \rightarrow Y$	mapping from domain X to codomain Y
$f(X) \subseteq Y$	range of f
f^{-1}	inverse function
F	function family
f_k	instance of function family F
$Rand^{X \rightarrow Y}$	family of all functions of X to Y
$Perm^{X \rightarrow X}$	family of all permutations on X
h	hash function
H	hash function family
$p(n)$	polynomial in n
$deg(p(n))$	degree of polynomial $p(n)$
$L_n[a, c]$	running time function
$ord(x)$	order of group element x
$ord_n(x)$	order of x modulo n
Ω	sample space (i.e., finite or countably infinite set)

ω	elementary event
U_n	uniform probability distribution on $\{0,1\}^n$
$\mathcal{A}$	event
$\overline{\mathcal{A}}$	complement of event $\mathcal{A}$
$\Pr$	probability measure
$\Pr[\mathcal{A}]$	probability of event A
$\Pr[\omega|\mathcal{A}]$	conditional probability of ω given that $\mathcal{A}$ holds
$\Pr[\mathcal{A}|\mathcal{B}]$	conditional probability of $\mathcal{A}$ given that $\mathcal{B}$ holds
X	random variable
P_X	probability distribution of X
P_{XY}	joint probability distribution of X and Y
$P_{X_1 \ldots X_n}$	joint probability distribution of $X_1, \ldots, X_n$
$P_{X|\mathcal{A}}$	conditional probability distribution of X given that $\mathcal{A}$ holds
$P_{X|Y}$	conditional probability distribution of X given that Y holds
$E[X]$	expectation (or mean) of X
$E[X|\mathcal{A}]$	conditional expected value of X given that $\mathcal{A}$ holds
$Var[X]$	variance of X
$\sigma[X]$	standard deviation of X
$H(X)$	entropy of X
$H(XY)$	joint entropy of X and Y
$H(X|Y = y)$	conditional entropy of X when $Y = y$
$H(X|Y)$	conditional entropy of X when given Y
$I(X;Y)$	mutual information between X and Y
H_L	entropy of language L
R_L	redundancy of language L
n_u	unicity distance
M	Turing machine
S_M	space complexity of Turing machine M
T_M	time complexity of Turing machine M
$\mathcal{P}$	"polynomial-time" complexity class
$\mathcal{NP}$, co$\mathcal{NP}$	"nondeterministic polynomial-time" complexity classes
$\mathcal{PP}$	"probabilistic polynomial-time" complexity class
$\mathcal{ZPP}$	"zero-sided error probabilistic polynomial-time" complexity class
$\mathcal{PP}$-Monte Carlo and	
$\mathcal{PP}$-Las Vegas	"one-sided error probabilistic polynomial-time" complexity classes
$\mathcal{BPP}$	"bounded-error probabilistic polynomial-time" complexity class
A^f	distinguisher A that is given oracle access to function f
O^P	oracle for problem P
$\mathcal{M}$	(plaintext) message space
$\mathcal{C}$	ciphertext space

$\mathcal{K}$	key space
$\mathcal{E}$	family $\{E_k : k \in \mathcal{K}\}$ of encryption functions $E_k : \mathcal{M} \to \mathcal{C}$
$\mathcal{D}$	family $\{D_k : K \in \mathcal{K}\}$ of decryption functions $D_k : \mathcal{C} \to \mathcal{M}$
$\mathcal{T}$	authentication tag space
$\mathcal{A}$	family $\{A_k : k \in \mathcal{K}\}$ of authentication functions $A_k : \mathcal{M} \to \mathcal{T}$
$\mathcal{V}$	family $\{V_k : K \in \mathcal{K}\}$ of verification functions $V_k : \mathcal{M} \times \mathcal{T} \to \{valid, invalid\}$
Γ	access structure (employed by a secret sharing scheme)

About the Author

Rolf Oppliger received M.Sc. and Ph.D. degrees in computer science from the University of Berne, Switzerland, in 1991 and 1993, respectively. After spending one year as a postdoctoral researcher at the International Computer Science Institute (ICSI) in Berkeley, California, he joined the Swiss Federal Strategy Unit for Information Technology (FSUIT) in 1995 and continued his research and teaching activities at several universities in Switzerland and Germany. In 1999, he received the venia legendi[1] for computer science from the University of Zürich, Switzerland, founded eSECURITY Technologies Rolf Oppliger[2] to provide scientific and state-of-the-art consulting, education, and engineering services related to information technology (IT) security, and started to serve as an editor for Artech House's computer security series.[3] He has published numerous scientific papers and articles, as well as 10 books on security-related topics. He is a member of the Association for Computing Machinery (ACM), the Institute of Electrical and Electronics Engineers (IEEE) Computer Society, the International Association for Cryptologic Research (IACR), and the International Federation for Information Processing (IFIP) Technical Committee 11 (TC11) Working Group 4 (WG4) on network security.

---

1   The *venia legendi* (also known as Habilitation) is the formal statement of a university that an academician is qualified to act as university lecturer or principal investigator. It is mainly used in German-speaking (European) countries. The formal status of an academician holding a venia legendi is the one of a Privatdozent (PD). The status of a PD is similar and comparable to the one of an adjunct professor in many other countries.

2   http://www.esecurity.ch, http://www.rolf-oppliger.com, or http://www.rolf-oppliger.ch.

3   http://www.esecurity.ch/serieseditor.html.

Index

Non-repudiation in Electronic Commerce, Jianying Zhou

Outsourcing Information Security, C. Warren Axelrod

Privacy Protection and Computer Forensics, Second Edition, Michael A. Caloyannides

Role-Based Access Controls, David F. Ferraiolo, D. Richard Kuhn, and Ramaswamy Chandramouli

Secure Messaging with PGP and S/MIME, Rolf Oppliger

Security Fundamentals for E-Commerce, Vesna Hassler

Security Technologies for the World Wide Web, Second Edition, Rolf Oppliger

Techniques and Applications of Digital Watermarking and Content Protection, Michael Arnold, Martin Schmucker, and Stephen D. Wolthusen

User's Guide to Cryptography and Standards, Alexander W. Dent and Chris J. Mitchell

For further information on these and other Artech House titles, including previously considered out-of-print books now available through our In-Print-Forever® (IPF®) program, contact:

Artech House
685 Canton Street
Norwood, MA 02062
Phone: 781-769-9750
Fax: 781-769-6334
e-mail: artech@artechhouse.com

Artech House
46 Gillingham Street
London SW1V 1AH UK
Phone: +44 (0)20 7596-8750
Fax: +44 (0)20 7630-0166
e-mail: artech-uk@artechhouse.com

Find us on the World Wide Web at:
www.artechhouse.com